Religion, Revolution, and English Radicalism

Religion, Revolution, and English Radicalism

Nonconformity in Eighteenth-Century Politics and Society

JAMES E. BRADLEY

Associate Professor of Church History
Fuller Theological Seminary

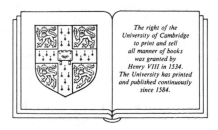

The right of the
University of Cambridge
to print and sell
all manner of books
was granted by
Henry VIII in 1534.
The University has printed
and published continuously
since 1584.

CAMBRIDGE UNIVERSITY PRESS

Cambridge

New York   Port Chester

Melbourne   Sydney

Published by the Press Syndicate of the University of Cambridge
The Pitt Building, Trumpington Street, Cambridge CB2 1RP
40 West 20th Street, New York, NY 10011, USA
10 Stamford Road, Oakleigh, Melbourne 3166, Australia

First Published 1990

Printed in Great Britain at the University Press, Cambridge

DA 480
B72
1990

British Library cataloguing in publication data
Bradley, James E.
Religion, Revolution and English radicalism:
nonconformity in eighteenth-century politics and society.
1. Great Britain. Social life, 1714–1830
I. Title
941.07

Library of Congress cataloguing in publication data
Bradley, James E. 1944–
Religion, revolution, and English radicalism: nonconformity in
eighteenth-century politics and society / James E. Bradley.   p.   cm.
Includes bibliographaical references.
ISBN 0 521 38010 3
1. Dissenters, Religious–Political activity–England–
History–18th century. 2. Religion and politics–England–
History–18th century.   3. Great Britain–Politics and
government–18th century.   4. Radicalism–England–History–18th
century.   5. England–Church history–18th century.   I. Title.
DA480.B72 1990   90–33078   CIP
941.07–dc20

ISBN 0 521 38010 3 hardback

For the students in Beijing and Prague,
who in 1989 led the struggle against oppression
and advanced the cause of human rights
through their suffering

When mankind are once instructed in their natural rights and privileges, they will not only complain but struggle to get clear of oppression. Wise men know what it is to obey just laws, but will never tamely submit to slavery and bondage.

The Rev. James Murray
Sermons to Asses
Newcastle upon Tyne, 1768

What arrogance is it for men to pretend to be Lords over God's heritage, when Christ said, *One is your Master, even Christ; and all ye are brethren?*

Sermons to Doctors in Divinity,
Being the Second Volume of
Sermons to Asses
London, 1773

Contents

Preface   *page xi*

List of Tables, Figures, and Maps   *xvii*

Abbreviations   *xx*

Chapter 1. AN INTRODUCTION TO RELIGION IN EIGHTEENTH-
CENTURY POLITICAL CULTURE   1

Nonconformity, Pro-Americanism, and the Evolution of
English Radicalism   7
Nonconformity, Whig Historiography, and Party Continuity   18
Religion, Social Class, and Economic Motivation in Modern
English Society   31
Political Ideology, Political Behavior, and Historical Method   39

PART ONE

THE LEGAL STATUS, SOCIAL STRUCTURE, AND IDEOLOGY OF
NONCONFORMITY

Chapter 2. NONCONFORMITY, THE LAW, AND SOCIETY   49

The Law and the Unity of 'the Dissenting Interest'   50
The Social Status and Social Equality of Dissent   61
The Corporation Act and the Practice of Occasional Conformity   69
The Test Act and the National Government   80
The Legal Sources of Dissenting Politics   84

Chapter 3. NONCONFORMITY IN POLITICS: INFLUENCE
AND INDEPENDENCE   91

The Demography of Dissent and Parliamentary Politics   92
Dissenters and Electoral Politics: Deference, Influence, and
the 'Water Spout of Freedom'   96
The Dissenters and Political Independence   106

vii

Contents

The Dissent-Low-Church Alliance and Whig Parties in the
Constituencies 113
The Social Sources of Dissenting Politics 118

Chapter 4. THE DISSENTING PULPIT, POLITICAL IDEOLOGY,
AND AMERICAN INDEPENDENCE 121

The Eighteenth-Century Pulpit 122
The Dissenting Pulpit and Dissenting Ideology 127
The Philosophical and Theological Sources of Dissenting
Politics 133
Natural Right, the Ancient Constitution, and English History 142
American Resistance: 'One of the Best Causes in the World' 147
The Justice of Resistance to Unlawful Authority 154

Chapter 5. THE DISSENTING PULPIT AND POLITICAL
RADICALISM IN ENGLAND 159

Opposition to the King and Government 159
The Dissenting Pulpit and the Relationship of National to
Local Politics 167
The Dissenting Pulpit on Social Stratification and Political
Oppression 174
The Dissenting Pulpit, Independence, and Deference 182
Practical Strategies for Reform Through Associations and
Petitions 185
The Influence of Dissenting Ideology on Elections 189

PART TWO

POLL BOOKS, PARLIAMENTARY POLITICS, AND NONCONFORMITY

Chapter 6. THE DISSENTING INTEREST AND THE AMERICAN
CRISIS IN BRISTOL 195

Bristol, Burke, and the Origins of the Whig Interpretation
of Party 196
Local Politics and National Issues 203
The Local Framework: Chapels, Clubs, and Societies 205
The National Framework: Contests, Candidates, and
Political Issues 209
The Religious and Social Dimensions of Party 220

Contents

Chapter 7. THE DISSENTING VOTE AND ELECTORAL
INDEPENDENCE IN BRISTOL AND GREAT YARMOUTH   224

The Electoral Behavior of the Dissenting Laity in Bristol   226

The Electoral Behavior of the Dissenting Laity in
Great Yarmouth   239

Political Consistency, Socio-economic Status, and Religion   243

Chapter 8. DEFERENCE AND THE DISSENTING VOTE IN
NEWCASTLE, LIVERPOOL, HULL, AND COLCHESTER   255

Newcastle upon Tyne and Secular Radicalism   255

Political Issues, Local and National   258

The Ideology of Radicalism   262

Electoral Behavior in Newcastle   265

Liverpool, Sir William Meredith, and the Rockingham
Whigs   274

Popular Political Ideology in Liverpool   279

Party Politics without Party Organizations   283

Kingston upon Hull and Corruption   289

David Hartley and his Constituents   292

Colchester and the Congregationalists   298

Charismatic Leadership and Parliamentary Elections   309

PART THREE

PETITIONS FOR PEACE, NONCONFORMITY, AND POPULAR
POLITICS

Chapter 9. THE PETITIONS OF 1775: POPULAR POLITICS
AND THE AMERICAN CRISIS   315

The Petitioning Agitation of 1775   316

Petitions and Public Opinion   326

The Leadership and Organization of Popular Politics
in 1775   330

The London Association and Newcastle upon Tyne   337

Liverpool and the Lancashire Petition   342

The High Church and Local Politics in Coventry   346

Nonconformity and Local Politics in Colchester,
Taunton, and Nottingham   349

Charismatic Leadership and Popular Politics   358

Contents

Chapter 10. THE PETITIONERS OF 1775: LAW, SOCIAL STATUS, AND RELIGION   360

Corporations and Custom-Houses   361

Popular Politics and Socio-economic Rank   371

Religion, Revolution, and Radicalism   385

Eighteenth-Century Political Structures and the Failure of Dissenting Leadership   395

The Interdependence of Religious and Economic Motivation   399

Conclusion   410

Appendix 1: NOMINAL RECORD LINKAGE AND LETTER CLUSTER SAMPLING   431

Appendix 2: OCCUPATIONAL STRUCTURE AND SOCIO-ECONOMIC STANDING   436

Bibliography: Manuscript Sources and Poll Books   447

Index   453

Preface

In the early 1930s Herbert Butterfield wrote perceptively concerning the distortions of the Protestant view of history, noting how nineteenth-century Whig historians judged previous centuries in light of their own notions of morality and progress. Lewis Namier had just published his magisterial work on the structure of eighteenth-century English politics, and these volumes almost completely demolished the teleological, progressive scheme of the Whig historians. Namier had effectively produced the revolution in outlook that Butterfield had merely sketched, but there remained in Namier's version of Hanoverian England one outstanding, progressive group in the body politic, namely, the Protestant Dissenters. Butterfield had demonstrated that Protestant religious ideology was perhaps the single greatest cause for anachronism in English historical literature, but using the new techniques of structural analysis, Namier discovered that most vestiges of party continuity in English boroughs could be traced to the Dissenters, and he believed that 'almost the only men who about 1770 held the modern British view of the Empire were the English Dissenters'. Although nineteenth-century Dissenting historians were a major source of the Whig interpretation, their eighteenth-century forebears had escaped Namier's searching critique unscathed. According to Namier, it was 'in the spirit of the Dissenters alone' that a solution to the Imperial problem could be found.

In the ecclesiastical version of the Whig interpretation, the Tories and High-Church Anglicans were always the reactionary villains, and the Dissenters and Whigs were invariably the moral, farsighted heroes. The first half of the equation has been largely corrected by Norman Sykes and recent research. In the Birkbeck Lectures of 1931–33, Sykes revealed the serious distortions in the Victorian version of the Georgian church, but no study of eighteenth–century Nonconformity has approximated Sykes' analysis of Anglicanism. Apart from regional studies, no account of Nonconformity even hints that the Dissenters may have been as involved in political treating as their Anglican counterparts. Clearly, a study is needed that applies the techniques of Namier and Sykes to the Nonconformists; we need to know how the Dissenters were actually affected by the Test and Corporation Acts, and how they behaved during the crucial decades of the American Revolution. Anthony Lincoln and others have studied the political and social thought of the Dissenters, but their political behavior has remained largely unassayed. This book examines the Nonconformists during a critical generation of change when they were dramatically transformed from loyal supporters of the government to its most outspoken, radical critics.

The American Revolution was the first modern war fought primarily for secular ends in which the role of religious Nonconformity can be quantified with precision. Before the age of the democratic revolution, the vital records of individuals within specific religious groups were poorly kept and of limited value, but in the 1760s and 1770s the Nonconformist registers of births and baptisms proliferated for legal reasons, and these documents provide us with the names and occupations of thousands of individual Dissenters. Extensive and continuous runs of published parliamentary poll books are also available for the first time only in the second half of the eighteenth century. The Dissenting elite are well-known for their contribution to the radical ideology of the Commonwealthman tradition, but despite the fact that vital records enable us to study the political action of the average layman, the behavior of the laity has been almost totally neglected. Traditionally, local political factions in England had articulated their ideological differences through such verbal expressions as handbills and newspaper articles, usually published anonymously. These peaceful means of political expression, combined with elections and election-eering, had, by the early eighteenth century, largely replaced acts of violence (although when religious issues were especially prominent in elections, people sometimes still reverted to force). But in the 1770s, the populace increasingly turned to such unsanctioned and potentially seditious forms of protest as the public petition. Signed petitions to the Crown over the Middlesex Election Affair and the American crisis represent the first nationwide political (as opposed to commercial) popular protests. For the first time in England, the common people moved from behind the traditional mask of anonymity and signed their names to political documents. At the moment in history when these individuals assumed a public identity, the hitherto undifferentiated mass of the people become more personal and far more politically potent. The events of the age of the American Revolution thus signal the further expansion of popular political culture, an increase in the value placed on the individual's political opinion, and the further development of radical techniques of resistance.

Historians, however, have traditionally depicted England as particularly stable in the 1770s and public opinion universally supportive of the crown. This conservative interpretation of English politics is supported by the formidable school of Sir Lewis Namier. Three of Namier's projected volumes on *England in the Age of the American Revolution* were completed by John Brooke, Bernard Donoughue, and Ian Christie, but the volumes for the period 1775–1780 were never attempted. By examining only the general elections of 1774 and 1780 it was possible to conclude that America was not a politically divisive issue. But Donoughue and Christie were largely undiscerning with regard to popular political culture and their conclusions for the period before 1775 and after 1780 were often considered valid for the entire war. Even John Brewer, who has contributed a great deal to the renewed interest in popular culture, depicted the steadily expanding progress of popular politics in the 1760s and 1770s in terms of cycles of advance and regress. But this picture of the halting development of the 'alternative political nation' is partially a result of the neglect of popular politics in the 1770s. It also reflects the neglect of the religion that gave coherence to radical ideology and energy to radical behavior.

The writings of Namier, and most recently the works of Ian Christie, John Cannon, and J. C. D. Clark have supplied convincing arguments for why reform was so slow in coming to England, but it now needs to be explained how the progressive forces in society led to any change at all. While the radicals who worked for reform were in a minority, and while they accomplished little in their lifetime, they do point toward the future and help account for the peaceful movement of England into the modern democratic world. Progressive leaders and their followers were present in only a few boroughs, but however rare, they were the very elements of society that help distinguish England from other nations of Europe. When the true dimensions of radical behavior in the decade of the 1770s are appreciated, a far more steady evolution of radicalism will be seen. This study, therefore, attempts to illumine the religious dimension of the origins of English radicalism during the central and most neglected period of the American Revolution.

The social and political characteristics of Nonconformity throughout the eighteenth century will be outlined, but the book concentrates on the years 1754 to 1784. This period extends over six general elections, and it enables us to examine the Dissenters as government Whigs under George II, and then trace their growing opposition to the government in a highly agitated revolutionary setting. Latent political and social divisions appeared during the revolution that in ordinary, peaceful circumstances remained invisible. The focus upon the period of a single generation is thus necessary for three closely related reasons. The vital records and political documents of thousands of individual Englishmen are available in a wide variety of boroughs for the first time. The Revolution evoked the Dissenters' political opinion, and as a result, they wrote prolifically on the topic; it was a crisis that engaged the best thought of the elite. Finally, to measure the political behavior of the average Dissenter it is necessary to examine an issue that would rivet the attention of the laity; a seismic shock of revolutionary proportions was the only phenomenon that could be expected to affect voters and petitioners in more than one eighteenth-century constituency at a time. But even in the most populous open constituencies, including those first analyzed by Namier, namely, Bristol, Newcastle, Nottingham, and Coventry, and even in a highly politicized revolutionary setting, structural impediments sometimes militated against a clear expression of popular opinion. Unsanctioned forms of political expression were therefore far more responsive to public opinion and political divisions. Where the parliamentary election fails, the popular petition will show that there were indeed two 'parties' in the nation that were widely dispersed, and these groupings reacted to political questions of authority very differently, not in each case involving Whigs and Tories, but often related to the distinction between Churchman and Dissenter, the elite and the lower orders. This book is accordingly organized in three parts: the first part examines the legal hindrances the Nonconformists had to overcome and establishes their political independence through a study of the sermons and political pamphlets of the Dissenting ministers. The second part turns to the established channels of expressing one's political voice and examines parliamentary elections and the behavior of the Dissenting laity in six boroughs. The third part investigates the more sensitive, yet hitherto little known expression of public opinion, the popular petition. These data, available for the first time in the 1770s, allow the earliest possible analysis of religion at the polls in any western country, and they take us into the less familiar terrain of popular social protest.

During the past ten years, the controlling theme of my research has been the question of historical causation; is it possible to demonstrate that religious ideas influence political behavior? For most of this period I struggled under the influence of Sir Lewis Namier, but have come increasingly to believe that if properly qualified, a convincing argument for both the importance and the influence of religious ideology can be sustained. It is not possible, however, to understand religious ideology in isolation from social and economic forces, and thus the eighteenth-century cultural context of Nonconformity has required almost as much attention as the Dissenters' sermons and pamphlets. This broader social context has taken me into territory I was ill-prepared to traverse, and without the expert advice of a variety of scholars, I would have certainly lost my way.

Four scholars in particular have influenced my work. In part one I am indebted to the writings of Colin Bonwick of Keele University who was the first to examine the Dissenters' radical ideology in depth; even at those points where I depart from his interpretation, I am often dependent upon his insights in formulating my thesis. The second part of the book depends a great deal on the innovative methods of analyzing poll books developed by John Phillips. Dr. Phillips gave many weeks of his time to this project, always with a remarkably gracious good will; chapters seven and eight are heavily indebted to his expertise in record linkage and poll book analysis and also upon the technical advice and programming genius of Dr. Charles Wetherell of the Laboratory of Historical Research at the University of California, Riverside. Work at the Laboratory was made possible by a generous grant from the National Endowment for the Humanities. Finally, the organization and much of the inspiration of part three is modeled upon George Rudé's analysis of the Middlesex election petitions and petitioners found in his book, *Wilkes and Liberty*.

I have benefitted a great deal from the counsel and advice of mentors and colleagues who read drafts of this book at various stages of its completion. The comments and corrections of Colin Bonwick, H. T. Dickinson, University of Edinburgh, G. M. Ditchfield, University of Kent, and Michael Watts of the University of Nottingham were invaluable. Each of these scholars helped me to discern weak lines of argumentation and provided useful suggestions for revision; Dr. Watts also allowed me to read and cite an important chapter from his forthcoming, second volume of *The Dissenters*. Frank O'Gorman of the University of Manchester read an early version of the book, and subsequent conversations with him were most helpful; John Money of the University of Victoria and John Walsh of Jesus College, Oxford, read the entire typescript as well and offered highly constructive criticism. Any errors of fact or interpretation that remain are my own. Several scholars helped me with specific technical matters, and they deserve special thanks: Henry P. Ippel of Calvin College, Judith A. Pullen of Bristol, Mrs. D. M. Olsen of Tigard, Oregon, Penelope J. Corfield, Bedford College, University of London, Elizabeth Baigent, School of Geography, Oxford, Clive D. Field, the John Rylands University Library of Manchester, and Mr. Darsie Rawlins of Penn, Buckinghamshire. Frank O'Gorman's *Voters, Patrons, and Parties: The Unreformed Electoral System of Hanoverian England, 1734-1832* (Oxford, 1989) and Peter Virgin's *The Church in an Age of Negligence: Ecclesiastical Structure and Problems of Church Reform, 1700-1840* (Cambridge, 1989) came to hand too late to be utilized in this study, but the former should be consulted on the artisans in relation to independency, and the latter on clerical magistrates.

Numerous librarians and archivists have given generously of their time and energy, in particular, Mrs. Janet Barnes of Dr. Williams's Library, Ms. J. Haskett at the Public Record Office, Kew, Mary E. Williams, City Archivist, Bristol Record Office, and Geoffrey Langley, County Reference Librarian at the Central Library, Bristol. I should also acknowledge the assistance of the staff and librarians of the British Library, the Public Record Office, Chancery Lane, the Institute of Historical Research, the Central Libraries at Newcastle upon Tyne and Colchester, the Liverpool Record Office, the Herbert Art Gallery and Museum, Coventry, and the Nottingham Record Office. In this country I have enjoyed the privilege of examining rare books at the Widener, Houghton, and Andover-Harvard libraries at Harvard University. Yale University Library, and the William L. Clements Library also supplied valuable materials. John Dickason, Librarian of McAlister Library at Fuller Seminary, assisted me a great deal with books on interlibrary loan and materials on microfilm, and the staff of the Huntington Library, particularly Mary Wright, Virginia Renner, and Doris Smedes, were most gracious and helpful. My greatest debt with respect to resources, however, is undoubtedly owed to the Genealogical Society of Salt Lake City; the branch libraries in Pasadena and

Glendale requisitioned hundreds of vital records on microfilm, and I am particularly thankful to Paul F. Smart, supervisor of the British Reference Department at Salt Lake City, and James and Evelyn Allard of Glendale for their kind and consistent interest in my research.

Finally, extracting thousands of names and occupations from parish and non-parochial registers would have been painfully tedious (actually, next to impossible) without a whole cadre of graduate assistants who gave of their time, and kept their eyes on the stretch, for what to them must have often seemed a fruitless endeavor. Janet Gathright heads the list, for she not only spent the most time with these monotonous documents, she shared the pain of my doubts about the feasibility of the project from its inception. Janet also helped set a high standard of accuracy that was followed by Barry Miller, Michael and Dawn Heisler, John and Cynthia Simpson, Kevin Dodd, Arthur Carranza, and Amy Plantinga Pauw. Devin Calhoun graciously volunteered to collate several thousand Anglican parish register entries, and David Wilkerson did an expert job of entering the poll book data into a computer, and to them, and my graduate assistants, I am forever indebted. I should also acknowledge the assistance of Grant Millikan who helped design the graphs. The encouragement that emanates from the word processing department at Fuller Seminary is truly remarkable; Sandy Underwood Bennett, David Sielaff, and Janet Gathright deserve much praise for their typing, editing, and proofreading skills, but even more for their sustaining good humor. The selection of type and the page design and composition reflect the good taste of David Sielaff, and David also produced computerized versions of the two maps. The sabbatical program at Fuller Seminary makes travel and research abroad not only feasible, but enjoyable, and Robert Meye, the Dean of the School of Theology, has always provided me with just the right combination of incentive and encouragement. As always, I am thankful to my wife and family for their support and interest in my work over the years.

List of Tables, Figures, and Maps

Table 2.1	Anglican and Dissenting Occupational Structure at Liverpool	*page* 63
Table 2.2	Anglican and Dissenting Occupational Structure at Newcastle upon Tyne	64
Table 2.3	Anglican and Dissenting Occupational Structure at Kingston upon Hull	65
Table 2.4	Anglican and Dissenting Occupational Structure at Bristol	66
Table 2.5	Dissenting Occupational Structure Compared to the Electorate	67
Table 3.1	Proportion of Dissenters Voting for Whig Candidates Compared to the Anglican Whig Vote	109
Table 6.1	Bristol Election Results: 1754–1784	211
Table 7.1	Straight Party and Cross Voting in Bristol	227
Table 7.2	Partisan and Floating Vote in Bristol	230
Table 7.3	Anglican and Dissenting Clerical Vote in Bristol	234
Figure 7.1	Partisan Vote of Bristol Dissenters and All Other Voters	235
Table 7.4	Proportion of Dissenters and Other Electors Who Maintained or Changed Their Orientation to Government	237
Table 7.5	Denominational Proportion of Vote for Opposition Candidates	238
Figure 7.2	Partisan Vote of Yarmouth Dissenters and All Other Voters	242
Table 7.6	Partisanship of New and Experienced Voters in Bristol	244
Table 7.7	Occupational Structure of the Electorate in Bristol	246
Table 7.8	Occupational Structure of the Electorate in Great Yarmouth	247
Table 7.9	Occupational Structure of Bristol and Great Yarmouth; Nonconformist Voters Compared to Other Voters	248
Table 7.10	Areal Distribution of the Electorate in Bristol	249
Map 7.1	Distribution of Dissenting Population in Bristol	250

Table 7.11	Areal Distribution of the Opposition Vote in Bristol	251
Table 7.12	Areal Distribution of the Partisan Vote as a Proportion of the Total Vote	252
Table 8.1	Newcastle upon Tyne Election Results: 1774–1780	257
Table 8.2	Straight Party and Cross Voting in Newcastle upon Tyne	267
Table 8.3	Consistent Partisan and Floating Vote in Newcastle upon Tyne	269
Table 8.4	Occupational Structure of the Electorate in Newcastle upon Tyne	272
Table 8.5	Liverpool Election Results: 1754–1784	276
Table 8.6	Straight Party and Cross Voting in Liverpool	283
Table 8.7	Consistent Partisan and Floating Vote in Liverpool	284
Figure 8.1	Partisan Vote of Liverpool Dissenters and All Other Voters	286
Table 8.8	Occupational Structure of the Electorate in Liverpool	289
Table 8.9	Kingston upon Hull Election Results: 1768–1784	291
Table 8.10	Straight Party and Cross Voting in Kingston upon Hull	294
Table 8.11	Consistent Party and Floating Vote in Kingston upon Hull	296
Table 8.12	Occupational Structure of the Electorate in Kingston upon Hull	296
Figure 8.2	Partisan Vote of Kingston upon Hull Dissenters and All Other Voters	297
Table 8.13	Colchester Election Results: 1768–1784	300
Table 8.14	Straight Party and Cross Voting in Colchester	302
Table 8.15	Occupational Structure of the Electorate in Colchester	303
Table 8.16	Consistent Support for Candidates in Colchester: 1780–1781	305
Table 8.17	Consistent Support for Candidates in Colchester: 1781–April 1784	305
Table 8.18	Consistent Support for Candidates in Colchester: April 1784–July 1784	306

Table 8.19   Proportion of Support for Government
Candidates by Colchester Residents and
Outvoters   307

Figure 8.3   Partisan Vote of Colchester Dissenters and
All Other Voters   308

Table 8.20   Proportion of Vote by Candidate in Colchester   309

Map 9.1   Geographic Distribution of Petitions and
Addresses Concerning America, 1775–1778   320

Table 10.1   Occupational Structure of Petitioners and
Addressers   374

Table 10.2   Nonconformist Signers of Petitions and
Addresses   390

Table 10.3   Nonconformist Signers of Addresses at Sudbury,
Plymouth, and Barnstaple   395

Table 10.4   Nonconformist Petitioners' and Addressers'
Occupations and All Other Petitioners' and
Addressers' Occupations   400

Table 10.5   Combined Occupations of Nonconformists
and All Other Petitioners' and Addressers'
Occupations   402

Abbreviations

BGAST	*Transactions of the Bristol and Gloucestershire Archeological Society*
BHST	*Transactions of the Baptist Historical Society*
BIHR	*Bulletin of the Institute of Historical Research*
BQ	*The Baptist Quarterly*
Burke Correspondence	*The Correspondence of Edmund Burke.* Gen. ed. Thomas W. Copeland; vols. 3, 4, Cambridge, 1961, 1963, ed. G. H. Guttridge, John A. Woods.
CH	*Church History*
CHST	*Transactions of the Congregational Historical Society*
CJ	*The Journals of the House of Commons*
Commons, 1715-1754	Romney Sedgwick, *The House of Commons, 1715-1754*, 2 vols., London, 1970.
Commons, 1754-1790	Sir Lewis Namier and John Brooke, *The House of Commons, 1754-1790*, 3 vols., London, 1964.
ECS	*Eighteenth-Century Studies*
ED	*Enlightenment and Dissent*
EHR	*English Historical Review*
FHSJ	*Journal of the Friends' Historical Society*
Fortescue	*Correspondence of King George the Third from 1706 to December 1783*, ed. Sir John Fortescue, 6 vols., London, 1927-28.
HJ	*Historical Journal*
HLQ	*Huntington Library Quarterly*
HMC	Historical Manuscripts Commission
HO	Home Office
JBS	*Journal of British Studies*
JEH	*Journal of Ecclesiastical History*
JIH	*Journal of Interdisciplinary History*
JMH	*Journal of Modern History*
JRH	*Journal of Religious History*
MH	*Methodist History*
Parl. Hist.	T. C. Hansard, ed., *The Parliamentary History of England ... to the Year 1803*, London, 1806-20.
PHSEJ	*Journal of the Presbyterian Historical Society of England*
P & P	*Past and Present*
PRO	Public Record Office
RG	Registrar General
TRHS	*Transactions of the Royal Historical Society*
UHST	*Transactions of the Unitarian Historical Society*

Abbreviations

VCH	Victoria County History
WHSP	Proceedings of the Wesley Historical Society
WMQ	William and Mary Quarterly

NEWSPAPERS

Bath Chron.	Bath Chronicle
Bath J.	Bath Journal
Brist. J.	Felix Farley's Bristol Journal
Cam. Chron.	Cambridge Chronicle
Chelm. Col. Chron.	Chelmsford and Colchester Chronicle
Cumb. Pacq.	Cumberland Pacquet
Gen. Eve. Post	General Evening Post
Glos. J.	Gloucester Journal
Hamp. Chron.	Hampshire Chronicle
Kent. Gaz.	Kentish Gazette
Leeds Merc.	Leeds Mercury
Leics. Nott. J.	The Leicester and Nottingham Journal
Lond. Chron.	London Chronicle
Lond. Eve.-Post	London Evening-Post
Lond. Gaz.	London Gazette
Man. Merc.	Manchester Mercury
Morn. Chron.	Morning Chronicle and London Advertiser
New. Chron.	Newcastle Chronicle
North. Merc.	Northampton Mercury
Norw. Merc.	Norwich Mercury
Nott. New. J.	Creswell's Nottingham and Newark Journal
Pub. Adv.	Public Advertiser
Read. Merc.	Reading Mercury and Oxford Gazette
Sal. Win. J.	Salisbury and Winchester Journal
Suss. Week. Adv.	Sussex Weekly Advertiser
Worcs. J.	Berrow's Worcester Journal
York Cour.	York Courant

1

An Introduction to Religion in
Eighteenth-Century Political Culture

The study of religion in the field of eighteenth-century English politics is beginning to enjoy a renaissance. One colloquy on Hanoverian England involving seven specialists reached the consensus that religion was of 'vast importance' to the politics of the period.[1] More recent investigations have also appealed for renewed attention to religion, and valuable work on Nonconformity in the electorate and Anglican political theory is currently emerging.[2] The increasing awareness of the importance of religion arises from its close relation to a wide variety of topics, including the origins of English radicalism, the longstanding debate over party politics, and the role of class in the emergence of modern society. With respect to the first topic, the impact of Nonconformity on pro-Americanism and on the evolution of political radicalism has not been adequately appreciated. To this date, the ideology of the Nonconformists has

---

1 John Cannon (ed.), *The Whig Ascendancy* (New York, 1981), pp. 192–3. No major study of eighteenth-century Nonconformity has appeared since the publication of Anthony Lincoln's *Some Political and Social Ideas of English Dissent, 1763–1800* (Cambridge, 1938).
2 John Phillips, *Electoral Behavior in Unreformed England: Plumpers, Splitters, and Straights* (Princeton, 1982), pp. 287, 293, 296, 305; J. A. W. Gunn, *Beyond Liberty and Property: The Process of Self-Recognition in Eighteenth-Century Political Thought* (Kingston and Montreal, 1983), pp. 164–85; J. C. D. Clark, *English Society 1688–1832: Ideology, Social Structure and Political Practice during the Ancien Regime* (Cambridge, 1985), pp. 31, 43, 195, 320, 375. The term Nonconformity is interchangeable with Dissent and embraced the Presbyterian, Congregationalist, and Baptist denominations. Sometimes Quakers were included in this designation. Little attention will be given in this study to the distinction between Particular (Calvinistic) and General (Arminian) Baptists, or to the Presbyterian drift into Unitarianism; the only Quaker community studied here is that of the Bristol Friends. The major points of difference between the denominations related to polity, where the Presbyterians differed from the Congregationalists and Baptists, and to baptism, where the Presbyterians and the Congregationalists were aligned against the Baptists. These differences seemed insignificant, however, when the denominations were confronted with the restrictive legislation of the Cavalier Parliament. For theology see C. Gordon Bolam et al., *The English Presbyterians from Elizabethan Puritanism to Modern Unitarianism* (Boston, 1968); W. C. Braithwaite, *The Second Period of Quakerism*, 2nd edn (Cambridge, 1961). For the colonies, see William Cathcart, *The Baptists and the American Revolution* (Philadelphia, 1876); Arthur J. Mekeel, *The Relation of the Quakers to the American Revolution* (Washington, 1979).

only been accounted for at the level of the history of ideas, and the question of the place of ideology in relation to economic factors has not been sufficiently examined. The relationship of the Dissenters' social status to the purported oppressive nature of the law has never been studied; in fact, while the contribution of religion to radicalism is often assumed, the entire social question has received only the most superficial attention.

The debate over party in the eighteenth century centers around the question of political principles in relation to organized party continuity. The Dissenters were faithful government supporters in the first half of the century and were viewed by virtually all observers alike as quintessential Whigs. The purported uniformity of their reaction to the government's American policy in the 1770s therefore raises the issue of party continuity in an acute form. Whig historians made Nonconformity the linchpin for their argument that during the 'Tory' years of the reign of George III the 'Whig party' maintained its integrity through the leadership of the Rockinghams at the top, and the Dissenting voters at the bottom. Modern research has effectively demolished the notion of a revived Tory party, but the religious component of a perceived resurgence of authoritarianism in Church and State requires further investigation. The study of Whig historiography in its religious dimension may also contribute to the debate over a deferential versus a participatory model of politics, and it necessitates a discussion of the connection between local issues and national politics.

A fresh examination of religion during the American Revolution will reveal new and abiding divisions in English society, both religious and economic, and these fissures may inform the question of social class and help explain the slow evolution of democracy. While there was no rebellion in England, the populace was sufficiently stirred by events in the colonies to expose the lineaments of society to our view. Through the study of religion and such expressions of resistance to government policy as public petitions, we can discern lines of cohesion in some social groups and divisions between others. For example, in times of political disturbance one might expect to find a strong affinity between those in the legal profession and the clergy of the Established Church, and yet historians of Nonconformity have seldom appreciated the importance of these connections.[3] The common threat of Nonconformity at home and rebellion in the colonies brought the shared interests of law and the Established Church vividly to light, and to many urban artisans, the new expressed unity of these elite groups appeared to be especially threatening. But why did the divisions usually remain latent, and what were the underlying social forces that kept some interest groups united? Part of the answer lies in the religion that was so central to eighteenth-century England.

---

3 Historically, lawyers and clergymen have not always acted together, but on the structural unity of the interests they represent, see the preface to the *Journal of Law and Religion* 1 (1983), by Michael Scherschlight and Wilson Yates.

In the period of the American Revolution, some segments of English society, albeit a minority, contested contemporary perceptions of a hierarchical
religious and social order. This study will demonstrate that in addition to the
Nonconformists, there were a substantial number of Anglicans who opposed
the government, and since political disaffection transcended denominational
distinctions, it is not possible to construe Anglican orthodoxy as a monolith in
support of the State. The study of this minority, however, is not intended to be
understood as offering an interpretation of English society as a whole; although
such a survey will illumine one principal cause of social change, it will place
the establishment in Church and State in a slightly different and more ominous
light than traditional accounts, and it will reveal new elements of freedom and
flexibility within the social order. In short, the study of Nonconformity in the
eighteenth century provides new evidence for the open-ended structure of society that sets England apart from other nations of Europe.[4] The three topics of
radicalism, party continuity, and social divisions will each require considerable
elaboration, and throughout the following discussion the competing themes of
political independence and deference, religious and economic motivation, and
local and national issues will be highlighted.[5]

A fourth concern of this study is the perennial question of the relation
between ideology, motivation, and political behavior. The issue of the causa-
tive role of ideas is an integral part of each of the three major themes of the
book. In the debate over party, one must distinguish between the mental reality
of party, the language of party, and actual party organizations, but the connections between these facets of corporate political action also require attention.
Similarly, in the evolution of radical opposition, the rhetoric of the leaders and
the perceptions and fears of their opponents are important aspects of the
radicals' self-understanding and behavior. Finally, in the ongoing debate over
class and class consciousness, one must have constant recourse to the distinction between the discourse of class on the one hand, and the actual class, or
class-like divisions in society, on the other. In a small number of urban settings
it is possible to bring together evidence that reveals both the ideological orientation and the political behavior of a sizeable minority of people and we can
thereby examine in some detail the interdependence of eighteenth-century
political and religious ideas and political action.

4 On this highly debated issue compare C. B. Macpherson, *The Political Theory of
Possessive Individualism* (Oxford, 1962), and Roy Porter, *English Society in the Eighteenth Century* (London, 1981), who find more openness than Lawrence and Jeanne C.
Fawter Stone, *An Open Elite? England 1540–1880* (Oxford, 1984), John Cannon, *Aristocratic Century: The Peerage of Eighteenth-Century England* (Cambridge, 1984), and
Clark, *English Society.*
5 H. James Henderson, 'Quantitative Approaches to Party Formation in the United States
Congress: A Comment', *WMQ*, 3rd ser., 30 (1973), 307 for helpful statements concerning the need for caution when using dichotomous classification.

The word religion is used in this study to denote a phenomenon that is much broader than doctrine or theology. Beliefs about God may be neither clearly formulated nor faithfully adhered to, and in this inchoate form they are often of secondary importance to politics; where religion influences political behavior, habit and convention are often more important than doctrine. Religion, to be sure, refers to conviction, but convictions are sometimes held without a clear or convincing rational basis.[6] The Dissenters, however, were extremely clear on two pivotal doctrines: the authority of the Bible as against the authority of tradition, and the nature of the gathered Church as independent from the Establishment. Christians of all denominations shared certain basic assumptions about these doctrines, but the Dissenters' distinctive emphases gave their teachings special relevance with regard to both their self-identity and their political behavior. The Dissenters' congregational polity provided a longstanding and abiding orientation against a hierarchical conception of society; their more egalitarian religious practice anticipated by many years their radical opposition to political oppression. When at length they turned against the government, the Dissenters claimed to derive their authority directly from God and his revealed Word, as well as their ecclesiastical tradition. While some so-called 'rational' Dissenters derived their political views in part from their heterodox theology, the common heritage of a radically separated ecclesiastical polity was controlling for both the 'rational' and the orthodox alike.

The strength of the Dissenters' conviction is accounted for at one level by the human capacity to attach values to God, God's 'revelation', or 'eternal' truth.[7] But the Dissenters' political convictions were also held firmly because of their experience of legal repression; in many locales they were excluded from the inner circles of power. The Dissenters' distinctive experience in legal, social, and political matters thus interacted with theological and ecclesiological principles, and the product was far more potent than private religious beliefs. A Dissenter need not have been particularly pious or theologically acute for his religion to have had a profound impact on his politics. Religion should not be reduced to social causes, but as James Obelkevich has said, it is unintelligible apart from them.[8] The religion of the Dissenters is therefore understood in this

6 The ideological roots to Dissenting politics are both secular and religious; many Dissenting ministers were indebted to Locke, and most of them praised his work, but Locke himself was heavily indebted to religion. See John Dunn, *The Political Thought of John Locke* (Cambridge, 1969), pp. 51, 121, 207, 213. In addition, the Dissenters' specific political convictions were also informed directly by reading the Bible, as we shall see in chap. 4 below.

7 See Bruce Lincoln, 'Notes Toward a Theory of Religion and Revolution', in Bruce Lincoln (ed.), *Religion, Rebellion, Revolution* (New York, 1985), pp. 266–8 for a good recent review of the sociology of religion.

8 James Obelkevich, *Religion and Rural Society: South Lindsey 1825–1875* (Oxford, 1976), p. 313. George Rudé's seminal *Ideology and Popular Protest* (New York, 1980), pp. 13–38 provides a theoretical framework for my understanding of the relationship between theology (Rudé's 'inherent ideas') and self-identity related to the social setting

study as a set of firmly held convictions about the nature of moral and political authority; these convictions differed from other people's political convictions by their deep grounding in different ecclesiastical, political, and social experience.

The concept of revolution as an explanatory device is as controversial as the concept of religion, but it is used in this study merely as the conventional means of referring to the colonial events of 1765–83. Recently, scholars have examined the distinction between revolution and rebellion with fruitful results.[9] There were scattered episodes of disorderly behavior in England, including riots and strikes, but clearly the nation did not experience anything approximating a classic revolution. If, however, eighteenth-century English Dissenters never advocated an armed uprising and never overtly rebelled, their thought and actions were deemed rebellious by many observers, and they did contribute directly to the evolution of radical ideology and the development of advanced political methods; strictly speaking, they manifested the characteristics of a religion of resistance rather than a religion of revolution. The terms 'radical' and 'radically' were used in the eighteenth century in the sense of going to the root of things, and the words were applied both to political ideas and political structures. Clearly, then, if ideas can be described as 'radical', we can speak without anachronism of the origins of English 'radicalism', though to be sure, the latter term only emerged in the nineteenth century. The Dissenting ministers and their congregations were genuinely radical insofar as they sought to reveal the root of contemporary problems by locating the source of their difficulties in what they considered the oppressive social and political structures of Hanoverian England.[10]

('derived ideas') and the way the two converge to form popular ideologies.

9 Lincoln, 'Notes Toward a Theory', pp. 268–81. J. C. D. Clark, *Revolution and Rebellion* (Cambridge, 1986), pp. 3–4 prefers rebellion over revolution, and suggests that even during the American crisis there was little that was genuinely revolutionary in English politics, pp. 97–8.

10 I utilize here the rather loose, contextualized understanding of radicalism as the ideology of the excluded who seek to change existing political structures. John Brewer, *Party Ideology and Popular Politics at the Accession of George III* (Cambridge, 1976), pp. 19–20. Brewer's work on the emergence of radical activity in the 1760s is the best general treatment of the early period; see also his 'English Radicalism in the Age of George III', in J. G. A. Pocock (ed.), *Three British Revolutions: 1641, 1688, 1776* (Princeton, 1980), pp. 338–9. For earlier, sporadic Tory radical activity and ideology see Marie Peters, 'The "Monitor" on the Constitution, 1755–65: New Light on the Ideological Origins of English Radicalism', *EHR*, 86 (1971), 706–27; Linda Colley, 'Eighteenth-Century English Radicalism Before Wilkes', *TRHS*, 5th ser., 31 (1981), 1–19, esp. pp. 15–16 on the radical Tory contribution to Wilkite radicalism; and H. T. Dickinson, 'The Precursors of Political Radicalism in Augustan Britain', pp. 63–84 in Clyve Jones (ed.), *Britain in the First Age of Party, 1680–1750: Essays Presented to Geoffrey Holmes* (London, 1987), who examines recent literature. For the complexity of the synthesis of Wilkite radicalism and the breakdown of religious continuities, see Philip Jenkins, 'Jacobites and Freemasons in Eighteenth-Century Wales', *Welsh History Review* 9 (1979), 399–404; for social continuities with the 1740s, see Nicholas Rogers, 'Aristocratic Clientage, Trade, and Independency: Popular Politics in Pre-Radical West-

Nonconformity, however, was not a unified movement and neither was radicalism.[11] The majority of Dissenters were clearly pro-American in orientation, but many were evidently indifferent to political matters, and a few were outspoken defenders of the government's American policy. Similarly, while historians continue to disagree over the nature, extent, and significance of radicalism, they have increasingly come to recognize the complexity of the movements between 1760 and 1790, their loose associations, and the diverse motives and aims of the leaders. Some studies, for example, have emphasized the ideological and religious motivation of radicals, while others have greatly illumined the social and economic context of radicalism.[12] This book does examine unifying themes and structures, but it makes no attempt to survey the entire variety of opinion and movements within the broad, complex, and sometimes contradictory history of radicalism. The focus, instead, is upon the contribution of urban Dissent to a form of radicalism that reached deeply into the ranks of skilled urban artisans. Though religion is the primary concern of these pages, the quantitative data from the petitions and addresses provides confirmation of the qualitative evidence adduced by John Brewer and others on the social and political fissures that were opening afresh in the 1760s and 1770s.

minster', *P&P* 61 (1973), 70–106.

11 I began to document the diversity of Dissent in 'Whigs and Nonconformists: "Slumbering Radicalism" in English Politics, 1739–1789', *ECS* 9 (1975), 1–27; for the divisions of Dissent over specific issues see John Stephens, 'The London Ministers and Subscription, 1772–1779', *ED* 1 (1982), 50, 52, 54–5, 57; John Seed, 'Gentlemen Dissenters: The Social and Political Meanings of Rational Dissent in the 1770s and 1780s', *HJ* 28 (1985), 301, 323; and K. R. M. Short, 'The English Regium Donum', *EHR* 84 (1969), 63.

12 For ideology, see Colin Bonwick, *English Radicals and the American Revolution* (Chapel Hill, 1977); and John Gascoigne, 'Anglican Latitudinarianism and Political Radicalism in the Late Eighteenth Century', *History* 71 (1986), 22–38; Clark claims to have gone deeper than others in locating a source of political disaffection in heterodoxy. See *English Society*, pp. 281, 292–3, 311, 332–3, 373–4, 378, 423, and J. C. D. Clark, 'On Hitting the Buffers: The Historiography of England's Ancien Regime. A Response', *P&P* 117 (1987), 204. But Clark and Gascoigne are only the most recent in a long line of scholars who have located the intellectual origins of radical ideas in heresy. Caroline Robbins, *The Eighteenth-Century Commonwealthman* (New York, 1968), pp. 335–56; Russell E. Richey, 'The Origins of British Radicalism: The Changing Rationale for Dissent', *ECS* 7 (1973–4), 191; Bernard Semmel, *The Methodist Revolution* (New York, 1973), p. 70; H. T. Dickinson, *Liberty and Property: Political Ideology in Eighteenth-Century Britain* (New York, 1977), pp. 197–205; Donald Davie, 'Disaffection of the Dissenters under George III', pp. 347, 349 in Paul J. Korshin and Robert R. Allen (eds.), *Greene and Centennial Studies* (Charlottesville, 1984). This debate will be reviewed in a forthcoming article entitled 'The Ideological Origins of English Radicalism: Heresy, Orthodoxy, and Polity'. For more material motives, see Brewer, 'English Radicals in the Age of George III', especially pp. 334, 356; Brewer concentrates on the pervasive growth of credit, the changing nature of the tax burden, and the increasing importance of statute law.

NONCONFORMITY, PRO-AMERICANISM, AND THE EVOLUTION OF ENGLISH RADICALISM

The importance of Nonconformity for the origins of modern radicalism is now widely recognized. Anthony Lincoln's early intuitive insights on the genius of Dissenting thought were elaborated more fully by Caroline Robbins and worked out in detail by Colin Bonwick.[13] Bonwick demonstrated the profound influence of the American Revolution on both Nonconformity and the origins of English radicalism and fully analyzed the political thought of Richard Price, Joseph Priestley, James Burgh, and Newcome Cappe. The Dissenters were friends of America and advocates of parliamentary reform, but while they were 'radical', it is now clear that the majority were neither levelers nor republicans.[14] Historians commonly make a distinction between the old, Commonwealthman radicalism of the 1760s and 1770s, and the new, more thoroughgoing artisan radicalism of the 1790s; this categorization represents a 'major faultline' in the history of radicalism.[15] According to the prevailing conserva-

13 Lincoln, *Some Political and Social Ideas of English Dissent*; Robbins, *The Eighteenth-Century Commonwealthman*; see the chap. 'The Contribution of Nonconformity', pp. 221–71; Colin Bonwick, 'English Dissenters and the American Revolution', in H. C. Allen and Roger Thompson (eds.), *Contrast and Connection: Bicentennial Essays in Anglo-American History* (Athens, Ohio, 1976), pp. 88–112; and *English Radicals*. On the influence of the American Revolution on English radicalism, see also Margaret and James Jacob (eds.), *The Origins of Anglo-American Radicalism* (London, 1984).

14 Bonwick led the way in this reinterpretation. See *English Radicals*, pp. 21–3, 53, 100, 101, 108; 'English Dissenters and the American Revolution', pp. 106–7, 109. For similar views, see Ian Christie, *Wilkes, Wyvill and Reform* (London, 1962); and Clark, *Revolution and Rebellion*, pp. 97–8.

15 Bonwick, *English Radicals*, p. xxi. Bonwick distinguishes between (1) Commonwealthman radicals, (2) Wilkite radicals, (3) Bentham's Utilitarianism, and (4) Paine's working-class radicalism, *English Radicals*, p. xiv. Similarly, Brewer distinguishes between the Dissenters and the Commonwealthman tradition on the one hand, and the Society of Supporters of the Bill of Rights and the Wilkites on the other, 'English Radicalism', p. 343. The paradigm that contrasts the old radicalism of the Commonwealthmen and Wilkites with the new artisan radicalism of the 1790s is pervasive. See Bonwick, *English Radicals*, pp. ix, 18–19, 131–2, 134, 163, 216–19. Bonwick's thought is based on the standard studies of Simon Maccoby, *English Radicalism, 1786–1832* (London, 1955); Carl B. Cone, *The English Jacobins* (New York, 1968); E. C. Black, *The Association* (Cambridge, Mass., 1963); E. P. Thompson, *The Making of the English Working Class* (New York, 1963); and John Cannon, *Parliamentary Reform, 1640–1832* (Cambridge, 1973). On p. xiv Bonwick does say that Wilkism was a bridge between the Commonwealthman tradition and artisan radicalism, to the extent that Wilkes utilized Commonwealthman ideology and involved artisans. But the contrasts are emphasized over the connections. Recent studies accept this viewpoint. See Joseph O. Baylen and Norbert J. Gossman (eds.), *Biographical Dictionary of Modern British Radicals* (London, 1979), pp. 2–3; Edward Royle and James Walvin, *English Radicals and Reformers, 1760–1848* (Lexington, Ky., 1982), do a little with continuities, but still date 'the rise of popular radicalism' from the 1790s, pp. 48–9. Similarly, H. T. Dickinson sees contrasts in *Liberty and Property*, pp. 232, 240, and especially pp. 246–7, but observes some continuities in 'The Rights of Man in Britain: From the Levellers to the Utopian Socialists', pp. 78–9, 82–3 in Günter Birtsch (ed.), *Grund- und Freiheitsrechte von der ständischen zur spätbürgerlichen Gesellschaft* (Göttingen, 1987). Clark, *English Society*, pp. 290–345. John Sainsbury, *Disaffected*

tive interpretation, Commonwealthman radicals were characterized by moderation, both with respect to their ideas and their political methods. Dissenters
were middle and even upper class in orientation and defended the social stratification and hierarchical structure of English society. Since they were themselves persons of property, they 'shared the values of a socially differentiated
community' and thereby had little to say about social inequality. They championed the legal and constitutional equality of right, were strongly loyal to the
State, and were dedicated to working within its constitutional framework.[16]

Other historians have argued that radical ideology was more advanced and
that its popular manifestations were more disruptive. The studies of George
Rudé, John Brewer, and H. T. Dickinson departed from the more conservative
interpretation by stressing the innovative aspects of the radicals' thought and
the deeper social penetration of their views. H. T. Dickinson, for example,
contrasted the radicalism of the 1760s in its extra-parliamentary character to the
earlier Country opposition and emphasized the leaders' willingness to go
further than the Revolution settlement. Like Bonwick, he relied on the most
well-known intellectuals, but he found a more thoroughgoing radicalism in this
period because he also examined newspapers, as did Brewer.[17] The regional
and local studies of John Money, Nicholas Rogers, Peter Marshall, and
Thomas Knox also revealed a more advanced and more influential radicalism,
though these reassessments have dealt mostly with the radicalism associated
with Wilkes, rather than the Dissenters and Commonwealthmen. The evidence
adduced in the present study provides additional support for this second interpretation of radicalism.

Patriots: London Supporters of Revolutionary America 1769–1782 (Kingston and
   Montreal, 1987), having discussed the London artisans' radical activity, hints at the
   connections with the artisan radicalism of the 1790s, pp. 164–5.
16 Bonwick, *English Radicals*, pp. 243, 11, 15–18, 35, 47, 95, 124, 256, 260, 265; Clark,
   English Society, pp. 289–93; Sainsbury, *Disaffected Patriots*, pp. 80–2. The idea of a
   moderate religious influence in politics is also characteristic of studies of religion in the
   colonies. Alan Heimert, *Religion and the American Mind* (Cambridge, Mass., 1966),
   p. 361, notes the moderation of the theologically liberal. See also Rhys Isaac, *The
   Transformation of Virginia 1740–1790* (Chapel Hill, 1982), p. 193, on the Baptists.
17 Dickinson, *Liberty and Property*, pp. 195–6, 204–5. Much of the divergence of
   interpretation is related to the kind of evidence examined and whether the study focuses
   upon politics at court or popular politics. Compare, for example, Ian Christie, *Wilkes,
   Wyvill and Reform*, with John Brewer, *Party Ideology and Popular Politics*, and more
   recently, Brewer, 'English Radicalism in the Age of George III', where he deals at length
   with the middling orders, with Ian Christie, *Wars and Revolutions, Britain: 1760–1815*
   (Cambridge, Mass., 1982), pp. 63–79. Sainsbury finds socio-economic divisions in
   London, but argues that organized support for the colonies, with 'few exceptions' like
   Bristol, was confined to London, *Disaffected Patriots*, pp. 69, 164. Unfortunately, this
   book went into print with reference to only two books, and no articles, published since
   1978; the studies of Thomas Knox, Peter Marshall, John Phillips, and Linda Colley are
   ignored, and John Money's studies are unassimilated. Ironically, these more sophisticated local studies have done the most to undermine the Namierian approach.

Commonwealthman ideology is properly distinguished from the earlier Tory and Country opposition. On the one hand, several facets of Commonwealthman radicalism were similar, if not identical, to the Country opposition of the Walpole years; for example, a desire for greater accountability in government through such measures as the removal of placemen from Parliament and more frequent elections was common to both traditions.[18] The rhetoric of independence and the constant denouncing of corruption were also characteristic of both. But beginning with the Dissenting radicals of the period of the American Revolution one finds a more emphatic insistence on the contractarian basis to government and a greater emphasis on popular participation, particularly in associations.[19] Increasingly, the radicals stressed the independence of the individual elector, and more emphasis was put on a Member's responsibility to his constituents (in a way that Edmund Burke found totally unacceptable). There was a heightened suspicion of those in authority, particularly the magistrate and the judge, and a greater willingness to openly criticize them. The attempt to implement the principle of accountability, according to John Brewer, gave some coherence to the radicals' various grievances.[20]

In most previous studies of radicalism, however, Commonwealthman ideology is typified by its limited appeal to the masses. In fact, historians have argued that the moderation of the radical intellectuals is directly related to their narrow appeal for support to the middle and upper levels of society. Although the Wilkes affair presaged a 'new phase' in the development of Commonwealthman radicalism characterized by the attraction of more widespread public opinion, it continues to be widely assumed that the political movements of the 1760s and 1770s were unrelated to industrial unrest.[21] Similarly, the American

---

18 In *Party Ideology and Popular Politics* Brewer first drew attention to the Wilkites' inheritance from Toryism. For the significance of the County tradition for radicalism and an illuminating discussion of similarities and differences, see Brewer, 'English Radicalism in the Age of George III', pp. 329–31. Colley emphasizes the similarities in the tradition, particularly in extra-parliamentary organizations, clubs, and the desire for parliamentary reform, 'Eighteenth-Century English Radicalism', 6–7, 11, 13–14. See also Nicholas Rogers, 'The Urban Opposition to Whig Oligarchy, 1720–60', pp. 136, 145 in Jacob and Jacob, *The Origins of Anglo-American Radicalism*. J. G. A. Pocock, 'The Varieties of Whiggism from Exclusion to Reform', pp. 225, 245, 251–2, 256–8, in *Virtue, Commerce, and History* (Cambridge, 1985), discusses the interpretation of Tory and Commonwealthman radicalism but sees in the 1770s, a shift 'away from the polity of independent powers and toward the sovereignty of popular will', p. 258.
19 Brewer, 'English Radicalism', pp. 350–1.
20 *Ibid.*, p. 353. The use of Country ideology by the radicals of the 1760s and 1770s concerning credit was adapted to the circumstances of the urban setting; it did not involve a nostalgic look backwards, but a pragmatic concern to reduce business risk, p. 337. See also pp. 344–5 on continuing use of Country ideology, but the addition of new content for old terms.
21 Bonwick, *English Radicals*, pp. 117–18, basing his thought on Rudé, *Wilkes and Liberty*, pp. 103–4; Christie, *Wilkes, Wyvill and Reform*, pp. 223–4. Brewer, 'English Radicalism', offers a more balanced perspective, yet also stresses radicalism in the middle ranks, and Dissent's failure to engage in the 'cut and thrust' of politics, pp. 331–2,

crisis was not a socially divisive issue. Even though a consistent pro-Americanism was publicized by the Dissenting pulpit thundering forth the rhetoric of liberty, this language was unable to stir the populace at large. The leading authorities on English radicalism have emphasized that pro-Americanism involved only a handful of leaders and never reached deeply into the populace. George Rudé put the matter categorically and his viewpoint was subsequently accepted by other leading scholars: 'Pro-Americanism seems to have been confined to higher social circles and does not appear as an expression of popular opinion.' John Sainsbury has recently argued that the divisions between pro-Americans and loyalists in London were based 'to a large extent' on socio-economic differences, but he believed these divisions were confined to the metropolis. Thus even those scholars who have searched deepest for a social basis to radicalism have found little evidence for it in the mid-1770s. Colin Bonwick concluded that the radicals 'spoke for the middle orders of society, but their intended constituents resolutely ignored their call'.[22] In this view, the pulpit had little if any impact on public opinion; the Dissenting laity, in short, were unmoved by the progressive thought of the intellectuals. When Bonwick wrote in 1977 he could say with certainty that Manchester 'remained firmly loyal to the government' though he was puzzled over the loyalty of Nottingham and Taunton, both of which contained 'large dissenting populations'. He knew that London, Bristol, Liverpool, and Birmingham were divided, but he concluded ruefully that the majority of the people even in these cities supported the government.[23] As late as 1780, during the Association movement, 'There was no suggestion of any frustration of the lower orders: the days of artisan, let alone working-class radicalism were still in the future.'[24] The conservative interpretation of radicalism in the age of the American Revolution is thus characterized by three related themes: radicals were at once moderate in political ideology and conservative in terms of social goals, and their political methods

---

342-3. See also for modification of the conservative viewpoint, Walter J. Shelton, *English Hunger and Industrial Disorders: A Study of Social Conflict during the First Decade of George III's Reign* (Toronto, 1973), and John Stevenson, *Popular Disturbances in England, 1700–1870* (London, 1979).

22 George Rudé, 'The London Mob of the Eighteenth Century', in *Paris and London in the Eighteenth Century: Studies in Popular Protest* (New York, 1973), p. 315. Sainsbury, *Disaffected Patriots*, pp. 69, 119, 164. Bonwick, *English Radicals*, p. 244; see also p. 101. Dickinson, *Liberty and Property*, p. 246. Dickinson refers to the radicalization of 'the middle and lower orders', but adduces little evidence, 'The Precursors of Political Radicalism', p. 81. The opposition of the urban middling orders has been studied by Nicholas Rogers in a series of important articles; see, especially, 'The Urban Opposition to Whig Oligarchy 1720–60', pp. 132–48 in Jacob and Jacob, *The Origins of Anglo-American Radicalism.*

23 Bonwick, *English Radicals*, pp. 85, 274 note 37. Clark, *English Society*, pp. 344, 369.

24 Bonwick, *English Radicals*, pp. 131–2 citing Herbert Butterfield, 'The Yorkshire Association and the Crisis of 1779–80', in *TRHS*, 4th ser., 29 (1947), 72; Christie, *Wilkes, Wyvill and Reform*, p. 224; Cannon, *Parliamentary Reform*, p. 95.

were not sophisticated enough to provoke a response in the population at large.[25] They were, in short, an elite middle-class intelligentsia without a following.

This interpretation of moderate, Commonwealthman radicalism has not been seriously challenged because it is widely assumed that English society was fundamentally united during the American Revolution. Detailed research on parliamentary constituencies has only served to strengthen this viewpoint. Most work on constituency histories has been dominated by Sir Lewis Namier and his colleagues, so that it is commonly believed that what political divisions existed were mainly local in scope.[26] The belief that politics was in most cases properly confined to the local setting was pressed on even the largest, most open constituencies in England.[27] The psephological studies of the electorate have modified this dominant local orientation, but, somewhat surprisingly, the poll books themselves have to this date corroborated the notion of a unified society. Studies of the electorate in Norwich, Maidstone, Northampton, Lewes, Great Yarmouth, Southampton, and Bridgwater reveal no significant socio-economic divisions during the American Revolution.[28]

A second reason for the dominance of the conservative interpretation is that the study of radical ideology has been confined largely to the thought of a few prominent intellectuals. To this date, historians have only examined the theologically liberal ministers and therefore 'Dissenting political ideology' really

25 Not all of these elements appear in every study of radicalism; Sainsbury, for example, appreciates the advanced ideology of the London radicals, but he thinks that it had little impact outside the metropolis. But the Dissenters' political impotence is everywhere assumed; Robbins, *The Eighteenth-Century Commonwealthman*, pp. 225, 258; John Sainsbury, 'The Pro-Americans of London, 1769–1782', *WMQ*, 3rd ser., 35 (1978), 450; *Disaffected Patriots*, p. 81; Dickinson, *Liberty and Property*, p. 223; Brewer, 'English Radicalism', pp. 342–3; Geoffrey Holmes traces the absence of 'popular radicalism' in the eighteenth century to the lack of 'religious dynamism', *The Whig Ascendancy*, p. 194. As a graduate student I was not only influenced by Namier's two books on eighteenth-century politics; it is fair to say that I was under their influence. As a result, my first publication on Nonconformity and politics almost completely discounted the importance of ideology in contributing to political behavior. 'Whigs and Nonconformists', 24.

26 See the documentation in the introduction of James Bradley, *Popular Politics and the American Revolution in England* (Macon, Ga., 1986).

27 Ian Christie, *The End of North's Ministry, 1780–1782* (London, 1958), on Bristol, Liverpool, and Newcastle upon Tyne, pp. 82, 128, 142, 153; and on Norwich, *Commons, 1754–1790*, 1: 342.

28 Phillips, *Electoral Behavior*, pp. 263, 268, 270, 275, 144, 145; Bradley, *Popular Politics and the American Revolution in England*, Table 7.1. Thomas Knox, 'Popular Politics and Provincial Radicalism: Newcastle upon Tyne, 1769–1785', *Albion* 11 (1979), 224–41; 'Wilkism and the Newcastle Election of 1774', *Durham University Journal* 72 (1979–80), 23–37, finds some elements of socio-economic cleavage. Peter Marshall was the first to suggest that the American crisis divided society on an economic basis: 'Manchester and the American Revolution', *Bulletin of the John Rylands University Library of Manchester* 62 (1979), 173. Clark, *English Society*, pp. 112, 370, makes a good deal of his argument depend on the social cohesion of the electorate.

amounts to the ideology of a small heterodox elite centered mostly in London.[29] But many Dissenting ministers in the provinces not only articulated radical ideology; these preachers helped popularize and legitimize political dissent. The Nonconformists thereby acted as a political catalyst that gave focus and force to undefined discontent even among those who did not share their religious views. Research, however, has not yet extended to the ministers in the provinces, and as a result, their contribution to urban radicalism has remained obscure; thus a selective reading of moderate radical ideology has indirectly corroborated the notion of an economically and socially unified society. These oversights have had a profound effect on the historiography of radicalism: because there have been so few hints of socio-economic conflict, scholars have failed to relate advanced political ideology to socio-economic conflict. And since the mid-1770s have seemed so placid, there appeared to be no compelling grounds for linking the radicalism of the Middlesex election affair with the emergence of the Association movement. With the one exception of the radical movement in London, discontinuities have been emphasized over continuities.

As a result of these lacunae, no account of the origins of modern radicalism convincingly relates social discontent to religion and ideology. Bonwick utilized the sociological concept of 'internal aliens' to explain the Dissenters' progressive political stance, but his aliens were not socially alienated and their politics had little impact on the laity. Edward Thompson, who was primarily interested in economic motivation, also grasped the importance of religion, but because he found little evidence of actual political conflict, he took refuge in the image of a sleeping giant and described the radical Dissenters in this period as dormant, and 'slumbering'.[30] The neglect of the precise role of religion and religious ideology in relation to the socio-economic status of the radicals has come about in part through a methodological oversight; the study of political ideology has largely been separated from the study of behavior. Where we do find research on political ideology in relationship to popular political behavior, it has invariably been carried out at too general a level. Commonly the attempt is made to relate the two at the national level, and while numerous studies have illumined political ideology, the tendency in these works is to neglect people's behavior. For example, those scholars who focused on popular literature knew of the progressive preaching of Joshua Toulmin of Taunton and George Walker

---

29 Verner W. Crane, 'The Club of Honest Whigs: Friends of Science and Liberty', *WMQ*, 3rd ser., 23 (1966), 210–33. Richey, 'The Origins of British Radicalism', 179; Seed, 'Gentlemen Dissenters', 299–325; Clark, *English Society*, pp. 318, 320.
30 Bonwick, *English Radicals*, p. 12. Bonwick's acceptance of the impact of economic motivation is implicit in his book, but never consciously worked out. The higher social status of Quaker merchants, for example, led them to passivity with respect to government policy, pp. 87, 190; Thompson, *The Making of the English Working Class*, p. 30.

of Nottingham, and yet they despaired over the Dissenters' apparent lack of behavioral consistency and passed over the Taunton and Nottingham petitions for peace in 1775 signed by these ministers and their congregations. This inattention to local history led to a premature and highly misleading conclusion concerning political and economic divisions in society.

The preoccupation with literary sources and ideology means that the extent of pro-Americanism in the nation has been seriously underestimated and the penetration of radical ideology into the lower orders of society has not been fathomed. We can now show that the most important centers of Nonconformity in England, including Manchester, Nottingham, and Taunton, the western center of Commonwealthman ideology, were thoroughly riven over America, both religiously and socially, and Dissenting ideology was thus far from spent. On the other hand, studies of the political behavior of individuals have examined regions and even cities in detail, but these studies have been inclined to discount the importance of ideology. The consistent behavior of Norwich Dissenting voters, for example, can now be proven, but the preaching of the Norwich radical Baptist, Rees David, has gone unnoticed, and as a result, scholars have doubted whether religious ideology could account for electoral behavior.[31] However, both the ideas of the Dissenting elite and the intensity with which these ideas were held can be measured with some precision. It is possible in a variety of parliamentary boroughs to identify specific interest groups and connect the ideology of the leaders of these groups to the electoral behavior of the individuals who followed them. In addition, the absence of socio-economic divisions in the poll books does not mean that society was unified. Valuable as they are, poll books turn out to be too blunt an instrument to discern abiding economic and religious divisions in society.

The topic of radicalism raises the broader issue of the nature and extent of political divisions in English society during the last half of the eighteenth century. Extra-parliamentary political activity in the 1760s through the 1790s has been examined by John Brewer, John Money, Thomas Knox, John Phillips, and John Sainsbury, but abiding skepticism concerning the vitality of popular political culture prompts renewed attention to the decade of the 1770s.[32] The reality of popular protest in this period was documented in a previous introductory study, but it was not possible in that book to examine the

---

31 Examples of studies focused on ideology are Bonwick, *English Radicals*, Brewer, *Party Ideology and Popular Politics*, Dickinson, *Liberty and Property*, Gunn, *Beyond Liberty and Property*, and Clark, *English Society*. Regional and local studies are John Money, *Experience and Identity: Birmingham and the West Midlands, 1760–1800* (Manchester, 1977), and Phillips, *Electoral Behavior*. In his two articles on Newcastle upon Tyne, Thomas Knox has done the best work available on ideology and behavior; see also Sainsbury, *Disaffected Patriots*, pp. 8–15, 118–19; Bonwick, *English Radicals*, p. 85; Phillips, *Electoral Behavior*, p. 291.

32 Clark, *English Society*, pp. 346–8, 424; *Revolution and Rebellion*, pp. 98–100.

social and religious nature of the divisions in detail.[33] The present work confirms and extends my earlier findings and relates economic divisions in society to radical ideology. The religious dynamism that stimulated urban radicalism, and the economic inequalities and differences in security and status that sustained radical behavior, will now be examined at length. This study will thus attempt to measure the nature and extent of radicalism at four interrelated levels: radical ideology (particularly in sermons), contemporary perceptions, the radical behavior of the leaders of the petitioning agitation, and socioeconomic divisions.

The moderate radical ideology of the London Dissenting elite was not always representative of Dissenting ministers in the provinces; several of the provincial Dissenters went beyond the question of legal right to address the more probing issue of economic oppression and social injustice. A few of the more radical ministers even identified themselves with the oppressed poor of English society and their preaching had a direct and demonstrable impact on public opinion. In addition to the Dissenters' sermons and pamphlets, massive collections of election literature, including popular songs, broadsides, and squibs, will show that local politics, and local political and social divisions, were intimately connected to the political and constitutional issues associated with the American crisis. These handbills, posters, and notices, distributed and tacked up throughout the cities, were one important means by which people assimilated political ideas; earlier research on the electorate that implied that newspapers exhaust our information concerning articulate political awareness has seriously misled us.

The conservative interpretation has also obscured the genuine radical quality of opposition to the government in the mid-1770s at the perceptual level. The sermons and pamphlets of the Dissenting elite only touch the surface of the political discontent and suspicion felt at the local level. Events in the colonies in the spring and summer of 1775 deeply stirred people in England; even loyal Dissenters in this setting were suspected of sedition, and English pro-Americans were viewed with utter abhorrence and detestation. Contemporaries clearly interpreted the signing of petitions against the government's policy of coercion as a considerable political risk. The royal Proclamation of 23 August that declared the colonists in a state of rebellion demanded the divulgence of full information concerning 'all persons who shall be found carrying on Correspondence with, or in any Manner or Degree aiding or abetting the persons now in open Arms and Rebellion against our Government'. Numerous newspaper editorials expressed the opinion that extra-parliamentary meetings organized to petition against government policy fell under the stipulation of 'aiding and abetting' the colonists and were as a result invariably treasonous.[34]

33 Bradley, *Popular Politics and the American Revolution in England.*
34 For a full discussion of the risk involved in petitioning, see *ibid.*, pp. 112–17.

It was widely believed that one of the major causes of rebellion in the colonies was found in the factions at home that encouraged the spirit of opposition.

A second measure of the nature of radicalism is thereby supplied by eighteenth-century opinion; loyalists viewed English pro-Americans as extremely radical. Expressions of opposition to the government and social disorder of any kind were immediately linked in people's minds with the rebellious colonies. For example, in the midst of the violent sailors' strike in Liverpool in August, 1775, one correspondent wrote 'I could not think but we had a Boston here and I fear this is only the beginning of our sorrows.' Later, in the fall of 1775, signers of the county petition in favor of peace at Liverpool were called 'rebels to their King and Country', and 'licentious Sons of Liberty'. At Coventry, pro-Americans in 1775 were depicted as 'patrons of sedition' who advanced 'pernicious principles', and a year later, the pro-government party was still threatened not only by the 'Horror of a Distant Rebellion', but by the 'unparalleled outrages of a Domestic Insurrection'.[35] An editorial in the *Newcastle Courant* observed that 'A set of noisy turbulent spirits in this town, under the denomination (but highly prostituted character) of Patriots, have lately set on foot a petition to the throne, on the present state of American affairs, and got some hundreds of persons of the lower rank, and some of the late disappointed electioneering party here to sign it.' In the midst of the petitioning agitation in London, there were rumors that a Dissenting minister by the name of Riley had been conveyed to Newgate on charges of 'treasonable practices against the State', and one disaffected editor commented: 'our Newgate seems to be converted into a French Bastile'. Such perceptions as these threatened violence and sometimes actually turned violent. At Exeter, the Dissenter John Bowring, who had expressed his sympathy for the American cause, was burned in effigy by a mob in the cathedral close. Feelings in the city of Bristol concerning the war always bordered on violence, and the Dissenters were particularly vulnerable to mob attacks. In 1780 more than one hundred houses were damaged by a mob described as 'the friends of government' who thought that the city was insufficiently loyal.[36] The fears expressed by pro-government commentators in the press and the violence actually enacted against pro-Americans suggest something of the danger radicals faced when they spoke up and petitioned on behalf of the colonists' rights. The sermons of the Anglican clergy reinforce this impression of hostility and fear; the clergy throughout the American war

---

35 R. B. Rose, 'The Liverpool Sailors' Strike of 1775', *Proceedings of the Lancashire and Cheshire Antiquarian Society* 68 (1958), 85; for Lancashire and Coventry, see chap. 9 below.

36 H. T. Dickinson, *Radical Politics in the North-East of England in the Late Eighteenth Century* (Durham, 1979), p. 9; *New. Chron.* (4 Nov. 1775); A. A. Brockett, 'The Political and Social Influence of Exeter Dissenters and Some Notable Families', *Report and Transactions of the Devonshire Association* 93 (1961), 192; Peter Marshall, *Bristol and the American War of Independence* (Bristol, 1977), pp. 10, 18.

sought above all else to inculcate reverence for the governing authorities in the hope that right religion would stabilize the social order.[37]

The fears of the loyalists, however, were not merely chimerical. The Dissenters and other radicals engaged in activities, some symbolic, some seditious, and some thoroughly constitutional, that more than justified their opponents' apprehensions. A third dimension of radicalism is thus found in the actual behavior of the Dissenters in leading radical activity. At Nottingham the radicalism of the Dissenters extended to obstructing the enlistment of soldiers for service in America. At Newcastle in October 1775 radicals expressed their dislike of John Wesley's public support of the administration's American policy by parading his effigy through the town on an ass and then committing it to the flames. Richard Champion, a leading Quaker of Bristol, used such questionable tactics as organizing hecklers to attempt to throw a pro-government meeting into an uproar. It thus comes as no surprise that numerous newspapers reported that 'the Dissenters wish to subvert the constitution'. The Dissenting radical Joseph Towers insisted that the Dissenters adhere to 'old Whig principles', but, he admitted, they were stigmatized as 'factious, seditious, disaffected, and even rebellious'.[38] Above all, the radicalism of Nonconformity is seen in the prominent part the Dissenting leaders played in stimulating the petitioning movements of 1769 and 1775. At Bristol, Newcastle upon Tyne, and Coventry the radical leaders who promoted the Middlesex election petitions were the same leaders who struck out against coercive measures in the colonies; an examination of signatures on the documents of 1769 and 1775 thereby demonstrates clear continuity in radical leadership and program. The notion that Commonwealthmen produced no viable practical program of reform and that they can be usefully analyzed apart from the Wilkites needs to be revised. Further study of the relationship between denominational associations and the petitioning and association movements is needed, but it is now possible to show that provincial religious organizations like the Western Baptist Association and the Essex Congregational Union (combined with even older organizations like the Dissenting Deputies) well prepared the Nonconformists to utilize the most advanced methods of political protest available.[39] The Dissenters thereby pushed the constitutional means of resistance to their fullest

---

37 James E. Bradley, 'The Anglican Pulpit, the Social Order, and the Resurgence of Toryism during the American Revolution', *Albion* 21 (1989).

38 On Nottingham, Newcastle, and Bristol, see chap. 9. Joseph Towers, *Observations on Public Liberty, Patriotism, Ministerial Despotism, and National Grievances* (London, 1769), p. 5.

39 John Sainsbury has recently thrown considerable light on the connections between the Wilkites and the pro-Americans in London, *Disaffected Patriots*, pp. 15–18. The Nonconformists' associations are part of the much broader movement of voluntary associations and clubs in England. Brewer calls for further research in this area: 'English Radicalism', pp. 358–9.

extent, and though these activities were constitutional, in the context of rebellion in the colonies, they were considered by many to be seditious.

A final and most important measure of the nature and extent of radicalism is found in the relationship between political and socio-economic divisions. The signed petitions from the large boroughs turn out to be far more sensitive instruments for revealing socio-economic differences than poll books. Signed petitions also provide an excellent means of measuring how far into the populace the ideas of the elite reached. Previous studies of English public opinion during the war have argued that the government derived most of its support from the landed gentry and that most pro-American support in England came from merchants trading to America.[40] These theories must now be heavily qualified, and with respect to several specific boroughs, rejected. For example, at Bristol, Newcastle upon Tyne, Colchester, and Nottingham the majority of petitioners who opposed the government's American policy in 1775 and pleaded instead for conciliatory measures can be identified as shopkeepers and artisans, whereas the greatest number of coercive addressers were drawn from the ranks of the gentlemen and merchants. A good deal of work has been done on tradesmen and artisans in the earlier eighteenth century, and this research shows that before the 1770s, the discontent was expressed against oligarchic control in general terms with little or no challenge to the social base of oligarchy. Moreover, with the exception of London and Westminster, the appeal of the opposition was to 'honest' men of all ranks.[41] Now, however, under the tutelage of the Dissenters, the disaffection of the lower orders became more specifically political and far more widespread. This book will examine the radical ideology of the disaffected Dissenters and show how it appealed to some Anglicans and to a social stratum slightly below the middle-ranking Commonwealthmen. We will find that the telling characteristic in both the religious and the socio-economic data is its consistency from borough to borough. The support the middling ranks and artisans gave to the American Revolution in numerous urban contexts suggests that the radical-religious-economic nexus is the dominant, if not the controlling, trait of late eighteenth-century popular political culture, and these data thereby provide new evidence for a social base to political radicalism.

The social analysis of individual petitioners will show that signing a petition in favor of conciliatory measures in the fall of 1775 necessarily entailed taking a political position directly opposed to the king, Parliament, the town corporation, the law, and that other strong corporation, the Church. The reality of

40 Dora Mae Clark, *British Opinion and the American Revolution* (New Haven, 1930), p. 133.
41 Nicholas Rogers, 'The Urban Opposition to Whig Oligarchy', pp. 136–7. See also Nicholas Rogers, 'Aristocratic Clientage, Trade, and Independency', pp. 80–3; and 'Popular Protest in Early Hanoverian London', *P&P* 79 (1978), 85–7. For a different view, see Clark, *English Society*, pp. 321, 324; Clark, *Revolution and Rebellion*, p. 158.

these social and economic divisions provided convincing grounds for people's perception of a threatening radical movement; leaders in both local and national governments detected a serious challenge to law and order and this perception alone can adequately explain the shrillness of their response. A disproportionately high percentage of the Dissenting laity who heard the sermons of radical yet orthodox Dissenting ministers also signed the conciliatory petitions, thereby adding an ideological element to the social base of radicalism. The coherence between the sermons and the socio-economic divisions suggests that Nonconformists were not merely fighting old battles but anticipating modern values. While the older anachronistic assumptions of the Whig interpretation are to be avoided, a close reading of neglected documents demands an evolutionary conception of the development of English radicalism. Moreover, it can now be demonstrated that at least one branch of the radical critique had its origin in both orthodox Christian theology and economic discontent.[42]

This book will show that radical Dissenting ministers and laity in the provinces attempted to foster discontent among the lower orders as early as the mid-1770s and, more importantly, that there was a measurable corresponding response of disaffection precisely among lesser tradesmen and artisans. Thus despite some diversity in radical ideology and program, the popular political behavior of these middle and lower orders provides structural lines of continuity that connect the radicalism of the Middlesex election affair to the American crisis, then to the Association movement, and finally to the radicalism of the period of the French Revolution. Some of the developments thought to be new in the 1790s can now be placed squarely in the 1770s, and with this altered perspective, much of the apparent abruptness of the events of the later years disappears. The disparate assumptions, aims, and motives of radical leaders must be acknowledged, but it is now possible to discern important religious and social continuities. English radicalism in the age of the democratic revolution is not properly characterized by the categories of 'old' and 'new', but it is best interpreted in terms of a slow, continuous, and connected evolution.

NONCONFORMITY, WHIG HISTORIOGRAPHY, AND PARTY CONTINUITY

The belief that society was seriously divided on the basis of religion was first advanced by the Rockingham Whigs; the notion was taken up by the radicals themselves, and it was later developed at length by Whig historians. Nonconformity thus not only has a direct bearing on the debate over the origins of English radicalism, but has abiding significance for any discussion of party politics. But despite the importance of religion to the Whig explanation of eighteenth-century partisan politics, the role of Nonconformity in Whig histori-

---

42 On the inherent teleology of the Whig interpretation, see Brewer, *Party Ideology*, pp. 18–19, and Clark, *English Society*, p. 347.

ography has been almost totally overlooked.[43] The centrality of Nonconformity to the Whig interpretation of eighteenth-century party politics is, however, readily proven. W. E. H. Lecky and G. M. Trevelyan[44] maintained that there was a progressive and steady development in the evolution of democracy and that one vital force in this process was Protestant, non-Anglican Christianity.[45] In eighteenth-century England the Whig 'party' was naturally the party of progress, and for Lecky and Trevelyan it was distinguished above all by its alliance with Nonconformity; the Whig aristocracy and the commercial classes in alliance with Nonconformity composed the other two elements.[46] Lecky and Trevelyan relied heavily upon the understanding of party and party continuity propounded by Edmund Burke; Burke, in turn, was strongly influenced by his own experience of local Whig and 'Tory' parties at Bristol.

Modern critics of the Whig interpretation of party have seldom asked what these historians meant by the continuity of parties. Trevelyan was interested in 'real differences of principle or interest' in party structures and believed that the answer to the problem of continuity might be found in 'sound subconscious instincts'.[47] Moreover, Trevelyan focused upon the country as much as he did upon Parliament, and in addition, he looked to strictly religious concerns, such as the High-Anglican dominance of local government. It is hardly ever remembered that Trevelyan qualified his hypothesis – and it was never meant to be more than a hypothesis – by reference to local politics:

43 This is one of the few weaknesses of Brewer's otherwise excellent study, *Party Ideology*, pp. 29, 39. Clark, as well, passes over the religious component of Trevelyan's thesis concerning party and yet with the addition of a stress on heterodox Dissent takes the thesis up as his own. *English Society*, pp. 31, 38, 43.

44 It should be noted that not all Whig historians saw Nonconformity in the same light as Lecky and Trevelyan; Horace Walpole, a founder of the Burkean view of eighteenth-century politics, and G. S. Veitch, a historian of parliamentary reform, are exceptions. Similarly, John R. Green, *History of the English People*, 4 vols. (London, 1880–3), 4: 122, 125, 140; and William Hunt, *The History of England, 1760–1801* (London, 1905), p. 264, do not make any connection between 'the Whig party' and Dissent, though both have very little to say about Nonconformity in general.

45 G. M. Trevelyan, *A History of England* (London, 1926), pp. 474, 615; and his *Romanes Lectures* of the same year, 'The Two-Party System in English Political History', in *An Autobiography & Other Essays* (London, 1949), pp. 183–99. W. E. H. Lecky, *A History of England in the Eighteenth Century*, 2nd edn, 8 vols. (London, 1878–90), 1: 177–81; 187–93.

46 In the period from 1715 through 1760 the 'Nonconformists were able to keep the Whig party in power' (Trevelyan, *A History of England*, pp. 501, 534). Trevelyan also said that 'class divisions and social instincts' were the basis of the two parties, 'The Two-Party System', p. 184. The commercial classes and the Whig aristocracy, Lecky notes, were potentially corruptible, but no such potential is mentioned in his discussion of the Dissenters, though, of course, there were many Dissenters in commerce (*A History of England*, 1: 182, 202; 202–8). For a lengthier treatment of the Whig interpretation, see my article 'Whigs and Nonconformists', 1–7.

47 Trevelyan, 'The Two-Party System', p. 185. Elsewhere he refers to the 'inner history and structure of party', p. 184.

The dualism of the English religious world and the disabilities imposed on Dissenters, form a large part of the explanation of the peculiarly English phenomenon of two continuous political parties in every shire and town of the land, surviving even when obvious political issues seemed asleep or settled, or when the programmes of the two parties seem in certain important respects to have been exchanged.[48]

Continuous oral tradition in the eighteenth century, Trevelyan reminds us, could be potent; and though the memories of people were often confused, England then was a 'slow-moving, stable society, of long-enduring local pieties and loyalties and customs'. He spoke, for example, of the Tories' 'strong dislike' of religious Dissent on the one hand, and their 'respect' for tradition, law, and order on the other. Trevelyan was thus portraying 'party' in a very loose sense, and he actually contrasted the eighteenth and nineteenth centuries and made no claim to describe eighteenth-century parties in terms of nineteenth-century realities.[49] He did claim to discern 'party continuity', but he certainly did not mean to locate modern party organizations in the eighteenth century, nor did he insist on ideological continuity in the sense of clearly articulated principles. 'Party' for him did not connote an organized parliamentary group that pursues political power and office; rather, continuity was located in a general political ethos and people's attitudes toward such matters as established authority, religious toleration, and the need for reform. Still, the conclusion that Lecky and Trevelyan overstated their case is unavoidable. The politics of the majority of boroughs in England for much of the eighteenth century had nothing to do with principles and even less with the terms Whig and Tory, and it was precisely such exaggerations in the Whig interpretation that led to a vigorous reaction.

Sir Lewis Namier's greatest accomplishment was effectively to destroy the notion of a mid-century two-party system based on ideology.[50] The idea of two parties in Parliament understood in the modern sense of party is now rightly discredited; the old party labels Whig and Tory cannot be applied simply, with self-evident meaning, to Parliament or any administration in the age of the American Revolution.[51] It is incontestable that no general election

48 *Ibid.*, pp. 192, 198.
49 *Ibid.*, p. 186.
50 Lewis Namier, *England in the Age of the American Revolution*, 2nd edn (London, 1961), pp. 32, 171–9, 195–8; 'Monarchy and the Party System', in *Personalities and Powers* (London, 1955), pp. 32–5; and 'Country Gentlemen in Parliament, 1750–84', in the same volume, pp. 64–5. He also demythologized the Whig legend concerning political corruption and the use of secret service money in *The Structure of Politics at the Accession of George III*, 2nd edn (London, 1957), pp. 212–14, 218. He effectively scotched the idea that there was a revolution in government at the accession of the new king in *The Structure of Politics*, pp. 158–73; *England in the Age of the American Revolution*, p. 154; 'Monarchy and the Party System', pp. 18–25. And he gave a new character to George III in 'King George III: A Study of Personality', in *Personalities and Powers*, especially p. 55.
51 John Brooke has written the finest available survey of the old party labels, Whig and

was fought on a national issue related to party; only rarely did national issues arise in the local setting. But these emphases have led to a distortion of two facets of eighteenth-century political reality: party coherence at the local level was sometimes based on ideology, and party continuity over a period of several elections can be discerned in some open constituencies. In the *History of Parliament* the only thing believed to give any meaning to borough politics is repeatedly construed as merely local in scope. When corporation interests formed over against anti-corporation factions the only significant points of difference were thought to be local, economic, or status related. When Dissenting opposition parties were observed at odds with Anglicans, the conflict was construed nonideologically as a contest for power and position only. Naturally, then, party continuity was neglected because merely local issues were episodic and not normally connected by ideological threads over time. But on this viewpoint, religion, though alluded to, was not appreciated for its organizing and rationalizing power, nor were the principles of the Dissenters taken very seriously.

The work of C. E. Fryer contributed directly to this neglect. Whereas Namier had at least recognized that Dissenting voters often formed an 'interest' that contributed to party conflict,[52] Fryer's Harvard dissertation and his published articles attempted to dissolve the connection between Dissenting religion and Whig party politics altogether. First he challenged the notions of the Whig historians by asserting that Dissenters had neither sufficient numbers nor adequate influence to form a significant electoral bloc in support of the Whigs.[53] With Fryer, as with the school of Namier generally, religion and public opinion stood and fell together; in an article on the general election of 1784 Fryer was so confident of the absence of public opinion that he dared any future historian to find evidence of the people's choice in support of Pitt.[54] Having eliminated the religious and ideological component of party, he could then deny any vestiges of genuine public opinion. The Namierian critique has been so influential that even those who have been most assiduous in their

Tory, and the labels clearly lacked meaning at Westminster after 1754. *Commons, 1754–1790*, 1: 184–203. But to say that 'it was universally recognized around 1754 that the old party denominations of Whig and Tory no longer corresponded to political realities and that the issues which formerly distinguished them were dead' overstates the case, p. 186.

52 Namier, *The Structure of Politics*, p. 137; see also pp. 90, 113, 125, 206. See *England in the Age of the American Revolution*, p. 110. Namier rejoiced when he found evidence of the Dissenters' compromising their principles. See *England in the Age of the American Revolution*, p. 110; *The Structure of Politics*, pp. 125, 206.

53 Charles E. Fryer, 'English Church Disestablishment: A Statistical and Sectional View, Being Mainly a Study in the Development of the Political Influence of Dissent since 1688', Harvard University Ph.D. thesis, 1906. 'The Numerical Decline of Dissent in England Previous to the Industrial Revolution', *American Journal of Theology* 17 (1913), 233.

54 C. E. Fryer, 'The General Election of 1784', *History* 9 (1925), 223.

search for issue-oriented politics at the national level have sometimes capitulated concerning local politics,[55] and in those few cases where local parties based on religious affiliation are discerned, the idea of genuine ideological continuity with the issues of the early eighteenth century is still discounted.[56] It is true that these phenomena can only be found in a handful of boroughs, but where ideological and behavioral elements do converge, we have evidence for the reason why the Whig interpretation emerged in the first place.

This study does not purport to find national party organizations or anything that approximates to a modern two-party system; any attempt to reintroduce a Whig interpretation is futile. In many boroughs there were no Dissenters at all, in other constituencies the Dissenting laity were politically supine, and in yet a third small group of boroughs, Dissenting patrons controlled voters in the interest of the government, even during the American Revolution. But in several large open constituencies the Dissenters formed a powerful electoral bloc and were politically progressive, and in these constituencies they acquired a reputation that has misled subsequent interpreters. Local political conflict in a small number of boroughs during the American crisis cannot be understood apart from the old party labels and the connection to national issues. The relevant point for the current debate on Georgian politics is the way in which the religious component contributed to the use of these labels and ultimately to the development of Whig historiography.

The study of party and party continuity in the early reign of George III has recently enjoyed a remarkable rebirth that takes us considerably beyond old Whig and new 'Tory' interpretations. This duly chastened and modified understanding of party politics has focused upon three related areas: there is new evidence of structural continuity among Whig leaders in Parliament; one finds the life of the Tory party extended into the 1760s and a new appreciation of the importance of authoritarian ideology in the reign of George III related to High Anglicanism; and scholars have discovered increased levels of partisanship in some boroughs connected to national issues. Each of these new emphases requires brief comment in order to place the study of religion in this new, more congenial historiographical context.

First, parliamentary factions have been analyzed with great success by Frank O'Gorman, who has also demonstrated the existence of meaningful party groupings. It is now possible to argue that the imperial crisis contributed directly to an increasingly definable opposition party in Parliament. America came to be the one main issue around which otherwise contentious factions could rally, and recent scholarship has convincingly revived certain facets of

55 Frank O'Gorman, *The Rise of Party in England: The Rockingham Whigs, 1760–82* (London, 1975), p. 319; 'Fifty Years After Namier: The Eighteenth Century in British Historical Writing', *The Eighteenth Century* 20 (1979), 118.
56 Phillips, *Electoral Behavior*, p. 117.

the old interpretation of the Rockingham Whigs. The Rockinghams' contribution to the beginning of a party system of parliamentary government is found in their legitimation of party as a political reality and the coherence of the Newcastle-Rockingham party traced through the second Rockingham administration.[57] But the Rockinghams were notoriously weak in popular politics and a constituency party in the electorate that could be said to have an important link to Westminster never developed. The Dissenters were, however, widely dispersed in the electorate, and the intellectual elite assumed a significant role of leadership in alerting the nation to the political issues concerning America. Moreover, a petitioning movement to rally nationwide Dissenting support had just concluded in 1772, and as astute a politician as George III feared that an issue with national implications might arouse the Dissenters into formidable opposition in numerous constituencies. Was there any substance to such a fear? Could the Dissenters across the country actually be marshalled in such a way that their vote at a general election would tell? Among the Dissenters in some constituencies there was a definite reaction to the colonial policies of George III and this opposition bears a strong resemblance to the new opposition of the old corps Whigs. This book will examine the ways in which the Dissenters contributed to local party politics in selected boroughs and show how these local parties in turn related to the national crisis over America.

57 On Whig party continuity see Brewer, *Party Ideology and Popular Politics*, pp. ix, 5, 14, 84; O'Gorman, *The Rise of Party*, pp. 20–1, 190–1, 224, 320; and *The Emergence of the British Two-Party System, 1760–1832* (London, 1982), p. 14. This new interpretation of party has been and will continue to be contested. For the literature on party before mid-century, see James E. Bradley, 'Nonconformity and the Electorate in Eighteenth-Century England', *Parliamentary History* 6 (1987), 237; see also J. C. D. Clark, 'A General Theory of Party, Opposition and Government, 1688–1832', *HJ* 23 (1980), 295–325. Compare the strictures in Linda Colley, *In Defiance of Oligarchy: The Tory Party 1714–60* (Cambridge, 1982), pp. 263–67. For a recent review of the literature on party and on the perception of the importance of religion in party formation but without significant development of the idea, see Clark, *Revolution and Rebellion*, pp. 144–63. Brian Hill, who is largely dependent on the work of O'Gorman and Colley, has recently argued that even at mid-century 'a basically two-sided alignment existed' and that the 'main elements of the Whig party went into opposition from the end of 1762 and that at the same time the Tory party largely went into support of successive ministries acceptable to George III'. *British Parliamentary Parties, 1740–1832* (London, 1985), p. ix. Ian Christie first addressed the issue in 'Was There a "New Toryism" in the Earlier Part of George III's Reign?', pp. 196–213 in *Myth and Reality in Late-Eighteenth-Century British Politics* (London, 1970); Christie recommended the use of the term 'Conservative', rather than 'Tory', p. 213. He recently counted the number of Members who could reasonably be called Tory and concludes there is no evidence in Parliament for a resurgence of Toryism, 'Party in Politics in the Age of Lord North's Administration', *Parliamentary History* 6 (1987), 47–67. But compare Mary Kinnear, 'Pro-Americans in the British House of Commons in the 1770s', University of Oregon Ph.D. thesis, 1973, p. 89, who found a strong continuity between supporters of the administration's American policy in the Parliament of 1774–80 and previous support of Bute, Bedford, and the 'King's Friends'.

The ideological basis to Whig party continuity has recently received considerable attention. H. T. Dickinson, in particular, has emphasized the rational, ideological coherence of the Rockingham platform and its connection with earlier Whig principles.[58] G. M. Ditchfield has undertaken a most detailed investigation of the religious issues of the Parliament of 1768–74, and he concluded that the contentious religious debates of the 1770s signalled a partial return to the conditions and issues of the 1730s. Ditchfield also examined national party continuity and Whig ideology in relation to the agitation over the repeal of the Test and Corporation Acts and showed that there was a demonstrable connection between M.P.s' support for repeal, parliamentary reform, and the Whig opposition.[59] Ditchfield's discovery of a Dissenting parliamentary interest or lobby numbering some 150 members in the period 1787–91 provides the best evidence yet adduced for an ideological component to the reemergence of parliamentary parties. But the most surprising evidence for an ideological basis to late-eighteenth-century politics has arisen from an unsuspected source, namely, High-Anglican political ideology.

A major pillar in the Whig interpretation of party was the belief in a revival of Toryism based on High-Anglican political theology. Just as a more sweeping radicalism can now be discovered among the Dissenters, a more thoroughgoing authoritarianism has recently been discerned among supporters of the crown, and it too was grounded in religion.[60] The earlier notion of unified

58 Dickinson, *Liberty and Property*, pp. 206, 208–9; Dickinson traces ideological continuity from the Chathamites, to the Rockingham Whigs, to the younger Pitt, to Charles James Fox, p. 221. See also Brewer, *Party Ideology and Popular Politics*, throughout.

59 G. M. Ditchfield, 'The Subscription Issue in British Parliamentary Politics, 1772–79', *Parliamentary History* 7 (1988), 47; G. M. Ditchfield, 'The Parliamentary Struggle Over the Repeal of the Test and Corporation Acts 1787–1790', *EHR* 89 (1974), 553–4, 558, 563. See also for the later period, 'Repeal, Abolition, and Reform: A Study in the Interaction of Reforming Movements in the Parliament of 1790–6', in Christine Bolt and Seymour Drescher (eds.), *Anti-Slavery, Religion, and Reform: Essays in Memory of Roger Anstey* (Hamden, Conn., 1980), p. 104.

60 Burke put the case most forcefully in a letter to Fox in 1777. 'There are most manifest marks of the resurrection of the Tory party... The Tories do universally think their power and consequence involved in the success of this American business. The Clergy are astonishingly warm in it – and what the Tories are when embodied, united with their natural head the Crown, and animated by their Clergy, no man knows better than yourself.' *Burke Correspondence*, 3: 383; Burke to Fox, 8 October 1777. Nothing approximating the numerous studies of the French *curés* exists for England, yet it can be argued that the Church was one major source for stability in this period. G. M. Trevelyan, Norman Sykes, E. P. Thompson, and Paul Langford have all emphasized the importance of certain aspects of the 'confessional state', recently expounded synthetically by J. C. D. Clark. Clark's work is valuable on the union of Church and State and the resurgence of High Anglicanism in the reign of George III; he ably shows that High Anglicanism was far more than 'mindless authoritarianism'; and he provides good insights on the king as the head of the Church. *English Society*, pp. 134–41, 195, 199, 306. He does not distinguish sufficiently between ideas of the divine *origin* of monarchy and divine *right*, understood as non-resistance and passive obedience (pp. 123–4, 126, 130, 150, 157, 174–7, 206, 216–35). Compare the discussion of High Anglicanism in Gunn, *Beyond Liberty and Property*, pp. 164–79. On the historic distinction between High Churchmen

Anglican clerical support for the government faced the same fate at the hands of Namier and his colleagues as the belief in the continuity of party; it was flatly denied. Writing in 1964 John Brooke said, 'There does not appear to have been any specific Anglican attitude towards the American War or any other aspect of policy', and he concluded, 'No clear-cut attitude emerges among the lower clergy.'[61] Recent research in three complementary areas suggests that there was indeed a revival of a Tory mentality in the reign of George III. This new authoritarianism was typified by a desire to strengthen respect for government, particularly the crown, and it emphasized trusting the political judgment of social superiors. These themes were particularly discernible in the Anglican clergy and there was a corresponding resurgence of authoritarianism in the law. J. A. W. Gunn and J. C. D. Clark, for example, examined Anglican political treatises published during the American Revolution that depended explicitly upon previous Tory tracts.[62] The question of a new Toryism in the reign of George III was also addressed directly and convincingly by a fresh examination of Anglican sermons; the conservative political ideology thus found expression in Fast and Thanksgiving Day sermons preached across the land.[63] The importance of the pulpit for the question of a popular ideological base for party, understood loosely, and for the question of ideological continuity is thereby underscored for a second time. Finally, both Tory political treatises and High-Anglican sermons contributed to the scores of addresses favoring coercion that were presented to the king in 1775. Paul Langford[64] demonstrated

and Low Churchmen centering in the Convocation controversy see G. V. Bennett, 'Conflict in the Church', p. 166 in Geoffrey Holmes (ed.), *After The Glorious Revolution, 1689–1714* (London, 1969).

61 John Brooke, *Commons, 1754–1790*, 1: 115. See also Christie, 'Was There a "New Toryism" in the Earlier Part of George III's Reign?', where there is not one allusion to the Church.

62 Gunn, *Beyond Liberty and Property*, pp. 164–79; and Clark, *English Society*, pp. 216–35. On the clerical J.P.s' zeal in criminal prosecutions in one county, see Diana McClatchey, *Oxfordshire Clergy, 1777–1869: A Study of the Established Church and the Role of the Clergy in Local Society* (Oxford, 1960), pp. 178–201.

63 Henry Ippel, 'Blow the Trumpet, Sanctify the Fast', *HLQ* 44 (1980), 55, and 'British Sermons and the American Revolution', *JRH* 12 (1982), 191–205. In the midst of the trauma of the war, there was something of a rapprochement between old Whigs and old Tories, but in their common defense of the status quo, striking differences on how best to justify the authority of the State emerged. Moderate Anglicans, like Beilby Porteus, made a traditional Whiggish appeal to the balanced constitution; High Anglicans, like George Horne and Myles Cooper, advanced views of the supreme power of monarchy that can only be called 'Tory'. See Bradley, 'The Anglican Pulpit'.

64 Paul Langford, 'Old Whigs, Old Tories, and the American Revolution', *The Journal of Imperial and Commonwealth History* 8 (1980), 106–30. 'The polemical importance of the search for clear Whig and Tory identities was strongly felt by contemporaries', p. 107; see also Bradley, *Popular Politics and the American Revolution in England*; Linda Colley, 'The Apotheosis of George III: Loyalty, Royalty and the British Nation, 1760–1820', *P&P* 102 (1984), 111; and Margaret E. Avery, 'Toryism in the Age of the American Revolution; John Lind and John Shebbeare', *Historical Studies* (Melbourne), 18 (1978–9), 24–36.

how the earlier expressions of attachment to the crown found among old Tories were expressed in the mid 1770s in terms of support for the authority of the king in Parliament. The Anglicans who signed petitions in favor of coercive measures received their political training from the sermons of the Anglican clergy who maintained the principal ideas of their Tory forebears. These three sources combined substantiate the idea of a genuine resurgence of loyalist opinion in the period of the American Revolution, and this recrudescence of authoritarianism is inexplicable apart from essentially religious ideology.

Beginning with the pioneering work of John Brewer and John Money, students of regional and local political culture have taken the study of popular ideology far beyond the constituency histories of the *History of Parliament* and have begun to transcend the local–national bifurcation that was so characteristic of the school of Namier. Money's study of Birmingham demonstrated just how profoundly local issues were tied to the national crisis of rebellion in the colonies, and his research proved that local politics had a controlling ideological component that contributed to deep fissures in society.[65] In two critically important articles on Newcastle upon Tyne, Thomas R. Knox found the same political sophistication and party continuity in the north of England that Money found in the west midlands.[66] John Phillips' examination of parliamentary elections in four boroughs over a forty-year period proved the existence of impressively high and steadily increasing levels of partisanship. More importantly, Phillips documented a connection between Whig Members of Parliament and Nonconformist voters.[67] The growth of local party politics in these larger, more open constituencies, though atypical, provides a rational and convincing local counterpart to the other recent studies that discern an early reorganization of party politics at Westminster.

These reassessments of the nature and role of party politics are compatible with Trevelyan's hypothesis concerning a bifurcation of the political nation in terms of political ethos. When we look beyond parliamentary elections to popular politics and petitions, his belief in the reality of two basic approaches to authority and toleration related to religious convictions in the nation at large

---

65 John Money, *Experience and Identity: Birmingham and the West Midlands*. For a historiographical survey of the issue of province and center that hints at the importance of religion, see Clark, *Revolution and Rebellion*, pp. 45–67; for a creative discussion of the Dissenters' contribution to cosmopolitanism, see Bonwick, *English Radicals*, pp. 27–52.

66 Knox, 'Popular Politics and Provincial Radicalism', and 'Wilkism and the Newcastle Election of 1774'.

67 Phillips, *Electoral Behavior*. Similarly, the examination of local parties in the early eighteenth century are related to religion and religious differences. See Geoffrey Holmes, *Religion and Party in Late Stuart England* (London, 1975), and W. A. Speck, *Tory and Whig* (London, 1970). See also, for the late eighteenth century, Ditchfield, 'Repeal, Abolition, and Reform', pp. 104, 115–16.

turns out to be remarkably accurate. The petitions to the crown in 1775 over the specific question of political authority exposed the pervasive reality of these mentalities. This study will show that the absence of parties in the electorate can by no means be construed as indicating the absence of strongly felt political convictions based on an ideology that transcended local affairs. It is true that in many boroughs the Whig interpretation does not fit political reality, particularly if politics is confined to parliamentary elections; in the majority of parliamentary boroughs the Dissenters had no significant influence on elections. Moreover, partisan behavior in even those boroughs where there were numerous Dissenters reached a low point in the middle years of the century. But in overreacting to the Whig viewpoint, the Namierian critique extended too far.

Namier and those who adopted his views not only neglected popular political ideology in some boroughs, but overlooked the centrality of religion in a number of smaller boroughs, such as Abingdon, Hertford, and St. Albans.[68] Ian Christie even tried to exorcize the Whig demon from the most open boroughs; he forced the idea that politics was controlled by local, nonideological interests on some of the largest boroughs in England, including Bristol, Norwich, Liverpool, Worcester, and Newcastle upon Tyne. But the rigid bifurcation between local and national issues fails in at least two ways. First, it is too simple. Local issues were often interpreted in the light of national issues, and national issues were seen through the lens of local concerns. The school of Namier largely neglected popular election literature, but this literature holds considerable promise for linking local, national, and imperial issues. Conversely, studies of the influence of ideas have often neglected the provincial setting that was the locus of the common person's life and interest; from the local perspective, a national crisis might be focused and even magnified. Thus when a town corporation expressed abhorrence at the rebellion in the colonies it was making a statement reflecting local concern for law and order and at the same time expressing interest in the future of the empire. The new national and international issues of the 1760s and 1770s thus might be interpreted through a local framework that would heighten their importance locally, and then through the local framework they were linked to the ideological themes of the period before 1750. These means of transcending 'provincial introversion' were expressed most clearly in those circumstances where religious convictions remained strong, because the strongest political convictions of the earlier period were those associated with High Anglicanism on the one hand, or Nonconformity on the other. Secondly, the conservative interpretation measured the importance of national issues by the standard of success. If those radicals who defended the Middlesex electors or championed peace with the colonists made a poor showing at the polls, then clearly local interests were 'more important' to

68 On these boroughs see Bradley, 'Nonconformity and the Electorate', 236–61.

the electorate than national issues.[69] The rule of the majority resulted in stifling evidence for the early emergence of both partisan politics and urban radicalism. Certainly, in the majority of boroughs, local affairs did predominate and there is no lack of illustrative materials to prove the pervasive reality of deference and political treating, even among the Dissenters. But these emphases of the dominant interpretation have resulted in a serious imbalance.

Historians have discovered new elements of party politics in both the first and last decades of the century, and these discoveries are almost without exception related to religion. The search for party continuity at the local level and the attempt to connect local and national issues must now be extended into the 1770s and 1780s. Since in the eighteenth century itself, religion was always viewed as one touchstone of party, it is surprising that the question of religion has not figured more prominently in the discussion of party in this period. By themselves, the Dissenters were not a formidable electoral force, but they were always associated in the electorate with Low-Church Anglicans. What then distinguished the non-Dissenting or Anglican Whigs from the Tories? Early in the century the answer was ready at hand; it was found in one's perspective on the Established Church. In the first two decades of the century most Anglicans who voted Whig were denoted 'Low Churchmen', while those who voted Tory were called 'High Churchmen'. This Low-Church perspective entailed support of toleration for Protestant Dissenters and the corollary of opposition to the king's involvement in the affairs of the Church. The High-Church Anglicans, on the other hand, were against toleration and more committed to the king's role as head of the Church. By mid-century, politicians continued to understand the Low-Church Anglicans in this light: the alliance of Low-Church Anglicans with Nonconformists was at the heart of most definitions of Whiggism. Some Commonwealthman Whigs and some Nonconformists came to oppose Walpole and the Pelhams and a few wished to abolish all Anglican privileges,[70] but in those constituencies where there was a strong High-Anglican party, the Low-Church Anglicans and the Nonconformists normally voted in concert.

Eighteenth-century politicians, therefore, viewed the Dissenters as an important force in the electorate and consistently associated with the Whigs. The Duke of Richmond, for example, described the Dissenters in 1772 as 'a weighty body of men' who throughout England 'are very powerful, and who stick pretty much together'. He thought that their religious principles and the

---

69 This triumph of the vested interests, couched in terms of ideological and cultural hegemony, is advanced by Clark, *English Society*, p. 19 and throughout.

70 For this threefold classification of parties that takes religion seriously by placing ecclesiastical issues squarely in the midst of high politics, see Stephen Taylor, 'Sir Robert Walpole, the Church of England, and the Quakers' Tithe Bill of 1736', *HJ* 28 (1985), 53, 58–9, 71–4. Much work is needed on 'Low-Church' parties; the following chapters merely hint at one possible direction for research in the constituencies.

Rockinghams' political principles were so very similar that they would 'most probably' make us 'generally act together'.[71] The pamphlet literature on the Whig party consistently identified the Dissenters with the Whigs, and the importance of this fact has been neglected for too long.[72] But perhaps most conclusively, the poll books reflect remarkable coherence among Dissenting voters on behalf of Whig candidates. In fact, the first attempt to analyze the motivation of individual voters proved the consistency of the Dissenters as Whigs: at Abingdon in 1734, 1754, and 1758 and at Shrewsbury in 1747, local agents went to the trouble to determine the religious affiliation of each voter and then printed their names in the poll books with an asterisk identifying all Dissenters.[73] The Dissenters were thus understood by contemporary politicians as an independent and important electoral bloc.

If the Whig notion of a national Whig party grounded in ideology was exaggerated, we still must attempt to account for the exaggeration. The Dissenters were unusually conscious of the national political scene; the first national canvass of a party within the electorate was a survey of the Dissenting vote conducted throughout England in 1715–29.[74] In addition, the Nonconformists were the first group in England to form a permanent political lobby known as the Dissenting Deputies. When these facts are considered along with the electoral analysis of the Dissenting vote in boroughs such as Abingdon and Shrewsbury, we see that the Dissenters were at once a national body that could reflect national concerns, and they were composed of many local congregations that, because of their potential as a voting bloc, riveted the attention of local politicians. The Dissenters agitated nationally on behalf of the repeal of legal strictures in 1734, 1736–9, and again in 1772–3, and in 1775, we have what amounts to a national agitation in the petitioning movement against the government's American policy. The Dissenters comprise a body of people with a national consciousness, which was nationally dispersed, yet whose influence was expressed locally. The most common phrase used by contemporaries to describe the Dissenters as a political entity was 'the body of Dissenters', and this phrase is laden with implications for the electoral history of England. The dual characteristics of national dispersion and local cohesion will be examined in this study in some detail.

71 Richmond to Rockingham, 26 April 1772, quoted in O'Gorman, *The Rise of Party*, p. 291.
72 See, for example, *The Balance: or the Merits of Whig and Tory* (London, 1753), and *The Contest* (Newcastle, 1774). Further details on Low-Church Anglicans and their connections with Dissent will be found in chap. 3. Clark has rightly called attention to the importance of Anglican political religion, but he has underestimated the contribution of moderate Churchmen to political thought. This neglect arises from a failure to distinguish adequately between High Churchmen and moderates. See *English Society*, pp. 136, 138, 229, 288–9, 302–3, 305–6, 315.
73 Chap. 2 below.
74 See Bradley, 'Nonconformity and the Electorate'.

The importance of the political unity of 'the Dissenting interest' for modern English historiography can hardly be overemphasized; it is both the basis for the Whig interpretation of party continuity and the foundation for one of the most well-accepted explanations of the origins of social class.[75] This book will demonstrate that before the accession of George III, the Dissenters' consistent support of the government was one of the most dependable features of the political landscape. The idea that many prominent Nonconformist ministers and the laity shifted as a body to a relatively unified anti-government stance in the 1770s is also of the utmost importance. There is considerable evidence to corroborate this notion; as a voting bloc the Dissenters' allegiance changed dramatically from support of government candidates to anti-administration candidates in Bristol, Norwich, Great Yarmouth, Northampton, and possibly other boroughs.[76] When it appeared that the Dissenters across the land had turned resolutely against the government, it seemed to numerous observers, including Edmund Burke, that one important body of people in the electorate had maintained its Whig principles while the government had taken a new and very threatening authoritarian stand.[77] Similarly, the Anglican clergy's new-found loyalty for the king was bound to be interpreted in terms of a resurgence of Toryism, and these events were very conducive to a revival of the old party labels at the local level.

Such developments do not add up to a vindication of the Whig interpretation of party continuity, but they certainly help explain the origins of the Whig interpretation. The specific origins of the Whig interpretation of party in the reign of George III will be traced to Burke's affiliation with the prominent and powerful 'body of Dissenters' in Bristol. As the principal architect of the revived Whig party, Burke believed that the Dissenters formed the moral core of the party and constituted perhaps the most important part of middle-class opinion.[78] In fact we will find that only when religious issues interlocked with political issues did religion become highly divisive and politically potent. These conditions will be documented in several local settings where issues of authority were at stake and then correlated to the national setting during the debates over the Quebec Act and the issue of representation during the Revolution.

---

75 For the first, see Trevelyan, above; for the second, Harold Perkin, *The Origins of Modern English Society, 1780–1880* (London, 1969), p. 353.

76 Phillips, *Electoral Behavior*, pp. 293, 296 and chaps. 6 and 7 below.

77 Phillips notes the changed orientation of the Dissenters after 1774, but does not show how this implies a principled consistency to partisan commitment at the local level. *Electoral Behavior*, pp. 18, 118–19, 121.

78 Trevelyan, 'The Two-Party System', p. 193; *Burke Correspondence*, 3: 383; Burke to Fox, 8 October 1777.

RELIGION, SOCIAL CLASS, AND ECONOMIC MOTIVATION IN MODERN ENGLISH SOCIETY

English Nonconformity is not only important for explaining the origins of modern radicalism and the emergence of partisan politics; some scholars have understood Dissent as 'the midwife of class.'[79] Isaac Kramnick has gone so far as to say that the Dissenters were 'the major modernizing agent' that played 'the decisive role' in transforming England into the 'first bourgeois civilization'.[80] The broader implications of this study are therefore found in an examination of the way that religious, economic, and communal forces contributed to the evolution of modern English society. The study of English Nonconformity bears directly on the perennial question of the nature of historical causation. Many well-known theories have been advanced concerning the relationship between religion and social change, including those of Marx, Weber, and Troeltsch. New, more encompassing views of human motivation are emerging that understand political behavior in both its economic and religious dimensions, and we now require more empirical evidence to test and weigh these social theories.[81]

Marxism is by far the most influential explanation of political motivation, and while much of Marx's social thought still recommends itself, his views on religion are now considered far too simplistic. Religion is less predictable than Marx believed, and it is no longer possible to think of the ideas of religion as epiphenomena, or mere projections of deeper economic motivation. Anyone with even the briefest acquaintance with English political thought knows that from the sixteenth century onwards, religious arguments were used against political authority as well as in support of it.[82] Hannah Arendt's understanding of religion as 'politically without consequences and historically futile' has, in light of recent developments in Latin America, Africa, Iran, and Poland, been

---

79 The phrase is Harold Perkin's, *The Origins of Modern English Society*, p. 196. See also Thompson, *The Making of the English Working Class*, p. 56.

80 Isaac Kramnick, 'Religion and Radicalism: English Political Theory in the Age of Revolution', *Political Theory* 5 (1977), 505; see p. 530 for a list of major works on Dissent and the Industrial Revolution. Clark agrees with Kramnick on the importance of Dissent, but understands its impact very differently, *English Society*, pp. 69, 74, 424.

81 See Robert Forster and Orest Ranum (eds.), *Ritual, Religion, and the Sacred*, Selections from the Annales, vol. 7 (Baltimore, 1982), for a wide range of studies on the relationship between individuals, communities, and the sacred. Scholars have increasingly given more prominence to theology in accounting for social protest and revolution. See Helmut Koenigsberger, 'The Organization of Revolutionary Parties in France and the Netherlands during the Sixteenth Century', *JMH* 27 (1955), 336; Peter Blickle, Hans-Christoph Rublack, and Winfried Schulze, *Religion, Politics and Social Protest: Three Studies on Early Modern Germany* (London, 1984), Dale Van Kley, *The Damien's Affair and the Unraveling of the Ancien Regime, 1750–1770* (Princeton, 1984); W. R. Ward, 'The Relations of Enlightenment and Religious Revival in Central Europe and in the English Speaking World', *Studies in Church History* 2 (1979), 281–305.

82 One thinks of the sixteenth-century political theorist John Ponet and the seventeenth-century Independent radical John Goodwin.

rendered utterly passé.[83] The comparative and more empirical studies of Bruce
Lincoln and his colleagues have demolished the remaining vestiges of the
Marxist critique of religion as the opiate of the people, and in its place, new,
more convincing theories are now advanced.[84] Generally speaking, modern
works have shown that religion can be Janus-faced in its social and political
expressions; it may at times contribute to the support of the social order, but the
same religion may suddenly turn into a force for change.[85] Submission to the
established order may be the dominant characteristic of a religious group for
generations, and yet submission to the higher authority of God can necessitate
resistance to the government when it attempts to usurp this higher authority.
Scholars are also currently emphasizing the importance of the interaction
between socio-economic forces, ideology, organizational structures, and
charismatic leadership.

The complexity of the role of religion in English society is also increasingly
acknowledged, particularly in the studies of E. P. Thompson, Harold Perkin,
W. R. Ward, and James Obelkevich. Thompson recognized the social importance of old Dissent for the eighteenth century and emphasized its contribution
to progressive political ideology. He understood Dissent as a stimulus to free
inquiry and popular political expressions of opposition, and he believed that the
Dissenters' frequent 'collision, schisms and mutations' nurtured the self-interest of the lower orders. The Dissenters, Thompson wrote, 'carried the principles of self-government and of local autonomy to the borders of anarchy'. The
anti-authoritarian intellectual tradition of eighteenth-century Dissent also nurtured the radical thought of such prominent eighteenth-century leaders as
Thomas Spence, Thomas Paine, and Thomas Hardy.[86] Harold Perkin's theory

83　Hannah Arendt, *On Revolution* (New York, 1963), p. 19. Similarly, E. J. Hobsbawm,
　　The Age of Revolution, 1789–1848 (New York, 1962), who says, 'In the ideologies of
　　the American and French [Revolutions] for the first time in European history, Christian-
　　ity is irrelevant', pp. 261–2. Daniel H. Levine, however, in *Religion and Political
　　Conflict in Latin America* (Chapel Hill, 1986), has shown how religion has strength-
　　ened political radicalism and revolutionary commitment, p. 16.
84　Lincoln, *Religion, Rebellion, Revolution*, pp. 266–83, for a thoroughgoing discussion
　　of changing theoretical frameworks. See also Richard C. Trexler, 'Reverence and
　　Profanity in the Study of Early Modern Religion', pp. 245–69 in Caspar von Greyerz
　　(ed.), *Religion and Society in Early Modern Europe, 1500–1800* (London, 1984).
85　See Gunther Lewy, *Religion and Revolution* (New York, 1974), pp. 555, 582.
　　W. R. Ward, 'Power and Piety: The Origins of Religious Revival in the Early
　　Eighteenth Century', *Bulletin of the John Rylands University Library of Manchester*, 63
　　(1980), 252 has shown clearly that theology must be related to specific social and
　　regional contexts; the same theology may have different effects given differences in
　　surroundings.
86　Thompson, *The Making of the English Working Class*, pp. 30, 39. Thompson argued
　　that the role of Methodism in the eighteenth century was negative because it reinforced
　　the control of the paternalistic establishment, and old Dissent tended to be viewed as
　　progressive only to the extent that it was theologically liberal. W. R. Ward in *Religion
　　and Society in England, 1790–1850* (London, 1973) saw Methodism in far more
　　progressive terms; similarly, James Obelkevich shows how religion promoted modern

of the relation of religion to class is more precise than Thompson's, but it is also based on literary, qualitative evidence. Perkin understood Dissent as the midwife to class in the nineteenth century and depicted religion's assistance to the parent of class in three ways. Sectarian religion emancipated people from 'the dependency system' of the ruling elite in Church and society by providing a viable alternative to the Establishment in Church and State. Second, it provided a model of class organization; when old Dissent pursued its own 'middle-class ends' such as opposing Church rates, it behaved as a 'class organization', and its participation in larger issues, such as parliamentary reform, helped transform interest groups generally into class group organizations. Third, by providing an example of the benefits of nonviolent opposition, it contributed to nonviolent class conflict as 'an analgesic against the pains of labour'.[87] Perkin's study lacked empirical substance, but further examination of Dissent in the eighteenth century will confirm and extend his concept of religious midwifery. Heretofore, the contribution of specifically religious ideology has not been sufficiently appreciated, nor has the interdependence of religious and economic motivation in producing opposition to the perceived oppressions of the Church, the law, and the government been understood. The studies of Thompson and Perkin supplied useful insights, but their works lacked a comprehensive character, and as a result, they failed to take ideology, office holding, and social status equally seriously, and they did not give adequate attention to the interaction of these elements.[88]

The purported exclusion of Nonconformists from local and national office by the Test and Corporation Acts is widely believed to be the reason why they went into industry and science in such large numbers; the law thereby provided the mechanism of marginality that simulated their energetic contribution to the middle and upper classes.[89] But the actual working of the law in relation to the

---

attitudes toward life and work in *Religion and Rural Society*, p. 203.

87 Perkin, *The Origins of Modern English Society*, pp. 196, 207–8, 347. Perkin, like Thompson, tends to reduce Dissent to 'a sublimated form of vertical social antagonism', and thereby takes neither theology nor ideology seriously. He believes that resentment toward the higher orders was 'diverted' into religion, pp. 34–6. Clark understands the importance of Dissent for the destruction of the *ancien regime* in terms of its rapid growth in the early nineteenth century, but he has not examined the social nexus of Dissent, *English Society*, p. 89.

88 Alongside the class arrangements that functioned relative to the social order, Weber placed the interlocking reality of social status. See Max Weber, 'Class, Status, Party', in C. Wright Mills (ed.), *Images of Man* (New York, 1960), pp. 121–35.

89 Perkin, *The Origins of Modern English Society*, p. 71; Thompson, *The Making of the English Working Class*, pp. 57–8; Kramnick, 'Religion and Radicalism', p. 508; Crane, 'The Club of Honest Whigs', 227. Philip Jenkins found little evidence that the exclusion of Tories from the center of high politics promoted their heavy involvement in industry, 'Tory Industrialism and Town Politics: Swansea in the Eighteenth Century', *HJ* 28 (1985), 123. Weber's thesis has recently received some qualified support; for the seventeenth century see Gordon Marshall, *Presbyteries and Prophets, Calvinism and the Development of Capitalism in Scotland, 1560–1707* (Oxford, 1980); David Little, *Reli-*

Dissenters has not been sufficiently examined, and more research on the proportion of manufacturing Dissenters in relation to Anglican manufacturers is needed. Arguments about the oppressiveness of the Test and Corporation Acts commonly lack the necessary context of local history and are often advanced with little reference to the social status of Nonconformity. The notion that the Dissenters were excluded from office might have led historians to examine whether their social status was one immediate cause of their political orientation, but remarkably, this question has hardly been posed, much less answered.[90]

In the search for social divisions in eighteenth-century England, R. S. Neale has suggested that we will have to be satisfied with literary evidence painstakingly derived from 'diligent search of newspapers and bits and scraps of paper'.[91] It may be true that in order to identify class *consciousness* verbal evidence of the common people's opinion will be required, but to establish the existence of social stratification related to political differences, other sources are showing great promise. We have seen that little evidence for conflict between social ranks has been discovered in the eighteenth-century electorate, in part because complicating matters such as a candidate's lack of a clear political stance often muddled the choice of individual voters. More hope for divulging latent social divisions is found in popular documents of political protest. Petitions to the crown form an alternative political pole centered around the single issue of the use of force in coercing the colonies. In addition, rich sources of ideological expression among Dissenters and occupational data of the same people allow us to probe the problem of the relationship between material and ideological causation in history, and this, in turn, may raise the discussion to a higher, more empirical level.

Nothing like a well-developed class structure is discernible in eighteenth-century England. George Rudé has rightly appealed for an open, undogmatic approach to the study of early modern popular ideology and behavior since the evidence does not fit a straightforward Marxist understanding of class conflict,

gion, Order, and Law (Chicago, 1984); and for the eighteenth, David Pratt, *English Quakers and The First Industrial Revolution: A Study of Quaker Communities in Four Industrial Counties – Lancashire, York, Warwick and Gloucester, 1750–1830* (New York, 1985).

90 K. R. M. Short in 'The English Indemnity Acts, 1726–1867', *CH* 42 (1973), 368, has begun work on the law; on Dissenting manufacturers in relation to Anglicans, see Everett E. Hagen, *On the Theory of Social Change: How Economic Growth Begins* (Homewood, Ill., 1962), p. 294. Three regional studies that have begun the social analysis are Charles I. Wallace, Jr., 'Religion and Society in Eighteenth Century England: Geographic, Demographic, and Occupational Patterns of Dissent in the West Riding of Yorkshire, 1715–1801', Duke University Ph.D. thesis, 1975, Albion M. Urdank, 'Dissenting Community: Religion, Economy and Society in the Vail of Nailsworth, Gloucestershire: An Economic, Tenurial, Social and Demographic Study, 1750–1850', Columbia University Ph.D. thesis, 1983; and David Pratt's work cited above.

91 R. S. Neale, *Class in English Society, 1680–1850* (Totowa, N.J., 1981), p. 189.

nor does it conform to traditional idealist accounts.[92] Recently historians have adopted a sophisticated use of the term 'community' and applied it to early modern social aggregates that predate the emergence of discernible class lines. It might be argued that the word 'community' connotes too much with respect to the self-consciousness and organization of artisans and shopkeepers, though Craig Calhoun insists that 'conscious goals in the minds of participants' are not necessary for cooperation.[93] But changing attitudes toward political authority and hierarchy can now be documented precisely among identifiable middle and lower ranked social groups and these attitudes can be related directly to conscious and articulate political expressions. This book provides quantitative evidence that masses of people were divided on a socio-economic basis concerning the American crisis; urban social antagonism related to political conviction was thus a reality in the mid 1770s. This struggle of divergent, relatively well-defined groups of people would appear to be a harbinger of genuine class or group conflict, and one of its principal components was religion. It is therefore possible to document the same early formation of communal behavior and possibly even class consciousness among English artisans that Gary Nash found in the colonies.[94] The petitions to the crown of 1775 reveal more than 'fleeting expressions' of social solidarities and they suggest that community divisions had already advanced beyond the 'stage of infancy'.[95] At least some urban artisans were able to transcend the fear of repression and move beyond anonymity, and the religious ideology of the Nonconformists served as an important stimulus to these actions. The Nonconformists never actively abetted armed resistance to the government, nor did they advocate social upheaval. But if English Dissenters in the period 1754–84 represented a religion of resistance rather than a religion of revolution, the Dissenting pulpit publicly advanced views that were considered politically

92 Rudé, *Ideology and Popular Protest*, pp. 13–38.
93 See Craig Calhoun, 'Community: Toward a Variable Conceptualization for Comparative Research', p. 110 in R. S. Neale (ed.), *History and Class: Essential Readings in Theory and Interpretation* (Oxford, 1983); Calhoun's comments are directed to the early nineteenth century, but they have relevance for urban discontent in the 1770s as well; see his *The Question of Class Struggle* (Chicago, 1982), pp. 149–82. For the earlier activity of urban artisans, see note 41 above and chap. 10 below. Calhoun notes that populations which mobilized for political activity were 'socially knit together through local communities or craft groupings', p. 180. For R. S. Neale's critique of Calhoun, particularly with respect to his failure to value the influence of ideas in shaping communities, see Neale, *History and Class*, pp. 289–91. But Neale's reasons for insisting on retaining Marxist language are not convincing.
94 E. P. Thompson, 'Eighteenth-Century English Society: Class Struggle without Class?', *Social History* 3 (1978), 149. The notion of community springing from religious differences has been established for the nineteenth century; Obelkevich, *Religion and Rural Society*, pp. 313–31. Gary Nash, *The Urban Crucible: Political Consciousness, and the Origins of the American Revolution* (Cambridge, Mass., 1979).
95 E. P. Thompson, 'Patrician Society, Plebian Culture', *Journal of Social History* 7 (1974), 398.

disruptive and in some cases actually became disruptive.[96] It will be important to distinguish between prudent expressions of loyalty and political behavior that was considered disorderly. Additionally, as agents of change, religious and economic factors seem to have been complementary rather than competing and an attempt will be made to evaluate the relative importance of each. But the nonrevolutionary nature of English religion in this period must be accounted for as well.

If Dissent served as a stimulus to class, paradoxically, religion also delayed violent class antagonism.[97] A more thorough examination of Dissenting religion reveals new dimensions of the openness of English society and goes some distance toward explaining its slow, relatively stable, and nonviolent evolution. Even in an age of revolution, English society was not as repressive as E. P. Thompson and the Marxists believed. A survey of the social structure of Dissent and an examination of the practice of office holding will show that Nonconformity both contributed to and benefitted from an open society that gave the impression, if not the substance, of freedom to many people. This study will demonstrate that the law in relation to the Dissenters actually operated in a remarkably benign manner. From the standpoint of comparative studies, religion helps us see how different England was from other early modern nations, and how pluralistic it was in the very midst of the aristocratic dominance recently depicted by John Cannon and Jonathan Clark.

The toleration of Nonconformity, therefore, reveals just how open eighteenth-century English society was, and Nonconformists thereby contribute to our understanding of why England itself did not experience revolution. If England was stratified by a patrician elite and a clerical intelligentsia at the top, these institutions were not sufficiently rigid to deter rapid social change or provoke political upheaval at the bottom. Although the Dissenters often perceived the establishment as an oppressive force, in fact they enjoyed freedom of worship and freedom of political expression to an unusual degree; their ministers were not denied the opportunity to preach political sermons, even when they bordered on sedition. If the Dissenters wished, they were relatively free to advance in the government itself, both locally and nationally, and they

---

96 Bruce Lincoln, 'Notes Toward a Theory of Religion and Revolution', in *Religion, Rebellion, Revolution*, pp. 275–6. Lincoln has advanced a useful theoretical framework and suggests that a religion usually lacks revolutionary potential when ancillary economic or legal pressures are absent. See also Alan D. Gilbert, 'Methodism, Dissent and Political Stability in Early Industrial England', *The Journal of Religious History* 10 (1978–9), 391–2.

97 Perkin observed that in emancipating people from 'the dependency system' religion delayed the hardening of society into overt class antagonism, *The Origins of Modern English Society*, p. 196. He saw this, however, primarily in terms of the enormous growth of Dissent in the late eighteenth and early nineteenth century. 'And the existence of numerous competing sects, which was more characteristic of Britain than of any other European country, provided a sequence of stepping stones by which the emancipated individual could make his way from the church to any position of Christian belief ... '

did so, particularly in the local setting, in surprisingly large numbers. Some ministers conformed to the Establishment and became Anglican priests. In addition, the Dissenting laity were free to voice their opposition to government policy in a variety of concrete expressions, including voting and petitioning. It is possible to demonstrate that Nonconformists also enjoyed relatively equal economic opportunity compared to Anglicans, and during the revolutionary crisis itself there was a notable absence of any real economic distress in England. Skilled urban artisans who may have felt oppressed appear to have taken a lesson from the Dissenters and seem to have vicariously appreciated the advantages many Nonconformists enjoyed.

The relationship between the Dissenters and this much larger body of Anglican and possibly secular Whigs who became disaffected with the government's American policy will require special attention, with a focus upon the potential ideological and economic links between the two groups. If religious ideology explains much about the progressive politics of the Dissenters, it does not explain all. Even with the handicap of the Test and Corporation Acts, the ideology of Nonconformity was not sufficient in itself to create a viable pattern of resistance to the government. Two additional ingredients were invariably needed: an issue that focused their concerns, such as the American crisis, and charismatic leadership to articulate their views. In those boroughs where the Dissenters lacked outspoken leaders, an absence of potent political opposition generally prevailed. But it appears that a third ingredient may have been determinative: the attainment of a middling level of socio-economic standing. There was thus a dynamic interaction between middle-class Dissenters who saw in the radical issues of the age a greater opportunity for pursuing legal equality and higher social status, an issue such as the American crisis to focus their attention, and the leadership of the elite to provide an ideology that both motivated and justified their behavior. But from the broader standpoint of social studies, the most important fact is that these expressions of opposition among the Nonconformists galvanized the political convictions of a numerous body of artisans.

In a handful of boroughs it is possible to discern how the mechanism of religion worked in relation to social discontent among non-Dissenters. The Bristol Dissenters, for example, were higher on the socio-economic scale than Dissenters in other boroughs, and they were also more economically advanced than most Anglicans in Bristol. Their status and wealth seem to help account for their greater level of political activism and their outstanding voting consistency. The behavior of the Bristol Dissenters suggests that a strong representation in the middle level of society had to be attained before it was likely for masses of people to act consistently together. The religion of the Dissenters involved sufficient strength of conviction that it made them a divisive force in elections, but to have a broader impact on non-Dissenters, their opposition had to be linked to socio-economic discontent. While the poll books often obscure this link, the petitions to the crown reveal a community of interests between Dissenters and non-Dissenters and Anglican artisans across a variety of urban settings. The American crisis did not stir discontent among the lowest orders of society, but rather among those who were improving their status and had the energy and leisure to pursue political interests. The ideological and social affinities between these artisans and the Dissenters thus require detailed examination. The evidence from Bristol corroborates Perkin's notion that religious cohesion antedates social cohesion, but it extends his findings by suggesting that religion and religious ideology worked in tandem with economic discontent and were really only effective when allied with it. Even at Bristol, however, the economic inequality was not serious enough to lead either Dissenters or Anglicans to actual rebellion.

The thesis expanded at length in the following chapters posits two interrelated aspects of the Dissenters' political life: the Dissenters' strong political self-identity was based on their religious ideology and legal status, and this in turn contributed to a social affinity with Anglican and possibly secular artisans that helped forge a political alliance. While the Dissenters' self-identity was essentially ideological, the alliance with the Anglicans was based on shared social and economic values; combined, these elements led the Dissenters, artisans, and Low-Church Anglicans to act together and their unified behavior provides one key to radicalism and partisan politics in some constituencies well into the nineteenth century. The link between Nonconformists and artisans will provide new insights into the role of religion in the early emergence of group consciousness and class struggle. The ideological and economic motivation behind political behavior cannot be neatly isolated, though it can be argued that religious ideology enjoyed a certain temporal priority. The religion of Dissent stimulated the discontent of many non-Dissenting artisans, and the temporal priority of religion can be demonstrated in numerous boroughs by the consistency with which the Dissenting elite, whether lay or clerical, took the lead in opposition to the government.

At the moment in Western history when the pursuit of happiness in this life had begun to supplant concern for one's soul in the life to come, religion still stood at the heart of much political contention. If the American Revolution was the first revolution to develop essentially along secular lines, and if the ideology of revolution had become secularized, the political behavior of many individuals was still largely determined by religion. This book, however, is not an attempt to explain English politics strictly in religious terms. Religion was in fact only a small facet of eighteenth-century politics; in many parliamentary boroughs Dissenters were not even numerous enough to have a chapel, and in Parliament itself, Dissenters throughout the eighteenth century were numerically insignificant. In the majority of boroughs there is no evidence of either political radicalism or social antagonism. Nonconformity has, however, been used to support a wide variety of political and social theories and this book represents an attempt to investigate the factual basis to these theories.

POLITICAL IDEOLOGY, POLITICAL BEHAVIOR, AND HISTORICAL METHOD

The most obvious defect in the Whig interpretation of Hanoverian England is that it examines political ideology primarily on the basis of literary sources, and since the accuracy of these documents remains an unsettled issue, one may always question the relation between ideology and actual behavior and dismiss ideas as mere propaganda. An excessive reliance on literary evidence is particularly characteristic of those studies of Nonconformity that have examined the ideas of the elite. Conversely, the greatest weakness in the modern conservative school is that it deals principally with social structure and behavior. In this case, the genuineness of serious ideological conviction is always in doubt; the conservative interpretation remains susceptible to the critique that as long as people's own avowals of political principle are discounted, their motivation can always be reduced to self-interest. Most books on eighteenth-century English politics continue to focus either on political ideology or popular or electoral behavior. Just as studies of radical ideology have neglected behavior, students of the social status of Dissent, such as E. D. Bebb, Alan Gilbert, and David Platt, have not attempted to relate social standing to political action. This book will attempt to show the reality of a dynamic interaction between ideology, social status, and behavior. The philosophical and methodological gaps assumed to exist between the social historian and the historian of ideas may possibly be bridged by concentrating on the religious ideology of a specific group of people and their political behavior in the context of a revolution.[98]

The religious, electoral, and economic data assembled here provide the basis for an approach to the study of the past that integrates social or structural, and political or ideological, concerns. Some scholars appear to believe that the task of relating the traditional interest in political ideas to the new interest in social history is impossible, or nearly so, due to the dominance of the latter.[99] Those engaged in the history of thought are not likely to suppose that important evidence for their discipline may lie in baptismal and burial registers, but undoubtedly one of the greatest puzzles in intellectual history is the question of

---

98 The division in the study of Dissent goes back to the 1930s; compare Anthony Lincoln's study of ideas with E. D. Bebb, *Nonconformity and Social and Economic Life, 1660–1800* (London, 1935). Gordon S. Wood called for a joining of the idealist and behaviorist approach to the study of politics in 'Rhetoric and Reality in the American Revolution', *WMQ*, 3rd ser., 23 (1966), 31. For more recent literature on the debate see Robert W. Fogel and G. R. Elton, *Which Road to the Past: Two Views of History* (New Haven, 1983).

99 Gertrude Himmelfarb, *The New History and the Old: Critical Essays and Reappraisals* (Cambridge, Mass., 1987), pp. 13–32.

how ideology and conviction are related to motivation, and how motivation in turn is transformed into behavior. It is one thing to trace the development of thought; it is quite another to measure and verify the effect of ideology in terms of human behavior. Historians of ideas have sometimes avoided questions of verification altogether because testing the utility or function of an idea appears to be at odds with the very ethos of the discipline.[100] Social historians, on the other hand, have been inclined to discount the causal force of ideas. In many specific local settings in England it will be found that an integrative approach to the study of history is not feasible because it necessitates the convergence of a wide variety of records, including poll books or signed petitions, birth and baptismal registers, and printed sermons or election ephemera. But in those boroughs where a full range of records is available, new dimensions of the complexity of human motivation are revealed. A serious attempt is made in this study to account for all of the causes leading to a pro-revolutionary attitude; Brewer's concentration on the non-electoral evidence for radicalism found in newspapers is thereby brought into closer relationship with Phillips' work on the more formal, institutional yardstick of poll books. When these sources are combined and examined in a variety of circumstances, the results suggest that religious, intellectual, economic, and social factors were often complementary rather than competitive; religious ideology was integrated with legal proscription and social inequality in such a way that together, these elements became conducive to independent, if not rebellious, political behavior. The diversity of materials necessitates a diversity of approaches, including the use of traditional narrative, intellectual history, and social and statistical analyses. The results of this research suggest that the variety of theories about political behavior have been unnecessarily narrow and exclusively preoccupied with one kind of evidence to the neglect of others.

Even the most sanguine defender of the influence of ideas in history does not believe that ideology is always, in every instance, equally important in explaining behavior. The role of popular ideology is only convincingly defended in terms of the occasional, perhaps unpredictable, influence of ideas. But detractors are inclined to discount the notion that ideas are ever influential, even in those circumstances where one might expect to find them playing a large role, such as in a revolution. And what is true of ideas in general is even more the case with religious ideas. The best students of political ideology are still often skeptical about the actual influence of specifically religious ideology.[101] Yet if the social historian wishes to see 'the mind put back in history', as Rudé termed it, then it will be necessary to 'trace the origins and course of the ideas

---

100 The most well-known example is found in the writings of Jacques Barzun, but see also David Hempton, *Methodism and Politics in British Society, 1750–1850* (Stanford, 1984), p. 26.
101 Bernard Bailyn, 'Religion and Revolution: Three Biographical Studies', *Perspectives in American History* 4 (1970), 85; Isaac, *The Transformation of Virginia*, p. 168.

that "grip the masses" (Marx's phrase)'.[102] Earlier discussions of the role of ideas in history were carried on at too simple a level, as if ideology could be neatly separated from events, or as if ideas had a direct causal force. Trygve Tholfsen, like Rudé, has significantly advanced the debate by insisting on the necessity of understanding ideas as an integral part of any event.[103] Political ideas do not arise in isolation from the culture, nor do they cause events in the same way that one motion causes another in the mechanical world. The social context of the ideas, the ideas themselves, and their function in stimulating and justifying behavior must be examined together.

These methodological and philosophical insights, however, have as yet not been applied to the ideology of the pulpit. A sermon was a public statement of political principle that took the preacher and his congregation far beyond their internal private convictions. Past treatments of Nonconformity have dealt with the written correspondence and private musings of the Dissenters, but little has been done with the ministers' sermons. In contrast, this study goes to the pulpit and the public oration, where we know that the laity heard, and in some cases read, the political thought of the preachers. Then we will turn to how the laity behaved. The focus of this book is thus on the public and their actions, rather than the preachers and their thoughts. As a public statement, the sermon was itself a political event, designed specifically both to inform and motivate the behavior of the laity; similarly, a speech at a county meeting called to petition the crown involved both ideology and behavior. The preacher and the public speaker at one and the same time articulated, acted out, and stimulated opposition to the government. It may be that the congregation's or the crowd's favorable response led the speaker to a more advanced statement of his principles in public than he had ever made while writing to a colleague or preparing a sermon in the quiet of his study. Here, ideology and behavior cannot possibly be separated. The ideas that the leaders held cannot appropriately be construed as mere ideology; preachers never merely 'held' certain ideas, but preached them, and this was an act that could in itself be considered treasonous in a revolutionary setting, since it entailed swaying the opinion and influencing the behavior of the populace against the government.[104] The literature published

---

102 George Rudé, 'The Changing Face of the Crowd', p. 203, in L. P. Curtis, Jr. (ed.), *The Historian's Workshop. Original Essays by Sixteen Historians* (New York, 1970). For an early expression of the principle of 'correlation' (the idea that all historical events must be understood together, as interrelated) see Ernst Troeltsch, *The Absoluteness of Christianity and the History of Religions* (1901), trans. David Reid (Richmond, Va., 1971), p. 9.

103 Trygve Tholfsen, *Ideology and Revolution in Modern Europe: An Essay on the Role of Ideas in History* (New York, 1984), pp. 6–7, 65, 154, and see the extensive review of the literature in chap. 1.

104 On the importance of charismatic leadership see John Baxter, 'The Great Yorkshire Revival, 1792–6: A Study of Mass Revival Among the Methodists', *Sociological Yearbook of Religion in Britain* 7 (1974), 46–76.

during elections reinforced the politics of the Dissenting pulpit, and thus two discrete types of printed sources will be analyzed in relationship to political behavior. The massive output of popular literature at contested elections at Bristol, for example, is exceeded only by London and Westminster, and yet both sermons and broadsides have remained largely unassayed. Political ideology, in all of its forms, is certainly part of the political event and the two cannot be related in a simple cause and effect nexus. The interconnectedness of thought and behavior as constituting a continuous political event is the only satisfactory way of explaining eighteenth-century popular politics.

In the preparation of this study, the question of historical method has been as prominent in my mind as the political issues themselves. Accordingly, the organization of the book is designed to show one way in which the study of ideology might be brought into closer relationship to the study of behavior. Previous works have seemed to suggest that the Nonconformists' religious convictions contributed directly to radicalism, but Part One will examine the legal, social, and ideological sources of radical Dissenting politics and show that social and legal conditions profoundly influenced the Dissenters' religion and their self-understanding. This investigation of the social and legal context helps explain the moderation that Bonwick found to be so characteristic of the Dissenters.[105] These chapters will study the Nonconformists' social standing in relation to Anglicans by a comparison of Dissenting and Anglican occupational structure. Since it is widely believed that the Test and Corporation Acts served as the operating mechanism for the emergence of radicalism, party, and class, the law in relation to the Dissenters' practice of office-holding must be examined in detail; indeed, the entire field of law in relation to religion is a subject that requires much further study. The Dissenters did not become radicals or bourgeois industrialists solely because they were excluded from office, because in fact, many of them enjoyed the benefits of office; in relationship to the Dissenters, English society and English law were remarkably tolerant. The first chapters in this section will show various reasons why Dissenters should *not* have been interested in expressing opposition to the government. Their behavior in some boroughs was typified by a pattern of deference, and in others, they consistently maintained their independence despite the enjoyment of office and place. Thus it is inappropriate to argue that the theological viewpoints of the Dissenters were a grand rationalization for their social distinctives, for they were able in many cases to transcend powerful social encumbrances, and at some risk to themselves, articulate their opposition rhetoric.[106] Their

---

105 Bonwick, 'English Dissenters and the American Revolution', pp. 108–9. The extent to which the Dissenters conformed to the social conditions of the day, however, means that Bonwick's concept of their self-identity as 'internal aliens' must be carefully qualified, *English Radicals*, p. 12.

106 The social science concept of boundary maintenance does not apply very effectively since the Dissenting elite were attempting to encourage political change. Robert F.

remarkable ability to maintain their political independence and develop a radical program is set forth in a study of the sermons of five provincial Dissenting ministers. The ministers' political ideology is then placed in the context of local history and local political interests in an attempt to account for the deeper feelings and more radical politics of some of the provincial leaders.[107]

Part Two investigates the political behavior of the Dissenters in six parliamentary boroughs where the American Revolution was raised as a political issue. The preaching of the ministerial elite is here related directly to the political behavior of the laity in their respective congregations. Entire monographs on single boroughs are now emerging, and such studies will add more detail than is possible to investigate here.[108] Boroughs differed from one another dramatically in the eighteenth century, and perhaps the greatest single need in the study of religion and politics is the examination of the Dissenters' political behavior under different local conditions. John Phillips found some variation in his study of four boroughs, but more variety yet is required. Bristol, Great Yarmouth, Newcastle upon Tyne, Liverpool, Kingston upon Hull, and Colchester will provide the complexity necessary to grasp the broader contours of religious influence. Records are richest for the large freeman boroughs, yet because of their very size, if a project is to be completed within a reasonable period of time, the number of cases must be carefully limited. These six boroughs were chosen on the basis of strenuous requirements concerning the available data; each borough must have a sufficient run of poll books during the period of the American Revolution to detect the possibility of change of behavior over time; each must have adequate non-parochial registers with occupations listed; and each must have returned candidates who at a minimum expressed an interest in the imperial crisis.[109] It must be granted that these boroughs are themselves unrepresentative of the tremendous range of borough constituencies, but the variety that is achieved offers the possibility of the first analysis of the electoral behavior of specific denominations within

Berkhoffer, *A Behavioral Approach to Historical Analysis* (New York, 1969), pp. 176–87. Recent work on the sociology of religion is less inclined to reduce religious developments to social causes, at least in a deterministic manner. Charles Y. Glock and Bryan Wilson, for example, no longer assert that sects inevitably develop into denominations. See Bryan Wilson, *Religion in Sociological Perspective* (Oxford, 1982), p. 98.

107 On the value of local history as a 'medium through which to investigate popular radicalism' see Knox, 'Popular Politics and Provincial Radicalism', 226. See also W. R. Ward's study, 'Power and Piety'.

108 I have in mind the works of G. S. DeKrey and John Sainsbury on London, Nicholas Rogers' forthcoming study on London and Bristol, and Thomas Knox on Newcastle upon Tyne.

109 At some point in the eighteenth century, Dissenters, or the friends of Dissenters, contested Bristol (Isaac Elton and Edmund Burke), Liverpool (John Hardman and William Meredith), Hull (Henry Hoghton and David Hartley), Colchester (Stamp Brooksbank and Alexander Fordyce), and Great Yarmouth (Henry Beaufoy and William Beckford).

Nonconformity.[110] It was also thought useful to examine precisely those boroughs in which urban radicalism merged with the issue of America, but where the political nature of the parliamentary contests has been denied.[111] Record linkage and statistical analysis of individual voters was accomplished with computer assistance with further attention in these chapters given to the social status of the Nonconformists.

The subject of this study is not electoral behavior in general terms: voter turnout, the effect of voting experience, and the penetration of the electorate into the population at large will be considered only as they bear on the Dissenting vote. However, questions concerning levels of partisan and cross voting and longitudinal analysis of the electorate over time must be addressed, for the Dissenters' behavior cannot be understood apart from these broader electoral developments.[112] But there has been no attempt here to penetrate to the level of individual behavior in municipal politics, and the related question of the interdependence of municipal elections and parliamentary politics is left for later research. These chapters seek to discern political consistency within identifiable minorities. Since the prior sweeping condemnations of the unreformed electorate have combined 'enlightened' and 'unenlightened' voters indiscriminately together, there is some value in attempting to isolate those voters who acted on the basis of political conviction.

The *History of Parliament* identified the political orientation of most candidates on the basis of one of two sources: parliamentary division lists and the judgment of political managers. In many cases the Member's voting record in Parliament and the private opinion of the elite are the only evidence we have. But numerous voters, particularly in the populous boroughs, saw the candidates through the eyes of the local writers of pamphlets, squibs, songs, and broadsides – popular sources that the *History of Parliament* has largely ignored. This popular literature put the aspiring M.P. in a political context for the average voter, and it was the primary means by which voters could connect men to measures. Collections of election literature and newspaper essays and notices will occupy a correspondingly large place in this study. The election

110 Bonwick notes that English and American Baptist correspondents were less politically oriented than Presbyterian and Congregational transatlantic correspondents, *English Radicals*, pp. 33, 273, note 14. But this study will show strong radicalism among Baptists at Bristol and Norwich.

111 Wherever Christie looked he found the same thing: parliamentary contests were dominated by local issues. But this can be shown to be related to the type of evidence that he examined. See on Newcastle, Nottingham, and Worcester, *The End of North's Ministry*, pp. 142–5, 145–7, 147–51. Colley observes the presence of extra-parliamentary Tory radical dissidence in these boroughs, 'Eighteenth-Century English Radicalism', 5, 15–16.

112 Phillips, *Electoral Behavior*, serves as a model for Part Two of this book and should be consulted for issues concerning the electorate and such technical topics as balloting procedures, swearing of oaths, etc. But whereas Phillips came to the Dissenters through a study of the electorate, this book comes to the larger electorate through a study of Dissenting voting behavior.

literature at Bristol, Newcastle, and Liverpool proves that the voters had a sophisticated awareness of their representatives' voting records in Parliament on issues of national importance. An examination of popular election literature is especially needed, not only because Namier and his colleagues have neglected it, but because it is the principal means by which one may connect parliamentary candidates with the policy of the administration, or with the opposition, and tie this ideological thread to local factions.

The Dissenters will also be examined in less than optimal local circumstances because it has not been adequately underscored before that the restrictions of the unreformed electorate influenced the Dissenters as well as the Anglicans. Dissenting voters were not only influenced by others, but in some circumstances, they were willing to use their influence to sway Anglican voters. Attention will also be given to the socio-economic status of voters; Newcastle upon Tyne is particularly valuable in this regard because the electorate illustrates social divisions related to radicalism, quite apart from the electoral influence of the Dissenting laity. For a variety of reasons, however, the progressive political ideology of the Dissenting elite did not have a measurable impact on the laity's voting in the majority of boroughs studied in Part Two.

Part Three will examine the popular petitions and the petitioning agitation of 1775. George Rudé and Thomas Knox began the task of analyzing the social background of the Middlesex petitioners, and Peter Marshall, John Sainsbury, and John Phillips have begun work on the American petitions.[113] The popular agitation over coercive measures in 1775 penetrated the populace in England as profoundly as the movement over the Middlesex election affair, and it did so over a longer period of time. The articulate spokesmen, such as Price and Priestley, have received almost as much attention as John Wilkes, but no one has studied the connection between the Dissenting elite and the laity on the order of Rudé's examination of the period 1768–74. A preliminary study of five small boroughs revealed marked religious and socio-economic differences between those who petitioned and supported peace and those who voiced support for the government.[114] While the poll books from Colchester, for example, revealed only minor cleavages in the electorate, the petitions over the American crisis point to deep and abiding religious and socio-economic divisions in society. The petitions will allow us to quantify the impact of religious ideology on urban society for the first time, and they will also reveal the economic motivation of many petitioners and suggest the reality of incipient class struggle. This study is limited, however, to the emergence of urban radicalism in its religious dimension in the period after the Middlesex election

113 George Rudé, *Wilkes and Liberty* (Oxford, 1962); Knox, 'Wilkism and the Newcastle Election of 1774'; Marshall, 'Manchester and the American Revolution', 168–86; Sainsbury, 'The Pro-Americans of London'; and John Phillips, 'Popular Politics in Unreformed England', *JMH* 52 (1980), 599–625.
114 Bradley, *Popular Politics and the American Revolution in England*, pp. 188–9.

affair; it will not deal with rural England on the one hand, or the topic of industrial unrest on the other.[115]

It can hardly be surprising that the political cleavages in England related to the American Revolution were caused in part by socio-economic differences, yet until now the presence of these differences over any national issue have largely been denied. The artisans and shopkeepers who supported the Americans cannot be viewed as moderate, backward oriented Commonwealthman radicals. The socio-economic data from Bristol, Newcastle upon Tyne, Nottingham, and Colchester suggest that these pro-American artisans were oriented in an independent, upwardly aspiring direction. In an earlier article on the topic of Nonconformity and radicalism, I suggested that it was overly optimistic to suppose that 'men always act upon their convictions, that a Presbyterian is a Dissenter before he is a merchant'.[116] At that time I had little inkling of the inveterate independence of the Dissenting ministry. For example, the attitude of Thomas Davis, pastor of the Reading Baptist chapel, was anything but deferential; while experiencing political pressure from the local parish priest in 1776 he wrote: 'The world rages, the devil roars, and the doctor of our parish said he would silence me if he went to the King in person, and the Bishop of London is his friend. I said they might tell him, if he had a mind to silence me he must take out my tongue'.[117] We now know a great deal about the patronage and influence of kings and bishops, but scholars have failed to grasp how the 'rebellious' disposition of ministers like Davis appealed to the lower orders, and how such a sharp and discontented tongue was translated into radical behavior by the Dissenting pulpit. It has taken a decade of research even to begin the task of measuring the relation between ideology and economic elements, and the picture that emerges is at once more complex and less predictable than I had imagined.

115 On the former, see Alan Everitt, 'Nonconformity in County Parishes', *Agricultural History Review*, 'Supplement', 18 (1970), 178–99; and *The Pattern of Rural Dissent: The Nineteenth Century* (Leicester, 1972); and on the latter, C. R. Dobson, *Masters and Journeymen: A Prehistory of Industrial Relations, 1777–1800* (London, 1980), on the militancy of labor, particularly in the cloth industry at Bristol, Taunton, and Tiverton. See also note 21 above.

116 Bradley, 'Whigs and Nonconformists', 13.

117 William Legg, *Historical Memorials of Broadstreet Chapel, Reading* (London, 1851), p. 50.

PART 1

The Legal Status, Social Structure, and Ideology of Nonconformity

2

Nonconformity, The Law, and Society

The Act of Uniformity required that every clergyman, schoolmaster, and fellow of a college accept the Book of Common Prayer, and all ministers were to receive episcopal ordination. The act became law on St. Bartholomew's Day, 24 August 1662, and immediately some 1,700 clergy were ejected from their livings.[1] The term Nonconformist was applied quite naturally both to these ministers and the congregations that gathered around them with the result that the former denominational distinctions that divided the Dissenters suddenly became less important. There were several attempts to 'comprehend' the Dissenters within the establishment in the 1670s and 1680s so that the distinction between Anglican and Dissenter, particularly the Presbyterians, was sometimes blurred nearly to the point of extinction. But the legislation of the Cavalier Parliament contributed more toward the Dissenters' self-definition and their self-conscious unity than all other efforts combined. Later generations would refer with disdain to the 'fatal Bartholomew Act' or the 'cruel Act of Uniformity', and with pride to those worthy gentlemen who had put principle above preferment and left the Church.[2] For many Dissenters the Act became a badge of honor and the touchstone of their self-understanding; it remained a major cause of their unity and independence well into the nineteenth century.

Volumes have been written on the legal status of Dissent as defined in the statutes of the realm, but very little research has been done on the way these laws were applied in everyday life.[3] While the actual working of the law has been repeatedly neglected,[4] the letter of the law has been made to appear more

1 14 Car. 2, c. 4. *The Statutes*, rev. edn (15 vols., London, 1870–8), contains the statutes referred to hereafter. Robert S. Bosher, *The Making of the Restoration Settlement: The Influence of the Laudians, 1649–1662* (London, 1951), p. 5; Douglas R. Lacey, *Dissent and Parliamentary Politics in England, 1661–1689* (New Brunswick, N.J., 1969), p. 19.

2 Josiah Thompson (ed.), *History of Protestant Dissenting Congregations*, 5 vols., 1772—, MS. 38.7–11, 1: 146; 3: 9 (hereafter cited as Thompson, History). In other places it was referred to as 'the famous year 1662' or 'the infamous Act of Uniformity'. *Ibid.*, 4: 58. On the definition of Dissent after the ejection, see 'The Gradations and Criteria of Dissent', in Lacey, *Dissent and Parliamentary Politics*, pp. 15–28.

3 Ursula Henriques, *Religious Toleration in England, 1787–1833* (Toronto, 1961), and Richard B. Barlow, *Citizenship and Conscience: A Study in the Theory and Practice of Religious Toleration in England During the Eighteenth Century* (Philadelphia, 1962).

4 N. C. Hunt, *Two Early Political Associations: The Quakers and the Dissenting Deputies*

stringent than it was so that modern studies continue to assume that the Dissenters were excluded from local office by the Corporation Act and from Parliament and high office by the Test Act.[5] To discover how the law was applied is admittedly a difficult task because circumventions of the law were usually covert. Dissenters often spoke of political activities as unwanted entanglements, though they continued to become 'entangled' whenever it served their interest. On those occasions when they agitated for repeal of the restrictive legislation they exaggerated the practical hindrance of the law and thereby implied that they had never actually circumvented it. Custom and convenience, however, are often more powerful than law, both when the law is harsh and when it is lenient, but especially when it is lenient. The practice of occasional conformity and other circumventions of the law must therefore be studied in the context of the actual oppression the Dissenters experienced, including both real and imagined restrictions. We will find that the perception of inequality and oppression was possibly more influential than their actual exclusion from office. An examination of the Nonconformists' occupational structure will show that they enjoyed a great deal of social freedom and considerable occupational status. The widespread practice of office holding in the municipalities suggests just how thoroughly they were socially assimilated by the mid-eighteenth century, yet their frequent expressions of independence in parliamentary elections reflect an abiding sense of unity and a strong group identity. Neither of these apparently contradictory facets of their political life can be understood apart from a fresh examination of their legal status and social standing in relation to Anglicans.

THE LAW AND THE UNITY OF 'THE DISSENTING INTEREST'

The legislation of the Restoration period was the principal cause of the Dissenters' political unity in the eighteenth century. The Corporation Act of 1661 was designed to keep seditious persons from holding seats on town corporations; it was conceived to alleviate Royalist fears that the Dissenters would dominate local government and return significant numbers of M.P.s from those boroughs where the corporation influenced parliamentary elec-

    in the Age of Sir Robert Walpole (Oxford, 1961), p. 126 says the practical position of
    Dissent before the law is 'difficult if not impossible to assess with complete certainty'.
    Henriques, *Religious Toleration in England*, p. 15. K. R. M. Short, 'The English Indem-
    nity Acts, 1726–1867', *CH* 42 (1973), 371, note 3, calls for further study on 'the
    incidence or discipline of occasional conformity.'
  5 Charles F. Mullett, 'The Corporation Act and the Election of English Protestant
    Dissenters to Corporation Offices', *Virginia Law Review* 21 (1935), 642; Russell E.
    Richey, 'The Origins of British Radicalism: The Changing Rationale for Dissent', *ECS*
    7 (1973–4), 179; John Cannon (ed.), *The Whig Ascendancy* (New York, 1981), p. 208;
    Roy Porter, *English Society in the Eighteenth Century* (London, 1982), p. 187.

tions.[6] In about thirteen percent of the boroughs the franchise rested with the corporation members alone, and in these constituencies, a small number of men (usually ranging from eighteen to thirty-two) returned representatives to Westminster. The boroughs where the franchise was held by a small number of freemen should be added to the corporation boroughs, since the corporation or borough patron could influence elections through controlling the creation of 'honorary' freemen. When these two borough types are combined, the total number of English constituencies where the corporation could potentially influence elections rises to about thirty-five percent of the whole.[7] The Cavalier Parliament believed the Dissenters were numerous enough to warrant legislation that required candidates for local office to take the 'several oaths of supremacy and allegiance' and receive 'the sacrament of the Lord's Supper according to the rites of the Church of England' one full year before election to office. Conscientious Dissenters were thereby excluded from office holding in all incorporated towns and denied the right to vote in parliamentary (though not municipal) elections in roughly one-third of the boroughs. It must be emphasized, however, that this legislation made no attempt to determine whether the Dissenters inhabited those seventy-odd boroughs, it could not anticipate their willingness to conform occasionally to qualify for office, and it left the franchise intact in all county and two-thirds of the borough constituencies. The Test Act (1673) was directed principally at Catholics but impinged on Dissenters as well. It accomplished for civil and military offices under the crown what the Corporation Act did for the municipalities, with the exception that the sacramental test was not enforced until three months after the officeholder was actually installed.[8]

The Act of Toleration (1689) is often described as a 'grudging concession', since the penal legislation was not repealed by it.[9] This act did exempt the Dissenters from the penalties inflicted by the former legislation, provided that they took the new oaths of allegiance. It permitted them freedom to worship if

---

6 13 Car. 2, stat. 2, c. 1. The full title is 'An Act for the Well Governing and Regulating of Corporations.' Lacey, *Dissent and Parliamentary Politics*, pp. 19, 30, 35, 37.

7 Based upon the assessment of borough constituencies in *Commons, 1715–1754* and *Commons, 1754–1790*. This includes freeman boroughs with electorates under 500 and these figures are approximate, since some corporations in the medium sized freeman boroughs wielded great influence. *Commons, 1754–1790*, 1: 20, 27. See note 62 below. There are minor differences of classification between the volumes of the *History of Parliament* for the first half and last half of the century.

8 25 Car. 2, c. 2. The Test Act did not apply to noncommissioned army or navy officers, nor to such 'inferior offices' as overseers of the poor, or surveyors of highways (see clause XVII). See Hunt, *Two Early Political Associations*, pp. 120–9. Two other laws worked considerably more hardship on the Dissenters: The Conventicle Act (1664) and the Five Mile Act (1665). These acts effectively dispersed the laity and silenced ministers in centers of population. 16 Car. 2, c. 4; 17 Car. 2, c. 2. A second Conventicle Act in 1670 mitigated the harshness of the penalties, but gave wider powers of enforcement.

9 E. N. Williams, *The Eighteenth Century Constitution, 1688–1815: Documents and Commentary* (Cambridge, 1970), p. 6.

their ministers subscribed to thirty-four of the Thirty-Nine Articles.[10] The doctrinal compatibility of the Anglicans and the Dissenters is emphatically underscored by the Dissenters' willingness to subscribe to the remaining articles; they did not chafe under this requirement until late in the eighteenth century when the drift into Unitarianism was becoming widespread, particularly among Presbyterians. The 'penalties' of the Test and Corporation Acts, however, were not among those from which they were exempted. In addition, the Dissenters were required to meet in unlocked buildings, pay tithes, and register their assemblies with the local bishop, archdeacon, or justice of the peace. Despite these limitations, Macaulay was undoubtedly correct when he wrote that the act 'removed a vast mass of evil without shocking a vast mass of prejudice'.[11]

If the Act of Toleration was lenient, it clearly did not permit any church or group of churches to qualify as a serious rival to the Established Church. The Presbyterians quietly dropped their proposed scheme of national synods and became congregational in polity; the distinguishing mark of Presbyterian polity was hereafter reduced to the ordination of ministers. This had the effect of endearing them to the Congregationalists, and following 1689 the denominations considered various ways to unite in the common cause. Expressions of unity can be found in a wide array of organizations, including the boards that were formed to collect funds designed to aid struggling congregations, ministerial associations, particularly in London, and above all, the Dissenting Deputies founded in 1732 for the common defense and protection of the Dissenters' civil rights. The Dissenting Deputies organized the movements for the repeal of the Test and Corporation Acts, they raised support for the legal defense of Dissenters, and they provided counsel on a variety of controversial subjects.[12]

The Toleration Act did not remove the previous penal legislation, but it did encourage a diversity of religious expressions. The Dissenters' new experience of freedom however, did not lead to their complete isolation from the Anglican Church. The frequency of the practice of occasional conformity so alarmed High Anglicans that when their party gained the ascendancy in the first years of Anne's reign, they were determined to conclude the unfinished business of

---

10 1 W. & M., c. 18. The full title makes these points clear: 'An Act for exempting their Majesties protestant subjects, dissenting from the church of England, from the penalties of certain laws.' Articles 20 and 34 through 36 dealing with rites and ceremonies, the traditions of the church, and ordination were not required; Article 27 on infant baptism was not required of Baptists.

11 Lord Macaulay, *The History of England from the Accession of James the Second*, (ed.), C. H. Frith, 6 vols. (London, 1913–15), 3: 1390.

12 Patricia M. Scholes, 'Parliament and the Protestant Dissenters, 1702–19', University of London M.A. thesis, 1962, pp. 89, 103, 110–14, 127–8; Russell E. Richey, 'Effects of Toleration on Eighteenth-Century Dissent', *JRH* 8 (1975), 352–3; Bernard Lord Manning, *The Protestant Dissenting Deputies*, (ed.), Ormerod Greenwood (Cambridge, 1952); Hunt, *Two Early Political Associations*, and Barlow, *Citizenship and Conscience*.

1689 and totally exclude the Dissenters from office. It took the Tories numerous attempts, several desperate ploys, and a considerable electoral victory in 1710 to obtain passage of the Occasional Conformity bill, and with it, the prospect of quashing the Dissenters' political influence seemed within their grasp.[13] But the accession of the first Hanoverian, the return of the Whigs to office, the Whig victory in the general election of 1715, and the failure of the Jacobite rising so decimated the Tories that they could not stop the Whigs from repealing the Act in 1719. To this date, neither the Tories, the Whigs, nor the Dissenters themselves had any solid information on the number of Dissenters nor the number of boroughs they inhabited. The legislation and much of the party rhetoric before 1719 was based either upon the exaggerated fears of High-Church Tories – Henry Sacheverell believed the Dissenters were everywhere – or the over-optimistic hopes of the Dissenters and Low-Church Whigs – Daniel Defoe estimated their strength in 1703 at an unbelievable 2,000,000.

The common theological heritage of the Dissenters and their shared political experience under the Stuarts combined to shape them into a single, well-defined religious tradition. The unifying agents of law, ideology, and experience led naturally to much intercommunion at the local level. The Dissenters continued to display numerous differences in doctrine throughout the eighteenth century and some disagreements over discipline and polity remained, but their underlying unity was more impressive and it was pivotal for their political history.[14] When describing the three denominations, contemporary Nonconformists spoke appropriately of 'the Dissenting Interest'; in the manuscript sources this phrase is found time and again.[15] The Dissenters of the three denominations, however, carefully distinguished themselves from both the Quakers and the Methodists. In neither the seventeenth nor eighteenth century is there any evidence that the three denominations combined with the Quakers for worship; in both doctrine and practice the Friends were far removed from other Dissenters. The Quakers also established their own separate political

---

13 10 Anne, c. 6. On the Occasional Conformity bill see Scholes, 'Parliament and the Protestant Dissenters', pp. 73, 81–2; and John Flaningam, 'The Occasional Conformity Controversy: Ideology and Party Politics, 1697–1711', *JBS* 17 (1977), 42–3, 52–3, 56–7 who treats it as an important political issue. The Whigs' opposition to the Schism bill gained them some credit with the Nonconformists. Geoffrey Holmes, *Religion and Party in Late Stuart England* (London, 1975), p. 15. Scholes, 'Parliament and the Protestant Dissenters', pp. 90–1, 96, 98, 107.

14 On theological points of agreement and fraternal cooperation between the denominations, see James E. Bradley, 'Toleration, Nonconformity, and the Unity of the Spirit: Popular Religion in Eighteenth-Century England', pp. 183–99 in Bradley and Richard A. Muller (eds.), *Church, Word and Spirit: Historical and Theological Essays in Honor of Geoffrey W. Bromiley* (Grand Rapids, 1987).

15 'A View of the Dissenting Interest in London... from the Year 1695 to the 25 of December 1731', (1731), MS. 38.18, (hereafter cited as A View, 1731), p. 2; Josiah Thompson, 'List of Protestant Dissenting Congregations in England and Wales', (1772–3), MS. 38.6, p. 1, (hereafter cited as Thompson List 38.6); Thompson, History, 2: 67, 74; 3: 82–3.

organization to work for relief from the burden of tithes. Nevertheless, at the local level of English politics, the Quaker vote was sometimes analyzed along with the three denominations and this suggests that they would normally act together on the side of the Whigs.[16]

The common legal status of the three denominations and the Quakers was expressed in terms of continuous pressure from the state, particularly at the local level. There were, for example, several notorious cases of the legal oppression of Dissent grounded on the Test and Corporation Acts. Perhaps the most well-known incident was the 'Sheriff's Cause', which began in 1739 when the city of London set about to build the new Mansion House. Some ingenious common councilman advanced the idea of passing a law that anyone who declined nomination to the office of sheriff should be fined £600. The city then began to nominate known Dissenters who refused to qualify for the office by taking the sacrament; these people were subsequently fined. The corporation of London raised the sum of £15,000 in twelve years by this method and it was not until 1767 that Lord Mansfield finally gave judgment in favor of the Dissenters.[17] This episode was, however, certainly an exceptional instance of injustice. It cannot be convincingly argued that the large sums raised in this case prove that occasional conformity was rare,[18] since the circumstances were coercive and bound to provoke a reaction.

Besides the more important matter of office holding and the threat this posed to the Dissenters' professional advancement, Nonconformists were often burdened by numerous minor legal nuisances.[19] Dissenters were excluded

16 Hunt, *Two Early Political Associations*, pp. 62–112. The Quaker vote is reported in the Evans List for Berkshire (100 freeholders), Cumberland (99 freeholders), Hampshire (27 freeholders), Hertfordshire (100 freeholders, and can influence about 80 churchmen). The number of hearers is noted for Westmorland, and voters for the boroughs of Hertford (32), and Durham (16). Their wealth and strength is noted for Bristol. John Evans, 'List of Dissenting Congregations and Ministers in England and Wales (1715–29)', MS. 38.4; pp. 5, 105, 49, 122, 35, 147 (hereafter cited as Evans List). See Bradley, 'Nonconformity and the Electorate in Eighteenth-Century England', *Parliamentary History*, 6 (1987), 236–61, for the trustworthiness of this list and the Thompson List. One rare instance of a Quaker meeting voting with the Tories is found at Hertford, *Commons 1715–54*, 1: 261. Before 1790 it is impossible to distinguish Methodist electors from other Anglicans.

17 Manning, *The Protestant Dissenting Deputies*, pp. 119–29.

18 Short, 'The English Indemnity Acts', 371.

19 An important series of articles by Charles F. Mullett can find little place for the lenient workings of the law. His comment, 'they could not secure the removal of the hydra-headed penal laws whose cruel embrace might at any time effectively suppress their activity', is typical. See 'The Corporation Act and the Election of English Protestant Dissenters to Corporation Offices', *Virginia Law Review* 21 (1935), 641–64; 'The Legal Position of English Protestant Dissenters, 1660–89', *Virginia Law Review* 22 (1936), 495–526; 'The Legal Position of English Protestant Dissenters, 1689–1767', *Virginia Law Review*, 23 (1937), 389–418; 'The Legal Position of the English Protestant Dissenters, 1767–1812', *Virginia Law Review* 25 (1939), 671–97; 'Lord Mansfield and English Dissenters', *Missouri Law Review* 2 (1937), 46–62; see also W. Gordon Robinson, 'The Toleration Act of 1689', *London Quarterly and Holborn Review* 187

from Oxford and could not take degrees at Cambridge by university statutes that were not abolished until 1854 and 1856 respectively; an act of 1871 removed tests for fellowships and other academic offices and degrees. Once at the university, however, students were not debarred from attending Dissenting meeting houses; we know of at least three instances of Dissenters attending Cambridge in the late eighteenth century.[20] Nonconformists were also prevented by the Toleration Act from teaching at the English universities, but the Cambridge Baptists could boast of one illustrious member in the 1770s who was also a professor of music in the university. 'Dr. Randel the present Professor of music in this University who worships with this people consist[ent]ly (except when his office in the University obliges him to be absent) hath ese:d [essayed?], all:d [altered?], and even comp[ose]d music for this assembly.'[21] Those Dissenters who wished to obtain university training were most often educated in Scotland; others went to the continent. Dissenters thus had their own alternate educational system in their excellent academies and in the universities of Scotland and the Netherlands, though they were occasionally given trouble by local authorities over the licensing of their academies.[22]

In some localities the denial of burial plots for the Dissenters in the parish churchyard proved a nuisance.[23] The prevailing practice, however, was for Dissenters to set aside a portion of their own church property for burials, either when the church was first built, or when it was enlarged.[24] Far more interesting are the numerous instances where local Anglican clergymen allowed the burial of Dissenters in the churchyard. In those cases where there was a genuine need for this form of relief, the practice seems seldom to have been denied; in the minutes of the Dissenting Deputies from 1732 to 1749, only two cases of Anglican refusal to allow burials in the churchyard were recorded.[25] But vicars could, and sometimes did, claim minor fees for deaths, burials, and churchings of Dissenters under section 6 of the Act of Toleration, even though

(1962), 178.

20 Since, technically, they could matriculate, but not graduate from Cambridge. William Wilberforce, *Correspondence,* (ed.), Samuel Wilberforce and Robert I. Wilberforce, 2 vols. (London, 1840), 1: 46.

21 Thompson, History, 1: 164.

22 *Ibid.,* 4: 232–3, 243, 300, 305. Philip Doddridge at Northampton, Joshuah Oldfield at Coventry, John More at Bridgwater, and possibly many others, experienced legal trouble related to the academies. T. Gascoyne et al., *A History of Northampton Castle Hill Church* (Northampton, 1896), pp. 21–2; Thompson, History, 4: 297, 170.

23 Robinson, 'The Toleration Act', p. 178.

24 All three denominations practiced this. Thompson, History, 2: 21, 212; 4: 20, 46, 50–1, 147, 172, 178, 254; 5: 61; the Thompson List, 38.6, p. 12. The Dissenters were apparently barred from burying their dead in the meeting house itself at Norwich. Thompson, History, 4: 19.

25 Thompson, History, 4: 223. In the same volume see pp. 238, 301, 323, 324, for instances of Dissenting ministers buried in Anglican churches. The Protestant Dissenting Deputies, Minutes, 2 vols. (9 November 1732–20 May 1791), MS. 3083–1, 1: 278, 311 (hereafter cited as Dissenting Deputies, Minutes).

the services were never rendered. At Castle Gate Congregational Church, Nottingham, for example, the Dissenters were threatened with burial fees even though the chapel had its own grounds. Church rates for the upkeep of the parish church and tithes were always galling, since the Dissenters received little or no benefit from them.[26]

The question of the legitimacy of weddings performed by Dissenting ministers was also troublesome. The possibility of persecution was definitely feared by the Baptists at Northampton, who, in 1709, agreed to contribute to a fund to be used in defense of their rights should any difficulty arise. The most famous incident in the eighteenth century arose at Wakefield in the Scott-Naylor suit. The case began in the Ecclesiastical court of York and ended in King's Bench in favor of the Dissenters in 1730. Nevertheless, as late as 1750, a Leicestershire man married in a Baptist meeting house was later indicted for living in adultery with his wife.[27] In 1753, Lord Hardwicke's Marriage Act required that all marriages (the Quakers alone excepted) must be celebrated in parish churches by Anglican clergy; it was not until 1836 that marriages performed by Nonconformist ministers were considered legally valid.

The Toleration Act required the registration of meeting houses with the bishop of the diocese or the Justice of the Peace, and this stipulation was considered oppressive. The Dissenting Deputies examined at least one case in which an Anglican clergyman refused to grant the appropriate certificates.[28] These instances of opposition, however, were rare, and there were several ways to meet the requirement. In Cambridgeshire the Dissenters faced a peculiar problem when, in 1764, the Bishop of Ely refused to grant any more certificates. Previously he had received the Dissenters' request and registered new meetings, but then he suddenly stopped the practice. 'The reason he assigned was that the Methodists had procured at his office several licenses (as his Lordship called them) and as they did not profess themselves dissenters, their Certificates were illegal and he could not protect them. To prevent any mistakes in the future, he determined to grant none.' The Dissenters therefore applied instead to the Quarter Sessions, and found that from 1764, they always

---

26 A. R. Henderson, *History of Castle Gate Congregational Church, Nottingham, 1655–1905* (London, 1905), p. 159. At Denton, Norfolk, the parish church got a shilling for every corpse buried in the Dissenting yard. Thompson, History, 4: 9. On church rates see Richard Alliott and Samuel McAll, *An Historical Account of the Congregational Church Worshipping in Castle Gate Meeting House, Nottingham* (London, 1856), p. 157; H. G. Tibbutt, *A History of Howard Congregational Church, Bedford* (Bedford, 1961), p. 18.

27 T. Arnold Culross, *The Jubilee of the Rev. J. T. Brown. A History of College Street Chapel, Northampton* (Northampton, 1893), p. 19; H. D. Roberts, *Hope Street Church, Liverpool* (Liverpool, 1909), pp. 59–60.

28 Mullett, 'The Legal Position of English Protestant Dissenters, 1689–1767', 398. Dissenting Deputies, Minutes, 1: 272. But this is found only once in the period 1732 to 1749.

'obtained them with ease'.[29] Some such avenue of recourse was usually available for those who sought it. But the situation at Cambridge illustrates another point; regional variations meant that the law could be applied with leniency, but it could just as easily be applied harshly. Regional differences thus contributed to the Dissenters' anxiety concerning the law.

A related requirement based on the same act insisted that ministers take the oaths of supremacy and allegiance to the crown. Another example from Cambridge shows how offensive this requirement came to be in the second half of the century. Robert Robinson, the Baptist pastor at Cambridge, reported the incident in his church book. 'In the year 1765 Will[ia]m Howel Ewin Esq[ui]re LLD, one of His Majesties [sic] justices of the peace in Cambridge advised the Dissenting ministers in the town to qualify as the Act of Toleration required.' Robinson felt that 'Dr. Ewin's advice was quite friendly, was sent by Mr. Ivat to me and was meant to preserve us from trouble on acc[oun]t of the omission.' Accordingly, Robinson and the local Congregational pastor went to the Quarter Sessions and took the required oaths in the presence of the earl of Hardwicke and several other J.P.s, for which the ministers received certificates. Writing in 1774, nine years after the incident, Robinson made the following comment: 'Had I seen the thing in the light I now do I might have thanked Dr. Ewin for his advice; but would have run all hazard rather than have qualified thus. Blessed be God for an High Priest who can have compassion on the ignorant and them that are out of the way.'[30] What had transpired in the period 1765 to 1774 that prompted Robinson so radically to change his attitude toward the law?

Before the period of the American Revolution, Nonconformist ministers had almost without exception voiced aloud their uniform appreciation for the English government. Warm expressions of loyalty and a due sense of the benefits enjoyed under the Hanoverians can be found in the writings of William Belsham, Richard Price, and Joseph Priestley.[31] Prior to the mid-1760s, the Dissenting elite did not often feel that the law was oppressive; in fact, it often seemed accommodating. The Riot Act of 1715 contained a clause that was designed to protect the Dissenters' chapels, and the government had made

---

29 Thompson, *History*, 1: 158–9, note 2. In 1800 at Wetheringsett, Suffolk, a local magistrate imposed the maximum penalty for the meeting house not being registered. Charles B. Jewson, *The Baptists in Norfolk* (London), p. 65.

30 Recorded in Thompson, *History*, 1: 168.

31 For Belsham, see Anthony Lincoln, *Some Political and Social Ideas of English Dissent, 1763–1800* (Cambridge, 1938), p. 22; Price is cited in J. C. D. Clark, *English Society, 1688–1832* (Cambridge, 1985), p. 316; Priestley, *An Essay on the First Principles of Government, and on the Nature of Political, Civil and Religious Liberty* (London, 1768), in *The Theological and Miscellaneous Works of Joseph Priestley*, (ed.), J. T. Rutt (Hackney, 1817–31), 22: 96. Lincoln refers to the Dissenters' political shift against the government in the decade 1768–78 as 'the central fact of dissenting politics in this period', p. 27.

adjustments to the law in 1722 to accommodate the Quakers' antipathy toward oaths. Dissenters were always free to seek seats in Parliament and a number roughly equal to their proportion of the population did so. If the consciousness of the need for greater political and legal independence was slow in developing among progressive ministers such as Robinson and Priestley, it also dawned slowly on the laity. By 1765, the Dissenters were two generations removed from the experience of Tory oppression under Queen Anne, and even the memory of the Forty-Five had by this time begun to fade. Laws that had formerly seemed to establish their liberty came by degrees to seem burdensome, but the failure to take full account of the changing social and political context has resulted in exaggerated and anachronistic statements about the 'oppressive' nature of the law under the early Hanoverians. The Dissenting laity had to be told that the law was oppressive, for their experience under George I and George II did not often teach them that it was. Wilkes, Fox, and the Dissenting elite in London and the provinces took up the task of education where Shaftesbury left off.

By 1774 Robinson was expressing a sentiment that reflected a widespread reorientation toward the government among his fellow Nonconformists. This reorientation had begun among some Dissenters, such as James Murray, Joseph Towers, and Joseph Priestley, as early as the mid-1760s. In the decade 1765–75 the debate with the colonies over the question of taxation began to stimulate interest in matters of political right and representation, and 'Wilkes and Liberty' became a slogan known all across the land. There is some evidence, though it is sketchy, that Dissenters were involved in the petitioning agitation over the Middlesex election affair.[32] Far more evidence is available concerning the Dissenters' dismay in the early 1770s at the defeat of the bill to relieve their clergy from subscription to the Thirty-Nine Articles and their alarm at the passage of the Quebec Act. Earlier, Dissenters perceived the Catholic menace as something that threatened government from outside; now they came to believe that they could find a pernicious sympathy for Catholicism within the government itself. Increasingly, they believed that their situation under George III was similar to that of their ancestors under Charles I, and, as later chapters will show, the Dissenters contributed directly to both the articulation and dissemination of the Whig myth of the early years of George III's reign. The depth of their disenchantment with the government at home was matched only by their growing sympathy for the colonists abroad. The bonds of affection that tied the Dissenters to the colonists had been established through generations of correspondence that revealed deep mutual interests, and thus the

32 Barlow, *Citizenship and Conscience*, pp. 132-6; Colin Bonwick, *English Radicals and the American Revolution* (Chapel Hill, 1977), p. 58. Wesley believed that religion was peripheral in the divisions of the 1760s. 'Free Thoughts in the Present State of Affairs' (London, 1768), *The Works of the Rev. John Wesley*, 3rd edn, Thomas Jackson, (ed.) (London, 1829-31 [reprinted, Grand Rapids, 1958-59]), 11: 27, 29.

attempts to establish episcopacy in the colonies were resented by the English Dissenters, and this in turn contributed to their growing hostility to the establishment.

While the American conflict was the principal cause that disengaged the Dissenters from their loyalty to the Hanoverians, a more strictly theological cause was also at work. As J. C. D. Clark has recently argued, the increasing number of Dissenters who adopted Arian or Unitarian views readily extended their critique of trinitarian thought to the orthodox Anglican establishment in general. But while not all Dissenters shared such liberal theological views, they all agreed on the biblical necessity of a separated polity, and it is likely that the shared characteristic of congregationalism, combined with the fear of episcopacy, was even more influential than heterodoxy. The antagonism to the establishment that had lain dormant for years in the Nonconformists' congregational polity became, under the influence of these events, explicit and outspoken. It took very little prodding to rekindle their mental habit of opposition into overt resistance; traditional Anglican fears that the Dissenters were inherently disruptive thus proved to be quite well-founded. The Dissenters began to demand once again the same legal equality for their separate organizations that the colonists claimed for themselves. Moreover, they represented a tradition that had already distinguished itself in the cause of liberty. By the mid-1760s, they had established a well-known pattern of opposition to unjust laws, and such innovative organizations as the Dissenting Deputies provided them with a powerful mechanism for political lobbying.

Previous accounts of eighteenth-century Nonconformity have thoroughly examined the Dissenters' progressive attempts to repeal the laws that burdened them, their association with radical politics, and their commitment to parliamentary reform.[33] The record of Nonconformity in these respects is indeed impressive. The Dissenting Deputies, for example, represented the three denominations in their numerous attempts to repeal the Test and Corporation Acts. That the first agitation against these Acts did not commence until 1732 suggests just how broadly satisfied the Dissenters were with Toleration, the Hanoverians, and the Whigs, but these first attempts met with defeat in 1736 and again in 1739. The Quakers, in the meanwhile, agitated against paying church rates and tithes and pressed a bill through the House of Commons in 1736 that was defeated in the House of Lords.[34] If the Dissenters were

---

33 See Manning, *The Protestant Dissenting Deputies*; Barlow, *Citizenship and Conscience*; Hunt, *Two Early Political Associations*; and Bonwick, *English Radicals*, chap. 7 on 'Religious Liberty'; James E. Bradley, 'Religion and Reform at the Polls: Nonconformity in Cambridge Politics', *JBS* 23 (1984), 55–78.

34 Manning, *The Dissenting Deputies*, p. 19; Hunt treats the means for attempting repeal in 1732 and has a detailed account of the agitation, *Two Early Political Associations*, pp. 128–9; 132–78; on the Quakers, see pp. 62–112. Stephen Taylor, 'Sir Robert Walpole, the Church of England, and the Quakers' Tithe Bill of 1736', *HJ* 28 (1985), 51–78.

minimally involved in the earliest issues surrounding John Wilkes, they were soon involved in radical politics; of the approximately twenty-five members of the famous Commonwealthman 'Club of Honest Whigs' in London, fully fifteen were Dissenting clergymen or schoolmasters. Dissenters were very active in the American crisis, as later chapters will show, and in the 1770s they also agitated against the necessity of subscribing to the Thirty-Nine Articles as stipulated in the Act of Toleration. In 1772 they circulated a petition that led to a bill to relieve Protestant Dissenting ministers and schoolmasters from subscription. The bill passed through the Commons in 1772 and again in 1773; it was supported by virtually all parliamentary factions, but it was twice rejected in the Lords. G. M. Ditchfield has recently shown that the Parliament of 1768–74 'witnessed more contentious religious debate than had appeared in the legislature at any time since the 1730s'.[35] In 1779 Dissenting ministers and tutors were finally granted protection under the Act of Toleration if they merely agreed that they were Protestants and accepted the Scriptures.

In the late 1780s the Dissenters once again dedicated themselves to seeking the repeal of the Test and Corporation Acts, but they were defeated in 1787 and 1789 by close margins, and with the coming of the French Revolution, the fifth and last bill on the subject during the eighteenth century went down to overwhelming defeat in 1790. Ditchfield has convincingly shown that the same Dissenting interest in Parliament that supported repeal also backed parliamentary reform. A close analysis of parliamentary division lists shows that the Dissenting lobby extended beyond the actual Dissenting representatives to embrace some 150 M.P.s and this group worked consistently over a period of years for liberal causes, including abolition of the slave trade.[36] These exertions on the part of Dissenters resulted in the production of several important theoretical works in the history of liberal thought, including Philip Furneaux's

---

35 Verner W. Crane, 'The Club of Honest Whigs: Friends of Science and Liberty', *WMQ*, 3rd ser., 23 (1966), 217–22; Barlow, *Citizenship and Conscience*, pp. 171–89; 203–9; G. M. Ditchfield, 'The Subscription Issue in British Parliamentary Politics, 1772–79', *Parliamentary History* 7 (1988), 47. John Stephens, 'The London Ministers and Subscription, 1772–1779', *ED* 1 (1982), 43–71. The so-called Feathers' Tavern petition sponsored by liberal Anglicans preceded the Dissenters' bill and may have doomed it by the association with liberal theology. See Norman Sykes, *Church and State in the XVIII Century* (Cambridge, 1935), pp. 381–4.

36 G. M. Ditchfield, 'The Parliamentary Struggle Over the Repeal of the Test and Corporation Acts', *EHR* 89 (1974), 553–4, 558; 'Repeal, Abolition, and Reform: A Study in the Interaction of Reforming Movements in Parliament of 1790–6', in Christine Bolt and Seymour Drescher (eds.), *Anti-Slavery, Religion, and Reform: Essays in Honour of Roger Anstey* (Hamden, Conn., 1980), pp. 104, 115–16. Ditchfield views the campaign as a substantial political and constitutional issue; see his 'The Campaign in Lancashire and Cheshire for the Repeal of the Test and Corporation Acts, 1787–90', *Transactions of the Historical Society of Lancashire and Cheshire* 126 (1977), 113. Ditchfield has now identified almost all of the M.P.s belonging to this 'interest'; see his 'Scotland and the Test Act, 1791: New Parliamentary Lists', *BIHR* 56 (1983), 69.

Letters to Blackstone (1771), and Robert Robinson's *Arcana* (1773). It must be emphasized, however, that there were conservative Dissenters in eighteenth-century England who resisted these 'enlightened' trends. The first agitation for repeal of the Test and Corporation Acts originated in Liverpool where numerous Dissenters held corporate office, but Liverpool Dissenters were profoundly divided on the propriety of repeal, and later in the century, another group of Liverpool Dissenters presented a petition to Parliament *against* relief from subscription to the Thirty-Nine Articles, fearing, they said, the influence of heresy.[37] Conservative instincts such as those of the Liverpool laity could have significant implications for the politics of Protestant Dissent.

THE SOCIAL STATUS AND SOCIAL EQUALITY OF DISSENT

The legal status of Nonconformity must be interpreted within the context of the social standing of the laity. Most work on the social structure of Nonconformity to date, however, has concentrated on the Quakers in the seventeenth century, the older denominations in the early decades of the eighteenth century, and Methodists in the nineteenth century. Occupational data has been compared with hearth tax returns and probate records among the early Friends. Though the samples are small and the results variable depending on the area that is sampled, the most recent study suggests that the early Quakers were socially distinct from their surroundings.[38] A broader denominational perspective was gained by Judith Hurwich's comparative study of Roman Catholicism in Warwickshire, whereas rural Dissenters were specifically singled out in

---

37 Hunt, *Two Early Political Associations*, pp. 126, 128, 195–7; Roberts, *Hope Street Church, Liverpool*, p. 292.
38 See below on the Bristol Quakers. Alan Cole pioneered in the social study of Dissent with his 'The Social Origins of the Early Friends', *FHSJ* 48 (1957), 99–118; and the best study to date is Richard T. Vann, *The Social Development of Early Quakerism* (Cambridge, 1969). See also Richard T. Vann, 'Quakers and the Social Structure in the Interregnum', *P&P* 43 (1969), 71–91; where he looked at Buckinghamshire Quakers, 1654–1740. Judith Hurwich, 'The Social Origins of the Early Quakers', *P&P* 48 (1970), 156–62 examined Warwickshire, but see the rejoinder by Vann, pp. 162–4, and Barry Reay, 'The Social Origins of Early Quakerism', *JIH* 11 (1980), 55–72. Vann's work suffers from failing to provide clear reasons for categorization and from a blurred distinction between wholesale and retail trade; he also compares occupations in a Gloucestershire muster roll with the occupations of Buckinghamshire Quakers, 'Quakers and the Social Structure', pp. 88–9. Hurwich helpfully distinguishes between urban and rural classifications but blends tradesmen and master craftsmen with no real reason given (p. 159). In a later article, 'Dissent and Catholicism in English Society: A Study of Warwickshire, 1660–1720', *JBS* 16 (1976), 24–58 she distinguished tradesmen and artisans a little more clearly, but ranked mercers and drapers with tradesmen (Appendix B, p. 56) and generally obscured wholesalers and retailers. Reay made the first real advance in occupational categorization in religious studies (p. 56). Clive D. Field has given passing notice to eighteenth-century Methodists in 'The Social Structure of English Methodism: eighteenth–twentieth centuries', *British Journal of Sociology* 28 (1977), 199–225.

Margaret Spufford's examination of Cambridgeshire.[39] The only study to utilize nonparochial registers for social analysis in the first quarter of the eighteenth century was Michael Watts' assessment of eight urban congregations. His conclusions, though stated tentatively, suggest that Presbyterians and Congregationalists were not significantly different in social status from the population at large. 'The presence of trade and industry, by freeing men from the social and economic pressure of the countryside, created conditions which were favourable to the growth and survival of Dissent, but within those manufacturing and commercial communities in which Nonconformity thrived, Dissenters were not distinguished by occupation or social status from the population at large.'[40]

All of the previous studies of Nonconformity have compared the occupational structure derived from non-parochial registers to the national estimates of Gregory King, Joseph Massie, or Patrick Colquhoun. But the comparison of local occupation structures to national Anglican averages is not very useful if one is particularly concerned to account for opposition politics on the basis of local inequalities or grievances. Carefully chosen samples from both parish and non-parochial registers where Dissenting congregations border Anglican parishes in the same cities should be far more illuminating, and urban historians have begun this comparative work. Utilizing broad descriptive occupational categories such as 'transport' and 'textiles and clothing' for their classification scheme, Langton and Laxton found that the differences between Anglican churches at Liverpool in the 1760s were greater than those between the Anglicans and the single Unitarian chapel they sampled.[41] Further examination

---

39 Judith J. Hurwich, 'Dissent and Catholicism', and Margaret Spufford, 'The Social Status of Some Seventeenth-Century Rural Dissenters', pp. 203–22 in Studies in Church History, 8; G. J. Cuming and Derek Baker, (eds.) *Popular Belief and Practice* (Cambridge, 1972). Spufford uses probate inventories for a small sample and makes the commonplace observation that distinctions in wealth between craftsmen and laborers, and between yeomen and husbandmen, were indeed real (p. 203, note 2).

40 Michael Watts, *The Dissenters: From the Reformation to the French Revolution* (Oxford, 1978), pp. 350–1, 353–4. Watts studies data from Chesterfield, London (Hand Alley), Norwich, Nottingham, Southwark (Court Yard), Bury St. Edmunds, Great Yarmouth, and Haverfordwest. The only other examination of the social status of Nonconformity is A. D. Gilbert's study of early nineteenth century Dissent and it is seriously flawed methodologically. While Gilbert has taken an adequate sample of the non-parochial registers (approximately 20,000 entries) and given a helpful denominational range, he counted the father's occupation each time there was an entry of birth, and his definition of what constitutes a general occupational category is too vague to allow for a comparison with Patrick Colquhoun. A. D. Gilbert, *Religion and Society in Industrial England: Church, Chapel, and Social Change, 1740–1914* (London and New York, 1976), pp. 62–5. It would have been helpful if Baptists had been distinguished from Congregationalists and if the 'professional' category had not been dropped altogether.

41 John Langton and Paul Laxton, 'Parish Registers and Urban Structure: The Example of late-eighteenth-century Liverpool', *Urban History Yearbook* (1978), 80–2, utilize the 1861 census classification which is not very useful for comparison to the previous studies noted above (notes 38–40).

of additional registers confirms their findings; Table 2.1 shows that the Liverpool Dissenters' occupational structure fell between the two Anglican

Table 2.1: *Anglican and Dissenting Occupational Structure at Liverpool*
(Percentage)

	St. George (Anglican)	St. Peter (Anglican)	Total Anglican
1. Gentlemen, Professions	8.5	2.6	4.8
2. Merchants	11.1	2.0	5.4
3. Shopkeepers	14.3	12.1	12.9
4. Artisans	38.5	51.5	46.7
5. Laborers	27.1	31.6	30.0
6. Other	.4	.1	.2
	N= 468	794	1262

	Kaye Street (Presbyterian)	Toxteth Park (Presbyterian)	Benn's Garden (Presbyterian)	Total Dissent
1. Gentlemen, Professions	2.0	11.1	2.8	2.9
2. Merchants	5.5	15.6	8.5	7.7
3. Shopkeepers	16.3	13.3	13.4	14.5
4. Artisans	42.0	26.7	35.7	37.6
5. Laborers	29.5	28.9	37.0	33.8
6. Other	4.7	4.4	2.8	3.5
	N= 343	45	544	932

parishes.[42] St. George's, however, had noticeably more men in the upper two categories than the Dissenters (the sample from Toxteth Park is too small to be significant) and this phenomenon may be related to the fact that St. George's was the preferred parish church of the corporation. Liverpool Dissenters, however, had clearly attained to the highest occupational levels; their numbers in the professional and merchant categories rivalled the number of Anglicans in these highest strata. The most obvious feature of the occupational structure at Newcastle upon Tyne (Table 2.2) is that the differences between the two Anglican churches are about as great as the differences between the Anglican churches and the Dissenting chapels overall. Here, the Dissenters had slightly

---

42 See Appendix 1 for a discussion of letter cluster sampling and Appendix 2 for the five-fold classification utilized here. Tables 2.1–2.5 utilize letter cluster samples, and Table 2.5 includes resident voters only.

Table 2.2: *Anglican and Dissenting Occupational Structure*
at Newcastle upon Tyne (Percentage)

	St. Andrews (Anglican)	St. Nicholas (Anglican)	Total Anglican
1. Gentlemen, Professions	9.6	4.2	6.8
2. Merchants	3.9	4.2	4.0
3. Shopkeepers	16.5	18.6	17.5
4. Artisans	48.1	54.7	51.4
5. Laborers	20.1	13.7	16.9
6. Other	1.8	4.7	3.3
N=	541	554	1095

	Silver Street (Scots Presbyterian)	Groat Market (Scots Presbyterian)	Carlisle Street (United Secession)	Total Dissent
1. Gentlemen, Professions	1.6	6.7	3.8	4.3
2. Merchants	2.0	3.3	.9	2.2
3. Shopkeepers	17.4	15.0	9.4	15.4
4. Artisans	49.0	41.1	52.8	47.9
5. Laborers	25.7	25.6	31.1	25.5
6. Other	4.4	8.3	1.9	4.8
N=	253	180	106	631

fewer men in the gentlemen/professional and merchant categories than the Anglicans, and slightly more in the category of laborer, and unlike Liverpool, the differences are statistically significant.[43] To the extent that occupational classification does reveal socio-economic rank, Newcastle Nonconformists seem to have stood in a less advanced social position than the Anglicans. The

43 In tables 2.1–2.4 using X^2, the differences in occupational groups between Anglicans and Dissenters are significant at .01 level of probability at Newcastle and Bristol, but not at Liverpool or Hull. Three chapels at Newcastle have too few people with occupations to be noticed individually, but the numbers are included in the total column: 39 occupations from Castle Garth (Scots Presbyterian) 38 from Close Chapel (United Secession) and 15 from Hanover Square (Unitarian). Combined, these three yield the following proportions: 1. 7.6%; 2. 2.2%; 3. 17.4%; 4. 52.2%; 5. 18.5%; 6. 2.2%.

The recorder of the Anglican register of St. Andrews Church was unduly fond of the catchall term 'yeoman'. From multiple entries for the same person described as yeoman on one occasion and given an actual occupation on another, it can be demonstrated that the term describes occupations in categories 3, 4, and 5 equally well. In the letter cluster sample covering the period 1765–88, the term was used to describe 121 people, a far greater proportion than in any other register. In Table 2.2 these 121 yeomen were simply excluded.

Table 2.3: *Anglican and Dissenting Occupational Structure*
at Kingston upon Hull (Percentage)

	St. Mary (Anglican)	Holy Trinity (Anglican)	Total Anglican	Bowl Alley Lane (Presbyterian)
1. Gentlemen, Professions	3.7	3.4	3.5	5.4
2. Merchants	2.6	2.3	2.4	5.1
3. Shopkeepers	19.5	17.7	18.3	16.3
4. Artisans	29.7	36.2	33.8	34.4
5. Laborers	44.2	39.5	41.2	36.6
6. Other	.4	.9	.7	2.2
	N= 462	787	1249	276

Presbyterians at Kingston upon Hull (Table 2.3) had a somewhat greater proportion in the highest categories, but once again, the differences between Anglican and Nonconformist are minimal. Watts' conclusions for the early eighteenth century seem to be corroborated by the data from these three boroughs for the period of the American Revolution.

The occupational data for Bristol are disappointingly sparse; only three of the twenty-one parish registers retained occupations in the period of the American Revolution and one of the three parishes was the ancient, centrally located, but very small parish of Christ Church.[44] Christ Church was structurally similar to the Dissenters from the standpoint of occupation, though the numbers are too small to be very useful (Table 2.4). But the occupational structures of the other two parishes, if they are at all representative, reveal striking differences when compared to the Bristol Nonconformists. With half of all Bristol Dissenters in the upper three categories, the Nonconformists had proportionately almost twice as many people in these groups as the Anglicans. The statistical evidence from the occupational data thus nicely corroborates the Dissenters' reputation for wealth noted in the literary sources.[45] What impresses one about the Bristol Dissenters, therefore, is the greater number of merchants, such as linen drapers and brokers, and the large number of shopkeepers or retailers of all varieties, including bakers, grocers, vintners, and tobacconists. Equally impressive is the very low number of laborers, such as carters and porters, at least in comparison

44 The parish register of St. Stephen records no occupations after 1783; additionally, it was considered the sailors' parish; even for a parish bordering the quay, there was a disproportionately large number of mariners. While St. Philip and Jacob was considered a poor parish, the majority of Bristol Baptists and Quakers listed with occupations were resident in this parish. The Presbyterians were most heavily concentrated in the parish of St. James. See chap. 7 below.

45 The Evans List, p. 146; see chap. 6 on the Bristol Dissenters.

Table 2.4: *Anglican and Dissenting Occupational Structure at Bristol*
(Percentage)

	St. Stephen (Anglican)	Christ Church (Anglican)	St. Philip and Jacob (Anglican)	Total Anglican
1. Gentlemen, Professions	4.2	3.5	1.5	2.4
2. Merchants	4.9	14.0	1.0	3.0
3. Shopkeepers	20.5	29.1	21.5	21.8
4. Artisans	30.3	34.9	51.2	44.3
5. Laborers	39.4	18.6	23.8	27.6
6. Other	.7	0	1.1	.9
	N= 307	86	736	1129

	Lewins Mead (Presbyterian)	Broad Mead (Baptist)	Friars and Temple St. (Quaker)	Total Dissent
1. Gentlemen, Professions	11.7	14.0	2.6	9.9
2. Merchants	13.4	6.5	10.2	9.7
3. Shopkeepers	24.9	24.5	44.6	30.3
4. Artisans	36.6	41.5	36.9	38.4
5. Laborers	13.2	13.5	4.5	10.8
6. Other	1.0	0	1.3	.7
	N= 197	200	157	554

to the populace of the parishes of St. Philip and Jacob and St. Stephen. It seems fair to conclude that the Bristol Dissenters were higher in socio-economic rank than some of the Anglicans in neighboring parishes and probably at least equal in status with the most economically advanced portions of the population in England.

Further insights on occupational structure may be gained by comparing entire Dissenting communities to the overall resident electorate of the boroughs (Table 2.5). The Bristol Dissenters' strength in the middle category of shopkeeper or retailer in comparison to Dissenters in other boroughs is particularly impressive relative to the electorate; these middle ranking Dissenters represent almost twice as many proportionately as the average Anglican congregation in other boroughs, and among the Bristol Quakers this group constituted almost

Table 2.5: *Dissenting Occupational Structure Compared to the Electorate*
(Percentage)

	Liverpool Electorate (1784)	Dissent Total	Newcastle Electorate (1774)	Dissent Total	Kingston upon Hull Electorate (1774)	Bowl Alley Lane (Presbyterian)
1. Gentlemen, Professions	5.2	2.9	2.5	4.3	11.5	5.4
2. Merchants	8.8	7.7	10.2	2.2	4.1	5.1
3. Shopkeepers	20.2	14.5	24.3	15.4	18.0	16.3
4. Artisans	61.7	37.6	55.2	47.9	46.2	34.4
5. Laborers	3.8	33.8	7.6	25.5	19.4	36.6
6. Other	.3	3.5	.2	4.8	.8	2.2
N=	955	932	815	631	898	276

	Bristol Electorate (1774)	Dissent Total	Colchester Electorate (1780)	Lion Walk (Congregational)
1. Gentlemen, Professions	8.7	9.9	8.4	10.7
2. Merchants	6.8	9.7	3.0	2.1
3. Shopkeepers	23.2	30.3	23.5	21.4
4. Artisans	50.8	38.4	55.5	51.5
5. Laborers	6.9	10.8	4.8	8.6
6. Other	3.6	.7	4.8	5.9
N=	1060	554	400	187

half of their numbers.[46] The very low proportion of laborers among Bristol Nonconformists is matched only by the Colchester Congregationalists. Of all the boroughs studied, only at Bristol and Colchester did the overall occupational structure of the Nonconformists approximate that of the freeman electorate; but in every large freeman borough examined, popular participation in elections was no more restrictive to the Dissenters from a social point of view than it was to the Anglicans.[47]

46 The Quakers at Poole, who were known to be wealthy, approximate the Bristol Quakers in the upper two categories with 3.4% in the Gentlemen, profession group, and 17.2% in the merchant group. See Table 7.4 in Bradley, *Popular Politics and the American Revolution in England* (Macon, Ga., 1986).
47 The comparison of Anglican and Dissenting occupational structures to the electorate reveals that unskilled laborers were seriously under represented in elections in the freeman boroughs of Newcastle, Liverpool, and Kingston upon Hull, but this affected Anglicans and Dissenters about equally (with the possible exception of Newcastle). Future work on the representative nature of the electorate relative to social strata must

At Bristol there were far fewer laborers among the Dissenters than there were at Liverpool and Newcastle. This discrepancy is especially telling at Liverpool and helps explain why so few Dissenters can be identified in the Liverpool poll books. Fully one-third of the Liverpool Dissenters were in the unskilled category, yet laborers comprised less than four percent of the entire electorate. On the other hand, this circumstance did not discriminate unduly against the Dissenters, since nearly an equal proportion of Anglicans were similarly excluded from voting. But Liverpool does contrast remarkably with Bristol. The tremendous strength of Bristol Dissent in the shopkeeping or retail category relative both to the electorate and to other urban Dissenters may help account for their consistent turnout at the polls. The occupational structure of the Bristol Dissenters would thus appear to have important political implications for the high level of their involvement in elections and possibly also their consistent partisan behavior. The very low proportion of laborers suggests that Bristol Nonconformists had moved further up the social scale than many Anglicans in Bristol and most Dissenters in other boroughs as well, and we will see in chapters 9 and 10 that this has important implications for the emergence of class-like divisions in popular politics.

The comparative study of the social status of Dissent across boroughs is therefore a valuable datum, since different levels of socio-economic attainment may have contributed to divergent attitudes toward social issues held by ministers and laity alike. For example, in a later chapter we shall see a genuine egalitarianism espoused by James Murray of Newcastle upon Tyne, and a far more moderate acceptance of social stratification by Caleb Evans of Bristol. It will not be possible to prove that socio-economic differences were the controlling factors for these political attitudes of the elite, but this evidence does help account for political expression at one level. If Murray and Evans were at odds on the need for social change in England, they were united in their sympathy for the colonists. Among the laity, there appears to have been a socio-economic threshold that must be crossed in order to allow the expression of opposition politics; the lack of laborers' involvement in the petitioning activity of 1775 examined in a later chapter suggests that economic independence was the necessary correlate of political independence. It cannot, however, be argued that economic independence necessarily stimulated radical political behavior; we will see below that some middle-ranking Anglicans were strongly loyalist in orientation. But the evidence does suggest that when combined, independent socio-economic status and 'independence' in religion could be politically potent.

compare Anglican registers to poll books. For a fuller discussion see John Phillips, *Electoral Behavior in Unreformed England: Plumpers, Splitters and Straights* (Princeton, 1982), pp. 189–93; and Frank O'Gorman, 'The Unreformed Electorate of Hanoverian England: The Mid-eighteenth Century to the Reform Act of 1832', *Social History*, 11 (1986), 40–4.

The most certain conclusion to be drawn from these occupational data, however, is that Dissenters held about as many professional, wholesale, and retail positions as Anglicans. Even at Liverpool, we find Dissenting lawyers, brokers, and goldsmiths, and thus Nonconformists, at least in the large urban centers, were clearly not inferior to Anglicans from an occupational standpoint. On the basis of this sample it seems likely that the occupational structure of urban Nonconformity at the time of the American Revolution was largely indistinguishable from that of Anglicanism; consistently greater differences are observable between communities of Dissent across several cities than between Dissenters and Anglicans. Any attempt to account for differences in the Dissenters' political behavior from borough to borough must therefore have constant recourse to their comparative occupational structure.

THE CORPORATION ACT AND THE PRACTICE OF OCCASIONAL CONFORMITY

The social status of the Dissenters appears to have had major implications for the Dissenters' opportunity for office holding and upward social mobility in the urban setting. While it is impossible to measure social mobility in the mid-eighteenth century, it seems certain that Dissenters were at least as economically mobile as Anglicans. These data will require a careful reassessment of the prevailing idea that the Test and Corporation Acts forced the Nonconformists directly into trade and industry.[48] The widespread practice of occasional conformity in order to qualify for office substantially alleviated the pressure to seek alternative occupations, and the actual occupational differences between Dissenters and Anglicans were, in any case, minimal. A fresh examination of the Dissenters' practice of office holding will put the matter in a new perspective.

After 1719 the sacramental test was still required as set forth in the Test and Corporation Acts, but if a Dissenter could reconcile the practice of occasional conformity with his religious convictions, then no office under the crown was barred to him. Besides occasional conformity, the law provided another legal loophole for Dissenters who wished to hold office. The first Indemnity Act was passed in 1726. The Corporation Act had stipulated that the sacrament must be received one year before election to corporate office; the Indemnity Act was designed to mitigate this requirement by allowing a person to qualify after

---

48 Watts, *The Dissenters*, 361. David H. Pratt, *English Quakers and the First Industrial Revolution: A Study of the Quaker Community in Four Industrial Counties–Lancashire, York, Warwick, and Gloucester, 1750–1830* (New York and London, 1985), pp. 119–27. My comparative study documents the atypicality of the Quakers. Moreover, Pratt wrote with no reference to the study of W. D. Rubinstein, who demonstrated the economic similarities of Dissenters and Anglicans on the basis of probate records: *Men of Property: The Very Wealthy in Britain Since the Industrial Revolution* (New Brunswick, 1981), pp. 146–59. For Tory industrialization and the issue of exclusion, see Philip Jenkins, 'Tory Industrialization and Town Politics: Swansea in the Eighteenth Century', *HJ* 28 (1985), 122.

taking office, thereby bringing the Corporation Act roughly into line with the Test Act. Recently it has been argued that the Indemnity acts, which were passed with a fair degree of regularity, were intended more for the careless Churchman than for the conniving Dissenter, but the data used to substantiate this claim are not impressive, and in some instances the Dissenters occasionally did benefit from the Indemnity acts.[49]

If there is little evidence to prove that the Dissenters actually used the Indemnity acts to qualify for office, it is certain that another act, passed earlier in the reign of George I, did allow them to qualify for holding corporation offices without taking the sacrament. In 1719 Lord Stanhope pressed through Parliament the Act for Quieting and Establishing Corporations.[50] This law provided that anyone elected to a town corporation, whose tenure was not questioned for six months thereafter, was freed from the need for any sacramental qualification and from any fear of prosecution. The law did not alleviate the initial risk of prosecution, but since most corporation positions were for life, this was a signally important modification of the Corporation Act. A mayor might be removed from office on this account, but such removal from one office did not affect his aldermanic status.[51] At least two avenues were thus open to the Dissenter who wished to sit on a town corporation: he could take the sacrament at the parish church, or he could ignore the law and take office 'with hazard' in the hope that no one would bring suit against him for six months. Where the Dissenters were numerous and where they were influential there was neither a legal nor a practical hindrance to their becoming aldermen; in such circumstances it appears that few people were concerned about their office holding and fewer yet desired to challenge them.

Opinion varied widely concerning the propriety of occasional conformity. Some Anglicans, like Jonathan Swift, were distinctly opposed to it, while Benjamin Hoadly, the famous Low-Church Bishop of Bangor, stoutly defended the practice; Thomas Tenison, Archbishop of Canterbury (1695–1715), even encouraged it. Generally, Presbyterians and Congregationalists were less opposed to occasional conformity than Baptists. Edmund Calamy (d. 1732), a well-known Presbyterian divine, argued that Dissenters were in fact united to the Anglican Church in faith and doctrine and should demonstrate their love for the Church by occasional communion with her.[52] Not all Dissenters, however,

---

49 Short, 'The English Indemnity Acts', 368.
50 5 Geo. 1, c. 6. David C. Douglas., *English Historical Documents, 1714–1783*, 12 vols. (New York, 1953—), D. B. Horn and Mary Ransom (eds.) (1957) 10: 394–5. Hunt, *Two Political Associations*, p. 125.
51 Short, 'The English Indemnity Acts', 372. Sheriffs and mayors, who were elected annually, still had to qualify for office by taking the sacrament, and the Test Act still applied to government office under the crown.
52 Richey, 'The Origins of British Radicalism', 183. Scholes, 'Parliament and the Protestant Dissenters', pp. 19–20; *A View*, 1731, p. 47. Short takes issue with the notion that Presbyterians and Congregationalists were more open to the practice, 'The English

shared Calamy's breadth of vision and in some settings there was a clear threat of ostracism from the community. The Baptists in London, for example, forbade the practice; under the date of 4 January 1743, the following entry is found in the minutes of the Ministers of the London Baptist Board:

Mr. Kenwood and Mr. Stinton came as Messengers from the Church under the care of Mr. Flowers [Unicorn Yard, London] with the following question, Whether a person ought to be continued in the fellowship of the Church who shall receive the sacrament in the Church of England to qualify himself for executing an office of trust or profit, when at the same time he does not incur [sic] any penalty if he refuses to accept the place to w[hi]ch he is elected – Present fourteen brethren. Agreed unanimously that it is absolutely unlawfull [sic] for any Member of a Gospel Church to commune with the Church of England on any consideration whatsoever.[53]

Such pronouncements as this, supported by fourteen Baptist ministers, combined with rare instances of discipline, have led historians to conclude that occasional conformity was infrequent.[54] The few examples of discipline, however, may just as certainly provide evidence that the practice was widespread, and it can be readily proven that numerous Baptist laymen held office, despite the disapproval of the ministry.

High-Anglican fears motivated the passage of the penal legislation and the anxiety of the Dissenters motivated movements for repeal; much of the rhetoric surrounding the eighteenth-century debate over the Test and Corporation Acts was thus based on subjective, emotionally laden perceptions. If the discussion is to be advanced, it will be imperative to discover the extent to which the participants' fears and perceptions comport with reality. By comparing the statistical and social data in two eighteenth-century surveys of Nonconformist congregations it is possible to determine the number of Dissenters that inhabited parliamentary boroughs and thus venture an analysis of the actual impact of the Corporation Act in the eighteenth century. The following survey of office holding will focus on parliamentary boroughs in order to determine how the law affected the Dissenters' influence in parliamentary elections; it should also provide a rough approximation of the prevalence of the practice of occasional conformity in non-parliamentary towns.[55]

Indemnity Acts', p. 371, but his evidence is scanty.
53 'The Baptist Board Minutes, 1724–June 27, 1820', *BHST*, 5 (1916–17), 24. For a case of discipline at St. Mary's Particular Baptist Chapel Norwich in 1786, see Charles B. Jewson, 'St. Mary's Norwich', *BQ* 10 (1940–1), 287.
54 Short, 'The English Indemnity Acts', 370, 374; the standard denominational histories draw the same conclusion; it is only the local chapel histories that reveal the actual incidence of occasional conformity.
55 While working on parliamentary boroughs, I discovered three instances of Dissenters holding office in non-parliamentary towns. As early as 1721 Stockport Cheshire had a Quaker mayor. There were Dissenters on the corporation at Bideford, Devonshire. At Netherton Dudley, a Baptist was first a bailiff, then in 1729, a mayor. George Unwin, *Samuel Oldknow and the Arkwrights: The Industrial Revolution at Stockport and Marple* (Manchester, 1924), p. 39; John Cox's 'Memoirs' in the *Transactions of the*

The strict enforcement of the Corporation Act would have had the most significant influence on parliamentary elections in the corporation boroughs and the small freeman boroughs. In the period 1715 to 1773, Dissenters were numerous enough in eighteen of the twenty-six corporation boroughs in England to have established chapels, and in these eighteen boroughs, they sat on the corporations of four.[56] But despite these corporation seats, they had little influence at Wilton after 1715, they were almost certainly discriminated against at Bodmin, and they were very weak numerically at Buckingham. However, with eight aldermen on the corporation at Tiverton in 1715 the Dissenters were very influential, and they also had a strong interest in the corporation borough of Devizes, even though in this case there is no record of their holding a single aldermanic seat.[57] The Dissenters were sufficiently numerous and they possessed enough wealth in five of the eighteen corporation boroughs that they might well have obtained office had they not been subject to legal restrictions.[58] But in the remaining eight boroughs, their very small numbers, the influence of a prevailing patron, and in the case of Salisbury, the erstwhile Royalists' dominance of the corporation, would have rendered them powerless quite apart from the Corporation Act.[59] Moreover, Nonconformists

Devonshire Association 29 (1897), 86–94; G. S. Hall, 'The General Baptist Church Netherton Dudley', *BQ* 29 (1982), 308–18. For further evidence of Dissenting magistrates in non-parliamentary towns see John Seed, 'Gentlemen Dissenters: The Social and Political Meanings of Rational Dissent in the 1770s and 1780s', *HJ* 28 (1985), 306–7; for Birmingham, see R. B. Rose, 'The Priestley Riots of 1791', *P&P* 18 (1960), 70.

56 The Evans and Thompson Lists show that there were no Dissenters in the remaining eight boroughs, or their numbers were so small that they had no regular meetings. For Dissenters on the corporation of Wilton, see R. B. Pugh and Elizabeth Critall, *A History of Wiltshire, VCH* (London, 1962), 6: 32; Geoffrey Holmes and W. A. Speck, *The Divided Society* (London, 1967), p. 122; for Bodmin, the Evans List, p. 15, shows one Presbyterian on the corporation. R. Ball, *Congregationalism in Cornwall* (London, 1955), p. 17; for Buckingham, see the Evans List, pp. 6–7; Richard W. Davis, *Dissent in Politics, 1780–1830: The Political Life of William Smith, MP* (London, 1971), p. 128; and for Tiverton, the Evans List, p. 30; Martin Dunsford, *Historical Memoirs of the Town and Parish of Tiverton* (Exeter, 1795), pp. 23, 146, 158, 162, 416, 444, 452.

57 On Devizes, see the Evans List, pp. 123–5; *A History of Wiltshire, VCH* 3: 123; 10: 295, 297. *Commons, 1715–1754*, 1: 614.

58 This observation is based on the seemingly higher than usual social status of the Dissenters at Andover, Christchurch, and Newport, Isle of Wight in Hampshire, Bury St. Edmunds, and Bodmin. See the Evans List, pp. 103–5, 108–11; Thompson, History, 4: 243, 245; J. Duncan, 'Bury St. Edmunds Independents—Early Prominent Members', p. 23; J. Duncan, 'The History of the Congregational Church in Bury St. Edmunds', 1962, pp. 103, 123; J. Duncan, 'The History of the Presbyterians in Bury St. Edmunds', 1961, pp. 69–70; all unpublished typescripts in Dr. Williams's Library; the Evans List, p. 15.

59 Calne, Marlborough, Truro, Banbury, and Scarborough were all heavily encumbered; Malmsbury and Harwich had very small Nonconformist communities. Bath was a relatively open corporation borough, but the Dissenters there were said to be 'of the poorer classes'. See the Evans List, pp. 123–5. On the other boroughs see the appropriate constituency histories in *The History of Parliament*, and the Evans List, pp. 15, 94, 128–31, 37–41; *Wiltshire, VCH*, 3: 120; 6: 107, 120–1; Jerom Murch, *A History of*

returned members to Parliament in three corporation boroughs where they resided (Wilton, Devizes, Tiverton), and a fourth (Saltash) where there is no record of Dissenting residents.[60]

Of all of the corporation boroughs inhabited by Dissenters, Devizes and Tiverton had by far the largest Dissenting communities with upwards of twenty percent of the population, and it was precisely in these two boroughs that they made the most significant inroads in office holding and politics. The very constituencies that have been thought to be the most oppressive to the Dissenters were in fact the most 'oppressive' to all Englishmen: of the eighteen corporation boroughs in which the Dissenters resided, only seven remained relatively free from government or private influence by 1790,[61] and from 1754 to 1790 there were no contests in eight of them and in three there was only one contest in the entire period. In the years 1715 to 1773 in five corporation boroughs alone there is solid evidence that the Corporation Act was the principal cause for the Dissenters' exclusion from office. Against all of the claims of denominational histories and Whig historians, it must be concluded that the law was not a major source of oppression in the corporation boroughs.

In freeman boroughs with small electorates, corporations often influenced elections through a variety of means and thus the Corporation Act might have had an indirect but important influence on Dissenters in these boroughs. From 1715 to 1773, Dissenters lived in twenty-nine of the forty-seven freeman boroughs with electorates under 500.[62] In twenty-three of these boroughs there is no current evidence of their having held local office. The Corporation Act may well have kept qualified Dissenters from involvement in municipal politics in several of these boroughs, though the lack of social data does not allow firm generalizations in this regard. In any case, it does not automatically follow that the law significantly influenced the Dissenters' role in parliamentary politics. In order to assess the latter, the numerical strength of the Dissenters in each of the boroughs must be determined and then compared with the independence and relative strength of the corporation. Fortunately, the number of Dissenting freemen for fourteen or nearly two-thirds of these boroughs was assessed in

---

the Presbyterian and General Baptist Churches in the West of England (London, 1835), pp. 139–40; the Thompson List, MS 38.6, pp. 38, 12; G. A. Moore, *The Story of Brown Street Baptist Church Salisbury, 1655–1955* (1955), pp. 12, 27; Wilton, Calne, and Malmsbury each lost one representative under schedule B of the First Reform Act, John Cannon, *Parliamentary Reform, 1640–1832* (Cambridge, 1973), p. 299.

60 John London for Wilton; Josiah Diston for Devizes; Dudley Ryder for Tiverton; Stamp Brooksbank for Saltash.

61 Salisbury, Bath, Bodmin, Andover, Malmsbury, Devizes, Bury St. Edmunds.

62 An analysis of the Evans and Thompson Lists indicates that few or no Dissenters resided in the remaining eighteen boroughs; in any case, in none of them was there an established meeting. In twenty of the twenty-nine boroughs they inhabited, the electorate numbered 200 or less, and in only one borough was it as high as 400. See *Commons, 1754–1790*, 1: 515–19.

1715. Thirteen were heavily encumbered by patrons in the period 1715–73 and two more were venal;[63] these fifteen boroughs were rotten enough that half of them were disfranchised or deprived of one member in 1832.[64] This leaves only eight boroughs and at the most ten, where the corporation was sufficiently independent to influence parliamentary elections, but the Dissenters were quite weak in several of these, and in others the Tories dominated the corporations.[65] Assuming the Dissenters had a social status equaling that of the Anglicans, and assuming they were not opposed by local Tory parties, they may have been genuinely discriminated against by the law in such a way that it would influence parliamentary elections at Totnes (where the Dissenters had 31 percent of the vote), Rye (with 45 percent of the vote), Shrewsbury (with 21 percent of the vote), and possibly Bewdley.[66] Thus in four small freeman boroughs the Dissenters were strong enough (with 20 percent or more of the vote) to have been electorally significant had they also held corporate office. But the Dissenters actually held corporate office in a greater number of small freeman boroughs than those in which they were excluded from parliamentary politics by the Corporation Act.

The Dissenters were politically active in four of the six small freeman boroughs where they sat on corporations.[67] At Lyme Regis the Presbyterian Henry Henly was mayor on four occasions, and in addition, recorder and M.P.

63 Namier's warnings concerning what constitutes 'nomination', 'influence', and 'possession', must still be heeded. Sir Lewis Namier, *The Structure of Politics at the Accession of George III*, 2nd edn (London, 1957), p. 144. Nevertheless, speaking roughly, the boroughs under patronage, either private or governmental, are Dartmouth, Plympton Earle, Liskeard, East Looe, Launceston, Lymington, Winchester, Malton, Hythe, Wigan, Kings Lynn, East Retford, Stafford; the two venal boroughs are Barnstaple and Hedon. Stafford was under patronage until the 1770s when it became venal. At Winchester the corporation had some independence and some influence, but was also influenced by patrons and after 1754 came under the complete control of the patrons. At Plympton Earle, Malton, and East Retford, the Dissenters had become so few that they disbanded their meetings by 1773. See the appropriate constituency histories in *The History of Parliament*.

64 Under Schedule A there was East Looe, Hedon, and Plympton Earl; under Schedule B, Liskeard, Hythe, Launceston, and Dartmouth. Cannon, *Parliamentary Reform*, p. 299.

65 The eight boroughs are Totnes, Okehampton, Rye, Boston, Morpeth, Shrewsbury, Wells, and Bewdley; only at Totnes, Shrewsbury, and Wells was the corporation free from patrons influencing at least one seat. Wigan and Hythe were opening up (in 1758 and 1768 respectively), and this would bring the total to ten.

66 At Okehampton they had only 10% of the vote, at Morpeth only 5%, at Hythe 6%, and very few votes at Wigan. At Boston and Wells the Dissenters were weak and the corporations were dominated by Tories. It is possible that the 'independent party' which emerged at Boston in the 1780s was linked to Dissent; but this is conjectural. The figure for Shrewsbury and the percentage of the Dissenting vote in the constituencies is based on data summarized in Bradley, 'Nonconformity and the Electorate'.

67 The other two boroughs, where there is evidence of their having held local office, were heavily influenced by patronage. On Chipping Wycombe see Richard W. Davis, *Political Change and Continuity, 1760–1885: A Buckinghamshire Study* (London, 1972), p. 128; the Evans List, pp. 6–7, 114–15; the Thompson List, 38.5, p. 35; 38.6, pp. 3, 34; on Guildford, see Thompson, History, 4: 290a.

(1722–48).[68] In most boroughs, the incumbency of a Dissenting mayor would suggest the likelihood of Low-Church sympathy, if not the actual presence of other Dissenters among the aldermen, since mayors were commonly co-opted from among the aldermen and only rarely elected by a vote of the freemen. The return of M.P.s at Poole was largely in the hands of the Presbyterian families of Henning, Tito, and Jolliffe, and these families often held corporate office as well.[69] At Plymouth the Dissenters had a very strong influence on the corporation and they possessed 36 percent of the freeholder and freeman vote in 1715; but while they served as channels of patronage and were therefore important to the borough's political life, there was only one parliamentary contest in the period 1701–80.[70] The four Portsmouth Dissenting families of White, Carter, Missing, and Mouncher held the mayoralty in the period 1715–90 for twenty-seven years and this led to interminable wrangles with High Anglicans. When an occasional legal suit was brought against the Dissenters for office holding, the attempts to oust them were sometimes made on the charge that they were not sacramentally qualified, but more often on strictly the question of who had the majority of the aldermen's votes. When the Dissenters were forced from office in March of 1775, the Low-Church vicar of Portsmouth, the Rev. Henry Taylor, was ousted along with them.[71]

Just as with the corporation boroughs, however, the characteristic structural restrictions upon popular participation did not keep Dissenters from influencing parliamentary elections, even when they were excluded from the corporation. Although the Dissenters did not hold office at Morpeth, they were active in a local independent movement against a constricting oligarchy in 1747–74, they occasionally returned Dissenting M.P.s at East Retford, Wells, and East Looe, and they were influential in electing Whig candidates at Shrewsbury and Okehampton. Altogether they influenced politics in at least eight small freeman boroughs where there is no record of their ever having held municipal office.[72]

In our period Dissenters inhabited sixteen of the seventeen medium sized

---

68 W. Densham and J. Ogle, *The Story of the Congregational Churches of Dorset* (Bournemouth, 1899), p. 371.

69 *Ibid.*, pp. 190–2, 196, 198, 260.

70 The Evans List, p. 30; R. N. Worth, *History of Plymouth* (Plymouth, 1871), pp. 134, 157; Murch, *A History of the Presbyterian and General Baptist Churches*, p. 500; Davis, *Political Change*, p. 128.

71 Richard J. Murrell and Robert East, *Extracts from Records... of Portsmouth* (Portsmouth, 1884), pp. 97, 273–4, 281–2, 285, 373–4, 376–80; Peter A. Taylor, *Some Account of the Taylor Family* (London, 1875), p. 251.

72 For Morpeth and East Retford, see the constituency histories and the biographies of M.P.s in the *History of Parliament*. On Shrewsbury, see Bradley, 'Nonconformity and the Electorate'; on Oakehampton, *Commons, 1754–1790*, 3: 422. George Speke sat for Wells, 1735–47, and on Speke's identity, see Densham and Ogle, *The Story of the Congregational Churches*, p. 371. See the *History of Parliament* for Sir Henry Hoghton, and for Samuel Holden who sat for East Looe. Dissenters were also returned for Queenborough and Higham Ferrers where the Dissenters never resided; see the biographies of Thomas Newnham for the former and those of John Lee and James Adair for the latter.

freeman boroughs with electorates of 500–1000 in 1754.[73] Theoretically the
corporations in these boroughs were less influential in controlling parliamentary elections than those in small boroughs, though in fact, patronage was
nearly as determinative here as elsewhere. Dissenters sat on the corporations of
at least two of these sixteen boroughs, Newcastle-under-Lyme and Ipswich.
Though medium in size, Ipswich was nonetheless still influenced by the
corporation, and since the Dissenters held municipal office there, this meant
influence for the Dissenters. In 1779 both bailiffs were Presbyterians, and as a
result, the corporation as a body attended the Sunday service of the Presbyterian chapel, though the maces were not allowed to be carried further than the
door, a remarkable instance of legal scrupulosity.[74] While the Dissenters were
apparently excluded from local office holding in the remaining fourteen
boroughs, they significantly influenced elections in several of them. Voting
statistics are available for only half of these boroughs in 1715. Seven of the
fourteen boroughs where Dissenters did not sit on corporations were heavily
influenced by private or government patronage in the eighteenth century, and in
three of these, the Dissenting congregations were so small as to have rendered
them insignificant electorally.[75] But in Maldon and Great Yarmouth, and also
in the venal borough of Sudbury, the Dissenters led revolts against dominant
patrons, not, it must be emphasized, against the Corporation Act.[76] Dissenters
also sat on the corporation of five small scot and lot boroughs and one small
freeholder borough. The Dissenting congregations at Bridport and Weymouth
and Melcombe Regis (the freeholder borough) were extraordinarily wealthy
and the Dissenters' involvement on these corporations is not surprising.[77]
Leominster Baptists not only sat as mayors and represented the borough as
M.P.s, but the Baptist M.P., George Caswall, also had the distinction of being
rebuked for bribery.[78]

73 This is determined from examining the Evans and Thompson lists.
74 A. Philip Hewett, *The Story of an Old Meeting House: A Short History of St.
    Nicholas... Ipswich* (Ipswich, 1960), p. 9.
75 Derby, Maldon, Rochester, Sandwich, Monmouth, Great Yarmouth, Ludlow. The
    Dissenting congregations appeared to have been very small in Derby, Rochester, and
    Ludlow. See the Evans List, pp. 18, 37–41, 53–6, 82–5; Thompson, History, 4: 163;
    the Thompson List, 38.6, pp. 12, 18, 24, 25.
76 On Sudbury, see William W. Hodson, *The Meeting House and the Manse* (London,
    1893), pp. 56–7; on Maldon see *History of Parliament*; on Great Yarmouth see Bradley,
    Popular Politics and the American Revolution in England, pp. 158–60.
77 On Bridport, Murch, *A History of the Presbyterian and General Baptist Churches*,
    pp. 254–5, 258; on Weymouth and Melcombe Regis, see Densham and Ogle, *The Story
    of the Congregational Churches*, p. 376.
78 On Leominster, see Bradley, 'Nonconformity and the Electorate'; and *History of Parlia-
    ment*. On the remaining scot and lot boroughs, for Lewes, see J. M. Connell, *Lewes, its
    Religious History* (Lewes, 1931), p. 60; for Bridgewater, Murch, *A History of the Pres-
    byterian and General Baptist Churches*, pp. 181, 188; Thompson, *History*, 4: 170 and
    Bradley, *Popular Politics and the American Revolution in England*, pp. 166–8 and for
    St. Ives, *History of Parliament*.

The large freeman boroughs were the most open of all the boroughs and have been referred to as 'the political barometers of urban opinion'.[79] The large freeman constituency was thus naturally the most open to Dissenters as well, and they inhabited all twenty-eight of these boroughs. At some point in the eighteenth century, Nonconformists sat on the corporation of ten, or more than one in three.[80] At Bristol, the Dissenters, including many Baptists, were involved in local government from the highest to the lowest offices. Between 1754 and 1784 eleven members of Lewins Mead Presbyterian chapel held the office of mayor, thus tying up the post for more than a third of the period. The unusually high occupational status of the Bristol Dissenters is thereby confirmed by their dominance in local politics. These and other prominent Dissenters held one of the two sheriffs' seats for fifteen of these thirty years, and between 1771 and 1776 they did so without a break. All of these officers were also aldermen and most of them did obtain certificates from the Quarter Sessions indicating that they had received the sacrament at an Anglican church.[81] Dissenters were from time to time disciplined or disqualified, but they ran about as much risk from disciplinary action by their own congregations as they did disqualification by the government. In 1779, Joseph Harford was disowned by the Bristol Quaker meeting for taking the oath (not the sacrament) in order to qualify as sheriff, and at Norwich, Simon Wilkin was disqualified for his religion in the shrieval contest of 1781. These were, however, exceptional cases. The wealthy town planner Jonathan Davey was made sheriff of Norwich in 1800 and he maintained his membership at St. Paul's Baptist chapel.[82] At Liverpool, in the period 1730 through 1760 four members of Benns Garden Presbyterian chapel were mayors, a fifth was a bailiff, and a sixth an alderman, though there was strong Anglican opposition to Dissenting office holding.[83] At Colchester before 1728 a number of Dissenters from Lion Walk Congregational chapel sat on the corporation and on at least four occasions served as mayors, two of whom qualified for the

79 *Commons, 1754–1790*, 1: 16.
80 They sat on the corporation boroughs at the rate of one in four; on small freeman boroughs, one out of five; and medium freeman boroughs, one out of eight.
81 O. M. Griffiths, 'Side Lights on the History of Presbyterian-Unitarianism from the Records of Lewin's Mead Chapel, Bristol', *UHST* 6 (1936), 122; the Evans List, p. 147. Quarter Sessions records are, according to Griffiths, available only through 1753. For Presbyterian aldermen, see RG 4/3507, 3570 under dates 1776, 1788; Baptist aldermen Page, Harris, and Dampier are found in burial registers RG 4/1829 for 1821 and 1801; RG 4/2871 for 1762.
82 P. T. Underdown, 'Burke's Bristol Friends', *BGAST* 77 (1958), 138, note 2. But it is noteworthy that 'disowned' Quakers often still identified with the meetings and had their children registered by Quakers. On Wilkin, see Phillips, *Electoral Behavior*, p. 165; see also note 52 above. The Presbyterians at Bristol were not averse to recording sheriffs in their registers. See under dates 1737 and 1752 of RG 4/1830, 2497. On Davey, see Jewson, *The Baptists in Norfolk*, p. 62.
83 Anne D. Holt, *Walking Together: A Study in Liverpool Nonconformity, 1688–1938* (London, 1938), pp. 111, 121.

office by becoming occasional conformists at St. Peter's Church. Since the mayor was also the returning officer at Colchester, the post of mayor was pivotal for parliamentary elections. Here, as in Portsmouth, the Anglican legal assault against the Whig corporation was not based on the Corporation Act (it could not be, since the Dissenters were legally qualified), but on a technicality in the borough charter.[84]

At Coventry the Dissenters had a majority of the aldermen in 1712 and as late as 1735 the Presbyterian chapel alone supplied eleven aldermen. That the Dissenting presence on the corporation continued into the nineteenth century is attested by the designation of several people as aldermen in the non-parochial birth and baptismal registers of the chapels.[85] In eighteenth-century Nottingham it was so common for the mayor to be a member of the Presbyterian chapel that the minister's vestry was named 'the mayor's parlor'.[86] The Dissenters often held the majority of corporate offices, they were all duly qualified sacramentally, and in 1777 they held all six aldermanic seats, as well as both offices of sheriff.[87] Presbyterians, Congregationalists, and Baptists alike held office at Nottingham and the combined influence of the Dissenters on parliamentary elections was profound. In anticipation of the general election of 1754, the corporation formed a committee 'for the purpose of exerting the Interest of this Corporation *against* the next Election for such Representative or Representatives to be chosen as are in the Interest of this Corporation'. Following the election the corporation voted to deny the annual gift of sixty pounds sterling to the rector of St. Nicholas parish church because he, the Rev. George Wakefield, had voted against the corporation candidate.[88] In every case we have documented, these officeholders came from wealthy, well-established meetings, and the Dissenters themselves were without exception gentlemen, esquires, attorneys, or merchants.[89]

84 E. A. Blaxill, *History of Lion Walk Congregational Church, Colchester, 1642–1937* (1938), p. 10; and *History of Parliament*.

85 Watts, *The Dissenters*, p. 483; T. W. Whitely, *The Parliamentary Representation of the City of Coventry* (Coventry, 1894), 1: 339; Irene Morris, *Three Hundred Years of Baptist Life in Coventry* (London, 1925), p. 26; John Sibree and M. Caston, *Independency in Warwickshire* (London, 1855), pp. 57, 62; RG 4/3315 West Orchard Independent Meeting under the dates, 1824, 1828.

86 Quoted in C. Gordon Bolam, *Three Hundred Years, 1662–1962* (Nottingham, 1962), p. 50. See Henderson, *History of Castle Gate*, p. 92. E. L. Guilford, (ed.), *Records of the Borough of Nottingham* (Nottingham, 1947), 7: 168, 188, 261, 274, 299–307, 409–18.

87 Guilford, *Records of the Borough of Nottingham*, 7: 102, 188, 412.

88 *Ibid.*, 6: 256, 258.

89 On the social status of Dissenters at Lewins Mead, Bristol; Benns Garden, Liverpool; Lion Walk, Colchester; Vicar Lane, Coventry, and High Pavement Chapel, Castlegate Congregational Chapel, and Friar Lane Baptist Chapel, Nottingham, see the Evans List, p. 147; Griffiths, 'Side Lights on the History of Presbyterian-Unitarianism', 122, Holt, *Walking Together*, pp. 117–25, Blaxill, *History of Lion Walk*, pp. 22, 10; Watts, *The Dissenters*, p. 483; Morris, *Three Hundred Years*, p. 26; Sibree and Caston, *Independency in Warwickshire*, p. 57; Bolam, *Three Hundred Years*, p. 52; Henderson,

Altogether, Dissenters at some point in the eighteenth century sat on the corporations of at least twenty-eight parliamentary boroughs, or one in five of every borough in which they had established meetings. Comparative social indices in the eighteenth century are notoriously difficult to obtain, but even this tentative and rough assessment reveals a close correlation between social standing and office holding among Dissenters. In those boroughs where Dissenters were poor they neither sought nor expected public office, but wherever Dissenters were wealthy they were influential, and where they were influential, they held office. Yet even in those boroughs where Dissenters were numerous and well-to-do they might still be barred from office by a local, landowning patron, and here again, local conditions must be examined to determine the reasons for the Dissenters' presence in, or absence from, office. At Marlborough, Lord Bruce (created earl of Ailesbury in 1776) controlled the nomination of members to Parliament in the second half of the century. His seat at Tottenham Park was five miles from the town, and his control of the corporation in 1771 was so great that the burgesses agreed to co-opt no new members without his consent. By 1783 there were only six burgesses left, and the new mayor, Charles Bill, who was also Ailesbury's agent and attorney, broached the topic of the creation of new burgesses to his patron. Bill thought that one or two Dissenters should be admitted to the corporation. The Dissenters were 'so considerable a part of the bettermost sort of people in the town', he wrote, 'that we have but little choice of persons who are decent enough to be brought into such a connexion, and are not in some other respect objectionable'.[90] Ailesbury ignored the mayor's advice – it would have made little difference to the political complexion of the borough had he taken it – and politics at Marlborough continued on the same basis of patronage that it had for decades. It is important to recognize that of the forty-four Dissenting Members of Parliament who sat at sometime in the period 1715–90, seven were returned for boroughs where there is no record of Dissenting inhabitants at all; four of

History of Castle Gate, p. 103; Alliott and McAll, *An Historical Account*, pp. 130, 158; John T. Godfrey and Jones Ward, *The History of Friar Lane Baptist Church, Nottingham* (Nottingham, 1903), p. 170. For the other five large Freeman boroughs on which Dissenters sat on the corporations see, for London, Herbert S. Skeats and Charles S. Miall, *History of the Free Churches of England, 1688–1891* (London, 1891), p. 276; Short, 'The English Indemnity Acts', 370; Watts, *The Dissenters*, pp. 265–6, 278; A. B. Beavan, *The Aldermen of the City of London* (London, 1913), p. 141; for Norwich, John Browne, *History of Congregationalism and Memorials of the Churches in Norfolk and Suffolk* (London, 1877), p. 281; Short, 'The English Indemnity Acts', 370; Jewson, *The Baptists in Norfolk*, p. 362; John Taylor and Edward Taylor, *History of the Octagon Chapel, Norwich* (London, 1848), pp. 32–4; for Dover, T. Timpson, *Church History of Kent* (London, 1859), p. 415; for Lancaster, J. H. Colligan, *Trinity Presbyterian Church, Lancaster* (Penrith, 1909), p. 9; for Worcester, John Noake, *Worcester Sects* (London, 1861), p. 104.

90 *Commons, 1754–1790*, 1: 419.

these were returned on the government interest, and three on the basis of private influence and patronage.[91]

Finally, the Dissenters might be numerous, have a relatively high social standing, face no dominant patron, and still be excluded from office by a local High-Church party.[92] In such an environment, Whig Low Churchmen fared as ill as Dissenters, and persecution tended to be local and political rather than national and legal. Eighteenth-century Dissenters were sometimes excluded from office, but the source of the exclusion was not principally the law sanctioned by the government. Persecution tended to arise from below, with no support from the state, and it was by and large social and political rather than legal in character. Numerous and complex factors commonly determine the office holding of any social or religious group, including their numerical strength, their social status, the pattern of patronage, local politics, and the law. Office holding among Dissenters must be studied in terms of these local structural conditions along with the principles of the state on the one hand and the principles of Dissent on the other. The Municipal Corporation Act of 1835 liberated the Dissenters from the worst abuses of the unreformed system, not the repeal of the Test and Corporation Acts in 1828. Nevertheless, the perceived inequities of the law were as important to the self-understanding of Dissent and its history as the actual practice of office holding. In fact, the law became more oppressive to the Dissenters precisely at that moment when the practice of occasional conformity and office holding were becoming commonplace.

THE TEST ACT AND THE NATIONAL GOVERNMENT

If the Corporation Act allowed the Dissenters to become aldermen and mayors, the Test Act prevented only the most conscientious from seeking a variety of posts in the excise and customs, in the military, and even in the Commission of the Peace. As with the Corporation Act, instances of scrupulous self-denial can be readily documented. John Meech, esquire and trustee of the Dissenting chapel at Weymouth and Melcombe Regis, was selected in February 1776 by his Majesty in Council to serve as one of the Sheriffs of Dorset; being a Dissenter, he refused to comply with the Test Act. Writing in June 1775, the Baptist historian Josiah Thompson recorded that Mr. Edmund

---

91 On the administration interest; Nathaniel Newnham, Aldborough; Thomas Newnham, Queenborough; Sir Dudley Ryder, St. Germans; Stamp Brooksbank, Saltash; on private interest, Richard Fuller, Stockbridge; John Lee and James Adair for Higham Ferrers. Six more Dissenters were returned for boroughs where Dissenters were very weak and declining: Richard Fuller, Steyning; John Raymond, Weymouth and Melcombe Regis; Nathaniel Gould, New Shorham, Nathanial Gould, his cousin, Wareham; John Deacle, Evesham; and John Bance, Wallingford. In these thirteen instances, Dissenting M.P.s did not rely upon Dissenting electors. See Bradley, 'Whigs and Nonconformists: Presbyterians, Congregationalists, and Baptists in English Politics, 1715–1791', University of Southern California Ph.D. diss., 1978, pp. 189–93.

92 The Evans List, p. 64; the Thompson List, 38.6, p. 10; and *The History of Parliament.*

Watkins, a Dissenting pastor at Blaine residing at Usk, Monmouthshire, and a man of considerable estates, 'was offer'd a Commission of the peace which he declined'.[93] That the Dissenters were offered such positions is noteworthy, and when they turned them down it was not uncharacteristic for Nonconformists, both then and now, to record such acts of self-denial with rejoicing. But it is also the case that Dissenters sometimes loudly lamented the legal restrictions they labored under, while at the same time they accepted office with relish. Martin Dunsford, wealthy sergemaker and radical politician of Tiverton, is one such example. Dunsford hated the Test Act: 'These dispositions', he wrote, 'and my utter abhorrence to employ any of the sacred institutions of religion to qualify for civil trusts or the offices of rank, power, or worldly interests, municipal or general, prevented my advancement to public office of influence, power, or profit, and exposed me to the opposition of every interested party in the emoluments of the world.' But then Dunsford added 'I served, notwithstanding, by general choice and approbation the office of Portreeve, three years, Overseer of the Poor, one, Collector of the Land Tax, one, and that of Church-warden, four successive years without submitting to one improper oath.' Dunsford failed to mention that he also sat on the Tiverton corporation from 1782 apparently until his death in 1802.[94] The position of Collector of the Land Tax could be profitable, and earlier in the century when the Tiverton corporation was temporarily dissolved, the entire direction of local government fell on the Portreeve, so it too was an influential post. Thus Dunsford did hold offices of influence and power, though his tenure was brief enough that he may not have turned them to profit.

A survey of eighteenth-century Baptist registers at Bristol reveals nine customs house or excise officers, and among the Presbyterians at Lewins Mead there were at least six. A supervisor of the excise at Bristol, Vincent Kenny, had his daughter baptized at Castle Green Congregational chapel in 1788.[95] Four customs house officers can be located in the Benns Garden register in Liverpool in the period 1770–92 and two each at Newcastle upon Tyne (Baptist) and Kingston upon Hull (Presbyterian/Unitarian).[96] The most

93 Densham and Ogle, *The Story of the Congregational Churches*, pp. 121, 381; Thompson, History, 5: 142.
94 Cited in M. L. Banks, *Blundells' Worthies* (London, 1904), pp. 92; Dunsford, *Historical Memoirs*, p. 258 note 225.
95 Baptists, John Marks, William Bartlett, Samuel Sanders, Robert Kaddy, Richard Awberry, James Bennett, William Eplott, Blaze Carter, and John Phillips, in RG 4/2871, 1827, 1826 and under dates (most are death dates) 1751, 1777, 1790, 1793, 1794, 1805, 1809, 1816, 1818. Presbyterians, Matthew Hale, Richard Lathrop, John Farr, John Ellison, Richard Hannah, John Harris, in RG 4/1830, 2497, 3507, under dates, 1729, 1742, 1764, 1765, 1772, 1783. For Kenny, RG 4/1792. Besides the aldermen and sheriffs noted above, Bristol Dissenters held a variety of local offices probably not requiring the Test; mayor's office, sheriff's office, 'ground sheriff', and vice chamberlain. See RG 4/1830, 2497, 2507 under dates 1743, 1784, 1785, 1797.
96 At Liverpool RG 4/1042 under dates 1770, 1771, 1792, 1795; at Newcastle, RG 4/2832

cursory sample of other registers reveals Dissenting excise officers at Great Yarmouth, Cambridge, Gloucester, Ipswich, Bath, Devizes, Barnstaple, Leominster, West Ham (Essex), Weymouth and Melcombe Regis, Lyme Regis, Southwark, and London.[97] Jeremiah Rudsdell was a member of Philip Doddridge's chapel in Northampton, and in 1773 he was the distributor of stamps for the counties of Northampton, Warwick, and Rutland. Joseph Clarke, another Dissenter, was also a distributor of stamps for Northamptonshire. At Bradford, Yorkshire, the Dissenter Richard Wheater was the collector of the land tax in 1797.[98] At least two instances of Dissenters holding a receivership, a potentially lucrative position, are found in the persons of Presbyterian Thomas Fenn of Sudbury who held the post for part of Suffolk, and Josiah Diston for Westminster and Middlesex, 1721–6. This initial survey demonstrates that the number of urban Dissenters holding minor government offices was proportionately as great as Anglicans who held such posts. In fact, at Bristol, there were more Dissenters in the excise office than Anglicans.[99]

Numerous Dissenters were employed by the government at Plymouth Dock. Francis Webb, a Unitarian, took up civil employment at Gravesend, 1768–77, without losing his identity as a Dissenter. The pastor at the Great Meeting at Chatham, Mr. William Harrison, was an officer in the Royal Dockyard until 1794. Walter Taylor, deacon at the Above Bar Congregational chapel at Southampton, was a prominent citizen of the borough and a government contractor for the Navy.[100] Wherever the Dissenters' jobs depended directly on the government as at Plymouth, Gravesend, Chatham, and Southampton, their occupations had implications not only for their legal status, but for their political influence as well. The same applies, albeit to a lesser extent, to positions in the military. The chapel histories fondly record the Dissenters' military support

under dates 1811, 1830; at Hull, RG 4/ 3572, under dates 1765, 1788.

97 RG 4/1973 under dates 1740, 1766; RG 4/3870 for 1726 and RG 4/2 for 1775; RG 4/768 for 1758; RG 4/1848 for 1764; RG 4/2347 for 1808 and 1811; RG 4/2591 for 1822 and 1824; RG 4/2026 for 1768; RG 4/730, 731 for 1741; RG 4/1068 for 1790; on Weymouth and Melcombe Regis and Lyme Regis for the years 1761 and 1787 see Densham and Ogle, *The Story of the Congregational Churches*, p. 371; for Southwark and London, A View, 1731, pp. 8, 48.

98 For these references see Gasquoine, *A History of Northampton Castle Hill Church*, p. 40; William Urwick, *Nonconformity in Hertfordshire* (London, 1884), p. 201; and D. J. Steele, *Sources for Nonconformist Genealogy and Family History* (London, 1973), p. 555.

99 Thompson, History, 5: 259–61; *Commons 1715–1754*, 1: 614. In the sample of Bristol occupations (see Tables 2.1–2.4) 4 of 1129 Anglicans were excise officers (.35%) as over against 16 of 554 Dissenters (2.9%); at Liverpool, 7 of 1262 Anglicans (.55%) versus 4 of 932 Dissenters (.43%); at Newcastle 5 of 1095 Anglicans (.46%) versus 2 of 631 Dissenters (.32%); and at Kingston upon Hull, 9 of 1249 Anglicans (.72%) versus 2 of 276 Dissenters (.72%).

100 Murch, *A History of the Presbyterian and General Baptist Churches*, p. 526; Worth, *History of Plymouth*, p. 68; on Webb, Murch, pp. 326–7; Timpson, *Church History of Kent*, p. 324; on Taylor, S. Steiner, *History of the Above Bar Congregational Church, Southampton* (Southampton, 1909), p. 101.

of the Hanoverians during the rebellions of 1715 and 1745, and among the leaders were numerous commissioned officers, all apparently granted exemption from the Test Act.[101] At Gloucester, Colchester, Cirencester, Sandwich, Lancaster, Leicester, and Canterbury, the number of military men found in the non-parochial registers is too great to list, but the vast majority of these would be noncommissioned, and thus not subject to the Test Act.[102] A few of these positions were, however, commissioned, but in either case, the Dissenters in the military were of necessity loyal citizens and defenders of the government.[103]

Finally, Dissenters were free to take up the practice of law, and many of them naturally became attorneys—one of them, John Lee, even became Attorney General—but it is somewhat surprising to find Dissenting judges, high sheriffs, and Justices of the Peace as well.[104] Sir Michael Foster, lawyer and Judge of King's Bench from 1745 onward, worshipped at Lewins Mead Chapel in Bristol. Samuel Heywood, Dissenter, was Chief Justice of the Carmarthen Circuit (1807–28), and Sir Henry Hoghton, Presbyterian M.P. of Preston, was Judge Advocate General from 1734–41. John Howard, the prison reformer and Congregationalist, had accepted office 'with hazard' in 1773 when he was nominated high sheriff of Bedfordshire. Samuel Shore was high sheriff of Derbyshire in 1761 and a magistrate in the West Riding of Yorkshire. Subsequently, Shore was active in the Yorkshire Association and the Society for Constitutional Information, and when he resigned his position as magistrate in 1787, it was not because of local or national pressure, but out of pique at the defeat of the Repeal bill.[105] Lancashire, in fact, had possessed

---

101 Roberts, *Hope Street Church*, p. 77; Holt, *Walking Together*, p. 114; Gascoyne, *A History of Northampton Castle Hill Church*, p. 33; on George Campbell, Captain in the Liverpool Blues in 1745, Holt, *Walking Together*, p. 118; on Sir William Middleton, 3rd Baronet, and Abraham Elton, *Commons 1715–1754*, 2: 11, 258; on Sir William Middleton, 5th Baronet, *Commons 1754–1790*, 3: 137; on Sir Henry Hoghton, *Commons 1715–1754*, 2: 143–4.

102 See, for example, for Gloucester, RG 4/768; for Colchester, RG 4/2907; for Cirencester, Dr. Williams's Library MS 38.88; for Sandwich, RG 4/938; for Lancaster, RG 4/2117; for Leicester, RG 4/3189; and for Canterbury, RG 4/936. See also Henderson, *History of Castle Gate Congregational Church*, p. 158; Ernest A. Payne, *College Street Church, Northampton, 1697–1947* (London, 1947), p. 20 note 8; Hewett, *Ipswich, The Story of an Old Meeting House*, p. 9; Duncan, 'The History of Presbyterians in Bury St. Edmunds', pp. 70, 73. The last two for soldiers or regiments of Scots Greys who would naturally worship with Presbyterians.

103 John Richy, a half-pay officer at Bristol and Robert Tomlinson a captain in the Royal Navy at Colchester. RG 4/1830, 2497, 3507 under date 1770; for additional army and navy posts at Bristol, most, if not all, non-commissioned, see under dates 1733, 1743, 1765, 1766, 1769, 1771, 1799. For Colchester, Blaxill, *History of Lion Walk*, pp. 21, 38.

104 For Dissenting attorneys see for Bristol, RG 4/1830, 2497 under dates 1749, 1761; for three attorneys at Liverpool, Holt, *Liverpool, Walking Together*, pp. 110, 122, 124; for Hull, C. E. Darwent, *The Story of Fish Street Church, Hull* (London, 1899), p. 199; for Norwich, Browne, *History of Congregationalism*, p. 271; for Taunton, Add. MSS. 32736 ff. 21, 22.

105 Murch, *A History of the Presbyterian and General Baptist Churches*, p. 112; Short, 'The English Indemnity Acts', 372; *Commons, 1715–1754* 2: 143–4; on Howard, see

several Dissenting Justices of the Peace since the 1690s. Among the monumental inscriptions in the burying ground of the Presbyterian chapel at Cirencester one finds the names of John Smith, esq., formerly of Aylesbury, and Thomas Smith, esq., formerly of Easton Grey, Wiltshire, both J.P.s. In the late eighteenth century at Birmingham, William Russell and John Taylor were wealthy Nonconformists and Justices of the Peace. There is also the remarkable instance of the Rev. William Williams of Lynn who was not only a Nonconformist minister but a Justice of the Peace as well.[106] A cryptic and regrettably brief allusion is found in the Evans List under the Presbyterian congregation at North Shields, Northumberland: 'One in the com[m]iss[ion] of peace, but cannot act.' In Henry Vowler's report on the state of Dissent in Devonshire dated 16 December 1716 it is reported: 'Not less than 20 Dissenters of estates and ability [capable] to serve in the commission of the peace.' Sir Henry Hoghton, besides holding the office of Judge Advocate General, was also a J.P.[107] Wherever Dissenters became J.P.s, it seems certain that their fellow believers were in large measure freed from most of the unjust burdens of the law.

THE LEGAL SOURCES OF DISSENTING POLITICS

Such examples of office holding as those examined in this study may always be considered exceptional, but the frequency of the practice of occasional conformity is great enough to warrant the conclusion that Dissenters were not excluded from corporations nor from government offices of trust principally by the law. When the Dissenters agitated against subscription to the Thirty-Nine Articles in 1772, George III wrote to Lord North, '... there is no Shadow for their Petition, as the crown regularly grants a *Noli prosequi* if any over-nice Justice of the Peace encourages prosecutions'.[108] What applies to school teachers in specific cases may also be applied to the broader experience of Nonconformists in general; when confronted with the Dissenters' proposal for repeal of the Test and Corporation Acts in the 1780s, the Duke of Portland,

Lincoln, *Some Political and Social Ideas*, p. 241; on Shore, Davis, *Dissent in Politics*, p. 41.

106 The Lancaster J.P.s are noted in Watts, *The Dissenters*, p. 360; for Cirencester, see Murch, *A History of the Presbyterian and General Baptist Churches*, p. 27; for Birmingham, Rose, 'The Priestley Riots', p. 76; for William Williams, R.J. Jones in 'Notes and Queries', in *UHST* 2 (1919), 96; who ponders 'What other instances are there of Nonconformist Justices of the Peace in the eighteenth century'? The wife of 'Mr. Constant' J.P. in Winburn Dorset in 1713 was a Dissenter, Thompson, History, 2: 76, and it is noted in the Evans List for Warminster, 'Of Estates sufficient for Justices, 4. Their totall [sic] value 90,000£'. The Evans List, p. 123. Similarly, for Bristol, 'And several have Estates fit for Justices of ye Peace', The Evans List, p. 147.

107 The Evans List, pp. 90, 31; *Commons, 1715–1754*, 2: 143–4.

108 Fortesque 2: 335. One case of this is actually documented. Prosecuted for keeping an Academy at Coventry, Joshuah Oldfield obtained a *noli prosequi* and was acquitted. Thompson, History 4: 297.

leader of the Rockingham Whigs, refused to help, since, he said, the law worked no practical hardship on the Dissenters.[109] Such sentiment can now be shown to have had some basis in fact.

The Test and Corporation Acts in the eighteenth century were not excessively repressive and this chapter has shown that the practice of office holding among the more well-to-do Dissenters reflected a surprising degree of social equality. At every level, the position of urban Dissenters relative to the government and society was actually improving; on the corporation, in the mayor's office, at the excise, and on the bench, Nonconformists took their places as readily as Anglicans. The benign neglect of the government had the effect, at least in some settings, of diffusing outspoken discontent, though it did not, as we shall see, fully satisfy the Dissenters. The government's approach to the Dissenters' office holding manifests another aspect of the English genius for pragmatism in social adjustment, and this characteristic almost certainly contributed to eighteenth-century social stability. Society was relatively open, Dissenters could hold office, and later chapters will attempt to show how their social attainments kept radical ideology from turning revolutionary. Moreover, the Dissenters may have provided an example to those Low-Church Anglicans, who like themselves, faced social or economic disadvantages. The Dissenters proved that with few exceptions, such as the Catholics, people of widely differing persuasions could attain to positions of trust if they enjoyed sufficient economic means. While the Dissenters provided the energy for numerous anti-corporation parties, it is well to remember that the majority of every anti-corporation party in England comprised disaffected Anglicans who coalesced around a Nonconformist core.

The myth that Dissenters were strictly excluded from offices of trust was constructed by the Dissenters themselves in the interest of reform in much the same way that T. H. B. Oldfield exaggerated the abuses of the unreformed electoral system. The Dissenters were not forced directly on to the margins by a harsh and repressive law requiring them to seek out new methods of industrial production, innovative techniques in education and science, and radical political discourse. It is true that a disproportionately large number of Dissenters were leaders in industry; Everett Hagen found nine times more English Nonconformists than Anglicans active as innovators in eighteenth-century industry, and W. D. Rubinstein's work in probate records has not altered this finding. Rubinstein does show that the total amount of wealth amassed by Anglicans and Dissenters was proportional to their share of the population. Hagen had systematically (and unjustifiably) excluded merchants, financiers, bankers, and big builders from his calculations. But, crucially, Rubinstein's research does nothing to discredit the connection between Dissent and invention; indeed it

109 Cited B. W. Hill, 'Fox and Burke: The Whig Party and the Question of Principles, 1784–1789', *EHR* 89 (1974), 22.

corroborates the alliance between Dissent and certain types of business endeavor, particularly industrial or manufacturing trades. On the question of the motivation of the Dissenters to go into industry, Rubinstein posits an Anglican avoidance of industries based on traditional status notions of landed society, on the one hand, and the Dissenters' exclusion from power and status, on the other, though he does not make much of the latter. He also finds some help in explaining these developments in the role of intermarriage and family networks, but this, in turn, is based on communal and theological identity, facets of reality that Rubinstein does not emphasize.[110]

The idea that marginalization produced by the law was a primary cause of industrialization falters on several additional grounds. First, Frederick B. Tolles showed that the Quakers in Pennsylvania, who were anything but excluded, were as diligent in business as those in England.[111] The vigor of the Dissenting communities in Bristol and Nottingham supports the same conclusion; their freedom suggests that the independent mentality of religious dissidents and their conscious historical and communal identity may be more important than the specific exigencies of local constraints, or even freedom from constraints. Secondly, Linda Colley and Philip Jenkins have recently discovered remarkable links between Toryism and industrialism that clearly call into question any facile connection between Dissent and industry. And whereas Colley accepted the notion of exclusion from politics as one basis for Tory motivation, Jenkins' most recent article discounts the utility of this explanatory device.[112] On the other hand, Michael Watts' extensive examination of Dissenting occupations in early nineteenth-century Britain reveals that the Dissenters were almost totally absent in the professions, and thus the long-term effect of the law, and in particular the statutes concerning education, may have had a profound impact.[113] In the eighteenth century, however, urban Dissenters were not underrepresented in any occupational category.

110 Everett E. Hagen, *On the Theory of Social Change: How Economic Growth Begins* (Homewood, Ill, 1962), pp. 296-7. Rubinstein, *Men of Property*, pp. 146–59, 162–3. While exclusion is necessary to Hagen's thesis, his overall explanatory scheme is overly psychologized. David Pratt, *English Quakers and the First Industrial Revolution* provides the best recent survey of the literature on Nonconformity and the Industrial Revolution, pp. 1-20. The marginalization thesis works best for the Quakers and the Unitarians because of the stronger sense of community in the former, and the strictures of the law regarding blasphemy for the latter. See Pratt, pp. 13, 139-40; and Raymond V. Holt, *The Unitarian Contribution to Social Progress in England* (London, 1938), p. 16. For Dissenters in science, see Crane, 'The Club of Honest Whigs', pp. 210-33.
111 Tolles, *Meeting House and Counting House: The Quaker Merchants of Colonial Philadelphia, 1682–1763* (New York, 1948), p. 49.
112 Linda Colley, *In Defiance of Oligarchy: The Tory Party 1714–60* (Cambridge, 1982), pp. 9–10, 147–8; Jenkins, 'Tory Industrialization and Town Politics', 105, 120, 122–3. Jenkins, however, offers little in place of the exclusion thesis; there is no discussion of specific 'Tory' ideas to account for industrialization.
113 Michael Watts' forthcoming second volume of *The Dissenters* examines the social structure of nineteenth-century Dissent.

If the actual exclusion from offices of trust does not fully account for the Dissenters' social and political behavior, we are forced to ask questions concerning their perception of the law, their mentality with respect to social realities, and their communal identity. Sociologists of religion have long recognized that a group's self-understanding is one of the most important factors for explaining its behavior.[114] Quite apart from the actual force of the law, the Dissenters' self-perception concerning social and religious identity informed and promoted opposition to the restricting statutes. The Dissenting elite who expressed the ideology of oppression and alienation—however exaggerated it was in fact—appear to have found real personal meaning in this ideology, and they seem to have been able to convince the laity of its truth. An examination of the Dissenters' actual behavior thus only reinforces the need to investigate their ideology and political rhetoric.

The oft-repeated conviction that the law excluded the Dissenters clearly helped shape their self-understanding, and it thereby indirectly contributed to an independent political and social outlook. The law addressed a wide variety of vital issues related to status and security, including the registration of the Dissenters' birth, their marriage, education, and finally, where they were buried. At each vital passage of life, the Dissenters faced a reminder of their unequal social status that did in fact have a powerful emotional impact. Moreover, some conscientious Dissenters who were unwilling to occasionally conform were excluded from local offices of trust, and the constant awareness of being required to pay for a parish system from which they received only dubious benefits was deeply resented by a group of people who despised waste in any form. Ministers, in particular, were constantly reminded of their inferior status by the need to obtain certification for their religious exercises. The threat of High-Church persecution remained a real possibility in some boroughs, and in others, Dissenting ministers made it their practice to remind the laity of the persecution of a former age. In this way, an independent mentality with a strong group identity came to be characteristic of many individual Dissenters. Among the minority who turned to Arianism or Unitarianism, a change in theological identity promoted a more vigorous commitment to social activism, and since the heterodox Dissenting elite were so adept at publicizing their views, their politics undoubtedly influenced the orthodox as well.[115]

The inequities in the Dissenters' legal status in society thus did stimulate political conflict, but it was a form of conflict that was largely nonviolent and enormously constructive. For example, when the Dissenters had the opportunity to seek repeal, their leaders struggled vigorously to change the law. This

114 Emile Durkheim, *The Elemental Forms of the Religious Life* (London, 1915).
115 Richey, 'The Origins of British Radicalism', 187–92 locates the changing rationale for Dissent primarily in a shift from theological concerns to matters of polity, and secondarily in the shift to theological liberalism. Clark adopts Richey's view, but puts the emphasis on heterodoxy, *English Society*, pp. 317-18.

struggle continued to shape both their identity and their unity; it led to an open discussion of political differences; and it contributed to various peaceful expressions of discontent and criticism of the government. The Dissenters became unusually sensitive to legal inequities—both those that bore directly upon them, and those that bore on others. The law was deemed oppressive enough in some locales, especially when combined with a tradition of High-Anglican opposition, that it provoked violent rhetoric and led the Dissenters to become extremely troublesome to borough patrons.

But paradoxically, the degree of the Dissenters' alienation in specific boroughs cannot be correlated directly to the strength of their political opposition to the government. At Newcastle upon Tyne, unlike Bristol, Liverpool, and other large freeman boroughs, the Dissenters were strictly excluded from the corporation. Additionally, one finds very few professional people among the Newcastle Dissenters, and a survey of the numerous registers of this very large Dissenting community reveals few people benefiting from minor government patronage. Such difficulties as the Dissenters faced at Newcastle evidently contributed to an empathetic understanding of American grievances, but it was no stronger than the reaction of the Bristol Dissenters who had achieved a considerably greater degree of social recognition and extensive office holding. The similarities in the behavior of the Nonconformist laity across several boroughs requires the investigation of both the ideological program that transcended local conditions and the role of charismatic leadership that is taken up in subsequent chapters.

The social status of Nonconformity combined with their increasing acceptance in society helps explain their proclivity for occasional conformity on the one hand, and their capacity for independent action, given the proper circumstances and adequate leadership, on the other. Good historians have interpreted the era in terms of the Dissenters' ideological contribution to the growth of liberty, but the actual course of the progress toward legal equality may now be placed in the setting of the Dissenters' gradual economic betterment and the widespread practice of occasional conformity. Based on this initial assessment of occupational data, we can say that the Dissenters' social status equalled that of the Anglicans in many urban centers, and in some boroughs, their status actually exceeded the Anglicans. Nevertheless, the Dissenters retained a number of characteristics that were strikingly unlike those of other groups who chafed under the same constrictions of the political and social system. Their strong group identity helped them focus their grievances, whether justly or not, on the law that gave them a second-class status. The evidence suggests that the Dissenters' experience of social and economic independence heightened, rather than diminished, the discontent felt over the remaining legal encumbrances. Dissenters did not agitate for repeal of the Test and Corporation Acts because they were wholly excluded from office; they were motivated to work for legal equality in part because they had tasted the spoils of office. The actual occurrence of office holding was found primarily in those boroughs where they had achieved some social standing, and thus it is likely that their improved circumstances motivated them to seek that degree of legal recognition and political prestige that was commensurate with the position they had begun to obtain in the social realm. Thus the *perceived* injustices of the Test and Corporation Acts remained a potent unifying force while the *practice* of occasional conformity allowed the Dissenters a large degree of participation in unreformed politics. Clearly, the wealthier the Dissenters became, the less they suffered, but as John Seed has recently pointed out, the 'feeling of insecurity and injustice, of symbolic exclusion and victimization was undoubtedly real'.[116]

Symbolic and psychological exclusion thus takes us to the heart of the matter. It was precisely the combination of the perceived oppression of the law, justified by the law's occasional enforcement, and the enjoyment of increased social equality and office holdings that provoked the Dissenters' reaction, and made them such a powerful force in both their expression of radical ideology and the use of popular political methods. Their perception of the ominous political developments in the reign of George III also made them unusually sensitive to the claims of the colonists. When their brethren across the sea began to speak out against the injustices of the government, the English Dissenters understood their rhetoric and took up the cause as their own. The betterment of structural conditions combined with the rhetoric of oppression and tyranny goes a long way toward explaining both the development of revolutionary events in the colonies, and the evolution of radicalism in England.

A candid recognition of the Dissenters' willing acceptance of place and their general compliance in the unreformed political system thus does not detract from their remarkable capacity to act on the basis of conviction. Rather, the radical political philosophy of many of the elite and the proclivity for independent action of many of the laity become all the more striking. Later chapters will show that the Dissenters' radical ideology could influence even those laymen who had occasionally conformed, yet who, despite all appearances to the contrary, maintained their religious identity as Nonconformists. Dissenters were taught to resist the putative unjust encroachments of government and to view the exercise of political force with suspicion. Some of their ministers, particularly those in the provinces, preached sermons that bordered on sedition, but they never took the ultimate step of advocating armed uprising. The oft-expressed fear that the coercion exercised in the colonies might be used at home never in fact materialized, and the economic conditions of the war years were never pressing enough to transform the Dissenters' discontent into open rebellion. Structural conditions also account for why a sizable minority remained

116 Seed, 'Gentlemen Dissenters', 316.

loyal to the government throughout the war. The long range significance of the Dissenters' social equality and their experience of office holding, therefore, may be found in the fact that the radicalism of the Dissenting pulpit never became explicitly revolutionary.

3

Nonconformity in Politics: Influence and Independence

The Dissenters experienced serious numerical decline after 1715 and this fact has contributed to the judgment that they were politically insignificant. C. E. Fryer made the first modern attempt to quantify the decline. In response to Richard Lodge's observation that since 1688 the Dissenters were the 'backbone of the Whig party', Fryer concluded that 'neither upon the ground of numbers nor of political influence can the Dissenters be assigned any such anatomical importance'.[1] This viewpoint has passed over into the body of common knowledge, so that one influential study of the Dissenters can say, 'they were also thought to be fast declining and thus politically unimportant'.[2] The anachronistic assumption behind such a statement is that numbers in eighteenth-century English politics counted for more than influence and patronage. In the decade of the 1770s, however, at the nadir of their numerical strength, the Dissenters exerted more political influence than they had fifty years before when they were far stronger numerically. Moreover, Fryer's statement ignores the critical issue of geography; a decline in numbers would have no bearing whatever on those boroughs where the franchise was tied to specific plots of land, and in several sections of England, Dissenters declined in the counties, but maintained their numbers in the large freeman boroughs. The failure of past treatments to keep numbers related to influence, and the concentration of population related to parliamentary boroughs, has seriously obscured the Dissenters' role in politics. The key demographic issues of social setting and regionalism must be carefully kept in the forefront of any attempt to reassess the meaning of the Dissenters' numerical decline.

1 C. E. Fryer, 'The Numerical Decline of Dissent in England Previous to the Industrial Revolution', *The American Journal of Theology* 17 (1913), 233; E. D. Bebb, *Nonconformity and Social and Economic Life, 1660–1800* (London, 1935), p. 43; John D. Gay, *The Geography of Religion in England* (London, 1971), p. 120. Yet *The History of Parliament* refers repeatedly to 'a strong local nonconformist community', a 'large Dissenting population', a 'Dissenting party', and most frequently, the 'Dissenting interest'. See *Commons, 1715–1754*, 1: 232, 273; *Commons, 1754–1790*, 1: 18, 210, 259, 319, 342.
2 Caroline Robbins, *The Eighteenth-Century Commonwealthman* (1959; reprinted, New York, 1968), p. 225. Many contemporary Dissenters observed the same.

THE DEMOGRAPHY OF DISSENT AND PARLIAMENTARY POLITICS

Statistics of religious bodies are notoriously biased and estimates of the population of Dissent in the eighteenth century are no exception. The civil registration of births, marriages, and deaths began only in 1838 and the first official religious census dates from 1851; as a result, the numerical strength of eighteenth-century Nonconformity has been the subject of considerable disagreement. A. D. Gilbert, for example, placed the low point of old Dissent in 1740 and argued that the Dissenters then comprised only half of their former strength. But at midcentury the data are unusually scanty, Gilbert and others have relied too heavily on the work of E. D. Bebb who wrote in 1935, and little use has been made of the manuscript sources of the 1770s.[3] Utilizing these sources, the decline of Nonconformity in the eighteenth century may be placed beyond dispute, but it was neither as precipitous nor as serious a problem for the Dissenters' political involvement as historians have believed.

Although the actual number of Dissenters in London and Middlesex is not available, the decline is registered in the loss of Dissenting congregations and in the loss of ministers. The total number of congregations of the three denominations dropped from 112 in 1727 to 72 in 1776, and the trend was one of persistent, unremitting decline.[4] The decrease in the number of ministers in the same period from 166 to 95 merely confirms these losses. Assistant pastors at such important London meeting houses as Salters Hall, Silver Street, New Broad Street, and Little Aliff Street were no longer needed in the 1760s. In a few congregations an upward trend in attendance may be discerned in the late 1770s, but there is no indication of a broad change for the better until the mid 1780s, and if anything, the increase in ministers without churches from 1771 to 1776 indicates a more serious decline, since this transpired while the population of London spiraled steadily upward.[5] While the London Dissenters

---

3 A. D. Gilbert, *Religion and Society in Industrial England: Church, Chapel and Social Change 1740–1914* (London, 1976), pp. 16, 215. On Bebb's highly misleading counting of congregations, see James Bradley, 'Whigs and Nonconformists: Presbyterians, Congregationalists and Baptists in English Politics' University of Southern California Ph.D. diss., 1978, Appendix I, 591–5. The best recent discussion of the early century is Michael Watts, *The Dissenters* (Oxford, 1978), pp. 491–510. See also M. W. Flinn, *British Population Growth, 1700–1850* (London, 1970), p. 50. For the difficulties involved in using the licensing records of chapels, see Barbara Donaldson, *The Registrations of Dissenting Chapels and Meeting Houses in Staffordshire, 1689–1825*, The Staffordshire Record Society, 4th series, vol. 3 (Kendal, 1960), p. xxvii; and Flinn, *British Population Growth*, p. 28, note 1. Yet these statistics have been used very uncritically. Fryer, 'The Numerical Decline of Dissent', p. 237. See also R. Currie, A. D. Gilbert, and L. H. Horsley, *Churches and Churchgoers: Patterns of Church Growth in the British Isles since 1700* (Oxford, 1977), pp. 23, 65, 154, 161.
4 Minute Books of the Body of Protestant Dissenting Ministers of the Three Denominations in and about the Cities of London and Westminster, 2 vols. (11 July 1727–11 April 1779) MS. 38.105–6. For a much expanded discussion, see Bradley, 'Whigs and Nonconformists', Table 1, p. 126 and Appendix II, pp. 603–7.
5 Phyllis Deane and W. A. Cole, *British Ecomonic Growth, 1688-1959: Trends and Struc-*

lost 35 percent of their congregations in absolute terms, relative to the whole, by 1776 it was closer to half. In terms of absolute denominational decrease, the Presbyterians lost 39 percent of their congregations, the Congregationalists 27 percent, and the Baptists 41 percent. Here, as in the provinces, the Congregationalists appear to have been more stable than the Presbyterians.

The decline in the nation at large was serious, but not as precipitous. In the early part of the eighteenth century the Dissenters comprised between five and ten percent of the population in eighteen, or almost half of the English counties, and these were predominantly in the south and southwest, the northwest, and the south midlands.[6] Only in Monmouthshire did they comprise over ten percent of the population. The Dissenters had never been strong in the southeast and the west midlands. However, by 1773 only nine, or one-fourth of the English counties, had five percent or more Dissenting population, and the bulk of these were in the agricultural south midlands.[7] In this period only four counties registered any increase relative to the population, four remained stable, and the remaining thirty-two decreased, sometimes two to three percentage points.[8] In almost every county there were some Baptist gains, but these were normally small congregations, and in only a few cases did they compensate for the losses of the Presbyterians and Congregationalists. Denominationally, the Presbyterians were predominant in the north and northwest, the Congregationalists were strong in the south midlands and East Anglia, and the Baptists were most numerous in the southeast and south midlands. In those cases where the overall decline is found to be retarded or reversed, it may be attributed either to the Congregationalists, or more often the Baptists. Sometimes, as in the south midlands, this was prompted by revival. The Presbyterians rarely experienced any growth, and since they were the most numerous of the three denominations in 1715, the so-called decline among Nonconformists was in fact most often Presbyterian decline. Altogether, the three denominations dropped from about five percent of the population in 1715 to four percent or slightly less in 1773. Throughout the century, the Quakers numbered less than one percent of the population, but they experienced the same decline as the other denominations.[9]

---

ture, 2nd edn rev. (Cambridge, 1967), p. 103, on the population of London and Middlesex.

6 For the geographic distribution of Nonconformity see the maps and analysis in Watts, *The Dissenters*, pp. 267–89. South and southwest: Hampshire, Wiltshire, Somerset, Devon; west midlands: Gloucestershire, Monmouthshire; northwest and north: Cheshire, Lancashire, Northumberland; north midlands: Nottinghamshire, Leicestershire; south midlands: Northamptonshire, Cambridgeshire, Bedfordshire, Berkshire, Hertfordshire, Sussex, and Essex.

7 Cambridgeshire, Bedfordshire, Hertfordshire, Essex, Gloucestershire, Monmouthshire, Nottinghamshire, Leicestershire, Huntingdonshire. Northumberland also had more than 5%.

8 Increasing: Monmouthshire, Northumberland, Huntingdonshire, Cambridgeshire. Stable: Westmorland, Durham, Leicestershire, Rutland.

9 John Evans, List of Dissenting Congregations and Ministers in England and Wales

Calvinists have often attributed the decline to the increase in Arminianism, Trinitarians have suspected the drift into Arianism, and Unitarians, in their turn, are inclined to blame 'dead' orthodoxy.[10] The first empirical attempt to answer this question was made in 1731 by the anonymous author of 'A View of the Dissenting Interest in London'. He attributed the loss to two principal causes; the Test Act, which drew many Dissenters from occasional conformity into 'stated communion' with the Anglican church, and the 'manifest growth of error', principally Arminianism and Arianism.[11] However, in the twenty-eight cases of Dissenting ministers who conformed examined in this study, only two were specifically mentioned as resulting in the dissolution of the church, though two others hint that the conformity of the minister led to a decline, and other cases probably did result in decline.[12] The problem should not be minimized, but because of the few numbers involved, it is doubtful whether conformity among the clergy contributed greatly to the loss of Dissenters. On the other hand, conformity among lay people, based on a variety

(1715–29), MS. 38.4, (hereafter cited as the Evans List). Josiah Thompson, List of Protestant Dissenting Congregations in England and Wales (1772–3), MS. 38.6, (hereafter cited as the Thompson List); Josiah Thompson, History of Protestant Dissenting Congregations, 5 vols., MS. 38.7–11 throughout (hereafter cited as Thompson, History). For a discussion of the composition and accuracy of these lists see James E. Bradley, 'Nonconformity and the Electorate in Eighteenth-Century England', in *Parliamentary History* 6 (1987), 236–61. The calculation for 1715 (5.2%) is based on auditors in thirty-four counties; that in 1773 (4.2%) is based on auditors in thirty counties. But the statistics for thirteen of these thirty counties are very sketchy, and the ten counties for which no auditors are given in Thompson's History may have been in a more serious state of decline than the ones for which he reports 'hearers'. See Bradley, 'Whigs and Nonconformists', tables 1–8, pp. 126–41 and Appendix I, pp. 588–602. Watts' estimate is based on the Evans' List and using the mean between the two lists of Charles Davenant and John Houghton, both in the 1690s, for the entire population by county, and making some allowance for missing data in the Evans List, he arrives at 5.49% for the three denominations in the early eighteenth century. See Watts, *The Dissenters*, pp. 272–6 and table XII, p. 509. This breaks down to 3.3% Presbyterian, 1.1% Congregational, .74% Particular Baptist and .35% General Baptist. Watts estimates that the Quakers comprised .73% of the population in the early century. On the decline of the Quakers, see p. 387.

10 See the helpful discussions in Frederick J. Powick, 'Apology for the Nonconformist Arians of the 18th Century', *UHST* 1 (1918), 101–28, and Watts, *The Dissenters*, pp. 364–89. On the rapid growth of Dissent in the late eighteenth century, see Gilbert, *Religion and Society*, p. 32–42.

11 'A View of the Dissenting Interest in London of the Presbyterian and Independent Denominations from...1695 to...1731', MS. 38.18, 1731, pp. 82–3 (hereafter referred to as A View, 1731). The line is from Arminianism to Arianism to Socinianism to infidelity to apostasy.

12 The Thompson List, 38.6, p. 25; Thompson, History, 2: 5, 9, 11, 19, 51, 77, 207; 3: 10; 4: 24, 27, 145, 163, 182, 230, 238, 240, 288, 292; the Evans List, pp. 22 (twice), 53, 64, 77, 78, 92. The author of A View, 1731, says he can document twenty instances of ministers conforming between 1718 and 1731. He argues, however, that the laity did *not* go over in the same proportion. A View, 1731, pp. 85–6. In the Minute Book of London Ministers there are nine instances among Presbyterians (some may be duplicated above) and none among Congregationalists and Baptists in the period 1727 to 1761. Minute Book of London Ministers, 1: 1–256.

of causes, appears to have been a more serious problem. The Dissenters' improved social status, combined with the negative influence of the social and legal discrimination associated with their religion, and the positive lure of respectability the Anglican Church offered, undoubtedly contributed to erosion. A loss of zeal for the earlier distinctives and a shift from evangelism to education also contributed to decline, but probably the greatest cause was the increased reliance on reason rather than revelation, and the concurrent inroads of doubt and scepticism.[13] All of these elements combined resulted in what Josiah Thompson aptly called 'that comm[on] operating cause in thinning assemblies', namely death.[14] Repeatedly the cause of decline is attributed to chapel members growing old and dying with none to replace them, and before the Great Awakening, the few attempts at evangelism were not adequate to counteract the general attrition due to death. The failure to attract new members may also be attributed to the significant extent of social assimilation the Dissenters experienced and 'rational Dissent's' notorious inability to appeal to the common person.[15]

The numerical decline of Dissent seriously affected the Dissenting vote in the counties, but in many parliamentary boroughs the Dissenters either maintained their numbers or may have actually increased relative to the population. Norfolk is a good example of how the consideration of a county's Dissenting population alone, without reference to localized centers of growth, may be greatly misleading. While the Presbyterians and Congregationalists were in a state of decline, the Dissenters in the two boroughs of Norwich and Great Yarmouth prospered throughout the century. They were described in 1774 as 'always leading churches in these 2 counties [i.e., Norfolk and Suffolk]'.[16] Similarly in Suffolk, although there was overall decline, Dissenters at least maintained their numbers in the two boroughs of Sudbury and Ipswich. In Nottinghamshire the Dissenters were probably reduced overall by half, yet the borough of Nottingham was virtually controlled by the Nonconformists. Despite the decline in Dorset, the two Congregational churches in the boroughs

13 For a full discussion of the impact of theological liberalism, see Watts, *The Dissenters*, pp. 386–92, 488–90. Other causes are the lack of popular talent in the pulpit, A View, 1731, pp. 1, 14, 29, 54; doctrinal disputes, Thompson, History, 3: 13; 4: 13, 156, 226; loss of faith and discouragement, Thompson, History, 4: 316, The Thompson List, 38.6, p. 21; wrangles over ministers or a rapid succession of ministers, Thompson, History, 4: 140, 173, 175, 226, 264; and finally, persecution and losses to Methodists, History, 4: 237, 174, 179, 227.
14 Thompson, History, 4: 9.
15 Something can be said for Troeltsch's theory of the movement from sects to denominations, although this does not account in every instance for decline. Geoffrey Holmes in 'The Achievement of Stability: The Social Context of Politics from the 1680s to the Age of Walpole', p. 5 in *The Whig Ascendancy: Colloquies on Hanoverian England*, (ed.) John Cannon (London, 1981), has a good summary of research on the stability of the population before 1742.
16 Thompson, History, 4: 245.

of Bridport and Wareham remained strong; each numbered about 500 in 1773. If Somerset lost numerous Dissenters, they maintained their strength in the borough of Taunton, and the same is true of Bristol in Gloucestershire. In Devon, the Dissenters in some boroughs such as Exeter declined with the rest of their brethren in the county, but it does not follow that the dismal loss of numbers in the southwest of England necessarily affected the political influence of Dissent in other boroughs. Cornwall, for example, had forty-four parliamentary representatives and was a county to be reckoned with in terms of politics, but never with respect to Dissent. In 1715 the Presbyterians had eleven tiny congregations, but by 1773 they, with the rest of the Dissenters, were nearly extinct. They never had been important in electoral terms as they comprised only 1 percent of the population in 1715.

In the course of the eighteenth century, the Dissenting communities in eighteen parliamentary boroughs dissolved entirely, but the loss of these boroughs had little, if any, effect on the Dissenters' relationship to the electorate. First, in fourteen of these cases the Dissenting interest was already extremely weak in 1715; statistics are available for twelve of the fourteen, and in these dozen boroughs the Dissenters totaled only 1240 auditors in 1715. In the remaining four, the corporation and freeman franchise would have hindered their activity under the best circumstances.[17] Thus the decline of Nonconformity, thought to be such a serious problem for the political importance of Dissent, must be studied in relationship to localized centers of growth. Moreover, Dissenters seeking seats in Parliament were by no means limited to constituencies where there was a strong Dissenting vote. Dissenting M.P.s were returned for six boroughs with very weak Dissenting support in the constituencies and for an additional seven boroughs where there is no record of Dissenting voters at all.[18]

DISSENTERS AND ELECTORAL POLITICS: DEFERENCE, INFLUENCE, AND THE 'WATER SPOUT OF FREEDOM'

By 1773, English Dissenters had established meeting houses in 125 of 203 parliamentary boroughs. In seventy-four boroughs, or nearly two-thirds of those in which they gathered for worship, they faced a variety of circumstances that seriously handicapped their political activity; in these boroughs, research has not been able to demonstrate that they had any significant effect on parliamentary elections. The causes for their impotence in these boroughs are for the most part those shared by the Anglican participants in the

---

17 Half of these boroughs were concentrated in Cornwall and Sussex. The fourteen are St. Ives, Fowey, Steyning, Arundel, New Shorham, Midhurst, Weobley, Petersfield, Thirsk, Malton, Wallingford, New Windsor, Peterborough, and Eye. The four are, Harwich, Bodmin, Launceston, and Plympton Earle.

18 See note 91 in chap. 2 above.

unreformed electoral system.[19] In twenty-six boroughs their numbers were so small as to render their vote ineffectual.[20] For example, in the burgage and freeholder boroughs the nomination to a seat was absolutely controlled by the owner of a majority of properties; even if the Dissenters were numerous in these boroughs, if they did not possess a majority of the burgages, they fared as ill as the minority of Anglicans. Many election contests were likely to be close, so a very small number of voters could swing the result, but in these twenty-six boroughs there is no evidence that the Dissenters ever voted together as a unified bloc. In an additional eighteen boroughs the Dissenters either habitually deferred to local patrons or their electoral independence was eroded by bribery.[21] In a third group comprising some thirty boroughs, the Dissenters were hindered in parliamentary politics by a combination of their low social status, patronage, and genuine legal restrictions related to the Test and Corporation Acts.[22]

19 For the way in which the franchise restricted popular participation in some boroughs where Dissenters were numerous, see the examples of Ashburton and Tavistock in my article 'Nonconformity and the Electorate', pp. 249–51. At Ashburton, the Dissenters owned 37 of the 190 burgages, but the owner of the majority controlled the borough. Similarly, at Tavistock, though the Presbyterians were very strong, the dukes of Bedford owned the majority of freeholds. For the influence of government patronage on the independence of the Dissenters' political behavior see the discussion of Plymouth in the same article (p. 251). There is no record in the Evans or Thompson Lists of Dissenting congregations in the remaining seventy-eight boroughs; it is obvious that some Dissenters may have lived in these boroughs, but the number was apparently not great enough to establish a congregation, and therefore we may assume that they were politically unimportant. Further work on licensing records may help identify these Dissenters.
20 In 1715, the Dissenters were a minority of electors in nine burgage and four freeholder boroughs: Ashburton, Horsham, Midhurst, Weobley, Whitechurch, Petersfield, Knaresborough, Pontefract, Thirsk, Tavistock, Weymouth and Melcombe Regis, Reigate, and Wareham. In seventeen scot and lot boroughs they were extremely weak numerically: Westminster, Southwark, Bridgwater, Milborne Port, St. Ives, Fowey, Penryn, Steyning, Arundel, New Shoreham, Wallingford, New Windsor, Dorchester, Peterborough, Eye, Stamford, and Tamworth. In thirteen medium and large freeman boroughs their interest was unimportant from an electoral standpoint: Kingston upon Hull, Evesham, Durham, Derby, Carlisle, Hereford, Lincoln, Maldon, Beverley, Lichfield, Bridgnorth, Ludlow, and Oxford. Wendover had a householder franchise; the small Baptist chapel is not listed by Evans, but may well have subsisted in 1715. The Thompson List, p. 3.
21 For the documentation of patronage in relation to the Dissenting vote at Cockermouth, see 'Nonconformity and the Electorate', (p. 249); patrons were also very influential at Okehampton, Westbury, Cirencester, and Kings Lynn; the Admiralty held sway in the cinque ports of Sandwich, Dover, Hythe, and Rye, and at Rochester and Plymouth; and money probably contributed to stifling the Dissenters' independence at Leominster, Barnstable, Honiton, Hindon, Great Marlow, Aylesbury, and Monmouth, for which, see the discussion below.
22 For genuine legal problems, see the discussion in chap. 2. The corporation boroughs include: Calne, Malmsbury, Salisbury, Wilton, Andover, Christchurch, Newport (Isle of Wight), Banbury, Bath, Bury St. Edmunds, Scarborough, Truro, Bodmin, Harwich, Buckingham, and Marlborough. Small freeman boroughs: Tewkesbury, Dartmouth, Totnes, Plympton Earle, Liskeard, East Looe, Launceston, Hedon, Lymington, Winchester, Bewdley, Guildford, Chipping Wycombe, and Newcastle upon Tyne, a large freeman borough that uniquely excluded Scots Presbyterians.

It can now be documented that the Dissenters exerted some political influence on elections in fifty-one boroughs, or one-fourth of the whole. The nature of the Dissenters' influence remains unclear in fifteen of these boroughs, but in these fifteen constituencies, their relatively large numbers, the openness of the boroughs, combined with the frequency, intensity, and closeness of contests, suggest that even a slight religious component could have swayed the results of elections.[23] Dissenting patrons were usually able to nominate the candidate to at least one seat in three constituencies,[24] and the Dissenting elite and the laity combined had a strong and occasionally determinative influence over one seat and sometimes both seats in thirty-three others.[25] An analysis of the type of franchise in these fifty-one boroughs reveals that the Dissenting interest in the eighteenth century was located primarily in the freeman boroughs, and this is a demographic fact of no little importance. In relation to the total number of parliamentary boroughs, the number in which the Dissenters had a significant interest was small; but in relation to the large, open boroughs, the proportion was impressive: the Dissenters wielded political influence sufficient to turn an election in twenty-five of the thirty-five large and medium-sized freemen boroughs with electorates of 500 or more voters.[26] This suggests the possibility that the frequency of contests in these boroughs was not only a function of their size and freedom from influence, but that it was also related to religion. In terms of popular political participation, the Dissenters' prominence in these open boroughs is more important than their geographical distribution, since the

23 This is not to say that these boroughs were free from patronage. Lord Gower had a strong interest in Newcastle under Lyme; but intense religious feelings disrupted politics in 1715 and again at midcentury. J. C. Wedgwood, *Staffordshire Parliamentary History from the Earliest Times to the Present Day*, 3 vols. (London, 1917–20), 2: 255. The fifteen include four large freeman boroughs; Canterbury, Chester, Gloucester, and Lancaster; two medium sized and three small freeman boroughs, Newcastle under Lyme, Ipswich, Wells, Boston, and Stafford; the householder borough, Minehead, and Bedford with a householder and freeman franchise; the scot and lot boroughs, Reading, Warwick, and Bridport; and Chippenham, a relatively open burgage borough.

24 At East Retford and Preston one seat was under the influence of Dissenting families, the Whites and the Hoghtons, respectively; at Ilchester, the Lockyer brothers regularly nominated candidates for both seats. In this group of fifty-one boroughs, the Dissenting communities at Minehead, East Retford, and Ilchester dissolved by 1773. Of these three, the only loss of influence to the Dissenters occurred at Minehead; the Dissenting patrons at East Retford and Ilchester proceeded in electoral matters as usual, with or without Dissenting electors.

25 The large freeman boroughs are; London, Bristol, Norwich, Liverpool, Colchester, Coventry, Nottingham, Worcester, Leicester, Exeter, Maidstone, and York; the medium freeman boroughs are, Great Yarmouth, Southampton, St. Albans, Hertford, Sudbury, Berwick-upon-Tweed, and Maldon; the small freeman boroughs are, Cambridge, Poole, Shrewsbury, East Retford, Lyme Regis, Portsmouth, and Morpeth. There were four householder boroughs: Northampton, Taunton, Preston, and Ilchester; four scot and lot boroughs: Chichester, Lewes, Abingdon, and Shaftesbury; and two corporation boroughs: Tiverton and Devizes.

26 *Commons, 1754–1790* classifies 'small' freeman boroughs in two ways; those with 500 or less, and those with 200 or less, (1: 513).

large boroughs included some two-thirds of England's entire borough electorate.[27]

Dissenters resided in all forty English counties and in fifteen they influenced one or more elections in the eighteenth century.[28] The Dissenters were particularly prominent in the reform movements of the last quarter of the century in Yorkshire, Northumberland, and Cambridgeshire, and as supporters of independent candidates in Essex and Leicestershire.[29] While the loss of the Dissenting vote in the counties was more serious than that in the boroughs, even at their strongest in 1715 the Dissenters comprised less than 5 percent of the county electorate in fifteen counties, and in these and an additional ten counties, there is no record of resistance to the dominant patrons.[30]

While the Dissenters were few in members, and while their potential for political independence was sometimes quashed by patronage, they remained politically influential for three reasons: they were thoroughly involved in local politics and learned to use the political tools of the age; they were attached to the central government through the mid 1760s and therefore formed a unified Whig electoral interest group; and, as a disciplined electoral bloc, they provided a core around which Low-Church Anglicans could rally. Each of these facets of their political involvement has been misunderstood and neglected, but of the three, the first has been most seriously distorted. In William Hogarth's *Four Prints of an Election* (1755) one character, and one character alone, stands aloof from the bribery that was not untypical of unreformed England – the pious Protestant Dissenter. In the plate entitled 'An Election Entertainment', the Dissenter is depicted turning away from the bribe, lifting his eyes to heaven, striking a posture of prayer, and rejecting the desperate pleas of his poor wife and child to take the election agent's money. Historians, almost without exception, have perpetuated this image of the incorruptible Dissenter.[31]

27 John A. Phillips, *Electoral Behavior in Unreformed England: Plumpers, Splitters, and Straights* (Princeton, 1982), p. 67. Phillips drew attention to the connection between Dissent and the frequency of contested elections, but did not emphasize the preponderance of Dissent in the freeman boroughs (p. 304). He did underscore the electoral importance of the large freeman and householder boroughs, and showed how the increase in the influence of patronage was concentrated in the southwest, and thus of limited importance to popular politics. On the geographical distribution, see Frank O'Gorman, *The Emergence of the British Two-Party System, 1760–1832* (London, 1982), pp. 78–9, and Bradley, *Popular Politics and the American Revolution in England* (Macon, Ga.), 1986.

28 Herts., Notts., Suss., Northamp., Somerset, Bucks., Lancs., Chesh., Staff., Northumb., Yorks., Camb., Essex, Leics., and Mon.

29 See Bradley, 'The Emergence of Opposition in the Counties', pp. 469–85 in 'Whigs and Nonconformists'.

30 Between 1715 and 1773, the Dissenters in only four counties registered any increase relative to the population.

31 Sean Shesgreen, ed., *Engravings by Hogarth* (New York, 1973), p. 86. See the chapter entitled 'The Contribution of Nonconformity' in Robbins, *The Eighteenth-Century*

Sir Lewis Namier very appropriately argued that 'corruption was not a shower-bath from above, constructed by Walpole, the Pelhams, or George III, but a water-spout springing from the rock of freedom to meet the demands of the people'. Recent research has substantiated the view that the practice of treating and even bribing electors was not as serious an encumbrance to popular political participation as was once believed.[32] Outvoters in particular, who came from some distance to cast their votes, expected their expenses to be paid, but in this, and other cases as well, treating commonly had about the same effect on both sides of a contest. That the Dissenters were involved in these practices can now be established beyond dispute, and in a few instances, treating clearly dampened their ability to retain their electoral independence. One measure of the significance of the extent of bribery among Nonconformists is the frequency with which Dissenting ministers warned the laity to avoid the temptation of the election agents' money.

Yet, treating, patronage, and sometimes outright bribery also contributed to the Dissenters' influence; for the most part, Dissenters worked comfortably within the unreformed system and used it to their own political advantage. The use of influence, of course, was not only legitimate, but expected. Sir George Savile, who was returned with Nonconformist support for Yorkshire and was himself a paragon of political virtue, gently chided his nephew, Richard Lumley Savile, when the latter expressed fastidious misgivings about using the family's political interest at Lincoln. The seasoned politician wrote in mild rebuke: '[It is] perfect Methodism in politics to talk of the Lumley interest at Lincoln rather as a curse than a blessing (not to be cultivated like an estate but got rid of like a mortgage).'[33] Despite popular opinion to the contrary, many Presbyterians, Congregationalists, Baptists, and Quakers were not 'Methodists' in politics, and they knew very well how to cultivate an interest. Any attempt to grasp the importance of Nonconformity in electoral politics must take seriously the Dissenters' use of political influence, treating, and to a lesser extent, even bribery.

The Dissenters' use of influence is as important for understanding their involvement in parliamentary elections as their occasional conformity is for grasping their role in municipal politics. Dissenting voters were influenced by wealthy Dissenting laymen far more often than they or their historians have

---

Commonwealthman, p. 269; E. P. Thompson, *The Making of the English Working Class* (New York, 1963), pp. 36, 51–2; Carl B. Cone, *Torchbearer of Freedom: The Influence of Richard Price on Eighteenth-Century Thought* (Lexington, Ky., 1952), p. 70; Sir Lewis Namier, *England in the Age of the American Revolution*, 2nd edn (London, 1961), p. 110; *The Structure of Politics at the Accession of George III*, 2nd edn (London, 1957), pp. 125, 206.

32 Namier, *The Structure of Politics*, pp. 103–4; John Phillips, 'The Structure of Electoral Politics in Unreformed England', *JBS* 19 (1979), 95–9.

33 *Commons, 1754–1790*, 1: 328.

wished to admit.[34] Well-to-do Dissenters scarcely expected the votes of their dependents to be used independently; their influence over their coreligionists was commonly the most important political tool at their disposal. The connection between Dissenters and business enterprise has long been recognized, but the implications of this connection for their political loyalties have been persistently ignored. The business interests of a Dissenter like Daniel Defoe, combined with his well-known political dirty work for the government, should have told researchers something about the possible conservative orientation of the Dissenting interest. Contemporaries noted the Dissenters' wealth at Cambridge, Exeter, Norwich and in other parliamentary boroughs; often a noticeable pride was taken in their material success.[35] At Cambridge, for example, it was said that the Presbyterians 'were not numerous, but they were rich'. In 1716 Henry Vowler observed in regard to Exeter that 'the influence of trading Dissenters [is] very extensive over their dependents in business', and he expected this influence to be translated into votes. Other examples may be cited: Thomas Dixon wrote from Whitehaven in 1717 that the 'Dissenters here by trade have such an influence on elections that with the Dissenters at Cockermouth, they turn them as they please'. The total wealth of the 3,500 Dissenters at Bristol was estimated in 1715 at £700,000. It will come as no surprise then that contemporary Nonconformists claimed that the 700 Dissenting voters in Bristol could 'by their estates and interest in trade' influence 100 more in the surrounding counties.[36] We have already noticed the Nottingham Dissenters' use of their position on the Corporation to influence the Nottingham election of 1754.

According to Lord Sandwich's agent at Portsmouth, the Dissenting families of White, Pike, and Carter had 'numerous connections and dependents' – so much so that they completely dominated local government and controlled parliamentary elections after 1780.[37] The Congregationalist voters at Hertford numbered 105, but it was claimed that they also influenced 124 Anglican voters in elections.[38] For the county of Hertford, Evans' correspondent observed, 'Churchmen, influenced in elections by the Quakers, in this county ab[ou]t 80'. A notice in the *Chelmsford and Colchester Chronicle* under 4 March 1768 appeared concerning Maldon:

The Dissenters who are free of this Borough are earnestly requested not to engage their votes or Interest for either of the three Candidates; and all other Dissenters, more particularly the

34 For the Dissenters' avowals of consistent independence see Bradley, 'Nonconformity and the Electorate', 249.
35 The Evans List, pp. 9–10, 31, 83–4.
36 *Ibid.*, pp. 9–10; 19–20, 31, 147.
37 *Commons, 1754–1790*, 1: 297–9.
38 The Evans List, p. 49. At St. Albans in 1722 there were 158 Low Churchmen who voted with the 129 Dissenting electors (99 Presbyterians, 16 Baptists, and 14 Quakers) and together they were able to sway elections over the 226 High Churchmen.

Clergy (tho' not free) are desired not to use any Influence in their Behalf, for Reasons that will be explained to them in five or six Days.[39]

Obviously the Dissenters found that their 'interest' or 'influence' was useful both with and without votes. In the early part of the century, for example, it was said that the government candidates in six boroughs in Devon were 'chiefly Supported by the Dissenters', though this can be shown to be an exaggeration.[40] At Minehead, however, 75 Dissenters could influence an additional 30 voters, giving them one-third of the total electorate, and in Northumberland 150 Dissenting freeholders at Newcastle upon Tyne could 'make about as many more votes as their own'.[41] In the eighteenth century, voters often behaved deferentially; 'trade' and 'estates' also meant political influence. The way wealthy Dissenters used their influence militates strongly against any idea that they were democrats. Thomas Dixon certainly had the right idea – influence, not votes, turned Cockermouth elections – but he failed to see, or refused to record, that this could as easily stifle the Dissenters' independence as help it, as Sir James Lowther was later to prove.

In several cases, it is possible to observe Dissenting politicians actually cultivating an electoral interest. When the Dissenting Member of Parliament, Nathaniel Newnham, set out to contest Ashburton, he did everything in his power to support 'the exploration of its manufactures', and this, he supposed, 'has procured me several staunch friends there'. It appears that Alexander Fordyce in the 1760s sought by gifts to gain the Dissenters at Colchester. Henry Hoghton's 'great interest' at Preston had to be cultivated just as others cultivated theirs, and he used gifts and 'benefactions' to do so.[42] The Dissenters did not rise naturally or easily above the political practices which were so characteristic of the age.

If, then, Dissenting M.P.s were willing to treat their potential electors, it is also clear that Dissenting voters were happy to be treated. William Praed, a parliamentary hopeful at Exeter, provided property for a Dissenting academy in 1760 just months before the general election: though he lost the election, the Exeter Dissenters voted for him.[43] Nathaniel Newnham complained that he did not want to sit for Bramber because living near to one's constituents was 'well-known to lead to endless trouble and expense;' he was thus positively trying to avoid 'democracy' in his reluctance to live near his constituents.[44] When the Duke of Newcastle used Newnham in 1743 at Aldborough, York-

---

39 *Chelm. Col. Chron.* (4 March 1768). On 11 March John Henniker announced his candidature.
40 The Evans List, p. 31. See Bradley, 'Nonconformity and the Electorate', 249–50 for a discussion of the boroughs in Devon.
41 The Evans List, pp. 99–102; 90.
42 *Commons, 1754–1790*, 1: 249; 277; *Commons, 1715–1754*, 1: 273.
43 Allan Brockett, *Nonconformity in Exeter, 1650–1875* (Manchester, 1962), 139; *Commons, 1754–1790*, 1: 253.
44 *Commons, 1754–1790*, 3: 199.

shire, to pacify the Dissenters at Lewes, Sussex, it is evident that the Dissenters themselves sometimes accepted the principle of 'virtual representation'.[45]

In addition to these more legitimate forms of material inducement and influence, money in the form of bribes was also used by Dissenting M.P.s. The practice can be documented at Colchester (Stamp Brooksbank, Presbyterian, 1727), at Leominster (George Caswall, Baptist, 1717, giving 20 guineas a vote), at Ilchester (Thomas Lockyer, 1754), at Shaftesbury (Samuel Touchet, 1761), at Preston (Sir Henry Hoghton, Presbyterian, 1727, 'two or three guineas a man'), and at Hindon (Thomas Brand Hollis, Unitarian, 1774, for 15 guineas a vote).[46] In the case of Caswall and Lockyer, legal charges were brought for their attempt to corrupt voters and Brand Hollis was actually sentenced and imprisoned for bribery. Besides these instances of Dissenting M.P.s giving money to voters, in the constituencies of Colchester, Leominster, Preston, Sudbury, Aylesbury, Barnstaple, Maldon, and Honiton it seems certain that the Dissenting electors themselves traded their votes for guineas. An analysis of the 1741 Leominster poll book reveals that bribery was probably the principal cause for the erosion of the electoral consistency of the Baptist vote.[47] In 1768 George Lewis Newnham, the son of Nathaniel Newnham, offered the corporation members of Nottingham, who were largely Dissenters, £2,000 outright as 'redress of grievance in the usual style', and, Newcastle's agent added, the 'bait was swallowed'.[48] The money was apparently never delivered, yet the incident illustrates how influence in some boroughs was purchased.

The Dissenters engaged in somewhat less than respectable political practices in several other cases. In 1727 at Bristol Abraham Elton paid his Tory

---

45 *Commons, 1715–1754*, 2: 293.

46 *Commons, 1715–1754*, 1: 495, 259, 534–5; *Commons, 1754–1790*, 3: 51–2; 534. *Commons, 1715–1754*, 1: 273. *Commons, 1754–1790*, 1: 416; 2: 113. On Thomas Lockyer's method of corruption at Ilchester, see the *Gloucester Journal* (11 December 1775).

47 See Bradley, 'Nonconformity and the Electorate', 251 for Leominster. For Colchester and Preston see note 46 above. At Sudbury the 400 Presbyterians were almost certainly involved in bribery; the Evans List, pp. 108–11. *Commons, 1715–1754*, 1:3, 27; *Commons, 1754–1790*, 1: 382. The Aylesbury Baptists expelled half their congregation in 1802 for taking 'bribes'. Richard W. Davis, *Political Change and Continuity, 1760–1885: A Buckinghamshire Study* (London, 1972), p. 70. The Presbyterians and Congregationalists made up nearly a third of the electorate at Barnstaple in 1715, and between 1739 and 1748 £7,000 was spent there on elections; in 1754 voters received between a half and a full guinea each. Treating may well have degenerated into outright bribery. The Evans List, p. 29; *Commons, 1715–1754*, 1: 548, 443, 406; *Commons, 1754–1790*, 2: 391; 1: 225. At Maldon the Dissenting leaders spent considerable sums for their choice of candidate in 1773, *Commons, 1754–1790*, 3: 225, 346; 1: 280. The Presbyterians and Baptists at Honiton may also be implicated by the notoriety of the corruption there. The Evans List pp. 25–31. *Commons, 1715–1754*, 1: 227; *Commons, 1754–1790*, 1: 254.

48 *Commons, 1754–1790*, 3: 199.

opponent £1,000 not to stand against him.[49] Coventry Dissenters put the city's charities to good political purpose; they also manipulated the returning officers, and at elections they got their enemies drunk and then put them to sea so they could not return to the poll in time to vote.[50] The Morpeth Presbyterian minister's political ally, Robert Trotter, won an election in 1774 through the intimidation of the returning officer – an act so blatant that he was unseated on petition.[51] The Presbyterian, John Coe, managed Maldon elections and channeled money just as ably and freely as any other agent, and it seems beyond doubt that Dissenters were recipients of the largess as well as Anglicans.[52]

Strictly speaking, this kind of political involvement might not impinge upon the issue of the Dissenters' political independence. It could be argued that favors and money flowed strictly between Dissenting hopefuls and Dissenting voters. Nonconformists, however, were involved in circumstances that do raise questions about the government's influence and in some cases even its control of the Dissenting vote. Unlike George Caswall at Leominster, who used his own money in exchange for Dissenting votes, the Dissenters sometimes received patronage from the government. A handful of individual voters were unquestionably influenced by minor government patronage, as we saw in the previous chapter, but on occasion the influence of the government extended to an entire body of Dissenters. Even at Taunton, which, because of its Dissenting academy, was known as the western center of Commonwealthman ideas, the Dissenters typically deferred to the government. Political lines at Taunton in 1754 were drawn from the Dissenters to the Presbyterian minister, from the minister to their patron, and from the patron to the government. The government then recommended the candidate and provided the money needed to contest the election. During the American Revolution, the government faced significant resistance from the Taunton Dissenters in 1775. The petitioning agitation against coercive measures may have contributed to the government's subsequent tactic. The government's election agent observed in 1781 that the principal cloth manufacturers were Dissenters, and to 'induce' them to decline from 'engaging in an opposition', the administration agreed to give £500 to the silk manufacturers, £300 to the woolen manufacturers, and 29s. each to 250 poor voters, and no opposition was forthcoming from the Taunton Dissenters at parliamentary elections thereafter.[53] The Dissenters clearly benefited from government patronage at Portsmouth, and indeed they expected it. The Dissenting patron at Portsmouth, John Missing, never lost sight, in his words,

49 *Commons, 1715–1754*, 2: 413; 1: 245.
50 T. W. Whitley, *The Parliamentary Representation of the City of Coventry* (Coventry, 1894), pp. 117, 145. *Commons, 1754–1790*, 1: 401; 2: 559.
51 *Commons, 1754–1790*, 1: 349–50; 2: 409–10.
52 *Ibid.*, 1: 280; 2: 135.
53 W. T. Laprade, (ed.), *The Parliamentary Papers of John Robinson, 1774–1784* (London, 1922), pp. 38–9; *Commons, 1754–1790*, 1: 372.

of 'that connexion which so long subsisted to mutual advantage' between the Dissenters and the Admiralty.[54] In 1781, while the American war was still intense, Missing specifically renounced the idea of any opposition out of 'mere dislike to the present ministry'. In fact, Missing made it clear that patronage flowed at Portsmouth in exactly the same channels as it did at Taunton, except that the ministerial intermediary was lacking. Opposition, in his view, was never to be pressed so far as to jeopardize the patronage; Missing and his colleagues were by no means willing to risk the loss of the advantages accruing from a connection with the Admiralty.

The same attitude toward the government may be found among the Dissenters at Maidstone. An appeal of the Nonconformists in 1761 begged the government for some material benefit that might 'heal their minds' after the Duke of Newcastle had made a serious political blunder.[55] We have seen that individual Dissenters were employed by the government at Bristol, Liverpool, Yarmouth and other boroughs, and government money was explicitly used to help support the Dissenting candidates for many years at both Coventry and Worcester.[56] In addition to the infamous *Regium Donum*, the Dissenters also received government patronage in specific counties; Capel Hanbury (M.P., Monmouthshire, 1747–65) was a staunch government supporter, and he received money from the secret service funds to be distributed directly to the Dissenting ministers – £100 paid annually, 1754–61. Sir William Middleton, Presbyterian M.P. for Northumberland (1722–57), received £800 annually from 1754 to 1757 from secret service funds, which undoubtedly sweetened the Dissenters, just as in Monmouthshire.[57] The Dissenters had a decisive influence in some settings precisely because they learned how to marshal their dependents, channel government patronage, and in a few notorious cases, line the pockets of voters. Without these political tools their influence would have been greatly reduced, and to suppose that they were politically effective without them is purely fanciful. Many individual Dissenters undoubtedly behaved in a highly ethical manner, but the moral superiority of 'the body of Dissenters' is a myth constructed by Whig historians to help preserve the

---

54 *Commons, 1754–1790*, 1: 297–9.

55 Namier, *The Structure of Politics*, p. 118.

56 Ian R. Christie, 'Great Yarmouth and the Yorkshire Reform Movement, 1782–1784', in *Myth and Reality in Late-Eighteenth-Century British Politics* (London, 1970), pp. 285–90; The Evans List, p. 149. Namier, *The Structure of Politics*, p. 88; *Commons, 1754–1790*, 1: 283; Whitley, *The Parliamentary Representation of Coventry*, p. 163; *Commons, 1715–1754*, 2: 61, 474–5, 494; *Commons, 1754–1790*, 1: 425–6.

57 On the *Regium Donum*, see K. R. M. Short, 'The English Regium Donum', *EHR* 84 (1969), 59–78. On Monmouthshire, see the Evans List, p. 81; *Commons, 1715–1754*, 1: 288; *Commons, 1754–1790*, 1: 338. The Monmouthshire Dissenters composed about 15% of the county voters. Ministers' incomes were normally supplemented rather than completely supplied, so it seems likely that a portion of the money reached the majority of the thirteen to sixteen ministers in the county. Namier, *The Structure of Politics*, pp. 217–18.

integrity of the Whig 'party'. This is not to say that the Dissenters in every instance failed to act independently.

THE DISSENTERS AND POLITICAL INDEPENDENCE

The crucial issue in all instances of the Dissenters' political involvement is the question of how the Nonconformists used their influence. The Dissenters' repertoire of deferential postures did not, on the whole, decrease their political significance, because, almost without exception, they exerted their energies on behalf of Whig candidates. In those cases where they themselves were susceptible to the influence of the government, they were remarkably discriminating in their deferential behavior and selective in their acceptance of bribes. The same government that was willing to treat had consistently defended the Dissenters' rights, and thus the Nonconformists were identified with the Whigs in a way that allowed them to maintain their political convictions with little actual compromise of principle. Before 1760, influence in all its forms usually served to cement the Dissenters' alliance with the Whig governments of George I and George II and mutual advantage to both the government and the Dissenters was the net result; the government got votes, and the Dissenters received patronage and protection. In the majority of those boroughs where Dissenters were politically active, they comprised the heart of local Whig parties, while their opponents commonly coalesced around High-Church Anglican factions.

In a few boroughs, however, the Dissenters joined together in temporary parties against other Whigs. These examples are exceptionally important because they show that the Dissenters did not always act solely on the basis of ideology in supporting government Whigs; when their local interests were threatened they would react on a more secularized basis of opposition to restricting oligarchy. At Northampton in 1768 the Dissenters challenged the monopolizing tendencies of the Montagu–Compton interest. At Berwick upon Tweed it was the tightening grip of Lord Northumberland that provoked a response in 1774. At Maldon the government itself was growing more restrictive, and the Dissenters attempted to win contests against secret service funds in 1773 and again in 1774 – all to no avail. At Morpeth the Dissenters reacted in 1757 when the advantages they had previously gained from selling the one seat they controlled were threatened by the Earl of Carlisle. Most of these instances of organized resistance took place in the late 1760s and early 1770s when the Dissenting ministers were just beginning to voice opposition to the government. In a handful of other boroughs where the Nonconformists normally supported Whig candidates they sporadically used their votes against the government; in Lewes, Chichester, Tiverton, and Sudbury religion clearly contributed to the persistence of party rivalry, but the added ingredient of the

Dissenters' independence contributed an element of indeterminacy that was both troublesome and irritating to those borough patrons who worked on behalf of the government. Local exigencies in these cases dictated a less friendly relationship to the Court than was characteristic of the Dissenters, though before 1760 their resistance was always temporary. The Dissenters were thus adequately unified and had a sufficiently solidified group identity that contemporaries believed they might, given the proper circumstances, turn against the government.[58] The Dissenters could thereby, at least theoretically, be linked together across the nation to form the disciplined core of an opposition party.

As separate, well-defined local interest groups, the Dissenters thereby made a major contribution to the evolving independence of the voter; in the practice of politics they often insisted that individuals should be able to elect whomever they wished. Dissenters characteristically resisted influence from above, whether in the crown, minister, or aristocratic clientage, and they sometimes overcame the temptations of bribery; they were widely known for their independence and frequently insisted on having their own way, both when the choice involved principle and when it involved material interest. They also contributed to the ideology of independence. While the independence of the individual presupposed a basic minimum of wealth, the Dissenters' arguments in favor of independence, as we shall see in later chapters, were less concerned with property than with the exercise of autonomous choice. For example, one leading Dissenter, Joseph Towers, observed in 1769 that 'When we reason only speculatively, it appears rational to suppose, that men in good circumstances, and of affluent fortunes, would be less liable to be influenced by corrupt motives, than those whose inferior situation seems to expose them more naturally to temptation. But experience often proves, that this kind of reasoning is uncertain and fallacious.' Those who possess much, often want more, and they are commonly enervated by luxury. 'Whilst, on the other hand, men of lower circumstances, of more moderate views and expectations, and of more regular and temperate manners, though they enjoy less property, often possess more independence of mind, and are more influenced by a virtuous affection to their country.' Both the practical and ideological contribution of Dissent to this new understanding of independence is well depicted at Southampton, where the Dissenting family of Bernard was actively involved in organizing and voting on behalf of the rights of the electors in the parliamentary elections of 1774 and 1790; in the latter election the independent party published a pamphlet entitled, *Independence! or a Correct LIST of the Independent Commercial Gentlemen Tradesmen Who Voted for Mr. Dawkins on the 17th and 18th June, 1790 in Support of the Glorious Independence of*

---

58 On the oft-repeated fears of the politicians that the Dissenters would unite against the government, see Bradley, 'Nonconformity and the Electorate', 236–7.

the Town of Southampton. Along with the radicals of the 1760s and 1770s, the Dissenters were pouring new content into the old country language of independence, property, and interest. As John Brewer has argued, the Dissenters and radicals adapted the country ideology to the circumstances of the urban setting, in part to explain, and possibly even to justify, their own participation in politics.[59]

But before 1760, in the majority of boroughs the Dissenters inhabited, the persistence of High-Anglican religious opposition at the local level, combined with the government's tolerance and protection at the national level, promoted a strong alliance between the Dissenters and the Whigs. The recurring possibility of persecution (brought vividly to mind in 1745), also contributed to the Dissenters' consistent orientation of support for the government. Five years after the Sacheverell riots, a 'noble crew' of Tories at Hertford identified the Church with Sacheverell and the Congregationalists with the Devil. In 1734 the Tories at Bishop's Castle likened Robert More to a Roundhead and damned both Puritans and Nonconformists. When a Tory candidate in Essex sought to make a show of his loyalty in 1759, he equated the Essex Whigs with 'Quakers, Presbyters, and Devils, etc'.[60] Religious differences between Dissenters and High Anglicans contributed directly to the extensive violence in the election at Taunton in 1754 and at Preston in 1768. At Birmingham there were riots against Wesleyans in 1751 and against Quakers in 1759. As late as 1780 the anti-corporation party at Coventry charged the Dissenters with having murdered 'Charles our King'.[61] Though the Dissenters sometimes asserted their independence against government candidates, there was not one constituency in England in which the Dissenters took a *consistent* stand against the government before 1760. The only instances of the three denominations ever voting with the Tories in the eighteenth century are found at Lewes in 1734

---

59 I first noted this contribution in 'Whigs and Nonconformists: Slumbering Radicalism in English Politics, 1739–1789', *ECS* 9 (1975), 25; on the use of the term independent, see E. P. Thompson, *The Making of the English Working Class* (New York, 1963), p. 467; Davis, *Political Change and Continuity*, p. 28; Sir Lewis Namier, 'Country Gentlemen in Parliament, 1750–1784', p. 60 in *Personalities and Powers* (London, 1955); and John Brewer, 'English Radicalism in the Age of George III', pp. 344–5, in J. G. A. Pocock, *Three British Revolutions, 1641, 1688, 1776* (Princeton, 1980). Dissent was not unique; Brewer shows the connection between clubs and independence as well, pp. 358–9; however, the Dissenters themselves formed a kind of club. Frank O'Gorman has also drawn attention to the centrality of the behavior and ideology of independence in an unpublished paper, entitled 'Popular Constitutionalism in the Eighteenth Century', History Workshop Conference, (1986). On Towers, see *Observations on Public Liberty, Patriotism, Ministerial Despotism, and National Grievances. With Some Remarks on Riots, Petitions, Loyal Addresses, and Military Executions* (London, 1769), pp. 27–8. On Southampton, see Bradley, *Popular Politics and the American Revolution in England*, p. 165.
60 *Commons, 1715–1754,* 1: 261; 2: 274; *Commons, 1754–1790,* 2: 486.
61 R. B. Rose, 'The Priestley Riots of 1791', *P&P* 18 (1960), 70; Whitley, *Parliamentary Representation of Coventry*, p. 180.

and Westbury in 1747. Of the twenty-five Dissenting M.P.s who sat in
Parliament before the accession of George III, only three could be considered
oppositionists. At Norwich in 1721 and at Shrewsbury in 1754 the Nonconformists explicitly declined opportunities to disrupt the current arrangement
where government Whigs were sitting. The Dissenters were so thoroughly
dedicated to the Hanoverians that they followed the government's lead, even
when the administration was at a low-point of popularity, as in the Excise
Crisis of 1733. Dissenters in at least thirty-four boroughs steadfastly
supported the Hanoverians before 1761, and this is unquestionably a modest
assessment of their overall support for Whig candidates.[62]

The nationwide support the Dissenting interest gave to the government may
be further illustrated by the consistent party vote that individual Dissenters cast
for Whig candidates in specific boroughs. Table 3 illustrates how consistently
individual Dissenters voted for Whig candidates at Abingdon, Shrewsbury,

Table 3.1: *Proportion of Dissenters Voting for Whig Candidates Compared to*
the Anglican Whig Vote (Percentage)

| | Abingdon | | | Shrewsbury | | Great Yarmouth | Bristol |
	1734	1754	1768	1734	1747	1754	1754
Anglican Whigs (as proportion of total Anglican vote)	53.2	32.1	43.8	50.0	45.2	47.5	50.3
N=	92	63	96	204	109	502	998
Dissenting Whigs	100	100	90.3	100	100	65.6	82.4
N=	52	37	31	39	39	59	62

Great Yarmouth, and Bristol.[63] Political coherence grounded in religious
affiliation thus provides further evidence for the Dissenters' potential for

62 Bradley, 'Whigs and Nonconformists', pp. 509, 581; on the Excise Crisis, see Paul
Langford, *The Excise Crisis: Society and Politics in the Age of Walpole* (Oxford,
1975).
63 For a lengthy discussion of Abingdon and Shrewsbury, see Bradley, 'Nonconformity and
the Electorate', 239–41, 243–5 and for Yarmouth and Bristol, chaps. 6 and 7 below.
Table 3 counts single votes as partisan, but it excludes all split votes. Abingdon was a
single member constituency, so there were no split votes; there were no split votes at
Shrewsbury in 1734 and only 2.1% of the voters split in 1747; 6.8% of the voters
overall split at Great Yarmouth in 1754, and 4% at Bristol. In my article on
'Nonconformity and the Electorate', the total number of voters at Shrewsbury in 1734
was based on the figures given in the *History of Parliament*; however, *A LIST of the*
Persons that Voted for Sir Richard Corbett Bart and William Kinaston and the votes for
Mytton and Lyster found in the manuscript S.P.L. Deed 46 utilized here, differ slightly,
though the proportions are not affected significantly.

independent action. In the first two boroughs contemporaries went to the trouble to identify each Dissenter who voted and then listed them in the poll books and placed asterisks next to their names; at Abingdon in 1734 and 1754, and at Shrewsbury in 1734 and 1747, all the Dissenters who voted, voted without exception for the Whig candidates. At Great Yarmouth the Dissenters were somewhat less disposed to support the government candidates in 1754, but this is certainly attributable to the fact that the anti-corporation party at Yarmouth was led by John Ramey, a disaffected Whig who was not associated with the Tories; under these circumstances, it is surprising that the anti-corporation party did not draw off even more Dissenting votes. The consistency of the Dissenters' support of government Whig candidates at a single election is matched by their consistent party orientation over several elections. At Abingdon, for example, seventy-seven individuals voted in both 1754 and 1768; among the Anglicans, nine out of fifty-nine voted for the Whig candidates in both elections, while sixteen out of eighteen Dissenters voted consistently Whig. At Shrewsbury, twenty-eight of the thirty-nine Dissenters voted in both elections for the Whig candidates, and thus none changed parties or split their votes, whereas of seventy-five Anglicans who voted Whig in 1734 and 1747, seven changed parties and one cast a split vote (10.7%). The Dissenters were thus only slightly more consistent than the Anglican Whigs at Shrewsbury, but this predictable bloc of voters nonetheless provided the decisive margin for the Whigs in 1747. Such consistency over a period of more than a decade would seem to justify the claim that the Dissenters possessed political 'backbone', and it certainly anticipates the consistency achieved by modern party discipline.

The Dissenters at Bristol were also more inclined to support the government than the Anglicans, and with impressively high levels of consistent party support in such populous and open boroughs as Bristol and Norwich, it is little wonder that religion was commonly viewed as the touchstone of local parties.[64] The Dissenters were thereby rightly known as government supporters in the first half of the eighteenth century. Most pamphlets on the topic of party identified the Dissenters with the Whigs, thus providing an important ideological counterpart to their perceived behavioral consistency. Even after 1750 the difference between Whig and Tory was almost always couched in religious terms, the Whigs being 'generally composed of the more moderate churchmen, and the main body of protestant dissenters'.[65] The importance of

---

64 For the consistency of the Dissenters' party support at Bristol, see figure 7.1 below. For Norwich, see Phillips, *Electoral Politics*, pp. 293, 95.

65 *The Balance: or the Merits of Whig and Tory, exactly weigh'd and fairly determin'd* (London, 1753), p. 4. The reprints of John Trenchard and Thomas Gordon contributed to this understanding. The link between the Tories and the High Church is equally pervasive. See the literature in J. A. W. Gunn, *Beyond Liberty and Property* (Kingston and Montreal, 1983), pp. 164–85.

the widespread contemporary identity of the Dissenters with the Whigs before the accession of George III helps explain the belief in party continuity grounded in ideology expressed throughout the century.

It is true that in the 1760s party distinctions were less consistently grounded in religion; characteristically, divisions centered around questions of foreign policy and domestic administration, particularly the economy.[66] Even then, however, the religious convictions that tended to orient a person's political proclivities were just below the surface. The political differences between factions were couched in terms of differing attitudes toward the exercise of authority, especially the king's authority, on the one hand, and tolerance toward religious Dissent on the other, and these attitudes in turn were still associated in people's minds with the High-Anglican tradition or the Low-Church and Dissenting tradition.[67] Moreover, an explicit emphasis on religion as the basis to party politics persisted in some pamphlets through the 1760s, though it was not viewed as the sole basis of party divisions.[68] Even when the utility of the terms Whig and Tory were denied, they were denied on the grounds that religious prejudices and animosities had subsided.[69] One anonymous writer urged in the interest of lessening party tensions that the annual commemoration of the 'martyrdom' of Charles I be abolished. He observed that in years past if one attempted to desist from celebrating January 30th, 'the Church would be in danger, and the nation would all turn Presbyterians. But we are now happily got above the prejudices of that sort: our present Bishops are Whigs, [and] are friends to liberty and the constitution'. But the same author candidly admitted that on January 30th 'the greater part' of the Anglican

66 *The Political Balance. In Which the Principles and Conduct of the Two Parties are Weighed* (London, 1965), p. 2. *Address to the Remaining Members of the Coterie* (London, 1765), pp. 10, 18.

67 *A Vindication of the Whigs Against the Clamours of a Tory Mob; With an Address to the City* (London, 1765), pp. 20, 24, 27. *The Political Balance*, pp. 9–10, 54; *A Full and Free Inquiry into the Merits of the Peace; with Some Strictures on the Spirit of Party* (London, 1765), pp. 154, 160. *An Address to the Remaining Members*, pp. 35–6, 40. *A Pastoral Puke. A Second Sermon Preached before the People Called Whigs by an Independent* (London, 1764), pp. 15–16. For connections between Cromwell and those who seek to weaken the throne, see *The Appeal of Reason to the People of England, on the Present State of Parties in the Nation* (London, 1763), pp. 5, 26, 30–1. *A Political Analysis of the War: The Principles of the Present Political Parties Examined* (London, 1762), pp. 56–8. Pamphlets that supported Bute's administration detested the Tory label; *The Political Balance*, pp. 9–10. *A Full and Free Inquiry*, p. 149, *A Political Analysis of the War*, pp. 28, 56; while opposition pamphlets tended to embrace the old terminology.

68 *A Parallel; Drawn between the Administration In the Four Last Years of Queen Anne, and the Four First Years of George the Third, by a Country Gentleman* (London, 1766), pp. 30–5; *A Dissertation on the Rise, Progress, Views, Strength, Interests and Characters, of the Two Parties of the Whigs and Tories* (Boston, 1773), pp. 17–18, 26–7, 35–6, 47–50, and on the 'low-churchmen' and Dissenting alliance, see pp. 51–2.

69 John Brown, *Thoughts on Civil Liberty, on Licentiousness, and Factions*, 2nd edn (London, 1765), pp. 91, 106; *A Letter to the Whigs, with Some Remarks on a Letter to the Tories* (London, 1762), pp. 13–14.

clergy are 'aukwardly [sic] tempted to preach against their own principles',
and that the memorial 'tends to perpetuate divisions among us, and is often
made, by the imprudence of the preacher, an occasion of raising party
contests, and of exasperating the minds of a neighbourhood against each
other'.[70] Trevelyan's allusion to 'long-enduring local pieties and loyalties and
customs' comes to mind. Linda Colley has remarked that 'Church versus
Dissent remained – and was to remain under the Hanoverians – the most
obvious way in which divisions in the constituencies mirrored and sustained
those at Westminster', and yet more precisely, it was Low Church and Dissent
versus High Church and Tory that went to the heart of much party conflict.[71]
Something of the strength of the religious basis to ideological continuity
between the 'parties' is found in the way that religious animosities, expressed
in the old party terminology, burst on the scene with such force over the subscription controversy in the early 1770s. These animosities were heightened
even further by the American crisis which elicited a revival of the old labels; in
places like Bristol and Newcastle upon Tyne, the religious basis to party
divisions was an oft repeated theme and the Dissenters were once again held
responsible for fomenting divisions.[72]

We will see that the Dissenters' identification with the Whigs, combined
with their reputation for political morality, had significant implications for their
behavior during the American Revolution. In marked contrast to the earlier
period, of the fifteen Dissenters who sat in Parliament after 1760, only two
supported the government during the American crisis, and the vast majority of
Dissenting ministers also became outspoken critics of the government.[73] If
'the Dissenting interest' as a body throughout the nation turned against the
government during the American Revolution, but at the same time continued to
vote for 'Whig' (now oppositionist) candidates at Westminster, a case might
be made for the consistent party behavior of at least a sizable minority in the
electorate. The Dissenters' material interests on the one hand, and their
independent principles on the other, could in this instance come into serious

70 *An Address to Both Parties* (London), pp. 16–18.
71 Linda Colley, *In Defiance of Oligarchy: The Tory Party, 1714–60* (Cambridge, 1982),
    p. 13. See also pp. 112, 130. Namier observed exactly the same thing in 'Monarchy and
    the Party System', in *Personalities and Powers* (London, 1955), p. 230. For an
    excellent study of the persistence and geographic sweep of High Anglicanism, see F.C.
    Mather, 'Georgian Churchmanship Reconsidered: Some Variations in Anglican Public
    Worship, 1714–1830', *JEH* 36 (1985), 255–83.
72 G. M. Ditchfield, 'The Subscription Issue in British Parliamentary Politics, 1772–79',
    Parliamentary History 7 (1988), 45–80. *Brist. J.* (10 Dec. 1774; 14, 28 Jan. 1775)
    advertisements for *A Dissertation on Parties; The Contest* (Newcastle upon Tyne,
    1774), pp. 11, 22; *Lond. Eve. Post* (11–14 Nov. 1775). During the Revolution, the
    connection between Dissent, the Whigs, and opposition to government was constantly
    reiterated in the newspapers.
73 Bradley, 'Whigs and Nonconformists', p. 547. Ten of the fifteen were in Parliament at
    some time during the period 1765–82.

conflict. The argument of popular political consistency is precisely the argument the Rockingham Whigs adopted when they insisted that the government of George III was behaving in a highly innovative and authoritarian manner. Because of the loss of poll books, however, the actual consistency of Whig voters can be documented in only a handful of boroughs. Nevertheless, these and other constituencies became the electoral base out of which the Whig interpretation emerged. But the Dissenters would have remained almost totally impotent by themselves. They could have influenced the outcome of only the closest contests, and they would have had no hope at all of influencing a general election were it not for the alliance they forged with Low-Church Anglicans.

THE DISSENT-LOW-CHURCH ALLIANCE AND WHIG PARTIES IN THE CONSTITUENCIES

The small numbers of Dissenters in many boroughs meant that if they were isolated from other electors, they would have little political influence, except in those contests where the parties were very evenly balanced. Two critical elements, however, helped compensate for their small numbers: their highly disciplined voting consistency, and the alliance with Low-Church Anglicans. In the mid-eighteenth century, the alliance between Dissenters and Low-Church Anglicans at the local level was everywhere assumed; in fact, it was the very basis for the definition of local Whig parties. At the national level, the association of the Dissenters with moderate Anglicans can be traced all the way back to the first and second exclusion parliaments.[74] In the following decades, and on into the eighteenth century, the support of Low-Church Anglican M.P.s was pivotal for the safety of the Dissenting interest. The division lists for repeal of the Occasional Conformity and Schism Acts, for example, illustrate once again the importance of this alliance.[75] The abiding importance of the association is proven by the similar configuration in Parliament in the 1780s identified by G. M. Ditchfield.[76] Informal cooperation of a nonpolitical

---

74 Douglas R. Lacey, *Dissent and Parliamentary Politics in England, 1661–1689* (New Brunswick, 1969), pp. 116–17, 123–31, 133–48. Much further work is needed on Low-Church Anglicans; here we will examine only the political implications of the behavior of moderate Anglican laymen.

75 Patricia M. Scholes, 'Parliament and the Protestant Dissenters, 1702–1719', University of London M.A. thesis, 1962, p. 162; see also John Flaningam, 'The Occasional Conformity Controversy: Ideology and Party Politics, 1697–1711', *JBS* 17 (1977), 38–62; Geoffrey Holmes and W. A. Speck, *The Divided Society* (London, 1967), pp. 3, 14. John Gascoigne, 'Anglican Latitudinarianism and Political Radicalism in the Late Eighteenth Century', *History* 71 (1986), 22–38 draws out the Low Church Anglican radical nexus.

76 G. M. Ditchfield, 'The Parliamentary Struggle Over the Repeal of the Test and Corporation Acts', *EHR* 89 (1974), 553–4, 558. See, also Reed Browning, *Political and Constitutional Ideas of the Court Whigs* (Baton Rouge, 1982).

variety between Low-Church Anglican clergy and the Dissenters was also fairly common in the eighteenth century.[77]

The most important facet of the Dissent-Low-Church party alliance for this study, however, is found at the local level, and the evidence for their political cooperation in the boroughs is fairly extensive. A contemporary of Josiah Diston, Dissenter and M.P. of Devizes in the early part of the century, said that Diston spared 'no pains or cost' to support the Low-Church party that subsisted in the borough. We have seen how the Low-Church vicar of Portsmouth, the Rev. Henry Taylor, cast his political lot with the Dissenting families of Carter and Missing and thereby contributed to the Dissenters' control of the borough. The Low-Church Dissenting alliance at Abingdon is graphically depicted in the poll book of 1754 where the name of the local vicar of St. Helens, Joseph Newcome, who led the opposition against the Tories, was followed immediately by the names of the 'Anabaptist Preacher' William Fuller, and the 'Teacher to the Quakers', Richard Rose. The Abingdon Whig party was thus defined in terms of the alliance between the Dissenters and the moderate Churchmen who voted Whig. Similarly at Shrewsbury, the vicar of St. Alkmond and a curate of St. Chad, along with the well-known Dissenting minister, Job Orton, and the majority of his Presbyterian congregation voted consistently for the Whig candidates both in 1734 and 1747.[78]

Two additional examples of the pivotal importance of this alliance for party politics are found in Hertfordshire. Except for the alertness of a contemporary Dissenting observer, the contribution of the Nonconformists to the success of the government's nominees at St. Albans would have been forgotten. The following note is found in the Evans manuscript and can be dated about 1722:[79]

High Ch. *Voters* for St. Albans   226

Low ch.	158
Presb.	99
Bapt.	16
Quak.	14
	287

---

77 Thompson, History, 1: 198; 4: 23, 76, 198, 235, 287; C. E. Darwent, *The Story of Fish Street Church, Hull* (London, 1899), pp. 107–8; Bradley, 'Whigs and Nonconformists', pp. 94–7, and 'Toleration, Nonconformity, and the Unity of the Spirit: Popular Religion in Eighteenth-Century England', pp. 183–99 in Bradley and Richard A. Muller, (eds.) *Church, Word, and Spirit: Historical and Theological Essays in Honor of Geoffrey W. Bromiley* (Grand Rapids, 1987).

78 *Commons, 1715–1754*, 1: 614; *An Exact LIST of those who Poll'd, Abingdon, 1754; A LIST of the Persons that Voted for Sr. Richard Corbett Bart. and William Kinaston* (Shrewsbury, 1734); 'The Poll for the Borough of Shrewsbury', *Shropshire Archeological Society Transactions*, 3 (1880), 221–38.

79 The Evans List, p. 48.

The total of Low-Church Anglicans when combined with the Dissenters gave the majority to the Whigs, and these figures graphically portray the basis to the vigorous party competition between Whig and Tory. That party rivalry was rife at St. Albans has long been recognized, but the religious base to this cleavage and the importance of the Low-Church Dissenting alliance has heretofore been neglected.

Both the Congregationalists and the Quakers had important political interests at Hertford. In addition to their own voters, who numbered 105, the Congregationalists could influence over 100 Anglicans; the Evans List notes 'in Hertford, of thos[e] who are not Dissenters, yet influenced by th[em] in Election, Voters for the County–10 – for the Borough–124'.[80] The Congregationalists along with their dependents thus comprised some 40 percent of the electorate, and the Quakers had an additional thirty-two voters. For the county of Hertford we find 'Churchmen, influenced in elections by the Quakers, in this county abt. 80'.

Henry Vowler, a resident of Exeter, described the Dissenters there in 1716 in the following terms:

In Exeter [there is] one Low-Churchman only to 3 Dissenters. The votes of Dissenters in elections [are] more than two to one of the Low-Church. And the Low-Church never undertook to vote above an eighth of the charges at any public election, the Dissenters advancing the other 7 parts. On the choice of 40 guardians for the new hospital erected in that city, anno 1700, when the law dictated that every voter should pay 2d. a week in their own right to the poor, the Whig Interest carried every Member. Nor could the High-Church with their utmost efforts reach above the half way in any of the 4 wards, to the votes by which the lowest guardian was chosen.

Vowler added wistfully, 'many of those reckoned among Low-Church were formerly Dissenters, and desirous to return again to them'. Vowler's comments are highly significant for what they imply. The Dissenters defined themselves distinctly from the Low Churchmen, but at the same time, they and the Low-Church party were willing to act together to oppose the High-Church party, and thus by definition the Whigs comprised the Low Churchmen and Dissenters. The Dissenters in this case formed the majority of the local Whig party, a group, Vowler believed, that could best be understood by its religious character. At Exeter the Dissenters explicitly identified themselves with the 'Whig Interest' and they identified the High Church with the Tories; as late as 1761, Thomas Sewell, a distinguished barrister and a favorite with the Dissenters, was nominated for Exeter 'in the interest chiefly of the Low Church party'.[81]

In 1715 John Noble, the pastor of a Congregational church in Bristol, delineated the political and financial strength of Dissent in the city. He concluded his account with a telling observation: 'And the strength of all the

80 *Ibid.*, p. 31.
81 *Ibid.*; The *Commons, 1754–1790*, 1:114; Namier, *The Structure of Politics*, p. 371.

Dissenters in Bristol may justly be reckoned much more than that of all the Low-Church-Party there.' Just as at Exeter, Dissenters were distinguished from Low Churchmen, yet they acted in league with them. In counting Bristol freeholders for Somerset, Noble computed fifty voters and observed that the 'Low-Church [are] not near that number'. Similarly, the Bristol voters for Gloucestershire among the Dissenters totalled seventy-two 'or upwards' and the 'Low-Church can hardly make up 30'.[82] Noble sought to make it emphatically clear that the Whig party at Bristol stood or fell with the support of Dissent. While he supposed that the interests of the Low Church and Dissent would normally coincide, the Dissenters in his view deserved credit for whatever degree of victory the Whigs might claim over the Tories. Obvious pride was taken in the wealth of Bristol Dissenters, and the wealth and influence was clearly tied to the present 'government', that is, the Whig government of George I. This same pattern is discernible in numerous other boroughs where there is little direct evidence for the alliance, but where the victory of government Whigs is inexplicable apart from Low-Church Anglican support. Sir Henry Hoghton and his nephew, both Presbyterians, represented Preston for fifty-three years in the eighteenth century. But the Preston Presbyterian church was only moderate in size and the Dissenters had a mere twenty-two votes in an electorate of about 700.[83] The environment was politically hostile to the Dissenters and the borough was strongly influenced by Tory country gentlemen. The Hoghtons were returned partially on the basis of their substantial property at nearby Hoghton Tower, but equally on the strength of Anglican support. Hoghton had been a deputy lieutenant of Lancashire and colonel of militia in the Fifteen, and the only alternatives to Hoghton in repeated elections were either Tories, or candidates with Jacobite leanings. In this setting, the Dissent Low-Church alliance was clearly an important factor, in repeated elections, for decisive Whig victories.

These illustrations portray the Dissenters as an independent bloc that could potentially act against the government. Nonconformists might occasionally oppose the policies of certain Hanoverian ministers, not necessarily upon the basis of national politics, but rather on the grounds of local exigencies. It is clear, however, that they were normally government supporters and developed a reputation as a unified local bloc of voters that could be counted on to oppose Tory candidates. After 1760, the distinctions between Low Church and High, Whig and Tory, seemed to loose their old, religious significance, certainly at the national level.[84] But recent research on the religious aspects of the legisla-

---

82 The Evans List, p. 147. Apparently Noble included the 2,000 Quakers 'who are generally well-affected to the present government', in this generalization.

83 *Ibid.*, pp. 59–63; The Thompson List, p. 19; *Commons, 1715–1754*, 1: 272; 2: 142. *Commons, 1754–1790*, 2: 142, 628.

84 For detailed studies that examine the tactical use of party and party labels at the national level, but that neglect religion almost altogether, see J. C. D. Clark, 'The Decline of

tion of the Parliament of 1768–74, particularly the subscription and *nullum tempus* bills, suggests that the old political concerns of High Churchmen on the one hand, and Low Churchmen and Dissenters on the other, even when they appeared to be dormant, were just below the surface, ready to erupt at any moment.[85] And where religious differences persisted in the boroughs, party labels were often preserved: when ideological differences become even more pronounced at the national level, as they did during 1775 over the colonies, so did the religious overtones of 'party'. Clearly, there was nothing approximating a two-party system at this time, and neither can we speak accurately of the revival of a 'Tory party'. But there was a resurgence of authoritarian political ideals and the true extent of the Dissent Low-Church alliance is accurately indicated by G. M. Ditchfield's analysis of the 'Dissenting lobby' in Parliament numbering some 150 M.P.s in the late 1780s. Ditchfield showed that this lobby represented constituencies with more voters than those of their opponents.[86] Dissenters, when allied with the Low-Church interest, clearly had considerably more electoral strength, particularly in the large open boroughs, than their numbers alone would suggest. Members of Parliament characteristically minimized religious differences when they went to Westminster, but their less sophisticated constituents often maintained their old religious loyalties at home. Low-Church Anglicans, as well as Dissenters, grounded their political orientation, at least in part, in religious or quasi-religious convictions. Moderate Churchmen were undoubtedly in some cases indifferent to religion, but they occasionally supported Dissenters out of conviction, and future research alone will enable us to separate their religious concerns from the purported growth of secularism.

Party, 1740–1760', *EHR* 93 (1978): 499–527, and his *The Dynamics of Change: The Crisis of the 1750s and English Party Systems* (Cambridge, 1982). Compare Frank O'Gorman, *The Rise of Party in England: The Rockingham Whigs 1760–82* (London, 1975). See also O'Gorman, 'Fifty Years After Namier: The Eighteenth Century in British Historical Writing', *The Eighteenth Century* 20 (1979), 111 where he insists on greater party continuity through the 1750s and into the 1760s than Clark, and O'Gorman, 'The Recent Historiography of the Hanoverian Regime', *HJ* 29 (1986), 1005–20. B. W. Hill's emphasis on ideological continuity in *British Parliamentary Parties, 1742–1832* (London, 1985), pp. 35–52 must be compared with Ian Christie's denial of continuity in Tory personnel after 1761 in the first half of 'Party in Politics in the Age of Lord North's Administration', *Parliamentary History* 6 (1987) 47–57. Of course, much of this debate hinges on the question of the meaning of party and party continuity. For example, on the question of party *issues* and continuity, compare Christie, 'Party in Politics in the Age of Lord North', 58–64 who argues that religion had ceased to be a 'bond of association', with Ditchfield, 'The Subscription Issue', and 'The Parliamentary Struggle over the Repeal'.

85 Ditchfield, 'The Subscription Issue', 47.
86 Ditchfield, 'The Parliamentary Struggle over the Repeal', 553–4.

THE SOCIAL SOURCES OF DISSENTING POLITICS

In numerous constituencies the Dissenters formed a body of electors whose political behavior was sufficiently predictable to enable Low-Church Anglicans to form a convenient alliance with them that had an impressive degree of stability. In chapter two we examined the social equality of Nonconformity with Anglicanism through a comparative study of occupational structures, but we observed that the abiding legal inequality of Dissent, combined with the actual practice of office holding, continued to exert an internal pressure that stimulated the ministerial elite to agitate for progressive political reforms. We have seen that the Dissenters' strong self-identity, grounded in ideological independence and reinforced by legal handicaps, led them to behave consistently in parliamentary elections. In addition to the Dissenters' ideological coherence as Whigs, the related trait of the reliability – even the predictability – of their behavior is crucial; they were for the most part a known entity in the electorate, and this characteristic allowed Anglicans who were generally sympathetic toward the Whig oligarchy and tolerant of the Dissenters to gather around them in an electoral bloc. If Dissenting religion stimulated the formation of local parties and provided an element of continuity from one election to the next, what was the mechanism by which the Low Church allied itself to Dissent?

The Exclusion crisis and the events surrounding the Glorious Revolution had firmly bound the interests of Anglican Whigs to those of the Dissenters. These affinities were further confirmed in the reign of Queen Anne, and then, for several generations in electoral politics, moderate, Low-Church Anglicans had found their only hope for victory over High-Church parties in the Dissenting vote. Ideologically, moderate Anglicans had traditionally been committed to toleration, and they were always more fearful of popery than Puritanism. Far from thinking that the Church was in danger from Dissent, they believed that Nonconformity played a crucial role in the preservation of the Protestant succession, and thus the alliance was strongly reaffirmed in both 1715 and 1745. From the Dissenters' perspective, the alliance in the electorate arose primarily from their practical need for political protection. At least through the midcentury, the Dissenters were relatively secure from Tory persecution, and while the various Whig administrations refused to grant them the full religious equality they desired, the Dissenters thrived, both socially and politically, under a policy of benign neglect. In some boroughs, constant pressure from High Anglicans helped cement the moderate Anglican-Dissent alliance; exclusion from corporations, for example, naturally led to numerous schemes of practical cooperation. Moreover, in a context in which some Tories and opposition Whigs were advocates of change and critics of government, it was natural for the Dissenters to ally themselves with moderate Anglicans; in these circumstances, they became defenders of both the national and the electoral status quo. Both Dissenters and moderate Anglicans thus felt satisfied with the Hanoverians, they vigorously defended the Protestant succession, took pride in their well-tempered constitution, and expressed some commitment to an extension of toleration, though never to the point of seriously jeopardizing the peace. Before the political tremors of the 1760s, Dissenters were in fact politically moderate and both their practice and ideology were wonderfully well-suited to the temper of moderate Anglicans. There appears to have been little if any social basis to the alliance; Anglicans and Dissenters of all occupational strata acted together in support of the Whig oligarchy.

The arrangement between the Dissenters, moderate Anglicans, and the government was so comfortable and secure that Nonconformists in numerous boroughs in the early eighteenth century were lulled to sleep, if not by the lure of government sinecures, then by the peace of political indifference. In such cases their potential for political radicalism was definitely eroded, a fact that can be documented in many smaller boroughs, such as Leominster, Portsmouth, and Sudbury. Yet remarkably, even in boroughs such as Portsmouth, where the Dissenters' influence appeared least enlightened and was clearly wielded on the side of self interest, the communal cohesiveness of the Dissenters was still a major component of their political power. Their behavior in electoral politics was so much training for radical politics; we will observe a very similar pattern of group cohesiveness and independence in the period after 1760 as well. By then, however, it was combined with a new proclivity toward resistance to the established authority of the central government.

If the Dissent Low-Church alliance was electorally significant in the period before the American Revolution, could the Dissenters lead a sizable body of Anglicans into opposition during the American crisis? Such a feat was not easily accomplished in parliamentary elections; even when political principles were clearly presented to the voters, in numerous boroughs the Dissenting vote made little practical difference in elections. Except in the most economically advanced and freest boroughs, such as Norwich and Bristol, the established structures of interest and influence, or the Dissenters' habit of voting for the government, or a combination of these elements, obstructed movement into a consistent stance of opposition to the government. But there are other means of measuring political convictions than parliamentary elections, and when we turn to popular politics we find a far more consistent pattern of behavior.

While the Anglican-Dissent alliance in the period before 1760 was grounded in both mutual interest and ideology, during the American Revolution we will find evidence for the emergence of a new basis for opposition politics. A more radical ideology was needed to attract Anglican support for pro-Americanism, and this ideology was espoused by a new breed of Dissenting charismatic leader. But the new opposition would also rally grass roots support linking radical ideology to expressions of socio-economic discontent. For example, when we examine the Dissenters' sermons and pamphlets we will see them actually encouraging Anglican artisans to resist the government. In order to guard against the encroachments of power, Joseph Towers believed that the 'inferior ranks' of the people must be politically engaged, and he hoped that they would imitate the conduct of the Middlesex electors.[87] Dissenters were very prominent as leaders of the popular agitation against the government's colonial policy, and this agitation manifested distinct social divisions. Nonconformity thus may indeed emerge as the midwife of class, and this is a complicated topic to which we will return in the last chapter. We can observe tentatively that the Dissenter's ideology of discontent, combined with a mutual experience of social inequality based on a perception of legal, and possibly economic, oppression, inclined many Low-Church Anglican artisans and some secularized artisans to cooperate with the Nonconformists.

But the new Dissent-Anglican artisan alliance of the mid-1770s only emerges to visibility through the study of popular petitions; it does not appear as an important aspect of electoral politics. Differences between electoral politics and popular politics can be traced to divergent structures that allow for more or less freedom of expression, to the influence of radical ideology derived from well-defined interest groups, and to social and economic fissures in society. While the average Dissenter proved incapable in many cases of rising above the restrictions of electoral politics, he did respond coherently in popular politics, and the elite provided charismatic leadership that does reveal abiding patterns of interest-group cohesion and a new commitment to radical principles. Disaffection did in fact run in subterranean channels that have heretofore been largely neglected; where parliamentary politics obscure the presence of two fundamentally opposed 'parties' in the nation at large, the petitions for peace betray their reality. Moreover, the grand theme of Whig political ideology and the more radical theme of opposition to social and economic privilege were explicitly worked out and connected in detail in the sermons of Dissenting ministers. Their sermons seem to have touched a responsive cord, not only in the hearts of the Dissenting laity, but in numerous lower ranking Anglican hearts as well. These expressions of popular radicalism must now be examined through an investigation of charismatic leadership and radical ideology, electoral behavior, and public petitions.

87 Towers, *Observations on Public Liberty*, pp. 28, 30.

4

The Dissenting Pulpit, Political Ideology, and American Independence

The Duke of Richmond, a prominent Rockingham Whig, observed in 1772 that the Dissenters' 'religious principles and our political ones are so very similar, and most probably will make us generally act together'.[1] The Dissenting pulpit will take us to the very heart of 'true Whig' ideology, it will demonstrate the convergence of religious and political principles, and it will illumine the way in which ideas contributed to consistent political action. The Established Church with the king at its head and its bishops in the house of Lords was still a major pillar of the state in the eighteenth century, and just as certainly as the political allegiance of the majority of the clergy was predictable, the religious independence of Nonconformity was readily transferred into politics.

There was nothing uniquely 'Nonconformist' about English pro-Americanism, but the Dissenters' tradition, their religious identity, and their legal status contributed to a far more consistent radicalism than that found among Anglicans. Bereft of the monetary support of the state and excluded from the advantages of the parish system, the Dissenting minister proclaimed 'the Word of God' from an elevated platform, and the act of preaching itself symbolized at once the minister's independence from the Establishment and his belief in the political importance of the proclaimed Word of God. Dissenting ministers during the American Revolution became outspoken advocates of religious and political independence and the Dissenting pulpit thereby provides us with one of the clearest expressions of political radicalism. The sermon remains perhaps the most neglected and yet one of the most important sources of political ideology in the eighteenth century.[2] Sermons also provide us with more than

1 Lord Albemarle, *Memoirs of the Marquis of Rockingham*, 2 vols. (London, 1852), 2: 224; Richmond to Rockingham, 26 April 1772.
2 For the literary genre and its importance see Robert Nye (ed.), *The English Sermon, 1750–1850* (London, 1976); James Downey, *The Eighteenth-Century Pulpit* (Oxford, 1969); James Gray, *Johnson's Sermons: A Study* (Oxford, 1972); Françoise Deconick–Brossard, *Vie politique, sociale et religieuse en Grande-Bretagne d'après les sermons prêchés ou publiés dans le nord de l'Angleterre 1738–1760*, 2 vols. (Paris, 1984). Harry S. Stout, *The New England Soul: Preaching and Religious Culture in Colonial New England* (Oxford, 1986).

ideology, because political preaching invariably involved ministers in political advocacy. Precisely because sermons represent a form of public discourse designed to change the listeners' behavior, they constitute a complex kind of evidence that at one and the same time embraces the ideology and action of the preacher as a public leader, and the assumption that the preacher's ideas and example will have some bearing on the behavior of the laity.

Candidates in eighteenth-century elections seldom made any attempt to clarify their political principles in public, and as a result few political speeches outside of Parliament have survived. Nothing approximating a national party platform existed, and acceptance speeches, or public statements upon a candidate's defeat, were almost unknown. Edmund Burke made a speech to his Bristol constituents during the general election of 1774, but this is notable precisely because it was so unusual; it is often considered to be the first illustration of a modern party platform. Another close approximation to a modern statement of political policy is found in Burke's address to the sheriffs of Bristol, but this, of course, was a conservative appeal for the right of an M.P. to act independently of his constituents. The harangues of popular candidates on the hustings in London, Middlesex, and a few other populous constituencies were frequent, but often very brief. Election handbills and pamphlets were designed to clarify one's party orientation and popular squibs addressed specific local or national issues, but developed theoretical foundations for political behavior were not typical of public expressions outside of Parliament. Some candidates, like David Hartley, wrote extended appeals to their constituents in the newspapers, yet this was hardly a widespread practice. Of all the possible avenues for disseminating political ideas, the pulpit provided one of the most influential political forums for leaders to expand upon their political convictions regularly and at length.

THE EIGHTEENTH-CENTURY PULPIT

The eighteenth-century clergy were the one minority within the nation that spoke to the public every week in extended discourses with developed theological and philosophical ideas. Dissenting and Anglican ministers alike preached many sermons of a specifically political nature, and these documents constitute a polemical and ideological base that helped shape the behavior of voters and stimulated popular expressions of opposition or loyalty to the government. When these sermons are combined with the other forms of popular election literature the ministers produced, it becomes clear that coherent and intelligible systems of politics were regularly presented to the public. Among the Dissenting elite, however, a minority of ministers were staunch defenders of the government's policy of coercion. Past studies of the role of English Dissent in the American Revolution have focused attention almost exclusively on a small – albeit important – group of radical intellectuals in London; it was not until 1938 that Anthony Lincoln first pointed out that sympathy for the American cause was not unanimous among the Dissenting leaders.[3] Several Dissenting ministers were not only loyalists themselves, but they also sought to elicit support for the government from the Dissenting laity. L.L. Peters, pastor of a Dissenting meeting at Newport, Gloucestershire, preached a sermon, published in Bristol in 1781, that encouraged support for the government. John Martin, Calvinistic Baptist minister in the chapel in Grafton Street, Soho, also preached in defense of the government, while the loyalism of Henry Hunter, minister at Little St. Helens, London, was outspoken and unqualified.[4] The list of leading Nonconformist opponents of the Revolution is growing; to Peters, Martin, and Hunter, one may add Job Orton of Kidderminster, John Handasyds of Newcastle upon Tyne, and a number of unnamed, yet to be discovered, ministers; Donald Davie has gone so far as to refer to these ministers as 'Tory Dissenters', a phrase that in the past would have appeared to some a contradiction in terms.[5] This is obviously a field that needs much further research,

3 Anthony Lincoln, *Some Political and Social Ideas of English Dissent, 1763–1800* (Cambridge, 1938), pp. 21–2, mentioned the loyalism of Edward Pickard and John Martin, but did not examine their thought. Lincoln also mentioned the Dissenting physician, John Aiken, who supported the government through 1778 (p. 25).

4 L. L. Peters, *The Voice of War; or the Present Posture of Public Affairs* (Bristol, 1781), p. iii. John Martin's *Familiar Dialogues Between Americus and Brittanicus: In Which the Right of Private Judgment, the Exploded Doctrines of Infallibility, Passive Obedience, Non-Resistance…* (London, 1776), is in direct response to the 3rd edn of Price's *On Civil Liberty*; see also, John Martin, *What Mean You by This Service: A Question Proposed and Discussed in a Sermon Preached on the late General Fast* (London, 1782), p. 28. Henry Hunter, *The Duty and Usefulness of Commemorating National Deliverances: A Sermon Preached… August 12, 1777* (London, 1777), pp. 6, 31, 36, 38. The only available study of any of these conservative Dissenters is a brief review of Martin's first pamphlet in Claude L. Howe, Jr., 'British Evangelical Response to the American Revolution: The Baptists', *Fides et Historia* 8 (1976), 43–4. None of the other loyalist Dissenters has been examined. There are a few comments on Martin in A. C. Underwood, *A History of the English Baptists* (London, 1956), p. 164. On Edward Pickard, see John Stephens, 'The London Ministers and Subscription, 1772–1774', *ED* 1 (1982), 43, note 2.

5 Colin Bonwick, especially, has been careful to give attention to the loyalist Dissenters in 'English Dissenters and the American Revolution', pp. 90–1; 109, note 3 in H. C. Allen and Roger Thompson (eds.), *Contrast and Connection* (Athens, Ohio, 1976). Job Orton, minister at Shrewsbury, Northampton, then Kidderminster, is mentioned by Donald Davie in a paper presented at the Annual Meeting of the American Society for Eighteenth-Century Studies at San Francisco, April, 1980, 'The English Dissenters in the Age of Revolutions' (p. 17). For John Handasyds, see the petition, Public Record Office, Kew, H.O. 55/12/6. John Rogers, a London minister, disagreed with the government's American policy, but opposed independence, as did many Dissenters. L. F. S. Lupton (ed.), *The Diary and Selected Papers of Chief Justice William Smith*, 2 vols. (Toronto, 1963), 1: 13. Two London ministers who opposed the colonists were referred to by John Rippon in Reuben A. Guild, *Life, Times, and Correspondence of James Manning and the Early History of Brown University* (Boston, 1864), p. 324; these may have been Martin and possibly Rogers, cited in Howe, 35. Donald Davie, *A Gathered Church: The Literature of the English Dissenting Interest* (New York, 1978), p. 127.

and it can be supplemented by an exploration of Dissenting laymen who opposed the Revolution; Israel Mauduit, a prominent Dissenting pamphleteer, is one good example.[6] And, while the majority of Dissenting M.P.s took the side of the colonists, there were a few members who used their influence on the side of the government, like Joseph and Thomas Lockyer.[7]

Leading loyalist Dissenters illustrate the fact that there is no necessary connection between religious nonconformity and political radicalism. Nevertheless, the vast majority of Dissenting ministers were clearly pro-American, and as a body, their political thought is sufficiently consistent to warrant an extensive examination of 'the Dissenting pulpit'.[8] Ample attention has been given to the most well-known radical Dissenters of London and Birmingham, but the Dissenting leaders of opposition in the provinces have not been examined in any detail, and their distinctive theological convictions have been neglected.[9] Edmund Burke, for example, observed that at Bristol the Dissenting preachers carried 'more weight' with the laity than in any other part of England.[10] But what was it precisely that the Dissenting ministers said to the laity? The printed sermons and political pamphlets of the most well-known Dissenting ministers in Bristol, Newcastle upon Tyne, Norwich, Taunton, and Nottingham provide detailed answers to this question.

Religion in eighteenth-century England has been called the supreme element that 'dominated and controlled' the radical mind.[11] The religious ideology of the elite, whether Anglican or Dissenting, was most often transmitted to the laity through the vehicle of the sermon, and so were radical, political ideas. The sermon was one of the few expressions of popular communication expressly designed to reach every social level of the populace, rich and poor, literate and illiterate. A sermon might be preached to a single congregation of Dissenters, but many sermons were also published. Since the sale of printed sermons was

6　See Bonwick, 'English Dissenters and the American Revolution', p. 90. According to Richard Price, Mauduit published an anonymous attack on the colonists.

7　After the Lockyers left Parliament themselves, the Lockyer nominees at their pocket borough of Ilchester were steadfast supporters of North. See *The Commons, 1754–1790*, 3: 32; 2: 289, 291–3, 666; 3: 452. On Samuel Touchet, Dissenter and author of the Townshend Duties, see *The Commons, 1754–1790*, 3: 535. Also Sir Lewis Namier and John Brook, *Charles Townshend* (London, 1964), pp. 174; 189–91. On Sir Henry Hoghton, who backed North to the end, *The Commons, 1754–1790*, 2: 628.

8　See Table 10.2 in chap. 10.

9　Caroline Robbins, *The Eighteenth-Century Commonwealthman* (New York, 1968), mentions Walker and Toulmin in passing, but does not allude to Murray, Evans, or David, pp. 232, 240, 361. Colin Bonwick, *English Radicals and the American Revolution* (Chapel Hill, 1977), refers briefly to all these leading Dissenters.

10　*The Correspondence of the Rt. Hon. Edmund Burke*, 4 vols. (London, 1844), 4: 270; Burke to Portland, 3 Sept. 1780.

11　Bonwick, *English Radicals*, pp. 14–15. On the fifteen Dissenting ministers in the 'Club of Honest Whigs', see Verner W. Crane, 'The Club of Honest Whigs: Friends of Science and Liberty', *WMQ*, 3rd ser., 23 (1966), 216–26 and chap. 2 above. In the early modern world, says Stout, the minister's voice was the only constantly vocal source of authority. Stout, *The New England Soul*, p. 4.

by no means restricted to the immediate congregation, in their published form sermons reached the population at large and became the common property of Anglicans and Dissenters alike. The minister's rationale for publishing his sermon was most often simply to inform and convince people of his views.[12] In some cases ministers explicitly intended to reach a broader range of people by publishing their sermons, and, paradoxically, they might even hope to appeal to the lower ranks. One Anglican minister, Robert Poole Finch, published his sermon because he felt that the lower ranks needed it, since they were being 'poisoned, corrupted and warped into a lack of submission to authority'. John Wesley felt a similar concern. He preached a sermon on 'How Far is it the Duty of a Christian Minister to Preach Politics?' and in an earlier treatise on the same topic lamented that 'every cobbler, tinker, porter and hackney-coachman' held political opinions and asserted them with too much assurance. Generally, as guardians of the social order, Anglicans felt it incumbent on them to preach on political topics. John Mainwaring, fellow of St. John's College, Cambridge, considered the Anglican clergy members of the state; they were concerned therefore in political matters and should 'declare their judgment on any question of political concern'. Nonconformist ministers, as watchmen of the public welfare, also felt a profound duty to sound the trumpet against perceived encroachments on civil and religious liberty.[13]

The radical Dissenting pulpit represented the position of a minority of Englishmen. Moderate Anglicans were more numerous and they espoused a political viewpoint that reflected a wider consensus; moderates were also clearly more accurate than Dissenter's in their depiction of high governmental practice. Anglican clergymen like Beilby Porteus, Bishop of Chester, and John Butler, first royal chaplain and then Bishop of Oxford, advanced a centrist position on the nature of English monarchy, the balance of the constitution in King, Lords, and Commons, and the nature of representation in the context of current imperial developments.[14] Nevertheless, extreme views on both ends of

12　Henry P. Ippel, 'British Sermons and the American Revolution', *JRH* 12 (1982), 193.
13　Finch, *A Sermon at St. Michael, Cornhill* (London, 1779), p. vi, cited in Ippel, 'Blow the Trumpet, Sanctify the Fast', *HLQ* 44 (1980), 46. Wesley, 'Free Thoughts on the Present State of Public Affairs' (London, 1768), and 'How Far is it the Duty of a Christian Minister to Preach Politics?' (London, 1782), *The Works of the Rev. John Wesley*, 3rd edn Thomas Jackson (ed.), (London, 1829–31 [reprinted, Grand Rapids, 1958–9]), 11: 18, 154, 355. Mainwaring, *A Sermon Preached before the University of Cambridge* (Cambridge, 1776), p. 1, cited in Ippel, 'British Sermons', 196; James Murray, *An Impartial History of the Present War in America*, 3 vols. (London, 1778), 1: 108–9; James Murray, *An Alarm without Cause* (Newcastle upon Tyne, 1780), dedicatory page.
14　For a much expanded discussion of these themes, see James E. Bradley 'The Anglican Pulpit, the Social Order, and the Resurgence of Toryism during the American Revolution,' *Albion* 21 (1989), and on the monarchy, see chap. 5 below. For the pervasive and abiding influence of High Anglican ideals, see F. C. Mather, 'Georgian Churchmanship Reconsidered: Some Variations in Anglican Public Worship 1714–1830,' *JEH* 36 (1985). On the number and influence of sermons in the Puritan revolution see Michael

the political spectrum worked powerfully to polarize opinion on the basis of old fears and apprehensions. Moreover, the conflicting views of High Churchman and Dissenter were sometimes found together in the same provincial town; local opposing pulpits set forth diametrically opposed ideologies that fuelled the flame of earlier rivalries. Suspicions based on the memory of events long past shaped and colored the movements of popular politics in the 1770s; such exaggerated and conflicting accounts typically led to further embitterment and misunderstanding.

Though the Dissenters were few in number, the pulpit gave them a far greater visibility and much greater political influence than their numbers alone would seem to warrant. One recent study examined all of the published general Fast Day sermons for the period 1776–82. Of the more than one hundred authors, the Dissenting clergy contributed about one-fourth of the whole, and if the Scots Presbyterians are included with the Dissenters, they comprised a third.[15] The sermons for the general Fast Day were far more than isolated ideological expressions; they were often associated with important social events. For example, in Newcastle upon Tyne at the general Fast in December 1776, the mayor ordered the distribution of handbills that no shop might be opened; contemporaries also noted that places of public worship were especially crowded on these days. Fast Day sermons were thus taken seriously and it is likely that the social impact was greater than other contemporary sermons. Printed sermons of all varieties, however, became public documents, eliciting comment, discussion, and rebuttal. They were often commented upon in the *Monthly Review*, the *Critical Review*, the *London Magazine*, and the *Gentlemen's Magazine*, and the comment provoked further published responses from the preachers.[16]

Recent surveys of the political thought of prominent Dissenters like Richard Price, Joseph Priestley, and Newcome Cappe, are thorough and convincing, but more attention must be given to the actual language of the Dissenting sermon

Walzer, *The Revolution of the Saints* (Cambridge, Mass., 1965), p. 325. On the social importance of the sermon in Hanoverian England, see Ippel, 'Blow the Trumpet', 43, and J. C. D. Clark, *English Society 1688–1832* (Cambridge, 1985), pp. 158–61, 231, 233. But there is little certainty about the number of people reached by printed sermons, Ippel, 'Blow the Trumpet', 47; see also, Ippel, 'British Sermons', 191–2.

15 Ippel, 'British Sermons', 192. Of the 116 authors identified, 72 were Anglican, 23 Dissenters, 12 Scots Presbyterian, 8 Evangelical, and 1 Catholic. Gayle Pendleton, 'Radicalism and the English "Reign of Terror": The Evidence of the Pamphlet Literature', *The Consortium on Revolutionary Europe* (1979), 197–8 found that of 349 authors whose religion could be determined, 39% were Protestant Dissenters and 45% were Anglicans. On the nature of national days of fasting and humiliation, the royal proclamation and public response, see also Ippel, 'Blow the Trumpet', 55–6. Ippel looked only at Fast Day sermons which probably tended to elicit the sermons of conservative Anglican preachers; similarly, these sermons in turn may have elicited more Dissenting opposition than other sermons.

16 Ippel, 'Blow the Trumpet', 53, note 40; 47, 49–50, 55–6.

since important historical conclusions have been made to rest on the purported hyperbole of the pulpit. Colin Bonwick, for example, argued that it was the injudicious language of Richard Price that gave Dissenters such a bad reputation during the American Revolution, and yet Price's language was a model of moderation compared to the Dissenting ministers in Newcastle, Nottingham, Norwich, and Cambridge.[17] Had the Duke of Richmond attended a meeting house in one of these cities, he would have been stunned at the language of the sermon, for on occasion, the Dissenting pulpit in the provinces reached far beyond the principles and the temper of the Rockingham Whigs.

THE DISSENTING PULPIT AND DISSENTING IDEOLOGY

Caleb Evans (1737–91) of Bristol was raised in the home of a Calvinist Baptist minister, and in 1759 he became his father's assistant in the pulpit of Broad Mead chapel.[18] As a Dissenting minister, Evans characteristically celebrated Guy Fawkes Day and the landing of William with a sermon that enthusiastically commemorated civil and religious liberty. Three of his 5th of November sermons have survived – *British Constitutional Liberty* (1775), *The Remembrance of Former Days* (1779), and *British Freedom Realized* (1788) – and together they provide a comprehensive survey of his political thought. These works rehearse the events of the Glorious Revolution and applaud English liberty in terms of the guarantee of life, property, and the freedom of conscience and inquiry; such rights, Evans believed, are based upon law, English statutes, representative institutions, and constitutional monarchy. Evans championed liberty and stood, as he said, in the tradition of the Sidneys, the Hampdens, and the Russells, and along with other Dissenting ministers, he

17 Bonwick, 'English Dissenters and the American Revolution', pp. 105–6, 108–9. Dickinson sees radical ideology as more advanced than Bonwick. For example, he gives us a more radical reading of Price's doctrine of popular sovereignty. However, like Bonwick, he stresses the moderate elements of the Commonwealthman radicalism with respect to the failure of practical reform; the satisfaction with a democratically elected House of Commons; the failure to challenge the mixed form of government; the lack of attack on monarchy and aristocratic privilege; and the failure to attend to the poor. H. T. Dickinson, *Liberty and Property: Political Ideology in Eighteenth-Century Britain* (New York, 1977), pp. 222–3, 246. On Robert Robinson of Cambridge, see James E. Bradley, 'Religion and Reform at the Polls: Nonconformity in Cambridge Politics, 1774–1784', JBS 23 (Spring 1984), 55–78.

18 J. G. Fuller, *The Rise and Progress of Dissent in Bristol* (London, 1840), pp. 186–92. John Evans, *The History of Bristol*, 2 vols. (Bristol, 1816), 2: 331. Evans was a Calvinist; he was theologically conservative on the authority of Scripture, the doctrine of substitutionary atonement, the deity of Christ, the Trinity, and he wrote vigorously against Arians, Socinians, and specifically the teachings of Joseph Priestley. See Caleb Evans, *A Reply to the Rev. Mr. Fletcher's Vindication* (Bristol, 1776), p. 23; *Remarks on a Letter Addressed to the Ministers* (London, 1789), pp. 10–11, 14, 16–19, 22, 29, 30; *The Scripture Doctrine of the Deity of the Son* (Bristol, 1766), pp. v, xix, xxii, 6–7, 10–11, 47–50, 51–4, 61; *The Law Established by the Gospel* (Bristol, 1779), pp. 25–6; *The Kingdom of God* (Bristol, 1775), pp. 7, 8, 10–11.

described his political viewpoints as 'liberal', meaning open, free, and tolerant.[19]

Evans' stature as a political commentator and his power as a charismatic leader came to light during the most publicized clerical debate of the revolutionary period.[20] In the very midst of the petitioning agitation of 1775, John Wesley published a plagiarized version of Samuel Johnson's *Taxation No Tyranny*. Evans' reply, under the pseudonym 'Americanus', was by far the most widely read and provocative response to Wesley, and it attacked him for his plagiarism, shameful versatility, and malicious intent.[21] Shortly afterwards, John Fletcher came to the defense of his wounded leader, whereupon Evans entered into battle with Fletcher, and subsequently also with Josiah Tucker, Dean of Gloucester. The focus of this debate was the question of taxation and the issue of actual versus virtual representation. In his defense of the colonies, Evans' pro-American perspective was outspoken and uncompromising.[22]

James Murray (1732–82) of Fans Roxburghshire was, like Caleb Evans, an orthodox Calvinist, and like Evans, he wrote several pamphlets against Wesley. He came to Newcastle in 1764 and his enormous popularity led to the establishment of an independent Presbyterian meeting and the building of a

19 Evans, *The Remembrance of Former Days* (Bristol, 1779), p. 38; *British Constitutional Liberty* (Bristol, 1775), p. 27 where Evans says 'To a feeling liberal mind, what is *life* without *liberty*?' George Walker, *The Duty and Character of a National Soldier*, 1779, in *Sermons on Various Subjects*, 2 vols. (London, 1790), 2: 440; and *Speech*, 1782, in *Essays on Various Subjects*, 2 vols. (London, 1809), 1: cxxiv, where he refers to 'the liberal spirit of Christianity'.
20 According to Thomas R. Adams, *The American Controversy*, 2 vols. (Providence, 1980), 2: 919–23, only Richard Price's pamphlet, *Observations on the Nature of Civil Liberty*, produced more responses than Wesley's pamphlet. These pamphlets were widely published in the newspapers; Wesley's 'Calm address', for example, was printed on a separate half sheet, and Evans' rebuttal was printed on two extra pages provided gratis, *Glos. J.* (9, 30 Oct. 1775). But the pamphlets were really overshadowed by the coverage of the debate in the newspapers. See Evans to Josiah Tucker, the Dean of Gloucester, *Glos. J.* (6 Nov. 1775); Wesley's letters concerning the debate are found in *Bath Chron.* (23 Nov. 1775); *Brist. J.* (2, 16 Dec. 1775); and Evans' letters are in *Brist. J.* (16, 23 Dec. 1775); other items rebutting Wesley are 'A Friend to the Constitution', *Brist. J.* (7 Oct. 1775); an essay in *Morn. Chron.* (30 Nov. 1775) and 'A Real Whig', *Lond. Eve-Post* (28 Oct. 1775). Against 'Americanus' (Evans) one finds 'A Middlesex Freeholder', *Morn. Chron.* (26 Oct. 1775) ('it will excite the Americans to continue in their independent notions') and Dean Tucker, *Glos. J.* (6 Nov. 1775) who believed Evans' work was disloyal to the crown.
21 Evans, *A Letter to the Rev. Mr. John Wesley* (London, 1775), pp. i, iv, 23, 24. For a complete survey of the debate with Wesley, see Evans, *Reply to Fletcher's Vindication*, pp. 4–23, and on his debate with Dean Tucker, pp. 91–103 of the same pamphlet. On John Wesley's *Calm Address*, see Frank Baker, 'The Shaping of Wesley's *Calm Address*', *MH*, 14 (1975), 3–12; Donald H. Kirkham, 'John Wesley's Calm Address; Response of the Critics', *MH* 14 (1975), 113–23; Albert M. Lyle, 'The Hostile Reaction to the American Views of Johnson and Wesley', *The Journal of the Rutgers University Library* 24 (1960), 1–13.
22 Evans, *Political Sophistry Detected, or, Brief Remarks on The Rev. Mr. Fletcher's Late Tract* (Bristol, 1776).

new chapel at High Bridge Street. He and his family had suffered under the Covenanters in Scotland, and thus from his youth he was steeped in libertarian principles.[23] Murray made his political debut with his *Sermons to Asses* (1768), a radical pamphlet that opened with inflammatory words reminiscent of the first line of Rousseau's recently published *Social Contract* (1762). 'A nation of slaves', wrote Murray, 'is a kingdom of asses'. 'All Europe – yea the greatest part of the world have couched down between these two burdens of civil and religious oppression.'[24] Murray wrote in the aftermath of the colonial resistance to the Townshend Duties and the agitation over the publication of the *North Briton* number 45, but his pamphlet appeared before Wilkes was elected for Middlesex (March, 1768). Murray's *Sermons to Asses* thereby preceded Joseph Priestley's influential *The Present State of Liberty in Great Britain and her Colonies* (1769) and easily rivaled this tract in importance; the pamphlet went through five editions and was reprinted in Philadelphia as late as 1774. Murray was thus one of the first Dissenting ministers to grasp the political implications of the discontent surrounding Wilkes and one of the first to speak out. His radical preaching nurtured the thought of the more famous Thomas Spence who attended High Bridge chapel and became one of Murray's most devoted followers.[25] A second political pamphlet that attacked the Established Church and particularly the Anglican clergy appeared in 1773 entitled *Sermons to Doctors in Divinity, Being the Second Volume of Sermons to Asses*.

In the mid-1770s Murray became deeply involved in parliamentary politics. On the eve of the general election of 1774, he published *The Freeman's Magazine* in Newcastle in which he advised voters to act independently at the polls. In the face of local magisterial oppression, Murray exhorted the freemen of Newcastle and other boroughs to stand firm: the freemen's 'natural rights are common', he averred, 'and their dangers equal'. Following the election, he published a poll book for the purpose of educating the electorate and stabilizing those voters who had wavered.[26] His warning to the king, EIKON BASILIKE

23 E. Mackenzie, *A Descriptive and Historical Account of... Newcastle upon Tyne*, 2 vols. (Newcastle upon Tyne, 1827), 1: 387–8. On his theology see his high view of Scripture, his understanding of original sin, the work and person of Christ, and an outspoken attack on Arianism, Murray, *An Alarm Without Cause* (Newcastle upon Tyne, 1780), pp. 5, 14, 15–16, 25, 26. On the nature of redemption see Murray, *Select Discourses*, 2nd edn (Newcastle upon Tyne, 1768), pp. iv, 10–12, 15, 16, 22, 29, 30 note, 33, 44, and Murray, *Sermons to Asses* (London, 1768), pp. 129, 130, 165, 168.

24 Murray, *Sermons to Asses*, pp. 4–5.

25 Bonwick, *English Radicalism*, pp. 59, 64–5 says that Priestley's tract was one of the earliest appeals on behalf of the colonists written by a Dissenter; and the other early work was John Fothergill's *Considerations Relative to the North American Colonies* (1765). H. T. Dickinson (ed.), *The Political Works of Thomas Spence* (Newcastle upon Tyne, 1982), p. viii.

26 *The Freeman's Magazine* (Newcastle upon Tyne, 1774), pp. 60, 74–5. On Murray's involvement, see his contribution to this volume, (pp. 86–8) 'by the author of Sermons to Asses', and Dickinson, *The Political Works of Thomas Spence*, p. viii. Murray, *The*

(1778) was written in the tradition of the mirror of princes, and a multivolume *An Impartial History of the Present War in America*, that was largely dependent upon the *Annual Register*, appeared in the same year. In addition to these strictly political works, Murray preached a series of sermons to his congregation that were later published, and he wrote several smaller tracts attacking his political opponents. Besides preaching on Sunday, he gave weekly public lectures with the goal of educating the people concerning their civil and religious rights; in 1779, for example, he lectured on the divine right of subjects to admonish their sovereigns. Two pamphlets against John Wesley's defense of the government's American policy were strongly pro-American in sentiment, and in *The Fast, A Poem* he argued that the powerful always oppress the poor. His *Sermons for the General Fast Day* (1781) include trenchant remarks on the corruptions of government, the superiority of natural law, the right of resistance to oppressive and unjust laws, and the justice of the American cause.[27]

Little is known of Rees David, the pastor of St. Mary's Baptist chapel, Norwich, but it is clear that he read and assimilated the political writings of James Murray.[28] He also had contacts with another leading radical Dissenter, Robert Robinson, of Cambridge; Robinson preached at David's ordination in 1779. The king's regular proclamations of an annual day of humiliation and fasting, combined with Murray's publications, finally provoked David to a vigorous public reaction to what he considered a repressive regime. In 1781 and 1782 he preached two sermons bordering on treason, both of which were subsequently published. David read Murray's history and interpreted events in America on the strength of Murray's presentation; his use of Scripture, his Calvinism, his love of satire, and his understanding of political authority, all show strong

27 For the literary genre of *EIKON BASILIKE* (Newcastle upon Tyne, 1778), see the introduction of Lily B. Campbell (ed.), *The Mirror for Magistrates* (Cambridge, 1938). On the authorship of *A Grave Answer to Mr Wesley's Calm Address* (1775), compare pp. 2–4 with Murray, *The Finishing Stroke to Mr. Wesley's Calm Address* (Newcastle upon Tyne, 1778), pp. 8–9, where the same detailed line of reasoning appears. Murray, *The Fast, A Poem* (1778); see also his *An Alarm without Cause*. On the topic of oppression, Murray, *Sermons for the General Fast Day* (London, 1781) hereafter, *Fast Sermons*; on which, see the exposition by Henry Ippel, 'British Sermons', p. 200. On his weekly lectures, see H. T. Dickinson, *Radical Politics in the North-East of England in the Later Eighteenth Century* (Durham, 1979), p. 7. See also Murray's *Sermons to Ministers of State* (Newcastle upon Tyne, 1781).

28 Charles B. Jewson says that from 1778 David fulminated against the American War, *The Baptists in Norfolk* (London, 1957), p. 55. St. Mary's was a Particular Baptist chapel. See Jewson, 'St. Mary's Norwich', *BQ* 10 (1940–1), 108–17; 168–77; 227–36; 282–8; 340–6; 398–406. On David's explicit dependence on Murray's *Impartial History*, see David, *The Hypocritical Fast* (Norwich, 1781), pp. 19, 20, 23. For a complete review of his Calvinistic orthodoxy, see David, *The Fear of God* (Norwich, 1782), pp. 4–9, and for a high view of the authority of Scripture, *Hypocritical Fast*, pp. 24, 26–7, 30.

affinities with Murray's thought.[29] David announced in the prefatory material of the first sermon that he had given 'public notice' of his plan to preach on *The Hypocritical Fast* a week in advance, but that 'the subject, and the method in which it was treated made a great stir in the city'. He was keenly aware that many would condemn the sermon, 'because it is chiefly political', but he proposed to publish it anyway in order to expose those who misrepresented it. There can be little wonder that it caused a stir, for David inscribed the sermon to 'all the Friends and Supporters of Civil Liberty' and began with the text of Scripture 'When the wicked beareth rule the people mourn' (Proverbs 29:2). He reminded his auditors that God opposes the cruelty of kings and their ministers toward their fellow creatures, and recommended that they 'Read the scriptural account of despotic kings and their servants, – consider their attempts to *oppress* and impose *taxes* on their subjects, contrary to justice and sound policy; – and forget not their punishment.'[30]

David's second sermon entitled *The Fear of God, the only Preservation from Temporal and Eternal Ruin* was no less inflammatory than the first. This sermon was dedicated to all the inhabitants of Norwich 'who have uniformaly opposed the destructive measures of administration against the Americans'. The title page began with the text of Scripture, 'Shall the throne of iniquity have fellowship with thee, which frameth mischief by a law? They gather themselves together – and condemn innocent blood', and continued, 'It is better to trust in the Lord than to put confidence in Princes' (Psalms 94:20; 118:9). He proceeded to examine the way in which the fear of God makes all earthly authorities relative. His affirmations of filial loyalty to the house of Brunswick hardly mitigated the radical quality of these sermons.[31]

Evans, Murray, and David were highly charismatic figures and they were all Calvinists, but Joshua Toulmin of Taunton and George Walker of Nottingham were theological liberals; Walker described himself as a 'cordial Arian', and Toulmin, who entitled one of his sermons 'The Unsuccessfulness of Christ's Ministry and his Reward with God' (1775) was a thoroughgoing Unitarian.[32] Toulmin (1740–1815) was the minister of Mary Street Unitarian Baptist chapel, Taunton, and he is most well-known as the editor of the works of Faustus Socinus; he was also an historian of note. He published only one sermon on America, though all of his writings took an advanced position on

29 See David, *Hypocritical Fast*, pp. 5, 7, 19; David, *Fear of God*, pp. 1, 2, 9, 13-14, 19-20.
30 David, *Hypocritical Fast*, pp. 4, 27. Here he cites 1 Kings 12:12–14. Ippel, 'British Sermons', pp. 200–1 and 'Blow the Trumpet', p. 50, gives some attention to *The Hypocritical Fast* but is unaware of how radical it is.
31 David, *Fear of God*, p. 11.
32 On Walker's theology, see his sermon 'On the Resurrection of Jesus Christ' where he distinguishes his views from Calvinism on the one hand, and Socinianism on the other, describing his own belief as 'a tempered Arianism'. *Sermons on Various Subjects*, 1: 216, 225, 227. On Toulmin's Unitarianism see *An Historical View of the State of Protestant Dissenters* (London, 1814), pp. iv, 448, 470–1.

civil and religious liberty, and we may safely assume that he espoused radical politics from the pulpit on more than one occasion. His homily on America, first preached to 'two societies' of Dissenters, was a lament that condemned the civil war that threatened 'ourselves, and those with whom we are united by all the tender charities of life' and he exhorted his hearers to pray for 'an happy reconciliation'.[33] While he condemned the government's policy of coercion and defended the just rights of the colonists, his radicalism, on the whole, was more temperate than that of Murray and David.

George Walker (1735–1807) was a native of Newcastle upon Tyne and as a child he attended Hanover Square Chapel. He carried on successful ministries at Durham (1757–61) and Great Yarmouth (1761–72), but always with a strong avocation in mathematics; while at Durham he completed his work on the *Doctrine of the Sphere* that was published in 1772. He settled in Nottingham in 1774 as pastor of the Presbyterian High Pavement chapel where he ministered until 1798, and in this period he became a confidant of Price and Priestley. Walker, like Murray, was actively engaged in parliamentary politics, first at Durham in 1761, where his political labors 'were deemed very instrumental to the election of the successful candidate', and he was subsequently complimented by the corporation with the freedom of the city. Later he was extremely active in the agitation over America. He drafted the petition from Nottingham in favor of reconciliation in 1775, led out as a speaker at a county meeting in the Association movement of 1780, and was also involved in parliamentary reform in 1782 and again in 1785. He was a major provincial leader in the movement for repeal of the Test and Corporation Acts in the late 1780s, acting as chairman of the associated Dissenters of Nottinghamshire, Derbyshire, and parts of Yorkshire. His position in Nottingham was unusually influential because most of the city magistrates were members of the High Pavement chapel.[34]

Walker preached at least three fast-day sermons (1776, 1778, 1784) and in the first two he concentrated on the moral degradation of England, though he alluded to a 'detested and ill-omened war' and reflected that he had come to think of his country as one thinks of the venerable dead. Walker was more outspoken in his opposition to the government in the last Fast-day sermon; he excoriated the 'wicked great men' who in the war with America had driven England to 'infamy and ruin'. He attempted to refute the notion that political

---

33 He wrote a history of the borough and a survey of Dissent from 1689–1705. Jerom Murch, *A History of the Presbyterian and General Baptist Churches in the West of England* (London, 1835), pp. 203–7; Toulmin, *Historical View*, pp. iv, 448; Toulmin, *The American War Lamented* (London, 1776), pp. 1, 3.

34 Mackenzie, *A Descriptive and Historical Account of Newcastle upon Tyne*, 1: 374–5. Walker, *Memoir*, in *Essays on Various Subjects*, 1: vii, xxiv, xliv, lxxi, lxxxii, lxxxv–lxxxvi, cxvii, cxli, clviii–clxiii.

wisdom and truth were annexed exclusively to any particular social rank.[35] At the height of the American conflict in 1779 he preached to the Nottinghamshire militia an incredibly audacious sermon. The preeminent duty of every citizen, including soldiers, said Walker, is to guard liberty, 'that Charm that Welcomes Toil and Poverty'. He exhorted the soldiers 'to watch with a jealous eye every encroachment of power' in each of the branches of government and concluded with a statement that bordered on sedition: 'You are the soldiers of the people more than of the crown.'[36] He developed his political ideas at the greatest length in three speeches at county meetings in Nottinghamshire called to encourage economic and parliamentary reform. Walker expressed tremendous confidence in the good judgment of the people and asserted the right of contributing to the laws by which one is governed, either in person or through a representative. Involvement in government was the common right of all, claimed Walker, and is 'inherent in the very idea of an English freeman'.[37]

THE PHILOSOPHICAL AND THEOLOGICAL SOURCES OF DISSENTING POLITICS

All five preachers fell squarely within the eighteenth-century Commonwealthman tradition. Each of them relied upon the same ideological sources as other, more well-known English radicals, and by any standard, they were highly learned and well-versed in political theory.[38] In addition to the biblical languages of Hebrew and Greek, they all knew Latin (with the possible exception of David), and Evans, Murray, and Walker read French as well. Their exposure to the best political theorists, both ancient and modern, was

---

35 Walker, *A Sermon Preached to a Congregation of Protestant Dissenters, 1776*, (London, 1777), p. 3; Walker, *A Sermon Preached to a Congregation of Protestant Dissenters*, 1778, in *Sermons*, 4 vols. (London, 1808), 4: 225; Walker, *The Doctrine of Providence*, 1784, in *Sermons*, 4: 260, 277.

36 Walker, *Duty of a Soldier*, pp. 429, 427, 431. Though this is radical, it was not as if Walker was preaching to troops destined for America. Major John Cartwright refused to bear arms against American liberties, but he felt an obligation to his country that led him to spend several years in active service in the militia. Bonwick, *English Radicals*, p. 89.

37 Walker, *Substance of the Speech of the Rev. Mr. Walker at the General Meeting of the County of Nottingham, Speech* of 28 October 1782 at Mansfield, in *Essays on Various Subjects*, 1: cxxvii; see also *Speech* of 1785 in the same vol., 1: clv.

38 Bonwick notes such sources as the European enlightenment, English common law, Scottish philosophy, seventeenth-century Commonwealthmen, and eighteenth-century Whig and libertarian thinkers, *English Radicals*, pp. 62–3. On the indebtedness of Price, Priestley, and Burgh to Trenchard, Gordon, and Bolingbroke, see Robbins, pp. 363–70. The discussions of Robbins and Bonwick are presupposed here; the terms 'Commonwealthman' and 'Real Whig' or 'True Whig' are used interchangeably. See Dickinson on the relationship between the old Country platform and the Rockingham Whigs on the one hand, and Wilkite and Wyvillite radicals on the other, *Liberty and Property*, pp. 208, 213, 215, 218, 221. The most iconoclastic recent account of English political thought is J. C. D. Clark's *English Society*, with its focus on the 'intellectual hegemony' of Anglican political theology, (pp. 64, 75, 90, 92).

extensive. Caleb Evans, for example, frequently cited 'the immortal Locke' and Montesquieu, but he also read Delolme and Benjamin Hoadly, and he relied on an impressive array of contemporary thinkers, including Chatham, Burke, Blackstone, and Camden, that 'truly noble peer'.[39] For his knowledge of American affairs, Evans looked to John Dickinson, the 'Cato of America' and his *Pennsylvania Farmer*, as well as Thomas Hutchinson, the late governor of Massachusetts. In addition, Evans had read the Latin classics; he referred occasionally to Seneca, Ovid, Virgil, and Cicero. Something of the distinctive thrust of Murray's radical political ideology is seen in his preference for Rousseau and Voltaire over against Locke and Montesquieu, although he did refer to 'the excellent Gordon'. Murray's love of political satire is betrayed by his affection for Juvenal rather than Cicero and Tacitus, yet above all other authorities, he relied on Scripture for his political orientation.

Toulmin and Walker also knew and relied upon the works of Locke and Montesquieu; in addition, the former cited the Whig historian Gilbert Burnet, while the latter appealed to Hénault. Walker exhorted the youth of Nottingham to follow the 'glorious deeds' of Hampden, Sidney, Falkland, and Locke, the truly 'venerable names of English story'.[40] Further, these preachers repeatedly depended upon works recently published by fellow Dissenting authors. Rees David's reliance on Murray is noteworthy since Murray was the only authority he cited in addition to the Bible. Richard Price's *Observations on the Nature of Civil Liberty and the Justice of our War with America* (1776) was particularly influential; Caleb Evans, Joshua Toulmin, and George Walker cited it extensively in their later works. Evans also praised the work of his fellow Dissenter Philip Furneaux and knew something about the literary labors of the Cambridge Dissenting radical, Robert Robinson.

In addition to these ancient and modern political writings, the Christian tradition itself contributed directly to the political thought of these five writers. A later chapter will demonstrate that the majority of pro-American Dissenting ministers and the majority of the laity were orthodox in their theological convictions, yet the orthodox sources of radical political ideology have largely been neglected. This neglect has been caused in part by scholars' assumption that interest in politics had taken the place of the Dissenters' passion for theology, particularly the so-called 'rational Dissenters'.[41] But even George Walker, a

---

39 The references are too extensive to annotate. On Locke, for example, see Caleb Evans, *Letter to Wesley*, p. 4; *Reply to Fletcher's Vindication*, pp. 32, 83; *British Freedom Realized* (Bristol, 1788), p. 14. John Louis Delolme wrote *The Constitution of England; or, An Account of the English Government* (London, 1775).

40 Walker, *Sermon*, 1778, p. 212; Toulmin, *Historical View*, pp. iii, 9, 513. Charles Jean François Hénault, French historian and orator (1685–1770).

41 Russell E. Richey, 'The Origins of British Radicalism: The Changing Rationale for Dissent', *ECS* 7 (1973–4), 179–92; Bonwick, *English Radicals*, p. 255. While recognizing the importance of theology, Bonwick does not draw out the way in which Christian doctrine was connected to politics, except in general, moral terms. Clark argues

liberal, believed that Christianity stimulated human progress and specifically promoted the growth of liberty. 'Christianity is, in its application to the human mind, favourable to liberty, to humanity, to generosity, to order, and to law'. Murray agreed that the Gospel never inculcated slavery, but rather liberty, 'and if this liberty were pursued in the manner it is recommended by Christ and his apostles, there would be no complaints of oppression, no slavery in nations, no convulsions in states, no commotions in kingdoms, nor tumults in society'. In speaking of the kingdom of God in a sermon before the Bristol Education Society in 1775, Caleb Evans said, in words not lost on the hearers, 'In this kingdom there are no oppressive statutes, no unrighteous laws, no sinful connivances, but *holiness to the lord* is the inscription written on it'.[42]

In the preaching of the orthodox pastors in particular, the authority of the Bible itself bulked large. For example, Rees David validated almost all of his political arguments with a citation from Scripture quoted in *en extenso*. For Murray, the 'sacred oracles' were the source of pure doctrine, and he was fully convinced of 'the divinity of scripture'. 'The New Testament', said Murray, 'is the *Magna Charta* of the Church, which is the kingdom of *Jesus Christ*; if once we make encroachments upon it, then the liberties of the *church* are at an end.' Murray made the political role of Scripture clear, when, upon citing a text from the book of Proverbs he observed, 'It would take a thousand Rousseaus to make one Solomon.' Evans said explicitly that the authorities for his political thinking were reason, Scripture, and the English constitution, and he urged that if Fletcher could prove that 'political slavery' was recommended in the pages of Scripture, it would shock his feelings and revolt his mind, but he would nevertheless promise 'the most absolute submission to it as a Christian'. The authority of Scripture, said Evans, must be revered 'above every other authority'.[43]

While such an approach to the authority of Scripture was common to Protestants, it had a keener edge in the mouths of these Nonconformists for two reasons: it represented the positive side of their rejection of church tradition, and it was irrevocably tied to the principle of private interpretation.

'religious heterodoxy was *conceptually basic* to radicalism in the ancien-regime sense', *English Society*, p. 293 note 63. He can demonstrate a connection in some cases: there was a link between the early eighteenth-century Deists' rejection of the traditional doctrine of God, their anti-clericalism, and their attack on monarchy (pp. 294–7). But to the extent that he believes that heresy exhaustively explains the roots of radicalism, he oversimplifies a complex development (pp. 277, 281, 317–18, 324, 330, 423). Clark alludes to the key issue of polity (p. 298), but does not pursue it, nor is there any mention of the orthodox Dissenters who comprised the majority of those Dissenters who were politically radical. This topic is examined at length in an article I am preparing, 'The Ideological Origins of English Radicalism: Heresy, Orthodoxy, and Polity.'

42 Walker, *Speech*, 1782, p. cxxiv; Walker, *Doctrine of Providence*, p. 253; Murray, *Alarm without Cause*, p. 10; Evans, *Kingdom of God*, p. 12.
43 David, *Fear of God*, pp. 9, 12; *Hypocritical Fast*, p. 5; Murray, *Sermons to Asses*, pp. 31, 66–7, 69, 70, 176; *EIKON BASILIKE*, p. 27; Evans, *Political Sophistry*, p. 9; *Reply to Fletcher's Vindication*, p. 51.

Therefore, those aspects of their theology that would contribute to their radical rhetoric and stimulate opposition to the government were eminently consistent with their doctrine of the church; the formal principle of authority was located outside of the institution of the Established Church and above the state, and thus ultimate matters of religion and politics were subject only to the interpretation of the individual, or the judgment of the congregation. Predictably, texts of Scripture that had traditionally been used to defend the state's authority, such as Romans 13, were interpreted in a radically different way.[44] The orthodox Dissenters, with their independent principle of church government expressed in a congregational polity, remained strictly trinitarian and were just as opposed to the government, indeed, perhaps more so, than their heterodox brethren.

In addition to the authority of the Bible, several Christian doctrines specifically informed their political thought. In each case, the doctrines, as doctrines, were the same as those they espoused earlier in the century when there was little hint of radicalism; in fact, the doctrines were not unlike those held by loyalist Dissenters. The real contribution of the radical ministers lies in the way in which they worked out their doctrines and applied them under the pressure of events in the colonies. The idea of God's sovereignty was controlling for the political philosophy of Evans, Murray, and David, and this doctrine was all the more important to them precisely because they derived it directly from Scripture, unmediated by Locke, Montesquieu, or any other modern thinker. Some radicals questioned political authority primarily in terms of the human dignity of the individual, or on the basis of the individual's autonomous reason, but the Calvinists questioned political authority in the name of a higher spiritual authority.[45] Thus the immediate corollary to the authority of Scripture was the authority of God over every earthly authority. This position was diametrically opposed to that of the High Anglicans who saw God's authority *in* the earthly authority; it was also opposed to loyalist Calvinist Dissenters who passively deferred to God's control of the political order. God, said Murray, is over kings; his laws are love, and his government, mercy. For this reason, when

---

44 Murray, *Finishing Stroke*, pp. 18–19 on Romans 13; and Evans, *British Constitutional Liberty*, pp. 6–7 on Paul's resistance to Roman authority in Acts 16. See also Evans, *Political Sophistry*, pp. 23–4.

45 The sovereignty of God as the basis for all authority, the relativization of every human law by divine law, and the resulting limited nature of secular authority, has a long history reaching back at least to Calvin and Knox. John T. McNeill, 'The Democratic Element in Calvin's Thought', *CH*, 18 (1949), 159–61. Calvin's oft expressed criticism of kings resulted in criticism of monarchical government generally. Richard L. Greaves, *Theology and Revolution in the Scottish Reformation* (Grand Rapids, 1980), pp. 170–2; Quentin Skinner, *The Foundations of Modern Political Thought*, 2 vols. (Cambridge, 1978), 2: 236–8. In the colonies, a clear link between Calvinism and the Revolution has been established for the middle colonies. John Beardslee, 'The Reformed Church and the American Revolution', in *Piety and Patriotism: Bicentennial Studies of the Reformed Church in America, 1776–1976* (Grand Rapids, 1976), and Alice Kenny, 'The Albany Dutch, Loyalists and Patriots', *New York History* 42 (1961).

Christians are advanced to power they are not 'exalted above the laws of Christ' for a 'Christian magistrate', if the title means anything, must be as humble, meek, and merciful as a Christian beggar. A Christian ruler is subject first of all to the Gospel and is bound both by his office and by his Christian character to Christian brotherhood.[46] Thus the proper reverential fear of God had tremendous political ramifications; this fear, said David, 'will teach us to disregard the commands of the greatest monarchs in the world, when they are contrary to the law of God'. The Dissenters also appealed to the Christian doctrines of creation and of final judgment to buttress their understanding of God's sovereignty. The Roman Catholic clergy treat people like asses, said Murray, and they are usurpers. 'Who gave them that right? Are not all men equally free? *Hath not God made of one blood all the kindreds of the earth?*' George Walker, who preached before the Nottingham corporation, averred that the magistrates will themselves one day enter a plea 'before the great Magistrate of the Universe', and therefore they should dread no offense as much as that of having offended God. Evans saw the connection between individual responsibility, toleration, and the final judgment very clearly: 'Can we answer for one another at the last day? Can we *really* think for one another now?'[47]

The Christianity of Caleb Evans, James Murray, and Rees David was traditional and orthodox, while George Walker and Joshua Toulmin espoused a more liberal view. Yet in every case, with the possible exception of Toulmin, these ministers interpreted the authority of Scripture and the sovereignty of God in a way that enabled them to limit and subordinate the authority of government. It is true, however, that some Anglicans had a similar understanding of Scripture and of the sovereignty of God, and one must therefore search deeper for the springs of the Dissenters' political radicalism. The distinctive contribution of Nonconformity to political radicalism is found neither in its orthodoxy nor its heterodoxy, but in its interpretation of human autonomy and ecclesiastical polity, and the application of these doctrines in a revolutionary setting. We have seen that the Dissenters emphasized the authority of Scripture and the right of private interpretation, but their independence was defined even more sharply by their doctrine of the church; their ecclesiology, in turn, dramatically influenced their attitude toward the state. The Dissenters' insistence on the liberty to think, act, and judge for themselves in all matters religious came to have a powerful effect on their approach to

---

46 Murray, *Sermons to Asses*, p. 119. He exults in the examples of judgment falling on evil kings drawn from the pages of Scripture, for example, Balak, King of Moab, and Ehud, slain by Eglon. See *Sermons to Asses*, p. 130, and *EIKON BASILIKE*, pp. 15, 27, 31–2; *Alarm without Cause*, p. 20.

47 David, *Fear of God*, p. 9; Murray, *Sermons to Asses*, p. 20; Walker, *Sermon*, 1778, p. 231; Evans, *Remembrance of Former Days*, p. 11; *The Death of a Great and Good Man Lamented and Improved* (Bristol, 1776), Sermon on James Rouquet, where we find that death is a leveller; high and low, rich and poor, great and small, all must die, p. 28.

government during the Revolution. Colin Bonwick has rightly argued that religion dominated the minds of the 'moderate radicals', and it was precisely because of their passion for theology that they were passionate about politics. This passion was most often expressed in terms of personal and ecclesiastical self-determination.[48]

The Dissenter's radical political theory was thus grounded primarily in polity, and only secondarily in theology. James Murray was the most articulate on the connection between egalitarianism, ecclesiology, and a critique of the state's authority, but Caleb Evans expressed the same principles, as did the majority of Dissenting ministers. Murray posited a radical disjunction between the Kingdom of God and the kingdoms of this world. On the basis of Christ's testimony before Pilate ('My Kingdom is not of this world'), Murray argued that no magistrate can have any jurisdiction over Christ's Kingdom without making himself a king above Christ: 'there can be no authority either *in* or *over his church,* but what he hath appointed by his *own* authority'. Truths contained in divine record are the laws by which God governs individual consciences and these laws cannot be subject to any human legislation. 'Even the Christian's obedience to *magistrates,* as *governors* of *civil society,* is founded upon express scripture precept'; and this is why Christians obey magistrates, 'not because *they themselves* require it. So little power have *magistrates over the church of God,* to *govern it,* or *make laws* in *it,* that they have not even a title to civil reverence from Christians, but what is *founded upon Christ's authority.*' Murray thus had a developed doctrine of two kingdoms: Christ's kingdom pertains to the salvation of souls, to conscience, faith, and obedience to God; the world's kingdom pertains to people's bodies and the laws of civil society. The two must remain distinct. 'As subjects of civil government they [Christians] are to mix with society, do the duties of men under the regulation of civil *policy;* – but as *Christians,* they have *another Lord,* and are governed by a *policy quite different.*'[49] Therefore the civil magistrate has no authority whatsoever in spiritual affairs.

Christ's authority is over all other authorities, particularly and exclusively over people's consciences; the unfettered conscience was thus the basis for the right of private judgment in religious matters. Those who understand the New Testament 'will reject *all dominion* over *their consciences,* but the *Lordship* of *Jesus Christ:* they will *laugh* at *clerical jurisdiction,* and *reject* all *religious*

---

48 Bonwick, *English Radicals,* pp. 14, 255; Bonwick said that the radicals 'transferred' their emotional needs from theology to politics, but this applies at best only to the so-called 'rational' Dissenters. The importance of Puritan ecclesiology for modern democracy is seen most clearly in A. D. Lindsay, *Modern Democratic State* (New York, 1962), pp. 117–18. See also Bonwick, *English Sermon,* pp. 12–13; and Isaac Kramnick, 'Religion and Radicalism: English Political Theory in the Age of Revolution', *Political Theory* 5 (1977), 511–12, who links the separation of church and state to restricting the role of government in economic matters.

49 Murray, *Sermons to Asses,* pp. 181–2, 183–4, 189.

dictators'. The best method of expelling heresy, for example, is teaching the truth; people are properly convinced and moved by evidence and no other power is needed.[50] On the basis of Christ's authority over the individual, on the strength of the principle of the priesthood of all believers, and on what he thought to be good scriptural warrant, Murray defended the practice of people choosing for themselves those who are to preside over them.[51] Christ's authority over the conscience of the individual leads naturally to a critique of the state. The idea of consent in church matters thereby becomes the basis for the idea of consent in civil matters, and in this way the ecclesiastical principles of the Dissenters had a direct bearing on their political principles. Ecclesiastical polity was the primary ground for political radicalism among orthodox and heterodox alike.

On the question of ecclesiastical appointment in the Church of England, and the corresponding lack of consent by the people, Murray observed,

Where is the reason of men *taking upon them* to represent people without *their consent*, and *impose* laws upon *them* which they never would have agreed to if they could have considered them? In this *alliance* all *the common Christians in England* are considered as so many *asses* for the *bishops* and *their clergy to ride upon* to *riches* and *preferment*. They first enter into an *alliance* without *their advice*, and take upon them to be *their teachers* without *consulting them*, and then they join in *making laws* to cause them to pay for *their service*, without so much as ever *giving them notice* till they are *called to pay*.

Murray believed that if people can judge for themselves in matters of ultimate consequence, then they certainly can judge for themselves in temporal matters, and thus the application to the civil realm was readily made: 'If men but enjoy the exercise of *common sense*, they will never meanly give up their right of private judgement to the will of oppressors.' '*Asses*, and worse than *asses*, surely you are, who either give up the cause of your *country*, or the rights of your own *consciences* to civil or religious *dominators*.'[52] Murray's rhetoric of 1768 rivals the inflammatory language of Thomas Paine, who wrote nearly a decade later.

Caleb Evans gave a simple rationale for Nonconformity, and most other Dissenters were in essential agreement with the principle he espoused: they were Dissenters, said Evans, not because they disagreed with the doctrine of the Established Church, but upon the principle of religious liberty. The Church, according to Evans, has no power to dictate in matters of faith, and people should insist on the liberty to think and act for themselves. Evans, like Murray, saw the connection between the congregation freely choosing its own minister and what he described as 'the truly constitutional principle, that the origin of power is from the people'. On the other hand, the radical implications of Dissenting individualism and ecclesiology were not always acted upon by all

50 *Ibid.*, pp. 40, 199, 200, 150–1.
51 *Ibid.*, pp. 57, 173, 175, 178, 201.
52 *Ibid.*, pp. 40, 194–5. One is bound to ponder whether Thomas Paine ever read Murray.

of the laity. Radical rhetoric failed to convince all the Dissenters, and this was particularly irksome when it pertained to one's own congregation. In his reply to Fletcher, Evans admitted that 'There are too many Calvinists and Baptists, some in the very society I serve, and several Baptist ministers with whom I am personally acquainted, who, through a mistaken view, as it appears to me, of our happy constitution and of the true meaning of the scriptures, contend earnestly for those very sentiments which you so strenuously defend.'[53] Murray, as well, admitted that 'There are many *simple slavish asses* among *dissenters*, who can without any *hesitation conform* to the *church*, and *take on* their *burdens* for some small *worldly advantage*, – or, to *please* their *friends*, *profanely tamper* with their *consciences*.' Yet though they were self-critical, these ministers viewed Dissenting politics as being essentially consistent with their religious principles. Dissenters had been friends to the house of Brunswick from the first; they had opposed two rebellions in England, and in the conflict with America they even yet 'endeavor to support the same principles, they did then'.[54]

Given the Dissenters' zeal for the Kingdom of God, for God's sovereignty and his rule, it is not surprising that they understood politics in moral terms. Although loyalist Dissenters and Anglicans as well approached public life in the light of morality, Dissenting radicals emphasized the moral implications of political behavior in such a way as to justify resistance to the government. We see, once again, that the contribution of Nonconformity is located in the radical use to which traditional doctrines were put. Political theory was, for these Dissenting ministers, a moral science: it involved the happiness of individuals, its end was the public good, and the nation's fate depended upon the public spirit and virtue of the people.[55] In each of these areas they viewed old England as corrupt almost beyond repair. With striking unanimity, all five ministers agreed on the characteristic sins of the age, in particular the loss of reverence for God manifested in the neglect of his worship and breaking the sabbath. This sin was the captain of them all, since, as George Walker put it, 'Irreligion cannot be a solitary vice.' The related problem of oath taking or swearing was commonly mentioned in this context. The catalog of vices also included

---

53 Evans, *The Scripture Doctrine of the Deity of the Son*, pp. xxvi–xxvii; *Remembrance of Former Days*, p. 11; *Political Sophistry*, pp. 28–9; *Reply to Fletcher's Vindication*, p. 85. The evidence concerning orthodox Dissenters demands a thorough-going reevaluation of Richey's article on the changing rationale for Dissent, 'The Origins of British Radicalism', pp. 188, 191-2.

54 Murray, *Sermons to Asses*, pp. 208, 44; *Finishing Stroke*, p. 20; Evans, *British Constitutional Liberty*, p. 14.

55 Walker, *Memoirs*, pp. xc, xci, viewed politics as a moral science. All statutes should be consistent with 'the moral attributes of God', Murray, *Fast Sermons*, p. 43. Bonwick observes that such laments of the radicals concerning the moral condition of England were commonplace, *English Radicals*, pp. 189, 255. Similar ideas of English decadence and desert of punishment are found generally in Commonwealthman theory. *Ibid.*, pp. 47, 114.

dissipation, drunkenness, debauchery, and excess in all its forms. But profligacy and luxury were especially heinous when found among kings, princes, and great men.[56]

The reason offered for the particular sinfulness of dissipation is revealing. People do not submit to bondage until they are first corrupt; slavery of the mind is thus the first form of physical bondage. As Murray put it, 'tyranny and dissipation have always kept pace together; but it must always be remembered also, that the latter is the parent of the former'.[57] Tellingly, oppression was also viewed as a sin by these radicals. This theme will be examined at length below, but it is well to point out that George Walker, for example, viewed English sufferings in light of neglecting 'that generous sympathy with the rights of human nature, that virtuous zeal in the cause of equal liberty and law', which our ancestors transmitted to us, and thus the rejection of civil liberty is put on a par with other sin. The war with the colonies was viewed specifically as the chastisement of God for the violation of such rights.[58]

Positively, these ministers stressed the importance of virtue, for 'where there is not virtue, there can be no liberty'. Walker urged that piety and public spirit are rightfully combined and called for 'a well informed public spirit'. For Walker, the moral principle is 'this little latent principle in the constitution of man', the neglect of which has led to the destruction of 'many a fine spun system of politics'.[59] Public virtue was characterized above all by vigilance, particularly the vigilance exercised in guarding liberty against the encroachments of arbitrary power. Diligence and industry were also a part of public virtue and these traits always entailed self-denial, temperance, and modesty.[60] Love of justice must be included in public virtue: 'It is the love of justice', wrote Murray 'that will make men dutiful and virtuous; the fear of punishment will make them servile but not honest.' Finally, independence of thought and action was at the center of public virtue and part of this independence was liberty itself. Just as indolence was a sin, attending to their own rights was a cardinal virtue: 'One cause of our present complaints, both as to *civil* and *religious* oppression, is, that *we look not to ourselves*, but think, as soon as

---

56 Walker, *Sermon*, 1776, pp. 25, 10, 12. See also Toulmin, *American War*, p. 11, and David, *Fear of God*, pp. 1, 16–17; *Hypocritical Fast*, p. 23; Walker, *Doctrine of Providence*, p. 271; *Sermon*, 1778, p. 216; Murray, *Fast Sermons*, p. 14.

57 Murray, *Fast Sermons*, p. 15; *Sermons to Asses*, pp. 19, 155.

58 Walker, *Doctrine of Providence*, pp. 259; 257–8. On oppression as a sin, see also David, *Fear of God*, pp. 16–17.

59 Murray, *Sermons to Asses*, p. 81. On virtue and politics, see *Sermons to Asses*, p. 115 and *EIKON BASILIKE*, p. 2, where Murray says only virtuous people enjoy liberty. Walker, *Providence*, pp. 271, 238.

60 Evans, *Reply to Fletcher's Vindication*, p. 72; *British Constitutional Liberty*, pp. 29, 32; Murray, *Sermons to Asses*, pp. 7, 11. Walker, *Sermon*, 1778, pp. 212–14. Isaac Kramnic, in particular, emphasizes the bourgeois ideology of Dissent (industry, frugality, reward for services rendered) as the heart of their contribution, 'Religion and Radicalism', 516–19.

we have elected civil or religious governors, we may fall asleep in pleasure, indolence, and inattention.'[61] Here Dissenters are encouraged to make a rational assessment of their own best material interests. Vigilance, self-exertion, and political independence were not only cherished traits in the Dissenters' own history and self-understanding; they were elevated by these Dissenting ministers to the status of cardinal virtues to be attained by everyone. It is difficult, I think, to exaggerate the importance of the link between religious independence and political independence understood in individualistic terms. Dissenters had always insisted on religious independence, but in the context of the American crisis, they made their theology do service in the cause of radical opposition to the government. This facet of their thought is seen most clearly in their understanding of natural rights.

NATURAL RIGHT, THE ANCIENT CONSTITUTION, AND ENGLISH HISTORY

Just as these Dissenters' political sources were substantially the same as those of other Commonwealthmen, their political and constitutional theory and their attitudes toward America were hardly distinguishable from other 'True Whigs'.[62] There was, of course, a number of variations and emphases between the five ministers, but while systematic unity is lacking, there is significant ideological agreement on major points. Together these ministers represent a clear, relatively coherent political philosophy that emphasized natural rights as the touchstone of English statecraft.

Following John Locke, the Dissenting ministers believed, taught, and preached that the 'actuating principle' of the English constitution 'was derived from, and founded upon, the primaeval rights of human nature'.[63] These God-

---

61 Murray, *Fast Sermons*, p. 7; *Sermons to Asses*, p. 77.
62 See Bonwick on the themes of natural rights, the corollary of liberty, equality, and freedom of conscience, praise for the English Constitution, the sovereignty of the people,
   government as a trust with the corollary of consent and contract, and the goal of
   government as the well being of the people, *English Radicals*, pp. 13, 16–17, 20, 49,
   51, 94–5. On the conspiratorial hypothesis, oppression in America leading to oppression
   in England, American virtue and America as an asylum of liberty, see *Ibid.*, pp. 119–24,
   91, 120. On the differences between Commonwealthmen, see *Ibid.*, pp. 4, 14, where Bonwick denies they had a 'logically integrated system' but does see ideological coherence.
63 Walker, *Speech*, 1782, p. cxix. The phrase 'natural rights of mankind', or some equiva-
   lents like 'eternal laws of equity' or 'common rights of humanity' appear often and are
   common to our five Dissenting ministers. Walker, *Sermon*, 1776, p. 18; Toulmin,
   American War, p. 15; David, *Fear of God*, p. ii, *Freeman's Magazine*, pp. 8, 74;
   Murray, *EIKON BASILIKE*, p. 33; Evans, *British Constitutional Liberty*, p. 8; Evans,
   Letter to Wesley, p. 5. William Stafford, *Socialism, Radicalism, and Nostalgia: Social
   Criticism in Britain, 1775–1830* (Cambridge, 1987), finds the social criticism of
   Thomas Spence and William Ogilvie, who wrote in the 1770s and 1780s, rooted in
   natural right theory, with later writers scarcely referring to natural right at all. Compare
   Clark's estimate of the importance of Locke and the 'contractarian tradition', *English
   Society*, pp. 50, 58, 89. The issue goes far deeper than questions of legitimation and
   allegiance; this theory *defines* personal freedom for the Dissenter.

given, self-evident truths, entail the right to life, liberty, property, and freedom of conscience. 'Slavery is a just reward to such as voluntarily give up their natural rights and privileges', said Murray. 'Such as do not value freedom and liberty deserve to be slaves. It is finding fault with the conduct of the Almighty to give up his prerogative to his creatures – such as voluntarily give up their rights and privileges given them by their maker, and submit to any human yoke, are next to atheists.' Since all people have the same frame and constitution, the same powers and capacities, they should not slavishly submit themselves to others. Evans distinguished at length between our civil liberty and our religious liberty in society, but located them both in 'our natural liberty'. 'To a feeling liberal mind', said Evans, 'what is *life* without liberty? We may indeed *breathe* in a state of slavery, but we can scarcely be said *to live.*' The freedom of speech is also emphatically viewed as a natural right. Rees David taught his congregation that Christians have an 'unalienable right', in the fear of God and with a due veneration for the king, 'to deliver their thoughts freely on the state of public affairs. The meanest subject of this empire claims this as his BIRTH-RIGHT; and our laws allow it just. What then, do we forfeit this natural privilege by becoming the disciples of Jesus?' The common people are themselves competent judges of 'the common rights of humanity'.[64]

The implications of natural right theory were far reaching, and the Dissenting ministers explicitly drew out these implications for the Dissenting laymen. First, since natural law was above positive law, one could obey government only in lawful things. Walker instructed the Nottinghamshire militia that God is above all, and obedience to him must be the supreme duty. The 'unwritten rule of government' in every Englishman's breast preserves the 'equal liberty of England'. It is superior to the laws, 'for law by a corrupt administration may be turned against the people for whom it was provided'. Walker admitted that 'these sentiments' may appear strange to some, but, he added, woe to us, if they seem strange. In arguing that the freemen in America have a right to vote for legislators in America, Murray said, 'This I do not say proceeds from nature, but from our laws, which give freemen this privilege. The principles of nature would carry us a great way further, and would teach us such doctrines, as societies accustomed to live in luxury would not endure.'[65] The influence of

64 Murray, *Sermons to Asses*, p. 8, 'Reason, and self-evident truth are the same, and all men can perceive it, unless blinded by prejudice, or when they wilfully shut their eyes through corruption', Murray, *Fast Sermons*, p. 17; Evans, *British Constitutional Liberty*, pp. 8–13, 15–18. Life and property are secured not only by natural rights, but by English statute as well, pp. 12, 27; David, *Fear of God*, p. ii.

65 Walker, *Duty of a Soldier*, pp. 437–8; on this same line of reasoning, see, David, *Fear of God*, p. ii; Murray, *Grave Answer*, p. 3. Actually, Murray takes this a little further. He contests the notion that the laws require kings, or that the king is the source of law. The existence of laws does not depend on 'any human regal authority'. God is the true ruler, and all government originally proceeds from him. God speaks to people about government in two ways: by the law of nature, and by positive precepts in Scripture.

this doctrine on the Dissenters' attitude toward the Americans was profound and will receive detailed attention below.

Second, natural right theory meant that the origin of power was located in the people, and since it came from them, it might revert to them. The complementary ideas of the consent of the individual and government as a trust are everywhere evident in the Dissenters' thinking. Evans admitted that all power is ultimately from God, but he urged that the origin of political power is immediately not from God, but the people. God did not ordain the particular form of government found in Britain. Since in several crucial respects the Dissenters stood outside the legal tradition, they were quick to observe that the particular form of government Great Britain enjoyed was not divinely inspired. They would concede that it was blessed by God, but it did not originate directly from him, and thus Evans can say, 'the origin of all power, under God' is the people. Every civil government is founded on mutual compacts between the governors and the governed, and therefore governors are 'accountable for any breach of their TRUST; and that as they have no power whatever but what the PEOPLE directly or indirectly gave them, the people are consequently no longer bound to submit to their power, than whilst it is exercised lawfully...' The people have never given the right to others to betray their privileges, or to destroy them; rather, they have always 'most religiously', kept this power 'in their own hands'. Walker even more forcefully asserted that governments 'are the depositories of a power originated from [the people] themselves, entrusted every moment for their benefit, and resumable at their pleasure, when the trust is wickedly and dangerously violated'.[66]

Third, the purpose of government was thought to be found in the good of the people, and this provided a standard by which to test every government. Toulmin preached this doctrine unequivocally; 'The end of men's uniting in society, is to guard and secure their own rights; not to strengthen each other for rapine and slaughter.' In every nation, David urged his Baptist congregation, the people have settled upon that mode of government 'which they thought most conducive to their happiness at large'. In his sermon on *British Constitutional Liberty*, Evans admitted that when people enter into society they part 'with some portion of our [their] natural liberty'.[67] But this is the only reference in these authors to the notion that people ever gave up part of their natural liberty, and we have seen that Walker positively taught that the power of the people is entrusted 'every moment' to the government. Similarly, Evans was

The 'execution' of this civil government from God is left up to the 'wisdom of society'. So there is nature on the one hand and there are 'divine positive laws', on the other, and only from these do we have human law. *Fast Sermons*, p. 24.
66 Evans, *Letter to Wesley*, p. 10; *Reply to Fletcher's Vindication*, pp. 67, 68–9, 71; Walker, *Duty of a Soldier*, pp. 426–7; David, *Fear of God*, p. 15.
67 Toulmin, *American War*, p. 4; David, *Fear of God*, p. 15; Evans, *British Constitutional Liberty*, p. 8.

somewhat more moderate than his fellow Dissenters when he called the end of government, 'good order and regularity'. But in the same sermon he also referred to the end of government as 'the safety and happiness of the people'.[68] While too much should not be made of these distinctions, since happiness entails order, in terms of emphasis, the radicals were more interested in happiness than in order.

These three principles of natural right theory were manifested concretely in the English constitution, and since the Dissenting ministers believed that the inhabitants of England enjoyed greater liberty under their well-tempered constitution than any other nation in the world, their political radicalism was accordingly moderated.[69] For most Commonwealthmen the tradition of liberty stretched back through ancient times to a pristine period of unsullied freedom. Murray was prepared to contrast the 'unrighteous decrees made by modern authority' with the 'ancient constitutional laws' and Walker believed that the 'primeaval rights' were 'at first uncontaminated with the servile maxims of aristocratic and monarchical governments'.[70] The idea of the ancient constitution was a common assumption in Dissenting thought, while the contrasting doctrine of a vicious state of nature was almost wholly lacking.

The vague mythical concept of the ancient constitution was made more specific by an appeal to history. Since Dissenting ministers viewed themselves as 'the Lord's Remembrancers', they felt it their duty frequently to rehearse the events of English history with their congregations. For Joshua Toulmin, the reign of William III had a peculiar relevance for Dissenters: 'These events are not only such as dissenters must feel a concern in, but they are connected with the history of the human mind, of the fluctuations of opinions, and of the progress of religious truth and of national felicity.' In his 5th of November sermon of 1778 entitled 'The Remembrance of Former Days', Caleb Evans argued that English history was important because it taught lessons on liberty and free inquiry. The history of past times 'calls upon the clergy of the establishment, and amongst the dissenters ... to disseminate with diligence and care the grand principles of Protestantism and free inquiry; the sufficiency of the

68 Evans, *British Constitutional Liberty*, pp. 9, 12. See the reference to 'honor and happiness', in Murray, *Fast Sermons*, p. 13.
69 Most thinkers moved from this theoretical base to the ancient constitution. Granville Sharp, who based his arguments on natural rights rather than legal privileges arising from colonial charters, was the exception. Bonwick, *English Radicals*, p. 74. On the ancient constitution in the Commonwealthmen, see Bonwick, p. 16. Bonwick believes that the rooting of these political principles in the specific postulates of the English constitution gave the radicals' thought a distinctive moderate hue. They supported the idea of stability and acceded to hierarchical structures in society and hence were reformers rather than root and branch radicals. *Ibid.*, pp. 12–13, 21.
70 Murray, *Fast Sermons*, p. 37. Walker, *Speech*, 1782, p. cxx. For the most extensive treatment of the ancient constitution, see, Walker's *Speech* of 1782, pp. cxx–cxxviii, and Walker, *Doctrine of Providence*, pp. 251–3. The basic concept is also found in Murray, *Fast Sermons*, p. 9; *Finishing Stroke*, p. 18; David, *Fear of God*, pp. 2, 16.

Scriptures, in opposition to traditions; and the right of private judgment, in opposition to ecclesiastical tyranny, and imposition upon the consciences of men'. Besides appealing to Scripture, Rees David advised his congregation: 'Attend to the history of your own country'.[71]

The pivotal events in constitutional history were thus a favorite theme of the Dissenting pulpit, and these events were interpreted within an unabashedly providential framework.[72] The historical emphasis entailed a constant reiteration of the principles of Magna Charta (which was, Caleb Evans insisted, 'an *acknowledgement* of the rights of Englishmen, not a *creation* of them'), the statutes of Edward I of 1297 and 1306 concerning taxation and representation, and the writ of *Habeas Corpus*.[73] The events of the Puritan Revolution were rather brazenly celebrated. Not surprisingly, the Dissenters damned 'the execrable Stuarts' and castigated the theory of divine right monarchy. David argued that the Hebrews' disobedience of Pharaoh and Daniel's disobedience to the king of Babylon proved that 'the doctrine of PASSIVE OBEDIENCE and NON-RESISTANCE is anti-scriptural, and absurd to the last degree'. Even more audaciously, the Dissenters held the regicides themselves up for praise. Murray applauded Oliver Cromwell and observed that in his time Englishmen began to 'claim liberty more perfectly'. Evans explicitly compared the struggle over ship money with the contemporary debate over representation, and Walker spoke in glowing terms of the piety and the 'zeal for manly liberty' of the soldiers of the Long Parliament.[74]

But of all these historic events, the Glorious Revolution itself held the most attraction for Dissenting ministers. The flight of 'guilty' James, the landing of 'that immortal hero' King William, the establishment of 'the rock of public liberty', the Bill of Rights, are all recounted in epic and heroic terms. At the Revolution, it was the people under God who 'transferred the sovereign power from King *James*, to that glorious patron of British liberty, King WILLIAM', and the many who were inactive in the event, implicitly consented with the main participants. 'It was a righteous cause; it was the cause of liberty, of religion, of general happiness; and God prospered it accordingly.'[75] The

---

71 Toulmin, *Historical View*, p. xviii; Evans, *Remembrance of Former Days*, p. 23; David, *Hypocritical Fast*, p. 27.
72 On the providential interpretation, see Walker, *Doctrine of Providence*, pp. 248–9; David, *Fear of God*, p. 28; Evans, *British Constitutional Liberty*, pp. 24–5.
73 Evans, *British Constitutional Liberty*, pp. 11–13; Evans, *Letter to Wesley*, p. 5; David, *Fear of God*, p. 19.
74 David, *Fear of God*, pp. 9, 13; *Hypocritical Fast*, pp. 26, 28; Murray, *Finishing Stroke*, p. 14; *Sermons to Asses*, p. 9; Evans, *Political Sophistry*, p. 15; *Letter to Wesley*, p. 20; Walker, *Duty of a Soldier*, pp. 416, 435; Walker, *Sermon*, 1776, pp. 7–8; see also Evans, *Remembrance of Former Days*, p. 21; *British Freedom*, p. 13; Toulmin, *The History of the Town of Taunton* (Taunton, 1791), p. 112.
75 Evans, *British Constitutional Liberty*, pp. 14, 24–5; *Reply to Fletcher's Vindication*, p. 83; *British Freedom*, pp. 9, 13; *Letter to Wesley*, pp. 10–11; Evans likens the overthrow of James II to that of Zedekiah, the wicked king of Israel, *British Freedom*, p. 10.

Revolution thus clearly established the contractual nature of government for the Dissenters, and the 'well-balanced constitution' of King, Lords, and Commons, emerged naturally from these events. The importance of balance between the branches of government 'to preserve the equipoise of power' is everywhere taken for granted, yet some, like George Walker, believed that there was a need for reform to protect the constitution from 'the encroachments of power', particularly in the executive branch. Evans as well praised the English constitution, found the liberty of the subject located preeminently in the House of Commons through the principle of representation, but refused to make even this constitution absolute, since Christ's design was not to support or destroy any particular form of government, including constitutional monarchy.[76] The Dissenters often praised the House of Brunswick for maintaining the principles of the Revolution, but there was one telling omission in all the Dissenters' defense of their esteemed constitution. There was no positive place found for the Established Church. While the Dissenters never mentioned the place of the Established Church in a positive light, to most Englishmen, the Church remained one of the great pillars and principal bulwarks of the state.

AMERICAN RESISTANCE: 'ONE OF THE BEST CAUSES IN THE WORLD'

The study of English pro-Americanism has recently advanced a great distance through the research of Colin Bonwick, Mary Kinnear, and John Sainsbury. Bonwick in particular has examined the 'remarkable congruence' between the thought of the English radicals and the Americans' arguments, and it is this coherent political ideology, in Bonwick's judgment, that qualifies the English radicals as pro-American, not that they were sympathetic to all that the colonists did or thought, nor that they supported independence. The English radicals understood the events of the late 1760s and early 1770s as a single constitutional crisis with two geographical arenas.[77] In England, the conflict over general warrants, followed by the massacre of St. George's Fields in

For David the idolatry of James II is like that of Ahab, *Hypocritical Fast*, p. 26. For similar accounts of the Revolution, see Walker, *Duty of a Soldier*, p. 435; David, *Fear of God*, p. iii; *Freeman's Magazine*, p. i.

76 Walker, *Speech*, 1782, p. cxxv; *Speech*, 1785, p. cxliii. Evans, *Remembrance of Former Days*, pp. 7–9; *Letter to Wesley*, p. 5; *Reply to Fletcher's Vindication*, p. 54. Murray, as always, asserted the primacy of 'fundamental' laws and 'natural justice' and the law of God over the laws of Parliament. *Fast Sermons*, p. 21. David, *Fear of God*, p. 13; *Freeman's Magazine*, p. 1.

77 Bonwick, *English Radicals*, pp. 60–1, 52, 117–18; Mary Kinnear, 'Pro-Americans in the British House of Commons in the 1770s', University of Oregon Ph.D. diss., 1973; John Sainsbury, *Disaffected Patriots: London Supporters of Revolutionary America 1769–1782* (Kingston and Montreal, 1987). See also Bartholomew P. Schiavo, 'The Dissenter Connection: English Dissenters and Massachusetts Political Culture; 1630–1774', Brandeis University Ph.D. diss., 1976, and John Seed, 'Gentlemen Dissenters: The Social and Political Meanings of Rational Dissent in the 1770s and 1780s', *HJ*, 28 (1985), 319.

1768, the Middlesex election affair, the controversy over public reporting of parliamentary debates, and the Dissenters' failure to obtain relief for their clergy and school masters from submitting to the Thirty-Nine Articles, all appeared to be somehow cruelly related. In the minds of most radicals, these events were closely connected to developments in the colonies. The same government that denied the Dissenters relief at home attempted to establish Episcopacy in the colonies and was unnecessarily kind to Catholicism in Quebec. The Stamp Act, the Townshend Duties, the Boston Massacre, and finally the Coercive Acts, were all instigated by the same repressive regime that was undermining liberty at home.[78]

Liberty in Great Britain and liberty in the colonies were thus intimately connected, and as with other Commonwealthmen, the Dissenters viewed themselves as part of a trans-Atlantic community that stood on the verge of a precipice.[79] Caleb Evans believed that 'the great *American question*' had everything to do with 'the *British constitution*, and *British liberty* ... I had almost said, the very being of the British constitution and British liberty is involved.' Similarly, upon the occasion of the general fast day, James Murray exhorted his congregation, 'Would Britain wish to have her prayers regarded, and her fasting accepted in the sight of the Almighty, let her loose the bonds of wickedness that she has twisted, and break the chains that she has forged for her brethren abroad, and the subjects at home'.[80] The laws against the colonies were viewed as 'novel and hostile', and since the English government had 'so much injured' her brothers abroad, the Dissenters doubted whether Englishmen at home could expect better treatment.

Bonwick has properly emphasized the loyalty of the English pro-Americans. Most radicals were at once devoted to the monarchy and committed to the unity of the Empire, and as a result they neither incited the colonists to rebellion nor advocated republicanism.[81] Detailed attention to the writings of Price and Priestley, however, has left the impression that Dissenting radicals were consistently moderate and this has obscured the more anti-monarchical orientation of some Dissenting leaders in the provinces. While it is true that one finds

---

78 Bonwick shows how English radicals needed the Revolution to revive their cause, and they put it in an empire-wide context and even perhaps a universal context, *English Radicals*, p. 26. Schiavo, 'The Dissenter Connection' is especially good on the relationship between the Dissenters' attempts at repeal and the Anglicans' attempts to establish Episcopacy, pp. 521–2.

79 Bonwick, *English Radicals*, pp. 119–20. See chap. 2, pp. 27–52 where Bonwick elaborates on the means which nurtured this community: visits, correspondence, books, pamphlets, and sermons. See also Schiavo, 'The Dissenter Connection', pp. 465–520. Oppression in both the colonies and England seemed to be eminently threatening. See Murray, *Fast Sermons*, pp. 44–5; *The Fast: A Poem*, pp. 3–4, 6.

80 Evans, *Political Sophistry*, p. 14; Murray, *Fast Sermons*, pp. 45–6.

81 Bonwick, 'The English Dissenters and the American Revolution', pp. 107–9. Of course, Bonwick looks at Anglican radicals as well, but all of his samples of their thought underscore the moderate nature of their radicalism. See *English Radicals*, pp. 72, 100, 101.

due veneration for the king in almost every Dissenting sermon, it is imperative to distinguish between prudent rhetoric and genuine affection.[82] The five provincial leaders studied here were outspokenly pro-American. Writing in July 1776, Evans boldly called the American resistance 'one of the best causes in the world', and viewed himself as one of the 'patrons' of this cause. For Murray the war 'originated in injustice, has been carried on with folly and attended with disgrace and disappointment'. He believed that 'bonds of wickedness are twisted one year after another, and the nation groans in chains'. 'Ah Britain...' he continued, 'you are twisting cords of oppression, rather than loosing bonds of wickedness.' Rees David inscribed his sermon to the gentlemen and tradesmen of Norwich 'who have uniformly opposed the destructive measures of administration against the Americans; and to all the friends of civil and religious liberty in general...'. Even Joshua Toulmin, who was the most moderate of the provincial ministers, pondered, if, when the colonists recovered, 'the remembrance of past grievances and sufferings [won't] rouse the dormant spirit of courage and liberty, and urge them to new contests, to shake off a yoke to which they have yielded a forced submission?'[83] These sentiments were not whispered behind closed doors: they were proclaimed from the pulpit, and there can be no doubt that such pro-American sentiment fueled Anglican fears of sedition at home.

These Dissenting ministers consistently referred to the American colonists as their own brethren, and the war against the colonists was thought unjust. It was an 'unnatural war', a 'civil war', or a 'detested and ill-omened war' and the English government alone was to blame for all of the violence.[84] The motive for carrying on the war was simple; lust for power and riches was behind the coercive measures. Accordingly, the Dissenters recommended that the government abandon its short sighted aggressive policy and pursue conciliatory measures instead.[85] The colonists' behavior, on the other hand, was construed in a uniformly positive light, so much so that America was viewed as a political asylum 'for those in whom the spirit of virtuous liberty still lives'.

---

82 Sometimes the deference expressed to the king appears genuine, as in the case of Caleb Evans, *Letter to Wesley*, p. 24. Other times, such verbiage is but thinly-veiled contempt. See below on Murray and David. It is also true that the Dissenters did not often explicitly encourage independence from Great Britain. See Evans, *Letter to Wesley*, p. 16.

83 Evans, *Political Sophistry*, p. 35; Murray, *Fast Sermons*, p. 45; David, *Fear of God*, p. i; Toulmin, *American War*, p. 11.

84 Murray, *Fast Sermons*, pp. 43, 8, 45; *Finishing Stroke*, pp. 12–13, 6–7, 10; David, *Fear of God*, pp. 25, 10, 23; Walker, *Sermon*, 1778, p. 189, *Sermon*, 1776, p. 3; *Doctrine of Providence*, pp. 255–6; Toulmin, *American War*, pp. 3, 6; Evans, *Reply to Fletcher's Vindication*, p. 51; David, *Hypocritical Fast*, pp. 23, 29.

85 Toulmin, *American War*, pp. 3–4, 6, 20; David, *Fear of God*, pp. 10, 25; Evans, *Letter to Wesley*, p. 24. And why is it manifest that the grounds for the war are doubtful? 'Because the nation is divided concerning them, and the greatest number of individuals have always been against it', Murray, *Fast Sermons*, p. 41. Walker, *Doctrine of Providence*, pp. 255–6.

The ministers envisioned the future of America in a more positive light than the future of Britain.[86]

But far more important than the elite's pro-Americanism was their belief that the conflict with the colonists involved genuine political and constitutional principles. On the printed page and from the pulpit, the ministers repeated endlessly to their congregations that more was at stake than a conflict of interests; the Americans contended for freedom of conscience, representation, and self-government, matters that went to the very heart of English liberty.[87] The political principles that most agitated the minds of English Dissenters emerged out of the debate over taxation and representation, and the related issue of the right of resisting oppression. While the Quebec Act was an important symbol to the Dissenters of the administration's true religious orientation, it did not attract as much attention as the controversy over representation. To be sure, developments in Quebec were an ominous sign both from the standpoint of encouraging Catholicism and vesting too much authority in the king, but the Act merely threatened the loss of liberty, whereas in the eyes of the Dissenters, the coercive legislation of Parliament actually infringed upon both chartered and natural rights.[88]

For the provincial Dissenting minister, the American conflict centered around the right of consent and the exercise of representation. Evans and Murray reacted vigorously to John Wesley's contention that the king had the power to tax his subjects without their consent. Basing his thoughts squarely on Locke, Evans argued that the right of granting one's own property and the freedom of not having it disposed of without one's consent is the 'very Soul and vital Spirit' of the English constitution, 'the grand palladium of British Liberty, and the bulwark of Freedom'. Murray agreed. Such unqualified power in a sovereign would destroy 'all elections, all parliaments, and all rights to property and life'. Wrapped up in the idea of consent was the virtue of independence: 'judging for ourselves of the real exigencies of the state', as Evans put it, or granting

---

86 The colonists are vindicated in the issue of the Stamp Act and the Quebec Act, Evans, *Letter to Wesley*, pp. 16, 18–20, while the English are chastised for their attempts to monopolize trade. Evans, *Reply to Fletcher's Vindication*, p. 57. On America as an asylum, see Walker, *Sermon*, 1778, p. 225; *Doctrine of Providence*, p. 266; Murray, *Finishing Stroke*, p. 122.

87 Toulmin, *American War*, p. 10; Evans, *Political Sophistry*, p. 32; Murray, *Fast Sermons*, pp. 40, 45.

88 See chap. 5 below on the Dissenters' anti-Catholicism. Murray viewed the 'Canada Bill', 'that worst than Trojan Horse' as the beginning of the toleration of Catholicism in England, *The Lawfulness of Self-Defense Explained and Vindicated* (Glasgow, 1780), p. 26. This pamphlet is a slightly different edition of *An Alarm without Cause*. See also Murray, *Impartial History*, 1: 474 where he does call the Quebec Act unconstitutional. Evans depicts the authority the Quebec Act gave the king as ominous, and conducive to despotism. Evans, *Reply to Fletcher's Vindication*, p. 72; also, *Letter to Wesley*, p. 16. Similarly, Toulmin, *American War*, p. 16. Bonwick treats the subject of representation at length, but does not emphasize the right of resistance when the principle of consent is denied, *English Radicals*, pp. 59–64; 144–6.

their property 'by their own act alone', in the words of Toulmin.[89] The idea of consent was based on both natural law and English statute, but these ministers reminded their readers that it was also grounded in the structure of English government. England's well-balanced constitution placed the power of giving and granting money in the House of Commons alone; the king and the House of Lords could neither frame nor alter a money bill, but only assent to it.[90] The right of consent was exercised in practice through duly appointed representatives, and political power was thereby harmonized with political liberty. But all the Dissenters agreed that while it was constitutional for Parliament to tax Englishmen at home, it was not constitutional to tax the colonists.

The principal reasons for this denial of the right of Parliament to tax the colonists was that the Americans were not represented in Parliament. The Dissenting ministers demonstrated a sophisticated understanding of the nature of the franchise in England, and they readily granted that those Englishmen who had never obtained the vote were still virtually represented in Parliament. Evans often reiterated three points relative to virtual representation in England: First, anyone with the smallest amount of property might acquire a voice in the legislature if he chose. Granted, people were by no means equally represented, and this was, in Evans' eyes, 'an acknowledged defect in the constitution'. But the capacity to qualify with a forty shilling freehold was not viewed as onerous. Second, the right of representation existed in fact no matter how few chose to exercise it. Third, and most important, non-voters had an actual power in the control of their property because they were taxed in common with the representative himself. 'Were it not for this important controlling power, every non-voter would be a slave.' But none of these circumstances subsisted for the colonists and thus the Dissenting ministers took serious issue with the claim that Americans were virtually represented in Parliament.[91] Instead, the colonists were and should be represented in their own respective houses of assembly, since the colonial charters gave them the responsibility of raising their own revenue.[92] Thus well into the war, taxation without representation was the

---

89 Evans, *Letter to Wesley*, p. 4; Murray, *Grave Answer*, p. 1; Evans, *Remembrance of Former Days*, p. 10; Toulmin calls this granting of their property a 'natural' right, *American War*, p. 15, and 'a great barrier of liberty'. A statute of Edward I also secured both life and property from lawless invasion through the idea of consent. Evans, *British Constitutional Liberty*, p. 11.

90 Evans, *Reply to Fletcher's Vindication*, p. 36; *Remembrance of Former Days*, p. 10; Murray, *Grave Answer*, p. 1; Walker, *Duty of a Soldier*, p. 426.

91 On the county and householder franchise, see, Evans, *Letter to Wesley*, p. 7; see also pp. 12, iv–v, 13; *Reply to Fletcher's Vindication*, p. 38; *Political Sophistry*, p. 5. See the same ideas in David, *Hypocritical Fast*, p. 19; Walker, *Duty of a Soldier*, p. 426.

92 Evans, *Letter to Wesley*, pp. 7, 14–15; *Reply to Fletcher's Vindication*, pp. 47–8. Murray, *Grave Answer*, pp. 1, 2, 4. The right of the colonial assemblies to make a grant of their own money to the treasury was upheld by most other radicals like John Fothergill, Arthur Lee, Joseph Priestley, and Granville Sharp. Evans, like Price, held to the distinction, often called into question, between taxation and trade legislation, and

pivotal political issue for the Dissenting ministers, and they viewed Parliament's assertions of absolute sovereignty as both unconstitutional and unjust. Taking other people's property and lives without their consent was consistently and repeatedly called slavery. In Murray's judgment, the mother country had turned into 'a cruel stepmother', and thereby forced the Americans to throw off the yoke of slavery. Dissenters who were accustomed to the burden of legal restrictions were naturally sensitive to all forms of political oppression; the radical principles that had lain dormant in their thought for two generations, emerged, under these circumstances, with fresh life. 'Slavery', said Evans, 'considered in its principle, does not depend upon the treatment of the slave, for if he is deprived of his liberty, and is at the disposal of another, he is equally a slave when treated well as when treated ill'.[93]

The language of liberty and slavery, however, was not strong enough. These ministers brought the political issues home to their congregations in unmistakably clear terms through dramatic stories found in the Bible. When read audibly and in their entirety, these dramas reveal something of the impression the Dissenting pulpit left on the average layman. Several examples of the biblical narrative need to be examined at length for the modern reader to appreciate the powerful effect of eighteenth-century preaching. In a sermon of 1778 in the tradition of a mirror for princes, Murray told the story of Eglon, the corpulent and wicked king of Moab, and described his ultimate demise at the sword of Ehud. When Eglon was slain, the sword entered his bowels and Scripture records, 'the dirt came out', a line with which Murray made fine play. Ehud had formerly submitted to the taxation of Eglon but Murray observed that these taxes were laid upon Israel unjustly.

He, no doubt, grudged to give away the substance of his country to a government where the people were not represented. These taxes were imposed, and not left to Israel's discretion. It was hard enough to be so used. There is little reason in taxes imposed by right of conquest; but when robbers, that are stronger than we, demand our purse, there is no other safe way but to deliver. This is as much as can be said for any unjust taxations; they are no more than political robberies, committed by persons in power upon those who have not might to oppose them. Very likely the king and people of Moab might pretend that they had taken Israel under their protection, and were not obliged to protect them for nothing; they therefore might pretend that they had a right to impose taxes upon them.

Such oppression, however, was nothing more or less than a 'yoke of slavery'. The sword of discipline should be thrust into the center of an overgrown government, 'though much dirt may come out by the operation'. Murray cautioned in conclusion, 'though I would not wish to see a poor *Moabite* feed

allowed Parliament the right to the latter. Evans, *Reply to Fletcher's Vindication*, p. 46.
93 Murray, *Finishing Stroke*, p. 20; Evans, *Reply to Fletcher's Vindication*, pp. 35, 30, 38; Evans, *Letter to Wesley*, p. 13; *Remembrance of Former Days*, p. 10; Murray, *Grave Answer*, p. 2; *Fast Sermons* p. 48. The works of Harry Stout, Ruth Bloch, and Donald Weber on the rhetorical nuances of colonial sermons have no counterpart in English scholarship.

crows upon a gibbet, yet it would certainly be but just that such as have swallowed more than their proper share of national emoluments should be obliged to restitution'.[94] With publications such as these, it is remarkable that Murray escaped prosecution for seditious libel.

Rees David provided his Dissenting listeners with an explicit and extended comparison between the conduct of Ahab, a despotic king of Israel, and 'our conduct toward the Americans'. First, Ahab wished to take from Naboth his birthright 'contrary to the express command of God', and, adds David, 'So did we want the Americans to give up the best part of their birthright, I mean, *civil liberty,* when we endeavor to *tax* them contrary to their charters.' Second, Ahab attempted to purchase the vineyard from Naboth offering its full value in money. 'So did we pretend that it was very reasonable to tax the Americans, because we have laid out so much money in protecting them, and many gave more credit to this, than they ever did to the gospel of Christ; forgetting that the Americans did more than was expected of them in the last war.' Third, as Ahab declared Naboth a rebel, so we 'upon finding the Americans would not tamely give up their *liberty,* declare them *rebels.* And the ministry to support their old design – found a considerable majority of the S-ns of B-li-l in the late inglorious House of Commons, to maintain the charge of rebellion brought against them.' Finally, just as the eyes of Ahab were on the vineyard, since the Americans had been declared rebels, 'our eyes have been fixed on the enjoyment of their *estates*; and therefore we have done all in our power to destroy them, by *killing, scalping* and *starving* the inhabitants'.

David concluded his homily by noting the differences between the court of Ahab and the government's conduct toward the Americans. Ahab's ministers first proclaimed a fast then declared Naboth a rebel, but 'our virtuous *ministry*' did not fast 'until they found by wretched experience that heaven and earth were fighting against them'. Now, he noted, we have had five fasts and the gist of the prayers respecting 'our brethren in the *New World* is "O Lord, kill the Americans, or else they will kill us for our cruelty toward them" '. In the second place, the wicked queen Jezebel was behind the 'hellish scheme' against Naboth, whereas our queen has had nothing to do with America; the ministry planned it and executed it. Next, Ahab appeared to be successful; he finished the whole affair in one day, with no apparent cost to the nation, but by mismanagement and obstinacy the ministry have added millions to the national debt and disgraced the English name. Finally, Ahab got the vineyard, but we will not get the object of our desire. Ahab displeased the Lord and brought ruin upon himself and his family, and David concluded with the admonition, 'Let this be a warning to every denomination of people against hypocrisy'.[95]

---

94 Murray, *EIKON BASILIKE*, pp. 29, 21. Evans, too, compared the English government to a 'highwayman'. Evans, *Political Sophistry*, p. 15.
95 David, *Hypocritical Fast*, pp. 18, 20, 22, 25. The background to this story, David

THE JUSTICE OF RESISTANCE TO UNLAWFUL AUTHORITY

It is now well-established that few Dissenters explicitly defended the concept of colonial independence, but this emphasis upon their moderation has obscured a fundamentally important point.[96] While the Dissenters did not advocate a program of independence, they did advocate the justice, indeed the necessity, of resistance to the government, and it is remarkable that this aspect of their thought has been largely neglected. On the authority of Holy Writ, and by simple, unmistakably clear stories of good versus evil, these Dissenting ministers taught their congregations that the appropriate response to the government's colonial policy was to resist established authority. Their viewpoint on the justice of resistance influenced their approach to domestic politics as well, and it seems to have contributed to the political independence of the Dissenting laity. The ministers' emphasis on the duty of political resistance to government thus requires renewed attention, not only because it has been overlooked, but precisely because it goes to the heart of their radicalism.

The most prominent theme of the Dissenting ministers' political theory was the constantly reiterated distinction between lawful authority on the one hand, and unjust or oppressive statutes on the other. Since most Dissenters had never accepted the justice of the penal legislation that limited their freedom, their sensitivity and unanimity on this point is understandable, and they were dedicated to teaching the laity its importance. Naturally they praised the British constitution and expressed support for hereditary monarchy, but they always insisted upon the pivotal qualification that the people possess the right to resist unjust authority. In short, 'Just government and allegiance are reciprocal.'[97] A careful exegesis of Romans chap. 13 and 1 Peter chap. 2 led Caleb Evans to the conclusion that it is the will of God for people to submit to government only insofar as it represented lawful authority and promoted the general good. The distinction between unwritten fundamental law, which includes in itself the end of government as the good of the people, and positive law enacted by government, was maintained by Murray, David, Walker, and Toulmin as

reminds his readers, is the commandment of God in Scripture, 'The land shall not be sold forever, for the land is mine', Lev. 25:23.

96 Bonwick, 'The English Dissenters and the American Revolution', p. 103. Again, this conclusion is derived from dependence on Priestley, Price, and Thomas Hollis, to the neglect of other Dissenters. Bonwick dismisses the fears of the Anglicans as unjustified with respect to the subversiveness of Dissent. 'The actual record of liberal Dissent was one of determined loyalty throughout the Revolution', p. 103. 'It is safe to say that at no point did Dissenters encourage American separatism', p. 104. Dickinson notes that the radicals went much further than Locke on the right of resistance, allowing the people to dissolve a government that did not protect their political rights, *Liberty and Property*, pp. 78, 199. On the doctrine before Locke, see Skinner, *The Foundations of Modern Political Thought*, 2: 347–8. Compare Clark, *English Society*, pp. 47–8, 207.

97 Murray, *Finishing Stroke*, p. 15; *Alarm without Cause*, p. 30; Evans, *British Freedom*, pp. 21–3; *Political Sophistry*, pp. 4–5.

well.[98] Since the power of a government is of all powers most liable to abuse, it must be constantly and vigilantly guarded, and when it ceases to be exercised on behalf of the good of the people, it thereby ceases to be good and may be resisted.

The Dissenting ministers also agreed that resistance to unlawful authority is itself lawful.[99] Evans asserted that

> The only question on the subject of *resistance* is, whether we resist a *lawful* or an *unlawful* authority: if a *lawful* authority, our resistance is *sinful* in a very high degree; but if it be an unlawful authority we resist, our resistance is glorious, though if there be no prospect of success, it may be rash and imprudent, and a quiet submission more eligible.

And who is to be the judge of when resistance is needed? Evans placed the determination of the answer to this question in the people. 'They cannot *resist* the supreme power, without at least supposing themselves *oppressed* by it.'[100] 'Those who obey the fundamental laws of government cannot be rebels', said Murray, though he added 'it is manifest that legislators that make laws contrary to natural justice and the law of God may be guilty of rebellion'. In his poem, *The Fast*, Murray put the following verse in the mouth of God.

> All just dominion hath its base in right,
> And shines self-evident like beams of light:
> Man's lusts apart, all mankind must agree,
> That only righteous power proceeds from me.
> None need dispute who has a right to rule,
> The god of wisdom ne'er appoints a fool.
> When fools wear crowns, and tyrants' sceptres sway,
> Then subjects sin not though they disobey

98 Evans, *Reply to Fletcher's Vindication*, pp. 52, 59, 60, 65; Murray, *Alarm without Cause*, p. 20; David, title pages of *Fear of God* and *Hypocritical Fast*; Walker, *Duty of a Soldier*, pp. 437–8; Toulmin, *American War*, p. 14.

99 For the lengthiest discussion of the right of resistance, see Evans, *British Freedom*, pp. 16, 21, 26–7. Evans based the right of resistance on Locke and the Glorious Revolution, Evans, *British Freedom*, pp. 14–15, and on Montesquieu, Evans, *Reply to Fletcher's Vindication*, p. 18. Evans repeatedly noted that on the basis of the principles of the Glorious Revolution, people resumed the power they originally gave when it is not exercised for their good. *Letter to Wesley*, p. 11; *Political Sophistry*, p. 17; *British Constitutional Liberty*, p. 21. But scriptural teaching was also heavily relied upon; Evans, *Reply to Fletcher's Vindication*, pp. 59–60, and Murray, *Finishing Stroke*, p. 15 on Romans 13; Murray, *Alarm without Cause*, p. 23 on the sixth commandment; on the basis of Paul's appeal to Caesar, see Murray, *Alarm without Cause*, p. 17. On the basis of the text of the Old Testament see David, *Fear of God*, title page. See also, Walker, *Duty of a Soldier*, pp. 426–7 and David, *Fear of God*, p. 18.

100 Evans, *Reply to Fletcher's Vindication*, pp. 54, 59. Evans here was a little more outspoken in 1776 than he was in his sermon of the previous year, *British Constitutional Liberty*, p. 21, where he says that resistance 'would be made as a *last recourse* and when the *probable evils* of resistance are overbalanced by the *certain evils* resulting from a pusillanimous submission'.

In yet another sermon Murray advised,

Laws that are unfriendly to the temporal interests and general good of society; laws that are made to exalt a few to power and dignity, by sponging, squeezing, and oppressing all other ranks of people, though contrived by angels, and executed by saints, are bands of wickedness, which [people] may suffer for transgressing, but can never sin in disobeying'.

Such oppression, however, is often compounded by the fact that the subjects 'are not allowed to be judges of their own abilities'.[101] Murray thereby brought the political implications of the principle of self-determination to the explicit awareness of his congregation and the reading public.

If resistance to oppression was justified, these ministers were equally certain that the oppression itself was always sinful. Dissenting pastors thus not only assured their congregations that it was not sinful to resist oppressive political authority, on occasion, they positively encouraged it as a duty. 'When mankind are once instructed in their natural rights and privileges', wrote Murray, 'they will not only complain but struggle to get clear of oppression. Wise men know what it is to obey just laws, but will never tamely submit to slavery and bondage.' Evans taught that when political authorities become ministers of darkness tending toward evil, 'the very *same reason* binds us to a *resistance* of them, as would otherwise engage us for *conscious-sake* to obey them'. In a later sermon, following the American Revolution, Evans went so far as to say that resistance to the usurpation of liberty is not only lawful, 'but highly virtuous and praise-worthy, and will most assuredly be crowned with the approbation of God and of all good men'. Conversely, submission to a wicked hereditary tyrant is so far from being a duty, it would be a 'great sin'.[102]

These sentiments were radical precisely because they were applied to the American colonists for the purpose of vindicating them. These five Dissenting ministers in the provincial urban setting explicitly instructed their congregations that the authority exercised by the English Parliament over America had become an unlawful authority, and neither reason, Scripture, nor the constitution bound the colonists to submit to it. When the trust placed in government is abused, as it was in America, the people have a right to resist, said Evans, and 'to resume the power into their own hands, and to endeavor to entrust it for the future to those who may make a better use of it'. The colonists were, according to Murray, not in reality rebels, but they were only 'created' rebels 'by the modern omnipotence of Parliament'. The present government, at least since the time of the Stamp Act, was 'more regulated by private interests and ambition, than justice and faith'. Toulmin, as always, was more moderate and put the issue in the form of a question. 'Shall we derive our hope of being happily

---

101 Murray, *Fast Sermons*, p. 22; *The Fast, A Poem*, p. 7; *Fast Sermons*, pp. 43–4. The same point is made in Murray, *Alarm without Cause*, pp. 6, 15, 21.
102 Murray, *Sermons to Asses*, p. 153; *Reply to Fletcher's Vindication*, p. 66; *British Freedom*, pp. 25–6.

delivered from impending evils, from our innocence in the present world? Can we, in the face of Heaven, declare we are not the first aggressors? I will not answer this question; I refer it to your own judgment and knowledge to decide it.'[103]

The Dissenting ministers took the Americans' side on most important issues, ranging from the Stamp Act, to the Boston Tea Party, to the coercive legislation, to seeking aid from France. Evans, for example, argued that in laying a tax on 'their unrepresented brethren' in America, Parliament sought to wield political power for their destruction, not their good; it attempted to exercise power never entrusted to it. This attempt was leading to

the destruction of that which is infinitely dearer to them than their lives, I mean their LIBERTIES. Their *religious* as well as *civil liberties*. They are not so stupid as not to know, that should an absolute despotic power be once established over their purses, they would be in a miserable plight to undertake the defense of their consciences.

Additionally, the destruction of tea was not an act of rebellion. 'For it can be no act of rebellion to resist laws that are contrary to the essential constitution of an Empire', said Murray. 'It was as much contrary to the laws of the British Empire for people to bring tea to America with a new tax upon it, as for them to throw it into the sea.' David included in the nation's wickedness and in uniting king and people in the threat of judgment, besides personal sins, such as swearing and drunkenness, the American war. 'That we are also engaged in a cruel and unjust war, is not to be denied. And it is very evident from the language of the people in every corner of the kingdom, that they consider it so.' The colonists were in the right to resist 'our design of enslaving them' and therefore they cannot be blamed for turning to France. 'They were willing to save themselves from *slavery*, in the best manner they could.' The Barons of King John offered the English crown to Prince Louis of France, and the Americans have not gone as far as these who 'laid the foundations' of English liberty in Magna Charta.[104] Finally, Murray warned that

It once happened that the violent measures of a Laud ruined both himself and his sovereign, and overset the whole fabric of episcopacy. Perhaps if such measures are again pursued, the next blow will be a total annihilation of the whole system; for mankind will not always endure an order of men that cannot enjoy their dominion and power without having it drenched in blood.[105]

---

103 Evans, *Political Sophistry*, pp. 15, 17; Murray, *Fast Sermons*, p. 37; Toulmin, *American War*, p. 14. Toulmin offers as reasons for the injustice of coercive measures, Englishmen inciting colonial slaves against their masters; popery established in Canada whereby papists are given weapons against Protestants; also vesting political power in the hands of a few men 'independent of the choice of the people'. All of this suggests that government is 'arbitrary and despotic', pp. 15–16.

104 Evans, *Reply to Fletcher's Vindication*, pp. 65–66; Murray, *Finishing Stroke*, p. 8; David, *Fear of God*, pp. 16–17, 18–19. On the use of coercive measures, see *Hypocritical Fast*, p. 12.

105 Murray, *Finishing Stroke*, p. 21.

It is little wonder that John Wesley thought the Dissenters' principles, if put into practice, 'would overturn all Government and bring in universal anarchy'. It is little wonder that John Fletcher accused the Dissenters of 'dangerous politics' and believed that they 'crowned King Mob' in their defense of the Americans and thereby seditiously encouraged 'groundless discontent'.[106] Nor is it any wonder that a dominant – perhaps the dominant – theme of the Anglican pulpit during these years was the obedience owed to government and the need for a stable social order.[107]

Eighteenth-century Nonconformists were increasingly well-informed about their own self-interests and the interests of society. Anyone with even a superficial acquaintance with sermons and provincial newspapers will attest to this emerging consciousness. But the Dissenters were clearly mistaken concerning the malevolent intent of the ministers of George III, and they advanced a radical understanding of the constitution that was considerably to the left of the mainstream. Anglicans readily commanded the majority opinion in the nation. Nevertheless, Nonconformists set forth a coherent and compelling vision that was at variance with the dominant Anglican vision and that was, in several respects, forward looking. Increasingly, the Dissenters did calculate rationally concerning their own material goals, though to be sure, they often used religious arguments to support their vision for the future. Dissenting ministers in the provinces argued that the people themselves were the best judges of their own abilities, and they were thus outspoken defenders of Lockean thought and more. They believed that independence, not subjugation, was the natural state of humankind, and what the Dissenters claimed for themselves, they claimed for others. Later chapters will show that the majority of English pro-Americans were Anglicans, not Dissenters, and yet the Dissenters provided both the dominant ideology of opposition and the bulk of charismatic leadership for the pro-American agitation. Nonconformists thereby offered a persuasive alternative political ideology and a clear example to numerous middle-level Anglicans who aspired to the same economic and religious self-determination that the Dissenters wished for themselves.

106 John Wesley, *Journal* in *Works*, 4: 70 under 14 April, 1776. John Fletcher, *A Vindication of the Rev. Mr. Wesley's 'Calm Address to our American Colonies:' In Some Letters to Mr. Caleb Evans* (London, n.d.), p. 17; Fletcher, *American Patriotism Further Confronted with Reason, Scripture, and the Constitution* (Shrewsbury, 1776), p. 38.
107 Bradley, 'The Anglican Pulpit'.

5

The Dissenting Pulpit and Political Radicalism in England

Having trained their congregations in the moral duty of opposing the government's authority in the colonies, each of the five Dissenting ministers attempted to influence the laity's understanding of government at home. Criticism of the government's American policy broadened readily into an all-embracing critique of the authority of English government, both national and local. Provincial Dissenting ministers were far removed from the centers of influence and power in London, and unlike their more prominent brethren in the metropolis, they had little contact with the great men of the age. The ideology of the Rockingham Whigs appealed to some of these ministers, but others, like James Murray and Rees David were even more advanced in their political and social views than the radical intelligentsia in London, and they were also orthodox trinitarian Christians. The provincial ministers' isolation from the central government, and, in many cases, from opposition politicians in Westminster, seems to have contributed to an even greater sense of alienation than was common among Dissenters. Their more radical views, therefore, may have been stimulated in part by their freedom from even the faintest hope of emolument or favor. Though he was a confidant of Price and Priestley, George Walker spoke with contempt concerning the 'Great Ones' of the age, the putative 'representatives of God'. At the same time, the Dissenters' radicalism was intensified by local grievances. Far from diverting radical sentiments, local issues seem to have heightened them and provoked an even more thorough-going contempt for centralized authority than was typical of Commonwealthman Whigs. The national crisis over America was interpreted through local issues, and local matters in turn were elevated in importance by finding hints of larger, more universal political significance in them.

OPPOSITION TO THE KING AND GOVERNMENT

The provincial Dissenting ministers' antipathy for the king and his ministers suggests something of the extent of their radicalism. The dominant interpretation, however, depicts the Nonconformists as moderate defenders of

159

monarchy; they were only republican in the loose sense that held that the purpose of government was the good of the citizens. They would deny, of course, that the monarch was infallible and, along with many others, they insisted that the king was always accountable. But Colin Bonwick reminds us that as late as 1777 and 1778, John Cartwright and Granville Sharp urged the citizens of London to petition the crown to pursue peaceful measures in the hope of possibly reestablishing union, and this is thought to demonstrate that the radicals had no sympathy for the republicanism of the Americans.[1] Recent studies have examined the crown in relation to the unity of the empire and have attempted to account for why English pro-Americans continued to make their appeals to the king for so long.[2] In fact, however, the colonists also appealed to George III long after they had lost confidence in Parliament.

But little has been written in detail about the English radicals' attitude toward the crown, and even less is known about the provincial Dissenters' approach to the government. In the mid-1770s, criticism of the king in any form was still a dangerous undertaking, and the prospect of prosecution for pro-American sympathies was a sobering matter. Such English radicals as Granville Sharp, Catharine Macaulay, and Richard Price feared for their liberty, especially after the suspension of Habeas Corpus in 1777. John Almon expurgated the strongest criticism of George III from his edition of Thomas Paine's *Common Sense* because of the risk involved in publishing it.[3] The writings of James Murray, Rees David, and George Walker were at least as sympathetic to the Americans as the advertisement concerning the fallen Americans that led to the arrest, imprisonment, and conviction of John Horne Tooke, and these three ministers' hostility toward monarchy matched quite well the feelings of Thomas Paine.

The radical Dissenting pulpit, however, espoused a minority position that was considered idiosyncratic and dangerous by most Anglicans. But within Anglicanism as well, one finds a wide spectrum of political conviction, ranging from radical to highly reactionary. Since attitudes toward the crown often served as a touchstone of one's political orientation, a brief examination of the Anglican clergy's understanding of monarchy will provide one means of

1 Colin Bonwick, *English Radicals and the American Revolution* (Chapel Hill, 1977), pp. 21–3, 108. He finds only about eight 'democrats' among the radicals. Bonwick believes that far from 'stimulating alienation from the existing political system,' the American Revolution encouraged the Dissenters' acceptance of the 'fundamental principles' of the constitution. Bonwick, 'English Dissenters and the American Revolution,' in H. C. Allen and Roger Thompson, (eds.), *Contrast and Convection* (Athens, Ohio, 1976), p. 106. This view, however, seems to equate the 'existing system' and the 'fundamental principles', and the Dissenters were dedicated to showing the difference.

2 James E. Bradley, *Popular Politics and the American Revolution in England* (Macon, Ga., 1986), chap. 2. Jerrilyn Marston, 'King and Congress: The Transfer of Political Legitimacy from the King to the Continental Congress, 1774–1776', Boston University Ph.D. diss., 1975, chap. 4.

3 Bonwick, *English Radicals*, pp. 87–8, 41.

surveying this diversity and it will place the following analysis of the Dissenters' sermons within a wider context of critical discourse. A sizeable minority of clergymen definitely exalted monarchy, so high, in fact, that they may reasonably be called 'Tory', if not Jacobite, in sympathy and expression. Thomas Nowell, for example, praised the Stuarts, and many contemporaries thought that Miles Cooper extravagently exalted the virtues of 'regal Government'; similarly, the archbishop of York, William Markham, affirmed his 'allegiance' to 'the king's sacred majesty', while John Coleridge explicitly approved the divine right of kings and boldly celebrated the 'sacred character' of his monarch.[4] These sermons usually provoked vigorous rebuttals from Whig or Dissenting opponents, for it was still clearly unsafe to openly advance Jacobite views. Another group of clerics, well represented by Josiah Tucker and Henry Stebbing, said little that could be construed as divine right theory, though they definitely wished to see respect for the crown strengthened.[5]

The majority of Anglican sermons were either silent on the subject of monarchy, or they were entirely conventional , one could even say 'Whiggish', in their expressions of loyalty to the crown. Beilby Porteus and John Butler are two good examples of this moderate Anglicanism. Both men championed the Whig interpretation of the Puritan and Glorious Revolutions, but while defending the policy of coercion, they were moderate in their praise of George III. Other clergymen, such as John Thomas, Thomas Dampier, East Apthorp, Thomas Maurice, Andrew Burnaby, and Cornelius Murdin put forth only conventional expressions of loyalty for George III.[6] The language relating to

---

4 Thomas Nowell (King's Professor of Modern History, Oxford), *A Sermon Preached before the Honourable House of Commons ... Jan. XXX 1772*, cited in J. A. W. Gunn, *Beyond Liberty and Property: The Process of Self-Recognition in Eighteenth-Century Political Thought* (Kingston and Montreal, 1983), p. 170; Myles Cooper (President of King's College N.Y. and fellow of Queen's College, Oxford), *National Humiliation and Repentance Recommended ... in a Sermon ...* (Oxford, 1777), pp. 2, 13, 23; William Markham, *A Sermon Preached before the Incorporated Society for the Propagation of the Gospel ...* (London, 1777), pp. 13, 19, 23–5; John Coleridge (Vicar of Ottery, St. Mary, Devon), *Government Not Originally Proceeding from Human Agency, but Divine Institution ... Shown in a Sermon ...* (London, 1777), pp. 6, 8, 9–10. For a much fuller discussion of these sermons, see James E. Bradley, 'The Anglican Pulpit, the Social Order, and the Resurgence of Toryism during the American Revolution', *Albion* 21 (1989).

5 Josiah Tucker (Dean of Gloucester), *Four Tracts, Together with Two Sermons, on Political and Commercial Topics* (Gloucester, 1774); 'Sermon 1. On the Connection and Mutual Relation between Christian Morality, Good Government, and National Commerce', pp. 17–18; Henry Stebbing (Chaplain in Ordinary to his Majesty), *A Sermon on the Late General Fast ...* (London, 1779), pp. 8–9, 13.

6 Beilby Porteus (Bishop of Chester), *A Sermon Preached at the Anniversary Meeting of the Sons of the Clergy ...* (London, 1776), p. 12; *A Sermon Preached before the Lords Spiritual and Temporal ... Being the Day ... observed as the Day of the Martyrdom of King Charles I* (London, 1778) pp. 14–15; John Butler (Bishop of Oxford), *A Sermon Preached before the Honorable House of Commons ...* (London, 1777), p. 16; *A Sermon Preached before the House of Lords ...* (London, 1778), p. 9; John Thomas (Bishop of Rochester), *A Sermon Preached before the Incorporated Society for the*

monarchy in the Anglican sermons thus reflects a political spectrum. Numerous clergy explicitly denied that they held to passive obedience and non-resistance, and yet even these ministers were on the side of strengthening respect for royal authority; a few of them were willing to place the king's authority over that of Parliament. Given the nature of established religion and the political agitation of the war years, these emphases were at once perfectly natural and readily susceptible to exaggeration by the Rockingham Whigs, radicals, and Nonconformists. But there was a significant body of clergymen whose Tory views have not been exaggerated. Thomas Nowell, Myles Cooper, John Coleridge, John Fletcher, George Horne, John Darwall, and possibly Richard Hurd, can rightly be called Tories because of the idea of the supreme power of monarchy that they espoused.[7] If there is little evidence for a new Tory party, there was an impressive resurgence of Tory ideas in the Anglican pulpit.

Clearly, then, neither the High Anglicans nor the Dissenting radicals accurately represented the dominant view of monarchy. While moderate Anglicans advanced the central and most convincing understanding of monarchy, others, on both sides of the center, misconstrued contemporary governmental practice. On the one hand, the Dissenters were undiscerning with respect to the Establishment; they failed to understand or appreciate the clear distinctions within Anglicanism. From their perspective, the sermons of High-Church clergy made the whole of the Anglican Establishment appear threatening. The point of view of many High Anglicans was equally undiscerning; it allowed for no distinction between moderate Dissenters and radical Dissenters and had little appreciation for the Whiggish moderation of the majority of Anglicans. In fact, however, moderate Anglicans not only represented the majority opinion in the nation, their political ideas corresponded most closely to political reality at the highest

Propagation of the Gospel ... (London, 1780), pp. 20, 25; Thomas Dampier (Prebendary of the Cathedral Church of Durham), *A Sermon Preached before the Honorable House of Commons* ... (London, 1782), pp. 22, 23; East Apthorp (Vicar of Croydon), *A Sermon on the General Fast* ... (London, 1776), pp. 8, 17, 19; Thomas Maurice (University College, Oxford), *A Sermon Preached at the Parish church of Woodford ... on ... the Day Appointed for a General Fast* (London, 1779), pp. 6, 8, 12; Andrew Burnaby (Vicar of East Greenwich, Kent), *A Sermon Preached before the Honorable House of Commons* ... (London, 1781), pp. 13–14; Cornelius Murdin (Vicar of Twyford and Ouzlebury), *Liberty When Used as a Cloke of Maliciousness ... A Sermon* ... (1776) in *Three Sermons, Preached on the Three Preceding Fast Days* ... (Southampton, 1779), p. 6.

7   For Nowell, Cooper, and Coleridge, see note 4 above. John Fletcher (Vicar of Madeley), *American Patriotism Further Confronted with Reason, Scripture, and the Constitution* (Shrewsbury, 1776), p. 36; *The Bible and the Sword* (London, 1776), pp. 11, 18–19, 20, 22; George Horne (President of Magdalen College Oxford and Chaplain in Ordinary to his Majesty), *A Sermon Preached before the Honourable House of Commons* ... (Oxford, 1780), p. 17 for very mild views of kingship; but for Horne's patriarchalism, see Gunn, *Beyond Liberty and Property*, pp. 168–9; John Darwall (Rector of Walsall), *Political Lamentations Written in the years 1775 and 1776* ... (London, 1776), pp. 4, 8; Richard Hurd (Bishop of Lichfield and Coventry), *A Sermon Preached before the Right Honourable House of Lords* ... (London, 1777), p. 16.

levels of the government. For example, unlike the Dissenters, they never felt the need to adopt the Whig myth of the early years of George III's reign. On the other hand, Anglican theory respecting the social order and the benign intent of magistrates was, to many lower ranking Anglicans, less persuasive than the political views of the Dissenters. Thus any analysis of Dissenting ideology must be placed within a wide spectrum of discourse that assigns an appropriately relative importance to their radical theory and its historical accuracy.

Avowals of loyalty to George III, of course, were not uncommon among Dissenters. Evans and Murray both cited the maxim in British politics that 'the king can do no wrong', and Evans in particular was quick to swear his allegiance to the House of Hanover, as were David and Walker.[8] Whigs were friends to the monarch, claimed Evans, and attached to the king, and for that reason they were no less 'the friends of American liberty'. Such friends of civil and religious liberty, 'whether Churchmen or Dissenters (for the cause of freedom is a common cause), are *upon principle* the friends of *King George*, whose throne is founded on *public liberty* and form'd for its support'. The Dissenters' loyalty to the crown in principle, however, was grounded in the idea that government is a trust and the king is under the law. 'The whole community are his superiors', wrote Murray, 'though individuals are his subjects, when he observes the law'.[9] Similarly, British kings must answer to the end of government which is the good of the people. True friendship to the House of Hanover, therefore, necessarily entailed rejecting the doctrine of passive obedience and non-resistance to the crown. The 'mutual contract between King and people' these Dissenters claimed, was the basis for the people's affection for the king.[10]

Walker, Murray, and David went further than other Commonwealthmen in their criticism of the crown. 'I am no republican, no enemy to monarchy', said Walker. He reverenced the prince

8 Evans, *A Reply to the Rev. Mr. Fletcher's Vindication* (Bristol, 1776), pp. 33–4, 81–2; Murray, *Sermons to Asses* (London, 1768), pp. 28, 50; David, *The Fear of God* (Norwich, 1782), pp. 13, 16, 26; Walker, *A Sermon Preached to a Congregation of Protestant Dissenters*, 1778, in *Sermons*, 4 vols. (London, 1808), 4: 189.

9 Evans, *Reply to Fletcher's Vindication*, p. 82; *British Constitutional Liberty* (Bristol, 1775), p. 22. Murray, *Sermons for the General Fast Day* (London, 1781), p. 25 (hereafter, *Fast Sermons*). The notion that the king has no peers and cannot be tried by his subjects is 'a maxim of human invention', said Murray; God alone is an 'infallible' legislator. See further on law being above the king, Evans, *British Constitutional Liberty*, p. 22; *Reply to Fletcher's Vindication*, p. 28; David, *The Hypocritical Fast* (Norwich, 1781), p. 6.

10 Evans, *British Freedom Realized* (Bristol, 1788), pp. 16, 21, 26–7; *Political Sophistry detected, or, Brief Remarks on the Rev. Mr. Fletcher's late Tract* (Bristol, 1776), p. 22; *Reply to Fletcher's Vindication*, pp. 26, 82; *A Letter to the Rev. Mr. John Wesley* (London, 1775), p. 11; Murray, *Fast Sermons*, pp. 25, 31; David, *Hypocritical Fast*, pp. 7, 16; David, *Fear of God*, p. 16.

who is willing to be the instrument of public happiness, and wishes not to move beyond the line in which power may safely and usefully be confided to a poor mortal. But kings are no gods of my adoration; they weigh not a feather in my scale against the public good; I do think the democratic or popular part of the constitution, to be the essence, the soul of the whole; I do think the safety of the people to be the supreme law, the supreme object; and that if kings, or whatever exalted individuals, will not enter, cheerfully enter, into this benevolent view, they ought to be considered and treated as mere expedients of public good, and be made subservient thereto.

Murray as well viewed the king as only a *'public servant* to the community', and barely concealed his contempt for 'superiors' who lived in transgression of both human and divine laws. The conduct of the government during the American Revolution brought Murray to the very edge of treason; the actions of the ministers of George III forced him to conclude, in his words, that the sovereign 'is but a child in conduct'. On the strength of 1 Samuel 8:5, David told his Baptist auditors that 'civil government may be maintained with great propriety without a King'. Many republics of Europe, he believed, also proved this. It was well to remember, David said, that 'regal authority' was clearly a token of God's indignation at the Jews. He concluded rather lamely by observing that this statement was not intended to reflect ill on those who preferred monarchical to republican government.[11]

Both Murray and David dwelt at length on the wicked kings of the Old Testament. Murray was enamored with the example of Eglon, the wicked king of Moab, and liked to reflect on the result of his death: 'I should beg the delicate reader's pardon, for making mention so often of dirt and nastiness; but as it is the excrement of kings and great men, I hope I shall be excused: This is not *common dirt'*. In Murray's fast-day sermons, Newcastle Presbyterians heard a lengthy disquisition on Rehoboam and Amaziah, the sons of Solomon, to prove that monarchs had been called to account by the people and to show 'what power' God had lodged in the people's hands. Rehoboam and Amaziah refused to redress the Israelites' grievances and the results were disastrous. Murray drove the lesson home: 'The complaints of the people are not to be trifled with; for if princes will not relieve them, they will themselves, and the Almighty will help them do it.' In his polemic against wicked monarchs, Murray also utilized the example of Zedekiah's claim to dominion, and he cited the illustration of Elisha's opposition to the king of Israel to show that it is no sin to resist royal authority.[12] David rehearsed the wickedness of Ahab and reviewed with his congregation the deliverance of the Jews from Pharaoh, 'that

11 Walker, *The Doctrine of Providence*, in *Sermons*, 4: 273–4; Murray, *Fast Sermons*, pp. 20, 28, 5; David also cites 1 Sam. 12:19, *Fear of God*, p. 12. Furthermore, David depicts Naboth, who resisted the king, positively as 'a republican', *Hypocritical Fast*, p. 16.

12 Murray, *EIKON BASILIKE* (Newcastle upon Tyne, 1778), pp. 29-30, 13; *Fast Sermons*, pp. 26–8; based on 1 Kings 12, and 2 Chron. 5; *The Fast, A Poem* (1778), pp. 13–15; *An Alarm without Cause* (Newcastle upon Tyne, 1778), p. 21; see 2 Kings 6:32.

DESPOT'. He reminded his Dissenting auditors that the Israelites 'took thirty-two Kings on this side of Jordan and destroyed them'. More to the point, the Lord himself helped the Israelites; he gave their enemies into their hands, for 'he has a right to dispose of all the kingdoms of the earth'. 'God does not regard the persons of wicked Kings any more than the meanest of his subjects.' David also mentioned Saul and recounted the details of the destruction of both him and his family. But sensing the dangerous tendency of his thought, David claimed that he did not intend to reflect negatively on 'the Royal dignity among any free people'.[13]

Even more radically, Murray taught his congregation the positive doctrine that the government itself may be rebellious. 'With regard to the charge of faction and rebellion which arbitrary rulers bring against the people, it may be returned upon themselves, where these crimes are oftener to be found than among the people.' Basing his teaching on Isaiah 1:25, Murray argued that princes were rebellious when they were the companions of dishonest persons who take what does not belong to them, or when they take more than what is justly due to them. It is also dishonest 'to promote or procure laws, that make it legal to give them more than the people can afford', yet in ancient Israel, princes were involved in such practices. 'Those who obey the fundamental laws of government cannot be rebels, though it is manifest that legislators that make laws contrary to natural justice and the law of God may be guilty of rebellion.' Second, princes were rebellious when they selfishly sought after rewards. Third, rebellion among princes was present when the laws were applied with partiality: the fatherless and widowed were either neglected, or made to feel 'all the force of penal laws when they were guilty', while those with influence were excused. Murray then concluded that princes can be rebels, and pondered whether or not they should be punished like other rebels, and if so, who should lawfully punish them: 'This question requires a little caution', he wrote, 'and must be determined by Scripture'. He sagely observed that he would leave to the Tories whether or not there was any difference between trying kings and princes for rebellion or punishing them without trying them.[14]

The most violent, inflammatory language against the government was reserved for the ministers of George III. Evans taught the Bristol Baptists that 'if we are not to be allowed to reason upon the conduct of *administration*, without being supposed guilty of personal disrespect to the *king*, farewell English liberty'. Murray adopted and preached the myth of Lord Bute's machinations and the secret cabinet. From his first political pamphlet in 1768 throughout the American war he kept up a constant harangue against the ministers of the crown – bloated, childish, cursed sycophants, who serve their own selfish ends. Through their 'uncontrollable power' these ministers 'often

13 David, *Fear of God*, pp. 1, 10–11, 13–15.
14 Murray, *Fast Sermons*, pp. 20–3.

raised such discontent in the nation as nearly threaten a revolution in government; ... neither colonies nor allies can put confidence in a corrupt, selfish administration'. At Norwich, David blamed the ministers' 'satanic advice' alone for the loss of America, and Nottingham Presbyterians heard from the pulpit that the administration's American policy in 1778 was 'the last act of public shame'.[15] As was true of opposition rhetoric in general, the administration was attacked for its dissipation and luxury that resulted in untold additional expense to the nation, and for its failure in political wisdom. Even the unsuccessful attempts at peace were laid wholly to the ministers' political ineptitude. Joshua Toulmin, who was somewhat less critical than the others, distrusted the political ability of the cabinet as well.[16]

While the Dissenting ministers placed no hope in the ministry, they still had some confidence in Parliament. 'A virtuous parliament is the security for a virtuous administration', said Walker. But the Dissenting elite also recognized the need for reform and worried about the corruption of elections. If the king was not above the law, neither was Parliament omnipotent, and these Dissenters readily admitted that there were defects in the present system of representation.[17] For example, the amount of time between elections was too great; the Septennial Act was itself thought to be a 'monster of corruption'. While they recognized that there was much corruption at the center of government, the bribery, treating, and high cost of elections at the periphery were also severely censured, and it was not uncommon for the ministers to exhort their people to shun bribery and choose worthy representatives.[18] Dissenting ministers thereby encouraged their congregations to be critical of the national government, and this criticism was applied directly to the king, his ministers, and Parliament. The Dissenting pulpit fostered critical reflection and independence of attitude with respect to every level of the central government.

15 Evans, *Reply to Fletcher's Vindication*, p. 34. Murray, *EIKON BASILIKE*, pp. 9, 12. See also *The Freeman's Magazine* (Newcastle upon Tyne, 1774), p. iii; *Sermons to Asses*, p. 99; *Fast Sermons*, pp. 2, 10, 30. In *The Fast*, p. 20, Murray likened Lord North to Sejanus, the 'prime minister' of Tiberius Caesar who fell into disgrace. David, *Fear of God*, p. 26; Walker, *Sermon*, 1778, p. 225.
16 Walker, *A Sermon Preached to a Congregation of Protestant Dissenters, 1776* (London, 1777), pp. 8, 29–31; *Sermon*, 1778, p. 216; *Doctrine of Providence*, pp. 259–60; David, *Hypocritical Fast*, pp. 7, 17–18, 23, 30; *Fear of God*, pp. 22, 25–6; Murray, *Fast Sermons*, p. 32; Toulmin, *The American War Lamented* (London, 1776), p. 10.
17 Bonwick notes the radical call for more equitable representation, annual Parliaments, and place bills. In addition, the American crisis contributed to the demand for parliamentary reform. *English Radicals*, pp. 23, 128–9. Walker, *Doctrine of Providence*, p. 275. On Parliament as not omnipotent, see Evans, *Letter to Wesley*, pp. 7–8; *Reply to Fletcher's Vindication*, pp. 65–6, 72. Murray, *A Grave Answer to Mr Wesley's Calm Address* (Newcastle upon Tyne, 1775), p. 1; David, *Hypocritical Fast*, pp. 15, 20.
18 Walker, *Speech*, 1775, in *Essays on Various Subjects*, 2 vols. (London, 1809), 1: clv; David, *Hypocritical Fast*, p. 20. Walker, *Substance of the Speech of the Rev. Mr. Walker at the General Meeting of the County of Nottingham* (London, 1780), p. 5; *Sermon*, 1776, p. 13; *Sermon*, 1778, pp. 221–2; Murray, *The Fast*, p. 8; *Sermons to Asses*, pp. 78–86, 89, 99.

THE DISSENTING PULPIT AND THE RELATIONSHIP OF NATIONAL TO LOCAL POLITICS

Most previous analyses of radical ideology have focused attention upon the political principles that applied to government broadly. The radical response to local institutions and symbols of authority has not been examined, and little attempt has been made to illumine the connection between local and national governments. In part this is related to the fact that only leading London intellectuals have been examined in detail. The provincial Dissenting ministers, however, are especially important because they linked local to national political issues. Colin Bonwick has argued that the Dissenters had a unique cosmopolitan outlook that emphasized universal matters of moral and political duty; they constantly drew attention to what they considered to be the proper destiny of the nation and empire. The recent scholarly interest in the trans-Atlantic and more extensive application of Commonwealthman ideology is very valuable in that it highlights the analogy between the colonists' position in the empire, and the Dissenters' own position, 'as an interest group pressing for Parliamentary and religious reform at home'.[19] But if Dissenters could link themselves as an interest group to imperial concerns, they could certainly see the connections between local and national politics.

James Murray at Newcastle, Rees David at Norwich, George Walker at Nottingham, and Joshua Toulmin at Taunton not only addressed the king in their political sermons; they all addressed the local magistrate, the clergyman, and the lawyer. They perceived the importance of local government in relation to their own political liberty, and more importantly, they believed that the oppression arrayed against them ranged from the highest to the lowest levels of ordered society. The oppression was of a piece. R. S. Neale has recently focused attention on an eighteenth-century pictorial criticism of ruling elites. William Hogarth's print entitled *Some of The Principle Inhabitants of Ye Moon: Royalty, Episcopacy and Law (1724)* well summarizes one craftsman's view of the nature of establishment oppression.[20] Power, for Anglicans like Hogarth, was concentrated in the Crown, the Church, and the Law, and these three institutions were in some sense a unified source of oppression. The same concern was expressed by the Dissenters: they experienced oppression descending upon them from the city corporation, the Anglican Church, the Quarter Session, and the rich and titled. When we probe below the level of the national government, we find in the thought of provincial leaders a far more

---

19 Bonwick, *English Radicals*, p. 58; see also pp. 12–13, 27–8. Bonwick sees that both the Dissenters and the colonists represented 'discontented interest groups' but inadequate attention has been given to local forms of oppression and to the way that ideology interprets and sometimes justifies interest. See J. C. D. Clark, *Revolution and Rebellion* (Cambridge, 1986), pp. 45–67.

20 R. S. Neale, *Class in English History: 1680–1850* (Totowa, N.J.), 1981, pp. 158–60.

encompassing radicalism that readily connected general political theory with local political structures that were felt to be oppressive.

Murray dedicated his sermon on the 'Lawfulness of Self-Defense' to the mayor of Newcastle in 1780, Francis Forster, Esq., and in it he exhorted local magistrates to attend to their duty and in particular to show no partiality in the discharge of their office. 'They ought to have no respect of persons, nor regard the rich more than the poor, but do justice to everyone. This will create them true esteem, and make them respected by all ranks of persons.' The conflict between the burgesses and corporation over the town moor in Newcastle led him to assert that the freemen of Newcastle were deserted and opposed by their magistrates. At Norwich, David drew a direct comparison between 'ministerial influence' at the national level and the recent undue influence exerted 'in the election of a Magistrate, not a great way from Norwich'. Walker too, addressed the Nottingham magistrates, the greater part of whom 'are the accustomed hearers of the preacher'. The reason magistrates are raised above others and committed with powers by the community is to contribute to 'public happiness', and the community thus 'demands a generous and magnanimous return for the trust it has reposed'. Though the majority of the Nottingham aldermen were Dissenters, Walker admonished them and expressed the same concern over their possible connections with the administration as David. 'Have magistrates, those immediate depositories of public order, law and manners, been wisely chosen; and the paltry view of serving some ministerial purpose, for carrying on the low work of a party, been cheerfully surrendered to the greater concerns of public sobriety, integrity and virtue?' Toulmin expressed identical concerns at Taunton, though not in a sermon. Following the successful outcome of the electoral petition of the popular candidates in 1775 he observed 'this determination gave great satisfaction to the country as well as to that part of the town, who had asserted their own privileges against the combined influence of the minister and the corporation'. He cited with approval the names of the local leaders who were active in supporting the petition and concluded:

It would be the dignity of all bodies corporate to confine themselves within their peculiar province, which is administration of justice, and the maintenance of a good police. Neither the constitution of the nation, nor that of such a borough as Taunton, invests them with any specific prerogatives in elections: but there they are on a level with any other townsman and fellow-citizens. As to the interference of the minister at an election, instead of being sought to give weight to a party, it ought to be rejected and opposed as inimical to our constitution and liberties; as transgressing the bounds of his province, and converting the power, which the people possess in the right of election, to control the crown, into an engine affecting the views and spreading the influence of the crown, to their own injury, if not ruin.[21]

21 Murray, *The Lawfulness of Self-Defense Explained and Vindicated* (Glasgow, 1780), dedicatory page. This pamphlet is a later edition, with additions, of *An Alarm without Cause*. See *Alarm without Cause*, p. 29; *Freeman's Magazine*, pp. 66, 89. In the prefa-

Of the five Dissenting ministers studied here, Caleb Evans alone had little or nothing to say concerning the local magistrates, possibly because so many Dissenters sat on the corporation at Bristol.

It was not the mere exercise of political authority in the local setting that offended these Dissenters. Their criticism repeatedly centered around three related phenomena: the connection of local officials with the administration, local corruption and influence, and the frequent wedding of secular and ecclesiastical authority. An Anglican dominated corporation at odds with a minority opposition party guided by a core of Dissenters was a characteristic feature of the large boroughs, and Dissenting ministers observed with some apprehension these monopolistic tendencies of their Anglican opponents. At Great Yarmouth the Anglican minister, Samuel Cooper, preached a sermon in defense of the government's American policy in 1782 and it was subsequently printed at the request of the mayor of Great Yarmouth. At Liverpool, St. George's Anglican Church was the preferred church of the corporation and it always sustained a unique relationship to the aldermen. At Newcastle upon Tyne, for the general fast of 13 December 1776, during which spiritual support for the government was solicited by Anglican clergymen, the mayor ordered handbills to be distributed that no shops might be opened.[22] Arrangements such as these greatly offended Dissenting ministers. Wherever there was an alliance of Church and state, clergymen assumed the prerogative of magistrates, and magistrates in turn enforced the dignity of ministers for the end of riches and preferment. In this way both became '*lords* over the *people*'. People became exposed to a double danger: they were exposed to the hearty curses of priesthood, or to the severe punishment of the magistrate. Murray believed that this danger led invariably to fear, and fear bred servility.[23] In any case, the Anglican Church forged yet another link between local and central government, and this was all the more odious precisely because it was based on religious authority.

This mixture of religious and secular authority was particularly offensive to Dissenters and led then to outspoken opposition to the secular power of the Anglican Church, the union of Church and State, the Test and Corporation Acts, and, 'Popery' in all its forms.[24] But it has not been adequately appreciated

tory material to the *Freeman's Magazine* Murray promises to deal fairly with magistrates but also to expose their 'oppressions' whenever present, p. vii. David, *Fear of God*, pp. 19–20; Walker, *Sermon*, 1778, pp. 227–30; 195; Toulmin, *The History of the Town of Taunton* (Taunton, 1790), pp. 90–1.

22 The incidents at Yarmouth and Newcastle are cited in Henry Ippel, 'British Sermons and the American Revolution', *JRH* 12 (1982), 193; 'Blow the Trumpet, Sanctify the Fast', *HLQ* 44 (1980), 53, note 40.

23 Murray, *Sermons to Asses*, pp. 155–6.

24 The important topic of the anti-Catholicism and intolerance of the Dissenters will not be examined here. John Sainsbury, *Disaffected Patriots: London Supporters of Revolutionary America 1769–1782* (Kingston and Montreal, 1987) has a good discussion of anti-

before that the Dissenters' opposition to the Anglican Church manifested itself in a vigorous anti-clericalism that was yet another facet of their radicalism. Their anti-clericalism was expressed in the local setting, but its importance lies in the connection between the Church and the national government. The local Anglican Church was viewed by some Dissenters as but another arm of the central government connected to it through the bishops in the House of Lords. The local Anglican priest was a symbol of authority and an ever-present reminder of the oppressive national Church and its restrictive laws. Anti-clericalism had been characteristic of Dissent throughout its history; it was nurtured by John Locke and other Whig writers such as John Trenchard and Thomas Gordon who were outspoken in their criticism of the Church.[25] Unlike continental anti-clericalism, however, there was little hint of rationalism or heresy in the Dissenting ministers' critique of the clergy; Evans, Murray, and David remained thoroughly orthodox in their Christian convictions. If heterodoxy is not an appropriate description of the theology of these Dissenters, their church polity, because of its radically separated nature and its anti-clerical tendencies, might rightly be called heteropraxis.

The debate over the American crisis stimulated frequent comment on matters of Church and State. The Dissenting ministers, even the most radical, often expressed thanks for the degree of freedom of worship they did enjoy, but they were not content with their legal status, and with every word of praise they uttered for the Hanoverians, they issued a plea for an extension of liberty.[26] Many Dissenting ministers had signed the petition for relief from subscribing to the Thirty-Nine Articles in 1772–3. Dissenters were chary of creeds in any form, but they were particularly opposed to an enforced adherence to a set of doctrines they might or might not agree with, and they often said so in the pulpit. Sacramental qualification for office was equally offensive since they

Catholicism in relation to pro-Americanism (pp. 156–8). Catholicism as a 'most horrid superstition', is a pervasive theme in their sermons; Catholicism has relevance to this discussion because of its purported tendency toward despotic, arbitrary rule; it was often viewed as a logical extension of Anglicanism. The Dissenters believed the alliance of Anglicanism with the state could become oppressive just as Catholicism had. See Evans, *The Kingdom of God* (Bristol, 1775), p. 11; *British Constitutional Liberty*, pp. 16–18; *The Remembrance of Former Days* (Bristol, 1779), pp. 14–15, 20, 27, 30; Murray, *Sermons to Asses*, p. 16; David, *Fear of God*, pp. 7, 12, 19; Walker, *Memoir*, in *Essays on Various Subjects*, p. xliii. Priestley was one of the few Dissenters who advocated toleration for Catholics. Bonwick, *English Radicals*, p. 201. On the contribution of these attitudes toward the Gordon Riots, see Murray, *The Lawfulness of Self-Defense*, pp. 27–8 where he encourages the Protestant Association, and Philip Hughes, *The Catholic Question, 1688–1829: A Study in Political History* (London, 1929). Martin Fitzpatrick has recently written extensively on the subject.

25 David L. Jacobson, (ed.), *The English Libertarian Tradition* (Indianapolis, 1965). See also Peter Gay, *The Enlightenment: An Interpretation, I: The Rise of Modern Paganism* (New York, 1966), pp. 371–80.

26 Murray, *Sermons to Asses*, p. 27; David, *Fear of God*, p. 13; Evans, *British Constitutional Liberty*, pp. 15, 20.

believed that people were accountable to God alone for their religious concerns. Evans and Walker were later active in behalf of the agitation for repeal of the Test and Corporation Acts.[27] Public statements concerning their legal status however, do not begin to plumb the depths of the Dissenters' anti-clericalism.

Evans' attitude toward the Church was mild, but he was suspicious of the higher clergy, the 'mitered prelate', and charged that some of Dean Tucker's 'Reverend Brethren' had encouraged coercive measures in America. He recalled the Sacheverell riots and feared that in the midst of the American crisis, 'high-churchmen' might once again become persecutors in England. Walker's contempt for the clergy of the established Church was only thinly veiled. He, like Evans, recalled how the clergy in a former era had preached the 'courtly doctrine' of passive obedience, and now he doubted whether the 'Great Ones of the Church' gave adequate attention to the morals of the people. The clergyman ought to attend to the care of his flock 'as well as the care of his fleece', but instead they spend their time 'parading at the palaces of the great'. David, the Baptist, was more radical. He believed that the Reformation in the reign of Henry VIII was merely 'a change in the form of popery'. The 'right reverend Fathers in God' had by their sermons encouraged the American war, and instead of charging the parish for the printed prayers that accompanied the day of fasting, such formal prayers should have been distributed gratis 'by way of atonement for the distress into which the nation is brought by their advice'.[28]

Murray, however, was by far the most violent opponent of clerical privilege; he attacked the 'Dignitaries of the Church of England' at every conceivable point. The servile language of passive obedience was the language of Balaam's ass, which in times past was '*brayed* out of pulpits'. Murray believed that the Anglican Church in alliance with the state was 'the *principle cause of civil* and *religious oppression* wherever it takes place'. The Church's requirement of tithes was oppressive, as was their exacting of fees of all kinds. 'Ah ye *priests*! Ye make us pay for all things; ye catch us as soon as we come into the world, and ye never lose sight of us until we return to dust. Our mothers must pay for bearing us, our fathers for having us baptized. When we are married, and when we are buried, ye must be paid.' The ready supply of money from the

---

27 Murray, *Sermons to Asses*, pp. 28–9, 147, 149, 151, 161–2, 205–6; *Alarm without Cause*, p. 21; *EIKON BASILIKE*, pp. 33–4; *An Impartial History of the Present War in America*, 3 vols. (London, 1778), 1: 414, 423. On Evans, see Bonwick, *English Radicals*, p. 210; on Walker, chap. 4 above. On the American stimulus to English attempts at repeal, Bonwick, *English Radicals*, pp. 189, 197–201.

28 Evans, *The Death of a Great and Good Man Lamented and Improved* (Bristol, 1776), p. 10; *Reply to Fletcher's Vindication*, pp. 102, 87–8: Wesley warned Evans that the Dissenters' inflammatory language might well provoke a High-Church reaction. See *Calm Address to the Inhabitants of England* (1777), *Works* 9: 129–40; Walker, *The Duty and Character of a National Soldier* in *Sermons on Various Subjects*, 2 vols. (London, 1790), 2: 435; *Sermon*, 1778, p. 194; *Sermon*, 1776, pp. 18, 29; David, *Fear of God*, p. 12; *Hypocritical Fast*, p. 11.

people led to the added abuse associated with wealth and profligacy. A '*self-denied minister of Jesus Christ*' is always to be preferred to a 'rich diocesan'. The bishops have seared consciences, 'stupified through voluptuousness', and on every hand Murray found haughty churchmen fond of power. The clergy further abused the power they were given in spiritual courts, and the alliance with the state corrupted the clergy from the lowest levels to the highest, particularly the bishops in the House of Lords and the clergy at St. James. 'To so low an ebb of estimation are the clergy in general sunk, that the *inferior* are contemptible, the *dignified* shunned as supercilious, and *Bishops* considered by all ranks, from noble Lords to the meanest mechanics, as the most *useless* order of men in the realm.'[29] There could be little doubt that those authorities in England who took the trouble to read Dissenting sermons like these viewed them as disruptive and serious threats to stability in both Church and State. Here we begin to discern the true extent of the Dissenters' radicalism.

The Dissenters' critique of the law was almost as sweeping as their criticism of the Established Church. The authority of parliamentary statutes and their execution were at the heart of the American Revolution, and in a later chapter we will see that the legal profession gave almost unanimous support to the pursuit of coercive measures in the colonies to enforce the law. These data corroborate John Brewer's contention that the radicals' criticism of the uncertain workings of the law was related to the traders' desire to reduce liability by calculating risks. But past studies have neglected two crucial areas that bear directly on the origins of radicalism: the Dissenters' unusual sensitivity to questions of legal equity, and the way in which their anti-clericalism could be connected with criticism of the legal system and its vast areas of jurisdiction. The Dissenters, of course, valued the law as a safeguard and normally worked within its framework; but their own interests would have been served better by less discretionary power and more equality and regularity. And, since law and its enforcement was one of the central ideological concerns of the Dissenters, it is not surprising that they extended their concern over the Test and Corporation Acts to the Coercive Acts and finally to the perceived harsh operation of law in general. Many Anglican clergymen and many city magistrates were also Justices of the Peace, and therefore radicals like Murray and David had little difficulty in locating the source of the legal oppression they experienced in the same lust for power they perceived in the Church and the corporation. More important to this discussion is the fact that some Dissenters saw the same oppression working at both the national and local levels. Beginning with his

29 Murray was more radical in this respect than Priestley, Caleb Evans, and Robert Robinson. See Bonwick, *English Radicals*, p. 200; Murray, *Fast Sermons*, p. iii; *Sermons to Asses*, pp. 160, 193; on tithes, see *Sermons to Asses*, pp. 53, 55, 207; on wealth, pp. 58–9, 114, 166, 172, 196–7; on spiritual courts, pp. 198–9; on corruption in high places, *Fast Sermons*, p. iv; *Lawfulness of Self-Defense*, p. 27; and for the last quote, *Lawfulness of Self-Defense*, p. 26.

first political publication of 1768 and continuing throughout his career, Murray was critical of 'courts of justice', wherever justice misfired. He lamented the prevalence even in England of subjects oppressing one another: 'They are like the *fishes of the sea*, the *great* devour the *small* – only with this difference, that we are devoured by law'. The American war only intensified his concern. We overlook vice, warned Murray, while

modern statutes, and unconstitutional decrees, are quickened with the utmost energy of power, and executed with the iron hand of rigour. Is the same regard paid to Magna Charta, the Petition of Rights, the Bill of Rights, and the Union Settlement between the two nations, that is paid to the Boston Port Bill, the Restraining Act, and the Canada Popish law? If our ancient statutes are founded in justice, these modern laws are undoubtedly subversive both of justice and equity.

On the same page Murray noted the identical disregard for justice at the local level. 'This appears to be our case at the present. A man will be prosecuted with rigour for killing a hare, or suffering a dog to follow him, when he will be permitted to transgress the moral law with impunity.' Thus people 'produce laws' for the purpose of oppressing others; 'muddy legislators' exaggerate 'modern statutes, and enforce them by the severest sanctions'.[30]

These Dissenters insisted on another crucial point: Justice is not complicated. It is infinite folly in legislators to suppose that laws can be binding on the conscience of men that are not 'immediately founded in justice'. Justice is a 'cardinal virtue' that even Cicero, the heathen, declared to be self-evident. The laws '*are* and *ought* to be the objects of every man's judgment'. Thus Murray lumped various manifestations of injustice together, explicitly condemning the oppression of judges, attorneys, and lawyers alike, with the added corollary that the public themselves have the necessary wisdom to determine basic questions of justice. Murray was one of the few Dissenting ministers to make such a sweeping indictment of the practice of the law, though Rees David also recognized that the law and the mere appearance of equity and justice could be used to conceal 'the most worthless, wicked and hardened wretches' in the

30 John Brewer, 'English Radicalism in the Age of George III', p. 348 in *Three British Revolutions: 1641, 1688, 1776*, (ed.), J. G. A. Pocock (Princeton, 1980). On the debate over the extent of the oppressiveness of criminal law in the eighteenth century compare Douglas Hay, 'Property, Authority, and Criminal Law', pp. 17–63, in Douglas Hay, et al. *Albion's Fatal Tree* (New York, 1975) with John Langbein '*Albions* Fatal Flaws', *P&P* (1983); 96–121, and Peter King, 'Decision-Makers and Decision Making in the English Criminal Law, 1750–1800,' *HJ* 27 (1984), 25–58. Langbein and King, while convincing, do not deal with contemporary perceptions of law. Murray, *Sermons to Asses*, pp. 49, 50; *Fast Sermons*, pp. 38–9, 9. Paul Lucas in 'A Collective Biography of the Students and Barristers of Lincoln's Inn, 1680–1804: A Study in the Aristocratic Resurgence of the Eighteenth Century', *JMH* 46 (1974), 227–61 demonstrates an increasingly strong alliance between clergymen and lawyers in the later eighteenth century. On the 'new legalism', see also Alison Gilbert Olson, 'Parliament, Empire and Parliamentary Law, 1776', p. 314 in *Three British Revolutions*, and note 80 in chap. 10 below.

land.[31] These and other Dissenters as well saw the corporation, the Anglican Church, and the Quarter Session, as different manifestations of the same government and equally dangerous as potential oppressors, particularly in the political setting of the 1770s.

The ministers' political preoccupations were neither merely local in scope, nor were they confined to the nation; rather, as the previous chapter has shown, the Dissenters were passionately concerned with universal questions of liberty and justice. The ministers' well-informed vision clearly extended as far as the British empire – indeed as far as humanity. But political experience at the local level shaped and strengthened their views of the nation and empire, and events in the larger world in turn influenced their understanding of local affairs. The radicalization of Nonconformity in the 1770s and 1780s thus contributed a prophetic voice to a broader general trend that would one day see the end of provincial introversion. This was a prophetic voice precisely because it did stimulate resistance to the central government, not only on the basis of local interests, as was common in the past, but now on the grounds of political principle. The question of the exact influence of Nonconformity in affecting a broader, more ideological and cosmopolitan outlook among local communities will remain debatable, but there can be no question that the provincial ministerial elite themselves transcended merely local interests and concerns. This transcendence is seen in their consistent opposition to oppression at every level of political authority, and in their equally consistent emphasis on the moral duty of the nation and the humane purpose of its constitution. A further facet of their all embracing political vision is found in their concern for the lower orders of society.

THE DISSENTING PULPIT ON SOCIAL STRATIFICATION AND POLITICAL OPPRESSION

Previous studies of English radicalism have insisted that radicals in the era of the American Revolution had little to say about social inequality. Of the two postulates of natural right theory they championed, liberty and equality, the emphasis clearly fell on the former; the only equality advanced by the radicals was a theoretical equality in the sight of God, or an equality of right.[32] The

---

31 Murray, *Alarm without Cause*, p. 23; *The Fast*, pp. 15, 22. Elsewhere Murray notes that we commit common thieves to the gallows. 'Where lies the difference between stealing from individuals and robbing the public; alas, poverty must suffer while rich overgrown Moabites are privileged to rob'. *EIKON BASILIKE*, p. 22. David, *Hypocritical Fast*, p. 14.

32 Bonwick, *English Radicals*, pp. 16–18, 256, 260. H. T. Dickinson, *Liberty and Property* (New York, 1977), p. 240. Bonwick attributes this moderation to two things; the radicals were drawn from the middle ranks and enjoyed the benefit of a stable society (p. 11); their theology emphasized the relationship of man to his creator 'making them less aware than they might otherwise have been of the conflicts possible between one social class and another' (p. 256, see also p. 15). The exact opposite may in fact be the

Commonwealthmen studied by Bonwick were middle class in orientation and while deploring corruption in the upper ranks, found virtue uniquely attached to themselves and their associates of moderate means. Different classes within a single kingdom were viewed as sharing the same interests and concerns.[33] Even radicals like Granville Sharp, who expected divine judgment for such moral abuses as the toleration of slavery, accepted the hierarchical structure of society.[34] Previous studies of English radicalism thus have found little evidence of concern about social injustice or oppression in the Commonwealthman tradition. This moderate radicalism of the 1770s is therefore commonly distinguished from the artisan radicalism of the 1790s. But to say that Commonwealthmen accepted the hierarchical character of society in which they lived implies that they found little to criticize in eighteenth-century social arrangements, or that they actually encouraged a deferential attitude among the poor. Such studies, however, have examined only the more well-known intelligentsia, while in the provinces, the obscure elite actually encouraged political independence and discontent with one's lower social standing. We have seen that James Murray did manifest a sensitivity to the oppressed, lower orders, and this sensitivity was also shared in varying degrees by a number of his colleagues. Since many Dissenters were acutely aware of the social inequalities of eighteenth-century society, their social thought has implications not only for the evolution of radicalism, but also for the question of the emergence of class consciousness; in several of the provincial Dissenting ministers we detect a startling note of hostility toward the aristocracy.

George Walker preached to a group of well-established wealthy Dissenters; among his auditors at High Pavement chapel were most of the Nottingham magistrates. His early sermons show a distinct awareness that he was

case: the more orthodox, and thus the more concerned with traditional theology, were actually most engaged in social critique. Recent attention has been paid to popular perceptions of order and disorder in the colonies. However, even in Virginia, social conservatism contributed to the limited scope of the 'evangelical revolt', among the Baptists. There was no Baptist attempt to wrest control of the central political system and no tendency toward leveling. Rhys Isaac, *The Transformation of Virginia 1740– 1790* (Chapel Hill, 1982), pp. 168–9, 171–3.

33 Bonwick, *English Radicals*, pp. 47, 95. Bonwick bases this assertion on Richard Price's *Observations on Civil Liberty*, and his *Importance of the American Revolution*.

34 Bonwick, *English Radicals*, pp. 48, 124. This, despite the fact that Sharp's later scheme of 'frank pledge' was based on equality of land holding, and he was concerned for the poor (pp. 162, 170). Sharp, like Murray, believed that the monopoly of land in the hands of a few families was one of the greatest causes of social inequality. English radicals did praise the relatively even distribution of property in the new world (*Ibid.*, p. 163). John Jebb was more radical than others in his rejection of property qualifications for the vote and John Cartwright, Wilkes, and the Duke of Richmond were more advanced than most in their advocacy of universal suffrage, but Cartwright presupposed a deferential society (*Ibid.*, pp. 18–19). But despite this, it is believed that there was no artisan involvement in the radicalism of the 1770s. (See *ibid.*, pp. 163, 134, 18–19, 131–2.) Pauline Maier, *From Resistance to Revolution* (New York, 1972), pp. 246–63, discusses at length the possibility of an uprising in England.

addressing a social elite, and at first he both accepted and encouraged a deferential attitude among the lower orders. Even the style of his sermons reflected his preoccupation with the higher strata; his sermons were elaborate and florid and thought to be unsuited to 'the lower sort of people'.[35] But between 1776 and 1784 his approach toward the poor, their virtues, and their political wisdom changed dramatically. As the American war progressed and his own political thought matured, his critique of the upper ranks became increasingly bold, and he sought finally to encourage the lower orders and extend to them the dissatisfaction that he felt with the government. Unlike James Murray, Walker made no practical proposals for the amelioration of social inequality, but he came to champion the political independence of the lower ranks in terms that were rightly considered disruptive.

Walker's early encouragement of deference among the poor is readily documented in his Fast-day sermon of 1776, but it is well to remember that by this date he had already taken the lead in the Nottingham petition of the previous year expressing opposition to the government's coercive measures. He praised 'reverence' for the magistracy and held up the necessity of people's 'respectful deference to their superiors'. He distinguished the 'higher ranks' of people from 'the middle' and from 'the lower walks of life', and directed specific and different aspects of his sermon to each of these three orders. Sin, of course, was 'equally within the reach of the highest and the lowest', since 'every class of the community' was affected by it.[36] He did allude to the possibility of aggression: he depicted 'the higher ranks' rioting 'in the spoils of the honest and industrious tradesmen', and while he exhorted those with influence to look with a 'more careful eye' over those who are 'your dependents', he did condemn the bartering of votes.[37]

Through 1778 Walker continued to accent the stratification of social groups, but by this date he believed that rank was merely a social convention. He was increasingly suspicious of the tendency toward oppression found among the 'Great Ones' and he only accepted their leadership in politics with reluctance. 'In a society familiarized to the distinction of ranks, the condescension of the Great is, I fear, the only possible cement of the more equal multitude, and necessary to give stability and dignity to their movements.' Walker's criticism of the upper ranks and their corruption bordered on contempt and contributed directly to suspicion of their motives.

35 See, as an example, Walker, *Sermon*, 1776, p. 25; and the comment in his *Memoir*, p. xxx in *Essays on Various Subjects*.
36 Walker, *Sermon*, 1776, pp. 46, 10, 15. The word 'class' is interchangeable with 'rank'. The 'higher ranks' are also called 'the polite and gay', and referred to as the 'more elevated stations of life', pp. 26, 44; the middle rank he also calls, 'the intermediate classes' who partake of 'the general range of better life', pp. 31, 44. He finds the decline of religion 'throughout every rank of the community', p. 15.
37 *Ibid.*, pp. 34, 49, 13. Since 'the principles which regulate the manners of lower life are few', religion is 'the only security of virtue' amid the populace, p. 45.

But we forsooth are another race of men! The conduct of the Great is above our comprehension, and above our censure. They are to us the representatives of God, to be worshipped with a silent adoration, and viewed not with too curious eyes. Covered with, what in an ordinary mortal we should call, corruption, we are to believe them as immaculate as the falling snow; and, like the vice-regent of God at Rome, that no inconsistencies in their private character can vitiate their public function. Or it may be, that initiated into the arcana of government, they view religion only as a creature of human policy; an instrument of state to govern that wild beast, the Mob; but think none of her documents to be directed to them.

On the other hand he had high praise for the virtue and understanding of the lower ranks, and this contributed to his confidence in their political ability.

I turn my eyes from so sickening a view, and direct it to those humbler walks of life, from which every thing great and good has generally sprung; which, however tainted with the general corruption, are not yet wholly to be despaired of; in whom increasing apprehensions may have awakened a more generous spirit of repentance; who are the invigorating soul of the community; and whose return to God and to their duty may give the law to their superiors and force them to assist in saving their country.[38]

By 1779, Walker had advanced considerably further; his address to the militia was far more radical. Here, the distinction in social ranks, while allowed, was no longer cast in a positive light but treated as humiliating and degrading.

Alas! it is too true, there is a proneness to servility, which the humiliating distinction of ranks insinuates by degrees into the most liberal communities, that makes us shrink from such sentiments [as the superiority of God over every earthly authority and the law over the king]; and there is a malignancy in power, however acquired, that is ever ready to frown upon such sentiments, and, with all the grimace of prudence, whisper that they are dangerous, invidious, and hardly to be brought forth in even the last extremities.

He defended the independence of the individual in the strongest possible terms.

Every Englishman feels that his property, his home, his thought, his speech, are his own, controlled by no lordly superior; that he can walk on God's earth with as erect a countenance as the proudest man that breathes; that he bows only to the laws, to which the greatest bow; that he enjoys an equal protection from injury; and, if he but doffs his hat to title and wealth, it is a matter of grace and favour.

Distinctions of rank in English society then must be seen as matters of grace, not social obligation, and Walker proceeded to insist that the equality of men, which is an equality of right, means that no personal differences or advantages of rank can give the possessor 'any authority' over the personal rights of another, no matter how weak the latter may be. All so-called 'superiors' are, according to Walker, 'mere expedients of public utility'.[39]

In his speeches of 1780 and 1782 Walker expressed tremendous confidence in the political judgment of the people and despised the criticism of 'those who

38 Walker, *Sermon*, 1778, pp. 190, 182–3, 191–2, 198.
39 Walker, *Duty of a Soldier*, pp. 438, 423–5. Elsewhere he calls social distinctions of superior, inferior, 'distinctions of utility, artificial arrangements for a common good, often abolished when the exigence ceased', *Speech* of 28 October, 1782 in *Essays on Various Subjects*, 1: cxxi.

move in a higher sphere'. Again in a sermon of 1784 he denied that political wisdom was annexed to social rank. In this sermon he observed that many of 'our rulers and great men' have viewed 'the mass of their fellow subjects' as 'easy and willing prey'. But Walker was quick to assert that he did not share 'their views on the people'; he recommended that the hunted be let out of the pit intended for their destruction and turned instead on the hunters.[40]

How pervasive was this contempt for the aristocratic ideal? The extent of these views in the mind of the political nation is impossible to gauge, though it is well to remember that the sermons and speeches of Walker were not only preached, but published. Joshua Toulmin and Caleb Evans, however, took a less advanced position than Walker, at least in their published sermons. They both acknowledged the reality of 'orders and ranks of men' and Evans encouraged the recognition of the social distinctions 'which providence has wisely ordained among men'. Both men were more careful to distinguish between the aristocratic ideal, which they accepted, and its debasement, which they deplored. 'Without subordination in society', Evans wrote 'the advantages of pleasures in society would, in great measure, be lost'. But he insisted that the rich and titled have no monopoly on virtue. Evans argued that the laborious curate may be greater than his 'exalted Diocesan', and the 'honest industrious, pious day-laborer, greater than the richest, proudest man in the universe, that is dishonest, indolent, and wicked'. Since outward greatness is a mere shadow compared to true inward greatness of mind, Evans posed the question whether respect was due to outward greatness when the inner substance was lacking. The answer was an emphatic 'no'. 'All the homage we may pay to false, pretended greatness, which has nothing real in it, but is altogether, imaginary, is a dishonor to real greatness, and a wicked attempt to level and destroy that most important of all distinctions, the distinction between virtue and vice, real goodness and proud impudent hypocrisy.' Evans criticized Wesley because of his very 'low idea' of the 'power of the people', and held instead that the poor are 'free agents' and if they are free from the influence of others should be given the vote. Fletcher, in turn, condemned Evans' viewpoint as inevitably levelling and aiming to 'crown *King Mob*'.[41]

Murray took a very advanced position on social issues and was the most outspoken advocate of the cause of the poor among the Dissenting clergy. He clearly sought to develop the same class or community consciousness in them

---

40 Walker, *Speech*, 1780, p. 2; *Speech*, 1782, p. cxxxv; *Doctrine of Providence*, pp. 260, 277–9; by 1785 he claimed the higher ranks were more corrupt than the lower, *Speech*, 1785, p. cxlv.

41 Toulmin, *American War*, p. 19; Evans, *The Death of a Good Man*, pp. 8–9; *Letter to Wesley*, pp. vi, 9–10; *Political Sophistry*, pp. 7–8, 11; Fletcher, *American Patriotism Further Confronted with Reason, Scripture, and the Constitution* (Shrewsbury, 1776), pp. 60, 129; Fletcher, *A Vindication of the Rev. Mr. Wesley's 'Calm Address to our American Colonies'* (London, n.d.), p. 16.

that he himself possessed.[42] Whereas the social assimilation of the Dissenters at Bristol may have contributed to Evans' moderate critique of the higher classes, at Newcastle, both Murray and his parishioners were largely excluded from social recognition and political power. Murray presupposed the legitimacy of master-servant relationships, honor and obedience to lawful magistrates, and he thereby accepted a social hierarchy of inferiors and superiors. But he was not at peace with these distinctions; he encouraged resistance to every form of injustice and vigorously pursued greater social equality for the poor. For example, he observed in a moderate tone that if all one's subjects were living in ease, the ease of the government should be in proportion, but since many were pining away in poverty, the government itself should regulate its expenditures more rigorously. In some of his writings, Murray would insist that there was no need 'to pursue leveling practices, to obtain this end; for moderation in the great would keep the poor from distress without raising them equal to the high, or bringing them below their dignity'.[43] But Murray at his more radical recommended a scheme of land nationalization that was indistinguishable from that of Thomas Spence. He vigorously attacked those who ruled without mercy by their wealth, and damned the 'long rob'd gentry' for their compliance with the government's policy that used religion to veil their aggression. The strong, in his view, were constantly devouring the weak. Powerful and ambitious men 'consider all the inferior ranks of mankind made for no other purpose than to serve the ends of their pride, folly, and ambition'. 'It is amazing', Murray observed, 'how the inferior degrees of mankind look up to those above them, from the scullion in the kitchen to his Grace's waiting servant. It is no uncommon thing to find all the imitations of high life below stairs, as many as low life above'.[44]

Since there was 'little difference between making men slaves, and taking away from them the means of living', Murray was particularly concerned about the oppression of taxes and tithes. The 'honest poor' were obliged to support the voracious lusts and appetites of courtiers and placemen. 'To support a swarm of these impure locusts, the virtuous labourer and honest tradesman must be burdened with taxes beyond all reasonable bounds'. By taxes and penalties the rich prevent the poor from hunting, reading newspapers, and riding in stagecoaches. With a brilliant insight that anticipated Marx, Murray observed that the public would be deprived of the labor of the poor if the rich

42 For comparison to a more conservative position see D. O. Thomas, 'Francis Maseres, Richard Price and the industrious poor', *ED*, 4 (1985), 65–82.
43 Murray, *Alarm without Cause*, pp. 27–9; *The Finishing Stroke to Mr. Wesley's Calm Address* (Newcastle upon Tyne, 1778), p. 16.
44 Murray, *Sermons to Asses*, pp. 79-86; *The Fast*, pp. 10, 22; *Fast Sermons*, pp. 6, 48; for additional references to the higher ranks 'oppressing the inferior ranks of mankind' see *Fast Sermons* pp. 1, 48 (Drawing on Isa. 58:5–6); *Alarm without Cause*, p. 29; *EIKON BASILIKE*, p. 25.

let them do such things.[45] Tithes, just like taxes, were particularly oppressive to the 'common people'. 'The common people are notwithstanding [European princes' rejection of the papacy] still oppressed with two burdens. The Prince lays upon them a burden of taxes at his pleasure, and the *Clergy* fits another to make it balance fairly.' Murray lashed out at those who 'love to make a *monopoly* of *privileges*'. Tithes, of course, were especially offensive to Dissenters who derived no benefit from them. 'If it be law, it is not *justice* to make persons pay for other people's *provisions* ...' With marvelous irony, Murray quoted 1 Cor. 3:22 and observed that it can be truly said of the priests of England, 'All things are yours'. The leading men of this world use religion as an engine of state policy because they know that 'the common people' will otherwise resist their authority.

In the eighteenth century, the leaders of English Nonconformity understood the protean force of religion: true religion gave virtue to the people necessary for sound politics. But religion could also be used falsely to enslave the people. Murray thought the oppression arising from taxes and tithes was pervasive; he saw their baneful influence at all levels, both local and national, and he depicted the poor 'in all parts of Britain' groaning under a heavy load.[46] Murray's thought was characterized throughout by stark polarities: rich, poor; property, propertyless; titled, non-titled; privileged, oppressed.

Murray's scathing indictment of the wealthy and the titled was almost always connected to the vindication of the virtue and wisdom of the lower ranks. As a group, the poor were virtuous. 'Although many vain men in high life despise the poor on account of their meanness, and generally speak disrespectfully of them, yet many of the poor are incapable of doing such mean actions as some of their superiors in rank are capable of: they have in general a truer sense of conscience, and are better acquainted with God.' Murray proclaimed from the pulpit that 'in times like these in which we live, the prayers of the poor are the

---

45 Murray, *Fast Sermons*, pp. 48–9; *The Teacher of Common Sense; or Poor Man's Advocate* (Newcastle upon Tyne, 1779), pp. 67–8. The authorship of this last pamphlet has been attributed to Murray: Thomas R. Adams, *The American Controversy*, 2 vols. (Providence, 1980), 2: 677, but recently to Thomas Spence, H. T. Dickinson, (ed.), *The Political Works of Thomas Spence* (Newcastle upon Tyne, 1982), p. x. If Murray was not the author he certainly contributed to this pamphlet. This is attested by the fact that he has the only signed essay in the collection, p. 59, and it seems to be further substantiated by comparing the eighteen queries 'all proposed by the Rev. J. Murray', pp. 59–61, with the queries of 'the Teacher of Common Sense', p. 1. The idea of using Dean and Chapter lands to ease the burden of the poor was Murray's idea advanced as early as 1768 in *Sermons to Asses*, p. 198. At this early stage he also asserted that possessions should be viewed as trusts for which we are accountable, *Sermons to Asses*, pp. 96–7. For further references on the oppression of taxes on 'the poor mechanic' see *Sermons to Asses*, p. 101; window and candle tax, *Sermons to Asses*, p. 47, and taxes on houses 'so grievous upon many poor families', *Fast Sermons* pp. 10–11. Murray suggests that taxes be lessened, provisions be made cheaper, or money more plentiful, *Sermons to Asses*, pp. 48–9.
46 Murray, *Sermons to Asses*, pp. 14, 28, 52–3, 55, 113; *Fast Sermons*, pp. 26, 44.

only prayers that the Almighty regards', whereas such promises are not made in Scripture to the 'noble and the rich'. But even more importantly, the poor were wise, and they did possess genuine insight into political matters. Walker shared this same viewpoint: he thought of the lower ranks as the invigorating soul of a community that alone can administer support to a suffering country in time of crisis. Of the government enforced fast, Murray said, 'If the devisors of the fast only heard what the common people say concerning it, it would astonish them. They make many shrewd remarks upon it.' In a discussion of the word 'undo' found in Isaiah 58, Murray took issue with the lord Bishop of London's translation: The word undo is 'exceedingly proper, and is well understood by the judgment of the common people: they make use of it to signify total ruin, and when they say anything will *undo* them, they mean it will ruin them. Therefore, all heavy, oppressive burdens must be unmade and not merely loosened ...' This comment illustrates at once his preoccupation with Scripture, his confidence in the common people, and his radical emphases. 'The lower ranks of men as they generally follow nature more nearly than those in high life seldom behave so unreasonably as those that call themselves their superiors: and with regard to objects of common sense, they are full better judges than the others.' Murray versified his viewpoint in doggerel:

> The poor man's interest, and his soul's as dear
> In my esteem, as those of prince or peer.
> Kings were appointed, legislatures made,
> Men's int'rests to preserve, not to invade.[47]

Rees David merely followed the lead of his mentor, rivaling Murray's invective but lacking his developed ideological foundation. Like Murray, he inveighed against 'men in power' who 'oppress, debauch, and ruin the innocent' and he included political oppression in his catalogue of sins, ranking it along with swearing, breaking the Sabbath, and drunkenness.[48] Similarly, he often expressed concern for the poor 'that are out of work in consequence of this war', and he held up justice and humanity as venerable virtues. The poor at large, he believed 'lived better before the commencement of this unnatural war, than many freeholders do', but now 'they suffer exceedingly', lack employment, and fast several times a week involuntarily. High taxes were also lamented, and like Murray, David held that the Lord especially favored the poor and would vindicate them. But this appeal to God was not a counsel of passivity since 'the lawful demands of the people' might also contribute to the release of the oppressed.[49] The anti-aristocratic tenor of the sermons of Walker,

47 Murray, *Fast Sermons*, pp. 50–1, 47, 17; Walker, *Memoir*, p. xci; Murray, *The Fast*, p. 8.
48 David, *Hypocritical Fast*, p. 9; *Fear of God*, pp. 16–17, 20.
49 David, *Hypocritical Fast*, pp. 11, 16, 29, 22, 27, 17–18; *Fear of God*, p. 22.

Murray, and David must be held in tension with the greater moderation of the writings of Evans and Toulmin, but they do, nevertheless, represent early expressions of an evolving radical egalitarianism. Moreover, the attack on the aristocratic ideal must be seen in conjunction with the ministers' anti-clericalism: the radicalism of the Dissenting pulpit clearly entailed a serious, coherent, and sustained challenge to the structure of society.

THE DISSENTING PULPIT, INDEPENDENCE, AND DEFERENCE

Walker, Murray, and David sought to foster a mentality of independent thought, not just among Dissenters, but specifically among the lower orders, including Anglicans. The explicit intention of their preaching was to motivate people toward the goal of changing their political behavior. Since these ministers had confidence in the good judgment of the people, including the poor, they encouraged independent thought and activity among the populace. In their sermons and published works they sought to bolster the self-confidence of the people they served; they encouraged them to help themselves, to be discriminating in judgment, and not to defer to the opinions of those of superior rank on the basis of rank alone. Once the people were aroused, these ministers sought to direct the laity's political activity into specific channels of resistance, both sanctioned and unsanctioned.

The Dissenting ministers' confidence in the people led them to encourage a mentality of independence rather than deference, and their exhortations often bordered on fomenting discontent. Evans agreed with Price and Priestley that a free government based on the consent of the governed tended to exalt the nature of man; it increased human dignity and incited men to emulate the best and pursue self-improvement. Political liberty for the Dissenter was understood as self-directed action, autonomous motivation, and this again worked against various forms of deference. Whereas Fletcher doubted the ability of the common people, in his words, 'to decide nice political questions' and discounted their understanding of 'the nature of the British government', Evans argued that the people can and ought to determine the legality of the actions of the government.[50] Walker was more outspoken. In a sermon of 1778 he preached against the passion 'for being all of one mould' and the 'sameness' this inevitably entails: 'Be above this servility then even in smaller matters, in the ornamental as well as the higher concerns of life; have a taste, a sentiment of your own; and think it rather a disgrace to wear the livery of the herd. Put no shackles on a free-born mind; however light, they are shackles still.' In 1784 he lamented, 'There was a time, when the meanest Englishman could judge of his country's welfare, and steadily and conscientiously pursue it.' Then Walker

---

50 Evans, *Reply to Fletcher's Vindication*, p. 69; *Political Sophistry*, p. 21. See also, *Reply to Fletcher's Vindication*, p. 71.

added, 'Your power of judgment is not diminished'; and therefore 'every moment' the people should examine the conduct of their representatives. He applauded the 'popular resentment' expressed toward a 'determined and desperate aristocracy', but he feared this resentment was ineffectual and proceeded to chastise his people for 'an undistinguishing idiot loyalty'.[51]

David recognized that such political discourses as he preached from the pulpit were bound to give offense: 'It is impossible for Ministerialists to approve of them; because they expose the infamous conduct of their patrons; and consequently tend to raise the just indignation of the people against them.' Thus when David described the American war as 'unjust', and encouraged the 'lawful demands of the people on behalf of the *oppressed*', he was self-consciously aware that this would result in nurturing popular opposition to the government.[52] Murray revelled in the role of radical politician. He forcefully sought to arouse discontent in his hearers through irony and mild abuse. In discussing the contemporary burden of taxes he said: 'All asses are not equally strong. – They should be burdened according to their strength and abilities.' Things necessary to life such as food and clothing should be gently taxed. 'The poor cannot well live with less necessary food than the rich, neither can they go naked.' He then attacked the window and candle tax. 'They enjoy no light but what pays duty to the government. I be mistaken, or perhaps they pay for their *windows* and *candles* but not for the light of them. – But the window, the candle, and the light are so nearly related, that in many cases we cannot well separate them.' Though he granted that there is 'no reasoning against power', he observed 'We may certainly complain with safety, even suppose we should not immediately receive redress.' Murray's sole purpose was to quicken the people's resolve.

We live under a government where grievances will be considered, *if faithfully represented*, and it is surely our own fault if we bear burdens. The burden is often *heavy*, and the cry *loud*, but proper means of redress are seldom pursued. It is to be feared we are not yet prepared for deliverance, for we do not apply for it earnestly, nor make use of *proper means*: we groan like *asses*, but do not bestir ourselves.

He held that to bear a civil burden tamely 'is an ass-like disposition' but 'when there is no remedy nor hopes of redress, it is christian-like to have patience, and to be obedient to the powers that are in being: but it is *stupidity* to couch down and take a burden'. Even freeholders, he thought, are far too prone to stoop down to 'any over-grown *duke* or *knight*'. Murray's condemnation of

---

51 Walker, *Sermon*, 1778, p. 224; *Doctrine of Providence*, pp. 274–5, 264–5. Walker even encouraged independence among soldiers; '… it is in the breast of a soldier to judge both of what is constitutional and what is legal; in such an alternative, a truly British army will refuse obedience even to the monarch on his throne'; one remains a citizen even as a soldier and is answerable to the law alone. *Duty of a Soldier*, p. 431, see also pp. 436–7. However, Walker was conservative to this extent; he viewed the love of property as a virtue, *Duty of a Soldier*, p. 418.

52 David, *Fear of God*, pp. ii, 10; *Hypocritical Fast*, p. 18.

deferential behavior was sweeping and applied equally from the highest to the lowest levels of government. 'What better is a *county*, a *city*, or a *borough*, than a *community of asses*, that suffer themselves to be cheated out of their privileges, by any *duke, knight,* or *'squire* that comes to *water them'*?[53]

Murray sought to enhance the people's self-esteem, alleviate their fear of independent behavior, and goad them to action. In his sermon on the occasion of the government fast he said: 'And should any tell them [the lower ranks] that they are not judges of their own rights and privileges, when they have plain statutes by which they [are] determined, they [should] consider them as ill designing persons who want to impose on them.' If there was indeed anything in government that the lower ranks were incapable of understanding, 'they were also incapable of yielding to it, because obedience depends upon knowledge of right and cannot exist without it'. Fear, too, was to be resisted, for we can see the ill effects of fear in the behavior of the courtiers of George III, 'who for fear of losing the royal favour, provoke a whole nation, and bring their necks to a block'. Among the people, fear is also debilitating; 'Fear, when it is a spring of action with respect to our superiors, produces servility without honesty, and makes men obey those who they do not regard.' Thus Murray sought to raise the aspirations of the people and defend their independence. 'May not poor people speak and write concerning their rights, though they may have little hopes of attaining them? Is it not hard, that they should both be deprived of their rights and of the liberty of complaining?' In a sermon in 1781 he boldly added divine sanctions to opposition to government; if the complaints of the people are not heard, the Almighty, said Murray, will help them obtain redress.[54]

Just as the defenders of the State Church, in the Dissenters' view, put little confidence in the people to learn the principles of Christianity directly from the Bible, so the defenders of English government foolishly denigrated the people's judgment in matters of State. Conversely, the Dissenters' rejection of the 'traditions of men' in religious matters contributed directly to their independent, thoroughgoing critique of contemporary political structures. By championing the independence of the humblest tradesman and highly esteeming the value of his choice, Dissenting ministers put the pulpit to much the same use as radicals put the press; both insisted upon the accountability of social 'superiors', and both were vehicles of securing this accountability.[55]

53 Murray, *Sermons to Asses*, pp. 46–8; 45–6; 72–3, 90, 80.
54 Murray, *Fast Sermons*, pp. 17–18; *EIKON BASILIKE*, p. 20; *Teacher of Common Sense*, p. 60; *Fast Sermons* pp. 27–8.
55 Murray, *Sermons to Asses*, pp. 176, 178. Brewer, 'English Radicalism in the Age of George III', p. 353 in *Three British Revolutions*.

PRACTICAL STRATEGIES FOR REFORM THROUGH ASSOCIATIONS AND PETITIONS

If the Dissenters were willing to work for reform within the existing structures of the English constitution, it is no longer possible to claim that they had no practical program of reform. In a political context dominated by a social theory that denied the value of popular participation and denigrated the people's political involvement as factious, Walker and Murray both articulated well-developed programs of popular resistance to government policy. In a speech on behalf of economic reform in 1780, Walker elaborated on the true characteristics of popular resistance, the sources of opposition, the nature of leadership, and the motives of the people. First, he argued that the practice of assembling and petitioning for the redress of grievances was not factious. 'Faction is a bugbear of ministers, the phantom with which they hope to fright the honest from looking with a too curious eye into their dark and wicked proceedings.' The ministers have committed 'crimes' and to be 'factious' is to be assured that we do not concur with them or abet their crimes. The 'first movers' in the petitioning agitation disavowed the charge, and the people were both convinced of the need to petition and disposed to do it. 'But I will venture to assert, that in all popular discontents, and even in those revolutions, which have often followed the too obstinate provocation of an injured people, the faction of a few never was nor in nature ever could be, the cause.' Even if the leaders of the petitioning agitation were factious, it was not faction that stirred the people's discontent. 'The great body of the people can see and feel for themselves; nor do they quit their repose, and set their face against the armed hand of government, unless irritated by severe and home-felt injuries.' If they are aroused to remonstrate 'against the misrule which galls them' they must be extremely cautious since the government has the advantage of force and 'one false step' may subject the petitioners to 'all its jealous terrours'. The people know this very well and therefore they are naturally reluctant 'to tread on this slippery ground'. For this reason it is not 'in human nature' for the people to be motivated by 'the wanton summons of a factious few, and I challenge all history to furnish one single instance of such a fact'. In addition, the discontent among the people precedes in time any ambition and interest among the leaders of popular resistance. The purpose for the remonstrance is 'the establishment of the public welfare'. Therefore, 'the discontents, the resentments, the interposition of the people' cannot be laid to the charge of 'a factious few'. The other criticism that the people's plea was ill-timed was depicted by Walker as even more ridiculous. They *are* ill-timed 'to the guilt which dreads a review, to the prodigality and corruption which will never be sated but with the last penny you have to give'. Walker concluded with the challenge that if the people were intimidated by the threats of the great, they would fall below the level of slaves, below 'the character of Englishmen' and 'the very character of men will not be left to you'.[56]

Murray made the same point as Walker on the source of popular opposition. Writing in 1768, just prior to the Middlesex election affair, he observed that oppression becomes especially burdensome when the lower part of mankind are not heard.

If they complain, they are not heard; if they resist, they are belaboured like *asses*; or if through *hunger* and *want* they should be compelled to rise up and relieve themselves, then they must wait the issue of a trial in some court of *justice* where the consequences are very visibly represented in some *late cases*. – Merciful Lord, would any people rise in mobs to disturb a peaceable nation if they could help it, who have been so ready in time of war to venture their lives for its safety? Nay, it is *pinching hunger* that is the cause of it. Some few there may be that join in riots without a cause; but the subjects of *Britain* love their *King* and *Country* too dearly to disturb their peace.

Later, in his fast sermons, Murray exhorted his hearers not to listen to rulers who seek to persuade the people that it is 'faction to oppose their measures, and treason to maintain their own rights'. As with Walker, the basis for Murray's encouragement of opposition was his confidence in the good judgment of the people. 'Rulers fondly imagine that the people are not qualified to discern the injustice of refusing their reasonable requests, and for that reason sport themselves with their petitions and remonstrances; but in this they display more their own want of judgment than the people do want of sense and understanding.'[57]

The Dissenting ministers not only recognized political conflict between social ranks, they fostered discontent, defended it against the charge of faction, and encouraged both traditional and extraordinary modes of seeking redress for grievance. First, they encouraged independent behavior in parliamentary elections and challenged their congregations to avoid every form of political influence, ranging from the pressure of the nobility to the lure of guineas. Murray repeatedly castigated the 'men of large fortunes' who 'treat their dependants like asses'.

But shall every dull d—e and heavy-handed k——t, whom providence has *curs'd* with a *large estate* have it in their power to impose one of *their friends* and creatures upon you for a member of *Parliament*, you may say, *farewel to liberty* and couch down under your burdens; like Issachar you will stand recorded in the *annals of future ages for asses*.

Similarly George Walker said that those who give their votes to knaves commit a crime: 'It is done for the poor draught of intemperance; for the wages of a day; for the hypocritical flattery of a dressed-out superior; for a promise; for a place of dependence and servility'. In this, says Walker to his Dissenting

56 Walker, *Speech*, 1780, pp. 6–8.
57 Murray, *Sermons to Asses*, pp. 49–50; *Fast Sermons*, pp. 18–19. David made the identical point against a charge of faction, *Fear of God*, p. 20; petitions are, he says, not factious, but 'the sense of the nation', 'the voice of the people'.

congregation, you betray yourselves. At Norwich, David focused on the problem of dependence in trade:

Many weak, but poor and honest men are threatened into compliance, on pain of losing their bread. And those brave men who are determined at all events to oppose ministerial influence, are sure in the end to be disturbed in their peaceable habitations: and care is generally taken to deprive them of all the favours, and customers (if in trade) that the opposite party can.[58]

To be really politically effective, voters must monitor the parliamentary performance of specific representatives, and even the person of very modest means can do this. Though Walker admitted his own rank was a 'happy mediocrity' and it might be thought that this 'does not entitle me to speak in so decisive a tone on these high and important subjects', yet he insisted that in choosing representatives, only 'ordinary talents' are required; '... it requires only an honest and virtuous intention, which is determined to pursue good, with enough of plain sense to detect the sophistry by which interested vicious men would blind the eyes of Britons, and lead them to the precipice'. At the approach of the general election of 1768, Murray believed that the whole nation knew who were '*the tools of the ministry*' in the last session of Parliament: '*Set a mark upon them*', he commanded, '*that ages to come may hold their memories in abhorrence*'. 'Would *England* desire to get free from some heavy and grievous burdens, which the poor, and even the middle ranks groan under, let them endeavour to make choice of men to represent them in parliament who will be as zealous to get them freed from oppression as their former representatives were to impose burdens upon them.' Murray also encouraged the close scrutiny of a Member's voting record in Parliament, and in 1774 he founded the *Freeman's Magazine* in Newcastle specifically for the purpose of motivating and educating the electorate and obtaining redress through turning the government incumbents out.[59]

The ordinary channels of parliamentary elections, however, were inadequate, precisely because the power to return many members was 'lodged in the hands of a few *monopolizers of privilege*'.[60] Dissenting ministers therefore often advocated the formation of political associations and the circulation and signing of petitions to Parliament or the crown. Significant petitioning movements against government commercial policy had been launched in the 1730s during the excise crisis, and again in the 1760s concerning the Stamp Act; the use of extra-parliamentary channels for seeking redress was therefore not without precedent. Contemporary critics, however, looked on such methods as extraordinary and fraught with dangerous potential for disrupting society,

---

58 Murray, *Sermons to Asses*, pp. 93, 102; Walker, *Doctrine of Providence*, pp. 276–7. See also, *Sermon*, 1776, p. 13; David, *Fear of God*, pp. 19–20.
59 Walker, *Doctrine of Providence*, pp. 277–8; Murray, *Sermons to Asses*, pp. 99, 101–2; *Freeman's Magazine*, pp. 56–7.
60 Murray, *Sermons to Asses*, p. 93.

especially in the period after Lexington and Concord. Nevertheless, the Dissenting ministers were strong advocates of extra-parliamentary political activity. In his fast sermon of 1778 Walker was aware of unrest among the multitudes and observed that if his hearers should despair of finding leaders, they must make themselves known to each other: 'assume a coat of the same colour', he said, which would be a public declaration of 'the common sentiment which animates you all'. Associating together would have the effect of dashing to the ground 'the insolence of the unprincipled, of the assassins of their country'. In addition to drafting the Nottingham peace petition of 1775 and the county association petition of 1780, Walker advocated petitioning on every possible occasion; through sermons and speeches he encouraged the expression of 'popular opinion', as he put it, in 1780 and again in 1782.[61] Murray, too, advocated from the pulpit popular opposition in the form of petitions. He repeatedly exhorted 'the whole body' of Protestant Dissenters 'to join in an *address* to the *parliament*' or the crown for the removal of their grievances. 'Instead of clamours against the court; instead of *mobs, riots*, and *commotions*, let the oppressed *ask orderly* and they shall receive', and if not, they will at least have the satisfaction that they are not asses. But Murray's concerns were not confined to the interests of the Dissenters. He found considerable reason for optimism in the recent popular petitioning agitation against the cider tax.

Those who opposed the *cider act*, and obtained the *repeal thereof* after it was passed, were truly *sons of liberty*. – They were like *Napthali, hinds set loose*; and not like *Issachar, strong asses couching down* and under unreasonable burdens and oppressions. We have certainly as good right to drink *beer* without *heavy excise*, as they have to *drink cider*.

Murray also used the repeal of the Stamp Act to stimulate his hearers into action. 'The Cyder counties have set you an *example*: they cried and they were heard. The *Americans* gained the *repeal* of the *stamp act* by a vigorous *resistance of oppression*. – Have the rest of *Britons* no burdens they want to have removed?'[62] David, Evans, and other Dissenters as well, also explicitly advocated putting forth petitions to the crown against current government policies.[63] In later chapters we will observe that the Dissenters across the land consistently took the lead in the petitioning agitation of 1775. Though others advocated the

---

61 On petitions, see the full discussion in Bradley, *Popular Politics and the American Revolution*. Walker, *Sermon*, 1778, p. 183; *Speech*, 1780, pp. 2, 4; *Speech*, 1782, p. cxxxv; *Memoir*, pp. lxxxvi, xcii.
62 Murray, *Sermons to Asses*, pp. 104–7, 63–5, 86, 100. See also *Impartial History*, p. 471.
63 David, *Fear of God*, p. 20; Evans, *Reply to Fletcher's Vindication*, p. 89. See also on the Taunton petition, Dean Tucker's challenge to the petitioners' logic, and Evans' defense, dated 27 October 1775. *Reply to Fletcher's Vindication*, 'Postscript', pp. 96, 98, 101. For earlier advocacy of petitions, see Joseph Towers, *Observation on Public Liberty, Patriotism, Ministerial Despotism, and National Grievances. With Some Remarks on Riots, Petitions, Legal Addresses, and Military Executions* (London, 1769), pp. 15–16, 19.

use of petitions on strictly secular grounds, the theological principle of the right of private judgment in these cases seems to have borne luxuriant fruit.

THE INFLUENCE OF DISSENTING IDEOLOGY ON ELECTIONS

Despite varying emphases and concerns, the political thought of Evans, Murray, David, Walker, and Toulmin was sufficiently unified to be characterized as pro-American and radical. But not all Dissenting ministers sympathized with the colonists, and it would thus be a serious mistake to think of Dissenting ideology as monolithic. We have seen that both Evans and Murray admitted that there were some conservative Dissenters in even 'the smallest *dissenting congregation*'.[64] More importantly, we have noted several Dissenting ministers, including L. L. Peters, Henry Hunter, and John Martin, who were loyalists and sought to inculcate support for the government among the Dissenting laity.[65] Martin not only preached support for the government, he based his political conservatism squarely upon his conservative theology, a theology that was indistinguishable from that of Evans, Murray, and David. He believed that due recognition of the exceeding heinousness of sin would lead one to 'a sense of his own rebellious tempers' and this in turn would invariably prompt one to submit to the authority of government; the person will then think of 'majesty without meanness, and of order without uneasiness and distress'. In every circumstance, Martin encouraged deference to superiors in matters of church as well as state. In short, the Americans' preoccupation with liberty was nothing other than 'fanaticism and folly'.[66]

Nevertheless, most Dissenting leaders were pro-American. Besides the five representative ministers studied here, the writings of well-known Dissenters like Richard Price, Joseph Priestley, Newcome Cappe, James Burgh, Joseph Towers, and Robert Robinson left the impression of a unified Dissenting party, and this perception was confirmed by the sermons and pamphlets of Andrew Kippis, John Fothergill, John Scott, Abraham Rees, Samuel Palmer, Samuel Wilton, Ebenezer Radcliffe, Benjamin Wallin, and William Turner. In addition, whereas a handful of loyalist Dissenters may be identified by a published sermon or two, the volume of written materials produced by the radicals far exceeded that of the politically conservative Dissenters. The signing of petitions by Dissenting ministers also proves that the great majority were pro-American; Dissenting ministers in the provinces were opposed to coercive measures in the ratio of thirty-two to one.[67] Finally, in chapter ten we will find a far more uniform response of the Dissenting laity in popular politics to the issues of the

---

64 Murray, *Sermons to Asses*, p. 44.
65 See chap. 4 above.
66 John Martin, *Sermons*, 2 vols. (London, 1817), on his Calvinism, 1: 107, 186, 189, 210–11; 215–16; 2: 299, 306, 447–50; on politics, 2: 140; 1: 182; 2: 545.
67 See Table 10.2 below.

American crisis in those boroughs that possessed a charismatic leader than in those boroughs where the laity were left to their own devices.

But when we turn to parliamentary elections, the diversity of Dissenting viewpoints suggests that the entire voting constituency of some congregations might be influenced to support the government in elections. We will find that while some churches were mobilized to support the politics of opposition, others stood steadfastly by the government; accordingly, the awareness of internal dissension and the difficulty of motivating voters to act independently at the polls prompted several attempts to rally a unified Dissenting vote at a general election. The earlier examination of Dissenting electoral behavior at Abingdon, Shrewsbury, Great Yarmouth, and Bristol suggested that the pattern of voting may have been habitual, but that it was consistent over a period of years, and that religious conviction contributed to that pattern. The habit of voting in favor of government candidates, however, seems to have bred a disinclination to oppose the government in a number of boroughs. But since the consistency of the Dissenting vote was based in part on a strong group identity, Dissenters as a body might be persuaded to take a stand against the government, and it is precisely this possibility that several Dissenting leaders hoped to take advantage of in 1774.

By the last quarter of the eighteenth century, general elections stimulated the production of massive amounts of political literature in the local setting, but national appeals to the electorate on the eve of a general election were still quite rare. It is possible to isolate only five such appeals for 1774, but of these, three were written by Dissenters.[68] This general election antedated by about one year the strong polarization in England over the American crisis. The Dissenters at Nottingham, for example, voted for government candidates through 1774, but by 1775 the majority petitioned against the government. Thus it was by no means clear that an appeal from progressive leaders like Benjamin Wallin, John Scott, and Joseph Priestley would have a uniform effect on the Dissenters, or indeed that it affected them at all. Though it was highly unlikely that national appeals from leading Dissenters could galvanize more than one community at a time, it seems significant that the elite even attempted it.

Benjamin Wallin, Dissenting minister at Maze-Pond Southwark, preached and published a sermon that connected America with the election and made an appeal for Dissenters to vote according to their consciences. In *The Popular Concern in the Choice of Representatives* he noted that the general election of 1774 was a 'truly critical juncture'. He warned his hearers that there was a 'connection between a right improvement of the present juncture, and our possession of everything dear, even to the freedom of preaching the Gospel'. Previously there were 'able common-wealth's men' to direct us and defend our

---

68 See Adams, *The American Controversy*, 1: 221, 222, 228, 327, for all of these but the sermon by Wallin.

liberties, but now, he lamented, there is once again just reason to complain, since 'evil men' have ascended to 'the seat of authoritative direction'.

All means in our power must succeed our prayers for the restoring our state. At this instant we can do more than barely remonstrate to God and the King. Our cries and complaints are deceitful and vain, if we are slothful, or foolishly neglect the opportunity in providence of acting for ourselves; let us up to the business in hand; now is the time to step forward and bear our part in the choice of a Senate who may revive and defend us.

He recommended that the people vote 'honestly' with a view to the good of their country, but also that the Dissenters 'exert our influence in favor of those who may be wise and good counsellors'.[69] A Quaker, John Scott, challenged the well known government pamphlet of Samuel Johnson entitled *The Patriot*; he attempted to destroy Johnson's contention that opponents of the court could not be patriotic, and he urged the electors to vote independently.[70]

Joseph Priestley's pamphlet attracted the most attention of all the national appeals. He claimed that the reason the administration was so hostile to the Americans was because the colonists, especially in New England, were 'chiefly Dissenters and Whigs'. Rather than take up arms, Priestley urged the Dissenters of England to avoid 'all undue influence' in the election but 'strenuously exert yourselves to procure a return of men who are known to be friends of civil and religious liberty'. He advised the Dissenters to examine the past conduct of Members of Parliament and base their vote on that conduct; if they had 'promoted the corrupt measures of the court' they should be avoided. Priestley admitted that he almost despaired because of the problems of placemen, patronage, and bribery, but since freedom and 'independence of mind' were so much at issue in 1774, he hoped that by admonishing Dissenters to eschew even the hint of bribery, he might persuade them to vote against government candidates.[71]

While these appeals for national electoral unity are impressive, Priestley's concern for freedom from bribery, a concern often voiced by other Dissenting ministers as well, betrays the fact that local interests, the practice of occasional conformity, and difficulties with the structure of the unreformed system could impede action on behalf of the perceived best interests of the nation and seriously damage the Dissenters' potential for influencing an election. For all of their avowed independence, the Dissenters faced enormous obstacles, both in

69 Wallin, *The Popular Concern in the Choice of Representatives* (London, 1774), pp. 2, 24, 35.
70 Scott, *Remarks on the Patriot. Including Some Hints Respecting the Americans: With An Address to The Electors Of Great Britain* (London, 1775), p. 5. It was intended for the general election but not published until after it. On the authorship of this pamphlet, see Adams, *The American Controversy*, 1: 327.
71 Priestley, *An Address to Protestant Dissenters, on the Approaching Election of Members of Parliament with Respect to the State of Public Liberty in General, and of American Affairs in Particular* (London, 1774), pp. 8, 9, 11. It was published in at least three places in America; Adams, *American Controversy*, 1: 228.

the weaknesses of human nature common to the race, and in the anomalies of the unreformed system. The Dissenting ministers in the provinces believed that the love of ease and the love of pleasure made people slaves: Murray meditated on the fear the superior ranks could instill in the lower orders, while Walker expressed concern that petitioners would be intimidated.[72] The constant exhortations and warnings of the Dissenting elite betray just how difficult it would be to enlist the Dissenting laity in a steady opposition. There was, however, no other coherent well-defined body in the eighteenth-century electorate that even approximated the Dissenters for the possible influence they could wield in elections.

These chapters have sought to underscore the importance of the outspokenly public nature of Dissenting opposition; Nonconformist ministers encouraged both Dissenters and those who did not share their religious views to oppose the government. The open criticism of the government was undoubtedly emboldening, and it was designed to be so. The plainness of the ministers' address was intended to show that the common person could understand the purported intricacies of public policy. The Dissenting pulpit thus bred a plain but contentious style of public discourse that seemed to offer to many people freedom from control, whether social or political. Additionally, Dissenters were clearly demonstrating that there was no self-evident connection between Christian faith and submission to government or deference to social superiors. Dissenting ministers thereby undercut the traditional and most well-known theological basis to a government that relied on Established religion. On the general Fast Day at Nottingham, for example, two messages were starkly juxtaposed in public: The Anglican minister, Thomas Prentice, preached and attempted to enforce the "Scripture-Precept of Subjection to Civil Government" while George Walker proclaimed the duty to criticize, oppose, and if necessary, resist the unjust encroachments of power – all in the name of religion.[73] When Christian ministers within a single city took fundamentally opposed political viewpoints, more rancorous and open debate was almost bound to follow, and even orthodox Dissenters thereby contributed to the polarization of society and ultimately to the secularization of politics.

---

72 Murray, *Sermons to Asses*, p. 10; *EIKON BASILIKE*, pp. 18–19; Walker, *Speech*, 1780, p. 8; Murray, *Impartial History*, p. 471; *Sermons to Asses*, p. 93, 79–86.

73 We find the same pattern of support for the government from the Anglican pulpit in Colchester, Great Yarmouth and other boroughs, while the local Dissenting community offered an alternative understanding of the relation of Christianity to politics. See the Anglican sermons of Nathaniel Foster, Thomas Howe, Samuel Cooper, William Hunter, and others in Adams, *The American Controversy*.

PART 2

Poll Books, Parliamentary Politics, and Nonconformity

6

The Dissenting Interest and the American Crisis in Bristol

The national appeals of Priestley and Wallin went considerably beyond sermons in support of the Americans, for they attempted, whether successfully or not, to influence the laity just before a general election. Could such entreaties, when focused upon national issues, penetrate the electorate? In the eighteenth century, the results of a general election had little if any influence on national policy, yet the Dissenters were the most widely dispersed interest group in the electorate and feared by politicians as a potentially disrupting force. Clearly by the 1760s and 1770s it made little sense to talk about 'Whigs' and 'Tories' at Westminster, but in these decades a recognizable opposition party did emerge in Parliament; though the Rockingham Whigs never developed into a popular party, they attempted to win the support of the voters in several populous constituencies. The Duke of Richmond not only identified the religious principles of the Dissenters with the Rockingham Whigs, he expected the Nonconformists to behave consistently in the electorate.

The relation between national issues and local parties can thus only be adequately addressed by examining a variety of large, open constituencies. Division lists in the House of Commons over the American crisis have been carefully scrutinized,[1] but political divisions in England's large freeman boroughs have not yet received the attention they deserve and are commonly dismissed as merely local in scope. The reason for this lies in part in the small number of constituencies that were contested over America, and it is usually held that in those boroughs and counties where the colonial crisis was debated, it was construed as only one of many issues. In the general election of 1774, for example, support for candidates who opposed the government's American policy was found in only fourteen boroughs and three counties; even in these constituencies it has generally been held that America did not play an important role in the minds of electors.[2] The motivation of electors has therefore been

---

1 *Commons, 1754–1790*, 1: 75; Mary Kinnear, 'Pro-Americans in the British House of Commons in the 1770s', University of Oregon Ph.D. diss., 1973.
2 Bernard Donoughue, *British Politics and the American Revolution* (London, 1964), pp. 177–200; John A. Phillips, *Electoral Behavior in Unreformed England: Plumpers,*

treated with some skepticism and the impression left from past studies is that electors in even the most populous urban constituencies were apathetic concerning the colonies.

Not every segment of the populace, however, can be included in these generalizations. If it is true that only a small number of boroughs manifested any pro-American feeling, within these boroughs, well-defined groups can be isolated that did take a strong and consistent stance on America. When the entire voting electorate is in view, no general election in the late eighteenth century can be construed as a contest between the government and the opposition.[3] But many individual borough contests were exactly that, contests between government and opposition, and though local issues were important, it is possible in some constituencies to examine local parties in relation to parliamentary divisions. The borough of Bristol is one such constituency.

BRISTOL, BURKE, AND THE ORIGINS OF THE WHIG INTERPRETATION OF PARTY

Bristol was, in Edmund Burke's words, 'the second city in the kingdom'. In the mid-1770s it boasted 55,000 inhabitants, and the electorate of more than 5,000 made it the third largest urban constituency in England, after London and Westminster. During the American Revolution Burke represented Bristol as Member of Parliament, and he was, by any standard, the city's most illustrious representative.[4] In his many pronouncements on English Nonconformity, Burke claimed that his views were based on his 'own observation',[5] and these generalizations were largely informed by his first extensive exposure to religion at the grassroots in Bristol in 1774. Moreover, the Whig interpretation of party was intimately connected to a positive appraisal of the Rockingham Whigs, and Burke himself was the chief Whig theorist who had labored longest in the defense of the Rockinghams. He thought he perceived a clear relationship between the Dissenters and the Whigs and his claims for the political influence of Nonconformity were sweeping. Late in his career he urged Charles James

Splitters, and Straights (Princeton, 1982), pp. 143–4.

3 *Commons, 1754–1790*, 1: 86.

4 *Burke Correspondence*, 3: 115: Burke to his sister, 2 Nov. 1774. Bryan Little, *The City and County of Bristol: A Study in Atlantic Civilization* (London, 1954), p. 327. James Sketchley's estimate of 35,440 in 1775 appears to exclude the suburbs, *Sketchley's Bristol Directory* (Bristol, 1775), p. 120. On the lack of population growth from 1735 to 1775 and the increases between 1775 and 1801 see Peter T. Marcy, 'Eighteenth Century Views of Bristol and Bristolians', in *Bristol in the Eighteenth Century*, ed. Patrick McGrath (Newton Abbot, 1972), pp. 17–18; Patrick McGrath, 'Bristol Since 1497', in *Bristol and Its Adjoining Counties*, ed. C. M. MacInnes and W. F. Wittard, 2nd edn (London, 1973), p. 208, note 1. On the franchise which allowed freemen and freeholders to vote and on the electorate see Peter T. Underdown, 'The Parliamentary History of the City of Bristol, 1750–90' University of Bristol M.A. thesis, 1948, p. 10; *Commons, 1715–1754*, 1: 244; *Commons, 1754–1790*, 1: 283.

5 *Burke Correspondence*, 6: 83; Burke to Richard Bright, 18 Feb. 1790.

Fox to work to attain the support of the Dissenters, 'who are already, I fancy, inclined to come over to you'. Burke believed that the influence of the Dissenters was found not at court, but in the constituencies; he described them as 'a set of Men powerful enough in many things, but most of all in Elections'.[6]

The Dissenters' political activity at Bristol is important because their behavior, however atypical, shaped Burke's ideas about Dissent and party, and Burke in turn shaped the views of the nation and later Whig historians. His experience as a candidate and Member of Parliament for Bristol was associated with religion from beginning to end. Burke's earliest contacts with local correspondents concerning the possibility of standing for Bristol alluded repeatedly to the political strength of Bristol Nonconformity, and even before the election, his agents assumed that the Dissenters would behave as a unified voting bloc in his favor.[7] Burke's election agents and closest confidants at Bristol were themselves Dissenters; Richard Champion and Joseph Harford were well-known Quakers, and John Noble and Paul Farr were prominent Presbyterians (the latter was assistant treasurer and deacon at Lewins Mead chapel). Joseph Smith, another Presbyterian, was Burke's host during the 1774 Bristol contest.[8] Burke was thus surrounded by leading Dissenters and it was from them that he formed his opinions concerning the political behavior of the laity.

Burke was also heavily involved with the Dissenters in extra-parliamentary politics. In the petitioning agitation at Bristol in 1775 he observed, 'The dissenters are in general perfectly well disposed. The most leading Ministers will do as they ought. Nine tenths of the Quakers will act in the same manner as I have been assured by one of the most influence amongst them.'[9] His experience with Bristol Dissenters was reinforced by other contacts with Nonconformists. When he wished to further the cause of petitioning in favor of conciliation at Nottingham, he wrote to the Presbyterian Mark Huish, and in thinking about

6 *Burke Correspondence*, 6: 15; Burke to Fox, 9 Sept. 1789.

7 *The Correspondence of the Rt. Hon. Edmund Burke*, 4 vols. (London, 1844), 1: 465–7; Dr. Thomas Wilson to Burke, 28 June 1774. 'The Quebec affair', said Wilson, 'has given an amazing turn within these three weeks to the tame dispositions of the Quakers and Dissenters who before that time were fast asleep ...' Richard Champion assured Burke that the Dissenters 'would indisputably declare for you'. Champion to Burke, 1 Oct 1774, 1844 edn. Richard Burke was certain that the Quakers were largely responsible for the success of Burke's nomination. *Burke Correspondence* 3: 65; Richard Burke to Richard Shackleton, 11 Oct. 1774. Burke later commented on the strength of the Dissenting contribution to his victory in 1774, 4: 271, Burke to the Duke of Portland, 3 Sept. 1780.

8 Peter T. Underdown, 'Burke's Bristol Friends', *BGAST* 77 (1958), 130–4, 137–41, 142–4, 147. Underdown is unclear on Noble's religious affiliation, but John Noble, esq. and merchant of St. James parish was definitely a Presbyterian. See RG 4/1830, 2497. Noble was successively sheriff, mayor and alderman. On Smith, see *Burke Correspondence*, 3: 119; Burke to Smith, 22 Feb. 1775. Harford became common councilman, then sheriff in 1779, and Smith followed him in both offices the next year. G. E. Weare, *Edmund Burke's Connection with Bristol, From 1774 till 1780* (Bristol, 1794), pp. 18, 111.

9 *Burke Correspondence*, 3: 208; Burke to Rockingham, 14 Sept. 1775.

finding someone to 'feel the pulse of the people' at Leeds, his mind turned naturally to the Quaker, Samuel Elam.[10] By 1780 Burke believed he understood the religious complexion of his Bristol constituents so well that he could distinguish between the degree of support from specific denominations.

> The presbyterians are in general Sound, and in our Interest. So are the Quakers, to about two or three; but the Quakers are not very active; and where interests are narrowly balanced, they are much inclined to caution. The Baptists and Anabaptists were originally disposed to Cruger and continue, through the means of one of their Ministers, (who is an Abingdonian &c. &c. &c.) much his friends, and ill enough affected to me. I had the most of them in the last Election rather upon the principle of Junction with Cruger than from any good liking to our politics.

Burke was somewhat less certain about the followers of Wesley:

> There is one Sect (if they may be so called,) behind; pretty numerous; and still more under the discipline of their Teachers than any of the rest – that is the sect of the Methodists. I am not yet quite certain what part they will take, except that negative certainty, that they will not take it for me.[11]

Just as his victory in 1774 has been attributed partially to the support of the Nonconformists, Burke's defeat in 1780 has been viewed as the result of their disaffection; the Bristol Dissenters reacted, it is held, to Burke's support for repeal of the penal legislation against Catholics.[12] Moreover, in Burke's famous speech in which he declined the poll – 'I canvassed you through your affairs and not your persons' – he dealt with the question of religion at most length. The Dissenting elite of Bristol, therefore, played a formative role in shaping Burke's understanding of the political influence of Nonconformity, and Burke's view in turn shaped major features of the Whig interpretation of eighteenth-century party politics. For this reason the political behavior of

---

10 *Burke Correspondence*, 3: 121, 129, 193; Burke to Huish, 22 Feb., 9 March 1775; Burke to Rockingham, 23 Aug. 1775.

11 *Burke Correspondence*, 4: 270–1; Burke to Portland, 3 Sept. 1780. The minister is undoubtedly Caleb Evans; the other reference is to the 4th Earl of Abingdon. On Wesley and the 1774 election at Bristol, see Caleb Evans, *A Letter to the Rev. Mr. John Wesley* (London, 1775), p. 23; John Wesley, *Works*, ed. Frank Baker, (Oxford, 1980), 25: 96, note 1. Burke may have believed that the Methodists were against him because of the supposed alliance between them and Cruger; but a letter of John Noble of 18 June 1780 suggests that Cruger and Wesley had fallen out over Cruger's parliamentary conduct. 4: 252; Noble to Burke, 18 June, 1780.

12 *Commons, 1754–1790*, 1: 285; 'Burke [in 1774] drew much of his support from the well-to-do Quaker merchants, while Cruger relied heavily on the poorer Methodists.' Burke's support of repeal of the penal legislation was said to have 'estranged many of the Low Church party, and caused many Protestant dissenters to regard him with suspicion'. Weare, *Edmund Burke's Connection*, p. 153. It is also supposed that the Wesleyans turned away from Burke, p. 132. Christie credits Burke's report to Portland of 3 Sept. 1780 and takes Champion's view of the strange alliance between Cruger and the Methodists at face value. Ian R. Christie, 'Henry Cruger and the End of Edmund Burke's Connection with Bristol', *BGAST* 74 (1955), 162. But this alliance remains problematic and will never be proven because of the absence of adequate Wesleyan registers.

Bristol Dissenters holds significant promise for unravelling the origins of Whig historiography. But there are additional reasons for turning to Bristol.

Next to London, Bristol had the largest and most diverse Dissenting community in England. Almost half of the chapels kept good records in our period and Caleb Evans not only preached politically oriented sermons during the Revolution, he also led his congregation at the polls. The political records of the borough are also exceptionally well preserved. The vote of Burke's chief confidant, Richard Champion, can be traced in the poll books of 1774, 1781, and 1784, but more importantly, Champion's brethren in the Quaker meeting he attended can also be analyzed and related to the commercial enterprise which so thoroughly engaged the Friends. The historiography of Bristol is also worth examining in detail because of parallel developments in other boroughs, and because it points so clearly to the need for an analysis of the electorate at the level of individual behavior.[13]

Bristol provides us with a microcosm of eighteenth-century political life insofar as it illustrates the way in which the nature of historical evidence and the interests of scholars can influence the interpretation of a constituency. Though the political life of Bristol has been the subject of massive research, conflicting interpretations of the borough in the period 1754 to 1790 remain unresolved. The earlier, pre-Namierian viewpoint emphasized political ideology, popular participation, and national party structure; following the work of Namier, scholars shifted to a stress on personalities, deference, and local needs. The first modern assessments of Bristol were based upon a cursory survey of a few of the broadsides that proliferated at Bristol elections. These scholars took the election literature at face value and gave full weight to popular party feeling. G. E. Weare and Ernest Baker, for example, told the story in terms of party conflict between Whigs and Tories. Weare wrote before the publication of Namier's research and characteristically linked the Whig theme of a two party system at Westminster with its counterpart in the constituencies to a belief in the moral superiority of the Rockingham Whigs on the one hand, and the resurgence of Toryism in the king's attempt at personal rule on the other. The Bristol elections of 1774 and 1780 were straight party battles fought on national issues; with Burke at its head, the Whig opposition contended against an oppressive Tory government over the issue of American liberty.[14]

---

13 For a general discussion of the participatory versus the deferential model, see W. A. Speck, W. A. Gray, and R. Hopkinson, 'Computer Analysis of Poll Books: A Further Report', *BIHR* 48 (1975), 64–5; and Frank O'Gorman, 'Fifty Years After Namier: The Eighteenth Century in British Historical Writing', *The Eighteenth Century* 20 (1979), 111–17. Norma Landau, 'Independence, Deference, and Voter Participation: The Behavior of the Electorate in Early-Eighteenth-Century Kent', *HJ* 22 (1979), 561–83, in calling for a modification of Speck's model, sees both participatory and deferential behavior in the electorate.

14 Weare, *Edmund Burke's Connection*, pp. x, xv, xvii, 10–11, 14–15, 18, 23, 30, 39, 121, 128–31, 162–3. Ernest Baker, 'Burke and his Bristol Constituency, 1774–1780',

This interpretation was based in part upon Weare's belief in a direct connection between political literature and partisan behavior. For example, Weare noted that Burke's 'A Short Account of a Late Short Administration' of 1766 and his celebrated 'Speech on Taxation' of April 1774 were widely distributed in Bristol before the general election of 1774. Through a simple cause and effect nexus between ideas and behavior Weare assumed that these pamphlets instructed the voters and contributed directly to Burke's illustrious victory.[15]

Peter Underdown and W. R. Savadge wrote more analytical histories of the borough and gave some recognition to Namier's accomplishments. Underdown was cautious about party alignments 'in the modern sense',[16] but the Whig tradition still controlled his interpretation of events; he and Savadge relied far more on Burke, Horace Walpole, and W. E. H. Lecky than Namier.[17] Underdown defended the ideological consistency of the two parties on the basis of the close working relationship between the Bristol M.P.s and the local political clubs, and the party ideology of political statements in newspapers.[18] Savadge did important research on the political clubs and amply demonstrated continuity in both ideology and leadership in the 1760s and 1770s, a point that was ignored in all subsequent treatments.[19] Furthermore, between elections Bristol voters instructed their Members over such issues as the Townshend

pp. 170, 171, 178, 181, 184–5, 203, 206, in *Essays on Government* (Oxford, 1945).

15 Weare, *Edmund Burke's Connection*, pp. xi, xv, xvii.

16 Underdown, 'Parliamentary History', pp. 60, 138, 286, 332–3; Underdown, 'Henry Cruger and Edmund Burke: Colleagues and Rivals at the Bristol Election of 1774', *WMQ*, 3rd ser., 15 (1958), 16, note 10.

17 Underdown, 'Parliamentary History', pp. 9–10, 36, 75–7, 91–2, 95–6, 177–8, 182, 193, 206, 211, 217, 228–9, 255, 257, 284, 286, 290, 307, 312, 324, 330. W. R. Savadge, 'The West County and the American Mainland Colonies, 1763–1783, with Special Reference to the Merchants of Bristol', Oxford University B. Litt. thesis, 1952, pp. 359, 396–402, 473–8 on Burke, Richard Champion, Walpole, and Lecky. While Savadge acknowledged Namier's accomplishment, the story of Bristol politics is still told in terms of Whig and Tory; 'of the reality and continuity of the conflicting loyalties there can be no doubt', p. 126. See also, pp. 110–11, 113, 125–6, 450, 463–4, 482, 491–2, 538, 549–50, 553. Savadge's thesis must be used with great caution; he contends at one point that national issues were far more important in Bristol than merely local concerns, yet he can say that individual contestants at Bristol carried far more weight than public issues. He is evidently not in control of his own material; for exaggerated statements and then contradictory observations, compare pp. 387, 426 with pp. 396–7; pp. 439–40 with p. 464; and p. 522 with 523. Savadge does not understand popular politics and his impressionistic analysis of the electorate and the Dissenting voters is wrong, pp. 127, 381, 393, 411, 554. Ronald H. Quilici, 'Turmoil in a City and an Empire: Bristols' Factions, 1700–1775', University of New Hampshire Ph.D. diss., 1976, provides a detailed account of the factions between merchants on the corporation, in the Society of Merchant Venturers, and in Lewins Mead Presbyterian chapel, but he ignores the larger Dissenting community and studies only the merchant voters. Remarkably, neither Underdown, Savadge nor Quilici examined the election literature, but relied instead on newspapers.

18 Underdown, 'Parliamentary History', pp. 155–64, 215, 254, 324, 404–7, 410–11.

19 Savadge, 'The West County', pp. 128, 378, 403, 364–5, 384, 553.

Duties, the Middlesex election affair, shorter Parliaments, economic reform, and opposition to the Fox–North Coalition.

Underdown and Savadge utilized the old party labels and relied upon the traditional Whig account of the changes at Court. With the accession of the new king, the time was appropriate for the 'revival in a new guise of the great Tory party which had been eclipsed and excluded from office since the death of Queen Anne'. Accordingly, the 'King's Friends' were appointed to office and the moment awaited 'to put the ultimate plan into operation'. By 1774 the Tories were ensconced as the 'Court party' under the king's personal rule while the 'Tory cabinet' derived its main strength from the landed gentry, and Parliament itself became a 'packed Tory' body.[20] The realignment of the central government meant that at the local level the Whigs were now oppositionists and the Tories were pro-government, and thus the ideological consistency between the borough voters, local party organizations, and national leaders, was maintained. Whig voters at Bristol and Whig leaders at Westminster were both involved in 'a Whig campaign to discredit the corrupt system of government of George III', and positively, Whigs, both national and local, sympathized with America and supported economic reform.[21] This ideologically based party system really only broke down in 1784 when the local Whigs found themselves supporting the 'Tory' government of William Pitt.[22]

Sir Lewis Namier, Ian Christie, and John Brooke brought a new complexity to this narrative, and with the introduction of fresh material, particularly the political correspondence of M.P.s and their agents, the old story could no longer be told in simple party terms. The purported connection between national and local political frames of reference was called into question by the introduction of personal and local factors. Namier's techniques and interests influenced the interpretation of many constituencies long before *The History of Parliament* was published and Bristol was no exception. Namier emphasized the fact that even though Bristol was politically organized, it treated its Members as agents to secure specific local interests.[23] Ian Christie examined the letters of Burke's agents in more detail than Namier; the Bristol elections of 1774 and 1780 were accordingly interpreted in terms of personalities and personal differences between leaders. While Christie recognized that the 1780 election was in some sense atypical, the Whig agents' attempts to avoid a

---

20 Underdown, 'Parliamentary History', pp. 95–6, 142, 177, 197, 206, 211. Savadge sees the government's policy as designed to keep the colonies in 'economic thraldom', 'The West County', pp. 161–2, 179, 254, 284, 292, 395, 432, 491–2, 558.
21 Underdown, 'Parliamentary History', pp. 297, 177, 230, 255.
22 *Ibid.*, p. 324. The Whig interpretation has recently been updated by Peter Marshall's pamphlet *Bristol and the American War of Independence* (Bristol, 1977), pp. 3, 6, 17, 20–1.
23 Sir Lewis Namier, *The Structure of Politics at the Accession of George III* (London, 1929, 2nd edn, 1957), pp. 88–91, 126. Quilici, 'Turmoil in a City', pp. 262, 266–70, reduces Bristol politics even further to a mere struggle for power.

contest through a compromise with their political opponents led him to deny any ideological grounding to politics and thereby to discount the connection between voting behavior and national issues.[24] Henry Cruger's determination to stand the poll by himself was motivated solely by his desire to win the election, and hence 1780 was anything but 'a straight fight between Tory friends and Whig opponents of the government'.[25] It was, in short, a contest between men, not measures. Underdown's articles of 1958 brought some balance to this interpretation of the 1780 election, but the interpretation oriented around the importance of personalities and influence generally prevailed.[26]

Although largely dependent on Underdown for details, John Brooke further advanced Namier's and Christie's interpretation. He played down the political characteristics of the two Bristol clubs and emphasized instead the discontinuity between the old Whig and Tory parties of the first half of the century and the new issues of the 1770s and 1780s. Brooke recognized the strength of the radical movement at Bristol, but stressed the controlling nature of local needs and the failure to link local matters to national issues. The grand themes in this reconstruction were twofold: Burke's inability to win his Bristol constituents over to the Rockingham party on the one hand, and the mercantile, selfish, unenlightened, and merely local interests of the voters on the other.[27] Characteristically, Brooke made only passing allusion to the political squibs and broadsides; he frequently depended on the opinion of election agents and faithfully recorded the amount of money spent on each election.[28] This interpretation seemed so convincing that even those interested in ascertaining the rise of party have conceded that local, economic matters were more important to Bristol voters in the 1770s than national, ideological issues.[29] Instead of a popular constituency with a rationally oriented electorate alert to national issues, Bristol politics had come to be viewed as dominated by local material needs and controlled by the personal animosities of the politicians. Namier, Christie, and Brooke subjected other politically vital constituencies such as Norwich, Great Yarmouth, Newcastle upon Tyne, and Liverpool to the same monotonous interpretation based upon the same kinds of samples from agents' correspondence.

Neither of the major interpretations of Bristol's political history has probed the popular side of Bristol politics adequately because neither made a serious

24 Christie, 'Henry Cruger', 155, 159.
25 *Ibid.*, pp. 160, 165, 168.
26 Underdown, 'Henry Cruger', 14–34; 'Edmund Burke, The Commissary of his Bristol Constituents, 1774–1780', *EHR*, 73 (1958), 252–69; and especially, 'Burke's Bristol Friends', 127–50.
27 *Commons, 1754–1790*, 1: 286–7, 289.
28 Brooke relies on Underdown's mistaken judgment that America was not a prominent issue in the election literature of 1774, and fails to note that Cruger was an American, a matter of no little importance to the Bristol voters.
29 O'Gorman, 'Fifty Years After Namier', 118.

attempt to understand the thought or the behavior of the electorate. Two additional dimensions need to be placed alongside the political manager, namely, the election literature and the behavior of the individual elector. A cursory study of political pamphlets alone predictably yielded an interpretation that emphasized the importance of ideology, while the study of agents' correspondence resulted in an emphasis on personality and intrigue. Yet both interpretations had a common theme: they focused upon the beliefs of the articulate elite rather than the ideology or behavior of the inarticulate voter. The first interpretation accepted the public statements of the leadership as accurate statements of fact, while the second utilized the private correspondence of the agents to throw doubt on the veracity of the leaders' public statements. The Whig interpretation on the one hand, and the school of Namier on the other, both accepted the perspective of the politicians, the one from the side of the Whig magnates, the other from the side of the government. Neither interpretation viewed political life from the perspective of the ordinary voter and both can be brought into balance only by addressing questions of popular ideology, the behavior of the electorate, and the social status and religious affiliation of individual Bristolians. This reassessment will not entail setting aside the private correspondence of the election agent, but rather interpreting it along with the insights that can be gleaned from tracing individual voters over time. By an analysis of election literature and voting behavior at successive elections, it is possible to penetrate a good deal further into party loyalty than through the traditional examination of local clubs. Since it was commonly believed that religion was one touchstone of party, an analysis of the religion of voters may contribute to new insights concerning political consistency and party continuity, and new patterns of radical political continuity may be revealed by linking petitioners and voters.

LOCAL POLITICS AND NATIONAL ISSUES

As with many populous boroughs, the Bristol electorate acted within two political frames of reference.[30] A strong tradition of local party rivalry was the most immediate and probably the most powerful influence on electoral behavior. At Bristol, Whigs and Tories in the first half of the century carefully distinguished themselves from each other by grounding their distinctive identities in local traditions which in turn were related to religious and political ideology; each party defended a separate political tradition and each gave its support to the respective political clubs. Local politics, however, could also be linked to

---

30 Underdown, 'Parliamentary History', pp. 332–3, 337 utilized the concept of frameworks, as did Phillips, *Electoral Behavior*, pp. 134, 140, 214, 216. The best treatment of Bristol before 1760 is Nicholas Rogers, 'The Urban Opposition to the Whig Oligarchy, 1720–1760', pp. 132–48 in Margaret and James Jacob (eds.), *The Origins of Anglo-American Radicalism* (London, 1984). See also Linda Colley, 'Eighteenth-Century English Radicalism Before Wilkes', *TRHS*, 5th ser. 31 (1981), 12, 15 on Tories joining the radical cause, and their use of radical tactics.

parliamentary politics, and national issues often constituted a second frame of reference. When, in the 1760s, the Bristol Whigs supported pro-government Members of Parliament, there was no conflict between local and national frames of reference. If a Member's political orientation at Westminster changed, or if the government changed and the representative remained loyal to the government, voters who believed their own local tradition to have remained the same might understandably take offense, although the question of a Member's responsibility to his constituents was a subject of considerable debate in this period, as Burke's famous *Letter to the Sheriffs of Bristol* demonstrates. As the volatile issue of representation came to the fore over the Middlesex election affair, and as the colonial situation degenerated, voters became increasingly alert to the political issues facing the nation. In populous open boroughs like Bristol, it might be possible that the national frame of reference would become more important to the voter than the tradition of local party rivalry. It might even be expected that former enemies would, in the face of national crises, be able to transcend their differences and unite in a new alignment on a national matter. On the other hand, it is equally possible that local partisan conflict could be understood as a microcosm of the larger national conflict, and in this case national issues might intensify local conflict and actually heighten the traditional lines of division. In fact it could be argued that *only* when local and national issues were believed to be politically linked could the local frame of reference be genuinely transcended. It is this last possibility that characterized political divisions at Bristol.

While the majority of eighteenth century boroughs betrayed few hints of such linkage, the prevailing interpretation of the unreformed electorate has even influenced the interpretations of populous, open boroughs like Bristol. Analyses of politics at Bristol have discounted the importance of any vital connection between local and national issues. Local matters, it is argued, played a far more important role than national issues, and, in the end, personalities appear to have been more important to the outcome of some elections than either local party loyalty or the American crisis.[31] Any analysis of Bristol politics in the period 1754 to 1784 must therefore give careful attention to local party organizations, national issues, and the personalities of Bristol representatives.

The various ways in which national issues could be linked to local politics will also require attention. Provincial newspapers were proliferating in the 1770s; news of events affecting the nation was thus more readily available than ever before and Bristol had two newspapers that advanced opposing political viewpoints.[32] Edmund Burke was a nationally known figure in 1774 and he

31 Sir Lewis Namier, *The Structure of Politics*, p. 89; *Commons, 1754–1790*, 1: 283–9; Christie, 'Henry Cruger', 155, 159; Quilici, 'Turmoil in a City', p. 258.
32 John Brewer, *Party Ideology and Popular Politics at the Accession of George III* (Cambridge, 1976), pp. 139–48; Peter T. Marcy, 'A Chapter in the History of the "Bristol Hogs". A Social and Economic History of Bristol 1740–1780', Claremont

explicitly attempted to raise the national awareness of his constituents. Dissenting ministers were also alert to the value of a national agitation for political change; in 1772 they concluded a national canvass for support for relief from subscription to the Thirty-Nine Articles. These ministers also viewed themselves as the chief defenders of the nation's liberties. On the other hand, local bodies concerned with law and order such as the Anglican Church and the city corporation, were especially sensitive to the threat to law they perceived in the colonial resistance to Parliament. Above all, the abundant election literature requires careful scrutiny, for it was the borough voter himself who reflected most seriously on the connection between his own political act and the future of his country.

THE LOCAL FRAMEWORK: CHAPELS, CLUBS, AND SOCIETIES

Bristol's electorate was so large and unwieldy that sophisticated political organizations developed early in the century, and political life traditionally revolved around two evenly balanced parties. But it was not merely the difficulty of managing a cumbersome electorate that led to political bifurcation. Religious differences contributed to the rivalry between Whig and Tory, and when the religious superstructure of these parties is recognized, both the coherence and the intensity of party feeling become more explicable.

By 1775, virtually every variety of English Dissent could be found in Bristol. In comparison to other boroughs, Bristol's Nonconformist community was not only diverse, but large and wealthy.[33] The Presbyterians at Lewins Mead, for example, were especially noted for their wealth. Presbyterians included many of Bristol's leading merchants and they were also unusually prominent as mayors in the period of the American Revolution; moreover, during the 1770s the Nonconformists treated one of the two sheriff's posts as their own. Lewins Mead was closely affiliated with a second, smaller Presbyterian chapel in Tucker Street, and the drift into Unitarianism seems not to have stifled Presbyterian growth; the Lewins Mead congregation built a new chapel in 1788–90 to accommodate the increase in membership.[34] The Baptists also experienced

Graduate School Ph.D. diss., 1964, appendix 1, on newspapers. Jonathan Barry, 'Culture and Society in Bristol, 1660–1760', Oxford University, D. Phil. thesis, 1985, pp. 69–128, 'The Impact of the Printed Word.' *Felix Farley's Bristol Journal* was the conservative organ; the *Bristol Gazette*, the Whig.

33 Josiah Thompson, (ed.), 'History of Protestant Dissenting Congregations', 5 vols. (1772 –) MS. 38.7–11, (hereafter cited as Thompson, History), 2: 151; Jerom Murch, *A History of the Presbyterian and General Baptist Churches in the West of England* (London, 1835), pp. 112–17; J. G. Fuller, *The Rise and Progress of Dissent in Bristol Chiefly in Relation to the Broadmead Church* (London, 1840), pp. 6–7; J. F. Nicholls and John Taylor, *Bristol Past and Present*, 3 vols. (Bristol, 1881), 2: 295; William Mathews, *The New History, Survey and Description of the City and Suburbs of Bristol* (Bristol, 1794), pp. 79–80; Little, *The City and County of Bristol*, p. 194.

34 O. M. Griffiths, 'Side Lights on the History of Presbyterian-Unitarianism from the

substantial growth in the eighteenth century. Caleb Evans' congregation, Broad Mead chapel, was the largest of three Baptist chapels, and it added new galleries in 1732 and 1746. In 1764 the entire structure was rebuilt and greatly enlarged. Relations between the Pithay chapel and Broad Mead were cordial (both were Calvinistic), while the third Baptist chapel in Callowhill Street offered a place of refuge for the General Baptists.[35] The Congregationalists were represented by a chapel in Castle Green, a group which was earlier denominated Presbyterian, but had broken from Unitarianism and become Independent.[36] It is a point of some importance for the political history of the borough that the Dissenters were not evenly dispersed throughout the population; the majority of Presbyterians, for example, resided in the northern parish of St. James, and the Baptists were found in greatest numbers in the eastern parish of St. Philip and Jacob.

The Bristol Quakers had two meeting houses, one in the Friars, and the other in Temple Street, and they, like the Presbyterians, were often noted for their wealth. Bristol was the home of the first building in England set apart for the followers of Wesley in 1739, and by 1773, Bristolians in Wesley's societies numbered 1,360 with four Methodist preachers. George Whitefield established a 'Calvinistical Methodist' work in Bristol in 1752 at his 'Tabernacle', and in 1775 Lady Huntingdon's connection opened a chapel in St. Augustine's parish.[37]

A survey of the Dissenting vote in the first quarter of the century revealed that quite apart from these newer, eighteenth-century 'Dissenters', old Dissent alone numbered about 700 voters; in addition, it was believed that 'many of these by their estates and interest in trade, can make as many as 100 more votes'.[38] The Dissenters thereby comprised nearly twenty percent of the resi-

Records of Lewin's Mead Chapel, Bristol', *UHST* 6 (1936), 122; for a full discussion of office holding see chap. 1 above. The new chapel could seat 1,000 people. Murch, *A History of the Presbyterian and General Baptist Churches*, p. 117. J. Latimer, *The Annals of Bristol in the Eighteenth Century* (Frome, 1893), p. 483.

35 Thompson, History, 2: 146–8, 137–8; Fuller, *The Rise and Progress of Dissent*, pp. 186, 233; F. Essex Lewis, 'Broadmead Records', *BQ*, 10 (1941), 225; Gordon Hamlin, 'The Pithay Chapel, Bristol', *BQ* 15 (1946), 378. On the Callowhill Chapel see Thompson, History, 2: 140–1; Fuller, *The Rise and Progress of Dissent*, p. 237; John Evans, *The History of Bristol, Civil and Ecclesiastical*, 2 vols. (Bristol, 1816), 2: 327.

36 John Evans, List of Dissenting Congregations and Ministers in England and Wales (1715–1729), MS. 38.4 (hereafter cited as the Evans List), p. 146.

37 The Evans List, p. 146; Nicholls and Taylor, *Bristol Past and Present*, 2: 288, 298, 303–4; Little, *The City and County of Bristol*, pp. 195, 197; Josiah Thompson, List of Protestant Dissenting Congregations in England and Wales (1772–1773), MS. 38.6 (hereafter cited as Thompson List), p. 106; Latimer, *The Annals of Bristol*, pp. 155, 421. Two groups of Protestants were not strictly English Nonconformists: A French chapel was begun in 1727 in St. Augustine's parish and in 1757 the Moravians, or United Brethren, opened a chapel in upper Maudlin Street, St. James parish.

38 The Evans List, p. 146. In 1715, Isaac Noble, pastor of the Castle Green chapel,

dent electorate and commanded even more votes by their influence. This religious contingent was large enough to be a decisive factor in contested parliamentary elections if its votes were used coherently as a bloc. The nature of the surviving chapel records allows only a small fraction of the Dissenting voters to be identified in the four surviving poll books. The non-parochial registers that include occupational data are in fact available for only six of the eleven chapels, and in some cases even these data are fragmentary.[39] However, the Dissenters that can be identified in the poll books voted so consistently that one may infer that the entire Dissenting electorate voted as a bloc, and it is this coherence that holds the most promise for explaining many of the vicissitudes of parliamentary politics in Bristol. In an early eighteenth-century political canvass of the borough, Isaac Noble, a Congregational pastor, believed that the Dissenting vote was stronger than that of the 'low-church party' but he assumed that the two groups would act in concert at the polls.[40]

The complexity of Bristol's political life was conducive to the early development of political clubs. With Dissenting and Low-Church support, the Whigs organized the Union Club in the 1730s at the Bush Tavern, while in the same decade, the Tories founded the Steadfast Society at the White Lyon. The Nonconformist leadership of the Union Club is well attested: of the fourteen committee members called to work out a compromise with the Tories in 1781, fully eleven were Dissenters.[41] Similarly, the consistent support the Anglican clergy gave to the opposing party is well attested in the poll books, and the election literature, as we shall see, utilizes the old party terminology well into the 1780s. These clubs attempted to organize the electoral interests of their parties, they sponsored candidates for Parliament, supported them financially, sent instructions, sometimes channeled patronage, and occasionally sought to influence national legislation. The records of the Steadfast Society indicate that it met regularly on a weekly basis, though its activities lapsed for years at a time in

estimated the Dissenters at Bristol as numbering between 5,800 and 6,300 (two estimates are given for the Baptist chapels) and the 'worth' of each congregation was estimated for a total of £1,200,000. The Evans List, p. 146. By 1816, Evans found it difficult to discern whether the Anglicans or the Dissenters were more numerous, *The History of Bristol*, 2: 99.

39 Records covering the appropriate years are available for Lewins Mead, Castle Green, the Broad Mead and Pithay chapels combined, and the Quakers (the Friars and Temple Street combined). For the Baptists, however, only about half of the entries in the two registers record occupations, and the Castle Green register begins in 1785, thereby allowing only a few links with the poll books.

40 The Evans List, p. 147.

41 Nine were Presbyterian, one a Quaker, and one a Congregationalist. Savadge, 'The West County', p. 130. For the prominence of Nonconformist leadership in 1774, see pp. 381, note 1, and 396. Roger's contention that the Steadfast Society broke significantly with its predecessor's High Churchmanship in 1737 is not convincing. It continued, for example, to insist on the Test Act. 'The Urban Opposition', 138–9.

the second half of the century. The records of the Union Club have not survived, but its history can largely be reconstructed from the correspondence of its spokesmen.[42] Some voters regularly expressed resentment over the club's nomination of candidates claiming that the caucus effectively disenfranchised them. Thus despite the fact that Bristol was more politically organized than most boroughs, there were many independent freemen who resented even this element of control and insisted upon maintaining the widest possible range of choices.

The clubs were naturally most active at election time, and their most important task was settling upon candidates for a contested election. The enormous expense of contests at Bristol, combined with the very real threat of a general disruption of society, led the clubs to a second, related duty, namely, the attempt to reach a compromise whereby each party would be satisfied with a single candidate. A compromise between the clubs was sought in 1754 and again in 1756, but in each case without ultimate success, and these two elections were said to have cost the Whigs alone £60,000. This enormous expense resulted in a more effective agreement in 1756 that was consolidated in 1766.[43] The agreement contributed to a lapse in the activity of the Steadfast Society from 1769–75. The club resumed its business in January 1775, but no satisfying reason has ever been advanced for why the local party did not introduce their organizational machinery in the contest of 1774. In early 1780 the club was once again in full-force; it was renamed the Loyal and Constitutional Club and much credit for the victory of the government candidates in this election must go to the excellent organization of this refurbished club. By 1781, the Union Club was also once again an important political organ, and attempts at compromise in both 1780 and 1781 should in no wise be construed as representing an absence of party rivalry, but rather its intensity.[44] Compromises were sought precisely because of the rage of the party, the threat of violence, and the exorbitant expense of contested elections. In the decade of the 1780s, the Union Club had more difficulty than the Loyal and Constitutional Club

---

42 Underdown, 'Parliamentary History', pp. 6–9; on the close relationship between the Steadfast Society and the 'Tory' Members see pp. 8, 45–6, 48, 54–5, 92, 179, 287, 291; on the Union Club, pp. 75–7, 85, 91. On the continuity of the political orientation and leadership of the clubs in the 1760s and 1770s, see Savadge, 'The West County', pp. 10–11, 127–31, 378–9, 381–2, 403, 406, 415, 465–7.

43 Underdown, 'Parliamentary History', pp. 44, 56, 93–4. See also Underdown's appendix which reproduces the agreements. Savadge, 'The West County', p. 354.

44 Underdown, 'Parliamentary History', pp. 179–80, 287, 304–5. *The Bristol Contest; Containing a Particular Account of the Proceedings of Both Parties ... in 1781* (Bristol, 1781), pp. 3–4; *Commons, 1715–1754*, 1: 85. Brooke emphasizes the discontinuity in clubs, suggesting little political continuity between the mid-century and the new issues of the 1770s and 1780s, pp. 284, 285, 288. Both clubs, however, could still be classed in terms of their stance relative to the government, and the discontinuity in organizations should not be overemphasized.

marshalling its independent supporters. Differences between the Whig candidates exacerbated this weakness, and accordingly, the Whigs were not able to return even a single candidate until 1784.[45]

The city corporation and the Society of Merchant Venturers constituted two of the most powerful interest groups in Bristol.[46] The corporation maintained a relatively even balance between the Whigs and their opponents, as did the Society of Merchant Venturers, and since both bodies comprised Dissenters and Anglicans, their political loyalties were never entirely predictable. The corporation leaned toward the Whigs during the American crisis while the Society of Merchant Venturers tended to favor the government. But the politics of these bodies changed according to the issue; the corporation produced a statement against the popular agitation over Wilkes in 1769, but it supported the second Rockingham administration in 1782.[47] The connections between these two interest groups and the local parties was also important. John Noble, Presbyterian, was not only one of Burke's local agents, he was a prominent leader of the Whig party in the corporation. Earlier in the century, the Dissenting Member of Parliament, Abraham Elton, was Master of the Merchant Venturers, but the different political persuasion of the Masters and Wardens from year to year illustrates the inability of any single party to gain absolute sway.[48] As lobbies for commercial, and occasionally, political causes, both bodies were politically divided, as were the majority of charitable societies in Bristol.[49]

THE NATIONAL FRAMEWORK: CONTESTS, CANDIDATES, AND POLITICAL ISSUES

Two Dissenters, Sir Abraham Elton, and his son by the same name, represented Bristol in the first half of the century, holding one seat continuously between 1722 and 1742. The elder Elton became one of the greatest commercial magnates of Bristol – Bristol M.P.s were always deeply involved in the

---

45 Underdown, 'Parliamentary History', pp. 306. *The Bristol Contest*, pp. 3–4. On the Whig independents, see *The Bristol Contest*, pp. 7, 12, 26–8, 28–9; Burke reported on the division between Cruger's supporters and his own in 1780 to Portland. *Burke Correspondence*, 4: 268–70; Burke to Portland, 3 Sept. 1780.
46 On the organization of Bristol's municipal government, Savadge, 'The West County', pp. 96–8, 555. For divisions on the corporation, see Quilici, 'Turmoil in a City', pp. 14, 188–229; on the Society of Merchant Venturers, pp. 142–80.
47 Underdown, 'Parliamentary History', pp. 23, 175, 177–8, 212, 226, 223, 241–2, 321. For a less convincing narrative of the political vicissitudes of the corporation and Society of Merchant Venturers, see Savadge, 'The West County', pp. 131, 475–6, 501–2, 522–4, 533–9, 546. The Whigs dominated the Common Council. Alfred B. Beaven, *Bristol Lists: Municipal and Miscellaneous*, (Bristol, 1899), p. 220.
48 G. E. Weare, *Edmund Burke's Connection*, p. 111; Beaven, *Bristol Lists*, p. 128; Savadge, 'The West County', pp. 98–105, 130.
49 Such groups as the Incorporation of the Poor, the Dolphin Society, the Grateful Society, the Colston Society, and the Society of St. Stephens Ringers.

commercial concerns of the local merchants – and he was created a baronet for his services on behalf of the government in the Rebellion of 1715.[50] Elton and son were each in turn sheriff, mayor, and aldermen of Bristol, and the latter became Master of the Merchant Venturers as well. In Parliament Abraham Elton Jr. was an opposition Whig until 1741 when he went over to the government side. The Whig monopoly, however, was not to last. Elton's running mate, John Scrope, lost his seat to a Tory in 1734, and from 1734 to 1756 one seat was held by the Tories. Once in power, the Tories developed a superior political organization, and after the death of Elton in 1742, the Tories were willing to accept an opposition Whig in his stead.

This turn of events meant that at midcentury Bristol Whigs had no dependable channel of government patronage reaching from Westminster. On the eve of the general election of 1754, members of the Union Club approached the Steadfast Society concerning a compromise over the two seats. Coveting both seats, the Tories refused, and the Whigs decided to fight, explaining that

> they had not a friend to whom they could apply for obtaining any favour from the great offices of state: – That a commercial city, such as theirs, stood in continual need of the interposition and assistance sometimes of the Treasury, sometimes of the Board of Trade, and sometimes of the Commissioners of the Customs, and the Excise.[51]

They settled upon Robert Nugent (later Lord Clare) largely because he had been an opponent of the monopolizing tendencies of London as a port and center of trade. Upon inviting Nugent, the Whigs agreed to help defray the expenses of a contest. Nugent refused to contribute any money, and so the Bristol merchants, 'in the first place the Quakers and Dissenters', raised the necessary funds.[52] The Tory candidates were Richard Beckford and Sir John Philipps, and in this, as in the following elections, the political orientation of the candidates was clear and well defined. Nugent was a faithful supporter of the Duke of Newcastle, then Bute, and finally Grenville, and as a result of these connections he came to be viewed as a time-server. Beckford, who stood as a Tory, consistently followed opposition measures in the House of Commons while Philipps had been a well-known Jacobite.[53]

---

50 For the biographical information, see the appropriate volumes in *The History of Parliament*. Savadge examines the merchants' connections with their members in most detail; his work is unsurpassed on the merchants' interests in politics and political lobbying techniques. He is also excellent on such matters as the bankruptcy of Bristol merchants as a result of the war, 'The West County', pp. 64, 74, 120, 302–3, 502–5. On the merchants' connections to Lewins Mead chapel, see Quilici, 'Turmoil in a City', pp. 7, 22, 165–6, 173–4, 220, 222, 254, 257–8.
51 Quoted in Namier, *Structure of Politics*, p. 88.
52 *Ibid.*, p. 203, note 4.
53 Table 6 is based upon the totals given in *The History of Parliament*; the poll books for 1756 and 1780 have not survived.

TABLE 6.1: *Bristol Election Results: 1754–1784*

1754		1756		1774	
Nugent (G)	2592	Smith (O)	2418	Cruger (O)	3565
Beckford (O)	2245	Spencer (G)	2347	Burke (O)	2707
Philipps (O)	2160			Brickdale (G)	2456
				Nugent (G)	293
				(Visct.Clare)	

1780		1781		1784	
Brickdale (G)	2771	Daubeny (G)	3143	Brickdale (O)	3458
Cruger (O)	1271	Cruger (O)	2771	Cruger (G)	3052
Lippincott (G)	2518			Daubeny (O)	2984
Peach (O)	788			Peach (G)	373
Burke (O)	18				

When Beckford died in 1756, both Nugent and his spokesman at Bristol, Josiah Tucker, tried to persuade the leaders of the Whig political organization to concede the seat to a Tory replacement. Tucker wrote to Dr. Nathanial Foster 25 February 1756 that 'a club of low tradesmen among the Dissenters' rejected any idea of a compromise and insisted on another Whig member in addition to Nugent.[54] Tucker was unable to forestall this ruinously expensive, and to him, senseless, endeavor. A Whig candidate was found, but even with Treasury support of £2,000 he was defeated. If the Tories were obstinate and greedy in 1754, the Whigs were equally so in 1756, and the Dissenters were perceived as adding an element of consistency, even inflexibility, to partisan politics. The two contests convinced both sides that thereafter a compromise would be expedient. Dean Tucker wrote in 1761: 'Our poverty and immense sums spent in former elections have done that toward reconciling us which reason and argument could not do.'[55]

The party rivalry was not easily extinguished, even though it became less obvious. In the period between 1756 and 1774, and thus over two general elections, the compromise between the two parties was maintained. As the old political clubs became inactive, a new radicalism emerged stimulated by the agitation over Wilkes. Nugent remained a government faithful, while Jarrit Smith, one of the founders of the Steadfast Society, maintained his reputation as a Tory (1756–68). Matthew Brickdale came in as a Steadfast Society nominee in 1768, but he took an independent line in the House, and even opposed the administration over Wilkes. Brickdale could therefore hardly be considered a traditional 'Tory'. But the conflict with America put a new

54 *Commons, 1754–1790*, 1: 289, note 4.
55 *Ibid.*, 1: 284.

complexion on local politics, and in this new environment both Nugent, now Viscount Clare, and Brickdale, came to support the government's American policy. By the early months of 1774 Brickdale was classed by John Robinson as 'hopeful', and received government money for the election in November.[56] Lord Clare had never altered his views to suit his constituents' wishes, and when Bristol electors favored the repeal of the Townshend duties, he defended the taxes and stood steadily in favor of the government's coercive policies. In the spring of 1774 he spoke repeatedly in the House against the colonists, comparing the rebellion there to the situation in Scotland in 1745, and his popularity in Bristol began to wane.[57] At the general election Lord Clare's supporters at Bristol were weak and divided, and he was forced to withdraw after the first day's poll.[58] This event provided the occasion for Edmund Burke's introduction to Bristol.

The election of 1774 developed into a three-way contest between Edmund Burke, Henry Cruger, and Matthew Brickdale, the government candidate. Burke's political views on America were well known by this date; he had been New York's agent since 1770. Cruger was born in New York and later traded with America, and he had become, in Lord North's words, a 'hot Wilkite'.[59] He ran as the candidate of the radicals at Bristol, but independently of Burke, and he and Burke were only returned after a long, arduous, and expensive campaign. Past accounts have made too much of the inability of Cruger and Burke to form a joint candidature. An agreement between the two committees was reached, and even though there was some cross voting, by eighteenth-century standards, it was not excessive. Cruger did on several occasions claim to stand alone, but numerous broadsides linked the two candidates and pleaded explicitly for two votes, since a plump for Cruger meant a vote for Brickdale.[60] The disagreements between Burke and Cruger led to more serious divisions later.

56 *Ibid.*, 2: 115 Underdown says Brickdale was a 'King's Friend' by 1774, 'Parliamentary History', p. 142.
57 *Commons, 1754–1790*, 3: 221; Underdown, 'Parliamentary History', pp. 98, 123. See Underdown's summary of the political reasons for Clare's loss of popular support, pp. 160, 166, 178–9, 191. For the publication of Clare's strong pro-government stance over America, *Brist. J.* (4 Feb. 1775).
58 Burke thought of the disciples of Lord Clare as the worst sort of 'Tories', since they were opposed to the Americans. Underdown, 'Parliamentary History', pp. 161, 217. On the opposition between Burke and Clare, see Peter Underdown, 'Edmund Burke, The Commissary', 254–6. For a lengthy account of this election by Richard Champion, see Champion Letterbook, 38083(4) April, 1775, pp. 374–408.
59 Underdown, 'Parliamentary History', on Burke, pp. 191–3; and on Cruger, pp. 163, 177, 182–9. On Cruger's strong defense of the colonies, see *Leeds Merc.* (3 Jan. 1775).
60 See 'Bristol Elections, 1774–1790. Addresses, Squibs, Songs', ref. B6979 (hereafter cited as 'Bristol Elections'), pp. 26, 28, 64, 73, 78, 87 and the advertisements of 8, 18 Oct., pp. 55, 59, 113. On Cruger's vow of independence, see advertisement of 8 Oct., and 'A Freeman', pp. 63, 49 in 'Bristol Elections'. Cruger's supporters were in favor of shortened Parliaments and some were chary of the association with Rockingham on that account; *ibid.*, pp. 54, 97, 105. But the supporters of the two candidates met together in a 'joyous, convivial manner' on more than one occasion. See *Brist. J.* (4 Nov. 1775).

The popular political literature of Bristol elections is extraordinarily rich; it is the main vehicle through which local politics can be connected to national issues; it establishes the conceptual framework that links the early century to the 1770s and 1780s; and yet this body of literature has remained almost completely unknown.[61] Much of this literature also served to reinforce the same political viewpoints the Dissenters heard in the pulpit; at every level of popular ideology a 'True Whig' viewpoint was reaffirmed in terms of suspicion toward the government, sympathy for the Americans, and the corruptions of Parliament and the ministry. Over one hundred pamphlets, broadsides, squibs, and songs emerged from the 1774 Bristol contest alone, and taken together, these documents clearly depict the political issues of the day.[62] The American controversy was by far the most prominent question agitating the minds of voters. Burke and Cruger's sympathy for America was the dominant theme throughout, and in light of both men's activities and reputations, this is hardly surprising. Burke arrived a week after the polls opened and began his campaign with a speech that is now considered one of the earliest examples of a modern political platform. In this address to the electors, Burke put himself in personal touch with the people over the American problem and urged upon his hearers the importance of working for a peaceful solution. Halfway into the campaign, Burke's earlier defense of the first Rockingham administration entitled 'A Short Account of a Late Short Administration' was republished and circulated in Bristol. In the preface to this tract Burke noted that he had 'preserved his attachment to the principles' of the first Rockingham administration inviolate.[63] Burke's association with the Rockingham party was repeatedly mentioned in the election literature by both friendly and hostile commentators thus drawing a close connection between his candidature, an opposition party at Westminster, and a great national issue.[64]

Cruger's American origins and his espousal of radical causes were well known at Bristol and frequently commented upon. 'You say Mr. Cruger is an

---

61 Underdown, 'Parliamentary History', omits any reference to the collection 'Bristol Elections', relying instead on the press, pp. 196, 204, 299–300, 335, and this results in his highly misleading statement: 'Yet the contest [of 1774] involved little discussion of the American issue at all'. Underdown, 'Henry Cruger and Edmund Burke', p. 33. See also Savadge on the 1774 election; 'The American Question, although it was the basic issue, was scarcely mentioned'. 'The West County', p. 404, and Quilici, 'Turmoil in a City', pp. 243, 258 who discounts ideology altogether.

62 Weare, *Edmund Burke's Connection*, pp. 28, 52–3, 55, 61–2, 73, has five additional items not found in 'Bristol Elections'. In addition to the broadsides, there were many short notices and articles in the press.

63 'Bristol Elections', pp. 91, 117; Henry Jephson, *The Platform: Its Rise and Progress*, 2 vols. (London, 1892), 2: 90–1. Burke's celebrated speech on American taxation of 19 April 1774 was also widely circulated in Bristol. Weare, *Edmund Burke's Connection*, p. xvii.

64 In favor of Burke, 'Bristol Elections', pp. 65, 143. Brickdale's pamphleteers also pointed out the Rockingham connection; *Ibid.*, pp. 34, 122, 137, 145.

American', wrote 'Philanthropos' – 'futile, disengenous [sic] objection. Hence he may have it more in power to be instrumental to a happy reconciliation between the mother country and her aggrieved settlements'. A number of secondary themes raised in this election were also related to America, such as the Quebec Act, which was viewed as both a political and religious issue.[65] Perhaps more importantly, the perceived attack on liberty abroad was believed to be threatening to liberty at home. In reflecting upon one of the 'most venal and profligate Parliaments' in English history, 'Cato' urged, 'Consider the many *unconstitutional* Acts of Parliament, that have been lately passed – Consider the abettors of them. And remember, that that Power which can establish *Taxation without Representation* in one Part of his Majesty's Dominions, may do it in *another*.' A 'Freeholder' had similar thoughts: Burke stood against the 'wicked, corrupt Ministry' that attempted to enslave us; 'He is the Man that boldly stood forth against that vile Boston Act.' These and other acts were 'shackles' intended for us by an 'abandoned Administration'. While considering the 'knavish' Stamp Act and the Quebec Act, 'The Jovial Huntsman' worried about his liberty, but felt confident that Burke and Cruger would work to repeal 'those cursed acts, that are so lately made'.[66] The appeal for shorter Parliaments came up occasionally, as did the principle of representation and the Members' responsibility to their constituents.[67] But the most frequently occurring theme was liberty: in broadside after broadside Burke and Cruger were associated with America, and America, in turn, was associated with civil and religious liberty.[68] Trade with America was not as popular a topic as liberty; commerce – a local issue – was specifically mentioned about as often as references to the destructive enactments of the 'last wicked Parliament'.[69] The election literature in favor of Burke and Cruger clearly reinforced the pro-American political orientation of the Dissenting sermons of Caleb Evans.

The majority of broadsides and pamphlets were written from the Whig side; in fact, less than one third of the extant documents supported Brickdale. The

---

65 *Ibid.*, p. 52; see also pp. 49, 71; on the Quebec Act, see pp. 23, 28, 43, 121, 171.
66 *Ibid.*, pp. 45, 87, 171.
67 On shorter Parliaments, Cruger's notice of 7 Oct., 'Philanthropos', 'Precaution', and 'Philo Veritas', pp. 47, 52–3, 114, 121 in 'Bristol Elections'. On the Members' responsibility, 'Cato', and Burke's speech of 3 Nov., pp. 45, 150–1, in the same volume. Religious allusions are found in the frequent references to civil and religious liberty, the connection between the Quebec Act and 'popery', and the attempt to associate Burke with either Catholicism or Quakerism.
68 See the broadsides and squibs by 'Delta', 'Consistency', 'A Freeholder', 'Sincerity', 'Briton', 'Philo Veritas', 'Civil and Religious Liberty', 'Britanicus', 'Cruger, Burke, and Liberty forever', 'The Remonstrance of Freedom', 'Free Representation', *ibid.*, pp. 71, 78, 87, 110, 120, 121, 125, 143, 146, 167, 169; see also pp. 55, 57, 73, 135, 141, and Weare, *Edmund Burke's Connection*, 'Reason Against Railing', pp. 61–2.
69 On trade, see 'Bristol Elections', pp. 15, 47, 52–3, 87, 14, 91, 123, 126, 171. References to the corrupt, wicked, and oppressive acts of the last Parliament are found on pp. 23, 35, 43, 45, 52–3, 64, 87, 143.

approach of Brickdale's supporters was mainly negative. They attacked Cruger's American origins arguing that this made him unfit to represent them, and they attempted to connect the Whigs with rebellion and religious Dissent.[70] Just as Burke was explicitly associated with the opposition at Westminster, Brickdale was associated with the government, though the local party apparently perceived that this was not likely to win many votes.[71] The Whigs clearly dominated the propaganda of this election with the theme of America and liberty, and this, combined with their superior local political organization, contributed to the eminent victory of both Whig candidates. But the use of the party labels was not prominent in this election, perhaps because the voters were slow to associate Whiggism with opposition at Westminster.[72]

Burke's *Letter to the Sheriffs of Bristol* made the affair with his intractable Bristol constituents famous.[73] In his eyes, all attempts to bring the electors around to a consistent support of the Rockingham Whigs failed, and Burke's disappointments have profoundly influenced the interpretation of Bristol politics. For example, in 1777 Burke wrote of the Bristol voters, 'Until I knew it, both by own particular experience and by my observation of what has happened to others, I could not have believed how very little the local constituent attends to the general public line of conduct observed by their Member.' In 1778 Burke argued in favor of trade concessions to Ireland, which was certainly a progressive policy, but his Bristol friends could not understand him. Harford and Cowles, the Quaker iron merchants, wrote to him to object: 'We do not find one amongst us who can declare in favor of thy sentiments under the present situation of things.' Burke had also strongly favored religious toleration and though he supported the Protestant Dissenters Relief Act of 1779, he received no praise for his exertions. But when he voiced sympathy for the Catholics and the harsh restrictions under which they labored,

---

70 *Ibid.*, pp. 27, 33, 51, 183; on Whigs, rebellion, and Dissent, pp. 122, 131, 137, 145, 175.

71 *Ibid.*, p. 99. Only two broadsides in this election urged a coalition between Burke and Brickdale, pp. 49, 115.

72 Underdown, 'Henry Cruger and Edmund Burke', p. 33; for the use of 'Whig' and 'Tory' see 'Bristol Elections', pp. 125, 174, 188. The election results were contested, for which, see *Brist. J.* (18, 25 Feb. 1775). Underdown examines the political issues between election years in great detail and there is little need to review these issues here. For the period 1754–74 see 'Parliamentary History', pp. 74–81, 155–65; for 1774–81, pp. 225–42, 276–83; for 1781–4, pp. 318–24, 330. For narrative accounts of the elections, see Savadge, 'The West County', pp. 137–54, 387–426, 549–9.

73 Underdown, 'Parliamentary History', p. 228. Burke's resistance to instructions from his constituents was one of the ideological differences that separated him from Cruger who welcomed instructions and campaigned, in part, on this issue. Instructing Members was also an issue at Norwich; Phillips, *Electoral Behavior*, p. 418. See the recent treatment by Paul Kelly, 'Constituents' Instructions to Members of Parliament in the Eighteenth Century' in Clyve Jones, (ed.), *Party Management in Parliament, 1660–1784* (New York, 1984), pp. 169–89.

and then condemned the Gordon rioters, he was severely criticized.[74] Burke regretted that he had ever sat for such a 'great busy place'.

Yet just before the general election of 1780, Burke took a political sounding of the Bristol electorate and concluded, 'our grand division is of Whigs and Tories'. Moreover, after he declined the poll and left Bristol for Rockingham's pocket borough of Malton, he himself supervised the restructuring of the Union Club.[75] The difference from the first half of the century was that 'Tories' were now ministerialists and 'Whigs' were oppositionists; many former Tories appear to have found in North a minister who would defend law, order, and the Church of England, rather than threaten them. Earlier in 1780, the Steadfast Society was revived under the leadership of George Daubeny as the Loyal and Constitutional Club, and it gave strong support to the government candidates, Brickdale and Henry Lippincott; the pro-government candidates received £1,000 from secret service funds in this election, and £5,000 in the 1781 by-election. Burke's unwillingness to respond to his constituents' whims, his lack of financial backing, and his inability to work effectively with Cruger were to prove disastrous in the 1780 election; he declined on the first day of the poll when it became clear that the government would push for both seats.[76] The newly reorganized Loyal and Constitutional Club proved most successful against the revived Union Club, and Brickdale and Lippincott, a prominent member of the former Steadfast Society, won easily. Samuel Peach, Cruger's father-in-law, had been put forward as a candidate with Cruger to attract his second votes, but this was to no avail. Cruger later claimed that he had been turned out because of his attachment to the Americans during the war.[77]

The supporters of Brickdale appear to have learned a great deal from the election of 1774. Their previous loss of both seats was due in part to their lack of adequate preparation. Accordingly, they planned for the election of 1780 well in advance, and as a result, the election literature, though far less voluminous than 1774, was dominated by the pro-government club. For example, in May of 1780, over three months before the election, the Steadfast Society purchased 5,000 copies of Wesley's *A Calm Address to our American Colonies*

---

74 *Commons, 1754–1790*, 1: 287; Peter Underdown, 'Bristol and Burke', in Patrick McGrath, (ed.), *Bristol in the Eighteenth Century*, p. 58.

75 *Commons, 1754–1790*, 1: 288. On the election of 1780 see Underdown, 'Parliamentary History', pp. 297–302; Christie, 'Henry Cruger', 160–5; on the Union Club, Underdown, 'Bristol and Burke', p. 59; and Underdown, 'Burke's Bristol Friends', 139.

76 *Commons, 1754–1790*, 1: 288. Underdown, 'Parliamentary History', p. 284. Personalities could count for more than issues, and in 1780 personalities were important. See Phillips, *Electoral Behavior* on this question at Maidstone, p. 156. But Christie has overstated the importance of the differences between Cruger and Burke, 'Henry Cruger', 159–60, 168, and because the election literature has been ignored, Savadge can say of the 1780 and 1781 elections: 'The fate of the war and of the American colonies was not an issue of these elections'. 'The West County', p. 548.

77 Underdown, 'Parliamentary History', pp. 301–2. On Peach's earlier involvement in Bristol radicalism in 1769, see p. 159.

for distribution to the electorate. Before the election, they also circulated a letter that Cruger had sent to Peter Wikoff in Philadelphia in July 1774 implicating him with the rebellion. In July, the club made arrangements to open the Merchant Hall for their election meeting in order to exclude the Whigs. The Whigs, in contrast, were plagued with difficulties; all attempts at a compromise with their opponents failed. The personal animosities between the agents of Burke and Cruger fatally weakened their cause, and ten days into the election, Cruger, like Burke before him, declined the poll.[78] The election literature continued to center around the American crisis, but in this contest it was oriented in favor of the government and patriotism. The war was still on, and this in itself put the Whigs at a considerable disadvantage. Supporters of the Loyal and Constitutional Club had learned the value of championing the high theme of 'rights' and thus the writers for Brickdale and Lippincott combined rhetoric on 'civil and religious rights', our 'constitutional rights' and 'our happy Constitution in Church and State', with patriotic appeals in support of George III and 'Old England'.[79]

The most frequently mentioned topic, however, was Cruger's supposedly treasonous letter to Wikoff. Dubbed 'Yankee Doodle', Cruger was held up to ridicule for his sympathy for America, and this strategy proved so successful that it was to dominate the by-election of 1781 when Cruger lost a second time.[80] The Whigs' central line of attack was against the fatal measures of the last Parliament, though they continued to associate themselves with 'liberty'. Finally, both sides gave a proportionately larger place in the literature to the Bristol poor than in previous elections, and this, too, was a harbinger of the by-election of 1781.[81]

Lippincott lived only a few months after the general election, and upon his death in early 1781, the Loyal and Constitutional Club orchestrated a by-election that led to Cruger's second defeat. In this contest, Cruger was supported by the Union Club, but his opponent, George Daubeny, the president of the Loyal and Constitutional Club, won handily (with substantial help from treasury funds). In Parliament, Brickdale stood steadfastly by North, and Daubeny was also outspoken in defense of North, and then North and Fox through 1783.[82]

---

78 *Ibid.*, p. 294, 295, 291; 'Bristol Elections', p. 239, Cruger declined on 18 Sept. There is no extant poll book of this election. Underdown, 'Parliamentary History', p. 300.

79 'Bristol Elections', pp. 197, 199, 229, 247. See also 'Crispin', 'A Friend to his Country', and 'No American', pp. 205, 211, 238.

80 'Crispin', 'A Journeyman', 'For the Benefit of a Declining Party', 'For the Benefit of an Expiring Congress', 'The Auction Room', 'The Lamantation of Yankee Doodle' (two versions), *ibid.*, pp. 205, 213, 233, 238, 243, 249, 253, 257. The Whigs, of course, attempted to defend Cruger; see pp. 201, 259.

81 *Ibid.*, pp. 201, 231, 245, 251, 258. See below on the poor. Trade was mentioned on only three occasions, *ibid.*, pp. 205, 213, 258.

82 Underdown, 'Parliamentary History', pp. 307–15; and Underdown, 'Burke's Bristol

The number of popular pamphlets and broadsides that have survived for the 1781 by-election is about a third greater than in 1774, and the Whigs once again dominated the use of the printed page. This was one of the most rancorous and violent Bristol elections of the century; riots resulted in the loss of two lives, and party animosities reached a new pitch of excitement characterized by the reemergence of the old party labels, Whig and Tory.[83] Ideological continuity with the past was a major theme: the pro-government propagandists associated the Whig interest with the Puritan Revolution and regicide; the Whigs, in turn, reminded the electors of the earlier Tory connection with the Stuarts and the 'Forty-Five'.[84]

The theme of America again dominated the election. The most frequently mentioned issue was Cruger's defense of the American colonists and his commitment to peace. The Whigs linked Cruger's name to liberty, willingly acknowledged his American origins, and reminded the voters of his record of opposition to the government in the last Parliament. But because of their opponents' jibes concerning rebellion and Dissent, the Whigs occasionally insisted upon Cruger's support for the present establishment in Church and State.[85] From the opposite side, Cruger was the American devil: 'Yankee Doodle' was responsible for confusion, riot, and bloodshed in both America and England. The most prominent piece of pro-government propaganda was Cruger's letter to Wikoff of July 1774 and the charge that he had promoted rebellion in Amer-

---

Friends', 140, where Joseph Harford's strong exertions on behalf of reunifying the Whigs are noted. Upon the dismissal of the Coalition, Brickdale and Daubeny stood by Fox and North; however, late in 1783, Robinson considered their support of the administration 'hopeful'. Underdown, 'Parliamentary History', p. 318.

83 'Justice' provides details on the riots and the loss of life, p. 379 in 'Bristol Elections', and see *The Bristol Contest*, pp. 127–9. All references to *The Bristol Contest* are to additional squibs, not duplicates found in 'Bristol Elections'. On the use of libel, threats, dirty tricks, and warnings not to riot, see 'Retaliation', 'Senex', 'The Consultation at the W. L. Club in Bristol', 'Cato', 'A Sincere Friend to his Country', pp. 369, 377, 393, 373, 385 in 'Bristol Elections' and 'Steady', 'True Blue', and 'To Mr. Lediard by N.W.', pp. 56, 71–2, 102–3 in *The Bristol Contest*. The use of the terms Whig and Tory is too pervasive to document exhaustively, but see, for example, 'Bristol Elections', pp. 321, 323, 331, 359, 363, 365, 399, 405, 409, and *The Bristol Contest*, pp. 2, 16, 34, 35, 55, 56, 69–70, 79, 109, 120, 130, 132, 140, 142, 149, 151–2. It is highly significant that on occasion, the term Tory was even self-ascribed: 'A New Song' wrote that if Cruger should win 'The true honest Tory no more shall look big/But be slave to *republican, traitor*, and *Whig*.' *The Bristol Contest*, p. 149.

84 'The Origin of a Shitsack', 'A New Song for the Bristol Blues', 'Bristol Elections', p. 407, and announcement, p. 62 in *The Bristol Contest* connect the Whigs to the Roundheads; broadsides on pp. 279, 285, 293, 299, 305, 397 of 'Bristol Elections' connect the Bristol 'Tories' to the Stuarts, Sir Robert Filmer, and the 'High Party' generally.

85 'Bristol Elections', pp. 268, 291, 321, 343, 351, 353, 357, 373, 397, 401, 283; *The Bristol Contest*, pp. 36–8, 41–2, 69–70, 83–4, 109, 118–19, 140, 141, 142, 147, 151, 152, 91–2, 97–8, 9, 12, 21; on Cruger on Church and state, 'Bristol Elections', pp. 331, 351, 359; *The Bristol Contest*, p. 132.

ica.[86] Daubeny, by contrast, was held up by his supporters as the defender of Church, king, and constitution.[87] The thrust of Daubeny's campaign was well summarized in a broadside which invited all 'True Britons' 'To drink a Health to the Friend of the King, and the Constitution, and the Downfall of Rebels Abroad, and Incendiaries at Home. *Stand up for the Church. Support a Fellow Citizen. No Yankee. No Compromiser'*. But to the Whigs, 'Jacobite George' was tainted by his reputation for seeking government places and his sympathy with popery. '*No* Frenchified *Englishman*! *No* Daubeny! *No* Popery!' was the cry of the Whigs.[88]

Not only were these national, ideological issues far more prominent in the election literature than trade, but the candidates, just as in 1774, were directly associated with either the opposition or the government at Westminster.[89] Voters were clearly interested in national affairs; 'An Indignant Elector' chided Brickdale for his absence from Parliament for the purpose of stumping for Daubeny and said: 'Is not Parliament now deliberating on the most momentous national concerns?' Observers also made an explicit connection between the political issues in this election and the electoral behavior of voters: 'No Rebel' wrote, 'I hope the poll will be published, that we may know who are the friends of OLD ENGLAND, and who are the *abettors* of *American rebellion* – the most *ungrateful* and *unnatural*, that ever disgraced the historic page.'[90] Although the Whigs were defeated by over 300 votes, they were encouraged by their comeback, and numerous comments were made concerning their new found unity and the happy prospects for the future.[91]

In 1784 Cruger stood for Bristol for the fourth and last time. Peach was once again advanced as a candidate to catch Cruger's second votes and both were sponsored by the Union Club. Brickdale and Daubeny contested this election as representing the Loyal and Constitutional Club, but by this date, Brickdale had attempted to distance himself from both Pitt and the Coalition, while Daubeny's political position after 1783 was far from clear. Cruger,

86 'Bristol Elections', pp. 271, 281, 301, 337, 339, 345, 375, 385, 401; *The Bristol Contest*, pp. 21–3, 26–8, 29–32, 43–8, 58, 62, 73, 76, 79–80, 95–7, 144–5, 148–9.
87 'Bristol Elections', pp. 301, 375, 401, 407; *The Bristol Contest*, pp. 14, 21–3, 44, 144–5.
88 'Bristol Elections', pp. 301, 303; see also pp. 286, 315, 321, 353, 361, 399, 401, 409, 267, 303, 335, 363, 387; in *The Bristol Contest*, pp. 17–18, 41–2, 50, 55, 77, 109, 56, 75, 118–19.
89 Cruger is seen as the proponent of trade in the following broadsides 'Citizen', 'Truth', notice, 'Patriae Amicus', notice of Feb. 12, 'Poll', in 'Bristol Elections', pp. 286, 321, 331, 343, 359, 372; 'Candour', p. 21 in *The Bristol Contest*. The following squibs and notices explicitly connect the candidate to the opposition at Westminster or to the government: 'Citizen', 'Pius IV', 'To the Point', in 'Bristol Elections', pp. 283, 363, 361; 'A Freeman', notice, 'Candour', 'A Tradesman', J. Docksey, Cruger's advertisement of 4 Sept. 1780, 'Amicus' in *The Bristol Contest*, pp. 9, 12, 21, 41–2, 69–70, 97–8, 142.
90 *The Bristol Contest*, pp. 117, 97.
91 *Ibid.*, pp. 37, 133, 142, 145, 148–9, 134.

though absent in America, was returned with Brickdale, and the party link to Peach turned out to be absolutely crucial, since Cruger beat Daubeny by a mere sixty-eight votes. Some rioting followed this election: a brickbat was thrown at Colonel Cruger (who was chaired in place of his brother), and Cruger's supporters proceeded to break the windows of the house from whence it came. Cruger devotees later attacked the headquarters of Brickdale and Daubeny at the White Lion and did some damage to the building.[92]

Comparatively few broadsides and pamphlets have survived for the 1784 contest even though the poll lasted from 3 April to 8 May and set a new record. The extant literature, however, does reveal a number of local political perceptions that are essential for understanding the behavior of the electorate. Brickdale and Daubeny were associated with the Fox–North Coalition, but more importantly, it was believed that Daubeny stood by the Coalition out of devotion to North, not Fox; Daubeny 'indissolubly adhered to the grand Aggressor and Destroyer even to the very last'. It was also observed that Cruger had supported Fox in the last Parliament, even though he now stood with Pitt.[93] Most of this literature centered around past loyalties, not the new government of Pitt, and the central issue continued to be Cruger's association with America. His opponents treated him as a traitor who had taken oaths of allegiance to the new colonial government; the letter to Philadelphia of 1774 was, at this late date, still believed to have some political capital.[94] His supporters defended his friendship with America and used the occasion to highlight his parliamentary opposition and the disastrous American policy of the previous ministry.

And I must do Justice to Mr. CRUGER'S Conduct, that he was endowed with a Discernment to forsee the fatal Catastrophe, and wished to guard the Nation against the Blow, as his Speeches in the House of Commons indicated even to the very last; and proved him to be a strenuous advocate for preserving the Dependence of *America* upon the Mother Country. And are we not to thank the *renowned Lord* in the celebrated *blue Ribbon*, and his nefarious Junto, for the loss of *America*? – For profusely lavishing the Public Money? – For the ponderous Load of Debt under which the Nation groans?

Cruger was viewed more as an opponent of North than as an advocate of Pitt's new supposedly 'Tory' administration. In Samuel Peach's speech of thanks to the voters for Cruger's victory, he reminded them that Cruger stood on 'genuine Constitutional Whig Principles'.[95]

THE RELIGIOUS AND SOCIAL DIMENSIONS OF PARTY

In addition to the more strictly political questions relating to the empire, religious and social issues were sometimes raised. In the four contested

92 Underdown, 'Parliamentary History', pp. 331–40. *Commons, 1754–1790*, 2: 282.
93 George Daubeny, p. 453 in 'Bristol Elections'; see also, David Lewis, Cruger's Committee, and 'An Addresser', pp. 425, 428, 443.
94 *Ibid.*, pp. 428, 441, 443.
95 *Ibid.*, pp. 453, 433, 439, 447. Cruger's support of the poor and trade are mentioned infrequently, p. 431.

elections of this period, pamphleteers often emphasized the strength of the Dissenting vote and described its use as a coherent bloc in favor of the Whigs. Burke's espousal of the repeal of penal legislation against the Dissenters was believed to have won their allegiance in 1774: 'the cause we are engaged in is the cause of civil and religious liberty, whether Churchmen or Dissenters', wrote 'Philo-Veritas'.[96] The Quakers' early enthusiasm for Burke was particularly stressed, probably in part because of the well-known religious affiliation of his political agents, Champion and Harford. Cruger also enjoyed Dissenting support; 'Cato' addressed him: 'You may depend upon it, that the major part of the Dissenters are and will be on your side'. It is a point of considerable interest to this study that contemporaries believed that the Dissenting pulpit was the means whereby the Dissenting vote was marshalled.[97] In addition, on several occasions, the Quakers were appealed to as a body specifically for the purpose of influencing their political orientation. Cruger's close relationship to the Dissenters was noted by both local parties, and just as Burke felt obliged to address the religious issue at length when he declined the poll in 1780, Cruger believed it was important to draw out the ideological significance of this association when he was defeated in 1781.

I shall be told, perhaps, that my friends are chiefly among *Dissenters* – Let me ask who were the *Whigs*, that had so principal a hand in bringing about what, even at this day is called *the glorious revolution*? The two first kings of the house of *Hanover* were not ashamed to acknowledge their obligations to the *Protestant Dissenters*, because their principles contributed to the establishment of that family on the throne.[98]

The specific contribution of Nonconformity to heightened party rivalry and the coherence of party was thus a frequent theme. This idea was so widely assumed that even when the partisan nature of a contest was doubted, it was doubted precisely because the Dissenters were allegedly divided. An 'Elector' wrote: 'and with respect to the late Contest [1774], has it been *Party* against *Party?* With what colour of reason can this be pretended, when it is so well known, that many Dissenters of each denomination, and even several of the Quakers voted for Mr. *Brickdale?*' 'Crito' thought that in 1774 party existed in name only, since the two clubs were 'confusedly intermixed with Dissenters of every denomination'.[99] Generally, however, the belief in an alliance between

96 *Ibid.*, pp. 121, 125, 103, 137, 135.
97 *Ibid.*, pp. 141, 143, 175; Cato, p. 373; see also p. 383. See 'Circumspection', pp. 21–3 in *The Bristol Contest*. 'Candour' in 'Bristol Elections', p. 357, answers 'Circumspection' denying that 'sedition and republicanism are enforced from almost every *dissenting* pulpit'. Burke himself held that the Dissenting pulpit at Bristol was extremely influential. *Burke Correspondence*, 4: 270; Burke to Portland, 3 Sept. 1780. 'A.B. to the People Called Quakers', 'A Serious Address to that numerous and respectable class of citizens denominated Quakers', in *The Bristol Contest*, pp. 79–80, 109–10.
98 Cruger's speech in *The Bristol Contest*, p. 132. See also on Cruger's association with Dissent 'An Enemy to Detraction', and 'Moderation', pp. 23, 109–10 in the same volume.
99 'Bristol Elections', pp. 95–6, 129.

the Nonconformists and Anglican Whigs prevailed.

Sometimes contemporaries commented on social divisions at Bristol, and a small number of broadsides and pamphlets alluded to an economic base to the vote. In 1754, Josiah Tucker thought that Nugent was supported by 'the mob', while Beckford and Philipps were backed by 'low and middling tradesmen'. In 1774, 'True Blue' and 'Civis' associated the Whigs with compassion for the poor, and 'A New Song' called the followers of Cruger *canaille*. The editor of *Felix Farley's Bristol Journal* worried about 'the multiplied distresses of the lower class of citizens' and feared the return of 'false disturbances and commotions'. The primary concern of the newspaper was thus 'the good order of Society'. Conversely, Brickdale was occasionally associated with property and there was thus some sense among contemporaries of a socio-economic division in the electorate.[100] One friend of Brickdale and Clare observed 'my connections are with the gentlemen, and we are determined to counteract and oppose the designs of the middling class of people and the vagabond tradesmen'.[101] The theme of Cruger's special concern for the poor continued in the election of 1780,[102] and it figured even more prominently in the by-election of 1781. In this contest, Cruger was either identified with the poor, or he was depicted as a friend of the people, while Daubeny, according to Whig propaganda, hated the poor and abused them as 'rascals'. The Bristol radicals formally espoused a platform of six principles in this election, including annual Parliaments. They also insisted that 'the poor man has an *equal* right, but *more* need, to have representatives in the legislature than the rich one'.[103]

When combined with the sermons of the Dissenting pulpit, the election literature from Bristol proves beyond a reasonable doubt that constitutional and political issues dominated the minds of electors. The only way that historians have been able to maintain the idea that trade and local interests were controlling is by ignoring the massive evidence of the election literature. A survey of the squibs, songs, and broadsides demonstrates the reality of a well informed and literate popular political culture. The idea that men, not measures, influ-

---

100 Underdown, 'Parliamentary History', p. 42; 'Bristol Elections', pp. 15, 23, 49, 176; *Bris. J.* (9 July 1774).
101 Dated 29 July 1774, cited in Weare, *Burke's Bristol Connection*, p. 23. Richard Champion wrote to Burke, 1 October 1774, that the lower sort of freemen were 'very numerous' and 'depend mostly on their Masters'. Cited in Savadge, 'The West County', p. 400.
102 'Bristol Elections', pp. 205, 209, 213, 224, 231, 251. But Lord Clare was certain that the Whigs had the 'superior weight of property' in 1780. *Commons, 1754–1790*, 1: 285. Burke thought he would have had the support of the 'most opulent' Whigs, p. 288.
103 'Bristol Elections', pp. 291, 293, 299, 303, 321, 335, 343; *The Bristol Contest*, pp. 9, 36–8, 104–5, 118–19, 140, 141, 151. For a republication of the radicals' 'Declaration' of 1781, see Marshall, *Bristol and the American War of Independence*, Appendix, pp. 24–5. In 1784, Cruger's support for the poor was mentioned infrequently. See 'A Freeman', p. 431 in 'Bristol Elections'.

enced the choice of electors and determined the outcome of elections at Bristol is far too simplistic; in the minds of voters, men stood for measures and the citizens explicitly and repeatedly associated candidates with specific administrations and their policies. But if popular ideology was articulate and sensitive to political issues, was it persuasive? Did it have any measurable effect upon the behavior of ordinary people?

7

The Dissenting Vote and Electoral Independence in Bristol and Great Yarmouth

From 1754 to 1784 the political persuasions of candidates for Bristol were well defined, and despite Burke's skepticism about the alertness of the voters, the issues raised concerning national politics seemed to be clearly understood by the electorate. With such well known and articulate leaders as Viscount Clare, Edmund Burke, and Henry Cruger, it would appear likely that at Bristol, if anywhere, the voters could understand the political orientation of the candidates and identify with it. This argument might be defended solely on the basis of the political literature produced by each party; the squibs, the pamphlets, and the notices in the press all attest to a degree of politicization that was matched by only a handful of boroughs in England. When this popular literature is combined with the sermons of the Dissenting and Anglican clergy and the sophisticated organization of the local clubs, we might well suppose that the electorate was enlightened, that the voters knew what they wanted, and that they knew how to achieve their political objectives. Similarly, the Dissenting laity, tutored by the progressive elite, might be expected to be especially active in political matters. This hypothesis may be tested by examining the extent of straight party voting as compared to cross voting in four Bristol elections, and then comparing these statistics to those found in other constituencies during the same period. This measure of partisan behavior is made by grouping electors for each contest into categories of 'party' and 'cross voters'. While this simple means of assessing partisan behavior is readily achieved, it is at once the crudest measure of party and the most susceptible to misinterpretation.[1]

In order to have meaning for partisanship, the categorization of 'party' and 'cross vote' presupposes two things: that the voters were presented with clear political options in their candidates, and that their vote clearly reflected their

---

1 Yet in the volumes of the *History of Parliament* this is the sole basis upon which generalizations concerning partisanship have been made. John Phillips, *Electoral Behavior in Unreformed England: Plumpers, Splitters, and Straights* (Princeton, 1982), pp. 218, 219, note 10, has shown how a high level of straight party voting could be accounted for on the grounds of patronage, corruption, or personality. This measure of electoral behavior, therefore, tells us nothing about the reasons for partisanship or the motivation of the electorate.

choice. The first condition of a distinct political option is more easily met than the second, for in any given election, not only the political orientation of the candidates, but also the number of candidates and the way they were paired could muddle the electors' choice. In English boroughs that returned two members to Parliament, each elector had two votes, and a double vote by its very nature militated against partisan behavior. In four-way contests where the two candidates declared a joint interest and did indeed run together, a high level of straight party voting might be achieved. A voter could be induced to cast both of his votes for one of the two sides, though partisan voting could never be taken for granted. If, however, two of the four candidates ran independently, as Cruger and Burke did at Bristol in 1774, there was often a greater pressure to split one's vote, or to cast a single vote or 'plump' for the favorite candidate. Moreover, in such a situation the initial grouping of the two independent candidates together as representing a 'party' means that on the basis of other data, a judgment has already been made concerning the weight that should be given to the candidate's avowal of independence. In the *Burgess Poll* of the Newcastle election of 1774, James Murray cogently explained these distinctions and thereby depicted contemporary assumptions concerning the difficulty of maintaining a 'party' vote.

He who polls for both these persons is called – a double vote. A junction of this kind commonly divides its opponents' friends, and some of them by such division, vote for one candidate of each party – this is what makes – a split vote. It sometimes happens for very good reasons, known only to the voter's self – that none but one candidate appears deserving of the suffrage he has to give, accordingly conscientiously gives his vote to one – this makes a single vote.[2]

The problem of the double vote became particularly acute in three-way contests. Here each of the three candidates might stand alone, and when this situation arises it is often inappropriate to group the voters into categories of partisan and split. Under such circumstances single voter could represent a partisan choice, but they could also represent a vote for a favorite, rather than a vote for a party. Such fine discriminations, however, can seldom be made in the eighteenth century. In those three-way contests where the electorate was polarized and one of the two parties put forth only one candidate, then a partisan vote for that candidate was of necessity a single vote. But the pressure to split one's vote in such a situation clearly increased. Often, of course, a single vote did suggest a higher level of party commitment than a double vote. When, for example, in 1780 Peach was brought in to catch the second votes of Cruger and thereby avoid the loss of votes to the government candidates, it

---

2 James Murray, *The Burgess Poll* (Newcastle upon Tyne, 2nd edn, 1775), pp. 7–8. Murray's use of party language is pervasive; for example, the use of the tally 'gives both parties equal spirits to exert themselves during the contest', p. 7. See Phillips, *Electoral Behavior*, pp. 5–6, 20–2, for the balloting process, swearing of oaths, and the nature of the double vote.

might be argued that this tactic betrayed a lack of real partisan commitment among those who voted for Cruger and Peach. Voters were, however, always reluctant to give up their second vote, and three-way contests usually did result in higher levels of cross voting. Finally, in two-way contests the possible options were greatly narrowed, and the vote was, by definition, fully 'partisan', though partisan voting had not in actual fact increased. For this reason two-way contests are not added into any measure of the average level of partisan behavior in a series of elections.

In the following analysis, a consistent or partisan vote is construed as either one or two votes for a party with one or two candidates. In three and four man elections, when a voter could cast two votes for a party but voted instead for one candidate alone, this single vote or 'plump' is still understood as a 'party' vote; incomplete party support is therefore still construed as partisan behavior.[3] Split or cross voting simply entails the casting of two votes across what were previously judged to be party lines. A large number of split votes thus calls into question the very existence of partisan behavior and will always necessitate a reexamination of the way the voters were grouped in the first place and a possible reinterpretation of the nature of the political contest. Given all of the peculiarities of the unreformed electorate it is still useful to group the electors into categories and attempt to measure the level of partisan behavior at each election.

THE ELECTORAL BEHAVIOR OF THE DISSENTING LAITY IN BRISTOL

The pattern of partisan voting in Bristol does, as one might expect, reflect the literary evidence already examined. (See Table 7.1.) The percentages for the 1754 election are especially impressive in light of the fact that it was a three-way contest. Fully 92.9 percent of all of Nugent's votes in 1754 were plumpers, a level that was not even approached by the supporters of Brickdale in 1774 (52.3%) or Cruger in 1784 (63.1%). The Dissenters on the whole were as partisan as the entire electorate – somewhat more so in the 1774 election and somewhat less in 1754 and 1784. The higher percentage of cross voting among Dissenters in 1784 may reflect the confusion of issues that was a product of the Coalition, a possibility that will be examined more carefully below. The Dissenters who plumped for Nugent in 1754 and Cruger in 1784 closely reflected the other electors (82.4% and 50% respectively). Evidently, an average party vote of 90.1 percent in the three elections of 1754, 1774, and

---

3 This usage has become conventional in psephological studies. Michael Drake, 'The Mid-Victorian voter', *JIH* 1 (1971), 484, note b., 486; W. A. Speck, W. A. Gray, and R. Hopkinson, 'Computer Analysis of Poll Books: A Further Report', *BIHR* 48 (1975), 87; Phillips, *Electoral Behavior*, p. 222. Speck, Gray, and Hopkinson found that contests involving three seats consistently increased the proportion of cross voting, and Phillips documented the same tendency. 'A Further Report', pp. 69–72; Phillips, *Electoral Behavior*, pp. 209–10, 214–23.

1784 represents a high level of partisan behavior, and this impression is strengthened by comparing these results to other constituencies.

Table 7.1: *Straight Party and Cross Voting in Bristol* (Percentage)

	1754	1774	1781	1784
PARTISAN	(3 way)	(4 way)	(2 way)	(4 way)
Electorate (other than Dissent)	96.3	83.8	100	90.2
Dissent	91.2	90.5	100	82.1
SPLIT				
Electorate	3.7	16.2	—	9.8
Dissent	8.8	9.5	—	17.9
Sample of Electorate, N=	1036	971	973	1089
Sample of Dissent, N=	68	95	106	112

Norwich was England's fourth largest urban center, and like Bristol, its size led to the early development of political organizations. In four elections at Norwich in the period 1761 to 1784 (two four-way and two three-way), John Phillips documented an average partisan vote of 90.6 percent.[4] Other large freeman boroughs show similar patterns of straight party voting during the American Revolution. At Liverpool, two three-way and one four-way contests between 1761 and 1784 yielded an average partisan vote only slightly less than that at Bristol (83.7%). At Newcastle upon Tyne a four-man contest in 1774 resulted in 94 percent of the voters using both votes in a partisan manner, but in the 1780 contest involving three seats, the partisan vote dropped to 46 percent. This dramatic change, however, did not reflect a lack of party conflict, but internal rivalry between radical candidates for the radical vote.[5]

Most eighteenth-century constituencies were less well-organized than Bristol, Norwich, and Liverpool. In Maidstone, Exeter, and Reading, personalities, patronage, corruption, uncertainty about a candidate's political persuasion, and in a few cases, even political issues, resulted in much lower levels of partisan voting. For example, Phillips found that voting in the five three-way Maidstone

4 Phillips, *Electoral Behavior*, pp. 204–6.
5 For Liverpool and Newcastle, see chap. 8 below, pp. 265, 283. The overall figures for Liverpool are, 91.6% in 1761; 78.5% in 1780 (both three-way); and 81% in 1784. The 1777 election at Newcastle was a two-man election. On the 1780 Newcastle contest, see Thomas R. Knox, 'Popular Politics and Provincial Radicalism: Newcastle upon Tyne, 1769–1781', *Albion*, 11 (1979), 240.

contests between 1761 and 1784 resulted in an average partisan vote of only 39.4 percent.[6] The 1761 election in Exeter was fought on party lines with only three of 1254 voters casting split votes, but unlike Bristol, there was no party organization in Exeter to sustain partisan behavior, and the elections of 1784 and 1790 evince a very different picture of the vote.[7] The 1784 poll book itself does not represent the three candidates grouped together in any fashion, but rather simply lists single and split votes for each one. Fully 33.6 percent of the electors cast single votes, and these were relatively evenly distributed between the candidates (14.9%, 6.8%, and 11.9%). In the 1790 election the three candidates might be grouped according to party, but this yields the result of consistent party support of 26.2 percent and cross voting of 73.8 percent. In constituencies that were not well organized, one election conducted along party lines might have nothing whatever to do with succeeding elections.

Reading was a scot and lot borough with an electorate of around 600. It was frequently contested, free from patrons, but very venal. Five poll books have survived for the period under study, and four of these elections were three-way contests.[8] The political issues, however, were not at all clear at Reading in 1754 and 1768. When one adds up the straight and the split votes, the proportion of partisan votes was higher in the elections where issues were less prominent than in those where clear choices were put before the electorate. In 1754, 71.1 percent of the vote was partisan, and in 1768, 71.5 percent, and in both elections there was little on the surface to distinguish the candidates politically. In 1774, however, when Francis Annesley offered the voters a clear alternative to the government over America, and in 1780, when Temple Luttrell stood as a strong opponent of North's administration, straight party voting dropped to 54.1 percent and 56.9 percent respectively, for an average of 63.4 percent over the four elections. This anomaly can be explained in part by the enormous sums of money spent at Reading to bribe electors. However, in 1774 the level of plumping for the government candidate on the one hand (17.2% of the vote) and the opposition candidates on the other (11.9%) suggests that one element in the electorate was oriented towards the issues, though this was not sustained in 1780.

These elections illustrate well the way that three man contests worked against partisan voting, but they also show that the lack of local political organization on the one hand, and bribery on the other, almost certainly militated against straight party voting. Moreover, while partisan behavior was normally greater in those boroughs that were politically organized and free from patronage and

---

6 Phillips, *Electoral Behavior*, pp. 204–6. After 1780, partisan voting at Maidstone increased in response to active local organizations.

7 *Commons, 1754–1790*, 1: 253; poll books for the 1761, 1784, and 1790 elections.

8 *Commons, 1754–1790*, 1: 211–12; poll books for the 1754, 1768, 1774, 1780, 1782 elections.

corruption, unusually high levels of partisan voting might be attained quite apart from the influence of political ideology.[9] Since the possible influences contributing to high levels of straight party voting are as various and complex as the differences between the boroughs themselves, it is necessary to turn to other, more analytical measures of partisanship.

A more penetrating test of partisan behavior may be made by examining the same electors over time. Longitudinal analysis of the electorate allows us to examine an individual's voting behavior on more than one occasion and this in turn provides insights concerning the extent of consistent partisan support.[10] On the basis of the preceding static assessment of straight party voting, the Dissenters at Bristol seemed to merely reflect the other electors. When, however, individual electors are examined for the degree of consistent party support over two elections, differences between Dissenters and other electors begin to appear. Table 7.2 depicts the partisan behavior of the same electors at two Bristol elections; the floating vote in this table includes only those who changed party; electors who split a vote in either election are noted separately.[11] Table 7.2 is organized on the basis of the candidates' association with the local clubs rather than their identification with the opposition or government at Westminster.[12]

9 Studies of different periods also provide useful comparisons. Levels of split voting in early eighteenth-century elections show a distinct decline over a period of years in constituencies where elections were frequent. In the first decade of the century, split voting dropped below 10% in Hampshire, Buckinghamshire, Westmorland, and Bedfordshire. W. A. Speck and W. A. Gray, 'Computer Analysis of Poll Books: An Initial Report', *BIHR* 43 (1970), 111; 'A Further Report', 69, 72, 87, 88. In the 1852 and 1857 elections in East Kent, levels of cross voting of 15.2% and 15% are thought by Michael Drake to be 'very small'. See 'The Mid-Victorian Voter', 486.

10 See Phillips, *Electoral Behavior*, pp. 212–13 for a good discussion of the meaning of a voter's identification with a party, as over against simply coherent political behavior.

11 Since the 1781 election is two-way, the options for the split vote of 1774–81 are necessarily restricted to split 1774 to party 1781; and for 1781–4, they are party 1781 to split 1784.

12 Nugent is classified as a Whig in 1754 as are Cruger and Burke in 1774, though the latter are in opposition; Brickdale and Daubeny are classed as Tories. In 1784 Cruger and Peach were still sponsored by the Union Club, even though by this date, Cruger was associated with Pitt. Just before the election in 1784 some Whigs perceived the apparent inconsistency of their now supporting a 'government' candidate and a resolution was passed at a meeting of Cruger's supporters at the Three Tuns in London to avoid the 'nominal distinction of parties by the appellation of Whig and Tory and blues and yellows which has long prevailed in Bristol'. But local party traditions were not to be expunged by a single resolution, and it undoubtedly worked to Cruger's advantage that the old labels were not so easily forgotten. Peter T. Underdown, 'The Parliamentary History of the City of Bristol, 1750–1790', University of Bristol, M.A. thesis, 1948, pp. 332–3. Against the resolution of Cruger's London supporters should be placed Peach's reminder to the local faithfuls that Cruger stood on 'genuine Constitutional Whig Principles'. 'Bristol Elections, 1774–1790. Addresses, Squibs, Songs', ref. B6979, p. 447, hereafter 'Bristol Elections'.

Table 7.2: *Partisan and Floating Vote in Bristol* (Percentage)

	1754-1774	1774-1781	1781-1784
PARTISAN (Union and Steadfast combined)			
Electorate	48.2	58.7	81.5
Dissent	56.2	76.1	82.6
FLOATING (Union to Steadfast or Steadfast to Union)			
Electorate	33.0	24.6	9.3
Dissent	18.8	12.0	2.3
SPLIT (Party to Split or Split to Party)			
Electorate	18.8	16.7	9.2
Dissent	25.0	11.2	15.1
Sample of Electorate, N=	197	528	637
Sample of Dissent, N=	16	71	86

In the local setting the pattern of increased partisan behavior that emerges in Bristol is parallel to that found in Norwich. This increase in partisan behavior over time is matched by an equally dramatic drop in the floating vote.[13] The lower level of consistent party support between 1754 and 1774 is in part explained by the length of time separating these elections. In the period 1774 to 1781, 58.7 percent of the electors other than those identified as Dissenters maintained a consistent party vote, which is comparable to Norwich, which reached about 52 percent during the same period.[14] But the high level of partisan activity reached by those electors who voted in 1781 and 1784 (81.5%) was not matched by voters in any other eighteenth-century constituency that has been studied heretofore. The even higher proportion of the Dissenters who voted consistently over two elections during the American Revolution and the concomitant low levels of their floating vote suggests a genuine affinity between religious orientation and partisan behavior. Consistency of partisanship is evidently related, at least in the case of the Dissenters, to religious

13 Speck and Gray initially interpreted a substantial floating vote as evidence of the freedom of voters from external pressure, but in their later research recognized that it could be a reflection of manipulation from above, 'An Initial Report', 112; 'A Further Report', 66. A large floating vote is also obviously a possible indication of a lack of political issues or convictions. See Phillips, *Electoral Behavior*, p. 228.
14 Phillips, *Electoral Behavior*, p. 232.

conviction. These data suggest that the Bristol Dissenters achieved a more disciplined party attachment earlier than the electorate at large, with the possible exception of the election of 1784 when a large proportion of Dissenters split their votes.

This evidence for increasing partisanship and higher levels of consistent party support requires a thorough reappraisal of Bristol's political life. Previous scholarship has failed to see the consistency of partisan behavior because of a narrow focus upon one, or at the most two, elections. On the grounds that the supporters of Cruger and Burke in 1774 were drawn both from the Whigs who disliked the existing government and the old Tories who were opposed to the sitting Members, Underdown argued that in 1774 there was 'an absence of any clear party alignment in the modern sense'.[15] It is true that 16 percent of the Whigs in 1754 supported the government ('Tory') candidate in 1774 and about an equal number of Tory voters in 1754 switched their support to Cruger and Burke. But the proportion of Whig voters in 1754 who voted for Cruger and Burke in 1774 was two times greater (31.5%) than those who changed parties between these two elections, and this represents an impressive substratum of consistent party support. This consistency, as we will see below, is also borne out by an areal analysis of Bristol voters. By identifying the party affiliation of individuals who voted in more than one election, and by identifying the party orientation of specific Bristol parishes, it is possible to argue that 'party alignment' in the modern sense was sometimes approximated in the eighteenth century, even when twenty years separated the elections.[16]

The disappearance of the 1780 poll book is a great loss, but a number of points may be advanced against Christie's contention that the Whig attempt to bring about a compromise in 1780 demonstrates the unimportance of political issues at Bristol.[17] First, because of the exorbitant cost and overall negative impact of party conflict, attempts at a compromise had been traditional.[18] Christie failed to note this tradition – a tradition that reflects not the lack of party spirit, but its ferocity. The elite had always tried to control partisan politics and would resort to caucus politics whenever they could, and thus an over reliance on the opinion of the elite has, in Christie's account, given too much prominence to caucus politics. Second, we have seen how the Steadfast

15 Peter T. Underdown, 'Henry Cruger and Edmund Burke: Colleagues and Rivals at the Bristol election of 1774', *WMQ*, 3rd ser., 15 (1958), 16 note 10.

16 The small number of voters that can be linked in the 1754 and 1774 poll books and the large complement of new voters in 1774 (to be examined below), require that these generalizations remain tentative. On the other hand, the great length of time separating the two elections makes the consistency of the few that can be linked all the more important.

17 Ian R. Christie, 'Henry Cruger and the End of Edmund Burke's Connection with Bristol', *BGAST* 74 (1955), 159–60, 168.

18 Underdown, 'Parliamentary History', pp. 56, 140, 304, 403; G. E. Weare, *Edmund Burke's Connection with Bristol, From 1774 till 1780* (Bristol, 1894), pp. 12–14.

Society prepared for this election five months in advance, and they did so with the best propaganda available – reprints of John Wesley's *Calm Address*.[19] Further, the Club's very unwillingness to sacrifice one candidate suggests that its supporters were ideologically committed to the government and its policies. Third, Underdown has clearly demonstrated that among Burke's agents at Bristol, Champion's hostility to Cruger was really exceptional; some of Burke's supporters were willing to work with Cruger.[20] In fact, Underdown concludes that Burke's 'more obsequious' followers often lacked a clear vision of the political scene at Bristol.[21] Fourth, Cruger's lack of support from Burke's friends may be accounted for as much in terms of a Whig capitulation to a well-orchestrated government landslide as in terms of dissension between the two Whig factions.[22] Personal differences did hurt the Whig cause in 1780, but Christie's reconstruction gives little place to the extent to which Low-Churchmen and Dissenters may have withdrawn over their disgust at Burke's support of Catholic emancipation.[23] In short, Christie's complete dismissal of the popular literature of the election, and his overreliance on Champion's narrowly focused hatred of Cruger, has resulted in a distinctly one-sided view of the 1780 election.

The same conservative denial of the importance of political issues has dominated the interpretation of the election of 1784. Commenting upon the apparent anomaly of Brickdale and Daubeny (both 'Tories') supporting the 'Whig' Coalition, and Cruger (a Whig) identifying with the 'Tory' Government of Pitt, while the Bristol voters of 1784 stood by the same candidates they had supported in 1781, Namier observed that 'party politics on a national scale did not as yet prevail even in places such as Bristol, which in appearance was politically organized'.[24] But politics 'on a national scale' had clearly prevailed at Bristol in 1774 and 1781, and it is a serious distortion to call the Coalition 'Whig' and Pitt 'Tory' when so many Whigs had reacted to the Coalition out of their feelings of revulsion toward North. From the local viewpoint, Brickdale and Daubeny were associated less with Fox than they were with North. Namier could not see the continuity between national issues and local parties during the

19 Underdown, 'Parliamentary History', pp. 291, 295, 302.
20 Underdown, 'Burke's Bristol Friends', *BGAST* 77 (1958), 128, 148.
21 *Ibid.*, p. 144.
22 Christie, 'Henry Cruger', 164–5.
23 Weare plays this issue up in *Edmund Burke's Connection*, p. 153, as does Underdown, 'Parliamentary History', p. 284; Underdown, 'Bristol and Burke', 58; in Patrick McGrath, (ed.), *Bristol in the Eighteenth Century* (Newton Abbot, 1972); 'Burke's Bristol Friends', 133–4.
24 Sir Lewis Namier, *The Structure of Politics at the Accession of George III* (London, 1929, 2nd edn, 1957), p. 91; Brooke makes an even stronger statement in *Commons, 1754–1790*, 1: 289. Underdown noted the same; 'The curious situation therefore existed in Bristol of Cruger's friends supporting the predominantly Tory government of Pitt, while those of Brickdale and Daubeny were adhering to the predominantly Whig Coalition of Fox and North ...' 'Parliamentary History', p. 324.

Revolution because even his highly analytical technique proved incapable of observing the political behavior of individuals and of specified interest groups within the electorate. The same Bristol Whigs who supported the Union Club's candidate in 1754 continued to view themselves as Whigs in 1774, though by then they had turned against Lord Clare. And if they were Whigs in 1774, they were even more strongly identified with the local party in 1781 and again in 1784 as the decline in the floating vote amply demonstrates. The local Whig party was in turn clearly associated with opposition at Westminster in 1774 and 1781, if not in 1784. In the wake of the Coalition's dismissal, issues of party loyalty were far less clear than they had been, and for that reason the general election of 1784 should not serve as the sole point of departure for the interpretation of partisan politics in any borough.

The continuity between national politics and local parties at Bristol is further illustrated by the way in which political ideology, religion, the use of the secret service funds, and the behavior of the average voter, converge. The reintroduction of Whig and Tory party labels in 1774 and their pervasive use in 1781 has already been documented.[25] References in the election literature to the 'Whig party', the 'Whig cause', or the 'Whig interest' are legion and almost rivaled by allusions to the 'Tories of Bristol', the 'true honest Tories', or the 'Tory-Administration'. 'A Member of the White Lion' wrote at length in 1781 concerning the evenly balanced strength of both parties and was principally concerned with 'our Interest as a Party',[26] and thus both groups understood themselves in terms of party. Accordingly, the opposition candidates in 1774, 1780 and 1781 derived their support from the local Whig organization, and the government candidates found their base in the Steadfast Society and the reconstituted Loyal and Constitutional Club. The role of ideology is most graphically displayed, however, in the radically altered orientation of the Anglican clergy and the Dissenting ministers. An ideological counterpart to the Dissenting ministers' support of the Americans is found in the Anglican clergy's support of the government candidates. The clergy, known for their Tory sympathies, voted overwhelmingly against the government candidate in 1754, and for the government in 1774 and 1781, while the Dissenting ministers turned unanimously to the Whig Opposition.[27]

25 See chap. 6.
26 'Bristol Broadsides', p. 323.
27 Other studies of the clerical vote have concluded that the Anglican clergy voted consistently 'Tory'. In fact, the most consistent body of electors in the counties were Anglican clergy. Speck and Gray, 'An Initial Report', 112. Phillips, *Electoral Behavior*, p. 286. At Bristol, the voting Dissenting ministers are, in 1754, John Diaper, Hugh Evans, Bernard Foskett, William Richards; in 1774, Caleb Evans, Hugh Evans; in 1781, Caleb Evans, Hugh Evans, John Estlin, Joseph Hoskins, James Davis, John Thomas, Thomas Wright; in 1784, Caleb Evans, John Estlin, Joseph Hoskins, James Davis.

Table 7.3: *Anglican and Dissenting Clerical Vote in Bristol*

	Anglican Clergy			Dissenting Ministers		
	Gov.	Opp.	Split	Gov.	Opp.	Split
1754	9	28	—	4	—	—
1774	42	6	3	—	2	—
1781	50	8	—	—	7	—
1784	2	13	—	4	—	—

The Church–Chapel cleavage in Bristol was grounded in both ecclesiastical and political issues; the Bishop of Bristol, Thomas Newton, characteristically dismissed Nonconformist principles as 'worse than Hottentots'.[28] It was probably this religious component of borough politics more than anything else that led Burke to exclaim in 1780, 'Our grand division is of Whigs and Tories', though this was standard opposition rhetoric.[29] The religious reorientation of the 1770s also stood behind some contemporaries' perception that the government had changed in an authoritarian direction, while local faithfuls maintained the age-old party traditions.

At the same time that the Anglican clergy turned to the government, the government's new departure, when viewed from the local angle, was made explicit by the redirection of secret service funds. For the first time in the century, the 'Whig' candidates in 1774 were denied financial support and large amounts of money were channeled instead to the local 'Tory' candidates; thereafter, the Loyal and Constitutional Club became the recipient of government election funds.[30] Any comprehensive analysis of borough politics thus must take into account local, national, financial, and religious issues, and only then is it possible to see why some observers associated the government's American policy with the resurgence of Toryism. Accordingly, it is highly misleading to argue that by 1774 the 'old type' of Tory was 'almost extinct' and that Brickdale, the so-called Tory, was indistinguishable politically from Clare, the so-called Whig, thereby discounting the importance of party labels.[31] The old party labels were grounded in religion and religion was anything but extinct. In Bristol the labels 'Whig' and 'Tory' had everything to do with how one understood both local and national politics, and religious

28 Quoted in Phillips, *Electoral Behavior*, p. 287.
29 Phillips found little use of the terms 'Whig' and 'Tory' in his study and he provides evidence for widespread contemporary objection to the terms, *Electoral Behavior*, pp. 116–18. He also minimizes the possibility of party continuities dating from the earlier period, pp. 117, 230. Clearly, Bristol was an exceptional case.
30 Large amounts of money also went to the government candidates in 1780, and Daubeny obtained a grant of £5,000 in 1781. Underdown, 'Parliamentary History', pp. 284, 315.
31 *Commons, 1754–1790*, 1: 284.

loyalties provide the most convincing evidence of party continuity. While the high degree of party continuity at Bristol is atypical, it clearly helps to explain Burke's understanding of party, and this, in turn, helps account for the origins of the Whig interpretation.

But the final verdict on the relationship of national politics to the Bristol electorate must be sought not in the actions of the elite, but in the political behavior of the voters themselves. The Bristol Whigs turned against the government in 1774, and the borough voter, far from demonstrating irrational behavior or merely local concerns, became increasing partisan precisely on national issues. This is best illustrated by the Dissenters themselves. When we look at the proportion of Dissenters who turned against the government in 1774, compared to all other Whigs, the differences are striking. Figure 7.1 shows how the well-defined local parties at Bristol related to the national political orientation of their candidates, and these data give strong support to two of

Figure 7.1

PARTISAN VOTE OF BRISTOL DISSENTERS AND ALL OTHER VOTERS

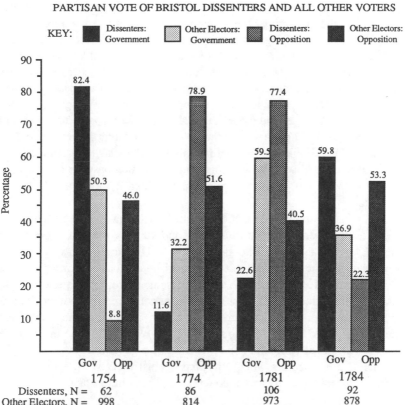

the main contentions of this book.[32] First, in those boroughs that were relatively free from external control, and where there was a developed tradition of party rivalry nurtured by religious differences, the voter could, and often did, transcend local issues and respond intelligently to national concerns. Second, where the Dissenting elite, whether clerical or lay, gave outspoken progressive leadership to the body of Dissenters, the majority of the laity might be expected to follow with consistent political behavior, even against what was previously judged to be a benign administration. When Caleb Evans went to the polls in 1774, 1781, and 1784, he voted for Henry Cruger, and his Baptist congregation, almost to a man, faithfully followed in his steps.

The dramatic reversals depicted in Figure 7.1 reflect the local political response to the changing political situation at Westminster. In 1774 and 1781 local Whigs viewed themselves as consistent, and merely responding to ominous reactionary changes in the government. The government was seen as increasingly repressive in 1774 and thus the Whigs, and in the first place the Dissenters, stood by their principles and voted against the government. In 1784, with the war at an end and the advent of a new administration associated with reform, they returned, at least momentarily, to the government (to the extent that a vote for Cruger was understood as a vote for the government). While it is true that the majority of voters turned against the government in 1774, the proportion of Dissenting electors compared to all other electors who changed their orientation toward the government shows that Dissenters were more consistently opposed to the American war than the Whigs in general. Proportionately 27.3 percent more of the Dissenters who voted, turned against the government in 1774 than all other 'Whigs', and this increased to 36.9 percent in 1781. Similarly, both before and after the war they supported the government more than other electors. These data demonstrate a clear relationship between Dissenting voters and the national issue of the American Revolution.

Further insight on the Bristol electorate can be gained by utilizing the categories of government and opposition and viewing the voters over time (Table 7.4). Here the steadfast opposition of the Dissenters who voted in two elections during the war stands out in comparison to other electors who voted in 1774 and 1781. Over twice as many Dissenters proportionately (67.6%) maintained their stance against the government compared to all other electors (30.3%). Also, the much higher proportion of non-Dissenting voters who were brought around to the government during the war is illuminating (20.1% versus 9.9%). Equally important is the return to the government in 1784 of the same Dissenting electors who had voted against the government in 1781 (61.6%). This undoubtedly had to do with the happy circumstance that Cruger

---

32 This graph excludes split votes which are displayed in Table 7.1 so the proportions do not total 100%.

was a known entity, and thus a vote for him did not entail the risk that might be involved with a new candidate who supported Pitt. But the high percentage of those Dissenters who voted on a partisan basis in 1781 and split their votes in 1784 (15.1%) and those who did move from government to opposition (20.9%), suggests that there was some dissatisfaction over Cruger's association with the government of Pitt. In any case, the majority of Dissenters at

Table 7.4: *Proportion of Dissenters and Other Electors Who Maintained or Changed Their Orientation to Government* (Percentage)

	1754-1774		1774-1781		1781-1784	
	Dissent N=16	Other N=197	Dissent N=71	Other N=528	Dissent N=86	Other N=637
Gov-Gov	12.5	16.2	8.5	28.4	0	5.0
Gov-Opp	50.0	29.9	2.8	4.5	20.9	52.6
Opp-Gov	6.3	18.3	9.9	20.1	61.6	28.9
Opp-Opp	6.3	16.8	67.6	30.3	2.3	4.2
Party to Split or Split to Party	25.0	18.8	11.3	16.7	15.1	9.3

Bristol were willing to return to the government after the American Revolution and this lends support to the widespread assumption that the Dissenters turned away from Fox in this election.[33] At Norwich the Dissenters supported a Foxite in 1784, but the situation at Bristol was significantly different and seems to comport better with the Dissenting vote at Northampton.[34] Pitt's early association with reform appears to have been very attractive to some of the Dissenters; we can observe this not only at Bristol and Northampton, but also at Great Yarmouth. There, in 1784, the Dissenters gave strong support to the outspoken Pittite, Henry Beaufoy, who had a Dissenting background, and thus it may be that the Dissenting support for the Coalition at Norwich was exceptional. The political affiliation of the Dissenters with a new alignment at Westminster – especially a grouping with as chequered a recent past as the Coalition – was evidently not as strong as their attachment to a cause such as the American Revolution. And, the local frame of reference at Bristol, as Namier believed, probably counted for more in 1784 than the turn of events at Westminster, though the majority of the Bristol Dissenters had the satisfaction of voting consistently with the local Whig club. There is convincing evidence

33 Robert A. Smith, *Eighteenth-Century English Politics* (New York, 1972), p. 155.
34 Phillips, *Electoral Behavior*, pp. 164, 294. Phillips observed that the Coalition 'rendered partisan ties less distinct' (p. 290) and suspected that it influenced Dissenting loyalties in the same way. Bristol Dissenters bear this out. See also pp. 213 note 5, 220.

that after 1784 at Norwich and Northampton, the Dissenters were moving increasingly away from the government, but whether this phenomenon was characteristic of other boroughs remains to be seen.

If the Dissenters' behavior at Bristol was predictable, the unity among the various Dissenting denominations was equally striking.[35] Before, during, and after the American crisis, the Presbyterians, Baptists, and Quakers voted together (see Table 7.5). Their vote for opposition candidates depicts considerable unity, but while the proportions are similar, nearly two times as many Baptists could be located in 1774 the poll book as Presbyterians, though the congregations were roughly the same size. These differences of voter turnout may well represent the mobilizing effort of Caleb Evans' pulpit.

Table 7.5: *Denominational Proportion of Vote for Opposition Candidates* (Percentage)

	Presbyterian	Baptist	Quaker
1754	6.5	8.3	16.7
1774	80.8	82.5	73.1
1781	72.7	81.6	71.9
1784	27.3	19.3	26.7

The pattern of Dissenting opposition found at Bristol in 1774 and 1781 is remarkably similar to that found at Norwich in 1780, an election in which America was a central issue. In Norwich the Dissenters who had supported the government in the 1760s turned against North's administration and there too, they were more consistently opposed to the government during the Revolution than the Whigs in general. At first they were as uniformly behind the government as other Whigs, but in the 1780 election, 63 percent of all the identifiable Dissenters who voted, voted against the government, compared to 45 percent of the remaining voters.[36] This pattern of early and strong Dissenting loyalty to the government turning to outspoken opposition to the government in the 1770s and 1780s suggests the presence of basic party continuities between the old Whiggism and a new progressivism redefined by the American war. Bristol and Norwich were two of Britain's largest and most prestigious urban constituencies. The Dissenters' conspicuous presence in both the municipal and the parliamentary politics of these two boroughs, combined with their age-long association with Whig politics, meant that the consistency of their behavior

35 This unity, it should be noted, lends support to the validity of the sample of Dissenting electors.

36 Phillips, *Electoral Behavior*, p. 292; only 21% of the identifiable Dissenters voted consistently for the government in 1780, compared to 42% overall.

probably influenced the self-definition of the entire local Whig party. Dissenters in both boroughs had outstanding charismatic leadership in the persons of Caleb Evans and Rees David. It is almost certain that these developments in such large boroughs influenced Burke's understanding of party. Though it is impossible to prove, it seems likely that Low-Church Anglicans who were willing to associate politically with the Dissenting interest derived an element of their own political cohesion from this association. Moreover, the election literature in both boroughs makes it quite clear that the local defenders of the government defined themselves over against the Dissenting branch of the Whig party.

The smaller boroughs of Northampton and Great Yarmouth confirm the patterns found in Bristol and Norwich, though without the corroboration of popular election literature. Northampton bears some resemblance to Norwich and Bristol despite the fact that the 1774 contest did not present a clear option to the electors over America. Here, 75 percent of all Dissenters supported an opposition candidate compared to 70 percent of all other electors. Generally the Northampton Dissenters were less unlike their Anglican Whig brethren than the Bristol and Norwich Dissenters and this may well reflect the influence of patronage.[37] But the pattern of strong Dissenting support of the government in the 1760s at Northampton turning to overwhelming support of the opposition in the 1770s is similar to that found elsewhere, and the same is true of Great Yarmouth.

THE ELECTORAL BEHAVIOR OF THE DISSENTING LAITY IN GREAT YARMOUTH

Great Yarmouth was a medium-sized freeman borough with some 800 voters. Frequent political contests suggest the presence of a viable opposition element, though unfortunately, little election literature has survived. The borough was heavily influenced by the Townshend and Walpole families who dominated the corporation, and the opposition in the second half of the century was centered in an anti-corporation party organized by the Nonconformists.[38] The Dissenting interest at Yarmouth was relatively small, though all of the old denominations were represented. The Gaol Street Presbyterian chapel was the largest congregation and it was the home of the prominent and politically active Hurry family. A Congregational chapel of unknown size subsisted throughout the eighteenth century; there were two Baptist meetings and an assembly of Quakers, but the birth and baptismal records of the Presbyterians and Quakers

---

37 *Ibid.*, pp. 294–6. Northampton had an inhabitant householder franchise.
38 *Commons, 1715–1754*, 1: 290; *Commons, 1754–1790*, 1: 340. B. D. Hayes, 'Politics in Norfolk, 1750–1832' University of Cambridge Ph.D. diss., 1958, p. 121. For a recent survey of the political history of Great Yarmouth during the American crisis and the repeated petitioning agitation there, see James Bradley, *Popular Politics and The American Revolution in England: Petitions, the Crown, and Public Opinion* (Macon, Ga., 1986).

alone have survived. Moreover, none of the four presiding ministers who were resident in the 1770s are known to have taken an aggressive political stance.[39] The small number of Yarmouth Dissenters, combined with the quiescence of the ministerial elite, meant that the Dissenting influence on elections would remain but slight. The lack of leadership among the ministers, however, was compensated for in part by the radical political activities of the Hurry family.

When the Dissenters first broached the possibility of opposing the Townshend–Walpole monopoly in 1768, they claimed that they had traditionally stood loyally by their Whig patrons.[40] The election of 1754 illustrates that the Dissenters were indeed one of the main bulwarks of the local Whig oligarchy; nearly two-thirds of all Dissenters voted for the government candidates compared to less than half of the remaining electors. In the late 1760s, however, an opposition party began to form against the Townshend–Walpole control of patronage; it was led by a small group of disaffected Anglicans on the corporation and ten of the town's leading Dissenters headed by Thomas Hurry.[41] This group was able to secure the resignation of the Townshend–Walpole agent, but the extent to which they took over the job of channeling patronage is unknown. In the general election of 1774 the same faction backed Sir Charles Saunders, a friend and supporter of Lord Rockingham and an opponent of the government's American policy, and William Beckford, son of the well-known London radical, but they were badly beaten and the poll book of this election has not survived. Signed petitions both for and against the government's coercive policy in 1775, however, have been recovered, and a comparison of these documents to the registers of the Presbyterian and Quaker chapels reveals the Dissenters' strong disapproval of the government's American measures.[42]

At a by-election in 1777 the leaders backed Beckford again, but they were able to marshal only part of the Dissenting vote and generally made a poor showing at the polls: Beckford received only 199 votes to Townshend's 502. Townshend was a steadfast supporter of North – he went in and out of office

39 John Evans, 'List of Dissenting Congregations and Ministers in England and Wales (1715–1729)' MS 38.4 (hereafter cited as the Evans List), pp. 83–5; Josiah Thompson, 'List of Protestant Dissenting Congregations in England and Wales, (1722–73)' MS 38.6 (hereafter cited as the Thompson List) p. 25; Hayes, 'Politics in Norfolk', p. 123; Ian Christie, 'Great Yarmouth and the Yorkshire Reform Movement, 1782–1784', in *Myth and Reality in Late-Eighteenth-Century British Politics and Other Papers* (London, 1970), p. 284. Of the Dissenting ministers, only John M. Benyon signed the conciliatory petition in 1775; See *Norw. Merc.* (9 Dec. 1775) and 'A View of English Nonconformity in 1773', in *CHST* 5 (1911–12), 271. The poll books were compared to the Presbyterian register alone. Though Hayes did no individual level analysis, he did observe that 'the great block-voting pressure group of Dissent was perhaps the most important single factor in politics'. 'Politics in Norfolk', p. 130. Hayes mentions the elections of 1774 and 1777 only in passing, pp. 196, 210.
40 *Commons, 1754–1790*, 1: 340.
41 Thomas Hurry-Houghton, *Memorials of the Family of Hurry* (Liverpool, 1926), p. 9. Hayes, 'Politics in Norfolk', p. 211.
42 Bradley, *Popular Politics and the American Revolution in England*, p. 192.

with him – and he was a staunch defender of the war against the colonies; he was returned unopposed in 1780. The independents' failure to contest the 1780 election was undoubtedly related to their overwhelming defeat in 1777 and the satisfaction they received from the other sitting Member, Richard Walpole, who voted consistently against North's administration. Christie's supposition that Walpole was unacceptable to the Yarmouth independents because he allowed whatever local influence he had to run in traditional government channels presupposes that the Dissenters were motivated purely by local concerns.[43] Patronage was important, as Christie has shown, but the independents petitioned for peace with America in 1775, for economic reform in 1780 – the same year as the general election – and again in 1782 and 1783 for parliamentary reform. The persistence and consistency of this popular political activity should not be lightly dismissed.

At Yarmouth, as in the other boroughs, the Dissenters supported the government more strongly than other electors before the Revolution, but during the American crisis the majority of Presbyterians turned against North's administration (see Figure 7.2).[44] The lack of well-established political organizations, the failure of clerical leadership, and possibly the power of patronage meant that many Dissenters remained satisfied with the government in 1777 (41.9%). But as at Bristol and Norwich, they were proportionately far more partisan in their orientation against the government than other electors. In 1784, the Hurry family introduced Henry Beaufoy to Great Yarmouth.[45] The Dissenters could hardly have found a more public-spirited, open-minded, progressive representative. Beaufoy came from a Quaker family and went to Nonconformist schools, but he later joined the Established Church and thus technically cannot be considered a Dissenter.

As an opponent of the Coalition, a friend of reform, and an outspoken advocate of Pitt, Beaufoy was so well received at Yarmouth in 1784 that upon a canvass, his opponent, Charles Townshend, withdrew. Beaufoy led the campaign for repeal of the Test and Corporation Acts (1787–90) and won a firm place in the affections of the Yarmouth Dissenters.[46] While Townshend had been opposed by the local opposition in 1777, and again in 1784, by 1790 he and the Dissenters seem to have been reconciled, for they and the vast majority of the electorate were willing to give one vote to Townshend and one vote to Beaufoy, resulting in an unprecedented proportion of cross votes.[47]

43 Christie, 'Great Yarmouth', p. 290. I found this line of reasoning acceptable in my article, 'Whigs and Nonconformists: "Slumbering Radicalism" in English Politics', *ECS* 9 (1975), 22.

44 The split votes in 1754 were 3.3% among the Dissenters and 7.2% among other electors; in 1790, 83.3% among Dissenters and 86.3% among other electors. The 1777 contest was a two-way contest.

45 Christie, 'Great Yarmouth', p. 294.

46 *Commons, 1754–1790*, 2: 73.

47 *Ibid.*, 3: 539.

Figure 7.2

PARTISAN VOTE OF YARMOUTH DISSENTERS AND ALL OTHER VOTERS

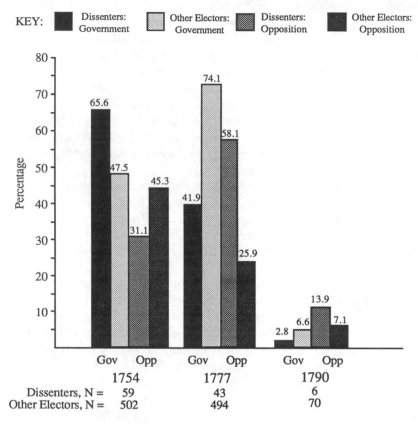

KEY: ▮ Dissenters: Government   ▨ Other Electors: Government   ▨ Dissenters: Opposition   ▮ Other Electors: Opposition

	1754	1777	1790
Dissenters, N =	59	43	6
Other Electors, N =	502	494	70

In the large freeman boroughs of Bristol and Norwich, and in a variety of smaller boroughs like Northampton and Yarmouth, the Dissenters' political behavior in the age of the American Revolution was strikingly uniform. First at the polls in the defense of the Whig ascendancy, the Dissenters turned to become the most outspoken opponents of the government's American policy. The Dissenting interest thereby provided the electoral base for a widespread sense of continuity in local politics, and at the same time, this interest gave birth to many of the exaggerations of Whig historiography.

The Dissenters studied here seemed to prove that Wallin's and Priestley's appeals did not fall upon deaf ears, but in other, less open boroughs, the Dissenters were largely politically impotent. Yet more is at stake than the Dissenting vote. By focusing attention on the Dissenters, we have detected a similar redirection of political loyalties on the part of a much larger body of Anglicans. The Dissenters' coherence as a voting bloc may have helped engage the Low-Church Anglican vote in opposition to the government, but there are other possible causes for the changed attitude of Anglicans. The overall increase in partisan behavior and the movement of many Anglicans into opposition may be attributed to religion, but it also may be related to economic causes. The organization of local clubs, the frequency of elections, the dissemination of popular literature, the religious ideology of the elite, and active leadership among the Dissenting laity finally provide only partial explanations for the increased partisanship and political consistency of the voters at Bristol and Great Yarmouth. The previous voting experience of electors and their socio-economic status must now be examined in detail, because in port towns in particular, one might expect that partisan cleavage during the American Revolution was related to commercial interests on the one hand and economic differences among the voters on the other.

POLITICAL CONSISTENCY, SOCIO-ECONOMIC STATUS, AND RELIGION

Modern studies of voting behavior characteristically examine both the frequency of the voters' electoral participation and their previous voting experience.[48] Increased levels of partisanship such as we have found at Bristol were commonly related to a party's ability to recruit new voters and attract and retain experienced ones. But because of the relatively small number of poll books available for this study, and because of the wide extent of time that often separated these elections, the value of an examination of voter experience is somewhat limited. However, in numerous boroughs – including Bristol – large numbers of new freemen were admitted just before a contest and thus some analysis of this question is required.[49]

In 1774 Cruger and Burke were slightly more popular with the new voters than the government candidate (Table 7.6).[50] Evidently, at Bristol, electioneering had a greater impact on voting behavior than in other eighteenth-century boroughs. Bristol's political managers were extremely dedicated, the clubs were highly organized, and the output of literature at election time was probably only exceeded by London and Westminster. In any case, these statistics bear out Brickdale's theory that Burke relied heavily on the recruitment of new voters.[51] Brickdale contested his loss on the grounds of the illegality of admitting new freemen, though his petition proved ineffectual.[52] In 1784 Cruger

48 Phillips, *Electoral Behavior*, p. 244 has a fine survey of the issues.
49 Bristol is a good example: 986 new freemen were admitted before the election in 1754; and in 1774, 2080 citizens became freemen a month before the election. On these statistics and the Durham Act which attempted to regulate the practice, see Underdown, 'Parliamentary History', pp. 41, 135, 191.
50 This table depicts the voters' experience in only one previous election.
51 G. E. Weare, *Edmund Burke's Connection*, pp. 80–6; 118–19.
52 See 'Bristol Elections', Burke's speech to the Electors, 3 Nov. 1774, pp. 147–151; 'Reflections on the Speech of Edmund Burke', 4 Nov. 1774, pp. 152–3; 'Atticus', 4 Nov.

(now government) continued to win more of his support from new voters than experienced voters, but once again, the differences are not dramatic.

Table 7.6: *Partisanship of New and Experienced Voters in Bristol*

(Percentage)

	1774			1781			1784		
	All Voters	Exp. Voters	New Voters	All Voters	Exp. Voters	New Voters	All Voters	Exp. Voters	New Voters
Gov	30.4	34.7	29.3	55.9	57.6	54.2	39.2	37.2	43.2
Opp	54.0	49.3	55.2	44.1	42.4	45.8	50.1	52.8	45.8
Split	15.6	16.0	15.5	—	—	—	10.7	10.0	11.3
N =	1066	213	853	1079	549	469	1086	723	301

Bristol, however, appears to have been exceptional in the eighteenth century. At Norwich and Maidstone, Phillips found that new voters were evenly distributed between the parties and that electoral experience had no measurable effect on voting behavior.[53] An analysis of new voters at Newcastle upon Tyne and Kingston upon Hull bear out his findings. New voters in Newcastle in 1777 and 1780 are considerably less distinguishable from experienced voters than those in Bristol, and at Hull in 1780 and 1784 no differences between new and experienced voters are detectable.[54]

Since Bristol derived its wealth and influence from foreign trade, it might well be expected that partisan conflict during the American crisis would have an economic base.[55] Contemporary Bristoleans often observed that religion was a cause of the polarization of the electorate, but sometimes they attributed the conflict to socio-economic causes. We have seen that in 1754, Josiah Tucker believed that Nugent drew his support from 'the mob', and in 1774 Brickdale's managers charged that Cruger was largely dependent on 'the middling class of people' and 'vagabond tradesmen'.[56] In the election literature of 1781, Cruger

1774, p. 155; 'Regulus', 16 Nov. 1774, p. 156; and anonymous, 23 Nov. 1774, p. 161.
53 Phillips, *Electoral Behavior*, pp. 245–6; 249–50. However, the duration of party support, not simply voting experience, did strengthen party loyalty, p. 251.
54 The only exception to these generalizations is the opposition vote at Newcastle in 1780 which was supported by a disproportionate number of new voters (43.8%), compared to the government (7.3%); 48.9%, however, of these new voters split their vote.
55 W. E. Minchinton, 'Bristol – metropolis of the west in the eighteenth century', in Peter Clark, (ed.), *The Early Modern Town* (London, 1976), p. 298.
56 Underdown thinks that the poll books do bear out Tucker's epithets of 1754 and that Cruger was indebted to the artisans in 1774, but he provides no summary of grouped trades, relying instead on individual occupations. 'Parliamentary History', p. 42; 'Henry Cruger', pp. 23, 33.

was frequently associated with the poor, though these connections were sometimes denied.

Any attempt at social analysis on the basis of occupational categories alone must deal honestly with the limited usefulness of such data, (see Appendix 2). While fine discrimination of social strata is impossible with this evidence, significant differences in occupational categories between two parties might point to underlying economic differences. Similar data have been used in a social assessment of the petitioning movement of 1775 where the coercive petitions were found to include a greater proportion of people in the professional and merchant category than the conciliatory petitions.[57] The following analysis will utilize the same categories, and, while recognizing the limitations of the data, it will set forth any evidence of social stratification that might have influenced partisan behavior.

At Norwich the Revolution was a political issue in 1780, but there was little evidence linking partisan behavior to socio-economic status, though the middling ranks were more supportive of the opposition than the elite.[58] Bristol, like Norwich, reflects socio-economic cleavages during the revolutionary period while there were virtually no differences between the parties before and after the Revolution (see Table 7.7). Nugent was slightly more dependent on the artisans in 1754 than his Tory opponent, but more importantly, Cruger and Burke in 1774, and to some extent, Cruger again in 1781, were more indebted to the lower orders than were the government candidates, while the latter drew proportionately more support from the highest category. Phillips found there was less social division between parties than between partisan and non-partisan voters at Maidstone and Northampton.[59] The same is true for Bristol in 1754 (though the number of split votes is very small) and in 1784, but not in 1774. In 1774 Brickdale received 25.7 percent of his support from the professional and merchant categories combined (categories 1 and 2), compared to only 9.5 percent for Cruger and Burke. The artisans favored the opposition slightly in both 1774 and 1781, and the shopkeepers gave strong support to the opposition in 1774. In an earlier study of five smaller boroughs I theorized that the sharpness with which the American Revolution was focused as a political issue in any given constituency was directly related to the polarization of the voters on economic grounds. Great Yarmouth, Cambridge, Southampton, and Bridgwater were divided politically during the American Revolution, but at Cambridge alone was the American conflict specifically raised as a political issue, and Cambridge showed greater signs of socio-economic cleavage in 1774 than the other three boroughs.[60]

57 See Bradley, *Popular Politics and the American Revolution in England*, p. 188.
58 Phillips, *Electoral Behavior*, pp. 144–5; 267. There was even less connection between occupational structure and voting at Maidstone, pp. 263, 268–71.
59 Phillips, *Electoral Behavior*, p. 269.
60 In 1774 at Bristol, the government candidates won only 30.4% of the overall partisan

Table 7.7: *Occupational Structure of the Electorate in Bristol* (Percentage)

	1754			1774		
	Gov.	Opp.	Split	Gov.	Opp.	Split
1. Gentlemen, Professions	4.3	6.2	11.4	16.7	5.0	6.0
2. Merchants	6.1	6.6	13.6	9.0	4.5	10.2
3. Shopkeepers	21.1	23.6	25.0	17.3	25.5	26.5
4. Artisans	55.5	49.1	34.1	46.0	54.5	47.6
5. Laborers	4.7	5.4	6.8	7.1	7.3	5.4
6. Others	8.3	9.1	9.1	4.0	3.1	4.2
N =	577	483	44	324	576	166

	1781			1784		
	Gov.	Opp.		Gov.	Opp.	Split
1. Gentlemen, Professions	10.6	6.7		5.4	8.5	9.5
2. Merchants	8.5	4.8		2.3	6.8	9.5
3. Shopkeepers	25.2	25.6		27.0	27.6	21.6
4. Artisans	47.3	54.8		52.6	50.0	56.0
5. Laborers	6.1	5.9		10.6	5.3	3.4
6. Others	2.3	2.1		2.1	1.8	—
N =	603	476		426	544	116

The occupational stratification of the voters of Great Yarmouth shows some similarities to Bristol, although the differences between the government and opposition parties are not statistically significant in 1777 (Table 7.8). As at Bristol and Norwich, the slightly greater support for opposition candidates among the artisans comports with what was found in a study of the petitioning agitation of 1775.[61] The voters in parliamentary elections were generally less susceptible to dividing over the American crisis on economic grounds than were the petitioners, but Norwich, Bristol, and to a lesser extent, Yarmouth do show some signs of socio-economic conflict. The differences, however, are

vote but they took 58.1% of the total gentry-professional group, whereas the opposition, with 54% of the total partisan vote won only 31.2% of the highest group; the merchants were less disproportionately spread out. But the opposition had 59.5% of all the partisan shopkeepers compared to only 22.7% won by the government candidates. Using X^2, the differences in occupational categories between parties are significant at the .01 level of probability at Bristol in 1774. On the smaller boroughs, see Bradley, *Popular Politics and the American Revolution in England*, p. 187. The data from Poole was inconclusive.

61 Bradley, *Popular Politics and the American Revolution in England*, pp. 188–9.

slight, and they fall far short of fully accounting for the intensity of party conflict, nor do they explain the rising levels of partisanship which were, it must be remembered, higher at Bristol in 1784 than in 1781.

Table 7.8: *Occupational Structure of the Electorate in Great Yarmouth*

(Percentage)

	1754			1777		1790		
	Gov.	Opp.	Split	Gov.	Opp.	Gov.	Opp.	Split
1. Gentlemen, Professions	13.8	4.9	9.8	15.8	4.6	25.7	17.1	10.8
2. Merchants	7.4	5.3	14.6	5.7	7.2	5.7	7.3	6.1
3. Shopkeepers	19.5	20.8	36.6	13.7	14.4	8.6	17.1	11.4
4. Artisans	36.7	38.6	24.4	38.6	51.2	28.6	29.3	50.4
5. Laborers	22.6	30.3	14.6	26.2	22.9	31.4	26.8	21.0
6. Others	—	—	—	—	—	—	—	—
N =	297	264	41	384	153	35	41	472

If partisanship at Bristol and Great Yarmouth is largely attributable to the stimulus of religion, is it possible to discern socio-economic motivation among the Nonconformists? At Norwich and Northampton there is evidence to suggest that the religious component of the anti-ministerialist party was genuinely religious and not merely economic differences in disguise; Dissenters were well-represented in each of the occupational categories.[62] But at Bristol and Yarmouth the more consistent support the Nonconformists gave to the opposition may be explained in part by their higher social standing. The overall structure of Bristol Nonconformity in relation to the electorate has already been investigated in chapter 2, and when we turn to the Dissenting vote we see the higher social standing of the Dissenters clearly reflected in their partisanship (see Table 7.9). Not unexpectedly, opposition Dissenters at Bristol had proportionately greater numbers than other oppositionists in the upper three occupational categories, and there were correspondingly fewer anti-government Dissenters among the artisans and laborers. Though not much should be made of the small numbers at Great Yarmouth, the same phenomenon appears to be present there, which is all the more striking because of the far greater propor-tion of artisans and laborers among the Presbyterians at Great Yarmouth.[63] Dissenters in the professional, merchant, and shopkeeper categories were

---

62 Phillips, *Electoral Behavior*, pp. 300–1. Phillips examined all Dissenting voters in each occupational category in the electorate, but he did not investigate the occupational structure of the partisan Dissenting vote.

63 Artisans, 31.2%; laborers, 43.8%. Bradley, *Popular Politics and the American Revolution in England*, p. 193.

apparently won over to political opposition more readily than Anglicans in the same ranks, which suggests that religion and socio-economic factors complemented each other.[64] The mutual reinforcement of religion and socio-economic status will receive further attention in a subsequent chapter on petitions. In parliamentary elections, however, it is clear that religion was far more important as a determinant of electoral behavior than socio-economic standing, a fact that can be placed beyond doubt by an areal analysis of Bristol parishes.

Table 7.9: *Occupational Structure of Bristol and Great Yarmouth; Nonconformist Voters Compared to Other Voters* (Percentage)

| | BRISTOL | | | | GREAT YARMOUTH | |
| | 1774 | | 1781 | | 1777 | |
	Dissent: Opposition	Other: Opposition	Dissent: Opposition	Other: Opposition	Dissent: Opposition	Other: Opposition
1. Gentlemen, Professions	10.7	4.2	8.5	6.3	20.0	1.6
2. Merchants	8.0	4.0	7.3	4.3	24.0	3.9
3. Shopkeepers	33.3	24.4	35.4	23.6	8.0	14.8
4. Artisans	45.3	55.9	45.1	56.9	40.0	53.9
5. Laborers	2.7	8.0	3.7	6.3	8.0	25.8
6. Other	—	3.6	—	2.5	—	—
N=	75	501	82	394	25	128

Through an areal analysis of Norwich wards and Northampton parishes, Phillips demonstrated a link between Nonconformity and partisanship with no corresponding connection between socio-economic structure and party. At Norwich and Northampton, 'religious differences emerge as the single variable corresponding to voting patterns'.[65] Similarly, at Bristol the uneven areal distribution of Dissent appears to have had a direct and controlling influence upon the borough's political history. Six of Bristol's Dissenting chapels were located in one of the city's twenty-one parishes, the large northern parish of St. James, and two more chapels were situated in the neighboring parishes of Castle Precincts and Christ Church.[66] Altogether, eight of the eleven chapels

64 Also, among the handful of Dissenters who supported the government in 1774 and 1781 at Bristol, there were fewer proportionately in the upper three categories than those who supported the opposition. This cuts against the evidence of the socio-economic motivation of conservative Dissenters derived from the petitions.

65 Phillips, *Electoral Behavior*, p. 301.

66 The six in St. James are Lewins Mead, Broad Mead, Callow Hill, the Friars, Wesley's Rooms, and Whitefield's Tabernacle. Castle Green was in Castle Precincts and the Pithay chapel was in Christ Church. Tucker Street (Presbyterian) and Temple Street (Quaker) were in the southern parishes of St. Thomas and Temple respectively; Lady Huntington's chapel was in the western parish of St. Augustine.

were thus concentrated in the northeastern half of the city, leaving only three of the remaining meetings in the southwestern parishes. For the purpose of analysis, these eight chapels are conveniently isolated by grouping eight of the northeastern parishes together. Approximately one-half of the voting population was located in the parishes east of High Street and northeast of the River Avon (see Map 7.1); beginning in the north and moving in a clockwise direction these parishes include St. James, St. Philip and Jacob, the out parish of St. Philip and Jacob, Castle Precincts, St. Peter, St. Mary Port, Christ Church, and St. John.[67] This division of the borough cuts diagonally through the middle of the central trading district and distributes some wealthy and some poor parishes in each of the two halves. The western most parish of St. Augustine, for example, was known for its wealthy residents, as were a number of northern parishes; conversely, each half had its poorer parishes, like Temple in the south and St. Philip and Jacob in the east.[68] This grouping reveals no significant differences in occupational structure of the electorate between the northeast and the southwest in any of the four elections under study (Table 7.10). Nor

Table 7.10: *Areal Distribution of the Electorate in Bristol* (Percentage)

	1754 North-east	1754 South-west	1774 North-east	1774 South-west	1781 North-east	1781 South-west	1784 North-east	1784 South-west
1. Gentlemen, Professions	4.0	6.7	7.5	9.9	8.5	9.3	5.6	9.2
2. Merchants	4.9	8.1	4.6	8.8	6.5	7.2	4.0	6.8
3. Shopkeepers	22.6	22.1	27.3	19.2	26.6	24.1	30.1	23.2
4. Artisans	53.6	50.2	51.2	50.5	50.3	51.0	52.6	50.6
5. Laborers	4.0	6.3	6.2	7.7	5.4	6.7	6.1	1.9
6. Others	10.8	6.7	3.3	3.8	2.7	1.7	1.6	1.9
N=	526	578	520	546	553	526	555	531

did the opposition draw a disproportionate number of wealthy or poor supporters from either half of the borough (Table 7.11). The northeastern parishes were, however, especially noted for their rapid growth in the mid- to late-eighteenth century, so much so that St. Paul's parish church was consecrated in 1787 to accommodate the expansion of the population in St. James.[69]

67 In 1754 these parishes polled 47.6%, in 1774 48.8%, in 1781 51.3% and in 1784 51.5% of the resident voters. St. Philip and Jacob out parish was first polled in 1784.
68 Underdown, 'Parliamentary History', p. 42. M. D. Lobel, (ed.), *Historic Towns: Maps and Plans of Towns and Cities in the British Isles, with Historical Commentaries, from Earliest Times to 1800*, (London, 1969), p. 17.
69 Lobel, *Historic Towns*, pp. 23, 25.

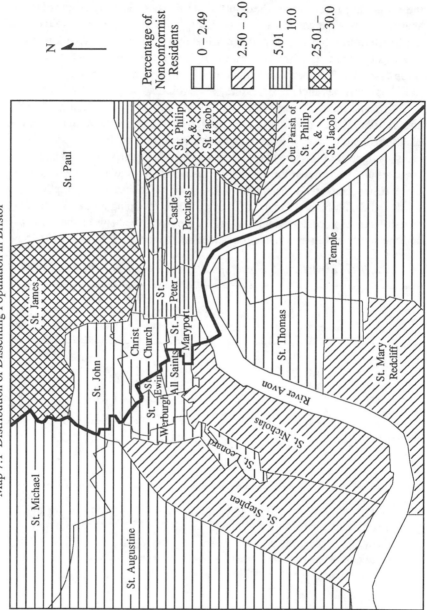

Map 7.1 Distribution of Dissenting Population in Bristol

Table 7.11: *Areal Distribution of the Opposition Vote in Bristol* (Percentage)

	1754 North-east	1754 South-west	1774 North-east	1774 South-west	1781 North-east	1781 South-west	1784 North-east	1784 South-west
1. Gentlemen, Professions	5.2	6.9	3.9	6.7	7.5	5.5	5.8	10.5
2. Merchants	5.2	7.6	3.6	5.9	4.4	5.5	7.1	6.6
3. Shopkeepers	23.2	23.9	30.3	18.8	24.5	27.5	31.7	24.3
4. Artisans	51.0	47.8	53.4	56.1	55.4	53.8	49.6	50.3
5. Laborers	3.6	6.6	6.2	8.8	6.1	5.5	3.3	6.9
6. Others	11.9	7.3	2.7	3.8	2.0	2.2	2.5	1.3
N=	194	289	337	239	294	182	240	304

The chapels were not only concentrated in these eight northeastern parishes, but so were the Dissenters themselves. A survey of the place of residence of more than 900 Dissenters reveals that 78 percent lived in these eight parishes, and the remaining 22 percent were dispersed in the thirteen parishes of the southwest. Not one of the southwestern parishes had 5 percent of the total number of Dissenters, and only three, St. Mary Redcliff, St. Stephen, and St. Nicholas had more than 2.5 percent. In each of the five denominations for which residential information survives, three-quarters or more of its adherents resided in the northeast.[70] Of the Dissenters who lived in these parishes, the Presbyterians, Congregationalists, and Calvinistic Methodists were most heavily concentrated in St. James, whereas the Baptists and Quakers were most numerous in St. Philip and Jacob. In descending order, Castle Precincts, St. Peter, and St. Mary Port were the next most heavily populated by Dissenters, with the least number found in Christ Church and St. John. Since, however, the Dissenters voted together irrespective of denomination, the specific denominational complexion of individual parishes is less important than the combined strength of Nonconformity in specific parishes.[71]

Most Bristol Dissenters thus worshipped in the northern and eastern parishes of Bristol, the great majority lived in the same parishes, and it will come as no surprise that the majority of them voted there as well. Of those Dissenters who

70 The Presbyterians (N=174) had 83.9% in the northeast; the Congregationalists (N=105) had 74.3%; the Baptists (N=216) had 75.5%; the Quakers (N=406) 77.6%; the Calvinistic Methodists (N=104) had 79.8%. This sample of Quaker residences was drawn from the registers of both the Temple Street chapel (Temple Parish) and the Friars chapel (St. James), and despite this, by far the largest proportion of Quakers resided in the northeastern parishes.

71 Of the 764 Dissenters located in the northeastern parishes, 38.4% resided in St. James, 33.8% in St. Philip and Jacob; the proportion dropped to 10.6% in Castle Precincts, 6.7% in St. Peter, 5.5% in St. Philip and Jacob out, and 2.6% in St. Mary Port.

can be identified in the poll books, 65.8 percent listed their residence in the northeastern parishes and the remaining 34.2 percent are recorded as voting in the southwest. This concentration of Nonconformity and the Nonconformist vote suggests that if the Dissenters did influence the politics of the borough, their influence should have been more pronounced in these parishes than elsewhere.

Support for opposition candidates in the period of the American Revolution was in fact consistently much stronger in the northeast. In the elections of 1774 and 1781, the northeastern vote was weighted in favor of opposition candidates by about 20 percentage points; 58.5 percent of the opposition vote was from the northeast in 1774, 61.8 percent in 1781, and in 1784, 62.9 percent of Cruger's support came from the northeast. (See Table 7.12.) In addition to the proportion, the consistency of this orientation is noteworthy, as is the change of the northeastern voters' allegiance between 1754 and 1774. At first the stronghold of government support, these northeastern parishes made a dramatic change in the period of the American Revolution. From the local angle, many voters undoubtedly perceived themselves as maintaining their principles and the Whig tradition; it was supposed, rather, that the government had changed its policies, and it was this which required a change in the voters' loyalties. The voting trends of specific parishes adds further weight to this argument.[72] In the

Table 7.12: *Areal Distribution of Partisan Vote as a Proportion of the Total Vote* (Percentage)

	1754		1774		1781		1784	
	Gov.	Opp.	Gov.	Opp.	Gov.	Opp.	Gov.	Opp.
Northeast	55.3	40.2	36.4	58.5	43.0	61.8	62.9	44.1
Southwest	44.7	59.8	63.6	41.5	57.0	38.2	37.1	55.9
N =	577	483	324	576	603	476	426	544

three elections of 1774, 1781, and 1784, Cruger topped the poll repeatedly in the northeastern parishes of St. James, St. Philip and Jacob, and Castle Precincts – the very parishes most heavily populated by Dissent – whereas the only southwestern parishes that gave a majority to Cruger on more than one occasion were St. Stephen and St. Leonard.[73] The Dissenters thus not

72 In 1774 many of the southwestern parishes gave a majority to Cruger and Burke, but it was precisely the northeastern parishes of St. Philip and Jacob and Castle Precinct which had the strongest government vote in 1754 that gave an overwhelming majority to the Whig candidates in 1774.
73 St. James faltered in 1781 when Daubeny won 50.8% to Cruger's 49.2%; otherwise, these parishes returned a consistent vote in all three elections. In 1781, overall, Daubeny won by 55.9% to Cruger's 44.1%, so St. James still returned a proportionately stronger

only voted for opposition candidates, but their presence in the city contributed directly to the Whiggish political complexion of the northeast half of the borough.

The Dissenters comprised twenty percent or more of the resident electorate in Bristol[74] – perhaps four times the national average – and they voted so consistently that it can be said with confidence that the Whig victories of 1774 and 1784 turned on their vote. (Burke won by only 251 votes in 1774 and Cruger won by 68 in 1784.) But the Dissenters also contributed to the overall partisan orientation of the electorate through their inflexible political line, local leadership in the persons of Champion, Harford, and Noble, dominance of the Union Club, and in the sermonizing of Dissenting ministers such as Caleb Evans. At Bristol, Nonconformity provided the political core around which a coherent Whig party was formed, and at Great Yarmouth they formed the core of the independent party through their leadership and partisanship.

The majority of the Whig party at Bristol, was, however non-Dissenting or Anglican, and the local political cleavage cannot be reduced to the religious element. Moreover, Dissenters at Bristol were themselves influenced by other extrinsic forces; in addition to the radical political ideology emanating from the Dissenting pulpit, Dissenters read election pamphlets and broadsides, many of which were undoubtedly written by Anglicans. The Union Club embraced Dissenters and Anglicans alike, although the Dissenters led the club. Yet the Dissenters continued to face discrimination, they were denied the legal equality of other Whigs, and these constrictions unquestionably contributed to their own identity. Insofar as Anglican Whigs were willing to be associated with Dissent in local politics, they were to some extent influenced by Dissent. This association almost certainly entailed an exalted view of the Revolution settlement, the Act of Toleration, and opposition to the principles of High Churchmen or any other form of perceived authoritarianism.

Before the American Revolution we have observed the Nonconformists' steadfast support at Great Yarmouth, Shrewsbury, and Bristol for the Whig governments of George II and George III. Phillips documented the same at Norwich, where 70 percent of the Dissenters voted for administration candidates in 1761, and at Northampton, a far less well-organized borough, where Nonconformists gave the government a majority of their votes in the 1768

Whig vote. In neither St. Stephen nor St. Leonard did the Whigs gain a majority in all three elections. A large proportion of Presbyterians (more than three times that of other Dissenters) made their residence in the out parish of St. Philip and Jacob, and this may help account for the overwhelming Whig victory in the parish in 1784.

74 Possibly more, because the 25% letter cluster sample of the electorate utilized in this study drew upon the records of only six of the eleven chapels in Bristol. From these six chapels a 25% sample yielded about 100 Dissenting voters. Thus using these sources alone, one could identify about 400 Dissenters in each contest, which, when doubled, amounts to 20% of the resident electorate.

election. Then, rather suddenly, Dissenting loyalty to the government collapsed, in some boroughs never to return. Only 20 percent of the Norwich Dissenters gave the government their vote in 1780 and a mere 5 percent were pro-government at Northampton in 1774.[75] Dissenters thus began to diverge dramatically from other voters precisely in the period 1768–80. Equally impressive was the shift to positive support for opposition candidates, and this was a continuous trend at Norwich, reaching a peak of 90 percent in 1802. Therefore the American war represents a period of decisive shift of electoral behavior for the Nonconformists, and the idea that this was motivated in part by the ideology of opposition emanating from the Dissenting pulpit would seem to be beyond dispute. In those cases where the ideology of the pulpit was lacking, as at Great Yarmouth, the aggressive leadership of the laity could supply the want of clerical direction. Moreover, since Burke understood Nonconformity as a crucial component of local Whig parties, his own evolving thought on the principled basis of party and local party continuity becomes readily explicable. While the Whig interpretation of party espoused by the Rockinghams was exaggerated and misleading, the well-spring of the theory can now be located in several of England's largest, most prestigious open constituencies.

But Nonconformity in Bristol and Norwich was in many ways unique. The Dissenters' large numbers, their prominent social status, their outspoken ministerial leaders, and their political tradition of opposition in the electorate could be matched by only a few other boroughs in England. The less consistent behavior of the Yarmouth Presbyterians suggests that local structural conditions, patronage, and in some cases, bribery, could lead to conformity in parliamentary elections – even among the Nonconformists. When we look for parallels to Bristol, Norwich, and Great Yarmouth in other cities we find that not in every instance did eighteenth-century political opposition and radicalism depend upon religion for its energy. We will also find, however, that in the very boroughs where electoral politics fail to reveal abiding political differences related to religion, an analysis of extra-parliamentary political expressions does demonstrate a consistent religious and socio-economic basis to popular opposition.

75 Phillips, *Electoral Behavior*, pp. 292–6.

8

Deference and the Dissenting Vote in Newcastle, Liverpool, Hull, and Colchester

The Dissenters at Bristol and Norwich contributed directly to party politics through increasing levels of partisanship and forging rational links between local structures and national issues. As a body, their political independence and the predictability of their behavior in these boroughs were matched only by one other group in the electorate: the Anglican clergy. At Great Yarmouth and Northampton, where party structures were less well developed, the Dissenting elite, whether lay or clerical, worked together with the Dissenting laity to shape what elements of partisanship were present. But further comparative study of other constituencies is needed to assess adequately the role of Nonconformity in atmospheres less conducive to political independence. Many questions remain concerning the alliance between Dissenters and anti-administration Anglicans, the precise role of the ministry in marshalling the Dissenting vote, and the deleterious influence of patronage and corruption. This chapter will examine the Dissenters in four additional boroughs where the American Revolution contributed to political polarization. Newcastle upon Tyne and Liverpool were both large open boroughs, free from corruption for the most part, shaken by the agitation over Wilkes, and susceptible to the rising tide of urban radicalism. Kingston upon Hull and Colchester were somewhat smaller and more easily influenced by patronage and corruption; political issues were characteristically less prominent in parliamentary elections, Wilkite radicalism scarcely touched them and little election literature has survived. The Dissenters at Hull and Colchester, therefore, might reasonably be expected to have found it far more difficult to transcend the entrenched political structures of these two boroughs.

NEWCASTLE UPON TYNE AND SECULAR RADICALISM

The Dissenting community in Newcastle upon Tyne was one of the largest in the north of England, though it lacked some of the rich diversity found in Bristol. Seven chapels belonged to the Scots Presbyterians: The Wall Knoll, Silver Street, Groat Market, Garth Heads, and Castle Garth chapels represented the majority of Scots Presbyterians in Newcastle, and in addition, there

255

were two smaller schismatic groups originating in Scotland known as 'United Secession' – the Carlisle Street and the Close chapels.[1] James Murray's High Bridge meeting was not officially affiliated with the Scots Presbyterians because Murray believed that every congregation was free to adopt whatever form of government it chose. The Scots chapels, however, were closely linked through the Newcastle Presbytery which, in 1783, included thirteen ministers. The members of these chapels were mostly natives of Scotland or their offspring; the suburb of Sandgate, for example, attracted the poor and industrious of Scotland, so much so that it required two meetings, the Wall Knoll and Garth Heads.[2]

Two Unitarian chapels subsisted in the eighteenth century, Hanover Square and Pandon Bank, and there was a group of Particular Baptists at Tuthill Stairs.[3] The Quaker meeting was situated in Pilgrim Street, and on 20 December 1742, the Methodists opened the Orphan House in Northumberland Street. (After Bristol, this was the second Methodist chapel built in England.)[4] The relations between the Scots Presbyterians and the English Dissenters appear to have been cordial, at least among the ministers.[5] The electoral strength of the Newcastle Nonconformists has never been estimated for the borough, however, we do know that early in the eighteenth century there were 150 borough inhabitants who could vote in county elections, and it was observed that these voters 'can make about as many more votes on their own'. Records with good

1 John Evans, 'List of Dissenting Congregations and Ministers in England and Wales (1715–29)' MS. 38.4, p. 89 (hereafter cited as the Evans List). In 1715 there were four Presbyterian meetings with a combined attendance of 1900, and one Congregational chapel with 100 auditors. In 1773 Thompson listed nine Paedobaptist and one Baptist chapel. Josiah Thompson, 'List of Protestant Dissenting Congregations in England and Wales', (1772–3) MS. 38.6, p. 27 (hereafter cited as Thompson List 38.6). Presbyterian growth in the eighteenth century is seen in that four of these chapels alone (Wall Knoll, Groat Market, Carlisle Street, and the Close chapel) could seat 2,500 people in the 1770s, E. Mackenzie, *A Descriptive and Historical Account of the Town and County of Newcastle upon Tyne, including the Borough of Gateshead*, 2 vols. (Newcastle upon Tyne, 1827), 1: 383–6, 390–1, 393–4.

2 Mackenzie, *A Descriptive and Historical Account*, 1: 387, 289, 383–4.

3 The Unitarian chapels merged in 1797 and a new, enlarged chapel was built in 1810 to seat 600 people. Mackenzie, *A Descriptive and Historical Account*, 1: 175, 178–9; 397. A. Hall, *Church of the Divine Unity, Newcastle upon Tyne: Two Hundred and Fifty Years, 1672–1922* (Newcastle upon Tyne, 1922), p. 12. Another Congregational chapel emerged in the early 1780s when the Postern chapel broke away from Silver Street.

4 Mackenzie, *A Descriptive and Historical Account*, 1: 382, 402. Forster Street meeting was gathered in the 1760s by the Sandemanians, a small secessionist sect of the Church of Scotland, p. 399.

5 William Turner, *A Short Sketch of the History of Protestant Nonconformity and of the Society Assembling in Hanover–Square, Newcastle* (Newcastle upon Tyne, 1811), p. 21. On the wealth and status of the Dissenters of Hanover Square, see John Seed, 'Gentlemen Dissenters: The Social and Political Meanings of Rational Dissent in the 1770s and 1780s', *HJ* 28 (1985), 303.

occupational data subsist for five of the Presbyterian chapels and one of the Unitarian chapels.[6]

Newcastle upon Tyne was a large freeman borough frequently contested by local members of merchant families, and in the first half of the century, the elections were oriented around Whig and Tory factions. Because of the enormous cost of contested elections, the parties agreed to a truce in 1747 whereby each group held one seat, and as a result, the borough was uncontested until 1774.[7] At the general election of 1774, Sir Walter Blackett, an erstwhile Tory and extremely popular representative, was paired with Matthew Ridley, sitting member for Morpeth and son of the other incumbent (see Table 8.1).[8] Blackett had held his seat for forty years, and from 1770 onward commonly voted with the government. The younger Ridley, however, was politically independent, though this did not hinder their joint candidature. Constantine Phipps and Thomas Delaval opposed Blackett on the grounds that he had refused to present a petition from his constituents in 1769 for the dissolution of Parliament; positively, the opposition candidates espoused radical resolutions concerning parliamentary reform. Phipps and Delaval also engaged the electors with promises to support the local freemen or burgesses who had recently concluded a controversy with the corporation over the use of the Town Moor, and subsequently, the local issue of the Moor has bulked large in historians' accounts of Newcastle politics. The 'magisterial' party of Blackett and Ridley was thus pitted against the 'burgesses' party of Phipps and Delaval, but the magisterial candidates were easily returned in a straight party contest with little cross voting. In 1775, Blackett and Ridley refused to present the Newcastle petition against the American war to the king, and Blackett began to lose some of his

Table 8.1: *Newcastle upon Tyne Election Results: 1774–1780*

1774		1777		1780	
Sir Walter Blackett	1432	Sir John Trevelyan	1163	Sir Matthew Ridley	1408
Sir Matthew Ridley	1411	Andrew Bowes	1068	Andrew Bowes	1135
Constantine Phipps	795			Thomas Delaval	1085
Thomas Delaval	677				

6 The Evans List, p. 89. Records from the Silver Street, Groat Market, Castle Garth, Carlisle Street, Close chapels, and Hanover Square were merged with the poll books.

7 *Commons, 1715–1754*, 1: 298; Sir Lewis Namier, *The Structure of Politics at the Accession of George III* (London, 2nd edn, 1957), pp. 95–9; *Commons, 1754–1790*, 1: 350–1.

8 *Commons, 1754–1790*, 2: 95; *The Burgesses' Poll* (Newcastle, 2nd edn, 1775) gives slightly different totals for 1774 (1432, 1411, 796, 678). *The Poll* (Newcastle, 1774) is utilized here. *The Burgesses' Poll* has a twenty-four page 'summary of the disputes' which is attributed to James Murray by the Central Library, Newcastle upon Tyne.

popularity.[9] From 1778 forward, however, Ridley opposed the administration over the American war, and in the new Parliament of 1780, he consistently voted for the opposition.

At the death of Blackett in 1777, the Newcastle radicals put forward another radical candidate, Andrew Bowes. Blackett's nephew and heir, Sir John Trevelyan, won the contest, but the margin was very narrow (less than 100 votes); the Newcastle opposition had clearly gained some local support. In Parliament, Trevelyan supported the government through 1779. The local radical faction was sufficiently consolidated in 1780 for Bowes to win a seat, though the sitting member, Sir Matthew Ridley, was still the popular candidate. Once in Parliament Bowes voted with the opposition over the American war and favored parliamentary reform in 1783.[10]

POLITICAL ISSUES, LOCAL AND NATIONAL

The standard account of these three elections has been written from the single narrow perspective of the purported trivial and merely local conflict over the Town Moor, and as a result, Newcastle politics have been subject to the same constricting interpretation as Bristol and Great Yarmouth. Namier and Christie concluded that 'non-political considerations' or 'at best local and personal issues, at worst hard cash', were more important in Newcastle than radicalism.[11] 'Importance' for the school of Namier was measured strictly in terms of the outcome of elections, the voting patterns of the electors were undifferentiated, and the minority party, with its far more interesting political involvements, was virtually ignored. Thomas R. Knox recently overturned this interpretation through a balanced integration of popular election literature, the Wilkes' petition of 1769, and poll books.[12] By utilizing these data, Knox demonstrated the prominence of local radical organizations and agitation, he proved there was a dynamic interrelation between local and national issues, and by measuring the consistency of individuals in both petitioning and voting, he highlighted the congruence between radical ideology and coherent political behavior.

By 1774 the local radical organizations had achieved a number of impressive victories. Political opposition to the corporation began in 1769 when the mayor

9 According to Namier, *Commons, 1754–1790*, 2: 96.
10 *Commons, 1754–1790*, 3: 563. Though against the government's American policy, he would not vote to condemn North's Administration. *Commons, 1754–1790*, 2: 107.
11 Namier, *Structure of Politics*, p. 96; Ian R. Christie, *The End of North's Ministry, 1780–1782* (London, 1958), p. 143. The entire period 1774–80 is interpreted in terms of purely local concerns. See also Christie's 'The Wilkites and the General Election of 1774', in *Myth and Reality in Late-Eighteenth-Century British Politics* (London, 1970), where somewhat more attention is given to local radicalism.
12 Thomas R. Knox, 'Popular Politics and Provincial Radicalism: Newcastle upon Tyne, 1769–1785', *Albion* 11(1979), 225–41; and 'Wilkism and the Newcastle Election of 1774', *Durham University Journal* 72 (1979–80), 23–37.

refused the burgesses the use of the Guildhall for a meeting over the Middlesex election affair. The radicals subsequently found another meeting place and produced instructions to their members in Parliament and a petition to the Crown, but the magistrates' characteristic resistance to these meetings was viewed by the burgesses as an attempt to oppress them. Support for the cause of Wilkes gathered strength in 1770 and the local oppositions' alertness to national events is seen in a published handbill of 29 September that associated the Newcastle city magistrates who 'wrestle from you' your 'natural Rights' with the ministry in London, described as 'a Set of the greatest Villains that ever surrounded the Throne of a Prince'.[13] In early 1771 the Wilkites agreed upon resolutions against corruption in Newcastle elections, and in the following year they formed the Constitutional Club of Durham, Northumberland, and Newcastle with the avowed purpose of preserving the memory of the Middlesex election and watching over the conduct of their representatives in Parliament. The club met quarterly in Newcastle with George Grieve as its chairman. In 1773 a number of the borough's companies agreed to impose a test on parliamentary candidates, and three additional clubs, all radical in orientation, were formed in preparation for the upcoming general election.[14] All this while, the political issues were kept before the public by the three established newspapers, and on the eve of the election, James Murray supervised the publication of *The Freeman's Magazine: or, the Constitutional Repository* and produced its first number in April 1774.[15] Stewards of the Newcastle companies met and nominated Delaval and Phipps and then proceeded to require both candidates to swear to support shorter parliaments, a new place bill, more equal representation, and recision of the Parliament's Middlesex election resolution.[16]

Knox thoroughly documented the ideological continuity in Newcastle politics leading up to 1774, but more importantly, he discovered a high level of behavioral uniformity whereby the debate over the Town Moor may be relegated to an appropriately subordinate, though not unimportant, category.

13 Knox, 'Wilkism', 24–5. For a short summary of these events see Knox, 'Popular Politics', 226–7. The Newcastle radicals' association with their metropolitan counterpart is seen in their support of the printers in the 'printers case' in London in 1771; George Grieve was first introduced to Newcastle politics over this issue. Knox, 'Wilkism', 25–26. On the interweaving of local and national concerns see also 36 and 'Popular Politics', 231, 233.

14 Knox, 'Wilkism', 26–7; 'Popular Politics', 227.

15 Knox, 'Wilkism', 27. *The Freeman's Magazine* proposed to present the 'Debate concerning the CAUSE of LIBERTY', i–vii. *The Freeman's Magazine: or, the Constitutional Repository* (Newcastle, 1774); on Murray's role see Mackenzie, *A Descriptive and Historical Account*, 1: 388, and his own contribution in *The Freeman's Magazine*, pp. 86–8, a humorous story 'by the author of Sermons to Asses'.

16 Knox, 'Wilkism', 28. *The Contest, Being an Account of the Matter in Dispute between the Magistrates and Burgesses, and an Examination of the Merit and Conduct of the Candidates in the Present Election* (Newcastle, 1774), pp. 29–30, attributed, by the Central Library, Newcastle upon Tyne, to James Murray.

He found that in all aspects of the local opposition, extending from the parliamentary candidates themselves to the lower level organizers of opposition politics, there was a single body of leaders, largely Wilkite in composition. First, both Phipps and Delaval had distinguished themselves as popular leaders in progressive politics. Phipps wrote *A Letter from a Member of Parliament to One of His Constituents* (1769) that defended the right of electors to bind their representative through instructions. Just before the election he spoke publicly of his opposition to the various measures of the administration, particularly the Quebec bill and the Middlesex election. Delaval's first association with Wilkism was his presentation of a petition to the king for the dissolution of Parliament (5 January 1770), and later in 1770 he chaired a meeting that produced a more strongly worded remonstrance to the king with a call for the dismissal of the ministers. Moreover, both candidates electioneered on the principle of a member's responsibility to his constituents.[17] Knox also discovered continuity of leadership at the level of local agents and organizers such as George Grieve, William Smith, and Nicholas Tyzack, who were involved repeatedly over the years in a variety of radical causes. Similarly, the association of these men with London radicals is carefully drawn out.[18]

Even more convincing was the continuity found in the coherent behavior of the rank and file; the petitioners over the Middlesex election affair in 1769–70 who were also voters in 1774, were proportionately more supportive of Phipps and Delaval than Blackett and Ridley.[19] In addition, the examination of occupational categories revealed a rational pattern of support in favor of radicalism; the same Newcastle companies gave a disproportionate share both to petitioners in 1769 and to opposition candidates in 1774.[20] Finally, the popular literature of the period integrated the local struggle against the magistrates with the national threat to liberty.[21]

17 Knox, 'Wilkism', 24, 28, 30, 31. Knox correctly discounts Phipps' and Delaval's subsequent conservative political associations, anachronistically played up by Namier and Christie.
18 Knox, 'Wilkism', 30–1. These men's connection with Wilkism and America in the petitioning agitation will be taken up in a later chapter. Sergeant Glynn was introduced to Newcastle by George Grieve to defend the rights of the freeman over the Town Moor. Knox, 'Popular Politics', 231.
19 The petitioners cast less than one fourth of the total vote in 1774 (24.2%), but they gave Phipps and Delaval more than one third of their votes (35.3%). The eligible freemen who had *not* petitioned in 1769 comprised nearly 40% of the vote (38.4%) and these non-petitioners gave Phipps and Delaval only a quarter of their votes (exactly 25%), Knox, 'Wilkism', 31 note 22. On the eve of the election in 1774, the editors of *The Freemans' Magazine* actually encouraged such consistency: 'every hand which signed the petition and remonstrance, will be against *S-- W----- B------* and Mr. *R-------y*' (p. 127).
20 Knox makes no judgments concerning a social division on these grounds. 'Wilkism', p. 31; 'Popular Politics', 235.
21 The explicit connection between developments at St. James and Westminster, on the one hand, where liberty was threatened by authoritarianism and corruption, and the increasing oppression of the magistrates at Newcastle, on the other, is even more pervasive than

The political conflict leading up to the general election of 1774 cannot be reduced to a simple matter of support or opposition to Wilkes,[22] but Knox demonstrated that Wilkism provided the catalyst for the local agitation surrounding the corporation and its privileges, and Wilkism accounts for the persistence of this opposition. Local issues were indeed important: the magistrates' denial of the Guildhall to the burgesses and their attempt to monopolize the Town Moor, combined with the sitting Members' resistance to instructions from their constituents go to the heart of the opposition's concern. But local expressions of Wilkism served to sharpened such genuine constitutional questions as the accountability of magistrates and representatives on the one hand, and the rights of burgesses on the other. The symbolic force of the struggle for control of the Town Moor is seen in the Company of Tailors' presentation of a gold signet ring to each of the committee members who had led the battle against the magistrates. Under the crystal of each ring 'Liberty' was represented stepping out of her temple with the words proceeding from her mouth *'Town Moor Safe, August 10th, 1773'*. On the inside of the ring was *Concordia parvea res cresunt*, 'By concord small things increase'; around the inner verge was 'Taylors' Company to ...' with the name of each member, and around the outer verge, the words, *Vox Populi Vox Dei*. In the cordwainers' hall a large board commemorated the victory with the words of admonition for posterity that 'oppression's iron hand ought ever to be legally resisted'.[23] The affair of the Town Moor, in short, was no mere squabble over the use of the Commons, but a conflict over the source of political authority and natural rights.[24] The electoral opposition of 1774 arose directly from these constitutional concerns.

Knox's revisionist interpretation of Newcastle is far more convincing than previous treatments, but it is insufficiently penetrating in two closely related areas: the ideology of radicalism and its social causes. His focus upon the Wilkite agitation rather than the American Revolution led to a failure fully to integrate local politics with national crises. Inadequate attention was paid to the popular literature read and heard by the electors in 1774, 1777, and 1780.[25]

Knox believes, 'Wilkism', 36. See *The Freeman's Magazine*, pp. i–vii, 29, 42–3, 74–5, 79, 81, 127–8, 149; Murray, *The Burgesses' Poll*, pp. 14, 24; *The Contest*, pp. 8, 12.
22 Knox reflects that Blackett and Ridley had voted with the opposition over Middlesex before 1770, 'Wilkism', 35.
23 Mackenzie, *A Descriptive and Historical Account*, 1: 672, 676.
24 Knox, 'Wilkism', 36; 'Popular Politics', 230–1; 233. Murray, *The Burgesses' Poll*, claimed that the guild, representing the burgesses, was superior to the Common Council which is 'a body of delegates in trust', 14. And thus the debate continued into 1775, but by then the colonial crisis attracted more and more attention.
25 Knox notes that such data are important, but not convincing in themselves, 'Wilkism', 28, 30; 'Popular Politics', 228. But the American crisis sharpened the political divisions at Newcastle more than Knox observes, and the popular literature is the means of linking leadership to the rank and file and of explaining rational or coherent behavior. Moreover, since Knox did not deal with the American crisis, he did not emphasize

The issue of the representative's responsibility to his constituents was by far the most important election issue, but already in 1774 the colonial situation was politically divisive. Moreover, the issues surrounding Wilkes merged readily with the opposition's attack on the government's American policy – an opposition that can be seen both in the popular literature and in the far greater consistency among individuals who voted and petitioned over America, compared to those who voted and petitioned over Wilkes.[26] In addition, Knox did not press very far into either the religious or socio-economic motivation of the radicals in their opposition to the government concerning America, and since, as we shall see, the religious explanation for the emergence of radicalism at Newcastle is inadequate when considered alone, it becomes all the more important to examine the occupational structure of electors and petitioners.

THE IDEOLOGY OF RADICALISM

The rich connotative language of liberty – both civil and religious – was pervasive in the election literature of 1774. For example 'Cassius' associated the 'court candidates' with 'arbitrary power' and 'despotic principles', and 'Marcus Aurelius' appealed to 'every true friend of liberty to support the burgesses' candidates'.[27] Before the election, the opposition displayed copies of Marat's *Chains of Slavery*, while the editors of *The Freeman's Magazine* cited Rousseau and the 'excellent' Thomas Gordon in support of their arguments.[28] The opposing parties were commonly denoted 'magistrates' and 'burgesses',[29] but one author, possibly Murray, defended at some length the appropriateness of using the old party labels 'Whig' and 'Tory'. The political conflict at Newcastle, he believed, was grounded in principle; the old designations were applicable above all because of the magistrates' reverence for royal and aristocratic authority and their hostility toward moderate churchmen and Dissenters. The burgesses were 'Whigs' because they understood their representatives to be trustees of the public good and were alarmed at the increasing power of the Crown.[30] These designations were also informed by

Ridley's changed stance on America and this leads to a lack of precision in his analysis of the 1780 election.

26 The petitioning agitation will be examined in detail in chap. 9.
27 *The Freeman's Magazine*, pp. 152, 162–4; See also 'A Hater of Tyranny', p. 168 and p. 179 on the same topic. *The Contest*, p. 18.
28 Knox, 'Popular Politics', 241; *The Freeman's Magazine*, pp. 56, 60.
29 *The Freeman's Magazine*, pp. vi, vii, 42, 60, 79, 111, 122; Murray, *The Burgesses' Poll*, pp. 11–12, 23; *The Contest*, pp. 15, 16–17, 31. The author of *The Contest* (see note 16 above) was at some pains to convince his readers that Blackett, as a favorite of the Court, was a Tory (pp. 2, 12, 13–17, 21, 23). He believed that the Hanoverians 'have turned or may turn tories' (pp. 12, 20). See also on Blackett as a Jacobite, the polemic against bishops, Scotsmen, and Jacobites being preferred at Court, *The Freeman's Magazine*, pp. 102, 103, 135.
30 *The Contest*, pp. 10–11.

the candidates' respective attitudes toward the colonial crisis.

In 1774 the Newcastle freemen were constantly reminded of the corruptions of the last Parliament, the failures of the current administration, the legislators' ill-conceived colonial measures, and the voting records of their representatives.[31] But it was the parliamentary voting record of the candidates in particular that brought the American issue explicitly before the public. The pamphlets repeatedly urged the electors to scrutinize the voting records of each candidate, and the local newspapers gave precise accounts of Members' votes.[32] We have seen that Phipps publicly declared his opposition to the Quebec bill when canvassing, but the opposition literature also censured both the government's American legislation and the sitting Members for supporting it. Blackett and the elder Ridley betrayed the burgesses' interests and 'sacred' rights 'these seven years past'.[33] The magistrates' 'unaccountably oppressive' behavior over the Town Moor, combined with the incumbents 'voting for, or being absent when most of the late unpopular acts were agitated in parliament', gave 'just and sufficient grounds for an attempt to turn both out of parliament'. On Blackett's parliamentary conduct, 'Junius' asked, 'Did he vote against the *Canada* Bill, and show his zeal against Popery, by supporting the protestant interest in the province of *Quebec*? Or did he assent, or remain silent, when the legislature was giving the most solemn sanction to the man of sin?'[34]

Phipps, on the other hand, 'voted against' the late unpopular acts and both he and Delaval were believed to adhere to 'the same principles with the independent free burgesses'.[35] Phipps voted on two occasions against the administration on Wilkes and 'against making K. Geo. as arbitrary over the lives and properties of the people of Quebec, as the King of France or Spain is over any part of their dominions – against shutting up the port of Boston, and ruining our own trade', and he firmly stood against sending a 'Papist governor' with a dozen regiments of 'well-meaning brave soldiers' to 'cut the throats of their

31 The Senate is depicted as devoid of representatives of virtue and honor, *The Freeman's Magazine*, pp. 95–7. 'Foreign and domestic affairs' are in disarray, while our Members in Parliament 'who ought to be the guardians of our natural rights, tread them under foot with impunity' (p. 31). The 'late measures of administration' have been advocated by men as zealous for absolute power as 'papists', 'jacobites' and 'nonjurors', (p. 163). In the same volume, references to the 'despotic measures' of the court or 'the present corrupt administration', or the 'wicked administration', are common (pp. 110, 132). Elsewhere, the Crown is viewed as aiming at absolute authority, *The Contest*, pp. 18, 29; *The Freeman's Magazine*, pp. vii, 16.

32 *The Freeman's Magazine*, pp. 161–2. It is easy enough, the editors urge, to distinguish between traitors and an 'honest supporter of the common liberties of mankind' (p. 75). The precision with which the local papers analyzed the parliamentary vote of Newcastle representatives is noteworthy. See *New. Chron.* (4 Nov. 1775).

33 *The Freeman's Magazine*, pp. 31, 95, 126. Return the same majority to Parliament, warns Junius, 'and your nation is ruined' (p. 128).

34 *The Contest*, p. 29; *The Freeman's Magazine*, p. 149. Such anti-Catholicism was hardly 'radical', yet it was characteristic of Murray's writings.

35 *The Contest*, p. 30; *The Freeman's Magazine*, p. 150.

fellow subjects'.[36] In short, the true 'leaders' of the burgesses' party 'are measures, not men'. The party claimed to invite Phipps 'not because he is Mr. Phipps, but because he has acted in the Senate, for these six years past, as they think he ought; and Mr. Delaval, from a firm belief he will do the same'.[37] As with Bristol and Great Yarmouth, it is remarkable that politics at Newcastle could have ever been construed as merely local in scope.

Colonial developments became more prominent and divisive following the election of 1774. The town's Philosophical Society debated the issue of the legitimacy of rebellion on more than one occasion, and decided in the affirmative.[38] The petitioning agitation of 1775 led Phipps, now Lord Mulgrave, to write a public letter renouncing the radicals' stance on America and declaring his own purpose to 'enforce the legislative authority of this country'. Consequently, when he thought of contesting the borough in 1777, he met with such a strong negative response from the Newcastle radicals that he declined to proceed.[39]

As the issues surrounding Wilkes faded and colonial matters came to the fore, the conflict over the Town Moor gained new relevance as a symbol associated with the colonists' struggles. Both friends and opponents of America used the Moor to drive home to the people of Newcastle the truth about the colonies. In 'The Squire and his Tenant: A Dialogue', which appeared in *The Freeman's Magazine*, the tenant observed, I have heard 'that our nation has not been over well used of late, by a very many of *those* who were appointed to take care of our rights and liberties'; and he proceeded to ask the squire, did 'you never hear, Sir, about certain *American* affairs, or charters, I think they call them, and about a *Newcastle moor*; and many such besides'?[40] The actions of the Newcastle magistrates and the those of the government in its legislation concerning Boston were of a kind: both were invasions of liberty that must be resisted.

Six years later, little had changed. In this election year an anonymous pamphlet was published at Newcastle entitled *A Short but Comprehensive Account of the Rise and Progress of the Commotions in America* (1780). It provided a thoroughgoing rebuttal to James Murray's *An Impartial History of the Present War in America* by attempting to prove that Presbyterian ministers were both the chief cause of rebellion in America and the driving force behind sedition in England.[41] To illustrate this thesis, and to bring it home to his Newcastle

---

36 *The Contest*, p. 37. Delaval is also believed to have opposed both the Quebec bill and the Boston port bill, (p. 36). For further criticism of the Quebec bill and sympathy for 'the Boston presbyterians', see p. 18.

37 *The Contest*, p. 18.

38 Knox, 'Popular Politics', 228.

39 *Gen. Eve. Post* (30 Nov.–2 Dec. 1775); Knox, 'Popular Politics', 230.

40 *The Freeman's Magazine*, p. 109.

41 *A Short but Comprehensive Account of the rise and Progress of the Commotions in America Wherein the Secret Springs and Causes thereof are discovered, by a person*

audience, the author of this pamphlet told the following story. A few miles from the city of New York, 'a kind of bushy common' had been peacefully used from 'time immemorial' by both 'church-people' and Independents or Presbyterians. A difference of opinion arose, however, whereby 'each party' claimed to have an 'equal right to put their cattle on the said common'. A certain Mr. Rogers, Presbyterian minister of New York, 'convened the Independents together in a secret manner', and encouraged them 'to claim the said common'. This secret advice being divulged, the minister 'lost the good opinion of the public', but only temporarily, since later he 'gave up the plain simple gospel' for the sake of 'politic preaching'. His preaching led to many becoming prejudiced 'against government', and 'drawn by him into a spirit of resistance'. The author's point, not easily lost on the inhabitants of Newcastle, was this: conflict over a town's commons in the new world (as in the old) was the means 'by which may be seen the disposition of certain ministers and people in America, who retain the same spirit as their ancestors did many years since in England'.[42] The citizens of Newcastle were invited to find the cause of political disruption, both local and national, in Presbyterian disaffection; they were also expected to find meaning in contemporary events through remembering the historical events 'many years since in England'.

ELECTORAL BEHAVIOR IN NEWCASTLE

Following the election of 1774, James Murray published a poll book with extensive annotations in the hope that those voters 'who are now uninformed, unconcerned and wavering, may, by reflection and experience, become more knowing, interested, and steady'. He clearly perceived the importance of an analysis of the results, and as he tallied the voters' place of residence and occupations, two characteristics began to stand out: the proportion of nonresident freemen voting for the magisterial candidates, and the social composition of the vote for the burgesses' candidates. Murray's listing of residences was designed to separate 'the spurious magistratical brats, from the legitimate Sons of Freedom', and his suspicions were confirmed when he found that an 'unexpected number of out-voters ... polled the three first days for the magistrates' candidates'. His examination of occupations revealed that among those who voted for Phipps and Delaval there was not '*one* lord, *one* baronet, *one* placeman, and the reader may be sure then, not one bishop, dean, priest, or deacon'. In Murray's estimation, two things lost the election: the burgesses

residing in America, from the beginning of the Year 1768, 'till the latter end of 1779 (Newcastle, 1780). On Murray see pp. 15–17, 23, 27, 29, 31–3; on the Presbyterian ministry, pp. 14, 30. The author characteristically equates Presbyterians and Independents, p. 10.

42 *A Short but Comprehensive Account*, p. 15. Mr. Rogers is otherwise unidentified and the role of the Presbyterians in the affair of the Moor at Newcastle has not been ascertained.

were 'crushed by their out-lying brethren – brethren! ignorant of, and consequently unconcerned at their wrongs', and the creation of new freemen before
the poll.[43]

Namier and Christie overlooked this evidence and thereby failed to grasp the
importance of the Newcastle outvoters – a group which comprised approximately a third of the total electorate. Knox was the first to actually count the
non-resident voters and his findings confirmed Murray's impressions. In
1774, the magisterial candidates won sixty percent of the vote from London
and other port cities, and eighty percent of the county vote; in 1777, Trevelyan
won only because he received two thirds of the county vote.[44] Against Murray,
however, Knox showed that the new freemen in 1774 were almost equally
divided between the parties.[45] But more importantly, Knox saw the value of
creating extended records of single voters over time, and by manually linking
the 1774, 1777, 1780 poll books, he discovered an exceptionally high level of
consistency in both parties. He found that for approximately half of the resident
voters who were shopkeepers and artisans 'a politics of opinion overrode the
traditional politics of interest', and his conclusions reveal that the past use of
aggregated election returns was superficial and highly misleading.[46]

Knox established the overall political coherence of the Newcastle electorate
and thoroughly explained the most important patterns in popular politics.
Bowes infiltrated the stronghold of magisterial support from the county in
1777, and though the radicals lost, it is now clear that support for their party
was on the increase in this period. The voting was also remarkably consistent;
seventy percent of those voting for Bowes in 1777 supported him again in
1780, and this accounts for more than half of his poll. Whatever losses Bowes
experienced in 1780 were caused by the competition between himself and
Delaval for radical votes.[47] Knox also discerned a social division between the
parties, which, though depicted in general terms, finds the magisterial candidates with a disproportionately large share of the voters in the gentry, professional, and merchant categories. Further work, however, is needed on the
softening of party lines after 1777, a comparative assessment of the floating

43 Murray, *The Burgesses' Poll*, pp. v, vi, 19, 22–4.
44 Knox excludes all those not listed in Newcastle proper, but in this study, 'residents'
include the communities contiguous to Newcastle that would have been influenced by
the political life of the borough. Further, numerous Presbyterians lived in the suburbs.
For example, many members of the Carlisle Street chapel lived in Sandgate, Gateshead,
Ballist Hills, Ouseburn, and Biker Bar. With this definition, out-voters accounted for
29.6% of the poll in 1774, 31.2% in 1777, and 33.4% in 1780. Knox, 'Popular
Politics', 238. 'Wilkism', 33 note 28. 'Socio-occupational' differences, Knox found,
were insignificant among non-residents. The 'county' support for the magistrates is thus
yet to be explained.
45 Knox, 'Wilkism', 29, note 16; 'Popular Politics', 236 note 22. This means that the
burgesses had a disproportionately large share of new voters.
46 Knox, 'Popular Politics', 238.
47 Knox, 'Popular Politics', 239–40.

vote, and a more extended analysis of the social and religious dimensions of partisanship.[48]

The high level of split voting in 1780 (see Table 8.2) may be accounted for on several grounds, not the least of which is the well documented difficulty of maintaining straight party voting in a three way contest. Ridley was the incumbent in 1780 and he was still a popular candidate; more importantly, by 1778 he had moved against the administration over its American policy. In June of 1780, three months before the election, Ridley presented the Association movement's petition from Cumberland to the House of Commons, although he never embraced parliamentary reform enthusiastically.[49] During the election, Murray proposed a test, or pledge, by which to bind the representatives to their constituents, thereby raising again the old standard of the popular party, but Ridley refused.[50] A vote for him in 1780 as representing the magistrates' party

Table 8.2: *Straight Party and Cross Voting in Newcastle upon Tyne*
(Percentage)

	1774	1777	1780
	(4 way)	(2 way)	(3 way)
PARTISAN			
Electorate (other than Dissent)	93.7	100.0	46.4
Dissent	100.0	100.0	28.5
SPLIT			
Electorate	6.3	0	53.6
Dissent	0	0	71.4
Sample of Electorate, N =	793	784	758
Sample of Dissent, N =	22	16	21

48 Knox rounds percentages to the nearest five points for the 1774 link to the 1777 poll book, though he does provide totals for all possible combinations in 1777 and 1780. But he pairs the votes in such a way as to slightly exaggerate the level of consistent party support from 1777 to 1780, and he does not make the floating vote for 1774–7 explicit, thereby neglecting a useful comparison. We are not told the basis upon which he samples the occupational data of 1774 ('Popular Politics', 237 note 23), nor the nature of his 'sample' of Dissenting registers ('Wilkism', 29 note 16). Finally, his manual linkage runs into trouble when he attempts a cross tabulation of voters in two elections with the third variable of occupation (240). The figures in the following analysis are based on the resident voters only and thus the same computations will differ slightly from Knox's.
49 Mackenzie, *A Descriptive and Historical Account*, 2: 659. Despite these changes, in Tables 8.2 through 8.4 Ridley is classed as representing the 'magistrates' party.
50 Mackenzie, *A Descriptive and Historical Account*, 2: 388.

may have made some sense, but he could not be classified as pro-administration. Clearly, there was less convergence between candidates, local issues, and national policy in 1780 than there had been in 1774 and 1777. The importance of the three candidates' relative uniformity of opinion concerning the American war has not been fully appreciated in past analyses of the 1780 election.

To complicate the voters' decision even further, Delaval and Bowes were not able to present a united front to the electorate. The suspicion that they were at odds with each other and competing for the radical vote is confirmed by the petition Delaval introduced against Bowes for bribery (not, it should be noted, against Ridley).[51] Further, there were two distinct groups within the electorate who might have been expected to provide plumps for Ridley who in fact were almost as prone to split their votes as the overall electorate. We have seen in other boroughs that the clerical vote may serve as a standard by which to judge political consistency. That the large number of split votes reflects the lessening of clear ideological options is substantiated by the confusion of the Anglican clergy and their unenthusiastic turnout in 1780. The twelve Anglican clergy who voted in 1774 voted unanimously for the magistrates' candidates, and the ten who voted in 1777 all voted for Trevelyan; but in 1780, while all seven cast at least one vote for Ridley, four paired Ridley with either Bowes or Delaval. The county out-voters also split a large proportion of their votes; 51.3 percent as compared to 54 percent overall.[52] Thus the tendency to split votes in 1780 was present among the clergy as well as the laity, and if it is true that the 'line between magistrates and radicals remained firmly drawn' in 1777, it is too much to claim that this line was firm in 1780, though the social basis to the vote, examined below, will reveal some consistent patterns among certain occupational groups.[53]

Nevertheless, an analysis of consistent party support over two elections suggests a highly committed core of supporters for both the magistrates' and the burgesses' party (Table 8.3). Despite the pressure to split their votes in 1780, nearly half (41.2%) of those who voted in both 1777 and 1780 did not do so and thereby demonstrated a strong attachment to their parties or candidates.[54] Nearly one out of five (18.2%) of the resident voters plumped for

---

51   Christie, *The End of North's Ministry*, p. 144. Knox, 'Popular Politics', only surmises that the two were not united, 239–40. For the crucial evidence, see *CJ* (20 Nov. 1780). At the same time, a petition of the burgesses was presented to the Commons 'on behalf of themselves' against Ridley for corruption, and they claimed that apart from bribery, more paired votes for Bowes and Delaval would have resulted. The issue of bribery certainly cannot be dismissed.

52   However, by this date London and the out-ports had come around to the radical candidates; 55.2% voted Bowes and Delaval and only 37.7% split their votes. Knox did not examine the outvoters in 1780.

53   As Knox does, 'Popular Politics', 229.

54   This group, representing 41.3% of the electorate, includes those who voted Trevelyan in 1777 and plumped for Ridley in 1780, and those who voted Bowes in 1777 and voted for Bowes and Delaval (either together or singly) in 1780.

Bowes, and 10.8 percent cast single votes for Ridley. This commitment is further illustrated by the significant drop in the floating vote. It should also be noted that the higher proportion of the floating vote 1774–7 (18%) may be interpreted as a radical inroad on the magisterial vote. Knox noted that in 1777 Bowes won over some former magisterial voters,[55] and in fact, he gained three votes from the magistrates' party for every one vote that the radicals lost to the magistrates.[56] Still, the consistent party support in both 1777 and 1780 is impressive and compares favorably with other well organized boroughs in the eighteenth century.

Table 8.3: *Consistent Partisan and Floating Vote in Newcastle upon Tyne*
(Percentage)

	1774–1777	1777–1780
PARTISAN (Magistrate and Burgess Combined)		
Electorate (other than Dissent)	75.1	41.2
Dissent	100	20.0
FLOATING (Magistrate to Burgess or Burgess to Magistrate)		
Electorate	18.0	4.8
Dissent	0	6.7
SPLIT		
Electorate	6.9	54.0
Dissent	0	73.3
Sample of Electorate, N =	638	580
Sample of Dissent, N =	12	15

Knox convincingly argued, however, that the split vote in 1780 does not reflect inconsistent or incoherent behavior. Firm supporters of the burgesses may be determined on the basis of the 1777 election, and thus Knox considered voters for Ridley–Bowes and Ridley–Delaval in 1780 who previously voted for Bowes in 1777 to be consistently in the burgesses' camp. The same logic applies to those who previously voted for Trevelyan and split their votes in 1780 and there is some evidence from those voters' occupations to confirm this association. On these grounds, Knox concluded that nearly three quarters (72.5%) of the electorate in 1780 voted in a politically coherent manner.[57] This proportion is certainly credible in light of the consistent party support achieved

55 Knox, 'Popular Politics', 239.
56 14.1% of the voters changed to Bowes in 1777, while only 4.2% changed to Trevelyan.
57 Knox, 'Popular Politics', 239–40.

between 1774 and 1777 (75.1%) and in light of the political similarities between the candidates.

If it can be shown that the voters behaved consistently with their respective parties' public pronouncements, the contribution of religion to partisan politics in Newcastle has remained obscure. On the eve of the 1774 election a published handbill requested the Dissenters to support Phipps and Delaval in light of their backing of the Dissenters' relief bill of 1772. Knox sampled Dissenting registers and concluded that the two factions 'split the Dissenting vote almost evenly'.[58] But the most striking feature of the Dissenters in Newcastle is not their political behavior, but their absence at the polls. The names of eleven resident Dissenting ministers can be isolated during the American crisis, yet unlike Bristol where the Dissenting ministers were active, not one of these ministers voted in the three elections.[59] Furthermore, these pastors were not politically quiescent: seven had signed the petition for relief from subscribing to the Thirty-Nine Articles in 1772, and at least four added their names to the petition against the government's American policies in 1775.[60] More than 700 Dissenting laymen from six chapels were merged with the poll books, but only twenty-two could be isolated in 1774, and this dropped to sixteen in 1777. Relative to the total population, the Dissenting community in Newcastle was very large and the laity should have had a considerable influence on elections, but if the proportion of voters from these six chapels is representative, the Dissenters comprised less than five percent of the resident electorate. In each election, the voting patterns of this tiny minority were almost indistinguishable from other voters, and if anything, the Dissenters favored the magistrates. In 1774, 45.5 percent of the Dissenters voted opposition compared to 33.4 percent overall, but in 1777 this dropped to 43.8 percent, compared to 49.3 percent overall, and in 1780, it was 19 percent compared to 35.2 percent overall. Apart from the publications of the Dissenting elite, particularly those of James Murray, and the leadership they offered during the petitioning agitation, the Newcastle Nonconformist laity contributed nothing at all to the partisanship of the electorate.

The Dissenters' lack of involvement in Newcastle elections is probably related in part to their lower social status. They were somewhat poorer than the population at large, with 25 percent of their membership in the laboring category compared to 16 percent in St. Andrews parish, and 10 percent in St.

58 Knox, 'Wilkism', 29 note 16. He sampled the records of the Ballist Hills cemetery, two Scots and two English chapels.
59 This applies to all the ministers of Scots churches, James Richardson, John Baillie, William Graham, James Shields, William Davidson, Andrew Ogilvie, and Robert Cowen, but also to James Murray and the English ministers, Samuel Lowthian, John Foster, Caleb Alder, and William Robson. (The ministers of the Quaker and Methodist chapels are unknown.) A number of William Robsons voted in each election, so a positive identification of this one minister is not possible.
60 'A View of English Nonconformity in 1773', *CHST* 5 (1911–12), 280.

Nicholas.[61] There were fewer Dissenting artisans and retailers and thus fewer men were qualified to join the Newcastle companies. But a more convincing explanation for the nonparticipation of both ministers and laity lies in the proximity of the borough to Scotland. In Newcastle, people were admitted to the freedom of the city in one of two ways: they could claim their freedom by servitude through apprenticeship, or by patrimony, on the strength of their father's freedom. In either case, the candidate was required to belong to the fellowship of one of the borough's companies.[62] But the majority, if not all, of the companies had rules against apprenticing Scotsmen, and some forbade their working in the city altogether. The ordinary of the fraternity of tailors ruled: 'It is ordered, as has been the custom time out of mind, that no brother of the fellowship shall let any Scotchman a work, under the pain of three shillings and four-pence'. These orders were repeated periodically in the eighteenth century, and some of the companies, such as the joiners, house carpenters, and masons, were even stronger in their denunciations of foreigners: in these three companies, Scotsmen could not be apprenticed, nor were they 'ever to be admitted into the company on any account whatever'.[63] A very small percentage of the Scots Presbyterians did vote, but they, and a number of the English Dissenters as well, were effectively disfranchised.[64] The felt makers, curriers, and armorers, for example, ruled in 1719 that no Quaker could be taken apprentice on pain of forfeiting £100.[65]

Contemporary explanations of the political cleavage in Newcastle accordingly focused upon social and economic differences rather than religion.[66] In the election of 1774, the burgesses were thought to be of 'mean and insignificant' social standing and it was said that the 'lower ranks of burgesses' execrated the magistrates as 'plundering villains'.[67] Newspaper articles referred to the opposition as the 'ragamuffin party' and some authors believed their

61 See chap. 2 above. The numbers are too small to be convincing, but a disproportionate number of those Dissenters who did vote were in the artisan and laboring categories in each election; 19 (86.4%) in 1774 (overall 62.8%); 13 (81.3%) in 1777 (overall 65.3%); and 16 (76.2%) in 1780 (overall 64.8%).
62 Mackenzie, *A Descriptive and Historical Account*, 1: 653; Knox, 'Wilkism', 24 note 2.
63 Mackenzie, *A Descriptive and Historical Account*, 1: 672, 692–3. Regulations against Scotsmen are also found in the following Companies: skinners and glovers, saddlers, tanners, smiths, fullers and dyers, weavers, barbers and surgeons, coopers, slaters, and plumbers, pewterers, and glaziers, Mackenzie, 1: 671, 673, 674, 677, 678, 689, 690, 691, 697.
64 The sample turned up eight voters in the Silver Street chapel and nine in the Groat Market.
65 Mackenzie, *A Descriptive and Historical Account*, 1: 696.
66 The *Short but Comprehensive Account* contained the usual rhetoric concerning Dissenters. In America, the Presbyterians, Seceders, and Baptists 'especially their ministers, were the people principally concerned in the American revolt'. And in England the ministers 'of different sects' have 'strained every nerve to foment and continue the rebellion in America, only out of a party spirit', pp. 29–30.
67 *The Freeman's Magazine*, p. 89; *The Contest*, p. 16.

primary support to be from 'the lower class of people'. The contest of 1774
was viewed, in short, as a conflict between laced waistcoats and leather
aprons.[68]

With 58.3 percent of the vote in 1774 (see Table 8.4) the magistrates' party
drew 86.4 percent of all resident professional and merchant voters, and in
1777, with 50.4 percent of the vote, they had 77.6 percent of the elite.[69] This
represents a greater socio-economic disparity between the parties than was
found at Bristol, Yarmouth, or Cambridge, and this emerged quite apart from
the stimulus of a Dissenting bloc of voters, though it may be related in part to
the radical rhetoric of James Murray. The most peculiar characteristic of the
magistrates' party is the uniformity of the merchants' support, whereas at
Bristol the merchants were somewhat more divided. Yet at both Newcastle and
Bristol, the retailers, and especially the artisans, were strongly oppositionist.
Equally striking is the lower number of laborers among the opposition; these
figures seem to suggest that the laborers were not politically engaged, or at least
they were not engaged by the radicals.

Table 8.4: *Occupational Structure of the Electorate in Newcastle upon Tyne*

(Percentage)

	1774			1777		1780		
	Mag.	Bur.	Split	Mag.	Bur.	Mag.	Bur.	Split
1. Gentlemen, Professions	3.4	1.0	2.0	4.0	1.3	2.4	.4	1.2
2. Merchants	15.4	2.1	8.0	14.9	4.3	17.9	4.4	14.0
3. Shopkeepers	18.9	33.1	24.0	16.9	28.2	17.9	28.8	20.2
4. Artisans	53.1	58.3	58.0	53.6	60.2	51.1	61.7	56.0
5. Laborers	8.8	5.5	8.0	10.6	2.0	9.5	4.7	8.6
6. Others	.4	—	—	—	—	1.2	—	—
Sample, N =	475	290	50	403	397	84	274	421
	(58.3)	(35.6)	(6.1)	(50.4)	(49.6)	(10.8)	(35.2)	(54.0)

The elections of 1774 and 1777 thus seem to reflect a genuine socio-
economic base to the political cleavage, and the 1780 poll confirms this division

---

68 Cited in Knox, 'Wilkism', 28–9.
69 Knox made some general observation on the social composition of the vote, noting the
preponderance of resident tradesmen and craftsmen among the supporters of Phipps and
Delaval in 1774, and their lack of support from the elite in 1774 (a 'little more than
10%') and in 1777 ('only a quarter'), but we do not know the basis of his sample except
insofar as he observes that 'the membership of whole companies has been omitted
because neither individual nor occupation patterns exist', 'Popular Politics', 237 note
23; 'Wilkism', 29, 33. While he admits that his percentages are only 'suggestive', they
are confirmed by this independent analysis.

in part for the 'consistent' voters. But the split vote in 1780 is also susceptible to further analysis on the basis of the occupational structure of the electorate. Knox observed that 'well over ninety percent' of those in the resident gentry, professional, and merchant category who had supported magisterial candidates in *both* 1774 and 1777 voted for Ridley and Delaval in 1780. He also showed that unusually consistent support for Ridley and Delaval in 1780 came from the artisans (a telling concession, in my judgment, that militates strongly against a socio-economic base to the 1780 election). He argued that the prominence of the elite who voted for Ridley and Delaval reflected 'political concerns focused on the nature of Bowesite support'.[70] That is, the elite wished to elect Ridley, but to avoid Bowes, they were forced to pair Ridley with Delaval. The elite thereby stood by Ridley and gave their second votes to Delaval in order to avoid the return of two radicals. Knox also averred that there was greater support from the tradesmen and craftsmen who had previously supported radical candidates for Ridley and Bowes, but he apparently could not press the analysis further with only manual linkage.[71] He argued, however, that some voters who paired Ridley and Bowes were genuine Bowesites who denied their second vote to Delaval. The first argument presupposes that the elite were more favorable to Delaval than Bowes, and the second suggests rather tentatively that the tradesmen and craftsmen favored Bowes over Delaval.

A closer scrutiny of the occupational data confirms the first of Knox's contentions. It is the case that consistent party support for Ridley and Delaval was drawn from the top two occupational categories; based on a comparison of the 1777 and 1780 elections alone, two times as many previous magisterial voters in the elite category paired Ridley with Delaval as paired Ridley with Bowes.[72]

Knox's second contention, however, is not fully borne out by the evidence. It is true that consistent Bowesites (plumps) were drawn in higher proportions from the tradesmen or shopkeeper and artisan categories than any other group, but a comparison of the 1777 and 1780 poll books proves that tradesmen and artisans who had voted for Bowes in 1777 were willing in 1780 to pair Ridley with Delaval in about the same proportion as they paired Ridley and Bowes (10.8% of all tradesmen and craftsmen versus 7.9%). Knox's use of occupational data in relation to the 1780 election rests too much weight on the unconvincing distinction between Delaval and Bowes, both radical candidates. With all three candidates in opposition over America in 1780 it is little wonder that the economic dividing line in this election was less pronounced, though the orientation of the elite in favor of Ridley remains impressive. The failure of the

---

70 Knox, 'Popular Politics', 239.
71 *Ibid.*, 240, where he admits that a conclusive analysis of the occupational group polling for Ridley and Bowes is 'very difficult'.
72 Trevelyan to Ridley–Delaval; 41.5% gentry, professional, merchant. Trevelyan to Ridley–Bowes; 18.5% gentry, professional, merchant.

Newcastle electorate, particularly the shopkeepers and artisans, to divide on a socio-economic basis when America was not a prominent issue indirectly corroborates the evidence from other large urban constituencies.

In Newcastle we have evidence of a strong and quite successful radical movement, influenced, if not led by the Dissenting elite. But ministers like James Murray had no measurable impact on the Dissenting laity in parliamentary elections, and at least some of the political division was caused by social and economic inequalities. As we found in an earlier study of Cambridge, progressive leaders using all the arsenal of radical ideology appealed to a populace that was socially and economically divided. If the differences between the parties' occupational structure reflect genuine economic inequality, then oppression by the elite, or at least the perception of oppression, is simply the best explanation we have for the reaction of the artisans and shopkeepers. In any case, their greater willingness to support radical candidates and express their opposition to the government's American policy is beyond dispute. But as in the case of Cambridge, the difficulties the Dissenters faced in the realm of parliamentary politics did not mean that they were excluded from all forms of political activity. A later chapter will show how the Newcastle Dissenters expressed their political opinion clearly and forcefully through the unofficial channel of petitioning. Their exclusion from parliamentary contests appears in fact to have contributed to their thoroughgoing involvement in extra-parliamentary politics and a rejection of their deferential posture.

LIVERPOOL, SIR WILLIAM MEREDITH, AND THE ROCKINGHAM WHIGS

In the first quarter of the eighteenth century three Presbyterian chapels constituted the whole of Dissent in Liverpool, but Nonconformity grew with the burgeoning population of the city, and by the 1770s there were eight Dissenting congregations.[73] By then Liverpool was competing in size with Bristol, and by 1800 it was arguably the largest provincial city in England.[74] The Presbyterians – distinguishable from Unitarians in name only – maintained three chapels in our period, and in 1763 they added a fourth. Of all the old denominations, they were by far the most conspicuous contributors to the borough's civic life. Benn's Garden had the largest share of 'the genteeler sort' of Nonconformist; in the 1730s through the 1760s four members were mayors, a fifth was a bailiff, and a sixth was an alderman. Like its counterpart at Lewins Mead in Bristol, this congregation had an impressive complement of

73 The Evans List, pp. 59–63. Including Toxteth Park near Liverpool with 249 auditors in 1715, the three congregations numbered 1407 hearers. By 1773, Thompson lists five additional chapels. Thompson List MS 38.6, p. 19.
74 Paul Laxton, 'Parish Registers and Urban Structure: The Example of Late-Eighteenth Century Liverpool', *Urban History Yearbook* (1978), 75. William Enfield's estimate was 34,407 in 1773, Laxton, 'Parish Registers', 83, note 6. James Sketchley, *Sketchley's Bristol Directory* (Bristol, 1775), estimates 35,440 for Liverpool, p. 120.

custom's house officers and it also was the spiritual home of John Hardman, M.P. for a brief period in 1754–5.[75] Kaye Street chapel and Toxteth Park meeting both flourished in the eighteenth century; the latter gave something of a conservative theological alternative to the more progressive Dissenters at Kaye Street and Benn's Garden. The experimental Octagon chapel, while vital in its congregational and liturgical life, lasted only a short while (1763–76), and when it closed, the members dispersed to the other Presbyterian chapels.[76]

Newington chapel was established in 1777 as the borough's one Congregational meeting, and though it was paedobaptist, it had theological affinities with the two Baptist meetings. One unnamed Baptist chapel at the end of Matthew and Stanley streets was matched by a much larger Baptist meeting in Byrom Street. The Friends had a meeting house on the west side of Hackins Hey and the Methodist chapel was situated in Mount Pleasant.[77] It cannot be proven that the Dissenters kept up with Anglican expansion since so little is known about the size of each congregation, but they certainly competed with the Anglicans in the addition of new churches – a competition that became even keener in the last decades of the century.[78] In 1715 the Presbyterians had 160 freemen or 16 percent of the electorate, but even with their growth and the addition of the Baptists, it is unlikely that they maintained this proportion of voters when the electorate increased to 2,000 in the 1770s.[79]

The characteristic feature of politics at Liverpool was the interminable conflict between the corporation and an independent party of freemen. In the first part of the century, the two sides were labelled 'Whig' and 'Tory', and the *History of Parliament* portrayed an Anglican corporation united against an independent party 'supported by the Dissenters'.[80] The politics of the borough

75 *A Picture of Liverpool* (Liverpool, 1803), p. 90; later situated in Renshaw Street. George Eyre Evans, *Vestiges of Protestant Dissent* (Liverpool, 1897), p. 135; see also George Eyre Evans, *Records of the Provincial Assembly of Lancashire and Cheshire* (Manchester, 1896), pp. 90–1, 100–1, 105–6; Anne D. Holt, *Walking Together: A Study in Liverpool Nonconformity, 1688–1938* (London, 1938), pp. 111, 121; on their social status, see pp. 117–25.

76 Kaye Street was later situated in Paradise Street, then Hope Street. H. D. Roberts, *Hope Street Church, Liverpool* (Liverpool, 1909), p. xvii; *A Picture of Liverpool*, p. 91. On Toxteth Park see Evans, *Vestiges*, p. 140. On the Octagon chapel, Holt, *Walking Together*, pp. 133–48; Evans, *Vestiges*, p. 139.

77 Roberts, *Hope Street*, p. 494. For the Baptists, Ian Sellers, *A History of Liverpool Baptists* (1960), p. 15, and *The Minor Churches: A History of Liverpool Baptists* (1962), pp. 2–3, and *A Picture of Liverpool*, pp. 92–3. By 1803 the Methodists had five chapels. On the Quakers, see James Touzeau, *The Rise and Progress of Liverpool from 1551 to 1835*, 2 vols. (Liverpool, 1910), 2: 543. There was also a Roman Catholic and a Sandemanian chapel, *A Picture of Liverpool*, pp. 91, 94.

78 Five Anglican churches were consecrated between 1744 and 1774 which graphically illustrates the growth of the city. *A Picture of Liverpool*, pp. 84–6.

79 The Evans List, pp. 59–63. *Commons, 1715–1754*, 1: 271; *Commons, 1754–1790*, 1: 317. Excellent records subsist for three Presbyterian chapels: Benn's Garden, Kaye Street, and Toxteth Park.

80 *Commons, 1754–1790*, 1: 317; *Commons, 1715–1754*, 1: 270–1.

in the second half of the century were increasingly dominated by the powerful Common Council, a self-elected and self-perpetuating body. For example, the Council worked hard to reduce the number of freemen, thereby keeping them under control. Occasionally, a Dissenter gained access to the Council, but generally, the corporation was steadfast in its support of the Church and the king.[81] But the office of mayor was, paradoxically, sometimes put to use in behalf of the independent party and there were other complicating factors in the borough's political divisions. It has been suggested that class differences may have contributed to political conflict, the wealthier citizens siding with the corporation party, and the poorer with the independents,[82] and thus both the religious and the political elements in Liverpool's political life require further investigation.

In 1754, John Hardman, member and pewholder at Benn's Garden Presbyterian chapel stood on the independent interest against the two corporation candidates (see Table 8.5).[83] His victory represented the largest majority of any contestant in the second half of the century, but with the loss of the poll book, the precise contribution of the Dissenting vote cannot be ascertained.

Table 8.5: *Liverpool Election Results: 1754–1784*

1754		1761	
John Hardman	1236	Sir Ellis Cunliffe	1163
Thomas Salusbury	746	Sir William Meredith	1138
Edward Lloyd	552	Charles Pole	1041
1780		**1784**	
Bamber Gascoyne Jr.	608	Bamber Gascoyne Jr.	954
Henry Rawlinson	572	Richard Pennant,	869
Richard Pennant	462	Baron Penrhyn	
		Banastre Tarleton	856
		Sir William Meredith	131

81 F. E. Sanderson, 'The Structure of Politics in Liverpool, 1780–1807', *Transactions of the Historical Society of Lancashire and Cheshire*, 127 (1977), 65–6. Sanderson estimates the freemen at 20% of the adult male population in 1734, 8% in 1761, and 3% in 1812 (68). He depicts the Dissenters as politically moderate (72). The offices of mayor and bailiff, while elective, were manipulated by the Common Council, and sometimes contests were avoided for several years.

82 *Commons, 1754–1790*, 1: 15.

83 John Hardman of Allerton Hall married Jane the daughter of Thomas Cockshutt, merchant, and son of alderman Cockshutt, a Dissenter. Holt, *Walking Together*, pp. 119, 121. For a brief biography that does not mention his religion, see *Commons, 1754–1790*, 2: 583.

Despite Hardman's overwhelming margin, the election led to serious rioting.[84] Hardman's parliamentary career was cut short by his death in December 1755 at which time Ellis Cunliffe took his seat without a contest. Charles Pole replaced Salusbury who died in the following year. Cunliffe and Pole were soon associated with the corporation party, and at the general election of 1761, they stood together as government Whigs.[85]

Joseph Clegg, merchant, late mayor, and member of Benn's Garden had, by 1761, already gained some notoriety for his defense of the independent party against the corporation. At the approach of the general election, Clegg led the movement to enlist Charles Townshend against the corporation members, but in the event, Townshend declined to stand.[86] The independents settled instead upon Sir William Meredith whom contemporaries depicted as the candidate most likely to free the burgesses from the oppression of the corporation.[87] Immediately after his election, Meredith set about to consolidate his position, and he turned to the Dissenters for assistance. Though elected on the strength of the independent party, Meredith well understood the importance of the office of Mayor: he wrote to Charles Jenkinson 12 October 1763, 'But without a mayor the rest of the corporation are insignificant and a Mr. Campbell, a friend of ours, is in nomination … But if we do not get a mayor now, Gascoyne or the Devil may come in for me.'[88] George Campbell, along with Hardman and Clegg, was a member of Benn's Garden; he was elected bailiff in 1756 and in 1763 he won the mayoral contest.[89] On 25 October, Meredith wrote to Jenkinson again: 'Everything turned out at Liverpool beyond my hopes. My friend was elected mayor, and the division among the gentlemen who opposed me so much greater than I expected, especially in the corporation, that no acts can be affected now, and the interest of my friends has now some reality and foundation …'[90] Meredith clearly linked the Whig interest at Liverpool to the politics of the Dissenting elite.

84 James A. Picton, *Memorials of Liverpool*, 2 vols. (London, 1875), 1: 184. Riots were common at Liverpool elections. For the general election of 1734 and the municipal election of 1757, see Touzeau, *The Rise and Progress of Liverpool*, 2: 492, 508–9; and for riots in the 1784 election, Ramsay Muir, *A History of Liverpool* (Liverpool, 1907), p. 225.
85 *Commons, 1754–1790*, 1: 317. On Cunliffe and Pole's joint candidature see *An Entire and Impartial Collection of all the Papers, etc., Published on Both Sides Concerning the Late Election at Liverpool* (Liverpool, 1761), pp. 3, 30; appeals to plump for Meredith were common, pp. 13, 33, 37.
86 Holt, *Walking Together*, p. 119 identifies Clegg. See the letters of 31 Oct.–19 Nov. 1760, concerning a movement to offer a third candidate in *A Genuine Collection of all the Papers, Addresses, Songs, Epigrams, and Acrostics printed by all Parties, During the late Contest for Representatives* (Liverpool, 1761), pp. 7–8 and Clegg's letter pp. 6–7. This collection is more extensive than *An Entire Collection*.
87 'Liberty requires' the contest. *A Genuine Collection*, pp. 8–11.
88 *Commons, 1754–1790*, 1: 318.
89 Holt, *Walking Together*, p. 111.
90 *Commons, 1754–1790*, 1: 318.

Meredith took office with the Rockingham Whigs in 1765, and consequently he had to stand for reflection, but the party in the corporation who opposed him could not find a suitable candidate to stand against him. When Cunliffe died in 1767, Meredith was able to bring Richard Pennant in without a contest and he and Pennant were returned unopposed at the general election of 1768.[91] On 6 February 1772, Meredith presented the petition of the liberal Anglican clergy against subscription to the Thirty-Nine Articles. He repeated this motion on two other occasions, and while it cannot be proven that this was a popular measure with his constituents, in other instances he carefully weighed their views, and it thus seems likely that his latitudinarian activities were prompted at least in part by the interests of his Liverpool constituents.[92] In 1774 Meredith and Pennant were returned unopposed and sat for Liverpool through 1780.

While representing Liverpool, Meredith became a leading opposition speaker in Parliament; for example, he opposed the government over general warrants and he was a critic of the government's American policy. In his *Historical Remarks on the Taxation of Free States* he supported granting concessions to the colonists, arguing that the Americans must be governed exactly as resident citizens are governed.[93] He took office under North in 1774, then resigned in December 1777 over the American crisis, and subsequently became even more outspoken against the government's American measures. Pennant, too, voted regularly with the opposition in Parliament; he spoke frequently on America, opposing the taxation of the colonists and supporting repeal of the tea duty.[94]

In the general election of 1780, Bamber Gascoyne, Jr., a local landowner with an estate at Childwall, stood with Henry Rawlinson, a merchant, on the corporation interest.[95] Since Meredith and Pennant were in opposition, during their tenure the corporation had often applied to Bamber Gascoyne, Sr., M.P. for Truro, and this connection was critical for the younger Gascoyne's success. The tide turned rapidly against Pennant, and he declined the poll on the fifth day of the election, but his parliamentary career was not over. In 1784, as a newly created Irish peer under the title Lord Penhryn, he stood singly against Gascoyne and the American war hero, Banastre Tarleton. Gascoyne had steadfastly supported the North administration, Tarleton's reputation was based on

---

91 Meredith said, 'Pennant knows who brings him in; he was adopted by my friends on Lord Rockingham's letter, and I cannot therefore doubt of his future conduct.' *Commons, 1754–1790*, 3: 262. Pennant was educated at Newcome's Academy, Hackney, and was thus possibly favorably disposed to the Dissenters.

92 *Commons, 1754–1790*, 3: 130–3.

93 Picton, *Memorials of Liverpool*, 1: 211.

94 *Commons, 1754–1790*, 3: 132, 262. After Meredith's defection to North, the Rockinghams did not receive him back.

95 Early in the contest, Gascoyne claimed to run independently, but the popular literature encouraged paired votes for himself and Rawlinson. *A Collection of Papers, Addresses, Songs, &c. printed on All Sides. During the Contest for Representatives in Parliament for the Borough of Liverpool* (Liverpool, 1780), pp. 22, 68, 69.

his attempt to suppress rebellion in America, while Pennant was, by this date, associated with Fox.[96] Pennant won his seat back, while Gascoyne took the other, thereby sealing an uneasy truce between the independent party and the corporation.

The corporation was, on the whole, a conservative body, which, during the period of the American Revolution, was associated with Anglicanism. It sustained an unusual relationship with the churches of Liverpool, and particularly with St. George's, which was known as the corporation church. The corporation regularly attended St. George's, it received the rents, paid minister's salaries, and occasionally even made modifications in the liturgy of the Sunday service. Consequently, the clergy of St. George's were always well remunerated.[97] The corporation's political pronouncements are thus in keeping with its dominant religious affiliation. The corporation's addresses concerning the Middlesex election affair in 1769, and against the colonists in 1775 and again in 1779, were extremely authoritarian, even for conservative bodies, and thus Campbell's mayorality and Meredith's ability to win over some of his opponents must be considered exceptional inroads into a conservative arena.[98] The power base of the corporation was thus readily consolidated, and its only weakness lay in the elective nature of its most powerful offices.

POPULAR POLITICAL IDEOLOGY IN LIVERPOOL

There were no formal political clubs at Liverpool around which the freemen might rally, but during an election, each party established its headquarters in a public house, published a variety of notices concerning meetings, and proceeded to generate massive amounts of literature for popular consumption.[99] In 1761 the political squibs and broadsides revolved around three topics, which, in order of prominence were, freedom from the corporation, the religious orientation of the candidates, and the African trade. Meredith and his friends carried this election on the theme of independence from the corporation's

---

96 *Commons, 1754–1790*, 2: 492; 3: 349, 262. Meredith's poor health prevented him from serious campaigning. On Tarleton, see *A Collection*, p. 68. Muir, *A History of Liverpool*, p. 224 says Tarleton stood on the 'Whig' interest in 1784. But he was hardly paired with Penhryn: Gascoyne–Tarleton received 19.4% of the vote; Penhryn–Tarleton received 9.5%.

97 Touzeau, *The Rise and Progress of Liverpool*, 2: 483, 519, 542. Touzeau notes that the corporation had a 'strong hold' on all the new churches erected in Liverpool, controlling both the appointment and terms of ministers, p. 545.

98 Printed in Touzeau, *The Rise and Progress of Liverpool*, 2: 547, 560, 575. Meredith continued to express surprise at his achievements at Liverpool. *Commons, 1754–1790*, 3: 131. Quakers had on occasion been forbidden the freedom of the town because of their refusal to swear to that part of the *freeman's* oath that concerned church rates, but in 1767 the magistrates eased this requirement, which illustrates another exception. Touzeau, *The Rise and Progress of Liverpool*, 2: 543.

99 *An Entire Collection*, p. 19; *A Genuine Collection*, pp. 16–17.

oppressive influence.[100] 'Amicus', 'Frabricius', and 'Britannicus', castigated Cunliffe and Pole for their attachment to the corporation and the services they rendered to municipal office holders. Cunliffe was a 'sort of Vice-Roy' ignorant of the interests of the burgesses and governed by a few gentlemen, while Pole in all of his parliamentary conduct was under the influence of the corporation.[101] In response, the writers for Cunliffe and Pole attempted to associate Meredith with Catholicism and Jacobitism, an allusion to his Tory past, and these charges raised the most volatile issue of the election.

At first the independent party vaguely applauded 'the happy Establishment, both in Church and State', but 'A Lover of Truth' opened up the religious issue with charges that Meredith derived some of his support from the Catholics. 'A Georgian' then reminded the friends of Meredith that 'the Protestant Dissenters of all Denominations' ought to be cautious 'in the Choice of Representatives'. Such aspersions were competently answered by 'Philo Patraie', 'Veritas', and 'A Burgess'.[102] Subsequently, however, a freeman purporting to be a 'Protestant Dissenter', published a letter in which he recounted a recent social gathering of Meredith's tenants at his estate in Bowden Parish. 'Several' Dissenters were present at this meeting and Meredith reportedly insisted that they all drink a toast to the words 'Down with the Rump'. This letter elicited the most rancorous exchange of the election, and it resulted in charges of libel and testimony being given before a magistrate.[103] Meredith's friends stoutly defended his commitment to the Dissenters, as did the writers for Cunliffe and Pole, but the damage was already done; the corporation party's ploy seems to have had the desired effect of dividing the Dissenting vote. In any case, both parties clearly discerned the potential electoral impact of a unified religious minority.

The candidates' past conduct in Parliament on commercial matters was closely scrutinized. The corporation candidates were praised for their attention to the American iron bill and the African trade, but the friends of Meredith contended that he was more consistent in his voting on trade and more convincing in his speeches than the sitting members.[104] The question of trade intensified in the following years as the situation in the colonies degenerated, and in the 1770s American affairs attracted more and more attention. The first political expression concerning America from Liverpool was the merchants' petition to

---

100 *An Entire Collection*, pp. 7, 8, 13, 22; *A Genuine Collection*, pp. 12–14. The language of party was present, but not prominent; Meredith, for example, is called a Whig. *An Entire Collection*, pp. 29, 48, 49.
101 *A Genuine Collection*, pp. 18, 22, 25–6, 35, 38.
102 *An Entire Collection*, pp. 74, 76, 81–2, 93, 95–8; *A Genuine Collection*, pp. 43–4, 45.
103 *An Entire Collection*, pp. 98–100. 'Veritas' responds a second time: Meredith is 'not a persecutor of Dissenters, but an able and willing advocate', pp. 101–2. For the charges and countercharges concerning this incident, see pp. 102–7.
104 *A Genuine Collection*, 'Meanwell', pp. 10–16; the friends of Meredith, pp. 17–22. See also, pp. 32, 34, 47–50; *An Entire Collection*, pp. 61–2, 99.

Parliament in the spring of 1775 against the recent coercive legislation.[105] In the fall of the same year, the corporation sent up an address in harmony with the government's coercive policy, but the Lancashire petition in favor of peace circulated in Liverpool and gathered considerable support. The savage seamen riots of 1775, the corporation's appointment of a police committee and curfew in 1777, and the garrisoning of the Yorkshire militia in 1779, suggest that the revolutionary war contributed to serious social unrest.[106]

Judging by the extant popular literature of the 1780 election, the constitutional matters surrounding the colonial crisis were by far the most important issues to electors.[107] It is thus patently wrong to suppose that local issues dominated this election and that America was unimportant politically.[108] The prominence given to the candidates' past conduct in Parliament on the one hand, and Bamber Gascoyne Sr's. long association with the corporation, on the other, prohibit such a conclusion.[109] Above all, the younger Gascoyne's candidature was based on the strength of his father's career, and this had the effect of connecting him to the blunderings of the North administration. 'Varro' depicted Gascoyne Sr. as a courtier: 'To him and the rest of our wise and upright ministers we owe all the blessings of the American war, to them we owe the decline of our trade …' and the increase in taxation, and impressment. But Gascoyne was also 'avowedly supported by the Corporation. It is well known that all bodies corporate have an insatiable appetite for this power [and it] wants a check instead of an increase'. 'Varro' thus discerned a natural affinity between the corporation and the ministry whereby both sought to increase their power, and he warned against becoming slaves to Mr. Gascoyne, slaves to the corporation, and slaves to 'Lord N'.[110] Another anonymous writer associated the 'little tyrant of Childwall Hills' with the Parliament that 'provok'd the

105 James Bradley, *Popular Politics and the American Revolution in England: Petitions, the Crown, and Public Opinion* (Macon, Ga., 1986), p. 22. See chap. 9 below on the Lancashire conciliatory petition.

106 Muir, *A History of Liverpool*, pp. 219–20.

107 *A Collection of Papers, Addresses, Songs* (Liverpool, 1780), pp. 6–7, 83. Trade is mentioned, but not as prominently as such matters as respect for law, or support for liberty.

108 Picton, Christie, and Sanderson appear to have been unaware of *A Collection of Papers, Addresses, Songs*. Picton, *Memorials of Liverpool*, 1: 219; Christie, *The End of North's Ministry*, pp. 83–4, 137–8; Sanderson, 'The Structure of Politics', 79–80. Christie even assures us that in 1780 at Liverpool 'Local newspaper reports give no indication that political arguments were publicly canvassed by either side during the election', (p. 138) as if this exhausted ideological resources.

109 Bamber Gascoyne Sr. developed a very close relationship to the corporation with political overtones that went beyond merely commercial interests. The corporation sent him thanks on 7 Oct. 1778 and again on 4 Nov. 1778 for 'his spirited conduct in defending the Merchants and Traders of this town when grossly attacked and publicly aspersed for their free gift to His Majesty last year, a means that could only be odious to those who feared its happy effect'. Touzeau, *The Rise and Progress of Liverpool*, 2: 574.

110 *A Collection of Papers* (1780), p. 25. The association of Gascoyne with the government was a recurring theme; a 'ministerial tool', a 'tool of state', guilty of 'aristocratic tyranny', pp. 64, 66.

Americans' without a soldier to support them and 'refus'd to hear the petitions of the Colonists' and then offered concessions that were derogatory to the honor of Britain. Gascoyne thus voted for schemes that repeatedly miscarried. A lengthy essay by 'A Freeman' portrayed for the voters an administration that has 'too long exercised the iron rod of oppression'. A 'most vile and corrupt junto' have engaged the nation 'in a cruel and unnatural war with our American colonies and two of the most powerful nations in the world'. Gascoyne is the son of a man who is subservient to 'an abandoned Premier' who has sought to put us in slavery.[111] In short, the last Parliament was corrupt and profligate and a change was long overdue.

Those in favor of Gascoyne and Rawlinson also examined the candidates' parliamentary conduct but came to the opposite conclusions. 'A New Song' depicted Pennant and Meredith as false to the king; they were traitors and friends to America. They were, after all, 'minority men', and they hurt their constituents by encouraging 'every enemy in the world' against them. 'Tom the Tinker' had heard that the independent party writer 'Varro' might be a Dissenting minister, but he was now convinced that he was an American spy, because 'Varro' referred to Meredith with respect – Meredith, who is 'the vilest incendiary'. Pennant was thereby associated with bondage and tyranny, while Gascoyne could be counted on for 'good laws'.[112] These ideological themes of law and order, support for the king and the Church, versus sympathy for the colonists and the rhetoric of liberty, are largely indistinguishable from those found in Bristol and Newcastle.

The friends of Pennant, however, stood by his parliamentary record. He was applauded for his opposition and described as a man who 'preserves his parliamentary conduct sound and untainted'. 'Pennant has only voted with the minority when it was in his country's best interest to do so'. He has shown real patriotism in his public character in Parliament by 'opposing every subject he thought liable to endanger the happiness of the state', and he can be trusted to enquire into the real causes of the late misfortunes. 'A friend to Varro' felt it necessary not only to justify Pennant, but to defend the anonymous independent writer against charges of being a Dissenter; Varro was a member of the Established Church; 'against the American rebellion (tho' he cannot think ministry entirely blameless in the affair)' and one who supports Pennant 'thro' principle only'.[113] The number of broadsides, songs, and squibs at Liverpool

111 *Ibid.*, pp. 27, 82–3.
112 *Ibid.*, pp. 68, 69, 72, 75.
113 *Ibid.*, pp. 25, 27, 74, 83. These references are only suggestive; for other political references to the colonial crisis that clearly prove that the Revolution was the dominant issue of the 1780 election and that the candidates were specifically associated with the government or opposition at Westminster, see pp. 8, 10–12, 13–14, 19, 28–9, 31–2, 33–4, 40–1, 50–1, 51–2, 53, 54, 56–7, 57–8, 62–3, 67–8, 70, 76, 84, 91–2, 92–4, 96. Meredith's pamphlet *Historical Remarks on the Taxation of Free States*, attracted detailed attention and penetrating comment in this election. See 'Old England', p. 43 and

almost rivalled the numbers at Bristol and Newcastle; here, as elsewhere, the lines were clearly drawn between candidates, political ideology, and national issues. Voters were required to make intelligent decisions on more than local issues.

PARTY POLITICS WITHOUT PARTY ORGANIZATIONS

The very low level of split voting in the three-way contest of 1761 suggests the political power of independent ideology (see Table 8.6).[114] Fully 45.3 percent of all votes cast were plumps for Meredith. This high proportion of single votes was not approximated in either 1780 or 1784: the plumps for Pennant reached only 12.6 percent of the total in 1784 representing a solid core of committed voters that secured his return. Even the high proportion of split votes in 1780, however, does make some sense. In the election literature, Gascoyne, not Rawlinson, was associated with both the corporation and the government, and as a result, Pennant was paired far more readily with Rawlinson than with Gascoyne (the former split vote counted for 18.8% of the overall vote, compared with 2.8% for the latter pair). Moreover, the split voting

Table 8.6: *Straight Party and Cross Voting in Liverpool* (Percentage)

	1761 (3 way)	1780 (3 way)	1784 (4 way)
PARTISAN			
Electorate (other than Dissent)	91.6	79.8	81.2
Dissent	90.8	59.5	78.7
SPLIT			
Electorate	8.4	20.2	18.8
Dissent	9.2	40.5	21.3
Sample of Electorate, N =	801	544	894
Sample of Dissent, N =	65	37	61

'A Friend to Old England', pp. 88–90. Though there was much bad verse and scurrility in many of the handbills, the ideological issues were clearly set before the electors. A more intelligent discussion of the political issues is hard to imagine.

114 The drop in the number who polled in 1780 may be related in part to the fact that on 4 June 1777, the corporation stopped all admission of new freemen on the basis of fines or purchase and henceforth allowed admission on the basis of birth or servitude. Touzeau, *The Rise and Progress of Liverpool*, 2: 571; Picton, *Memorials of Liverpool*, 1: 219–20; Sanderson, 'The Structure of Politics', 79. Thus in 1780, every potential voter was required to appear before a committee in the Exchange to prove his freedom. *A Collection*, pp. 26, 69, 73. In 1784, 284 freemen were admitted which was less than half those admitted in 1761. Touzeau, *The Rise and Progress of Liverpool*, 2: 522, 582.

dropped off somewhat in the 1784 contest and it must be remembered that this was virtually a three-way contest (Meredith obtained only 1.3% of the overall vote). In comparison to three-way contests in other boroughs, the Liverpool electorate in 1780 and 1784 represents a relatively well-organized and fairly disciplined body of voters.

An individual's consistent party support over two elections (Table 8.7) suggests that the Liverpool parties had some difficulty retaining support over time. The distance in time between the first two elections results in a very small number of identifiable voters, especially among the Dissenters. Nevertheless, the crucial statistic in this table is the floating vote for 1780–4 compared to the earlier period. It is true that there was a higher proportion of voters who split their votes in either 1780 or 1784 then 1761, but this must be placed over-against the greater proportion of consistent party voters. And since the 1784 election was, in effect, a three-way contest, these proportions compare favorably with other well-organized eighteenth-century constituencies like Newcastle.

Table 8.7: *Consistent Partisan and Floating Vote in Liverpool* (Percentage)

	1761–1780	1780–1784
PARTISAN (Government and Independent Combined)		
Electorate (other than Dissent)	35.3	52.7
Dissent	35.7	33.3
FLOATING (Government to Independent or Independent to Government)		
Electorate	35.3	14.5
Dissent	35.7	13.3
SPLIT		
Electorate	29.4	32.8
Dissent	28.6	53.4
Sample of Electorate, N =	133	332
Sample of Dissent, N =	14	30

On the grounds that Lady Penhryn's extensive hereditary connections in Liverpool were effectively put to use in 1784, Picton believed that in Penhryn's victory over Tarleton, 'Influence prevailed over popularity.'[115] The unproven assumption in Picton's conclusion is that apart from the outcome of the election, it can be shown that Tarleton was more popular than Penhryn. But it seems unlikely that Lady Penhryn's influence could account for so many single

115 Picton, *Memorials of Liverpool*, 1: 222.

votes: Penhryn received twice as many plumps as Tarleton.[116] More importantly, the independent party was able to retain its support between 1780 and
1784 just as consistently as the government candidates, which is somewhat
surprising in light of the purported prevalence of influence. Of those who voted
for Gascoyne and Rawlinson in 1780, 66.8 percent voted for the corporation
candidates again in 1784, compared to 68.9 percent of those who voted for the
opposition in 1780 and again in 1784. While the two parties retained their
previous supporters at about the same level, of those who had not voted in
1780, but did vote in 1784, Gascoyne and Tarleton took proportionately more
votes: 56.7 percent of the new voters as against 48.6 percent of the old, while
Penhryn took fewer, 24.5 percent of new as against 32.3 percent of the old
(excluding split votes). Thus one key to Penhryn's victory was his old
supporters. The belief that influence in 1784 counted for more than ideology
thus remains unproven. A final thread of evidence that supports the ideological
consistency of a large body of Liverpool voters is found in the petitioning
agitation of 1775. Consistent support for the government among a well defined
group of conservatives is discovered by comparing the coercive addressers
with the voters in 1780. Phillips demonstrated that 76.7 percent of the coercive
addressers who were also voters favored court candidates in 1780, compared
to 61.1 percent of the voters overall.[117]

The most striking feature of the Dissenting vote in Liverpool according to
Tables 8.6 and 8.7 is the greater preponderance of split votes and the lower
proportion of consistent party votes. The Liverpool Dissenters evidently voted
less coherently than other voters and when we turn to the particular party affiliation of Liverpool Dissenters compared to all other voters, these tendencies are
confirmed. Figure 8.1 shows the Dissenters as a mirror image of the other
electors with virtually no greater tendency to support the independent party than
others. In the 1761 election the near even distribution of the Dissenting vote
can be accounted for on several grounds. Cunliffe and Pole were government
Whigs and thus the contest was one of Whig versus Whig. Secondly, the
attempt in the popular literature to cast Meredith as a persecutor of the
Dissenters may have had some effect. These considerations, however, do not
explain the behavior of the Dissenters in 1780 and 1784. Meredith's commitment to the improvement of the Dissenters' legal situation, combined with
Pennant's record of opposition, should have endeared the Dissenters to these
candidates, but their voting behavior reflects no hint of such support. The

116 Penhryn received 26.2% of the whole as over against 13.6%. Even Gascoyne received
   only 20.6% of the electorate in plumps. Also, the occupational breakdown of Tarleton's
   vote does not show a disproportionate share of votes from the 'mob', as Picton believed.
117 Phillips, *Electoral Behavior in Unreformed England: Plumpers, Splitters, and Straights*
   (Princeton, 1982), p. 30, Table 1:1. Phillips' sample resulted in 55.7% overall vote in
   favor of court candidates in 1780.

Dissenting vote is all the more anomalous in that the vote of the Anglican clergy
was uniformly and predictably conservative.[118]

Figure 8.1

PARTISAN VOTE OF LIVERPOOL DISSENTERS AND ALL OTHER VOTERS

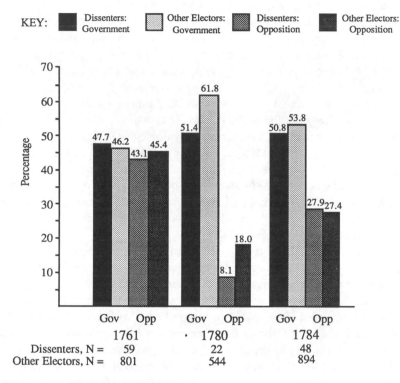

KEY:	Dissenters: Government	Other Electors: Government	Dissenters: Opposition	Other Electors: Opposition

Gov   Opp   Gov   Opp   Gov   Opp
1761   ·   1780   1784

Dissenters, N =   59   22   48
Other Electors, N = 801   544   894

The Dissenting laity's political behavior raises questions concerning both its
ideology and its social standing. That the Dissenting laity in Liverpool was not
engaged by radical political thought can be explained on several grounds. First,
at least one congregation, Benn's Garden, was known for its political conservatism. Despite the fact that Benn's Garden supplied leadership for the independent party in the 1750s and 1760s, there were no known progressive
leaders among the ministers. In the same year that George Campbell became
mayor, the minister of Benn's Garden, John Henderson, made a decision that
for the religious identity of the Dissenting layman can only be considered

118 In 1761, of the twenty-two Anglican clergy who voted, twenty-one voted Cunliffe–Pole,
     and only one plumped for Meredith. In 1784, of the eight identified in the poll book, six
     plumped for Gascoyne and two voted Gascoyne–Tarleton. I was unable to locate any
     clergy in the 1780 poll book; this may be due to the fact that the poll closed on the fifth
     day.

disastrous: he conformed to the Church of England.[119] Further, Anne Holt has identified two members of Benn's Garden who owned privateers and as many as fourteen other members who owned Guineamen that traded in slaves. Secondly, no Dissenting minister at Liverpool is known to have taken an anti-government stance during the American crisis, and as we shall see in the next chapter, Robert Lewin, the minister at Benn's Garden, effectively defended the government.[120] Not one of the fifteen identifiable Dissenting ministers who resided in Liverpool in this period voted in any of the three elections, though five did sign the petition of 1772–3 for relief from subscription to the Thirty-Nine Articles.[121] This apparent absence of concern over America comports well with the tolerance shown to privateering and the slave trade, for if the ministers failed to speak against these practices, it is not surprising that they would not give a clear trumpet sound over America. The evidence from the petitions studied below merely confirms this picture.

The Dissenters of Liverpool in the persons of Hardman, Clegg, and Campbell were clearly influential in supporting the independent party, but as at Newcastle, the elite leadership affected the voting laity hardly at all. While a few Dissenters were involved in office-holding, they were far less active in civic life than the Bristol Dissenters, and they were, on the whole, as low in socio-economic status as some of the poorest Dissenters in other boroughs. At Exeter, for example, the Nonconformists were numerous, but they composed the poorest element in the borough; what wealth the Exeter Nonconformists possessed was concentrated in the hands of a few bankers and cloth manufacturers. Given these structural conditions and the dominance of the city's local government by the High Anglicans, it is not surprising that the Exeter Dissenters had little influence on parliamentary elections.[122] We found similar circumstances at Newcastle; the lower economic standing of the rank and file Dissenter was combined with a situation where the few elite were excluded from municipal politics and this probably contributed to the lack of political consistency among the handful of Dissenting voters. With the one and telling exception of radical ministerial leadership, Liverpool is almost indistinguishable from Newcastle. Liverpool and Newcastle Dissenters reflected the lowest social standing of any group of urban Dissenters examined in this study, and it

---

119 Holt, *Walking Together*, p. 116. Henderson was Hardman's, Clegg's and Campbell's pastor, 1752–63, and then the first incumbent of St. Paul's Liverpool. George E. Evans, *Records of the Provincial Assembly*, p. 100.

120 Holt, *Walking Together*, pp. 154–5. William Roscoe, another member of Benn's Garden, began an attack on the slave trade in 1777 that appears to have had some influence, for by 1798, Holt finds only one owner of a slave ship left. But in the chapel histories, I have yet to find a record of a Dissenting minister taking a stance on the slave trade.

121 The Thompson List, 38.6, p. 263.

122 A. A. Brocket, 'The Political and Social Influence of Exeter Dissenters and Some Notable Families', *Report and Transactions of the Devonshire Association*, 93 (1961), 184–8. See chap. 2 above on the overall social status of Liverpool Dissent.

is entirely likely that this was a major cause of their lack of orientation in favor of opposition candidates. On average, one-third of the Liverpool congregations were composed of laborers, compared to only one-tenth at Bristol, and the laborers among the electorate at Liverpool amounted to only about one-twentieth of the voters. The evidence of the voting consistency of the Dissenters at Bristol contrasts markedly with the Dissenters at Exeter, Newcastle, and Liverpool, and the one characteristic shared by the Dissenters in the latter three boroughs was a lower overall socio-economic standing. There is, however, no confirmation for this thesis from the voting data itself; the occupational status of the conservative Dissenters who voted in Liverpool shows no discernible tendency toward higher (or lower) groupings in any of the elections.

In addition to the questions of religion, trade, the corporation, and America, the election literature occasionally reflected a contemporary belief that socio-economic differences contributed to political divisions. 'Theodosia' asserted that 'those of the lower class' are capable of judging for themselves in an election and therefore should not defer to their superiors. 'Philo-Patriae' also spoke in favor of the independence of 'the lower burgesses', while 'Plain Dealer' defended the integrity of the 'common people'.[123] In 1761 there were fears that plumpers for Meredith would be turned out of work, and in response, Meredith's friends promised to find them employment. Cunliffe subsequently attributed Meredith's victory to 'the present situation of the lower tradesmen (the great demand for journeymen rendering them independent of their employers)'. In 1780 only one broadside addressed the economic issue by linking plumps for Gascoyne with Esquires on the one hand, and laborers on the other.[124]

In fact there was little occupational difference between the parties (see Table 8.8).[125] The outstanding differences appeared in 1761 and in 1784 when the government candidates appealed more strongly to the elite: Cunliffe and Pole with 46.3 percent of the overall vote took 73.7 percent of the total gentlemen and professional category, compared to 14 percent given to Meredith, and in 1784 Gascoyne and Tarleton acquired 62 percent of the highest category and the opposition attained only 16 percent. The independents received slightly greater support from the artisans in 1761, but not in 1780 or 1784, and throughout the period the shopkeepers were relatively evenly divided between the parties. The 1780 election provides evidence that contradicts the thesis that the electorate would divide on a socio-economic basis when the American Revolution was a prominent issue. Not only did the Anglican clergy fail to

---

123 *An Entire Collection*, p. 78; *A Genuine Collection*, pp. 44, 46.
124 *An Entire Collection*, pp. 15, 37; *Commons, 1754–1790*, 1: 318; *A Collection*, (1780), p. 64. Gascoyne, however, was associated with protecting game in several broadsides, and this was clearly a 'class' issue.
125 However, using X^2 the differences in the occupational groupings between the government and independent parties are significant at .01 level of probability.

participate in this election, Pennant received a disproportionately high degree of support from the upper two categories. But it must be remembered that this election was cut short; Pennant declined the poll only five days into the election, and thus the poll book may not reflect accurately the socio-economic divisions. This lack of socio-economic division, however, is strikingly confirmed by the data from the petition and address examined in chapter 10.

Table 8.8: *Occupational Structure of the Electorate in Liverpool* (Percentage)

	1761			1780			1784		
	Gov.	Ind.	Split	Gov.	Ind.	Split	Gov.	Ind.	Split
1. Gentlemen, Professions	10.5	2.0	9.6	1.1	3.0	3.2	6.1	3.1	6.1
2. Merchants	6.2	9.9	20.5	2.3	11.9	9.6	7.4	12.6	7.2
3. Shopkeepers	22.7	20.2	19.2	22.3	22.8	24.0	21.3	16.0	23.2
4. Artisans	50.6	62.2	46.6	68.2	60.4	60.0	60.5	64.9	60.2
5. Laborers	9.5	5.6	4.1	5.6	2.0	3.2	4.3	3.4	2.8
6. Other	.5	—	—	.6	—	—	.4	—	.6
Sample, N =	401	392	73	355	101	125	512	262	181
	(46.3)	(45.3)	(8.4)	(61.1)	(17.4)	(21.5)	(53.6)	(27.4)	(19.0)

The Liverpool electorate reflected a comparatively high level of coherent political behavior, but with little evidence of a religious basis to the party division (the one exception being the Anglican clergy). The support the highest occupational category gave to government candidates in 1761 and 1784, however, is noteworthy. The behavior of the Dissenting laity may finally be attributed to a lower overall socio-economic standing and a failure in the leadership of the elite, though this will remain difficult to prove. The annual municipal elections for mayor and bailiffs meant that the freemen were constantly active, and in other constituencies, municipal elections have been shown to have had a controlling influence on the formation of local parliamentary parties. Municipal politics may therefore prove to be a fruitful area for future research. On the basis of what is currently known, it is possible to conclude that Nonconformity had little effect on the outcome of Liverpool elections. As with Newcastle, we are led to investigate more spontaneous and popular expressions of political opinion in order to take a sounding of the potential impact of Nonconformity below the surface of electoral politics.

KINGSTON UPON HULL AND CORRUPTION

The Dissenters in Kingston upon Hull were represented by only two chapels in 1715, but with the addition of three meetings by 1773, they may have kept pace with the overall population growth of the borough.[126] The Bowl Alley Lane Presbyterians comprised the largest and probably the most prestigious group of Dissenters; the chapel's historian was impressed with the wealth of the congregation in the 1750s, and while there is no record of municipal office holding, a few members held minor government posts.[127] With an attendance of 500, the Presbyterians alone could boast fifty voters in parliamentary elections, but this represented only about five percent of the electorate in the early part of the century. The Congregationalists were first situated in Dagger Lane, but in 1769 a conservative group seceded to Blanket Row. When the Blanket Row meeting built a new chapel in Fish Street, Samuel Thornton, future M.P. for Hull, subscribed £20 for the building, possibly in the hope of securing some votes.[128] The Dagger Lane Congregational meeting subsisted throughout the period, and two Baptist meetings were added sometime prior to 1773.[129] In comparison to the other boroughs in this study, the Dissenters at Hull were a tiny minority, and adequate registers subsist for only the Bowl Alley Lane chapel.

The freeman electorate of about 1,200 was unruly, expensive, frequently contested, and never safe.[130] An illustration of the difficulties the Dissenting interest faced at Hull arises out of a contest between two Whigs in 1724. George Crowle ran against Sir Henry Hoghton, a Dissenter who was backed both by the government and the corporation. This by-election was 'hotly contested', and Crowle maintained his supporters only at great expense; he finally won, polling 419 to Hoghton's 299 votes.[131] If the Dissenters in Hull did vote solidly for Hoghton, and if they did not take Crowle's money, then they were not strong enough by themselves to turn an election. On the other hand, some Dissenters may have been wooed by guineas.

In the second half of the century, the corporation, the body of merchants known as Trinity House, and the government, had enough influence when combined to return one member.[132] Lord Robert Manners was returned on this interest and sat uninterrupted from 1747 to 1782. A number of local luminaries also had some influence, including Sir George Savile, Lord Rockingham,

---

126 The Evans List, pp. 120–34. The Thompson List, 38.6, p. 41. A. E. Trout, 'Nonconformity in Hull', *CHST* 9 (1924–6), 81.
127 W. Whitaker, *One Line of the Puritan Tradition in Hull. Bowl Alley Lane Chapel* (London, 1910), pp. 95, 121; George E. Evans, *Vestiges of Protestant Dissent*, p. 108. See chap. 2, p. 82 above. On the wealth of Bowl Alley Dissenters, see Seed, 'Gentlemen Dissenters', 303.
128 C. E. Darwent, *The Story of Fish Street Church, Hull* (London, 1899), pp. 18, 19, 102, 118.
129 Darwent, *The Story of Fish Street*, pp. 19, 117; Whitaker, *Bowl Alley Lane*, p. 121. By 1789 there was a Methodist chapel, Darwent, p. 201.
130 *Commons, 1715–1754*, 1: 359–60; *Commons, 1754–1790*, 1: 435.
131 *Commons, 1715–1754*, 1: 596.
132 For the following account, see *Commons, 1754–1790*, 1: 435; 2: 593; 3: 524, 617, 107.

William Wilberforce, and the Thorntons. But corruption was also a complicating factor. Writing in 1792, Oldfield explained the situation.

For upwards of thirty years the candidates have paid the poorer order of voters two guineas for each vote. The number who took money was probably two-thirds of the voters. So established is this species of corruption that the voters regard it as a sort of birthright. Very few of the voters are independent of the higher ranks of people in the town.

This practice so incensed the pious Henry Thornton that when Manners' death left a vacancy in 1782, he refused to stand for Hull. With the government, local merchants, patrons, and their money all making an appeal for the Hull voter, Brooke concludes, 'political questions did not count for much'. The three-man contests, it is true, would lead predictably to a large proportion of split votes, but each of the candidates offered the average voter an unusually clearly defined political profile.

William Weddell had come in on Rockingham's and Savile's recommendation in 1766, and he consistently followed Rockingham in Parliament (see Table 8.9). Manners was steadfastly devoted to the government; he supported each successive administration (except Rockingham's), and North later praised him for his exertions on behalf of the government. The voters in 1768 thus returned both incumbents as though there was little to separate them politically. In 1774 Manners topped the poll, and David Hartley was returned with the blessings of Rockingham and Savile, thereby confirming the compromise of 1768. Hartley is of importance to this study because of his well-articulated stance on America; he spoke frequently on American affairs in Parliament and between 1775 and 1779 he made eight motions for conciliation with the colonies.

Table 8.9: *Kingston upon Hull Election Results: 1768–1784*

1768		1774	
William Weddell	774	Lord Robert Manners	1065
Lord Robert Manners	545	David Hartley	646
Thomas Lee	308	Thomas Shirley	581
1780		1784	
William Wilberforce	1126	William Wilberforce	806
Lord Robert Manners	673	Samuel Thornton	751
David Hartley	453	David Hartley	338

DAVID HARTLEY AND HIS CONSTITUENTS

In 1780 there were few men in England as devoted to conciliation with the colonists as David Hartley. Lord Robert Manners was equally devoted to the government, and William Wilberforce was an untried youth of twenty-one years, but with a large purse and a determination to enter Parliament. Wilberforce won the contest handily, at a cost of between £8,000 and £9,000, and yet Hartley complained that he had been turned out because of his pro-American stance in Parliament.[133] When Manners died in 1782, Hartley won the seat back without a contest, but in 1783, against Savile's advice, he adhered to the Coalition, though by 1784 he was not opposed to Pitt.[134] Wilberforce, on the other hand, opposed the Coalition and spoke vigorously against it. In 1784 Wilberforce was once again the popular candidate, while Samuel Thornton, Wilberforce's cousin, a committed Pittite and future member of the 'Clapham sect', easily took the second seat.[135] No popular election literature for Hull has survived, but the candidates presented the electors with exceptionally clear choices, and Hartley in particular insisted upon informing his constituents of his parliamentary conduct.

Many of Hartley's parliamentary speeches and motions were published separately in London and York, including his well known statement of 27 March 1775 on reconciliation with America.[136] It cannot be proven that his constituents read these documents, but in late 1778 he decided to present a series of letters concerning American affairs to the voters in Hull. His stated intent was 'to keep up that connection, which, in the very idea of representation, ought to subsist between the electors and the elected'.[137] Hartley proceeded with an extremely detailed account of his own parliamentary conduct

---

133 *Commons, 1754–1790*, 3: 633; 2: 593. Brooke discounts this claim.
134 Hartley took office under the Coalition, but only to work for peace. George H. Guttridge, *David Hartley, M.P. An Advocate of Conciliation, 1774–1783* (Berkeley, 1925), p. 300. After the 1784 election, he learned that Wilberforce would vacate the seat for Yorkshire, and he then approached the borough on the platform of support for Pitt and parliamentary reform. See David Hartley, *An Address to the right Worshipful the Mayor and Corporation, to the Worshipful the Wardens and Corporation of the Trinity House, and to the Worthy Burgesses of the Town of Kingston upon Hull*, (London, 1784), pp. 8, 12.
135 *Commons, 1754–1790*, 3: 636–7; 525.
136 See the list in Thomas R. Adams' bibliography, *The American Controversy* (Providence, 1980), 1: 288–91. See David Hartley, *Speech and Motions, made in the House of Commons on Monday, the 27th of March, 1775, Together with a Draught of a Letter of Requisition To the Colonies* (London, 1775), pp. 11, 17, 20. He argued that the colonies had been driven to resistance against their wills.
137 David Hartley, *Letters on the American War. Addressed to the Right Worshipful the Mayor and Corporation, To the Worshipful the Wardens and Corporation of Trinity-House, and to the Worthy Burgesses of the Town of Kingston upon Hull* (London, 3rd edn, 1778). 'It is because I value and esteem the confidence of my Constituents, and because I wish the continuance of it; for which reason I desire to lay my heart open to them, and explain every motive of my conduct', p. 31, dated 13 Sept. 1778. Guttridge calls this Hartley's most important writing.

over the past four years wherein he proved that he 'uniformly opposed the principles, and continuation of the American war'. Blame for the loss of the colonies was placed squarely on 'the violent and unrelenting measures' of the administration.[138] The first letter concentrated on the motions and protests of the opposition in each of the first three sessions of Parliament. A week later, the second letter examined the fourth session of Parliament and argued that the administration intended to establish an 'influential dominion' in the colonies with an independent revenue for the Crown uncontrolled by Parliament.[139] The third and fourth letters, which appeared at two-week intervals, defended the parliamentary opposition against charges of treason and proposed a plan of reconciliation.[140] Here, as in all his writings on America, Hartley vindicated the conduct of the colonists – their actions bear the mark of 'reluctant necessity' – while the administration was execrated – it was a 'ministerial war'.[141] Even this far into the conflict Hartley believed that the average Englishman opposed the war: 'The national sentiment of this country towards America is likewise still entangled in the bonds of antient affection.'[142]

Hartley's letters to his constituents went through eight editions, and in other publications leading up to the general election of 1780 he continued to make his views on America known. In late 1779 he brought his constituents abreast of his latest activities in Parliament and sought once again to persuade them to oppose the present government. 'Let America feel that the people of England are not their enemies', he wrote. 'Let them feel that they have no enemies in this country, but an implacable and vindictive ministry; and let the result be a reconciliation and federal union between Great Britain and America.'[143] He championed parliamentary reform as one means of relieving the 'national calamities',[144] and even after his loss in 1784, Hartley still appealed to 'the worthy burgesses' of Hull to examine his 'former conduct in Parliament' and make their choice for a representative on that ground.[145] The 1780 election thus provided the freemen of Hull – particularly the Dissenters – with a clear opportunity to prove their 'bonds of antient affection' for America, and yet,

---

138　Hartley, *Letters on the American War*, pp. 2, 19.
139　*Ibid.*, pp. 33–51, dated 24 Sept. 1778. He wrote a lengthy statement against the Quebec Act, pp. 45–50.
140　Hartley, *Letters on the American War*, pp. 53–68; 69–92, dated 11 Oct., and 29 Oct. 1778.
141　Hartley, *Letters on the American War*, pp. 71, 86.
142　*Ibid.*, p. 71.
143　David Hartley, *Two Letters from D. Hartley, Esq. M.P. Addressed to the Committee of the County of York* (London, 1780), p. 18. Here he addresses himself to the 'constituents' throughout the kingdom.
144　Hartley, *Two Letters*, p. 20. See also David Hartley, *An Address to the Committee of Association of the County of York, on the State of Public Affairs* (York, 1781), pp. 1, 22, 28.
145　Hartley, *An Address to the Right Worshipful* (1784), p. 14.

with the prevalence of influence and corruption, the election would also be a genuine test of the worthiness of their electoral behavior.

The electoral interests at Hull centered around local corporate structures and interest groups, but local political issues were few, and the borough thereby lacked a focal point around which political factions could rally. The characteristic conflict between a corporation and an independent party of freemen was altogether missing, and thus even the most rudimentary political organizations failed to develop. One symptom of this failure is the scant attention candidates gave to the need for presenting the voters with clear party options; in each of the three elections, little effort was made to yoke candidates and this resulted in high levels of cross voting (see Table 8.10). The majority of Hartley's votes, for example, were obtained in each election through the voters pairing him with other candidates who did not share his views: Manners in 1774 (44.5% of the overall vote), Wilberforce in 1780 (34.6%) and Wilberforce and Thornton in 1784 (21.2% and 15.3% respectively). Given the lack of party organization and the prevalence of bribery, it is not surprising that these voters refused to give up their second votes for the sake of political principle. Accordingly, the average number of plumpers amounted to only 7.5 percent of the electorate over the three elections; Hartley was never paired with another candidate in a compelling way and this undoubtedly contributed to the difficulty he had in winning an election.

Table 8.10: *Straight Party and Cross Voting in Kingston upon Hull*
(Percentage)

	1774	1780	1784
PARTISAN			
Electorate (other than Dissent)	47.1	62.4	63.7
Dissent	46.2	42.9	55.6
SPLIT			
Electorate	52.9	37.6	36.3
Dissent	53.8	57.1	44.8
Sample of Electorate, N =	872	748	728
Sample of Dissent, N =	26	21	18

Some elements of consistent political behavior, however, can be discerned even at Hull. The corporation and Trinity House almost certainly exerted their influence against Hartley in 1780 and 1784; both had sent strongly worded addresses to the Crown in support of coercive measures in 1775 and these activities were consistent with the conservative majority that voted against

Hartley in 1780. The address from the inhabitants of the borough in support of coercive measures presented to the king by Lord Robert Manners provides some confirmation of this supposition. Of those signers of the address who voted in the 1780 election, 65.4 percent voted for the government candidates in 1780, compared to 61.4 percent overall.[146] However, 34.6 percent of the addressers in 1775 who voted in 1780 were willing to give one vote to Hartley in that election, and this suggests a lack of ideological commitment over a period of time among a large group of voters. The Anglican clergy did deny Hartley their support after the 1774 contest. Three of the five who voted in 1774 paired him with Manners, but only one cleric linked the two in 1780 (the only clerical vote Hartley received) and none voted for him in 1784. America was clearly not an issue at Hull in 1774 and though Hartley was associated with Rockingham and Savile, his reputation on American affairs was yet to be made. As a result, electors had little difficulty linking him to a government candidate; the Manners–Hartley split vote accounts for almost half of the total in 1774. However, by 1780 Hartley's opposition stance was well known and Manners was just as thoroughly associated with Lord North; accordingly, the Manners–Hartley vote in this election dropped to 3.5 percent of the whole. Wilberforce was the untried candidate in 1780 and yet the majority of voters paired him with Manners (53.3%), presumably to avoid Hartley. To the extent that rational political choices and not influence determined the pairing of votes, Wilberforce was viewed as compatible with Manners, while Hartley was not. (Wilberforce is classified with Manners as a 'Government' candidate in these tables.) Wilberforce, however, was also linked with Hartley, but the Wilberforce–Hartley vote was reduced by over a third between 1780 and 1784 – a loss to Hartley that may be accounted for in part by the clarification of Wilberforce's political position. On the other hand, Hartley had neither the local influence nor the money of the other candidates, and there is little reason to doubt that these factors swayed numerous voters.

Consistent party support increased slightly among electors who voted in 1780 and 1784 (see Table 8.11); the absence of the floating vote is due to the very small number of consistent party votes (plumpers) for Hartley. The number of identifiable Dissenters who voted in more than one election is too small to be significant. A cross-sectional analysis of the occupational structure of the electorate also reveals little of importance (see Table 8.12). The number of plumpers cast for Hartley in these elections is so few that they are not recorded in the table. In 1774 there was virtually no distinction between the voters for Manners–Shirley on the one hand and for Manners–Hartley on the other, and in 1780 equally small differences between the electors' occupational groupings appear with the one exception of elite support for the government

---

146 For the Corporation and Trinity House addresses see *Lond. Gaz.* (10–14 Oct. 1775); 171 inhabitants of Hull addressed the Crown, 13 Oct., 1775; HO 55/8/4.

candidates. Again in 1784 the government candidates won considerably greater support from the gentlemen and professional group than did Hartley when paired with either Wilberforce or Thornton (76.1%, with 62.3% of the overall vote, compared to 23.9% with 36.5% of the vote). When we examine the occupational categories of voters who consistently supported government candidates over two elections compared to those who split their votes, the elite support for the government becomes more obvious. The consistent government supporters who voted in both 1774 and 1780 comprised 37.1 percent of the vote, but they had 54.2 percent of the entire body of gentlemen and those in the professions who voted in both elections; the remaining elite vote was spread out over a variety of split configurations. The proportion was less impressive

Table 8.11: *Consistent Party and Floating Vote in Kingston upon Hull*
(Percentage)

	1774–1780	1780–1784
CONSISTENT Electorate (other than Dissent)	37.1	45.2
FLOATING Electorate	0	0
SPLIT Electorate	62.9	54.8
Sample of Electorate, N =	456	417

Table 8.12: *Occupational Structure of the Electorate in Kingston upon Hull*
(Percentage)

	1774		1780		1784	
	Gov.	Split	Gov.	Split	Gov.	Split
1. Gentlemen, Professions	13.8	9.1	17.6	11.9	11.0	5.9
2. Merchants	4.2	3.8	1.3	5.1	.9	2.9
3. Shopkeepers	17.7	18.3	20.8	20.1	18.7	21.3
4. Artisans	47.2	45.7	40.8	43.0	45.8	50.0
5. Laborers	16.5	22.3	18.9	19.1	23.0	19.9
6. Others	.7	.8	.8	.7	.6	—
Sample, N =	407 (45.3)	475 (52.9)	472 (61.4)	293 (38.1)	465 (62.3)	272 (36.5)

for those who voted in 1780 and 1784 but still worth noting; with 45.2 percent of the vote, consistent government supporters composed 53.8 percent of the Hull elite. No other occupational category divulged any significant differences related to voting.

The very few Dissenters that can be identified seem to have succumbed to the same forces that operated on Anglican electors (see Figure 8.2). None of the five resident Dissenting ministers voted in any of the elections, though two signed the petition of 1772–3.[147] Not one Dissenter plumped for Hartley (and hence the opposition bar in the graph does not register in Figure 8.2) in 1780, but the 1780 poll book itself designates Emmanuel Sparkes as 'a Dissenting

Figure 8.2

PARTISAN VOTE OF KINGSTON-UPON-HULL DISSENTERS
AND ALL OTHER VOTERS

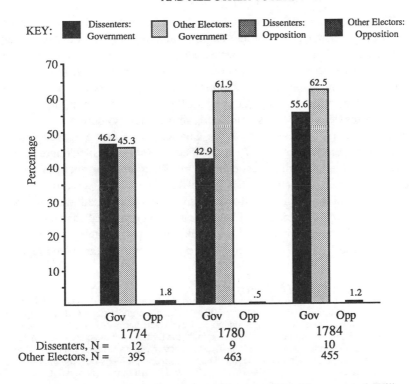

| KEY: | Dissenters: Government | Other Electors: Government | Dissenters: Opposition | Other Electors: Opposition |

	Gov	Opp	Gov	Opp	Gov	Opp
		1774		1780		1784
Dissenters, N =		12		9		10
Other Electors, N =		395		463		455

Minister' from Shore Ditch, London, and he voted for Manners and Wilberforce. The Dissenters were somewhat less supportive of the government

147 John Beverley and John Beatson, 'A View of English Nonconformity', 379.

candidates in 1780 than other electors and they gave the outspoken pro-American leader a little more support when linked with Wilberforce than other electors (52.4% of their vote as against 34.0% of other electors). Similarly, in 1784 the Dissenters were just a little more inclined to Hartley when combined with Wilberforce or Thornton than other electors (44.8% as against 36.3%) but these differences are hardly dramatic. Commenting on the political conservatism of the Dissenting ministry in this period, one of the chapel historians observed that the ministers were 'so absorbed in their strictly spiritual work, that numbers of them forgot their ecclesiastical principles'.[148] Numerous factors conspired to keep the Dissenters politically impotent including the lack of a tradition of local resistance to the corporation, the failure to develop political parties, the small number of Dissenters combined with the quietism of their leaders, and possibly the presence of political corruption.

COLCHESTER AND THE CONGREGATIONALISTS

The concentration of Congregationalists in Colchester and its environs was as striking a characteristic of the religious landscape of Essex as the preponderance of Presbyterians in Newcastle upon Tyne. Two large Congregationalist chapels were maintained throughout the eighteenth century, along with a Baptist meeting, but even greater numbers of Independents were found in the nearby towns of Bocking and Coggeshall.[149] Early in the century the resident and non-resident Dissenters combined were thought to comprise some 400 borough voters, and as late as 1790, Charles James Fox observed that the Dissenters were 'very powerful' at Colchester.[150] Lion Walk Congregational chapel was the borough's most eminent meeting; numerous members of this chapel had been elevated to municipal office. In addition, some well known merchant families, such as the Tabors, had become associated with the ministerial elite through marriage.[151] Helen's Lane Congregational chapel was more theologically progressive than Lion Walk, but approximately the same size, while the Eld Lane Baptist meeting was considerably smaller. Good registers

---

148 Darwent, *The Story of Fish Street*, p. 107.
149 The Evans List, pp. 37–41. There are two estimates for the Paedobaptists at Colchester in 1715; one is 1,200, the other, 1,500. At Braintree and Bocking there were nine Dissenting borough votes for Maldon and Colchester, but as it is unclear whether the Evans List intended to list nine votes for each, the figure is not included here. There was a 'Dutch' church at Colchester, and five Colchester M.P.'s were of Dutch or Flemish descent, but their relation to English Dissent remains problematic. *Commons, 1715–1754*, 1: 241; *Commons, 1754–1790*, 1: 276; 2: 535. All three congregations were still intact in 1773. The Thompson List, 38.6, p. 12.
150 In a letter to John Chubb just before the general election, cited in T. Bruce Dilks, *Charles James Fox and the Borough of Bridgwater* (Bridgwater, 1937), p. 30.
151 E. Alec Blaxill, *The Nonconformist Churches of Colchester* (Colchester, 1948), p. 17; Blaxill, *History of Lion Walk Congregational Church, Colchester, 1642–1937* (1938), pp. 18, 22.

subsist for only the Lion Walk chapel, but a handful of Congregationalists from the surrounding towns and villages can also be identified in the poll books.[152]

The Whigs dominated the mayoralty and thus influenced the representation of the borough until 1728, and in this period a number of Dissenters sat on the corporation; on at least four occasions they served as mayor.[153] In 1727, Stamp Brooksbank, a Presbyterian, made his political debut as Member of Parliament, and the Dissenters contributed to his victory – the Congregationalist Jeremiah Daniell was mayor and hence returning officer that year, but it was also claimed that Brooksbank was returned 'by the most notorious bribery and corruption'.[154] But between 1728 and 1740 the Tories held the mayorality, and as a result, the Whigs were eclipsed. The corporation was finally dissolved in the 1740s as a result of legal wrangles between the two local parties.[155]

After 1762 the corporation was reconstituted and politics were soon reestablished along corporation, anti-corporation lines, but now the Dissenters were excluded from power. An independent, anti-corporation party began to emerge in the late 1760s, and in approaching the general election of 1768, it canvassed the borough for support even before it had secured a candidate. First, 180 citizens pledged themselves to resistance and soon the party claimed to have the backing of 'upwards of Five hundred freemen'; it made an appeal on 12 February 1768 in the local paper for 'any Gentleman of Character' to stand as a candidate in opposition to the two corporation nominees. When the party finally found a candidate in the person of Scots Presbyterian Alexander Fordyce, four people, three of whom may be identified as Dissenters, including a trustee of the Lion Walk Congregational Church, announced their endorsement of him in the *Chelmsford and Colchester Chronicle*.[156] The ensuing

152 Lion Walk built a new chapel in 1766; with a membership of 169 in 1774, the auditory was probably at least twice as large. Blaxill, *History of Lion Walk*, pp. 19, 25. On Helen's Lane, see Blaxill, p. 8 and on the Baptists, Edward Spurrier, *Memorials of the Baptist Church Worshipping in Eld Lane Chapel, Colchester*, rev. by Joshua Thomas (Colchester, 1889), p. 17. Since the Congregationalists were so numerous in Colchester's environs, the Dissenting registers from Bocking, Braintree, Coggeshall, Dedham, Rockford, and Witham were compared to the poll books (the number of voters from these towns totalled 70 in 1781). The 'borough voters' in the following tables include these villages; the outvoters include numerous other towns in Essex and London.

153 As the returning office, the mayor had great influence on elections. *Commons, 1715–1754*, 1: 241; *Commons, 1754–1790*, 1: 276; 2: 535. See Blaxill, *History of Lion Walk*, p. 10 for the identification of these mayors. See also the discussion of office holding in Colchester in chap. 2 above.

154 This is the opinion of the borough historian, T. Cromwell, cited in *Commons, 1715–1754*, 1: 495. M. E. Speight discounts T. H. B. Oldfield's allegations of excessive bribery at Colchester, cited in Phillips, *Electoral Behavior*, p. 80.

155 See Blaxill, *History of Lion Walk*, p. 10; *Commons, 1715–1754*, 1: 495; 241.

156 *Commons, 1715–1754*, 1: 277; *Chelm. Col. Chron.* (12, 26 Feb., 11 March 1768). For the identification of John Baker (very uncertain because of the commonness of the name) and Bezaleel Bloomfield as Dissenters, see RG 4/2907; 1508. There was a second identical endorsement signed by Richard White and John Unwin. Neither Baker nor

contest was furious, and Fordyce spent £14,000 on the election, only to lose by a few votes.[157]

Table 8.13: *Colchester Election Results: 1768–1784*

1768		1774	
Charles Gray	874	Isaac Martin Rebow	566
Isaac Martin Rebow	855	Sir Robert Smyth	303
Alexander Fordyce	831	Alexander Fordyce	124
		Robert Mayne	12

1781		April 1784		July 1784	
Christopher Potter	639	Sir Edmund Affleck	665	Sir Robert Smyth	653
Edmund Affleck	571	Christopher Potter	425	Christopher Potter	382
		Sir Robert Smyth	416	Samuel Tyssen	26

The corporation candidates, Gray and Rebow, retained their seats throughout the 1770s and even avoided a contest in 1774. The conflict between the corporation and the freemen, however, remained unresolved; the peace of the borough was interrupted in 1775 when differences over the American crisis erupted. The corporation sent up an address favoring coercion, and the freemen, led by the Dissenters, circulated one of the larger petitions for peace emerging from a borough. In 1780, Gray retired and Rebow stood on the corporation interest with government support, but the other candidates' political orientation combined with an apparent absence of political issues have left historians puzzled.[158] Fordyce reluctantly decided to stand, although it is not clear that he still represented the independents, and after the polling had begun, Sir Robert Smyth unexpectedly joined the contest. Smyth was a strong proponent of the

Bloomfield signed the petitions of 1775 and 1776, but a Richard White signed the conciliatory petition, and John Unwin, possibly a Dissenter from Coggeshall, signed the coercive one (RG 4/2418). In the election Bloomfield and Baker plumped for Fordyce. There is no record of the vote of White, and a John Unwin, glazier for Colchester, voted for the government candidates. *The Poll* (Colchester, 1768). This makes the identity of Unwin very uncertain. In their endorsement they deplored the pressure put on the workers of the principal Bay-Makers and claimed that several workmen had actually been discharged.

157 This attempt led to his bankruptcy. When he returned to Colchester for the general election of 1780, he gained only 124 votes as compared to 831 in 1768. *Commons, 1754–1790*, 1: 277. Fordyce was the son of the provost of Aberdeen, was educated by Dr. Thomas Blackwell, a Presbyterian, and he 'supported a chapel for himself and his family' next to his mansion at Roehampton. His brother, James Fordyce, was the well-known Presbyterian pastor of Monkwell Street chapel in London.

158 *Commons, 1754–1790*, 1: 277.

Association movement and was the chairman of the Essex Committee.[159] He was returned with Rebow, and once in Parliament, he consistently voted in opposition until the fall of North.

Rebow died in 1781, and at the by-election, Edmund Affleck, a government supporter, stood against Christopher Potter, a government contractor. But Affleck was associated with the corporation, and Smyth, the reformer, lent his support to Potter. Affleck spent over £7,000 on this election (£2,000 of it secret service money), Potter more than £5,000, but Potter won by 68 votes, though he was unseated by a petition alleging bribery. In his short time in Parliament, Potter voted against the American War on 12 December 1781 and again on 27 February 1782.

By 1784 Smyth was, in Pitt's words, a 'zealous friend' of the new government and he received the standard £2,000 from secret service funds to contest the borough and thus his reputation as a reformer carried through 1784.[160] But Affleck also supported the new government, as did Potter, and thus all candidates could be construed as government faithfuls. Affleck and Potter won, but Potter's election was declared void, and he was required to stand against Smyth again in July, in which election Smyth gained a decisive victory. At the local level, Potter may have gained the favor of the independents, for by the second election in 1784, Smyth had the backing of the mayor and the majority of the corporation.[161]

The independents at Colchester, and in the first place, the Dissenters, put forth a well-defined united front in the elections of 1781 and 1784, and their quest for independence was even more animated in the second half of the decade. In 1788 the Dissenters were clearly the leaders of the independent party that put George Tierney forward against the government and the corporation. Tierney lost the election, but was seated through a successful petition, but when he returned to Colchester for the general election of 1790 he was severely beaten. In response he made a bitter public announcement to the 'independent electors' of Colchester.

That I failed of success is to be attributed to no increase of strength in the interest which opposed me, but to the cool, deliberate treachery of the Dissenters who formerly supported me. To them alone I owe my defeat, and to their conduct I can give no other name than that of treachery, because it never showed itself in the shape of open hostility, but wore the mask of friendship to the last.[162]

159 *Ibid.*, 3: 456.
160 *Ibid.*, 3: 456.
161 When he won in 1784 he noted 'A particular set of men, who professed much, have been defeated. I appeal with defence, gentlemen, how far the conduct of that faction has corresponded with the professions they made, and upon which I humbly solicited your assistance'. *Chelm. Col. Chron.* (23 April 1784). The aldermen voted 5 to 3 in favor of Smyth.
162 *Chelm. Col. Chron.* (12, 19 Dec. 1778; 4 June 1790); *Camb. Chron.* (3 July 1790). Tierney lost to George Jackson, 638 to 796; *The Poll* (Colchester, 1790).

The circumstances surrounding the Dissenters' change of heart have not yet been explained, but their potential importance as a voting bloc is well-attested in the earlier elections.

The only alternative to the government and corporation interest was found in the persons of Robert Smyth and Christopher Potter, and yet the high proportion of cross voting in the 1780s suggests that bribery, political confusion, and three-man contests rendered consistent political behavior difficult to maintain. Rational analysis of these elections is made even more intractable by the paucity of election literature and the scant attention given to these elections in the newspapers;[163] the election of 1780, for example, has been thought to have had nothing to do with national politics and is characterized by the 'shady manoeuvering' that went on before the poll.[164] But the elections of 1768, and 1780 may be usefully analyzed in terms of party and cross voting. Table 8.14 shows an impressive proportion of straight party voting among Dissenters and Anglicans alike in the three-man contest of 1768, but this level was greatly reduced in the election of 1780. The largest component of the split vote in 1780 was comprised of those who paired Rebow and Smyth (39% of the total), and while this certainly does represent non-partisan behavior, there were several minorities within the Colchester electorate that voted with increasing consistency in the 1780s.

Table 8.14: *Straight Party and Cross Voting in Colchester* (Percentage)

	1768	1780
STRAIGHT PARTY		
Electorate	73.5	46.8
Dissent	75.4	35.1
SPLIT		
Electorate	26.5	53.2
Dissent	24.6	64.9
Sample of Electorate, N =	831	363
Sample of Dissent, N =	61	37

The long association between the corporation and the government did have meaning for at least four distinct subgroups in the electorate: the gentlemen and professional group (including the Anglican clergy), the county outvoters, the

163 See, for example, Tyssen's verbiage in the second election; he entered the contest just before the poll closed to exult in the freedom of offering himself a candidate. *Chelm. Col. Chron.* (14 July 1784).
164 *Commons, 1754–1790*, 1: 277.

conservatives who had voiced support for the government's American policy, and the Dissenters. When the local issue of independence was prominent in 1768, the corporation candidates had the weight of property on their side; with 44.4 percent of the resident vote in 1768, Rebow and Gray attracted 69.6 percent of the gentlemen and those in the professions and this characteristic carried through the election of 1780 (see Table 8.15). In that year Rebow continued to receive steadfast support from the elite; among those who cast

Table 8.15: *Occupational Structure of the Electorate in Colchester* (Percentage)

	1768			1780		
	Gov.	Opp.	Split	Gov.	Opp.	Split
1. Gentlemen, Professions	8.1	2.3	3.4	18.8	9.1	2.3
2. Merchants	2.0	1.1	1.7	3.1	3.6	2.8
3. Shopkeepers	25.3	16.1	23.4	18.8	16.4	28.1
4. Artisans	52.0	65.5	62.6	46.9	63.6	58.5
5. Laborers	9.1	11.5	7.2	4.7	3.6	3.2
6. Others	3.5	3.4	1.7	7.8	3.6	3.2
Sample, N =	396	261	235	128	55	217
	(44.4)	(29.3)	(26.3)	(32.0)	(13.8)	(54.2)

	1781		April 1784			July 1784	
	Gov.	Ind.	Affleck-Smyth	Potter	Affleck-Potter, or Smyth-Potter	Smyth	Potter
1. Gentlemen, Professions	13.0	6.8	11.8	3.4	3.4	8.7	3.5
2. Merchants	3.4	2.4	3.4	—	1.3	2.8	.4
3. Shopkeepers	24.3	26.0	25.2	19.0	18.6	28.1	17.1
4. Artisans	48.0	57.1	51.1	77.6	67.4	49.3	69.7
5. Laborers	5.1	5.9	3.8	—	6.8	6.3	6.1
6. Others	6.2	1.8	4.6	—	2.5	4.9	3.1
Sample, N =	177	338	262	58	236	288	228
	(34.4)	(65.6)	(47.1)	(10.4)	(42.4)	(54.3)	(43.0

single votes for him (32% of the whole) were found fully 70.6 percent of the elite in Colchester. In 1781 Affleck attracted only 34.4 percent of the resident vote, but he had the support of exactly half of those in the gentlemen and professional category. The Anglican clergy – a litmus test for the presence of political issues in other boroughs – confirm the pattern of elite support for government and corporation candidates. Of the dozen clergymen who voted in

1768, only one voted for the independent candidate, Fordyce, and of the eight who voted in 1780, six plumped for Rebow.[165] The socio-economic status of the voters in 1784 adds an element of consistency to what might otherwise appear to be a confusing picture. In April 1784 Affleck paired with Smyth obtained three-quarters (75.6%) of the elite vote with 47.1 percent of the overall vote; and in July, with 54.3 percent overall, Smyth alone took 75.8 percent of the elite vote.[166] Smyth also won the support of 88.9 percent of all the merchants in July, thereby consolidating the support he had won from the corporation. It is not perfectly clear why the elite should have supported Smyth, given his known sympathy for reform, but it may have been related to a desire to avoid Potter.

This association of the corporation candidates with the Colchester elite accounts in part for the political consistency of a minority of voters that can be traced from 1780 forwards (see Tables 8.16–8.18). About one-third (32.3%) of the sixty-two people who plumped for Rebow in 1780 and Affleck in 1781 were in the gentlemen, profession, and merchant categories. This group comprised about half (47.6%) of all gentlemen, those in the professions, and merchants who voted in the two elections.[167] The same phenomenon is discernible among those who voted in 1781 and April 1784, though it is less pronounced (Table 8.17); none of the elite group who supported Affleck in 1781 were willing to give a vote to Potter in April, 1784 (in any combination), whereas about half of the small number of the elite who had previously voted for Potter were willing to give one vote to Affleck in the latter election. This fact supports the thesis of the elites' avoidance of Potter, though it does not explain it. We shall see below, however, that if the borough elite avoided Potter, the Dissenters were willing to embrace him. The elite support for Smyth is also evident in April of 1784, and in the second election of this year the elite continued to prefer Smyth over Potter; Smyth took 82.9 percent of the previous elite votes, whereas Potter obtained only 17.1 percent.[168] None of the other occupational categories revealed any particular political orientation, with the exception of the strong support Potter obtained from the ranks of the artisans.

---

165 In 1768 this includes four resident clergy and eight outvoters and in 1780 two resident clergy and six outvoters. The one vote for Fordyce was not a plump, but a vote paired with Gray.

166 The grouping of the April 1784 election in Table 8.15 is admittedly arbitrary, insofar as all three candidates could be classified as government supporters. In July 1784 Tyssen had only 2.6% of the vote and is not included in the table.

167 Only six resident voters who voted in these two elections voted for Mayne.

168 Only fourteen of the resident voters who had previously voted, voted for Tyssen in July 1784.

Table 8.16: *Consistent Support for Candidates in Colchester:*
1780–1781

		Dissenters	Other Electors	Gentlemen Professions, Merchants	Total Vote
Rebow–Smyth	–Potter	14	64	5	24.4
Rebow–Fordyce	–Potter	2	28	1	10.7
Smyth–Fordyce	–Potter	0	5	0	1.9
Rebow	–Potter	1	40	11	15.3
Smyth	–Potter	1	16	1	6.1
Fordyce	–Potter	0	2	0	.8
Rebow–Smyth	–Affleck	0	35	3	13.4
Rebow–Fordyce	–Affleck	0	12	0	4.6
Smyth–Fordyce	–Affleck	0	0	0	0
Rebow	–Affleck	5	57	20	21.8
Smyth	–Affleck	0	3	1	1.1
Fordyce	–Affleck	0	0	0	0
		23	262	44	100%

Table 8.17: *Consistent Support for Candidates in Colchester:*
1781–April 1784

	Dissenters	Other Electors	Gentlemen Professions, Merchants	Total Vote
Affleck –Affleck–Smyth	4	52	12	15.2
Affleck –Affleck–Potter	0	17	0	4.6
Affleck –Smyth–Potter	0	1	0	.3
Affleck –Affleck	2	44	6	12.5
Affleck –Potter	0	2	0	.5
Affleck –Smyth	0	3	3	.8
Potter –Affleck–Smyth	4	30	6	9.2
Potter –Affleck–Potter	1	70	5	19.2
Potter –Smyth–Potter	7	67	5	20.1
Potter –Affleck	0	8	0	2.2
Potter –Smyth	11	17	6	7.6
Potter –Potter	5	24	2	7.9
	34	335	45	100%

Table 8.18: *Consistent Support for Candidates in Colchester:*
April 1784–July 1784

		Dissenters	Other Electors	Gentlemen Professions, Merchants	Total Vote
Affleck–Smyth	–Smyth	5	75	13	21.0
Affleck–Potter	–Smyth	1	21	0	5.8
Smyth–Potter	–Smyth	6	42	5	12.6
Affleck	–Smyth	2	25	3	7.1
Potter	–Smyth	1	4	0	1.3
Smyth	–Smyth	13	14	8	7.1
Affleck–Smyth	–Potter	2	6	1	2.1
Affleck–Potter	–Potter	1	75	1	19.9
Smyth–Potter	–Potter	1	16	0	4.5
Affleck	–Potter	2	28	2	7.9
Smyth	–Potter	0	0	0	0
Potter	–Potter	2	39	2	10.8
		36	345	35	100%

A second body of voters was almost as consistently in favor of the government and corporation candidates as the elite, namely, the county outvoters. Just as at Newcastle, the outcome of Colchester elections was sometimes determined by the outvoters. Table 8.19 includes both the voters from small towns and villages in Essex and the sizable numbers from the larger urban centers of Ipswich and London. The London outvoters were almost indistinguishable from the vote of the residents of Colchester, and when they are excluded, the differences between county outvoters and Colchester residents is even more striking. For example, 63 percent of the 232 county outvoters in 1780 voted for Rebow, and 66.6 percent of the 530 outvoters in 1781 voted for Affleck. In some towns, such as Harwich, where the government had an overwhelming influence, the vote in favor of the government candidate (92% in 1781) is not surprising. Richard Rigby, whose estate was at Mistley near Colchester, ran the government side of this election and the unanimous vote of Mistley electors in favor of Affleck is also predictable. But it is difficult, if not impossible, to determine whether or not the dominant conservatism of the county outvoters was related primarily to patronage and influence, or to socio-economic standing – the majority of these voters were farmers and husbandmen – or, what is more likely, to a combination of factors.

Table 8.19: *Proportion of Support for Government Candidates by Colchester Residents and Outvoters* (Percentage)

1780		1781		April 1784	
Resident Voters	Outvoters	Resident Voters	Outvoters	Resident Voters	Outvoters
54.9	58.7	34.4	56.7	39.8	51.7

Comparison of the poll books to the petitions of 1775 reveals a high degree of consistency among a third group of voters. Colchester's past and future M.P.s took a clear position on America; the signatures of both Isaac M. Rebow, Recorder, and Captain Edmund Affleck, are found on the coercive address.[169] Among those who addressed the Crown in favor of coercive measures in America who also voted in 1780, 55.3 percent plumped for Rebow, as over against 32 percent of the overall vote, and only 26.3 percent of the addressers split their votes between Rebow and Smyth compared to 39 percent overall, thereby demonstrating that a small minority of voters was consistently oriented toward conservative issues and candidates. In contrast, 55.6 percent of those who petitioned for peace in 1775 and also voted in 1780 split their votes for Rebow–Smyth and only 27 percent of these petitioners gave single votes to Rebow. Only 4.8 percent of the petitioners gave plumps for Smyth (8.3% overall) and they were thus far less consistent than the conservatives.

At Colchester, as at Liverpool, the local Dissenting elite were actively involved in the independent party's assault on privilege, but at first they were unable to rally their brethren in the local cause of independence. The identifiable Dissenters in the 1768 election did not give consistent support to the opposition candidate; the partisan behavior of the Dissenters was not much greater than other voters (see Figure 8.3). The Dissenters behaved even less consistently in 1780; not only was the turn-out in this election low, more than half of the Dissenters that can be identified (51.4%) were willing to pair the corporation candidate, Isaac Martin Rebow, with the reformer, Sir Robert Smyth. However, in the two-man contest in 1781, when there was no temptation to split one's vote, the Dissenters voted overwhelmingly for Potter. They appear to have understood Potter as a clear alternative to the corporation candidate because when we analyze those who voted in both 1781 and 1784, we find that 82 percent of the Dissenters who voted for Potter in 1781 voted for

169 See HO 55/2/4; 9/4. Thirty-eight addressers can be found as resident voters in 1780, and sixty-three petitioners.

him or for Smyth in 1784, compared to 50 percent of non-Dissent; only 17.9 percent of the Dissenters who had previously voted for Potter were willing to give a vote to Affleck, compared to 50 percent of non-Dissent (Table 8.17). The total proportion of voters who avoided the corporation's candidate altogether in 1781 and 1784 is also somewhat surprising (35.6%), though this must be compared with the number (19.2%) who were willing to pair Affleck and Potter in 1784. Moreover, the only genuinely irrational pattern of voting among previous Affleck supporters (Affleck to Affleck–Potter or to Smyth–Potter or to Potter or to Smyth) was quite small (6.2%).

Figure 8.3

PARTISAN VOTE OF COLCHESTER DISSENTERS AND ALL OTHER VOTERS

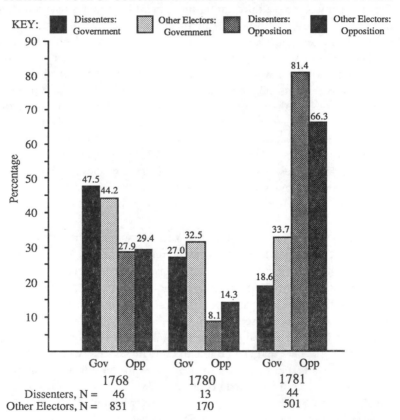

In April 1784 (Table 8.20) there was noticeably stronger support for Smyth alone among the Dissenters than other voters and a corresponding aversion to Affleck and Affleck yoked with Potter. The Dissenters' proclivity for Smyth was even more pronounced in July when they gave him 78 percent of their vote as over against 52.4 percent overall. This election shows that when confronted with a choice between Smyth and Potter, the Dissenters strongly preferred Smyth. Smyth was still identified with reform, but from the local perspective it was difficult to associate him with 'independence'; by July 1784 he not only had the support of the elite, five of the eight aldermen who voted in this election supported him. This does not mean that the corporation was perfectly happy with Smyth, but rather that they sought to avoid Potter. At the very moment the Dissenters were becoming more consistent, the Anglican clergy became less so. In April the clergy saw no problem in linking Affleck with Smyth (five out of eight did so), while in April they made a complete about-face from 1780; seven out of nine voted for Smyth.[170] Whatever degree of consistency the Dissenters achieved in this period was accomplished without the example of their ministers; not one of the three resident ministers, nor one of the nine in the surrounding towns, voted in any of the five elections.

Table 8.20: *Proportion of Vote by Candidate in Colchester* (Percentage)

	April 1784			July 1784	
	Electorate	Dissent		Electorate	Dissent
Affleck–Smyth	23.4	22.7	Smyth	52.4	78.0
Affleck–Potter	27.0	4.5	Potter	44.8	22.0
Smyth–Potter	17.0	20.5	Tyssen	2.8	—
Affleck	16.6	9.1			
Potter	5.7	31.8	N =	489	41
Smyth	10.3	11.4			
Resident Electorate N =	512				
Sample of Dissent N =		44			

CHARISMATIC LEADERSHIP AND PARLIAMENTARY ELECTIONS

Each of the boroughs studied in this chapter illustrates a different aspect of the characteristic difficulties the Dissenters faced in the electoral system of unreformed England. The Dissenters at Newcastle upon Tyne experienced genuine political repression. If a Dissenting community lacked a tradition of political participation, as at Newcastle, than obviously little could be expected from the Dissenters at elections. Here, an excellent run of non-parochial registers allows us to say with certainty that the Newcastle Dissenters did not vote,

170 In April 1784 four clergy were resident voters and four outvoters; in July, four were resident and five out-voters.

and yet a radical movement emerged full-blown quite apart from the activity of the Dissenting laity. At Liverpool, where it has long been held that the Dissenters contributed to the political division between Whig and Tory, the Dissenters in fact merely reflected the divisions and did little or nothing to influence them. Liverpool illustrates how, in the midst of a conservative political ambiance, an indifferent, or possibly even loyalist, ministerial elite could stifle the independent orientation of the laity. The Liverpool Dissenters' lower social standing may also have contributed to their political quietism. The Dissenters at Hull were too few in number to make an impact, and here, as well, they seem to have lacked the progressive leadership that might have mobilized their small potential. The influence of corruption on the Hull voter will remain difficult to assess, but it probably impinged on Dissenter and Anglican alike. At Colchester, the Dissenting vote gradually became more cohesive as the American war progressed, despite the lack of ministerial leadership at the polls. But as late as 1780, the Colchester Dissenting voters could not be relied upon to take a stance on principle against a government candidate. Wherever the American crisis failed to sharpen the ideological options placed before the electors in the persons of the candidates, there was consistently less evidence of division along religious lines, though some economic differences remained.

English Dissenters were potentially one of the most important independent elements in the eighteenth-century electorate, especially in the large, open freeman boroughs. But this chapter has made it evident that a voter's affiliation with a Dissenting denomination by itself meant very little. A local tradition of party conflict combined with charismatic leadership provided by either the Dissenting clergy or the laity were almost essential for marshalling and giving coherence to the Dissenting vote. It is a striking fact that none of the Dissenting ministers in Yarmouth, Newcastle, Liverpool, Hull, and Colchester voted in parliamentary elections, and only in Newcastle and Bristol was there a radical ministerial voice. The ministers' failure to lead the laity to the polls in the former boroughs helps account for their political inconsistency in parliamentary elections. Religion clearly contributed to pro-Americanism at Bristol and Great Yarmouth, but in places like Newcastle upon Tyne, what was lacking in religion was supplied by aggressive radical leadership among Anglicans fueled by economic differences that revealed themselves in political alignments. In both Bristol and Newcastle, a combination of the agitation over Wilkes and the crisis in America led to sharp political disputes; in the one case, much depended upon the Dissenting laity, in the other, very little.

But the outspoken tradition of radicalism at Newcastle can in part be attributed to the charismatic leadership and sermonizing of James Murray. At Norwich, Rees David was the clerical counterpart to Caleb Evans of Bristol and James Murray of Newcastle, and here as well, the laity were highly consistent in political behavior. In some boroughs, leadership by the laity was as vital as that of the ministers', though it was generally less effective. For example, apart from the Hurry family of Great Yarmouth, the Yarmouth Dissenters might have fared as ill as the Nonconformists at Hull. At Liverpool, Joseph Clegg was an active advocate of independence, while the leadership at Colchester fell to the layman, Bezaleel Bloomfield. But these efforts, with the exception of those of the Hurry family, were not sustained for a significant period of time. The Dissenters' reputation for independence, however, is clearly warranted; the majority of leaders, whether lay or clerical, were strongly disposed toward political independence, even though they faced enormous obstacles in mobilizing the laity's full potential.

One characteristic that does stand out in all of the boroughs examined in this study is the consistent support the wealthy and influential gave to government candidates (with the exception of Liverpool in 1780). In some boroughs, particularly Newcastle, this support was characteristic of the merchants as well. Local elites at Bristol, Yarmouth, Newcastle, Liverpool, Hull, and Colchester evidently saw their interest wrapped up with the strength of the central government. This pattern of elite support for the government during the American Revolution was even more consistent across boroughs than the support the Dissenters gave to opposition candidates. The rhetoric of radicalism concerning oppression that emanated from local interest groups, like the Dissenters and the Low-Church Anglicans who were excluded from High-Anglican corporations, takes on added significance in this light, and these data call for further examination of the possible interdependence of religious and socio-economic factors in popular politics. We might even expect that artisan electors who were weary of being beaten in parliamentary elections by local power brokers would respond with enthusiasm to any alternative, more popular form of political expression.

The constraints the Dissenters labored under at Newcastle, Liverpool, Hull, and Colchester suggest that the electoral workings of even the most open boroughs were often too cumbersome to adequately express people's political choices on a great national question. Fortunately, there is an alternative method of measuring public opinion in the eighteenth century that did not depend upon enfranchisement and was less susceptible to various forms of material inducement. Influence of a different kind wielded by charismatic Dissenting ministers at Bristol, Newcastle, Nottingham, and Taunton, might, in a more open political forum, finally become effective. Just as Mary Kinnear found that the nation was more responsive to the American crisis in the counties and larger boroughs, it might be expected that forms of political expression such as the public petition would provide a better index of public opinion and a more certain measure of the influence of ideology.[171]

171 Mary Kinnear, 'Pro-Americans in the British House of Commons in the 1770s', University of Oregon Ph.D. diss., 1973, p. 71.

PART 3

Petitions for Peace, Nonconformity, and Popular Politics

9

The Petitions of 1775: Popular Politics and the American Crisis

From the Stamp Act crisis in the mid-1760s until the popular reaction to the Fox–North Coalition in 1783, widespread political agitation in England erupted about every five years, and on three of these occasions it involved approximately 60,000 petitioners. The petitions to Parliament and the crown collected more than a quarter of a million signatures, a number that is roughly comparable to the total number of people who voted in the general elections of 1768, 1774, 1780 and 1784. Similar patterns between popular and electoral politics are also found by comparing the national distribution of parliamentary seats to the regional concentration of cities that petitioned the crown. In the age of the American Revolution, extra-parliamentary politics rivaled electoral politics in demographic terms, if not in influence.[1]

A minority of Englishmen believed that the government was unresponsive to the course of events and viewed the traditional channels of political expression as inadequate. They assumed, or at least hoped, that petitioning was a viable alternative that might influence the policy of the national government. The petitioners, however, made little attempt to influence public opinion at large; their pleas were easily ignored by the authorities, and, in the case of America, neglected by the opposition. Historians have carefully studied the Middlesex election affair and agitation over economic and parliamentary reform, but, since the mid-1770s were thought to be largely free from domestic disturbance, scholars failed to connect the movements of the 1770s and the 1780s. Seen separately and in isolation, these episodes of popular agitation were sometimes viewed as evidence that the political nation was uniformly conservative, apathetic, or corrupt. But when the petitions over America in the mid-1770s are related to previous and subsequent events, hitherto unperceived regional and ideological connections become apparent, and, taken together, these movements challenge the notion of a moribund national will.

---

1 A much expanded discussion of the petitioning agitation over America with full bibliographical references is found in James E. Bradley, *Popular Politics and the American Revolution in England: Petitions, the Crown, and Public Opinion* (Macon, Ga., 1986). For the actual number of voters in these elections see note 15 below.

George Rudé, John Brewer, H. T. Dickinson, and others have helped us understand the development of radicalism in terms of how it engaged public opinion and reached ever increasing masses of people. These scholars have shown that though the Rockingham Whigs failed in their stated objectives, their emphasis on the legitimacy of a formed opposition to the crown indirectly fostered extra-parliamentary radicalism that went far beyond their limited demands. In fact, the extension of radicalism into extra-parliamentary channels is one measure of its growth; the other traditional measure of the growth of radicalism is the increasingly progressive quality of its ideology, studied above in chapter 5. The neglect of the extension of radicalism between the Middlesex election affair and the Association movement has contributed to the belief that the Dissenters failed to launch a positive program of reform. New evidence concerning the petitioning agitation of 1775, however, demonstrates that the Nonconformists did in fact utilize the constitutional means of resistance to the fullest extent, and in so doing, they extended their radical convictions to a much broader audience. The following chapters will argue that the English petitions concerning the American Revolution do reflect popular opinion and that they are more sensitive instruments for measuring religious and economic divisions in society than poll books.

The Dissenting ministers at Bristol were exceptionally active in parliamentary elections, and a handful of politically active ministers can also be traced in some smaller boroughs, such as Abingdon. But a broad survey of poll books reveals that the ministerial elite were largely uninvolved in parliamentary politics; Dissenting ministers apparently failed to obtain the franchise in Great Yarmouth, Newcastle upon Tyne, Liverpool, Kingston upon Hull, and Colchester, and despite their interest in politics, not one Dissenting minister voted in these boroughs during the American crisis. Inevitably, there were numerous Dissenting laymen, probably the majority, who were similarly uninvolved in parliamentary politics, even though the American crisis was a highly divisive political issue. In fact, the Revolution was so divisive that in the fall of 1775, at least 40,000 people in England felt impelled to reach beyond the normal channels of political expression and make their opinion known to Parliament and the crown. Among these petitioners we will find a disproportionately large number of Nonconformists.

THE PETITIONING AGITATION OF 1775

John Encell of Bristol, grocer; James Fogo of Newcastle, shopkeeper; Joseph Brotherhood, frame-work-knitter of Nottingham; and John Clitsom of Taunton, grocer, were all Dissenting laymen, and although none of them voted during the American Revolution, they all watched with increasing concern as events in the colonies degenerated into war.[2] They listened to the exhortations concerning political liberty emanating from the Dissenting pulpit, and in the fall of 1775, they recorded their political concern at an alternative political 'poll'. Along with their pastors, Caleb Evans, James Murray, George Walker, and Joshua Toulmin, they, and thousands of others all across England, signed their names to petitions that opposed the government's coercive policy toward America, and pleaded instead for conciliatory measures. Dissenters at Colchester who lacked clerical leadership in parliamentary elections, and those at Newcastle, who were, for the most part, indistinguishable from other voters at the polls, stood out as staunch defenders of peaceful concessions in the petitioning agitation.

Petitions to Parliament were a normal avenue of popular political expression and the time-honored means of introducing legislation.[3] Petitions were also received in Parliament against existing laws, and Burke once described them as 'the only peaceable and constitutional mode of commencing any procedure for the redress of public grievances'.[4] Petitions to the crown, however, were an extraordinary form of popular expression exercised only when other, more common means of obtaining relief had failed. The right to petition the crown was part of the Revolution settlement guaranteed by the Bill of Rights, but this avenue of redress was never intended by its framers to function as a means of appealing to the crown against an act of Parliament.[5] In petitioning the king against the coercive legislation of Parliament, the petitioners of 1775 were unwittingly pitting the executive branch of government against the legislative, and since the king and his ministers had inspired the policy of coercion, there was hardly any hope of changing their perspective. Such considerations, however, had surprisingly little effect on the enthusiasm of those who now turned their attention to this alternative form of political expression.

In January 1775 English merchants from fifteen centers of trade petitioned Parliament on behalf of peaceful concessions to the colonists.[6] The majority in

2 For the identification of these individuals see RG 4/1826; Genealogical Society film no. 095016; RG 4/1588; RG 4/2937; HO 55/11/64; 28/19; 10/18; 8/3.
3 Sheila Lambert, *Bills and Acts: Legislative Procedure in Eighteenth-Century England* (Cambridge, 1971), pp. 52, 82, 87–105, and P. D. G. Thomas, *The House of Commons in the Eighteenth Century* (London, 1971), pp. 17–19, 57–60.
4 *Burke Correspondence*, 3: 208–9; Burke to Rockingham, 14 Sept. 1775.
5 Lois G. Schwoerer, *The Declaration of Rights, 1689* (Baltimore, 1981), pp. 14–16, 69–71.
6 On the growth of pro-Americanism before 1775, see Mary Kinnear, 'Pro-Americans in the British House of Commons in the 1770s', University of Oregon Ph.D. diss., 1973, chap. 1; Bradley, *Popular Politics and the American Revolution in England*, chap. 2; and John Sainsbury, *Disaffected Patriots: London Supporters of Revolutionary America 1769–1782* (Kingston and Montreal, 1987), pp. 3–21. London, Bristol, Norwich, Dudley, Liverpool, Manchester, Wolverhampton, Birmingham, Leeds, Bridport, Nottingham, Whitehaven, Huddersfield. Six places sent documents in support of coercive measures: Birmingham, Leeds, Trowbridge, Huddersfield, Nottingham, Poole. See *CJ* XXXV (1775), 71–3, 77, 78, 80–1, 82, 89, 90, 108, 123, 124, 139, 141, 144, 151, 164, 186, 198.

Parliament voted to disregard these petitions; accordingly, the documents were isolated in a committee which Burke aptly dubbed 'the committee of oblivion', and as a result, the merchants' complaints were never heard in Parliament.[7] The refusal to entertain any appeals concerning trade was grounded in the majority's determination to narrow the conflict to the single question of colonial submission, and on 7 February, Parliament declared the colonists in a state of rebellion.[8] Parliament's reluctance to reconsider the coercive legislation of the previous session led to a major shift in the people's approach to the government. From March 1775 forward, petitions from both the colonies and England were addressed to the crown, but George III was as opposed to peaceful concessions as the majority in Parliament. In April the king decided to receive no more petitions while seated upon the throne, that is, publicly, in his royal capacity; thereafter petitions were presented to the Lord in Waiting, or at the levee, and in either case, they were easily disposed of.[9] The evil of un-answered petitions became one of the colonists' major objections in their long litany of complaints against the English government.

News of the battles of Lexington and Concord reached England on 29 May, but it was not until 23 August 1775 that the king publicly declared the colonists in a state of rebellion. The royal proclamation of colonial rebellion elicited dozens of addresses to the crown expressing support of government policy, and the loyal addresses stimulated in turn an equally strong reaction in favor of peaceful concessions. Numerous charges in the newspapers were leveled against the administration for promoting addresses through bribery.[10] While such accusations appear to be unwarranted, it is evident that the government was not averse to using less flagrant forms of influence in order to elicit at least some addresses. As early as July, the Solicitor General, Alexander Wedder-burn, had urged Lord North to consider the utility of a royal proclamation against treason. He believed that 'Addresses from the Country in support of government, which are never worth solicitation, would soon follow unasked'. Two days after the royal proclamation, while writing to the king over possible means of encouraging army recruitment, Lord North observed, 'the cause of Great Britain is not yet sufficiently popular ...'[11] By the first week in September, North had received loyal addresses from Manchester and Lan-caster, and it was at this juncture that he recommended to the king a positive

7 *Parl. Hist.* 18: 173.
8 *Ibid.,* 18: 221–33; 265–92.
9 *City Addresses, Remonstrances, and Petitions to the Throne, Presented from the Court of Aldermen ... Commencing the 28th October, 1760, with the Answers Thereto* (London, 1865), pp. 36–7: Hertford to the Lord Mayor, 11 April 1775; Fortescue, 3: 235: George III to Lord North, 26 July 1775; p. 273: George III to Lord North, 23 Oct. 1775.
10 *Lond. Eve.-Post* (14–17 Oct. 1775); *Bath J.* (2, 9, 23 Oct. 1775); *Cumb. Pacq.* (19 Oct. 1775, 4 Jan. 1776); *Suss. Week. Adv.* (20 Nov. 1775).
11 HMC, *Tenth Report, Appendix, Part 6* (London, 1887), p. 9. Fortescue, 3: 249: North to George III, 25 Aug. 1775.

program of encouraging addresses:

As this spirit has sprung up spontaneously in Lancashire, Lord North submits to his Majesty whether it ought now to be encouraged, least [sic] the Lancashire addressers who have behaved so handsomely should think themselves neglected, and complain of being unsupported. If his Majesty is of that opinion, Mr. Robinson will privately endeavour to set on foot again the long projected address of the Merchants of London. One or two addresses may perhaps not be of much importance, but a general run of addresses just before the opening of Parliament will be of great service ....[12]

The king's response to the idea of a general run of addresses was positive.

The addresses and petitions concerning the American crisis were as numerous as the petitions which arose over the Middlesex election affair, and they represented an equally wide geographic area. But the petitions in favor of peace were considerably more radical than the petitions in defense of the Middlesex electors, and the American crisis was far more divisive than the issues surrounding John Wilkes. Rumors of colonial advances into Canada reached England in November, the same month in which the majority of these documents ascended to the throne. The petitions for peace thus arose when the conflict was well advanced and when all branches of government alike had declared the colonists in a state of rebellion. Considerable risk was involved in circulating and signing documents in favor of concessions, since in many people's eyes such acts were tantamount to encouraging rebellion.

The Middlesex election affair resulted in petitions from eighteen counties and twenty boroughs, but only two of these counties and four of the boroughs sent opposing petitions favoring the government.[13] The American crisis, however, prompted popular documents from eleven counties and forty-seven boroughs, and of these, five counties and twenty-one boroughs were so seriously divided that they sent signed, conflicting documents over whether coercive or conciliatory measures should be pursued.[14] The number of addresses in favor of coercion outnumbered the petitions for peace, but the petitions actually collected more signatures, since many of the addresses came from corporate bodies and were unsigned. Quite apart from the normal channel of parliamentary elections, at least 44,000 Englishmen were involved in popular agitation over America in the period 1775–8. If the petitions in the spring of 1775, and those from London and the counties of Cumberland and Kent are added, the total reaches about 60,000. This number approximates the actual turnout of voters in the general election of 1761, and if the petitions from Scotland and Ireland are

12 Fortescue, 3: 255: North to George III, 9 Sept. 1775.
13 George Rudé, *Wilkes and Liberty* (Oxford, 1962), pp. 112, 118. *Lond. Gaz.* (4–7 Feb. 23–7 May 1769).
14 See Tables 3.1–3.3 in chap. 3 of Bradley, *Popular Politics and the American Revolution in England*. Altogether, George III received over 200 appeals concerning America, and over half of these (109) came from England alone. All but three of the Scottish counties sent addresses, as did the majority of Scottish parliamentary boroughs. In Ireland only four towns addressed the throne; in Wales there were three.

9.1 Geographic Distribution of Petitions and Addresses Concerning America, 1775–1

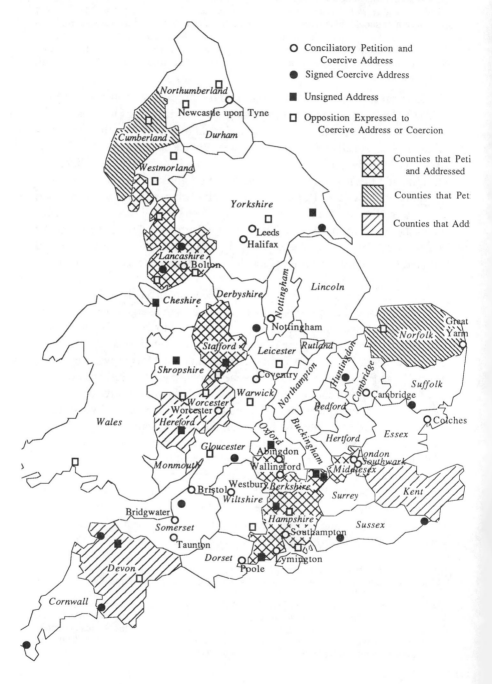

included, it equals the number that petitioned over economic reform in 1780, or the popular outcry against the Coalition in 1784 (see Map 9.1).[15]

Elsewhere I have argued at length that the resistance to the government's policy of coercion was pervasive and nationwide. In eleven cities that sent addresses only, and in seven others that neither petitioned nor addressed, there is solid evidence for disaffection with the government's measures.[16] Subsequent research has provided additional evidence of popular discontent at Hexham (examined below), Morpeth, Portsmouth, and Carmarthen. The well-known radical, George Grieve, spoke at the general meeting of freeholders at Morpeth in late July 1774 against the Northumberland candidates, Lord Algernon Percy and Sir John Delaval, and he appears to have won some popular support for the opposition. We know Portsmouth had a large contingent of Dissenters and that these Dissenters had established a comfortable arrangement with the government that worked to the advantage of both. But not all Portsmouth Dissenters were comfortable during the American crisis. While no independent petition against the American war emerged from Portsmouth, a contingent of at least seven citizens of the port, including the leading Dissenter, Sir John Carter, went to Winchester in the fall of 1775 and actively promoted the Hampshire petition for peace. Finally, at Carmarthen in South Wales, one newspaper reported that on account of the American war there was 'Animosity among the Inhabitants on Occasion of a Difference in Sentiments in Politics'.[17] Further research will undoubtedly reveal an even wider geographic sweep of discontent with the government's American policy.

The popular documents concerning America fall into two distinct categories; they either support the government and urge the use of coercive measures, or they express concern for the Americans and appeal for conciliatory measures. Typically, the addresses voiced their abhorrence of the rebellion in America and of those factions in England that had encouraged the spirit of opposition. The language, however, differs considerably from one address to the next, ranging from bellicose to irenic. The mayor, burgesses, and inhabitants of Bristol, for example, expressed their 'Astonishment' at the conduct of 'a few disappointed men, whose sophistical Arguments and seditious Correspondence, have, in great Measure, been the occasion of deluding your American Subjects into

---

15 *Commons, 1754–1790*, 1: 514. Counting the total voting constituency for contested English boroughs and adding the approximate number of voters; for the contested counties, the turnout for the general elections was 47,600 for 1761; a notorious low; 66,000 for 1768; 97,600 for 1774; 71,700 for 1780; and 79,900 for 1784. These estimates are undoubtedly high, and many voters polled in more than one election. On the other periods of agitation, Rudé, *Wilkes and Liberty* pp. 128, 211. Ian Christie, *Wilkes, Wyvill and Reform* (London, 1962), pp. 97, note 1, 122. Map 9.1 excludes the merchants' petitions of early 1775.

16 Bradley, *Popular Politics and the American Revolution in England*, chap. 3, tables 3.4, 3.5, and p. 84.

17 See *York Cour.* (2 Aug. 1774); *Morn. Chron.* (2 Nov., 1 Dec. 1775).

open Rebellion'. The reference to seditious, disloyal people at home was characteristic. The addressers testified to their 'Abhorrence of this unnatural Rebellion' and expressed their 'warmest wishes for the success of those measures your Majesty hath adopted in Support of the Legislative Authority of Great Britain over all your Dominion'. The Newcastle addressers used the same language of 'abhorrence and detestation', but they 'sincerely lament that an unjustifiable spirit of resistance is present in the American colonies'. The gentlemen, clergy, and merchants of Liverpool pledged their tribute of 'allegiance and fidelity to the best of Princes', while they castigated the 'open and daring contempt' for the legal authority of Parliament. Colchester addressers promised 'on every occasion to pay a due obedience to the Legislative Authority, and [to] defend your Majesties Person and Government to the utmost of our power'.[18] Support for George III and North's administration was thus commonly wedded to an expression of belligerence towards the colonists, and the use of force was encouraged with promises of local assistance forthcoming if necessary. Of all the addresses, only four equivocated on the use of force as the best policy, and even these allowed that force might be desirable.[19]

The majority of petitions in favor of peace explicitly stated that they were advanced in response to the misrepresentations of the coercive addresses; the petitioners sought to rectify the impression that the people were united in support of coercive measures. Burke drafted the petition from Bristol, and in the conclusion, he explained its necessity: 'lest it might be supposed, that by our silence we were consenting to the opinion and wishes for coercive proceedings'. He observed that the petitioners wished to clear themselves 'from any share whatsoever, in producing the calamities, which the present proceedings so inauspiciously begun, might yet bring upon this nation'. Petitioners at Newcastle also refused to sanction by their silence the infatuation of 'those interested men who have plunged an unhappy and united people into all the horrors of civil war'. The Lancashire conciliatory petition that circulated in Liverpool pleaded with the king to 'immediately put a stop to the dreadful and destructive consequences of a most unnatural civil war', while the Colchester petitioners simply appealed for the adoption of 'conciliatory measures'.[20] A handful of petitions can be attributed to the inspiration of Rockingham Whigs, and others are similarly moderate in tone,[21] but a number of petitions neglected the doctrine of parliamentary supremacy, and still others championed the natural as well as the chartered rights of the colonists, thereby witnessing to a more radical element in numerous boroughs.[22]

18 HO 55/11/9; 12/6; 28/20; 12/4.
19 Cambridge, Plymouth, Exeter, and Hereford, HO 55/10/16; 10/10; 11/7; 10/7.
20 HO 55/11/64; 28/19; 9/3; 9/4.
21 Those attributable in part to Burke and his associates are discussed below; see note 71.
22 Southwark, Taunton, Newcastle upon Tyne, Southampton, Lymington, Coventry, Leeds, Staffordshire, Middlesex, Worcester, and Wallingford. *Pub. Adv.* (4 Dec. 1775)

The ideological differences between addresses and petitions reflected considerable depth of feeling, and these differences illustrate how divisive the American issue had become by the fall of 1775. The differences were grounded in principle; the addressers consistently viewed the conflict as an 'unnatural rebellion', while the petitioners thought of it as an 'unnatural civil war'. Despite the relative clarity of the issues, and despite the simplicity of the choice put before the public, a number of contemporary observers were either skeptical about the motivation of the petitioners or doubtful whether the petitions reflected genuine political awareness. Those who spoke as critics of the administration's American policy disparaged the value of the pro-government petitions: they were invalid as expressions of political opinion since the signatures were thought to be obtained under the pressure of conservative, pro-government interests.[23] Conversely, those on the side of the government denigrated the anti-administration petitions and claimed that signatures were extorted at public meetings from men well versed in deception.[24] It was almost predictable that oppositionists would see this most representative form of political expression manipulated by the powers above, while those in power feared that such expressions were influenced by the rabble below. Neither side appears to have examined the petitions in any detail, and few on either side bothered to inquire further concerning the petitioners themselves. Both sides, in short, were motivated more by fear than by an open approach to the documents. What was the basis for these fears?

The practice of petitioning was not in itself a radical act; numerous controversies over such diverse issues as the excise and the cider tax resulted in widespread petitioning activity. In fact, on more than one occasion in the first half of the century, the Tories themselves had advocated the use of addresses or petitions.[25] But in interpreting the political significance of popular opposition, the immediate historical context is all important, and the petitioning activities of the opposition during the Middlesex election affair in 1769, the debate over the government's coercive measures in 1775, and the Association Movement of 1779–80 were often considered radical because of the context of the colonial rebellion and the related threat of domestic disorder. For example, during the Middlesex election affair, those who advocated petitioning the crown described themselves and the people as 'greatly dissatisfied', 'discontented with the public measures', and 'exasperated', but the opponents of petitioning thought the petitioners were 'factious, seditious, disaffected, and even rebel-

HO 55/8/3; 28/29; 11/20; 11/56; *Lond. Eve.-Post* (21–4 Oct. 1775); HO 55/21/39; *Lond. Eve.-Post* (12–14 Dec. 1775); HO 55/13/2; *Lond. Eve.-Post* (9–11 Nov. 1775); HO 55/28/21.
23 *Parl. Hist.* 18: 847; 1105–6; 719–20.
24 *Ibid.*, 18: 175, 186.
25 Linda Colley, 'Eighteenth-Century English Radicalism Before Wilkes', *TRHS* 5th ser., 31 (1981), 11, 13.

lious'. Some government supporters went so far as to argue that English subjects did not have a right to petition.[26] Similarly, during the Association Movement, petitions against stated government policy were often thought radical and abhorrent; critics of petitioning associated the practice with 'republicanism', and one anonymous observer felt certain that 'petitions, such as flow at this moment from the source of popular discontent', would inevitably obstruct the pursuit of the nation's best interest. 'Malcontents' thereby promoted 'the clamours of undescriminating faction', and while petitioning considered in the abstract might not lead to national inconvenience, the fear was that in war time, it would invariably embarrass the government.[27]

In the mid-1770s, opposition to petitioning was even more outspoken and intense. In the assemblies that met to petition Parliament in the period before Lexington and Concord, fears were commonly expressed about taking a stand in favor of the colonists, since the colonists had resisted the authority of Parliament.[28] But after Lexington and Concord, and following the royal proclamation of 23 August declaring the colonists in a state of rebellion, such perceptions became pervasive. In this context, petitioning the king on behalf of the Americans was associated with mob activity and was, accordingly, strongly resisted by loyalists. In the fall of 1775, feeling for and against petitioning ran high. 'Anti-Catalene', for example, expressed astonishment at those who petitioned, because by so doing they took an active part 'in favour of a rebellion'. 'At such a crisis as the present, the executive power requires the whole of that aid which is appointed to it by the constitution, and to withdraw any part of that aid, is in effect to withdraw that allegiance which is due in a state of civil society to legal government.' Such advocates of strong coercive measures abroad were very concerned about tumults at home, since 'The dispute, Sir, is no longer between America and Administration, it is a contention for power, with the people at large, and the meanest individual is deeply interested in the success of our troops.' As John Sainsbury has observed, 'Instead of simply supporting colonial dissent, the pro-Americans were now of course aligning

26 Joseph Towers, *Observations on Public Liberty, Patriotism, Ministerial Despotism, and National Grievances, with Some Remarks on Riots, Petitions, Loyal Addresses, and Military Executions* (London, 1769), pp. 5, 9–10, 11, 14; *The Contest* (Newcastle, 1774), pp. 23–4.
27 *Substance of Political Debates on his Majesty's Speech ... November 25th, 1779 ... with a Postscript on Petitions* (London, 1780), pp. 39–41.
28 See *Camb. Chron.* (7 Jan. 1775). In the House of Commons, Solicitor General Wedderburn clarified the change of concern from commercial to political issues in the spring of 1775 when he said that 'the legislative rights and powers of a nation, when flaunted and denied, especially by a people in actual rebellion against those rights was of far greater import than the question of the benefits to commerce and industry'. Despite the disruption to trade that might transpire, he insisted that 'an enemy in the bowels of the kingdom is surely to be resisted, opposed and conquered'. See Bradley, *Popular Politics and the American Revolution in England*, pp. 112–17 for a full discussion of the risk involved in petitioning.

themselves with armed opponents of the crown.'[29]

The language of the petitions themselves was highly stylized and conventional, but the speeches at the borough and county meetings where the petitions originated were often more spirited; here, viewpoints of opposing factions were articulated with precision and at length, and these speeches take us behind the petitions to the political commitments of the principal leaders. The tenor of some of these meetings was clearly threatening to observers on both sides of the debate.[30] The provincial press also made the political associations and proclivities of the petitioners manifest. Readers of local newspapers who also signed petitions were often well-informed concerning the political issues; week by week, reports of the debates in both Houses of Parliament were printed, as were such government documents as the royal proclamation and the activities of radical groups like the London Association. The linking of petitioning activity with the views of well-known radicals and their activities was thus unavoidable. For instance, notices of petitions appeared in the same columns of the newspapers as full reports of Wilkes' speeches in the House of Commons.[31] Radical organs like the *Newcastle Chronicle* and the *Kentish Gazette* repeatedly associated petitions with radicalism. Simons and Kirkby, Canterbury booksellers and editors of the *Kentish Gazette*, were strongly anti-government; their newspaper encouraged petitioning and associations and deplored addresses to the crown; 'So our glorious and popular administration are once again reviving the stale trick of *addressing*.' Yet the editors feared the government as well as hated it. 'The Ministry are determined to let slip the dogs of war at *home* as much as in America, on all those who either *in* or *out* of the House this session, dare gainsay their mandates.' Popular assemblies 'out of doors' called to petition the crown against its own stated policies were clearly associated with other acts of a radical nature. The *Kentish Gazette* rejoiced in resistance to recruiting for the American service, it celebrated the defection of commissioned officers in the army, praised the London Association as a 'laudable institution', and gave full and sympathetic accounts of the riots at Liverpool.[32] In the popular mind, people who petitioned were necessarily involved not only in exercising independent judgment against government policy, but actually

29 The debate at Poole is typical, see, *Sal. Win. J.* (30 Oct. 1775); see also popular opinion at Winchester and York, *Morn. Chron.* (15 Sept., 21 Nov., 1775). At York the bitter divisions over petitioning continued through the war, *York Cour.* (1 Aug. 1780). Sainsbury, *Disaffected Patriots*, pp. 90, 95.

30 See the speech of the Clerk of the Peace of the county in Hampshire *Morn. Chron.* (21 Nov. 1775); Thomas Wooldridge's speech in Staffordshire, *Worcs. J.* (2 Nov. 1775); and Sir Joseph Mawbey's speech at Southwark, *Pub. Adv.* (11 Nov. 1775). Wooldridge was associated with Wilkes and Mawbey was a member of the Society of the Supporters of the Bill of Rights.

31 See *Worcs. J.* (2 Nov. 1775).

32 *Kent. Gaz.* (6–9, 20–3 Sept. 1775); see the radical rhetoric of the essays by 'Publicola', 'Richlieu', 'An Englishman', 'A Patriot', 'Pistol', 'Titus', *Kent. Gaz.* (30 Aug–2 Sept., 2–6, 9–13, 16–20 Sept. 1775).

attempting to obstruct that policy, and herein lies the radical character of petitioning in a setting of Revolution.

Scholars who have doubted the threatening quality of radicalism in the
period of the American Revolution have failed to appreciate the ominous tone
of some of the meetings assembled to petition the crown, and they have not
taken the provincial and radical press seriously. The strength of popular
resentment toward established power structures has not been grasped. For
example, the radicalism of the *Kentish Gazette* is of a piece with the Dissenters
who told their congregations that the nation is sick of 'all mysterious crooked
politics'.[33] And since historians have known so little of the petitions in the fall
of 1775, the continuity of radical sentiment linking the Middlesex election affair
with pro-Americanism has been neglected. Such continuities in Parliament and
in London have received some attention; Mary Kinnear discovered a correlation
between the minority that voted with Wilkes and pro-American M.P.s in the
Parliament of 1774–80, but she found a 'clearer correlation between those who
opposed Wilkes and those who supported North'. John Sainsbury convincingly linked the London Wilkites to the pro-Americans and their programs.[34] In
the provinces, however, radical continuities are even more impressive. The
leaders in the petitioning agitation concerning the Middlesex election at Bristol,
Newcastle, and Coventry were the same leaders of the pro-American agitation
in these boroughs, and thus the commonplace observation among contemporaries that petitioning against the government's measures was associated with
radicalism should not be surprising. Like the agitation over Wilkes, the American petitions were put forth against the considered judgment of the nation's
leaders, but unlike the earlier unrest, they were put forth in the context of a
well-advanced and horribly threatening rebellion.

PETITIONS AND PUBLIC OPINION

The validity of these documents as genuine indicators of public opinion may
be addressed by comparing them to other instances of popular opposition, first
in terms of geography. Almost all of England's forty counties were touched by
the petitioning agitation, although the geographical provenance of the petitions
suggests important connections between parliamentary politics, popular politics,
and patronage. Of the four geographical areas of England classically described

33 George Walker, *The Doctrine of Providence*, 1784, in *Sermons* 4 vols. (London, 1808),
    4: 236. For a balanced discussion of the possibility of insurrection in England, see
    Sainsbury, *Disaffected Patriots*, pp. 98–106; insurrection was never likely, but it was
    hoped for by some London radicals, and feared by those in authority.
34 Kinnear, 'Pro-Americans in the British House of Commons', p. 94. For a fine
    discussion of both the ideological congruence and the historical continuities in leaders
    and techniques between pro-Wilkism in the 1760s and pro-Americanism in the 1770s,
    and parliamentary reform, see Sainsbury, *Disaffected Patriots*, pp. 15–18, 24–5, 31–42,
    52–4, 82–8, 112, 119, 146–7.

by Sir Lewis Namier, the southwest produced a disproportionately large number of popular documents during the American crisis. With only one-fourth of England's population, the southwest had nearly half (45.2%) of England's parliamentary boroughs; yet the majority of these constituencies were small and highly susceptible to influence.[35] From 1761 to 1790, 80 percent of the nation's increase in seats influenced by patronage occurred in the southwest.[36] Nevertheless, agitation over America in 1765 and again in 1775, over Wilkes in 1769–70, over economic reform in 1780, and parliamentary reform in 1782 was concentrated in the southwest. From 1765 to 1783 only 18.1 percent of all signed petitions for change come from the midlands, whereas 38.1 percent come from the patron dominated southwest.[37] This may be construed as partly the product of a fortuitous distribution of parliamentary seats; the higher proportion of boroughs in the area meant that there was a greater number of political contests at regular intervals, and this in turn may have resulted in a general heightening of political awareness. However, it also suggests that instead of stifling popular activity, patronage may have actually stimulated it by encouraging popular resistance. The greatest number of addresses from a single county came from the southwestern county most influenced by government patronage, namely, Hampshire, but in reaction, Hampshire also produced the greatest number of conciliatory petitions. It is also entirely possible that the geographic concentration of popular opposition was related to industrial unrest. C. R. Dobson has located a proportionately larger number of industrial disputes involving artisans in the southwest in the first half of the century.[38] Future research must entail a detailed examination of local politics in order adequately to evaluate the connection between patronage, labor disputes, and popular politics. In terms of geography, however, the petitioning agitation of 1775 fits rationally into a pattern of popular protest beginning with the Stamp Act crisis and extending through the Peace of Paris.

The petitioners may be compared to voters in parliamentary elections more directly. In his examination of five large freeman boroughs that petitioned in the fall of 1775, John Phillips found a strong relationship between voting in favor of government candidates and addressing the crown in support of coercive measures. At Coventry, Liverpool, and Nottingham approximately half of the electors voted for government candidates at the general election in 1774; but at Coventry, of those who voted for the government in 1774 and signed an address or petition in 1775, fully 93.4 percent signed the coercive address. At

35 Sir Lewis Namier, *England in the Age of the American Revolution* (London, 1930, 2nd edn, 1961), pp. 199–201; John A. Phillips, 'The Structure of Electoral Politics in Unreformed England', *JBS* 19 (1979), 84–8.
36 Phillips, 'The Structure', 84–5.
37 Bradley, *Popular Politics and the American Revolution in England*, Table 5.1, chap. 5.
38 C. R. Dobson, *Masters and Journeymen: A Prehistory of Industrial Relations 1717–1800* (London, 1980), pp. 15–29.

Liverpool and Nottingham the degree of consistency in political orientation was almost equally impressive (76.7% and 83.5% respectively). At Bristol 73.9 percent of the addressers supported court candidates and at Newcastle upon Tyne the same level of consistency was found among pro-government voters. Sainsbury discovered the same consistent political affiliation among London petitioners and addressers who were also voters.[39] Similar patterns of consistency in political behavior over time are found in two medium-sized and two small boroughs. Great Yarmouth and Southampton were subject to some influence, and yet the data from these boroughs comports well with what was found in the larger constituencies: 92.9 percent of the addressers at Yarmouth who were also voters, voted for the government candidate in 1777, and 93 percent of the Southampton addressers voted pro-government in 1774. There was, however, some inconsistency among the petitioners at Southampton; more conciliatory petitioners voted for the government candidates in 1774 than for the opposition candidate (48.7% to 32.9%).[40] However, while Montagu was clearly in opposition to the government in 1774, America was not a major issue in the election; moreover, it was always difficult to maintain a strict party vote in a three-way contest. In the small boroughs of Cambridge and Bridgwater, where one might expect to find more manipulation of political activity, there was some agreement between voters and petitioners, especially at Cambridge where America was a prominent issue in the election of 1774.[41] Even though a year or more separated the events of voting and petitioning, in large and small boroughs alike individuals behaved consistently in both political acts, and thus it seems reasonable to assume that they acted freely upon the basis of their own convictions. Against the opinion of Samuel Johnson, petitioners appear to have both understood and remembered the political content of the documents they signed.[42]

39 John A. Phillips, 'Popular Politics in Unreformed England', JMH 52 (1980), 618–20; Sainsbury, *Disaffected Patriots*, p. 119.
40 The poll books for these elections are at the Institute of Historical Research, University of London. The addresses and petitions are, for Yarmouth *Lond. Gaz.* (3–7 Oct. 1775), *Norw. Merc.* (9 Dec. 1775), *Lond. Eve.-Post* (21–3 Nov. 1775) and for Southampton, HO 55/11/20; 11/19.
41 Of the addressers, 88.5% who were also voters voted for the government candidates in Cambridge, and 73% of the Bridgwater addressers voted for the government candidates in 1780. Using X^2, the data from Yarmouth, Southampton, Cambridge, and Bridgwater yields a significant statistical difference at .01 level of probability. The strength of relationship between voting and petitioning, using Yule's Q is .86, .95, .77, and .69 respectively. See Bradley, *Popular Politics and the American Revolution in England*, pp. 172–3. For the Cambridge petition and address see *Camb. Chron.* (2 Dec. 1775); HO 55/10/15.
42 See the lengthy discussion of the petitioning process from the government's perspective in *The False Alarm* (1770) in Donald J. Greene, (ed.), *Samuel Johnson's Political Writings* (New Haven, 1977). Some observers were even associating the number of petitioners directly to the popularity of the government's measure, quite apart from the

A final test of the political consistency of addressers and petitioners is found by comparing the petitions to lists of subscribers to funds which supported wounded English soldiers and their families. A subscription was begun in London on 18 October 1775 and approved by the king. This subscription remained open through 15 January 1777 and was designed to aid the soldiers who were employed in his Majesty's service in America, and 'for succoring the distressed Widows and Orphans of those brave Men who have fallen or may fall in defending the Constitutional Government of this country'. The names of subscribers were printed every week in the London papers along with the amount they subscribed; lists subsist for London, Bristol, Leeds, Nottingham, and Poole.[43] In these five boroughs, between 22 percent and 70 percent of all subscribers also addressed the crown (an average of 46%) and of all those who addressed, an average of 24 percent subscribed to the government fund. Conversely, only .8 percent to 7.8 percent of the petitioners subscribed (an average of 3.3%). Thus many who addressed the crown in favor of coercive measures were willing to support the use of force with their fortunes, if not their lives, while the conciliatory petitioners, on the whole, were not. Popular support for coercive measures seems to have been given freely, one could even say enthusiastically, since the addressers who also subscribed, responded sooner than all other contributors considered together.

Finally, petitions represent public opinion in that they penetrated deeply into the populace. Previous studies of popular protests assumed that virtually all of the petitioners involved in the Middlesex election affair and in the movement for economic reform were also electors. This interpretation was recently overturned, and it now can be shown conclusively that petitioning offered an avenue of political expression to a considerable number of people who were not enfranchised. In his examination of six large freeman boroughs, Phillips found that an average of 51.8 percent of the signers were not voters in parlia-

---

question of external influence or the social status of the signers. With respect to Colchester it was observed, 'There were upwards of 500 respectable signatures to the above address [i.e. petition]. – The address which was lately presented from the same place, was signed by 125 only. – A proof that there, as well as many other places in the kingdom, a great majority of the people are quite averse to the American war.' *Camb. Chron.* (3 Feb. 1776). Clearly the popular will was becoming increasingly meaningful to some. For identical observations relating numbers to popularity, see *Lond. Eve.-Post* (30 Nov.–2 Dec. 1775), and Richard Champion to Portland, 5 Oct. 1775, Portland Papers, PWF 2, 718; and William Baker to Champion, 4 Oct. 1775, Champion, Letterbook, 38083 (4), p. 470.

43 For London, *Pub. Adv.* (25, 31 Oct.; 4, 8, 15, 22, 29 Nov.; 12, 27 Dec. 1775); *Gen. Eve. Post* (16–18 Jan., 6–8, 27–9 Feb.; 11–13 April; 7–9 May; 13–16 July; 17–19 Sept.; 1776); *Pub. Adv.* (15–29 Jan 1777). For Bristol, *Brist. J.* (23–30 Dec. 1775; 6, 13, 20, 27 Jan.; 3, 10, 17, 24 Feb.; 2, 9, 16 March; 13 April, 1776). For Leeds, *Gen. Eve. Post* (7–9 May 1776). For Nottingham and Poole, *Pub. Adv.* (12, 27 Dec. 1775). These lists were compared to the addresses and petitions from each borough. For further details, see Bradley, *Popular Politics and the American Revolution in England*, pp. 152–6.

mentary elections.[44] The number of petitioners actually exceeded the number of voters in many of the smaller boroughs, and many nonelectors were obviously involved in the non-parliamentary towns. A comparison of poll books to petitions in two medium-sized and three smaller boroughs further confirms Phillips' findings. On average, 62.7 percent of all petitioners and addressers in Yarmouth, Southampton, Cambridge, Bridgwater, and Poole were non-voters.[45] While approximately half of those who signed petitions and addresses from large, medium, and small boroughs were not voters, they were interested enough in the political issues raised by the conflict between the colonies and Parliament to risk signing their names to documents that were sometimes considered seditious.

THE LEADERSHIP AND ORGANIZATION OF POPULAR POLITICS IN 1775

The petitioning activity of 1775 fell short of an organized movement because there was little centralized leadership; no significant organizational structure either preceded or followed the agitation. The efforts of the Rockingham Whigs were centered in Bristol, while the London Association enjoyed one of its few successes in Newcastle, but an examination of the local leaders, their political connections, and the nature of their activities will show that these centralized attempts to influence popular politics were half-hearted and uncoordinated. A comparison of the American crisis to the nationwide agitation over Wilkes and the Middlesex election affair will reveal important continuities in the ranks of the leadership and their radical political tactics. But if opposition groups had found it difficult to present a unified front against the government in 1769, they were even more at odds in 1775, and the divisions among those who made a bid for popular support would, in the end, contribute not a little to their inability to influence government policy.

Popular radicalism in Bristol was enlivened in the late 1760s through the agitation over Wilkes. Samuel Peach and his son-in-law, Henry Cruger, organized meetings for instructing Bristol representatives (March 1769); they then established a radical 'Independent Society' and in July put forth a petition to the king on behalf of the Middlesex freeholders.[46] The Independent Society

---

44 Phillips, 'Popular Politics', 611.
45 Bradley, *Popular Politics and the American Revolution in England*, chap. 5, n. 70. As with the larger boroughs studied by Phillips, the proportion of non-voting petitioners was greater than the proportion of non-voting addressers, but the differences are not great enough to make valid generalizations about the disaffection of the unenfranchised. They are as follows: Yarmouth conciliatory, 77.3%, coercive 63%; Southampton, conciliatory 35%, coercive 23.2%; Cambridge, conciliatory 83.8%, coercive 72.9%; Poole, conciliatory 93.8%, coercive 50.9%; Bridgwater, conciliatory 46.7%, coercive 52.7%.
46 Linda Colley locates the main centers of extra-parliamentary dissidence in Bristol, Newcastle, Coventry, Norwich, Colchester, and the metropolis, 'Eighteenth-Century English Radicalism', pp. 15–16. By 1781, the Bristol radicals had clearly articulated the grounds upon which their insistence on annual Parliaments and equal representation was based:

adhered to such radical measures as shorter Parliaments, exclusion of pensioners from Parliament, lessening public expenditure, and conciliation with the American colonies. Richard Champion and Joseph Harford (both Quakers) were involved in the petitioning agitation (Champion wrote a rebuttal to Lord Clare's criticisms of the petition), but Champion was always wary of the 'lower ranks' and he withdrew when there was further talk of additional associations.[47] By 1772, the active radicals were Peach, Cruger, Harford, Samuel Span, and John Wallis; continuity in urban radical leadership is illustrated by the fact that they all signed the conciliatory petition concerning America. In the petitioning activity of 1775, however, Champion came to the fore, while Cruger and Peach, though they signed the petition, were less prominent. In the merchants' petitions to Parliament in the spring of 1775, and in the petitions to the crown in the fall, Champion took the lead under the direction of Burke.[48] Through Champion and his connections in Bristol, Burke secretly attempted to coordinate widespread popular resistance to the government in cities other than Bristol; it was the first and only time in his career that he genuinely embraced radical tactics.

Both in 1769 and 1775 Burke was the Rockingham party's leading proponent of popular opposition.[49] In January 1775 he was vitally involved in the petitioning activity in Bristol; he provided the 'heads' of the merchants' petition to Parliament and also had a hand in drafting the petition from the Merchant Venturers. Champion kept him informed of local developments, and Burke was also in close contact with the leaders in Nottingham and possibly in Leeds; by the fall of 1775 he was well versed in the petitioning process.[50] On 23

'That liberty, or freedom, consists in having *an actual share* in the appointing of those who frame the laws ...'. See Peter Marshall, *Bristol and the American War of Independence* (Bristol, 1977), p. 24. Marshall handles the political divisions at Bristol throughout the war, as does Underdown. See Peter T. Underdown, 'The Parliamentary History of the City of Bristol, 1750–1790', University of Bristol M.A. thesis, 1948, pp. 159–64, 226.

47 The rift between Cruger and Champion remained, although Harford was involved with the radicals in the instructions of 1772. Peter T. Underdown, 'Bristol and Burke', in Patrick McGrath, (ed.), *Bristol in the Eighteenth Century*, (Newton Abbot, 1972), p. 48. On Champion's attitude toward the 'lower ranks' see G. H. Guttridge, (ed.), *The American Correspondence of a Bristol Merchant, 1766–1776: Letters of Richard Champion* (Berkeley, 1934), pp. 49, 50, 65; Champion to Willing, Morris & Co., 13 March 1775, Nov. 1775; Hugh Owen, *Two Centuries of Ceramic Art in Bristol* (1873) p. 108.

48 *Burke Correspondence*, 3: 96: Champion to Burke, 10 Jan. 1775. Underdown, 'Bristol and Burke', p. 54. Thomas Hayes and John Mallard, both American merchants, were also actively involved, *Brist. J.* (14 Jan. 1775). The Bristol coercive address is HO 55/11/64; the petition is HO 55/11/9.

49 Rudé, *Wilkes and Liberty*, pp. 107–8, 120. *Burke Correspondence*, 3: 95, 98: Burke to Champion, 10 Jan. 1975; Burke to Rockingham, 12 Jan. 1775. W. R. Savadge, 'The West Country and the American Mainland Colonies, 1763–1783, with Special Reference to the Merchants of Bristol', Oxford University B. Litt. thesis, 1952, pp. 457–62.

50 *Burke Correspondence*, 3: 96, 202, 121, 129, 131: Richard Champion to Burke, 10 Jan. 1775; Burke to Champion, 12, 20 Jan. 1775; Burke to Mark Huish, 22 Feb., 9 March 1775; Burke to Champion, 9 March 1775.

August, the same day as the royal proclamation, he attempted to persuade Rockingham of the importance of obtaining support out of doors before Parliament met; Burke urged Rockingham to draw his friends together for a meeting where it could be examined 'whether a larger meeting might not be expedient'. He offered specific suggestions of three leaders who 'might feel the pulse of the people' and wondered whether it would be possible to do something 'in the Counties and Towns'. In response, Rockingham expressed deep skepticism about the 'generality of the Public' and he proposed a conservative alternative; the only 'proper' course of action would be for Parliament to petition the crown. Unlike the situation in 1769, neither a small nor a large meeting was ever held.[51] In mid-September Burke tried once again to persuade Rockingham of the importance of popular support through petitioning, and he candidly admitted he had taken matters into his own hands at Bristol: 'A trusty secret Committee is formed to digest Business, and to correspond with other Towns. I am persuaded that the movement of our City would be followed by that of twenty or thirty other places, and some of them of consideration.' He promised, however, not to proceed without his Lordship's approval. In response, Rockingham appealed to his earlier opinion: Nothing must be done until Parliament met.[52] When Burke received the letter of September 24 from Rockingham, he apologized for what he had already done. He acknowledged that he had also encouraged activity in London through William Baker, the organizer of the London merchants' petition, and we know from other sources that Baker attempted to coordinate activities with Champion at Bristol.

Burke was bitter over Rockingham's recalcitrance: 'My sole motive for attempting anything there [in London]', he explained to Rockingham, 'was to keep the City, now and forever, out of the hands of the Wilkes, Olivers, Hornes, Mascalls, and Joels – perhaps even out of the Talons of the Court.'[53] Thomas Joel was the secretary of the London Association, and on the same day Burke apologized to Rockingham, he wrote to the 'secret committee' at Bristol encouraging them to take actions not unlike those of the London Association.

My friends, employ your usual vigilance and activity. It never was more necessary believe me. It would not be amiss in the several Towns to which you have written to press anything further to your *Confidential Correspondents*. It is only to those confidential that we ought to press through though on the whole I agree with Paul Farr that our own standing forth and

---

51 *Burke Correspondence*, 3: 193–4: Burke to Rockingham, 23 Aug. 1775; pp. 205–6, Rockingham to Burke, 11 Sept. 1775. Rockingham's reservations in 1775 parallel exactly those he had in 1769. See Rudé, *Wilkes and Liberty*, pp. 108, 120.
52 *Burke Correspondence*, 3: 207–9, 210: Burke to Rockingham, 14 Sept. 1775; pp. 214–16, Rockingham to Burke, 24 Sept. 1775.
53 *Burke Correspondence*, 3: 223–4: Burke to Rockingham, 10 Oct. 1775. He also complained to Richmond that Rockingham's approach was an error (p. 219), Burke to Richmond, 26 Sept. 1775. On the radicals Richard Oliver, John Horne, Henry Maskall, and Thomas Joel, see Sainsbury, *Disaffected Patriots*.

[blank] will draw others out more than a thousand Letters. Take care not to propose your design in any company of which you are not previously assured of every man.

As late as 23 October, Burke wrote to Champion referring to 'our future operations'.[54]

The secret committee at Bristol comprised Richard Champion, Paul Farr,[55] and possibly others whose names cannot be traced, and while their correspondence to their confidential friends has not survived, it is possible to reconstruct some of their activities surrounding the petitioning agitation. Champion discussed every facet of his involvement with Edmund, Richard, and William Burke, ranging from the most advantageous time to present the petition, to its reception by the king, to the numbers in London in support of petitioning, the use of the press, the 'respectability' of the petitioners, the meaning of petitions – 'to distinguish us from our false brethren' – , and the political content of the speeches at the public meetings called for petitioning.[56] By the 1770s public meetings in large boroughs were organized along well defined and predictable lines and Champion published an account of the accepted procedures.[57] The leaders normally called for a public meeting weeks in advance by advertisements in the local newspapers that included the place, time, and purpose of the meeting. These advertisements often led to counter proposals at about the same time, and as a result, a well-publicized choice was presented to the public. The first order of business was the election of a chairman, followed by the main question concerning whether the assembly wished to petition, and the question was then brought to a vote. The meetings provided an occasion for extended debate of the issues involved, and often the arguments were far more technical (and sometimes more radical) than those found in the brief compass of the resulting document. The petition itself was drafted ahead of time, read twice to the assembly, and finally voted upon. Once the assembly agreed to the petition, it was determined who would present it and the document was signed by those present.[58] In other settings, the procedure for petitioning was altered, sometimes dramatically so. For example, closed bodies, like the Nottingham corporation, did not seek support outside of a select group, and they obviously proceeded differently from those meetings organized specifically to obtain as

---

54 Champion Letterbook, 38083 (4), Burke to Champion, pp. 454–5, also in *Burke Correspondence*, 3: 220–1, where the editor supplies 1 Oct. as the date. The blank space has not been supplied in any of the copies of this letter. *Burke Correspondence*, 233: Burke to Champion, 23 Oct. 1775.

55 Champion Letterbook, 38083 (4), Richard Burke to Champion, 17 Oct. 1775, p. 481.

56 See Champion Letterbook, 38083 (4) Edmund Burke to Champion, undated, p. 465; Richard Burke to Champion, 2 Oct. 1775, p. 466; same to same, undated, pp. 467, 468–9; William Burke to Champion, 13 Oct. 1775, pp. 473–4; Champion to William Burke, 14 Oct. 1775, p. 476.

57 Champion Letterbook, 38083 (4) p. 455, printed in *Gen. Eve. Post* (5–7 Oct. 1775).

58 This was the procedure followed at Bristol, Newcastle upon Tyne, London, and Cambridge, *Brist. J.* (30 Sept. 1775); *New. Chron.* (28 Oct. 1775); *Morn. Chron.* (4–7, 10–13, 17 Oct. 1775); *Gen. Eve. Post* (11–14, 21–3 Nov. 1775).

wide a public response as possible. In contrast, the meeting of the Lancashire freeholders, discussed below, was characteristically informal; discussion was more open and the outcome of the meeting less certain. The majority of boroughs in this study, however, followed a pattern similar to that found at Bristol.

The petitioning movement in Bristol began on 18 September, when, at the request of twelve citizens, the mayor, Charles Hotchkin, summoned a meeting of the corporation to address his Majesty. On the 21st, the number who attended the Council House was insufficient for a quorum, but those present determined to publicize a notice for an assembly of the citizens at large and set the date for the following Thursday. News of this projected meeting prompted Champion and two other merchants, Samuel Brailsford and John Fisher Weare, to organize a meeting at the Guildhall for Wednesday, the 27th. With Thomas Hayes, an American merchant, in the chair, this meeting passed a series of resolutions concerning the depressed state of trade and agreed to a petition to the crown that had been previously drafted by Burke. The next day the addressers met; with Charles Hotchkin in the chair, George Daubeny, president of the Constitutional and Loyal Society, spoke in favor of a loyal address, and then Thomas Symonds, an attorney, gave a lengthy statement against it. There was some heckling from those who supported peace, but the chairman was able to silence the disturbance and the assembly agreed to a loyal address.[59]

Champion not only organized the petitioning meeting, but he planned the disturbance in the meeting of the 28th. Since two of his own vessels were docked in Bristol, he had numerous dependents on hand; he planted four parties of his people – 'common people' – he called them, in the 'Tory' assembly in order 'to get the better of these blood thirsty Fellows'.[60] Having put his plan into action, he wrote to Portland that he expected the meeting to be 'very tumultuous', since 'a strong opposition' to the address would be made. As it turned out, the disturbance was not as great as Champion had hoped, since 'many' of our friends, 'from a false opinion of its not being genteel to disturb them kept away'.[61] Champion later published a misleading account of this meeting complaining of the irregularity of its organization; Hotchkin, he claimed, had merely assumed the chairmanship, and was never duly elected.[62]

59 Full accounts are found in *Brist. J.* (30 Sept. 1775) and almost all of the metropolitan and provincial papers. See Underdown, 'Parliamentary History', pp. 217–20, and Savadge, 'The West Country', pp. 482–95. On Symonds' speech, see *Brist. J.* (7 Oct. 1775); on the actual documents, printed with signatures, *Brist. J.* (14, 21 Oct. 1775).
60 Champion to Burke, 27 Sept. 1775, quoted in Peter T. Underdown, 'Burke's Bristol Friends', *BGAST* 77 (1958), 131–2. His reversal on the lower ranks is remarkable.
61 Champion to Portland, 28 Sept. 1775, Portland Papers, PWF 2, 715.
62 *Pub. Adv.* (4 Oct. 1775); *Lond. Eve.-Post* (5–7 Oct. 1775); *Gen. Eve. Post* (5–7 Oct. 1775); See Champion Letterbook, 38083 (4), 28 Sept. 1775, p. 455 and his full accounts to Portland, 27, 28 Sept. 1775, Portland Papers, PWF 2, 714, 2, 715.

The petition in favor of peace was deposited at the Bush Tavern in Corn Street for signing. But against Burke's explicit directions, Champion also carried it about to collect signatures. Burke had written earlier: 'When the thing is ready Let each take a district and bring in those who are willing to sign to some certain place. This is far better than to go from House to House.' Champion, however, reported to Portland, 'I have taken a great deal of Pains in going around the Town to procure the signatures of Tradesmen which exertions might lead me to a greater knowledge of the condition of Trade.' Despite such tactics, he could point to strong support from the corporation: 'Notwithstanding all of the boasts of the Tories, we had fifteen of the Corporation, the Mayor, two Sheriffs, three Aldermen, and Nine Common Councilmen.'[63] Champion was involved in other radical activities such as the dissemination of propaganda in the press. He had Burke's controversial letter to Hayes, the chairman, published in the Bristol newspapers, along with other political pamphlets outspoken in their opposition to the ministry. At Champion's behest, William Burke saw to it that the Bristol petition was published with signatures in the London newspapers.[64]

Issues surrounding the petitions and the practice of petitioning itself were highly divisive politically. The same week in which the documents were being signed, inflammatory papers were posted on several churches in Bristol declaring: 'All true churchmen are desired to unite in an address to the throne at the present alarming time; it being evident the Dissenters in general wish to subvert the constitution.'[65] The vituperative public exchange between John Wesley, Caleb Evans, and others was carried on in the context of the petitioning movement.[66] Heated and sometime lengthy essays appeared in the press under such pseudonyms as 'Scipio', 'An Englishman', 'Omega', 'An Addresser', 'A Lover of Truth', 'Obediah Steadfast', 'A Petitioner', and 'Diver'; in addition, the important letter, signed 'An Addresser', was printed and circulated by hand bills in the city.[67] These essays discussed the likelihood of petitions in England encouraging rebellion, the intention of the Americans, the nature of parliamentary authority, the Bostonians' destruction of property, and questions of virtual representation and taxation. The intelligence displayed in

---

63 Champion Letterbook, 38083 (4), Burke to Champion, 1 Oct. 1775, p. 455. Champion to Portland, 5 Oct. 1775, Portland Papers, PWF 2, 718. It is possible to actually identify eight, not nine common councilmen, who signed the petition. See chap. 10 below.

64 Champion Letterbook, 38083 (4), Burke to Champion, 20 Oct. 1775, p. 485; William Burke to Champion, pp. 471–2; Champion to William Burke, 14 Oct. 1775, p. 475.

65 *Lond. Eve.-Post* (28–30 Sept. 1775).

66 *Morn. Chron.* (26 Oct., 30 Nov. 1775). See also James Rouquet, a Wesleyan Anglican, but pro-American clergyman in Bristol, *Brist. J.* (21 Oct. 1775); Dean Tucker's differences with Burke and his signing of the address were also thoroughly aired. *Brist. J.* (28 Oct., 4 Nov. 1775); *Bath Chron.* (9 Nov. 1775); *Glos. J.* (23 Oct. 1775); *Lond. Eve.-Post* (12–14 Oct. 1775).

67 *Brist. J.* (23, 30 Sept.; 7, 21, 28 Oct.; 4 Nov. 1775); *Morn. Chron.* (8 Dec. 1775).

this debate, and the strength of the participants' convictions, clearly rival those attained in modern political discourse. Moreover, the political differences between the parties persisted. At the anniversary dinner celebrating the election of Cruger and Burke held in November 1775, constitutional toasts were drunk 'to reconciliation between Great Britain and her colonies', to the Lord Mayor of London (Wilkes), Lord Effingham (who had resigned his commission in protest against the government) and to 'the minority in both houses of Parliament, and success to their patriotic endeavors'. Yet when in December, Champion and Farr proposed to the Society of Merchant Venturers an alternative to the government subscription consisting of a collection for poor artisans in the city who were out of employment because of the dispute with America, the proposal was badly defeated. In the same month, a Court of Common Council agreed to present the freedom of the city to Lord North.[68]

Champion wrote to Portland late in September: 'The petition is so much approved of here, that I am in great Hopes it will be followed by many other places.'[69] But if the secret committee's activities in Bristol may be judged a success by the popular response to the petition, the impact of the correspondence with leaders in other boroughs is difficult to assess. The interaction between the committee and the London merchants is readily established and something of the excitement of a unified popular effort is communicated in Baker's letter to Champion of 15 October 1775: 'if anything occurs which is thought proper by the good people with you to move', he wrote, 'I shall heartily join in forwarding ... the Great Public Cause. There is no harm in being on the watch and ready to take advantage of such occasions as offer'.[70] But in addition to Bristol and London, it is only possible to trace the influence of Burke's centralized efforts in Abingdon, Berkshire, Westbury, and possibly Leeds, Nottingham, and Bridgwater. In Abingdon and Berkshire, it appears certain that the Earl of Abingdon and Lord Craven took the initiative with Burke's encouragement.[71] Sir James Lowther was apparently acting independently in his work on behalf of conciliation in Cumberland, as was Thomas

68 *Brist. J.* (11 Nov.; 16, 23 Dec. 1775).
69 Champion to Portland, 28 Sept. 1775, Portland Papers PWF 2, 715.
70 Champion Letterbook, 38083 (4), Baker to Champion, 15 Oct., p. 477; see also same to same, 25 Aug. 1775, pp. 440–1; 4 Oct. 1775, p. 470.
71 *Burke Correspondence*, 3: 121, 194, 234–5: Burke to Mark Huish, 22 Feb. 1775; Burke to Rockingham, 23 Aug. 1775; Rockingham to Burke, 2 Nov. 1775. See on Abingdon, Charles Ritcheson, *British Politics and the American Revolution* (Norman, Okla., 1954), p. 228, and on Berkshire, *Berkshire, VCH* (London, 1907), 2: 164; *Pub. Adv.* (29 Nov., 1 Dec. 1775). Sir George Savile presented the Newcastle and Halifax petitions, *Lond. Eve.-Post* (30 Nov.–2 Dec. 1775); *New. Chron.* (11 Nov. 1775). Lord Craven was at Coventry when the petition was circulated in early October. Lord George Cavendish presented the petition from Bolton to the king. *Lond. Eve.-Post* (14–16 Dec. 1775). But the actual role of these leading Rockingham Whigs in the agitation is difficult to determine.

Wooldridge in Staffordshire.[72]

Perhaps the greatest difficulty the Rockingham Whigs faced was the worsening political atmosphere; in any case, the possibility that these activities would be considered treasonous worried Champion. He wrote to Portland that except for the large number of local supporters, he could have been fearful 'as the first movers are often styled seditious'. By the end of October he told Burke that other business had made it difficult 'to look upon our friends', but added, 'they are ready for action'. Writing about the same time, Burke worried about the arrest of Stephen Sayre, and his comments make it clear how menacing the government had become. 'This is thrown out to discourage the Spirit of Petitioning from the main point.' Burke believed that Sayre's arrest and the rumor that the government might arrest 'two or three more' discouraged people from adding their names to documents that were possibly seditious.[73] These fears, combined with a lack of unanimity within the ranks of leadership, resulted in the Rockingham Whigs' only modest success.

THE LONDON ASSOCIATION AND NEWCASTLE UPON TYNE

The more radical political principles enunciated in petitions from other boroughs demonstrate that the narrower interests of the Rockingham Whigs were not able to embrace all of the popular opposition to the government. In contrast to the Rockinghams, the London Association had no scruples about working with committees of correspondence; it was the only other centralized organization that attempted to elicit popular support for conciliatory measures.[74] Under the leadership of Thomas Joel, the society met regularly at the Globe Tavern, Fleet Street, and published resolutions concerning their grievances against the administration and warnings against possible encroachments on the freedom of the press.[75] In late August, the Association gained considerable notoriety for sending printed circular letters to a number of boroughs appealing for the organization of provisional associations designed to defend British liberties. The letter recommended the formation of committees of

---

72 *Cumb. Pacq.*(2, 9, 16, 23, 3 Nov. 1775; 18 Jan. 1776); *Hamp. Chron.* (24–6 Oct. 1775).
73 Champion to Portland, 28 Sept. 1775, Portland Papers PWF 2, 715; Champion Letterbook, 38083 (4), Champion to Burke, 23 Oct. 1775, p. 487; Burke to Champion, 24 Oct. 1775, pp. 486–7.
74 For a detailed discussion of the London Association, see John Sainsbury, 'The Pro-American Movement in London, 1769–1782: Extraparliamentary Opposition to the Government's American Policy', McGill University Ph.D. diss., 1975, pp. 208–22, and *Disaffected Patriots*, pp. 106–13. Rumors of 'Associations' forming throughout England to defend the people's liberties appeared in late July. See *Lond. Eve.-Post* (29 July–1 Aug.; 5–7 Aug. 1775). Sainsbury is excellent on the extent to which the Association's activities were linked with treason, but his overlooking the articles of Thomas Knox (note 79 below) allows him to discount the Association's success in Newcastle. *Disaffected Patriots*, p. 108.
75 See *Lond. Eve.-Post* (9–12, 12–14, Sept.; 26–8 Oct. 1775); *Bath J.* (9 Oct. 1775); *Suss. Week. Adv.* (9 Oct. 1775).

correspondence, and, while no specific appeal was made for petitions, loyal addresses were condemned as conducive to oppression.[76] Letters were addressed to at least nine boroughs, but the response was unenthusiastic and the reason is not difficult to discern.[77] These circular letters were addressed to the mayors, not the populace, of these boroughs, and though some of the Association's deliberations were published in the newspapers, the appeal to the corporations demonstrates the radicals' concern for the support of the more respectable elements in society. This was a mistake of the first order, for all of the boroughs known to have received the letter sent addresses to the crown supporting coercion. In Newcastle upon Tyne alone was an association actually formed, and of the nine cities known to have received letters, only Newcastle, Nottingham, and Worcester sent petitions for peace.[78] It is thus entirely possible that the net effect of the London Association's efforts was to promote more support for government measures than sympathy for the Americans.

Radicalism at Bristol and Nottingham has long been understood to have had a religious component. But the religious element of popular politics at Newcastle, Coventry, Colchester, and Taunton has been neglected; in fact, even the broader radical element in the last three boroughs has received insufficient study. Of all the urban centers of radicalism outside London, most attention has been paid to Newcastle upon Tyne, but here as well, research to date has not concentrated on the contribution of the American crisis.[79] By 1775, Newcastle upon Tyne already had a well-developed tradition of local opposition politics and at its core was a vital and outspoken radical element. The addresses in

---

76 Printed in *Lond. Eve.-Post* (26–8 Oct. 1775).
77 See *Lond. Eve.-Post* (7–9 Sept. 1775); *Man. Merc.* (12 Sept. 1775); for Worcester, *Gen. Eve. Post* (5–7 Sept. 1775); *Lond. Chron.* (5–7 Oct. 1775); for Leicester, *North. Merc.* (18 Sept. 1775); for Lichfield see HMC, *Dartmouth Manuscripts*, 3 vols. (London, 1887–96), 2: 376–7, 376–7; for Salisbury, see *Sal. Win. J.* (11 Sept. 1775). At Leicester, the Association's appeal was almost certainly the main stimulus to the loyal address, and Dartmouth's tendering of thanks to the mayor of Lichfield may well have helped elicit the Lichfield loyal address. See HMC, *Dartmouth*, 2: 380, 393. For Manchester, see *Man. Merc.* (12 Sept. 1775); for Blackburn, HMC, *Dartmouth*, 2: 378, dated 28 Aug.; for Hull, see *Burke Correspondence*, 3: 216: Rockingham to Burke, 24 Sept. 1775; for Newcastle, see *Lond. Eve.-Post* (2–5 Sept. 1775); *Lond. Chron.* (7–9 Nov. 1775); *Bath J.* (11 Sept. 1775). It was often observed in the newspapers that the loyal addresses were promoted in response to associations formed against the government. See, for example, *Glos. J.* (18 Sept. 1775).
78 On Newcastle's connection with Wilkes, and by extension, the London Association, see *Gen. Eve. Post* (31 Oct.–2 Nov., 2–4 Nov. 1775); *Lond. Chron.* (2–4, 4–7 Nov. 1775).
79 Four independent analyses of Newcastle politics that converge to a remarkable degree appeared almost simultaneously; Thomas R. Knox, 'Popular Politics and Provincial Radicalism: Newcastle upon Tyne, 1769–1785', *Albion* 11 (1979), 225–41; 'Wilkism and the Newcastle Election of 1774', *Durham University Journal* 72 (1979–80), 23–37; H. T. Dickinson, *Radical Politics in the North-East of England in the Later Eighteenth Century* (Durham, 1979), pp. 1–24; John Brewer, 'English Radicalism in the Reign of George III', pp. 331–2 in J. G. A. Pocock, (ed.), *Three British Revolutions: 1641, 1688, 1776* (Princeton, 1980); and P.M. Ashraf, *The Life and Times of Thomas Spence* (Newcastle upon Tyne, 1983).

favor of coercion from Lancashire, combined with news of the formation of radical associations throughout the land, stirred considerable excitement in the fall, and in early October, a group of citizens approached the mayor for the use of the guildhall to address his Majesty.[80] The mayor declined to open the guildhall on the grounds of maintaining his own neutrality; as a result, the addressers never held a public meeting, though a document in support of coercive measures was subsequently circulated and ultimately gained the support of 168 inhabitants. The energy for this address was supplied by the nearly unanimous support of the corporation and the Anglican clergy.[81] The movement for conciliatory measures arose among the stewards of the incorporated companies who approached the mayor and met with the same rebuff as the addressers; following public advertisements in the newspapers, they and a numerous group of burgesses assembled at the Fourth-House on Monday 23 October. George Grieve was elected chairman and a petition was read and unanimously agreed upon. The assembly voted on letters of thanks to be presented to John Wilkes and Lord Effingham; the first, for asserting the right to petition the Throne, and the second for refusing to draw the sword against the Americans. William Smith then took the chair and read instructions to their Members in Parliament which were also agreed upon. The petition was to lie at Richard Swarley's Public House for one week; in the first five days it collected 800 signatures, and ultimately more than 1000.[82]

Just as at Bristol, the pro-American leadership in Newcastle had been previously involved in pro-Wilkes agitation. George Grieve was consistently involved in radical causes; he was a member of the Bill of Rights Society and had a hand in drafting the Society's program in 1771; he was active in organizing the Constitutional Club at Newcastle, and later he served as agent for the opposition in the by-election of 1777. It was thus natural for him to assume the chairmanship in the petitioning agitation over America. William Smith, like Grieve, had been active in opposition politics since 1771; he headed the Moor committee in 1774, and followed Grieve in the chair to instruct the Members of Parliament. He was also an active correspondent in the cause of the Americans. Nicholas Tyzak chaired the nominating meeting which put up Phipps and Delaval in 1774, and after the petitioning agitation, chaired the committee of 'the free burgesses and inhabitants' who petitioned against the American

80 *New. Chron.* (2, 16, 23 Sept.; 7 Oct. 1775).
81 Printed with signatures in *Lond. Gaz.* (21–5 Nov. 1775).
82 *New. Chron.* (21, 28 Oct. 1775); and many metropolitan and provincial papers. Printed in *New. Chron.* (18 Nov. 1775) and *Lond. Eve.-Post* (9–11 Nov. 1775), HO 55/28/19. 'Steady', observed that the address was 'hawked' about for three weeks and only acquired 168 signatures. *Lond. Eve.-Post* (30 Nov.–2 Dec. 1775); 'Humanus' said it was 'mendicant from house to house for five or six weeks, *New. Chron.* (9 Dec. 1775); and 'Veteran' noted the address lacked a head, (i.e., the mayor), and a chairman (i.e., no meeting was ever called). *New. Chron.* (4 Nov. 1775).

war.[83] In fact, of the nine prominent leaders in the agitation over Wilkes, eight signed the conciliatory petition over America, and four of the eight were among the first five signers.[84] These leaders had also been the prime movers in the opposition to the corporation over the Town Moor.[85] Nonconformists in Newcastle were not as prominent in the actual organization of petitioning as was Richard Champion at Bristol, but the Dissenting elite led their congregations from the pulpit. James Murray also published separate tracts, contributed to the debates conducted by the Philosophical Society, and in the Freeman's Magazine upheld the right of petitioning on the basis of a theoretically informed and sophisticated analysis of the Bill of Rights. If the Dissenting ministers were not involved in the elections, they turned out in force in the petitioning agitation.[86]

The Newcastle radicals' enthusiasm for the London Association is seen in the high praise this organization received in the *Newcastle Chronicle* and in the prominence given to Wilkes in the American petitioning agitation.[87] Little is known of the Newcastle Association, but there is evidence of its activity in the correspondence of Grieve and Smith with prominent leaders like Lord Mulgrave and the city's representatives.[88] Local interest in the American crisis stimulated a wide array of radical activities. The Philosophical Society was particularly active in debating such lively issues as whether or not the civil war in the reign of Charles I was similar to the contest with America, and whether limited monarchy or a republican form of government was preferable. The first question was unanimously carried in the affirmative, and a republic was favored over a limited monarchy by a majority of two. Local and national interests were brought together by the Society in December when it debated

83 Thomas R. Knox, 'Wilkism and the Newcastle Election', 30–1; *Lond. Eve.-Post* (11–14 Nov. 1775); *Pub. Adv.* (1 Dec. 1775); *New. Chron.* (30 Dec. 1775).
84 The nine identified by Knox are George Grieve, Thomas Maude, Nicholas Tyzack, Jaspar Harrison, William Smith, Thomas White, George Guthrie, Robert Reed, and Henry Gipson, and Gipson alone did not sign. Knox, 'Wilkism and the Newcastle Election', 23–4, 26, 30–1.
85 Seven of the Committee of Ten appointed by the Stewards in April 1771 to wait on the mayor signed; Smith, Tyzack, Bartholomew Kent, Thomas Maddison, Robert Michison, John Story, George Young. Four of the Committee of Six appointed by the Stewards in 1771 to look further into the affair of the Town Moor, signed; Smith, Maude, William Addison, and Matthew Laidler. Knox, 'Wilkism and the Newcastle Election', 25, note 6.
86 *The Teacher of Common Sense; or Poor Man's Advocate* (Newcastle, 1779), p. 59; *The Freeman's Magazine* (Newcastle, 1774), p. 50. See Table 10:2 in chap. 10 for the ministers. Ashraf believes that Murray actually initiated the meeting to petition, but the evidence is sketchy, *The Life of Spence*, p. 26.
87 On the formation of the Newcastle Association, the encouragement of other Associations, and the news of activities in London, see *New. Chron.* (2, 16, 23 Sept. 1775). On praise for Wilkes and full accounts of his speeches in the fall, *New. Chron.* (4, 11 Nov.; 9 Dec. 1775). Wilkes' and Effingham's public responses to the petitioners received widespread attention. *Lond. Eve.-Post* (4–7 Nov. 1775); *Gen. Eve. Post* (2–4 Nov. 1775); *Morn. Chron.* (6, 9, 11 Nov. 1775).
88 Grieve, *Lond. Eve.-Post* (11–14 Nov. 1775); on Smith, *Morn. Chron.* (2 Dec. 1775); *Pub. Adv.* (1, 7, 12 Dec. 1775).

'whether corporations are an advantage either to the places incorporated themselves, or to the kingdom in general': it was decided that they were 'disadvantageous to both'.[89] A Constitutional Club had been organized during the agitation over Wilkes, and it was active in the fall of 1775. The semi-annual meeting of the club was held at Sunderland on 6 December with Jaspar Harrison, an attorney and a signer of the peace petition, in the chair. Toasts were drunk to a long list of radicals, to the Rockingham Whigs, to success to 'all constitutional associations' and to the 'worthy petitioners of Newcastle'.[90] Although it has been argued that political issues were absent in the county contest of 1774, a year later the 'independent freeholders' of Northumberland met in Parker's Long Room in Newcastle to celebrate their eminent victory over prerogative, and at this dazzling assembly, the 'daughters of Liberty' were reported to have displayed their 'alacrity in a good cause'.[91]

During the week that the petition was being signed, Thomas Slack, publisher of the *Newcastle Chronicle* and a signer of the petition, printed a new edition of Marat's *The Chains of Slavery*.[92] To counter such radical propaganda, Thomas Saint, the editor of the *Newcastle Courant* and a signer of the address, published a separate edition of Wesley's *Calm Address* in the form of handbills, and, according to Slack, threw them 'into every home and shop in town, to depreciate the Americans and all that wish a reconciliation with them'.[93] On the evening of Thursday, October 26, 'there was a curious Procession through the principal Streets of Newcastle, of two Effigies mounted on Asses, which, on Enquiry were found to be intended for the Author of An address lately published, and a Tory Printer of that Place'. Wesley was mounted on the first ass 'with his face to the Tail, dressed in Canonicals, and his *"Calm Address to the Colonies"* painted on his Breast; the Word *Filmer* in large Characters, was fastened to one Shoulder, and *Hobbes* on the other'. On the forehead of the figure of Thomas Saint were written the words '*Ambition* and *Servility*'. The figures were carried in great pomp to the Flesh-Market, 'the usual place of executing such Criminals', and there they were committed to the flames, 'amidst the Shouts of the Multitudes by the Common-Hangman, who repeated the Words, *"Thus may every Traitor to his Country perish"* '.[94] When the royal

89 *New. Chron.* (30 Sept.; 28 Oct.; 9, 23 Dec. 1775).
90 On the formation of the Club in 1772, see Knox, 'Wilkism and the Newcastle Election', 26. *New. Chron.* (2, 9 Dec. 1775).
91 *New. Chron.* (23, 30 Sept.; 28 Oct. 1775); *Commons, 1754–1790*, 1: 348.
92 Earlier, Slack had encouraged people to read Lord Molesworth's preface to Hottoman's Franco-Gallia in order to learn 'the genuine principles of a real Whig'. *New. Chron.* (23 Sept.; 21, 28 Oct.; 4 Nov. 1775). Grieve knew Marat and may have encouraged the publication of his work.
93 *New. Chron.* (28 Oct. 1775).
94 *North. Merc.* (6 Nov. 1775); *New. Chron.* (28 Oct. 1775). Though much opposed to Wesley, Slack urged caution in this affair. 'These practices can only be founded upon persecuting principles and savour too much of the nature of the friends of the minister.' In London, there was a denial that the incident ever happened. *Lond. Chron.* (11–14

proclamation concerning colonial rebellion was read in the neighboring community of Hexham, the 'mob' viewed it as an 'enemy to liberty' and 'when it was put on the Town-cross, tarred and feathered it'.[95] Newcastle residents' opposition to the war sometimes went beyond symbolic acts of resistance to the government; their indignation at the servility of the Manchester address was so intense that some citizens threatened a boycott of goods manufactured at Manchester.[96]

Political divisions over the American crisis in Newcastle were thus deep and abiding. Those who met to petition the crown in October assembled again to celebrate their accomplishments in December.[97] The battle between the burgesses and the corporation which formerly drew its ideological component from Wilkes, now derived its energy from America, and the conflict seemed to be interminable. At the Court of Guild held in October, four burgesses loudly protested against the new mayor's unwillingness to hear their concerns, and they subsequently were charged by the corporation with riotous behavior and misdemeanors; all four had signed the conciliatory petition – Thomas Maude had signed second after George Grieve.[98] Local newspapers published the American papers and parliamentary debates, but the debate over petitioning stimulated additional political essays which examined many facets of the conflict itself, as well as the constitutionality of such popular expressions.[99] A more public and politically sophisticated discussion of the issues surrounding the Revolution would be difficult to imagine.

LIVERPOOL AND THE LANCASHIRE PETITION

Lancashire was deeply riven over the American conflict; the popular political response to petitioning and addressing spread rapidly throughout the county and was unusually rancorous. The county was nearly as divided as Hampshire, with contrasting petitions and addresses from Bolton and addresses from Liverpool, Manchester, Blackburn, Wigan, and Lancaster. On 11 September 1775, the corporation of Liverpool was one of the first to address his Majesty on behalf of coercive measures, 'expressing our Abhorrence and Detestation of all traitorous and rebellious Disturbers of your Majesty's Peace and Government'. The Liverpool inhabitants' address that collected nearly 500 signatures later in September was equally strongly worded. Alluding to 'the present

---

    Nov. 1775).
95 *Morn. Chron.* (3 Nov. 1775).
96 On the frequent criticism of Manchester, *New. Chron.* (16, 23, 30, Sept.; 7 Oct. 1775); *Lond. Eve.-Post* (7–10 Oct. 1775); *Lond. Chron.* (7–9 Nov. 1775).
97 *New. Chron.* (30 Dec. 1775).
98 Thomas White, Robert Michison, John Hewitson. *New. Chron.* (14 Oct.; 25 Nov. 1775).
99 See for example, the unsigned editorials in *New. Chron.* (2 Sept.; 21 Oct.; 11 Nov.; 9, 16 Dec. 1775); and 'J. W.', 'Juba', 'Humanus', and 'Veteran', *New. Chron.* (23, 30 Sept.; 2, 9, 23, Dec. 1775).

Phrensy of your Colonies', and 'the hand of Parricide lifted up against the Parent Country', the addressers promised to 'exert our best Abilities towards the Crushing every Rebellion, and silencing all Disaffection, that may be harboured in the Breasts of seditious and ill-designing Men, who, under the specious Mask of Liberty, attempt to deceive and seduce the minds of your faithful subjects'.[100] Though Liverpool did not put forth an independent petition for peace, owing in part to the recent violent seamen's strike, resistance to the two Liverpool addresses was expressed immediately in the newspapers;[101] however, it was not until early November, when the county petition emerged, that citizens were able to actually join in the protest. The city addresses and others from the north of England stimulated interest in a county meeting; advertisements directed to the attention of the 'gentlemen, clergy and freeholders of the County Palatine of Lancaster' appeared in the *Manchester Mercury* in late October over the signature of Sir Watts Horton, High Sheriff, and a meeting was set for 9 November.[102]

The gathering at the county hall at Lancaster was led by Lord Stanley, M.P. for the county; the Earls of Derby and Sefton and Messrs. Joddrell and Hornby spoke in favor of coercive measures. The leaders of the opposition were T. Butterworth Bayley, a Dissenter and prominent member of the Society of the Supporters of the Bill of Rights, Col. Richard Townley, and J. Dobson, all of Liverpool, and Abraham Rawlinson, opposition Whig and later M.P. for Lancaster. After speeches from both sides, the address was agreed upon by the majority in the hall, and the leaders of the opposition withdrew to a nearby public house where a petition was set forth.[103] The opposition Lords' Protest against the Address to the crown by both Houses of Parliament, signed by nineteen Lords, was published in some newspapers as a companion document along with the petition.[104] The address and petition were then circulated throughout the country; the petition was signed first at Liverpool, then Manchester, Rochdale, and eventually in London. The provincial newspapers published notices concerning where the documents might be signed; at Manchester, for example, the petition rested at Fletcher's Tavern until Saturday 25

100 *Lond. Gaz.* (12–16, 26–30 Sept. 1775).
101 *Lond. Eve-Post* (5–7 Oct. 1775). For contemporary details on the riots in Liverpool, see *Kent. Gaz.* (6–9 Sept. 1775). R. B. Rose, 'The Liverpool Sailors' Strike of 1775', *Proceedings of the Lancashire and Cheshire Antiquarian Society*, 68 (1958), 85.
102 *Man. Merc.* (24, 31 Oct. 1775).
103 Reports of the 9 November county meeting ranged from neutral, to pro-American, to pro-government. For the former see MS q 942. 73001 H 7, Samuel Hibbert Ware Miscellany; *Cumb. Pacq.* (16 Nov. 1775); *Lond. Chron.* (16–18 Nov. 1775); for the second, *Pub. Adv.* (18 Nov. 1775); *Lond. Eve-Post* (14–16 Nov. 1775); *Morn. Chron.* (22 Dec. 1775); for the last, *Gen. Eve.-Post* (12–14, 26–8 Dec. 1775); *Morn. Chron.* (29 Dec. 1775).
104 MS q 942. 73001 H 7. The Lord's protest says, in part, 'When we consider these things, we cannot look upon our fellow-subjects in America in any other light than that of freemen driven to acts of resistance by acts of oppression and violence'.

November and the address lay at Crompton's Coffee House.[105] The address ultimately collected over 6,000 signatures and the petition about 4,000; of the latter, it is possible to isolate 292 signatures in support of peace from Liverpool.[106] But unlike Bristol, Newcastle, and Coventry, where one finds a high degree of correspondence between radical leaders in 1769 and 1775, despite the activity of Bayley, no such correspondence in leadership is found at Liverpool. A comparison of the Middlesex election petition with the county petition for peace, reveals virtually no continuity among the signers.

The political nature of the debate in Liverpool and the radical quality of the pro-American position are revealed in a published letter from Liverpool dated 13 November.

Party matters at present run very high here. A county petition and address are both now handing about; the two parties belonging to which are extremely inveterate against each other. In consequence of these heats, there was the greatest confusion at the county meeting, held at the county hall at Lancaster, on Thursday the 9th of the present month.

Another account said, 'The county in general is all in a Ferment', and yet a third referred to the county as 'divided and distracted'.[107] A lively debate was carried on in both the provincial press and the London newspapers lasting until the end of December. The *Manchester Mercury* published accounts from both sides, including a lengthy defense by Richard Townley denying the charges that signers of the petition were 'rebels to their King and Country'. It seemed necessary to Townley and other supporters of the petition to depict the county meeting as 'the most *Tory* proceeding that ever was proposed', because they themselves had been branded by government defenders as 'factious demagogues', leaders 'who now call upon you [the people] to affront his Majesty and both Houses of Parliament; who call upon you to abet the foulest treason, and the most unnatural rebellion'.[108] Contemporary observers were thus keenly aware of local political divisions in England, and it is scarcely an exag-

---

105 *Man. Merc.* (14, 21 Nov. 1775). Advertisements for signing the Lancashire conciliatory petition in London appeared in *Pub. Adv.* (9, 13, 14, 15 Dec. 1775).

106 The Liverpool coercive address was published in *Lond. Gaz.* (26–30 Sept. 1775); the conciliatory county petition is in the PRO, HO 55/9/3. The Liverpool signatures are found on the first three skins of parchment; of the 292 Liverpool signatures, 13 are totally obscured. The county address and petition were two of the latest to be presented to his Majesty, the former by Sir Watts Horton, Lord Stanley, and Sir Thomas Egerton; the latter by Lord George Cavendish and Sir Michael le Fleming; *Man. Merc.* (12 Dec. 1775); *Lond. Chron.* (16–19 Dec. 1775); *Lond. Eve-Post* (16–19 Dec. 1775). For the Liverpool Wilkes' petition, see HO 55/4/3. Liverpool, Coventry, and Bristol divided over the Middlesex election affair, but Newcastle did not.

107 *Lond. Chron.* (16–18 Nov. 1775); *York Cour.* (21 Nov. 1775); *Morn. Chron.* (22 Dec. 1775); see *Pub. Adv.* (22 Nov. 1775) for further references to two 'parties', understood, of course, in the loose sense of political groupings.

108 *Man. Merc.* (14, 21 Nov. 1775); *Morn. Chron.* (22 Dec. 1775); *Gen. Eve. Post* (12–14 Dec. 1775). *Gen. Eve. Post* (26–8 Dec. 1775) refers to the 'insidious method [of petitioning] to gain such a barbarous and inhuman enjoyment' as the downfall of their leaders.

geration to say that they were as concerned about local expressions of due respect for authority on the one hand, and oppression by unjust authority on the other, as they were about affairs in America. In a speech in the House of Commons rebutting Lord Stanley, Temple Luttrell denied that the 'sense of society' at large on the colonial issue was to be decided by the addresses; it is not, he said, 'to be ascertained by the cry of a few Tory Justices, ductile Magistrates, huddled together by their creator, the Lord Lieutenant of the county, to approve of proscriptions and proclamations, devised in councils where he himself takes the head as President'.[109] The Lancashire petition was described by one government supporter in a way that betrayed the author's true concerns: 'though mild in its Pretentions, [it] is nevertheless calculated to Fan the Flames of Sedition, and keep alive that restless Spirit of Opposition, so destructive to Society, and serving only the Purpose of Faction and Discontent'.[110] The political issues surrounding both real and potential divisions in English society were far more prominent in Lancashire than the question of commerce, which was raised on only a few occasions.[111] Clearly the conflict had broadened beyond the simple question of the desirability of peace; the call for conciliatory measures was seen by local government supporters as tantamount to treason, while the recommendation for coercive measures was viewed by many as an invitation to the sway of arbitrary power.

Not unexpectedly, participants in the Lancashire debate over America appealed to historical precedents and examples. One signer of the address depicted his colleagues as 'free from every Idea of Slavery, and untainted with the Varnish of OLIVERIAN HYPOCRISY'. Comparisons were drawn with the Puritan Revolution where 'under the Sanction of Religion' the foundations of Church and State were sapped and the nation subjected to the 'tyrannical Usurpation of lawless Depredation'. Now, 'Similar Causes will always produce similar Effects; and it is only common prudence to suspect the Intentions of those licentious Sons of Liberty'.[112] The appeal to history was closely

---

109 Quoted in *Lond. Eve-Post* (31 Oct.–2 Nov. 1775). Luttrell claimed that on the basis of 'the intelligence I have been able to procure from a multitude of persons widely different in station and description, as by my own remarks in the congress of many a journey through the interior of this island during the summer season, that the sense of the mass of the people is in favor of the Americans'. Repeatedly it was denied that Lord Stanley was correct concerning the majority in Lancashire who supported coercion. *Pub. Adv.* (18, 22 Nov., 31 Oct. 1775).

110 *Pub. Adv.* (22 Nov. 1775).

111 For further fears of social upheaval see *Lond. Eve-Post* (31 Oct.–2 Nov. 1775) where Luttrell finds 'a radical decay of the constitution' and the kingdom 'shaken to its foundations', and *Gen. Eve. Post* (26–8 Dec. 1775) where there are fearful references in Lancashire to 'the original rights of mankind, independent of constitution and human laws'; and *Pub. Adv.* (28 Nov. 1775) where 'Violence, Folly, and Oppression' have shaken 'the most precious Jewel from the Crown of England'. Only two brief allusions to the economic stagnation of Liverpool were found in the newspapers. *Lond. Eve-Post* (5–7 Oct.; 9–12 Dec. 1775).

112 *Pub. Adv.* (22 Nov. 1775). In the same paper, 'A Protestant' compared the American

associated with a religious explanation of the social divisions. Referring to the county 'Addressers for Blood', a 'Lancashire Freeholder' charged that 'the Author of those christian-like Exhortations to Civil War and Blood, is – a Clergyman'. The 'Right Reverend Pastors' are depicted as 'almost unanimously voting and addressing' for the blood of the Americans. Conversely, it was widely believed that the Nonconformists, particularly the Quakers and Presbyterians, were active in promoting the petition for peace.[113]

THE HIGH CHURCH AND LOCAL POLITICS IN COVENTRY

The number and influence of Nonconformists in Coventry so impressed an anonymous observer in 1702 that he wrote: 'The majority of the heads of the corporation and the magistrates are now in ye sober men [i.e., the Dissenters], so it's esteemed a fanatick Town, and there is indeed ye largest Chapple, and ye greatest number of people, I have ever seen of ye Presbyterian way.'[114] In the early century the Dissenters had numerous aldermen and their presence on the corporation seems to have continued throughout the eighteenth century.[115] The franchise was in the freemen, and politics were conducted on a corporation, anti-corporation basis, but with a crucial difference; the corporation encouraged the Dissenters' involvement in municipal politics and excluded High Anglicans. Elections were so riotous and expensive that the country gentlemen avoided the borough. Because of the fragmentary nature of the registers, the number of Dissenting freemen cannot be determined, but they were an important force on the corporation; as a result, the Coventry corporation was a Whig island in the midst of a Tory sea. Under both Walpole and the Pelhams the corporation candidates generally supported the administration, and the Tory members consistently voted with the opposition.[116] It could, of course, be argued that boroughs like Coventry and Nottingham (discussed below) prove that the real structural issues were simply office holding, or political power and status, since the Anglicans who were out of office behaved exactly like excluded Nonconformists in other boroughs. But such an explanation would be forced to ignore an important body of evidence.

---

crisis to the '45', for the purpose of focusing on popery and arbitrary power.

113 *Pub. Adv.* (22 Nov. 1775); *Gen. Eve.-Post* (12–14, 26–8 Dec. 1775).

114 Quoted in T. W. Whitley, *The Parliamentary Representation of the City of Coventry* (Coventry, 1894), p. 117. The population is estimated at about 12,000 in 1754, so the Dissenters comprised about 9% of the whole. *Commons, 1754–1790*, 1: 400; *Commons, 1754–1790*, 1: 339.

115 For a full discussion of Dissenters holding office at Coventry, see chap. 2. Whitley, *The Parliamentary Representation of Coventry*, pp. 71, 140. *Commons, 1754–1790*, 1: 339. Michael Watts, *The Dissenters* (Oxford, 1977), p. 483. Irene Morris, *Three Hundred Years of Baptist Life in Coventry* (London, 1925), p. 26; John Sibree and M. Caston, *Independency in Warwickshire* (London, 1855), pp. 57, 62.

116 *Commons, 1754–1790*, 1: 340; 2: 82, 88–9, 290, 316.

From 1747 through 1761 the seats continued to be contested by the corporation and anti-corporation parties, and in this period each party ended up with one seat. Then, in 1761, a crucial realignment began to take shape. The corporation put up James Hewitt and Andrew Archer and with Dissenting support they won handily against the anti-corporation party's candidate. When they reached Westminster, the corporation's M.P.s voted against the government. Hewitt went into opposition over the Wilkes affair and became a frequent opposition speaker. Archer followed Newcastle and voted with the opposition on general warrants.[117] It cannot be proven that Hewitt and Archer voted as they did because the Dissenters at Coventry wished them to, but the ensuing elections and political wrangles prove that the Dissenters' loyalty to the Hanoverians had definitely shifted following 1761. This shift can be seen at the by-election of 1768. For the first time in the eighteenth century, government money was used against the corporation candidates, and it was apparently because Hewitt and Archer had been so troublesome.[118] The religious dimensions of this election are made obvious by the handbills issued by the anti-corporation party, declaring: 'No Corporation Slavery! No Nash!! No Two Thousand Pound Bargains!!! High Church – Glyn and Liberty! Now or Never!'[119] The cry for the High Church was in opposition to the Low Church and Dissent, and 'Glyn and Liberty' was obviously an answer to the corporation party's standard of 'Wilkes and Liberty', and Glyn won this election. In the next year, the petitioning agitation over the Middlesex election affair divided Coventry, just as it had Bristol. The radicalism of the corporation is graphically portrayed in the signatures of the pro-Wilkes petition of 1769; three aldermen and the future mayor were among the first ten persons to sign this document.[120]

From 1768 through 1774 the 'independent' party at Coventry continued to work for the rights of freemen in opposition to the corporation. Through adverse decisions in the Court of King's Bench, the corporation's power began to wane, and in the general election of 1774 it proposed only one candidate, Thomas Green, and he was badly beaten.[121] For the first time in nearly sixty years, the anti-corporation interest returned both Members. In this election there is no evidence that the anti-corporation candidates, Waring and Yeo, had government money backing them, but the government candidates definitely did in 1780.[122]

117 *Ibid.*, 1:79, 114–15; 2: 26, 559.
118 Whitley, *The Parliamentary Representation of Coventry*, p. 163. *Commons, 1754–1790*, 1: 401; 2: 505–6.
119 Whitley, *The Parliamentary Representation of Coventry*, p. 167.
120 HO 55/3/4.
121 *Commons, 1754–1790*, 1: 401; 3: 607; Whitley, *The Parliamentary Representation of Coventry*, pp. 169, 172.
122 *The Poll* (Coventry, 1774), p. 1.

348   *Religion, Revolution, and English Radicalism*

The coercive and conciliatory petitions at Coventry arose in the context of the first major defeat of the corporation party in the century. Never before had it lost both seats to the anti-corporation party, and while the eclipse of the corporation lasted only a decade, it was undoubtedly deeply resented. The circulation of the address and petition at Coventry thus reflected the party conflict that was already present, but it also contributed to it. Following notification of a meeting by the distribution of thousands of handbills, a numerous group of inhabitants assembled on 22 September and agreed to an address.[123] Just as in parliamentary politics at Coventry, religion was a prominent part of the American conflict. A certain unnamed Anglican clergyman drafted the address and his hand may be seen in the appeal the document makes to the king to support 'our admirable Constitution, both in Church and State'. Moreover, the cry 'the church in danger' was raised in the meeting and the High-Anglican tenor of the group is further discernible in the language of the address, which refers to those 'pernicious Principles, which the Patrons of Sedition have been industriously insinuating into the Minds of your Majesty's deluded subjects', its hopes to avoid 'partaking in their iniquity', and its promise to renounce 'all Fellowship with the Men of this Complexion'. It collected 159 signatures and was presented to the king by the two sitting members, Yeo and Waring.[124] The public meeting to petition the crown was held two weeks later at the King's Head in Coventry with Thomas Green, the former opposition candidate, elected to the chair (10 October 1775). The order of business followed the usual pattern, and since Lord Archer and Lord Craven were present, they signed the document first; it ultimately collected 406 signatures.[125] As at Bristol and Newcastle, the leadership of the conciliatory movement came from former Wilkites, in this case the pro-Wilkes corporation, and the Dissenting elite. Of the first ten names on the Wilkes' petition of 1769, five were among the first to sign the conciliatory petition.[126] After the names of Craven and Archer, those of the mayor, James Soden, the Steward of the Court, Thomas Green, and four aldermen immediately follow. Four names below the alder-

123 In Parliament, Lord Craven criticized the method of obtaining this address, charging that it was 'smuggled' up to the Court, *Parl. Hist.* 18: 719–20; he was rebutted by 'Peeping Tom', *Morn. Chron.* (14 Nov. 1775).
124 Accounts in *Lond. Eve.-Post* (7–10 Oct. 1775); *Morn. Chron.* (27 Sept. 1775); *Gen. Eve. Post* (26–8 Sept. 1775). The four clerics who signed were Joseph Rann, vicar of St. Trinity, James Eyre, John Priest, and F. Blick. The document is printed with signatures in *Lond. Gaz.* (26–30 Sept. 1775). An essay in *Morn. Chron.* (27 Sept. 1775) noted not one alderman signed it. On the clerical inspiration, see *Lond. Eve.-Post* (17–19 Oct. 1775).
125 Accounts in *Morn. Chron.* (19 Oct. 1775); *Lond. Eve.-Post* (19–21 Oct. 1775); *Gen. Eve. Post* (17–19 Oct. 1775). Green was, according to the hostile account in the *Morn. Chron.* 'a great man in the corporation'. Printed in *Lond. Eve.-Post* (19–21, 21–4 Oct. 1775). It was presented by Lord Craven when the Duke of Portland was at Court.
126 HO 55/3/4. John Clark, James Soden, Thomas Green, John Minster, and Thomas Collett.

men, one finds Posthumous Lloyd and Jacob Dalton, both Dissenting ministers. Here, as elsewhere, the petition and address stirred up considerable debate in the press, and as elsewhere, the issue was of more than passing importance.[127] A year later a second coercive address from the freemen and inhabitants was sent to the king expressing their 'Horror of a Distant Rebellion ... heightened by the unparalleled outrages of a Domestic Insurrection'.[128] By October 1776, eighteen names that had appeared on the conciliatory petition of October 1775 were now enlisted on the side of coercion, but this represents only 4.4 percent of the original petitioners, and it thereby reflects very little erosion of political conviction on the part of Coventry pro-Americans.

In 1780 the independent anti-corporation party's candidates were supporters of North, while the corporation put up Sir Thomas Hallifax and Thomas Rogers, a Presbyterian; both were oppositionists. Hallifax and Rogers won (against a considerable amount of government money), but were unseated by the House of Commons on petition. It would not have been difficult for the corporation party to believe that the central government was seeking to deprive them of their liberty, and these were exactly the terms in which the borough historian construed the struggle.[129] But the religious dimensions of the conflict have not been adequately underlined by past analyses. Since Rogers was only in Parliament for three months, his religion had more importance in the local than in the national setting and religion seems to have added to the intensity of party feeling.[130] He and his backers on the corporation and among the freemen gave added intensity to the party rivalry in Coventry. In the aftermath of the 1780 election, the anti-corporation Blues still identified the corporation Yellows with the issues of a century past. Grasping for threads of continuity with the past, they rhetorically stabbed at their opponents with the words, 'Though they may have forgot the thing,/ Who was it murder'd Charles our King?'[131]

NONCONFORMITY AND LOCAL POLITICS IN COLCHESTER, TAUNTON, AND NOTTINGHAM

The popular uproar over the Middlesex election affair did not lead to petitions at Colchester, Taunton or Nottingham, but local political issues that centered around corporation and anti-corporation factions did divide these boroughs. This pattern of local political conflict prepared the ground for the

---

127 *Morn. Chron.* (27 Sept.; 19 Oct.; 14 Nov. 1775); *Lond. Eve.-Post* (7–10, 17–19 Oct. 1775).
128 HO 55/11/65; presented 19 October 1776, signed by 239.
129 See Whitley, *The Parliamentary Representation of Coventry*, p. 163. It was not, according to Whitley, the Coventry Whigs who had changed, but the king and his 'Tory' friends. See also pp. 171, 175–7, and *Commons, 1754–1790*, 1: 402; 2: 567; 3: 673.
130 No record is left of his having voted or spoken in Parliament. The same applies to the brief tenure of Hallifax. *Commons, 1754–1790*, 2: 567; 3: 371. Neither is there any indication of how Rogers came to Coventry.
131 Whitley, *The Parliamentary Representation of Coventry*, p. 188.

divisions that opened afresh in the mid-1770s; each borough sent conflicting popular appeals to the crown concerning America. Little evidence of a radical tradition survives at Colchester; the borough was not deeply stirred over the Middlesex election affair, and the movement for independence seems never to have been successfully linked to radical ideology, though a previous chapter has shown how it was connected to the American crisis. However, social divisions in the town were widening in the 1750s through the 1770s, typified by the increasing wealth of the large clothiers and the development of the professions on the one hand, and decline in the cloth making industry resulting in pressure on smaller clothworkers on the other.[132] While the colonial issue divided Colchester, the language of the conflicting documents is mild by comparison to other boroughs, and differences over the question of coercion stimulated little popular literature on either side. The conciliatory petition does not contain any reference to the constitutional issue but merely pleads for the adoption and pursuit of conciliatory measures. Similarly, the rhetoric of the address is unexceptional, simply resolving 'on every occasion to pay a due obedience to the Legislative Authority, and defend your Majesty's Person and Government, to the utmost of our power'. The attempt to secure an address in support of the administration was underway at Colchester by the second week in October and seems to have arisen independently of any centralized government leadership.[133] The address derived its main support from the corporation; the mayor, Thomas Clamtree, the recorder, and the deputy recorder head the list followed by the alderman, assistants, and common council, although the clergy, as at Bristol, Newcastle, and Coventry, were equally prominent, with nine signatures.[134] The conciliatory petition was the only borough petition indicating that it drew support from the nearby towns. The petition itself notes that it originated from the gentlemen, free burgesses, and inhabitants of the borough of Colchester 'and places adjacent'.[135] It finally gained 509 signatures compared to the address with 125.

The leadership of the Dissenters in the petitioning movement at Colchester cannot be proven, but all the evidence points in one direction: the first signature on the first skin of parchment is that of Daniel Rudkin, deacon in the Lion Walk Congregational chapel, and heading the second column on the first skin is the name of Thomas Bingham, Congregational pastor of Dedham, followed by Isaac Diss, secretary of the Essex Congregational Union.[136] Given the high

132 On the Tory Charter Club in Colchester that did espouse radical Tory ideas, see Linda Colley, 'Eighteenth Century English Radicalism', 7; on the cloth industry, see Arthur F. J. Brown, *Colchester in the 18th Century* (Colchester, 1969), pp. 18–19, 28–9.
133 *Lond. Eve.-Post* (14–17 Oct. 1775); notice from Colchester, dated 14 Oct. 'Such bloody addresses', said the correspondent, 'deserve to be burnt by the common hangman'.
134 Printed in *Lond. Gaz.* (7–11 Nov. 1775); HO 55/12/4; Brown, *Colchester*, pp. 27–8 on the closed, conservative orientation of the corporation.
135 Printed in *Camb. Chron.* (3 Feb. 1776); HO 55/9/4.
136 On the Congregational Union, see E. A. Blaxill, *History of Lion Walk Congregational*

proportion of Congregational signatures from the county, it seems likely that Diss himself circulated the petition among the Congregational chapels in the surrounding villages: eighty Congregationalists from Bocking and Braintree, Coggeshall, Dedham, Rochford, and Witham signed the conciliatory petition, while only fifteen non-resident Dissenters can be identified as having voted in the five elections of 1768–84.[137] The large number of Anglican clergymen who signed the address may have contributed to provoking this response. In any case, the Dissenting ministers who were uninvolved in parliamentary politics, came out in force in popular politics; altogether six Dissenting ministers signed the petition, including John Barrett of Witham and Thomas Davidson at Bocking.[138] The high level of involvement among non-voters suggests just how important a form of popular political expression petitioning had become to many English citizens. The circulation of the petition in the countryside took some time; it was one of the last conciliatory petitions George III received, not reaching Whitehall until 29 January 1776.

At Taunton the Dissenting academy contributed to the vitality of Nonconformity, and the Dissenters' dominance of the woolen industry guaranteed their importance in the community. Caroline Robbins noted the prominence at the academy in the eighteenth century of the leading rational Dissenters, Henry Grove, Thomas Amory, and Matthew Warren, and commented that 'Taunton under three generations of such men, was one of the centers of commonwealth ideas in Western England'. Joshua Toulmin's chapel in Mary Street was a Unitarian Baptist meeting from which the Presbyterians of Tancred Street had seceded in the early eighteenth century. The Independents met at Paul's Meeting and there was also a small Quaker assembly in the borough.[139] Writing in 1769, Tobias Smollett was still impressed with the 'Puritanism' of the town. The franchise was in the inhabitant householders, and the Dissenters commanded a large part of the electorate. The borough remained open and elections were conducted on party lines; they were frequent and sometimes violent.[140]

Church, Colchester, 1642–1937 (1938), pp. 21, 61; and RG 4/1508; 1509; 2163.

137 Dedham is five miles north of Colchester and in the 1770s a number of inhabitants at Colchester had their children baptized in the Dedham Congregational Church, so there was known intercommunion between these churches. See RG 4/1511. Witham is about fourteen miles distant and Braintree about sixteen. The largest number of lay signatures outside of Colchester came from Coggeshall, about seven miles distant. Phillips found only 12.4% of the petitioners were enfranchised, yet many of the petitioners were not residents of Colchester. Phillips, 'Popular Politics in Unreformed England', 611.

138 In addition to Bingham, Barrett, and Davidson, Giles Hobbes of Lion Walk, and Thomas Stanton of Eldlane Baptist chapel. See Blaxill, *History of Lion Walk*, pp. 19, 23, 24 and RG 4/2907; 1510.

139 Robbins, *The Eighteenth-Century Commonwealthman* (New York, 1968), p. 251; Jerom Murch, *A History of the Presbyterian and General Baptist Churches in the West of England* (London, 1935), pp. 191, 194–5.

140 On Smollett see George H. Kite and H. P. Palmer, *Taunton: Its History and Market*

Political life at Taunton was characterized by rivalry between an Anglican-dominated corporation, often in alliance with neighboring country gentlemen, and an independent party comprised of Dissenters and Low-Church Anglicans. In the first half of the century the independent party with its nucleus of Dissenters worked in tandem with the government and repeatedly returned Whig candidates against Tory opposition.[141] The Dissenters and the government in 1754 were pitted against the gentry in a contest that cost the Administration £7,675 to secure a Whig victory. In this notoriously corrupt election the Dissenters worked assiduously to keep the borough from falling under Tory domination. Fifty-one leading Taunton Dissenters signed an address swearing to give their support to the candidate nominated by the government. They were clearly an important interest group in their own right and yet dependent on government money to maintain their influence. The Dissenters won the election, but the rioting that ensued was said to have contributed to the loss of several lives and the subsequent decline in the woolen industry.[142]

In the second half of the century the political interests were well described by one of the participants in Taunton politics, John Halliday; the principal manufacturers of Taunton, said Halliday, were all Dissenters and 'much at enmity with the corporation'. Since the corporation refused to admit any Dissenters into local government, opposition to the corporation's parliamentary candidate was most likely to arise from the Dissenters.[143] After the disruption of 1754, Taunton was uncontested for twenty years, but in this period a crucial realignment began to develop. In the late 1760s, the Dissenters moved out of the ambit of government influence, just at the moment that the corporation was being led increasingly under government control.[144] In 1774 Lord North became the recorder of Taunton, and in this position of influence, he sought

Trust (Taunton, 1926), pp. 5, 8; *Commons, 1754–1790*, 1: 317; *Commons, 1754–1790*, 1: 371. The Dissenters made up as much as two-thirds of the total population of Taunton. The reason more do not appear on the conciliatory petition is due to the fact that not all of the chapels retained registers.

141 Several of these Members were opposition Whigs, but the majority were steadfast supporters of government. One of the two opposition Whigs, Abraham Elton, was himself a Dissenter. In two cases at least, Whig candidates were said by contemporaries to have been returned 'on the dissenting interest': Francis Fane in 1734 and Robert Webb in 1747, *Commons, 1754–1790*, 2: 24; 1: 316; 2: 527.

142 See Namier, *England in the Age of the American Revolution*, p. 110. See also Namier, *The Structure of Politics at the Accession of George III* (London, 1929, 2nd edn 1957), pp. 125, 206; *Commons, 1754–1790*, 1: 372; Joshua Toulmin, *The History of Taunton in the County of Somerset*, (ed.), James Savage (Taunton, 1822), pp. 329, 375. The sum of money is based on the assumption that Maxwell contributed £3,000 and the secret service money was spent in addition, rather than to pay Maxwell back. Kite and Palmer, *Taunton*, p. 22. The list of Taunton Dissenters is in the British Library, Additional Manuscripts, 32736, f. 25, described as 'every substantial Dissenter in Taunton'.

143 *Commons, 1754–1790*, 1: 372.

144 It was Lord Thomond, former friend of the Dissenters, who gained control of the corporation and brought it over to the government side. He had some degree of success in this as early as 1764. *Commons, 1754–1790*, 1: 372.

with the aid of the corporation to bring in two ministerial candidates. In preparation for the general election of 1774, a local committee was formed to insure that the independent interests of Taunton would be represented, and it put forth two candidates against the government, John Halliday and Alexander Popham. Since government money was still available, North's candidates won the election, but in the end they were unseated when the House of Commons determined that the mayor, who was the returning officer, was guilty of bribery. Of the thirteen people who signed the petition to Parliament against the undue election, eight signed the conciliatory petition in 1775, and at least three of these were Dissenters.[145]

The local contest for power thus provides the framework for the petitioning agitation of 1775, but the conflict cannot be reduced to local differences. In fact, the colonial crisis clearly inspired the corporation interest and galvanized its determination to exclude Dissenters. The corporation met in the third week of September, and in common council assembled, agreed to a strongly worded address to the crown.[146] The language is significant: the address assured the king that the blessings of his reign would have continued

if unfortunately there did not exist here, as well as in America, men, who void of all principle are harden'd enough at the expense of every duty they owe your Majesty and their country, to become at once (under the masque of Patriotism) disrespectful to your sacred person, and disturbers of the public peace. Their machinations have driven headlong, the Americans into a rebellion, which cowardice only prevents their joining in.

The address concludes: 'the traitorous attempt to subvert its [i.e. the government's] legislative authority in America will never be submitted to'. In this address the focus of the corporation was almost as much upon the political setting at home as it was on the colonies. Similarly, the strength of the Dissenters' pro-American sentiment can be accounted for best when seen in the context of the traditional Whig-Tory political conflict, combined with the Dissenters' exclusion from the corporation – a corporation no longer in alliance with Tory country gentlemen, but rather with the national government.

In the first week in October two more documents circulated in Taunton; the one, inspired by the corporation, was signed by the mayor and aldermen, and collected 191 signatures; the other, supported by the opposition party, gathered 154 names.[147] The independent committee of 1774 had comprised six men,

---

145 *Commons, 1754–1790*, 1: 372. Eight of the names are supplied by the *Commons Journal*, five by Toulmin. Also on 30 Aug. 1775 the case of Alexander Popham against the mayor, Colonel Roberts, James Poole, and Mr. Sweeting, attorney of Taunton, for bribery came before the Nisi Prius Bar. Roberts and Poole were acquitted, but Sweeting was found guilty and fined £500. Poole and Sweeting had signed the coercive address. See *CJ* 35: 98, (6 Feb. 1775); Toulmin, *The History of Taunton*, p. 337; *Sal. Win. J.* (4 Sept. 1775).

146 Account in *Sal. Win. J.* (16 Oct. 1775); the corporation met on 22 Sept.; the document was presented by John Roberts, HO 55/10/1.

147 On the inhabitants' address (HO 55/10/3) presented on 6 October by J. Cabbell, see

two of whom were Dissenters, and five of these men signed the petition urging conciliation.[148] Moreover, of the fifty-one prominent Dissenters who promised the government their support in 1754, eighteen still survived in 1775 and signed the petition against the government; only one signed the address favoring coercion. These, the most well-to-do manufacturers and tradesmen in the town and thus the most qualified to hold corporate office, were the very ones excluded from participation in local government. From this perspective their opposition to the national government's coercive policy in America is readily understandable. But an important ideological element was present as well; Joshua Toulmin and two other Dissenting ministers supported the conciliatory petition. Commonwealthman ideology, inspired in part by the teachers at the academy at Taunton, may have contributed to the language of the 'Address and Supplication of the Inhabitants, and Principal Manufacturers of the Town of Taunton':

> We conceive that the Act of Navigation which has been recognized by our Fellow subjects in America secures all the Wealth of the Colonies to this Country. We apprehend that Your Majesty's just Prerogative may suffer some infringement by the revenue Laws being made in this Kingdom for the Colonies, which are not represented; because we conceive that Your Majesty alone has the Right of asking Aids from the Colonies; in the same constitutional Manner that Your Majesty receives Supplies from this Kingdom, and from Ireland; and because Your Majesty's sole Power to give the Force of Law to the acts of Provinces is the one principal Bond of Union between them and the whole Empire.[149]

The petitioners of Taunton adopted the arguments – indeed, the very language – of the colonists. The address is all the more remarkable when it is remembered that it appeared eight months before the colonists declared their independence. The Taunton petitioners understood representation as the heart of the issue, and the king was at one and the same time, subject to the Constitution and understood as the titular head of the empire, who in his person served to bind it together.[150]

The corporation of Nottingham was one of only two in the kingdom that sent a petition for conciliation, and the explanation for these pro-American expres-

---

Lond. Gaz. (3–7 Oct. 1775), where both addresses are printed. On the petition, (HO 55/8/3) see *Bath Chron.* (12 Oct. 1775) presented by Alexander Popham, one of their representatives, on 6 October, printed without signatures, in *Lond. Eve.-Post* (7–10 Oct. 1775). Eleven of the names on the original petition are totally obscured and cannot be recovered.

148 Toulmin, *The History of Taunton*, p. 337. The five were Joseph Melhuish, Luke and John Noble, John Clitsom, and Joseph Jeffries; the last two, Dissenters.

149 HO 55/8/3.

150 On the basis of the conciliatory petition at Taunton, it would seem that Bonwick has overstated his case. Dissenters, he says, 'were not little Englanders, nor did they find the exercise of military strength ipso facto repugnant; they were as concerned to promote Britain's commercial prosperity and global power as the most patriotic jingoist'. 'English Dissenters and the American Revolution', in H. C. Allen and Roger Thompson, (ed.), *Contrast and Connection: Bicentennial Essays in Anglo-American History* (Athens, Oh, 1976), p. 105. This is hardly the position of the Taunton petitioners.

sions is not difficult to discover. Although the aldermen were not unanimously in favor of peace, the Dissenters held the majority of corporate offices in 1775, and in addition, they controlled nearly a third of the votes in this large freeman electorate.[151] They were the main support of the Whigs in the first half of the century, but they had traditionally agreed to share one seat with the Tories. At the general election of 1747, however, the corporation stubbornly set itself to bring in two Whig candidates: John Plumptre (the sitting member) and Lord Howe. The leading Tories heartily resented not only this threat to 'their' seat, but also their 'total exclusion from every office in the governing part of this corporation'.[152] Here, as at Coventry, instead of Dissenters attacking a corporation dominated by Anglicans, Tories are found chafing under the influence of a Dissenting stronghold.

In 1747 the Whig candidates, Plumptre and Howe, were faced with an irate and powerful Tory opposition which supported Sir Charles Sedley. Plumptre was in considerable trouble: he had lost the support of an important local patron, and, 'to crown all', Plumptre reported, 'the Dissenters are leaving me apace'. He claimed that the reason was because he had 'at times, got in three or four Whig churchmen' to the governing part of the corporation, otherwise consisting chiefly of Dissenters, 'all brought in by my interest and money'.[153] Plumptre therefore decided to give up without a contest and the balance between Whig and Tory was restored; Sedley, the Tory candidate, and Howe sitting together. The commitment of the Dissenters to the government Whigs, combined with their willingness to discipline their representative when he offended them, is worth emphasizing. Upon Lord Howe's death in 1758 the corporation chose his younger brother, William Howe, later commander-in-chief in the American war. As in 1747, this was without consulting Newcastle and against his wishes, but there was no contest. In 1761 and 1768 John Plumptre, the former M.P.'s son, and Howe were returned unopposed.[154]

In 1774 a group of electors designated in the words of Rockingham as of the 'old Tory stamp' wearied of the Whig dominance, and 'displeased and dissatisfied that they had never been consulted' in the corporation's choice of two candidates, put up Sir Charles Sedley, who had been out of Parliament for twenty years. He was returned, top of the poll, and William Howe, supported by the corporation, came in second.[155] Thus while the corporation was powerful, it still could not control both seats even when it was still returning

---

151 They had 461 votes in an electorate of about 1,500. John Evans, 'List of Dissenting Congregations and Ministers in England and Wales (1715–1729)' MS. 38.4, p. 93. *Commons, 1754–1790*, 1: 301–2; *Commons, 1754–1790*, 1: 355. The interest of the Dissenters should not be thought of as a separate interest from that of the corporation.
152 *Commons, 1754–1790*, 1: 301–2. So said John Plumptre (see 2: 155).
153 *Ibid.*, 1: 302.
154 *Ibid.*, 1: 355.
155 *Ibid.*, 1: 355.

government candidates. In 1775 several burgesses brought suit against the corporation of Nottingham for the purpose of restoring to the burgesses at large the right of choosing six junior common councilmen to the corporation, a right of which they had been deprived since 1722. On 11 November 1775, a verdict was given in the Court of Kings Bench in favor of the burgesses.[156] If the Whig-Tory nomenclature had become obsolete in the country, religious differences made the terms credible in the borough, and this is underscored by the role the Dissenters played in the period of the American Revolution.

In the second week of October an address in favor of coercion circulated in Nottingham. The document abhorred the 'Spirit of Faction and Rebellion' and all the more, since the rebellion was carried on under the 'specious Pretence of Liberty'. 'We feel the necessity your Majesty was under in taking the Part you did in the Crisis of Affairs in America', and, the address continued, 'we offer you every Assistance in our Power'. The corporation was divided down the middle: three of the six aldermen signed this document and the first name on the address was that of the loyalist Dissenting alderman, Cornelius Huthwait.[157] Among the 230 signatures one finds the names of five Anglican clergymen. In response, a meeting of the corporation of Nottingham 'in common council assembled' took place on Friday, October 20 at the Guildhall. A petition 'in behalf of our American Brethren' was unanimously agreed to (Huthwait and the other two aldermen must have been absent), signed by the Town Clerk, and sealed with the corporate seal.[158] This petition warned against those who put forth the coercive address;

Permit us, Sir, to express our dread of the consequences of those addresses, which making a shew of peculiar Loyalty to Your Majesty and of distinguished Zeal for the right of the British Legislature; recommend an unyielding pursuit of Measures, which whether constitutional or not, if we may judge from present appearances, are perhaps as impractical as they are ruinous.

The document concluded with the observation: 'the hand of Force will never answer the wishes of the British Legislature'.

In the following week, a petition from the inhabitants was circulated, and finally obtained 328 signatures. The Dissenters on the corporation and the Dissenting ministers were both leaders in this endeavor. The document itself

---

156 *Leics. Nott. J.* (4 Nov. 1775); *Morn. Chron.* (13 Nov. 1775) *Records of the Borough of Nottingham, Being a series of Extracts From the Archives of the Corporation of Nottingham*, 9 vols. (Nottingham, 1882–1956), 6: x. The information was filed against Cornelius Huthwait, formerly mayor and Dissenter, and others of Nottingham who had allegedly 'managed the business of the town just as they chose'.

157 HO 55/11/27. The other two were Richard Butler and John Carruthers. See *Records of the Borough of Nottingham*, 7: 412. Printed *Lond. Gaz.* (21–4 Oct. 1775), transferred to the Earl of Rochford on 21 October.

158 HO 55/12/1. Accounts in *Lond. Eve.-Post* (24–5 Oct. 1775) and other metropolitan and provincial papers. Both petitions were presented by Lord Howe and Lord Edward Bentinck on 1 November. *Lond. Eve.-Post* (31 Oct.–2 Nov. 1775), both printed, *Morn. Chron.* (3 Nov. 1775).

was drafted by George Walker and the first signatures were those of the mayor and three aldermen who were all members of the High Pavement chapel. The Dissenting control of municipal politics is further seen in the fact that Smith Churchill and Tertius Dale, both signers of this petition, both Dissenters, were the sheriffs of Nottingham in 1776.[159] Altogether, eight Dissenting ministers at Nottingham were also unanimously in support of conciliation.[160] This petition, like many of the others, subtly reflected the local setting from which it emerged, for it gave a little more attention to the conservative trading interests of the town than some of the other petitions. After noting that the purpose of sovereign power is the welfare of the people, the petition continued: 'in this great National question, Sire, we decline the mention of our particular interest, the manufacturers of this late flourishing Town and neighborhood which are deeply affected by the unhappy differences with your American provinces; and will, we more than fear, be attended with irreparable injury to the Merchant and the Artisan'. The petition concluded: 'Victory cannot avert the mischief which it threatens, but returning peace carries no terror with it.'

The Dissenters maintained their stance against the government during the course of the war, and as the situation in America worsened, they became more outspoken in their resistance. On 21 December 1777 Lord Sandwich's agent, Thomas Rawson, wrote him from Nottingham: 'This town is without exception the most disloyal in the kingdom, owing in great measure to the whole corporation (the present mayor excepted) being Dissenters, and of so bitter a sort that they have done and continue to do all in their power to hinder the service by preventing as much as possible the enlistment of soldiers.'[161] After Sir William Howe returned to England in 1778, the erstwhile commander-in-chief voted with the opposition, though this did not satisfy the Nottingham Dissenters. By this date a number of George Walker's sermons against the

159 HO 55/10/18, printed with signatures in *Leics. Nott. J.* (4 Nov. 1775). See RG 4/1588; 137, and *Records of the Borough of Nottingham*, 7: 412. Cornelius Huthwait was the only Dissenting alderman for coercion. On Walker's role in drafting the petition, see *Memoir*, p. lxxxvi in George Walker, *Essays on Various Subjects*, 2 vols. (London, 1809).

160 The Dissenting ministers signing the conciliatory petition were: from High Pavement Presbyterian, George Walker, Peter Emans, Edward Williams, and Samuel Stratham; of Castle Gate Congregational, Richard Plumb and J. T. Alliston; of Friar Lane Baptist, Richard Hopper; and J. Simpson whose affiliation is unknown. See for the list of ministers who petitioned against subscription, 'A View of English Nonconformity in 1773', *CHST* 5 (1911–2), 274.

161 There was a meeting at Nottingham 22 July 1779 for raising voluntary companies to fight the colonists. *Commons, 1754–1790*, 2: 513. The Dissenters may have opposed this meeting as well. Major John Cartwright refused the offer of a lieutenancy under Howe because he would not coerce the Americans, and he was awarded the freedom of the town in July 1776. But later he trained the militia at Nottingham and was ready to defend his country. Cartwright lost the election of 1780, though he stood on a program of parliamentary reform. See Dora Mae Clark, *British Opinion and the American Revolution* (New Haven, 1930), p. 159.

government's policy in America had been published. Finally, in 1780 the Nottingham Dissenters rejected Sir William Howe for his conduct in America and selected Daniel Parker Coke; when Howe learned that he had lost the support of the Dissenters, he declined the poll.[162]

CHARISMATIC LEADERSHIP AND POPULAR POLITICS

Our examination of electoral politics at Newcastle, Liverpool, Hull, and Colchester suggested that the Dissenters failed to take a political position on the American crisis; they appeared, as Horace Walpole once said, to have been bribed, or to have simply desponded from the neglect of the opposition. Even leading historians of radicalism have chronicled a dreary record of the Nonconformists' political quiescence at Bristol, Nottingham, and Taunton.[163] Moreover, Taunton was Namier's leading example of a borough where the Dissenters themselves acquiesced in the system of patronage. But when one looks more closely at popular political radicalism outside the normal channels of political expression, striking illustrations of the Dissenters' independence appear. A recent survey of Fast and Thanksgiving Day sermons found that one in five of these documents espoused sympathy for the American cause,[164] and we can now show that such sermons had a rational counterpart in the behavior of the Dissenting laity.

Three common threads are found in each of the seven local episodes of political agitation over America studied in this chapter. In borough after borough, the American rebellion led people to reflect upon divisions in English society concerning the proper exercise of authority, the rights and liberties of the individual, and social, economic, and religious inequalities. The theme of the harmonious function and right ordering of society at home was nearly as prominent an issue as the rights and rebellion of the colonists abroad. The divisions in England were perceived to be primarily political in nature, not commercial; the questions that dominated people's minds had to do with the exercise of political power, or the threat, as one address put it, of 'domestic insurrection'. Second, the political nature of the debate is clearly illustrated by the constant appeal to historical examples in order to explain contemporary events. Meaning was sought in the parallels that history offered, particularly the Puritan Revolution, the Glorious Revolution, and the Rebellion in 1745; articulate spokesmen on both sides of the debate found their identity in the past. Though it was not often mentioned in the press, historical continuity was also

162 *Commons, 1754–1790*, 1: 355; 2: 233. Christie thinks it is quite 'unprofitable' to try to correlate the votes of Smith and Coke with the views of their electors. See I. R. Christie, *The End of North's Ministry, 1780–1782* (London, 1958), p. 116. This can only be because Coke said no man held the advice of his constituents more cheaply than he.
163 Colin Bonwick, *English Radicals and the American Revolution* (Chapel Hill, 1977), pp. 13, 85.
164 Henry Ippel, 'British Sermons and the American Revolution', *JRH* 12 (1982), 192.

found in the fact that the local leaders of opposition to the government over the Middlesex election affair at Bristol, Newcastle, and Coventry were the same people who took the lead against the government in 1775. Third, the connection with the past was related to the fact that religion was at the heart of political conflict. In each of these boroughs, charismatic Dissenters, whether lay or clerical, took the lead in opposing the government's American policy; where no Dissenting ministers could be found in the parliamentary contests of five boroughs, thirty-two ministers were involved in the petitions from seven boroughs. In every documented case of provincial borough inhabitants sending a petition to the king, the Dissenters were among the principal leaders of the opposition; with the exception of Newcastle, they were the principal leaders. The opposition to the government at Bristol, Newcastle, Taunton, and Nottingham was clearly focused and intensified by the charismatic leadership of Caleb Evans, James Murray, Joshua Toulmin, and George Walker. The stance of the Established Church on the one hand, and the concerns of the Nonconformists on the other, were not added to the debate as merely ancillary matters; in many people's minds, one's religion remained the most telling and predictable guide to one's political behavior. The unified themes of political power, history, and religion that emerge from the petitions of 1775 may now be examined through an analysis of the social and religious background of individual petitioners.

10

The Petitioners of 1775:
Law, Social Status, and Religion

Signed petitions to the throne hold significant promise for the study of popular behavior and radical politics. The popular documents of the Middlesex election affair, the American crisis, and the Fox–North Coalition have recently been used to demonstrate that petitioning reached much deeper into the populace than parliamentary elections. Through a comparison of individual petitioners and voters it is now possible to show that in the eighteenth century, the 'political nation' embraced at least 425,000 people, more than a third greater than previous estimates.[1] The petitions to the crown also show that the American crisis was a highly divisive issue. The English were far less enthusiastic about going to war with the colonies than most historians believed, and the common people were anything but politically apathetic. The American crisis divided more boroughs and counties than either the Middlesex election affair or parliamentary reform, and the petitions for peace suggest that the Revolution may have been one of England's least popular modern wars.[2]

If the American Revolution divided England, and if it was, as the critics of the ministry claimed, a cruel civil war, the basis for this division must be sought in the attitudes of individuals toward authority and how their attitudes in turn were formed by social status and religious affiliation. The background of individual petitioners alone will provide answers to the causes of pro-Americanism. My earlier investigation of Great Yarmouth, Southampton, Cambridge, Bridgwater, and Poole attempted to show that government influence, both national and local, along with economic and religious differences, helped to determine whether people supported the government's policies or pleaded for concessions. The identity of the petitioners in the ten boroughs examined in this chapter will serve to refine previous arguments and modify earlier conclusions.

The previous examination of small boroughs suggested that more attention should be given to the dynamic interplay between the petitioners' attitude

1 John A. Phillips, 'Popular Politics in Unreformed England', *JMH* 52 (1980), 616.
2 James E. Bradley, *Popular Politics and the American Revolution in England; Petitions, The Crown, and Public Opinion* (Macon, Ga., 1986).

360

toward law, their socio-economic rank, and their religion. For example, the overwhelming support corporations gave to the government is related to the question of constituted authority; local office holders seem to have identified their security with the security of the great national corporation sitting at Westminster. But since members of corporations were commonly the most opulent citizens in a community, the pro-government attitude of most corporations is also connected to socio-economic status. It would thus be extremely misleading to examine the addressers' ideological commitment to established sources of authority apart from their material motives. Neither would it be advisable to isolate the role of religion from material interests. We have noted the nearly unanimous support for coercion among Anglican clergy. The clergy themselves formed a corporate entity established by law that in the 1770s stood on the side of order and tradition. A religious counterpart to the community of interest formed between corporations and the House of Commons is found in the connection between the lower clergy in the English provinces, local magistrates, and the bishops in the House of Lords. On the other hand, the Dissenters revelled in their freedom from statutory restrictions, sometimes to the point of rejecting creedal formulations altogether. They defined their very existence in opposition to laws passed by Parliament and it is thus no coincidence that they often formed the nucleus of anti-corporation parties. Predictably, these anti-corporation parties possessed a natural affinity for agitation against the central government.

The individuals who addressed the crown were commonly criticized for being unduly influenced by city corporations on the one hand, or the central government's offer of patronage on the other. Conversely, the petitioners were commonly denigrated for their lower social origins and their association with Nonconformity. Both sides of the debate thereby candidly revealed important assumptions about the workings of eighteenth-century popular political culture; pro-Americans perceived their opponents in terms of social privilege and sinecures, while supporters of the government's American policy feared that social upheaval in the colonies, if left unchecked, might spread to England. It is a question of some importance why corporate bodies responded so uniformly to the American crisis; and, approaching the same question from another perspective, why anyone in eighteenth-century society would view an address from a corporation as oppressive and reprehensible.

CORPORATIONS AND CUSTOM-HOUSES

The single most conspicuous interest group that petitioned the crown in support of coercive measures was the town corporation. In the fall of 1775, at least thirty-three corporate bodies sent addresses to the crown appealing for submission to the supreme legislative authority of Parliament. The expressions of loyalty from the corporations were so overwhelming that Temple Luttrell, in a speech in the House of Commons, felt compelled to say, 'Sir, the sense of the society at large [on the colonial issue] is not to be ascertained by the signature of a score of Provincial corporations, under corrupt ministerial influence.'[3] Many of the addresses for coercion from boroughs that were divided were inspired by corporations, such as those from Newcastle, Colchester, and Southampton. The American rebellion thus elicited a far stronger response in support of the government from aldermen and common councilmen than from country gentlemen. The response is stronger in several ways. First, the contrast with the lack of enthusiasm among landed elements is striking. The only substantial country support came from Lancashire; the number of addressers in favor of coercive measures from Berkshire, Hampshire, Staffordshire, Herefordshire, Devon, and Worcestershire never rose above 380 people and averaged less than 225 signatures each. The petitions from the counties in favor of peace were far more impressive; the petitions from Berkshire, Hampshire, and Staffordshire averaged 1400 signatures each.[4] Moreover, research on pro-American Members of Parliament has shown far greater sympathy for the colonists among representatives from counties. In the Parliament of 1774–80

3 For Luttrell's speech see *Lond. Eve.-Post* (31 Oct.–2 Nov. 1775). The corporations are York, Beverley, Kingston upon Hull, Lancaster, Liverpool, Oxford, Chester, Gloucester, Hereford, Leicester, Exeter, Great Yarmouth, Lichfield, Taunton, Shrewsbury, Bewdley, Winchester, New Windsor, Andover, Christchurch, Leeds, Maidenhead, and South Molton. These twenty-three documents were the products of corporate acts, they were unsigned, and thus explicitly do not represent public opinion. For Beverley and Hull, see *Lond. Gaz.* (30 Sept.–3 Oct.; 10–13 Oct. 1775); for the remainder see HO 55/11/63; 11/2; 8/1; 10/8; 10/6; 11/5; 10/7; 11/3; 11/7; 10/2; 8/9; 10/1; 11/23; 8/23; 8/5; 11/67; 10/9; 11/28; 11/40; 10/14; 10/11. Ten additional addresses from the corporations of mostly small boroughs collected the signatures of some inhabitants and thus may be considered reflective of public opinion to a greater extent: Warwick, Cirencester, Wigan, Plymouth, Barnstaple, Huntingdon, Rye, Arundel, Helston, and Axbridge. See HO 55/9/1; 10/12; 8/34; 10/10; 11/83; 11/54; 10/15; 10/4; 11/37; 11/52; and Table 3.4 in Bradley, *Popular Politics and the American Revolution in England*, for the numbers involved. The prominence of ministerial support from corporations was often noted in the press, *Lond. Eve.-Post* (21–3 Sept. 1775); *New. Chron.* (14 Oct. 1775).

4 The address from Middlesex, while it has numerous signatures, can hardly be considered a county address. HO 55/12/8; 12/2; 21/40; *Lond. Gaz.* (12–16 Dec. 1775); HO 55/11/31; *Lond. Gaz.* (24–8 Oct. 1775); HO 55/12/9; *Lond. Eve.-Post* (23–5 Nov.; 12–14 Dec. 1775). See Bradley, *Popular Politics and the American Revolution in England*, Table 3.3 for the total numbers. The category of 'country gentlemen' requires further research. W. R. Savadge, 'The West Country and the American Mainland Colonies, 1763–1783, with Special Reference to the Merchants of Bristol', Oxford University B. Litt. thesis, 1952, notes that most of the fourteen leaders of the address at Bristol who presented the document to his Majesty were country gentlemen, and 'nearly all' belonged to the local 'Tory' club (p. 488). Champion, too, thought the Bristol addressers were mostly country gentlemen and former Jacobites, Champion to Portland, Portland Papers, 5 Oct. 1775, PWF 2, 718. Paul Langford, 'Old Whigs, Old Tories and the American Revolution', *The Journal of Imperial and Commonwealth History* 8 (1980), 124 has done the most to illume the old Tory connections of the country addressers, but an entire study needs to be done on the country petitioners.

more than half of the eighty county M.P.s were pro-American, a figure which represents nearly one-fourth of all pro-American members.[5] Compared to the response of the city corporations, the verdict of the countryside was only mildly in support of coercion.[6]

Secondly, the most forcefully worded statements of abhorrence of the very thought of rebellion came from city corporations. The corporation of Warwick contended that the colonists aimed at 'a total subversion of all Law and good Government' and addressers wished to express their 'utter abhorrence of the Authors and Abettors of such outrageous and Traitorous proceedings'. The mayor, recorder, aldermen, and inhabitants of Huntingdon swore that 'none of your Majesty's Subjects exceed us in Loyalty to your Sacred Person, or in Abhorrence of the Vile Machinations of those Disturbers of the Public Tranquility, who, by Various Means, have given Encouragement to the deluded Colonists to hope for Success ...'. The corporation of Axbridge, Somerset, expressed its astonishment to the king that: 'a set of Patricides should have risen up among your own people' and found in the colonies 'An Extreme of Wickedness unknown to past Times and Countries'. These corporations were concerned above all with 'seditious principles', and alluded repeatedly to the 'seeds of sedition' sown at home as well as abroad.[7] With the constant refrain of submission to law, the response of corporations to the crown suggests a pervasive concern with respect for properly constituted authority.

In the debate over America, corporations saw their own interests clearly at stake, but more importantly, they elevated local concerns to the level of principle by an appeal to ideology. At Bristol, for example, upon his resignation of the office of mayor, Charles Hotchkin explained his motives for calling the meeting to address the crown in the following terms:

The internal policy here has very little to do with the business of the State, yet whatever may tend to strengthen the hands of authority either supreme or subordinate is surely an object worthy of the attention of the most respectable corporation this day in the kingdom. It was from this consideration, that I wished to see a dutiful, affectionate and loyal address presented to the throne from the magistracy of this opulent and flourishing city, and presumed to call a house for that purpose.[8]

The same connection between local respect for law and concern to encourage national lawmakers is seen at Bewdley. The corporation not only addressed the

5 Mary Kinnear, 'Pro-Americans in the British House of Commons in the 1770s', University of Oregon Ph.D. diss., 1973, p. 71.

6 Popular wisdom on this point, typified by the comments of Dora Mae Clark, *British Public Opinion and the American Revolution* (New Haven, 1930), p. 133, needs to be modified.

7 *Lond. Gaz.* (3–7 Oct.; 28 Nov.–2 Dec. 1775). See also the addresses from the corporations of Lancaster, Leicester, Worcester, and Gloucester. *Lond. Gaz.* (12–16 Sept.; 24–8 Oct. 1775). The only stronger language is found in the addresses from Scotland, an irony which the radicals never tired of repeating.

8 *Brist. J.* (30 Sept. 1775).

crown in favor of coercive measures, it followed this corporate act by electing
Lord North a burgess of the borough, 'in consideration of his great and
meritorious services in his administration of the public affairs of this country'.[9]
The near unanimity among corporation members in favor of coercive measures
at Newcastle, Colchester, Liverpool, Worcester, Great Yarmouth, Southampton, and Taunton, is also impressive. It is not surprising that the American
conflict was a point of contention in the large freeman boroughs where the
rivalry between corporation and anti-corporation parties was endemic, but these
differences cannot be reduced to merely local antagonisms. Entrenched corporation interests were under attack in a number of smaller boroughs at this
same period of time; at Winchester the mayor won a victory over the inhabitants concerning the right of electing freemen, and as a result, it was believed
that 'the Constitutional Club lately called the Independent Goatum Club is
entirely vacated and dispersed'. On the other hand, there was a temporary victory for the independent party at Portsmouth in the fall of 1775 when the mayor
and leading aldermen deferred to popular pressure and thereby 'convinced the
inhabitants they are declared enemies to *monopoly*'.[10]

The opponents of the government's American measures very commonly
linked local oppression with the oppressions of the central government, and
these conflicts were couched in terms of political principle. The Newcastle
radicals envisioned a kind of oppressive chain of command, extending from the
Court of St. James, to the members of Parliament, and finally to the magistrates. In the opinion of Thomas Slack, the editor of the *Newcastle Chronicle*,
mayors, aldermen, and corporations 'are almost always mere tools of ministers, and clogs to public liberty'. The experience of local bullying over the
town moor evidently enhanced some people's awareness of the undue use of
force in the colonies. Newcastle radicals detested the corruption produced by
wealth; in high politics, public liberty was as readily destroyed 'with the
squeeze of a hand as with a point of the dagger', and this observation is
'equally applicable to corporations, and even to private families – where the

9　*Brist. J.* (25 Nov. 1775).
10　At Colchester, Coventry, Liverpool, Nottingham, Worcester, Exeter, Leicester, and
　　Norwich there was constant political conflict between the corporation and anti-
　　corporation parties. *Commons, 1754–1790*, 1: 15; 253. The first five sent both coercive
　　and conciliatory documents, and America was an issue in the last three as well. On
　　Portsmouth and Winchester, see *Hamp. Chron.* (20 Nov.; 9 Dec. 1775). The unanimity
　　of corporations in favor of coercive measures can in some cases be established from the
　　addresses themselves; in others, lists of corporation members were compared to the
　　addresses. For example, the Colchester Assembly Book, 1763–97, compared to HO
　　55/12/4 reveals that eight of ten aldermen, and twelve of eighteen common councilmen
　　signed the address; only four common councilmen signed the petition. The Yarmouth
　　corporation was the preserve of the Prestons, the Palmers, the Costertons, and the
　　Lacons, and these Anglicans excluded all those whose politics ran counter to their own.
　　B. D. Hayes, 'Politics in Norfolk, 1750–1832', Cambridge Ph.D. thesis 1958, pp. 120–2.
　　Five members of these four families signed the address; none signed the petition.

revenues are great, uncontrolable, and centre in a few hands, then the community soon sorts itself into two classes – slaves and tyrants!'[11] In the 1780 Liverpool contest one pamphleteer urged electors to vote against Bamber Gascoyne Jr. because of his close association with the corporation and its abuse of power in serving special local interests and 'Lord N'. 'It is well known that all bodies corporate have an insatiable appetite for this power [and it] wants a check instead of an increase.' After the Worcester corporation sent up an address in favor of coercive measures, an application 'by some respectable citizens' was made to the mayor for the use of the town hall, 'that the citizens might deliberate on a dutiful and respectful Petition to the Throne'. The mayor of Worcester refused this application, and at the meeting of petitioners at Tom's Coffee House which followed, it was resolved 'That the Mayor of this city, in having refused to the Citizens the use of their Town Hall, for the purpose of deliberating on a dutiful Petition to the Throne, has, by such refusal, deprived the Citizens of their just rights'. The injustice of the mayor's action, and the address of the corporation, which was said by the petitioners to be 'smuggled' up to the crown as a 'delusive' misrepresentation, were tied in the popular mind to the central government's producing the 'present unhappy disturbances in America'. The corporation of York was divided on the question of the use of force, and when an attempt to address the crown was defeated, one observer rejoiced that the city would send no address 'against the distressed colonists, whatever other deluded, unthinking, chains-forging corporations may be induced to do'.[12]

North was the recorder of the borough of Taunton, and when the anti-corporation party won a victory in 1775 over the corporation party's candidates in a contested election return, Joshua Toulmin noted that 'this determination gave great satisfaction to the country as well as to that part of the town, who had asserted their own privileges against the combined influence of the minister and the corporation'. Himself a signer of the petition for peace in 1775, Toulmin later wrote, 'Corporate bodies have not, in general, proved themselves the most exact and faithful trustees', and with the corporation of Taunton and Parliament in view, he concluded,

The evils arising from a body of men being separated from the community, united by an independent interest or divided by mutual jealousies, the abuse of power connected with such

11 *New. Chron.* (10 Oct. 1775); *The Contest* (Newcastle upon Tyne, 1774), p. 8. See also *New. Chron.* (9, 23 Dec. 1775) and *Freeman's Magazine* (Newcastle, 1774), pp. 42–3, 45.

12 *A Collection of Papers, Addresses, Songs, &c. printed on All Sides, During the Contest for Representatives in Parliament for the Borough of Liverpool* (Liverpool, 1780), p. 25; *Worcs. J.* (26 Oct. 1775). Full account of Worcester in *Lond. Eve.-Post* (9–11 Nov. 1775); *Morn. Chron.* (30 Oct. 1775). On York, see *Lond. Eve.-Post* (12–14 Sept. 1775) and for a similar attitude at York, reported in *Morn. Chron.* (15 Sept. 1775). This conflict at York continued; see 'Reasons Why No Member of the Corporation of York Should Join in the Addresses', (in the aftermath of the Gordon riots). *York Cour.* (1 Aug. 1780).

constitutions, and the advantages which a corrupt minister may derive from their influence, have been, in many instances too visible to escape the observation of the most careless.[13]

Just as local vested interests associated their values with Parliament and the crown, local opponents to these interests at Newcastle, Liverpool, Worcester, York, and Taunton were concerned not only with their own rights, but also the rights of their fellow citizens across the sea. A significant body of people who were excluded from the inner circles of power clearly resented their exclusion and felt alienated, but they expressed their concerns in political terms revolving around questions of right, trust, independence, and liberty.

These attacks on ministerial influence on corporations arose mostly from those boroughs where the corporation was largely united; not all corporations, however, were of one mind on the issue of America. The corporations of Cambridge, Portsmouth, Bridgwater, and apparently Poole, were divided over the use of coercion, and on each of these corporations some Dissenters held local office.[14] The same is true at Bristol, Coventry, and Nottingham. The presence of Dissenters on the corporation of Bristol is well attested. Three aldermen, two sheriffs elect, the mayor elect, and eight common councilmen signed the conciliatory petition, whereas the current mayor and sheriffs together with twelve councilmen signed the coercive address. While only three of the conciliatory office holders can be identified as Dissenters, the connection between the traditional Whig politics of the corporation and its openness to Nonconformity is beyond dispute.[15] Similarly at Coventry, at least a few Dissenters sat on the corporation throughout the eighteenth century. Five of the borough's aldermen signed the petition for conciliation, one of whom can be identified as a Dissenter, while none signed the coercive address.[16] Despite the corporation party's resentment over having lost the 1774 election, it cannot be argued that the Dissenters at Coventry came to the defense of the American

13 Joshua Toulmin, *The History of the Town of Taunton, in the County of Somerset* (Taunton, 1791), pp. 90, 64–5. For similar resentment at Nottingham, see *Leics. Nott. J.* (8 Nov. 1775); at Yarmouth, *Lond. Chron.* (5–7 Oct. 1775); but for a conflicting account *Morn. Chron.* (3 Oct. 1775).

14 On Cambridge, see HO 55/10/16, and *Camb. Chron.* (9 Dec. 1775) and James Bradley, 'Religion and Reform at the Polls: Nonconformity in Cambridge Politics, 1774–1784', *JBS* 23 (Spring 1984), 55–78; on Portsmouth, *Commons, 1754–1790*, 1: 298; on Bridgwater, HO 55/11/34. (Besides Nottingham, Bridgwater produced the only petition for peace from a corporation.) On Poole, W. Densham and J. Ogle, *The Story of the Congregational Churches of Dorset from their Foundation to the Present Time* (Bournemouth, 1899), pp. 191, 195 and HO 55/8/2; *Lond. Eve.-Post* (21–4 Oct. 1775).

15 On William Barnes and Thomas Deane, aldermen, and John Noble, sheriff elect, the Dissenters who signed the conciliatory petition, see RG 4/1830; 2497, 3507. The councilmen were located by comparing the petition to Alfred B. Beaven, comp., *Bristol Lists: Municipal and Miscellaneous* (Bristol, 1899).

16 John Clark is noted in the register as an alderman, RG 4/3315. See chap. 2 above on office holding in Coventry. The five aldermen who signed the petition are John Clark, John Minister, Thomas Collett, Thomas Daken, and Joseph Craner. See *Lond. Eve.-Post* (21–4 Oct. 1775) and *The Poll* (Coventry, 1774); one alderman signed the second coercive address in the fall of 1776: John Hewitt, HO 55/11/6.

colonists because of a history of repression, as might be argued for Newcastle or Taunton. On the contrary, the Dissenters shared freely in the Whig monopoly of power, and one might even have expected the corporation party to have remained faithful to the government. At Nottingham the alliance between Dissent and progressive politics was even firmer. Three aldermen and the mayor of Nottingham signed the conciliatory petition, and in addition, the two sheriffs for 1776 also signed. All six of these leaders were Nonconformists, and eight of the nine common councilmen who signed were also Dissenters. The three remaining aldermen signed the coercive address, of whom one was a Dissenter, but none of the remaining common councilors signed the address.[17] Not all Dissenters were able to transcend the lure of places and gifts, but many did maintain their ideological commitments in spite of such benefits; in these boroughs Dissenters were not excluded from corporate office and yet they strongly supported conciliation. In fact, in every known case where a corporation divided over America, a complement of Dissenters sat on the corporation.

The corporations of Coventry and Nottingham were thoroughly divided on the issue of using force against the colonists. But even more importantly, in both boroughs Anglicans were excluded from these corporations and had brought suit against them.[18] It might be argued that at Newcastle, Liverpool, Colchester, and Taunton, the Dissenters' pro-Americanism was related more to their exclusion from office than their political ideology. But that something more was at stake in these conflicts than oppression based on the Test and Corporation Acts is proven by the anti-corporation parties in Coventry and Nottingham. These parties were Anglican in composition and faced no legal restrictions in their pursuit of office (except, perhaps, the local ones imposed by Dissenting aldermen), and they did not oppose the central government concerning America. The power of religion is seen in the ability of the Dissenting corporation members at Bristol, Coventry, and Nottingham to side with the Americans despite a natural concern for their own status; in these boroughs, Dissenting ideology seems to have been more important than even local vested interests. While the role of local structures of power and status on the one hand, and the impact of the Test and Corporation Acts on the other, are important for understanding the divisions over America, they do not fully explain these divisions.

The other major charge brought against the addressers was that they were influenced directly by the central government through minor government

17 Mayor, John Fellows; aldermen, Humphrey Hollins, James Hornbuckle, Thomas Oldknow; Dissenting councilors, W. Bilbie, George Dodson, James Foxcroft, John Foxcroft, Mark Huish, Jonathan Inglesant, Thomas Sands, Matthews Whitelock. E. L. Guilford (ed.), *Records of the Borough of Nottingham*, 9 vols. (Nottingham, 1882–1956), 7: 412. RG 4/1588; 137; 1586; 3664.
18 See above, chap. 9.

patronage.[19] Crewe's Act of 1782 disfranchised custom officers, but before that date, they could vote in parliamentary elections and obviously they could also address or petition the crown at any time.[20] In a number of larger ports, the connection between revenue officers and the government is readily documented. At Bristol the collector of customs, Daniel Harson, signed the coercive address along with James Beckett, the collector of salt duties, Francis Hammond, the controller of customs, fifteen custom-house and excise officers, two land surveyors, and a tidewaiter. In the pro-government subscription at Bristol, the landwaiters subscribed £21 to the fund, and the names of Harson, Beckett, and others attest their loyalty a second time. In contrast, only one signature of a custom-house official could be located on the conciliatory petition.[21]

An identical pattern is found at Newcastle upon Tyne. An essay by 'Steady' in the *London Evening-Post* on the Newcastle addressers identified the business and political connections of eighty-six of what it termed 'the insignificant or interested individuals'. The signatures include those of Aubone Surtees, receiver general of the land tax for Northumberland, John Erasmus Blackett, paymaster of the Northumberland militia, and five custom-house officers.[22] The same story was repeated at Liverpool. The collector of customs, John Colquitt, two tax gatherers, James Foster and Stephen Tillingshaft, the collector of salt duties, Matthew Greenwood, the postmaster, a landwaiter, a riding surveyor, a deputy searcher and a great assortment of lesser custom-house

---

19 'A Petitioner For Peace' in Champion Letterbook, 38083 (4), pp. 526–7. 'Veteran' in *New. Chron.* (16 Dec. 1775); *Pub. Adv.* (19 Oct. 1775); *Hamp. Chron.* (16, 30 Oct. 1775); *Sal. Win. J.* (13 Nov. 1775). John Sainsbury, *Disaffected Patriots: London Supporters of Revolutionary America 1769–1782* (Kingston and Montreal, 1987), determined that at least 10% of the London pro-government addressers were government contractors; altogether, some 24% of the addressers had some economic connection with the government, pp. 115–16; see pp. 120–5 for a very fine discussion of the political implications of government contracts.

20 Betty Kemp, 'Crewe's Act, 1782', *EHR* 68 (1953), 258–63. Strictly speaking, officers in the Navy or Army, unlike excisemen and custom-house officials, held their places by law, not at the pleasure of the king. However, many servicemen undoubtedly supported the addresses because they were devoted to the military and because they were in government pay.

21 HO 55/11/64 and 11/9 compared to James Sketchly's *Bristol Directory* (Bristol, 1775). For the Bristol subscription, *Brist. J.* (30 Dec. 1775; 6 Jan.; 16 March 1776). John Harris, listed as a custom-house officer in the non-parochial register (RG 4/3507) signed both the petition and the address. Many additional local government officers, such as two sheriff's officers, signed the coercive address, but local organizations, such as the infirmary, seem to have divided about evenly. Abraham Isaac Elton, J.P. for the counties of Gloucestershire and Somersetshire, signed the address.

22 *Lond. Eve.-Post* (30 Nov.–2 Dec. 1775). In addition, Donald Cameron, half-pay lieutenant, and Edward Mosley, whose shipping was employed by the government, and William Lowes, J.P. for Northumberland signed. The names of five people who were connected in business, or dependents or relatives of those on the corporation, are also listed. The number of custom-house officials is corroborated by the address itself which lists occupations.

officers, altogether totaling twenty-four people, signed the coercive address.[23] In neither of these leading ports is there any significant connection between office holding and the conciliatory petitions; no office holders could be found on the massive Newcastle petition and only two were found on the document from Liverpool. The petitioners' oft-repeated boast of independence is thereby vindicated.

Revenue officers, placemen, and pensioners gave the ministry their support in numerous small boroughs as well, for example, at Poole, where the address obtained the signatures of eleven custom-house officers. But the most notable example of government influence was observed in the small boroughs of Hampshire. At Southampton there were nine custom-house officers who signed the address, in addition to assorted commissioned officers and a handful of government contractors. 'Spur' claimed that 'more than half' of the seventy-four subscribers to the address of Lymington were 'placemen in the Salts, Custom-house, Excise offices, Etc', and in the Hampshire county address with a mere 201 signatures, one critic observed the names of Commissioner Gambier of Portsmouth, Capt. Saxton, and 'nine other officers from the Custom-house at Cowes'.[24] In the smaller boroughs in particular, corporations not only channeled government patronage, aldermen were often themselves government placemen. Minor government office holders clearly favored the government, and there can be no doubt that the government influenced popular politics as well as parliamentary politics. This influence was felt most keenly in the small boroughs; the custom-house officers comprised less than 5 percent of all addressers in the large ports, and if the direct influence of the government is expanded to include the relatives of placemen, officers in half-pay, and those hoping for a place, it still cannot account for the majority of pro-government supporters.[25] Corporations and custom-houses, however, were almost without exceptions major centers of active pro-ministerial politics in the age of the American Revolution. Opposition to this power base is also readily demonstrated; John Brewer has drawn attention to the resentment of the middling sort against revenue officers who possessed threatening powers of entry, search, and seizure.[26]

---

23 HO 55/28/20 and HO 55/9/3 compared to *The Poll* (Liverpool, 1761) which lists custom-house officers and George T. and Isabella Shaw, *Liverpool's First Directory* (reprint of Gore's Directory for 1766, Liverpool, 1907). In addition, the overseer of the poor, an 'agent', the town clerk, and the town bailiff signed the coercive address.
24 For Poole, *Gen. Eve. Post* (5–7 Oct. 1775); for Southampton, *Lond. Eve.-Post* (28–31 Oct. 1775). On these two boroughs, see the full discussion in Bradley, *Popular Politics and the American Revolution in England*. For Lymington, see *Lond. Eve.-Post* (25–8 Nov. 1775); for Hampshire, *Morn. Chron.* (23 Nov. 1775).
25 At Bristol 2.2%; 4.1% at Newcastle, and 4.2% at Liverpool.
26 John Brewer, 'English Radicalism in the Age of George III', p. 339 in J. G. A. Pocock (ed.), *Three British Revolutions: 1641, 1688, 1776* (Princeton, 1980).

Most of the corporations that addressed the crown were unified in support of coercive measures. Addresses from other bodies established by law, such as the two universities, several groups of militia, and Justices of the Peace are also notable.[27] In most if not all of the boroughs that divided over the government's policy of coercion there was an ongoing struggle between those who enjoyed local office with all of its privileges, status, and benefits, and those who were denied these perquisites. The corporation, anti-corporation conflict resulted in legal wrangles in Coventry, Nottingham, and Taunton, and the only corporations that were divided among themselves were those which traditionally had allowed Dissenters to hold office. Government influence through minor patronage was important in influencing a minority of addressers at Bristol, Newcastle, and Liverpool, yet in the large boroughs, the government was not as influential as the local tradition of support for the established political arrangements. Research in the provincial urban centers does extend the insights of Nicholas Rogers on the anomalous tension between the growth of the political nation on the one hand, and the passivity of the humbler person, even in the more open constituencies, on the other. Local burgesses, common councilmen, and excisemen sometimes influenced the lesser sort; it was not only in London that the 'intricate webb of court and aristocrat clientage' penetrated the plebeian world with effect.[28] The custom house was one place where the provincial cities were not exempt from the network of court clientage extending out from London. The influence of local government, and in particular, local institutions of status and influence, were, however, probably more important in shaping pro-government convictions than direct government influence exerted through patronage, though, since most patronage was channeled through corporations, the two cannot be completely separated. Indeed, the gifts of the government undoubtedly gave energy to the ministerial convictions of many corporation members, or at least stimulated the hope of future reward. And whether this hope was related to strengthening the authority of local or national government, the basic motive remained the same. Those who enjoyed the privileges and the perquisites of office wished to keep them, and support for coercive measures was certainly viewed by most of these people as one means of maintaining the government's favor.

Those who were denied the rewards of government sinecures may have wished to enjoy them, though it is difficult to see how opposition to the government could have led in any way to participation in the spoils. Certainly some of those who opposed the government's coercive measures aspired to

27 For the Universities of Oxford and Cambridge, see HO 55/11/32; 11/53; for the First and Northern Regiments of the Devonshire Militia and the Northamptonshire Militia, HO 55/11/12; 11/17; 11/26; for the Devonshire J. P.s, and the J. P.s of the Tower of London and Precincts, see HO 55/11/68 and *Lond. Gaz.* (21–4 Oct. 1775).

28 Nicholas Rogers, 'Aristocratic Clientage, Trade and Independency: Popular Politics in Pre-Radical Westminster', *P&P* 61 (1973), 86–87, 106.

become aldermen, but the petitioners' lack of involvement with government patronage may suggest the reality of something more interesting than merely the limited number of available places; it may suggest a doctrinaire commitment to a politically independent orientation. In fact, the petitioners were less dependent on ruling bodies, both local and national, than were the addressers. But what did 'independence' mean to these people? If petitioners were independent of the structures of government, were they also economically independent? Further light is thrown on the motive forces of popular politics by examining the socio-economic status and religion of individual petitioners.

POPULAR POLITICS AND SOCIO-ECONOMIC RANK

An analysis of the occupational structure of the partisan vote at Bristol and Newcastle revealed significant socio-economic differences, but with the important exception of elite support for government candidates, at Liverpool, Colchester, and Hull the occupational analysis showed little difference between voters. This led to the hypothesis that the extent to which an election focused on the American controversy contributed directly to whether or not the electorate divided on socio-economic grounds. By comparing popular documents to poll books, directories, registers, and lists of freemen, it is possible to analyze the socio-economic standing of individuals who petitioned or addressed the throne. Previous studies were largely unaware of the petitions for peace, and they concluded on the basis of literary evidence alone that the lower orders were not pro-American; the smaller craftsmen, journeymen, and urban wage earners were not sufficiently radicalized to be supporters of liberty.[29] Using city directories and the popular petitions over America, however, Peter Marshall was able to show that Manchester 'divided along social and economic lines', though his occupational categories were not sufficiently precise to offer more than broad generalizations.[30] My previous examination of the petitioners who were also voters in Great Yarmouth, Southampton, and Cambridge led to the tentative conclusion that socio-economic status contributed directly to the political differences that divided the English populace over America. The strongest support for coercion came from the ranks of the elite, particularly

29 George Rudé, *Wilkes and Liberty* (Oxford, 1962), pp. 197–8; and 'The London Mob of the Eighteenth Century', p. 315 in *Paris and London in the Eighteenth Century: Studies in Popular Protest* (New York, 1963). See also Colin Bonwick, *English Radicals and the American Revolution* (Chapel Hill, 1977), p. 244, and John A. Sainsbury, 'The Pro-Americans of London, 1769–1782', *WMQ* 3rd ser., 35 (1978), 447; Sainsbury was the first to attempt an analysis of the occupational standing of London addressers and petitioners, but in his dissertation of 1975 and his article of 1978 he found few differences among the London signers. Closer analysis of occupations led him to a very different conclusion: the political divisions in London were 'to a large extent' socio-economic. *Disaffected Patriots*, p. 119.

30 See Peter Marshall, 'Manchester and the American Revolution', *Bulletin of the John Rylands University Library of Manchester* 62 (1979), 173.

those in the gentlemen, profession category, whereas shopkeepers and artisans provided the bulk of support for peaceful concessions.[31]

In a recent reevaluation of London addressers and petitioners, John Sainsbury found significant socio-economic differences between government supporters and pro-Americans. The London merchants were devoted to the government; of the identifiable addressers, fully one third were merchants, though only a small fraction of these were traders to North America. Many of these merchants were unusually wealthy and others were directors of moneyed companies who stood to profit by the war. On the other hand, 66 percent of the pro-American petitioners were lesser wholesalers, retailers, and craftsmen who were drawn from the same occupational categories as members of the London Association and the Common Council of London. These London tradesmen and artisans perceived themselves in terms of 'economic and political victimization by successive administrations', and Sainsbury does not shrink from calling this 'economic and class antagonism'. To the London retailers and artisans, True Whig ideology, with all of its attendant exaggerations, was eminently believable.[32]

Contemporary observers were convinced of the relationship between popular politics and economic motivation, and they spent a good deal of time arguing over the 'respectability' of those engaged in petitioning. The 'rank' or 'order' of people was commonly thought to be proven by their occupation or profession; one critic of the Bristol petition suggested

that those who signed the Petition, and those who signed the Address, may put the addition of profession, trade and calling, to their respective names, that the public in general, who are strangers to our town, may be in some degree able to judge who are the tag, rag, and bob-tail of it, and who have a real interest in its tranquility, trade, and commerce ....

Having taken this advice, another citizen of Bristol concluded that only 105 of approximately 1,000 petitioners were men of 'business' or 'property'.[33] The opponents of the petitions thus often claimed that the addressers were more affluent, and by implication, more responsible, but it was just as common to argue that the addressers were poorer and hence more dependent. The Manchester address, for example, was said to be signed 'in the lowest public-houses, by porters, labourers, carmen, and such like gentry'.[34] A more sys-

31 For Cambridge, Bradley, 'Religion and Reform at the Polls', 68; and for Great Yarmouth and Southampton, *Popular Politics and the American Revolution in England*, chap. 7.
32 Sainsbury, *Disaffected Patriots*, pp. 115–118, 19, 14; 44% of the addressers were tradesmen and craftsmen, but many of these enjoyed contractual links with the government. Sainsbury says the middling sort in London had 'a characteristic class consciousness', and he uses the language of 'lower middle class aspirations' without further discussion of what is intended, p. 43.
33 Lord Rockingham used the phrase 'ranks, professions, or occupations', *Burke Correspondence*, 3: 215, Rockingham to Burke, 24 Sept. 1775. 'A Lover of Truth', *Brist. J.* (21 Oct. 1775); 'Diver', *Morn. Chron.* (8 Dec. 1775).
34 *New. Chron.* (14 Oct. 1775). On the social status of petitioners and addressers generally,

tematic approach to the poll books and city directories of Bristol, Newcastle upon Tyne, Liverpool, Colchester, Coventry, and Nottingham demonstrates that those in favor of coercive measures were in fact representative of the higher ranks of society.

The prominence of the gentlemen and professions among the addressers (Table 10.1)[35] confirms what was found in the earlier examination of leadership. We have seen that certain professions, such as the Anglican clergy and custom-house officers, were consistently disposed toward coercion, and with the possible exception of Coventry and Nottingham, the occupational data show that the elite in general supported the government. Bristol, Newcastle upon Tyne, and Colchester almost exactly mirror the data for Yarmouth, Southampton, and Cambridge, with half to two-thirds of the support for coercion coming from the upper two categories, and two-thirds to three-fourths of the support for conciliation coming from the shopkeepers and artisans, particularly the latter. The majority of individuals for whom we have occupational data were voters, but in no election during this period were these people as polarized at the polls on social and economic grounds as they were in petitioning the crown concerning America. Gentlemen, esquires, and those in the

see *Pub. Adv.* (19 Oct. 1775). On the supposed higher rank of the addressers at Bristol and Coventry, see *Brist. J.* (21 Oct. 1775); *Gen. Eve. Post* (7–10 Oct. 1775); *New. Chron.* (14 Nov. 1775); on the perceived lower rank of the addressers at Bristol, Coventry, Southwark, Winchester, and Middlesex, see *Lond. Eve.-Post* (17–19 Oct. 1775); 'A Petitioner for Peace', in Champion Letterbook, 38083 (4), pp. 524–7; *New. Chron.* (28 Oct. 1775); *Morn. Chron.* (23 Nov. 1775); *Lond. Eve.-Post* (19–21 Oct. 1775).

35 The resident electorates in Table 10.1 are based on the 1774 poll books for Bristol, Newcastle, and Nottingham, and the 1780 poll books for Liverpool and Colchester. The petitioners and addressers were compared to the following volumes in order to identify the occupations of as many petitioners as possible. Bristol: *The Poll* (Bristol, 1774); *Sketchley's Bristol Directory* (Bristol, 1775); and the non-parochial registers; Newcastle: *The Poll* (Newcastle, 1774); *The Poll* (Newcastle, 1777); *Whitehead's Newcastle Directory for 1778* (Newcastle, 1778, reprinted in facsimile by J. R. Boyle as *The First Newcastle Directory*, Newcastle, 1889), and the non-parochial registers; Liverpool: *The Poll* (Liverpool, 1780); Shaw, *Liverpool's First Directory* (Liverpool, 1766); and the non-parochial registers; Colchester, the poll books of the elections of 1768, 1780 and 1784, and the non-parochial registers; Coventry: Joan Lane (ed.), *Coventry Apprentices and Their Masters, 1781–1806* (Stratford upon Avon, 1982), and both coercive addresses (1775 and 1776); Nottingham: *The Poll* (Nottingham, 1774). The Coventry poll book for 1774 does not distinguish voters' occupations, and the non-parochial registers at Nottingham do not record occupations. The 1774 Nottingham poll book does, however, list all eligible freemen, voters and non-voters, so the use of freeman lists is superfluous. On the Newcastle coercive address all the occupations are listed and summarized in Table 10.1, but only those in the letter cluster in Table 10.4. Common names that appear on both petitions and addresses were excluded; the names are thus unique. When two or more identical names appear in the poll books or directories, they were not matched with the petitions or addresses. See Appendix 1. These sources make it possible to identify as many as 57.4% of the Bristol addressers and as few as 25.8% of the Liverpool petitioners; the average (excluding the Newcastle address, which gives all but three of the occupations) is 42.7%. Using directories and poll books, Sainsbury was able to identify 51.8% of the London petitioners, *Disaffected Patriots*, p. 169.

Table 10.1: *Occupational Structure of Petitioners and Addressers*

	BRISTOL			NEWCASTLE UPON TYNE			LIVERPOOL		
	Entire Resident Electorate %	Conciliatory (%)	Coercive (%)	Entire Resident Electorate %	Conciliatory (%)	Coercive (%)	Entire Resident Electorate %	Conciliatory (%)	Coercive (%)
1. Gentlemen, Professions	8.7	27 (15.0)	103 (33.2)	2.5	10 (2.9)	51 (30.9)	1.9	15 (18.5)	64 (28.4)
2. Merchants	6.8	27 (15.0)	62 (20.0)	10.2	24 (8.4)	54 (32.7)	5.5	29 (35.8)	62 (27.6)
3. Shopkeepers	23.2	47 (26.1)	51 (16.5)	24.3	103 (29.9)	25 (15.2)	22.7	15 (18.5)	52 (23.1)
4. Artisans	50.8	76 (42.2)	86 (27.7)	55.2	192 (55.7)	35 (21.2)	65.1	21 (25.9)	47 (20.9)
5. Laborers	6.9	2 (1.1)	7 (2.3)	7.6	15 (4.3)	0 (0)	4.5	1 (1.2)	0 (0)
6. Others	3.6	1 (.6)	1 (.3)	.2	1 (.3)	0 (0)	.3	0 (0)	0 (0)

	COLCHESTER			COVENTRY		NOTTINGHAM		
	Entire Resident Electorate %	Conciliatory (%)	Coercive (%)	Conciliatory (%)	Coercive (%)	Entire Resident Electorate %	Conciliatory (%)	Coercive (%)
1. Gentlemen, Professions	8.4	13 (8.9)	31 (55.4)	5 (3.0)	8 (5.5)	4.8	26 (17.9)	29 (24.1)
2. Merchants	3.0	8 (5.5)	1 (1.8)	17 (10.1)	5 (3.4)	2.3	12 (8.3)	8 (6.7)
3. Shopkeepers	23.5	41 (28.0)	12 (21.4)	28 (16.7)	38 (26.0)	20.7	28 (19.3)	38 (31.7)
4. Artisans	55.5	68 (46.6)	9 (16.1)	118 (69.8)	93 (63.7)	71.4	79 (54.5)	44 (36.7)
5. Laborers	4.8	8 (5.5)	0 (0)	0 (0)	1 (.7)	.5	0 (0)	0 (0)
6. Others	4.8	8 (5.5)	3 (5.4)	1 (.6)	1 (.7)	.3	0 (0)	1 (.8)

professions who gave some support to government candidates in parliamentary elections gave exceptionally strong support to coercion; similarly, shopkeepers and artisans who had voted for opposition candidates were disproportionately in favor of conciliation compared to the addressers from the same occupational groups.

In a sample comprising half of the Bristol addressers, fully thirty gentlemen and fifteen esquires signed their names, a number that represents about ten percent of the total number of addressers. Among the elite who supported coercion at Liverpool there were fourteen gentlemen and esquires compared to only four who petitioned, while at Colchester, one finds the names of six gentlemen and ten esquires on the address. At Newcastle upon Tyne, in addition to the support for coercion among the corporation (fifteen common councilmen signed, along with eight aldermen, the recorder, town clerk, and sheriff), fifteen addressers (almost ten percent) classified themselves as 'gentlemen'. The independent party's allusion to 'magistrates and gentry' whose glory it seems to be 'to treat their inferiors as slaves' may be propagandistic, but it reflects deeply felt social antagonisms.[36] Some professions, such as medical doctors, occasionally appeared more frequently on the coercive addresses than on conciliatory ones (as at Coventry), but the numbers were too small to be statistically significant. Other professions, however, stand out, particularly at Bristol, Newcastle, and Liverpool, where the directories supply fuller information than the poll books. The most notable group is the legal profession.

That the conflict had a strong ideological component that united local and national politics is demonstrated by the uniform support for the government from city corporations and bodies charged with upholding the law, such as the Justices of the Peace. This thesis is confirmed by the nearly unanimous support for coercion that arose from attorneys. At Bristol some seventeen attorneys signed the coercive address, while only one signed the conciliatory petition.[37] Of 168 signers of the address at Newcastle, there were nine attorneys and barristers, whereas among nearly 1200 petitioners, it was possible to positively identify only six, and at Liverpool there were eight attorneys favoring coercion versus two who supported conciliation. Some attorneys, like Thomas Symonds of Bristol, who spoke against the Bristol address, Jaspar Harrison, radical leader at Newcastle, and James Clegg of Liverpool, had come around to pro-Americanism, but the weight of the legal profession was clearly wielded on the side of the government. At every level of jurisdiction, those with a vested interest in law and order encouraged the use of force to compel colonial submission to Parliament and the crown. The radical nature of this conflict is

---

36 Reference in *Commons, 1754–1790*, 1: 350–1.
37 The entire petitions and addresses at Bristol and Newcastle, rather than the letter cluster sample, were searched for clergy, attorneys, booksellers, and publicans, and at Bristol, merchants. The numbers cited in the text thus represent the full number based on the poll books, directories, and registers.

illustrated by comparing the American petitioners to the petitioners over the Middlesex election affair. Rudé found a great number of noblemen, J.P.s, and gentry who signed county petitions in favor of Wilkes,[38] but such accumulated status, wealth, and property is not to be found among those who, five years later, petitioned for peace.

The division among the merchants of Bristol, Newcastle, and Liverpool is noteworthy and comports well with the results of Sainsbury's research on the London merchants.[39] Entire commercial bodies, such as Trinity House at Hull, also addressed the crown in favor of coercive measures.[40] It has been widely supposed that most pro-American support in England came from merchants trading to America, whereas pro-government addresses came from traders to the continent, but this viewpoint greatly oversimplifies the nature of pro-Americanism.[41] American merchants such as Richard Champion and Joseph Harford, both Quakers, were indeed prominent in the petitioning process, but many merchants could not agree over the best method of restoring peace in America. Moreover, they were divided precisely over the issue of the necessity of maintaining Parliament's supremacy by force as the grounds for order and hence trade. The Westbury, Warminster, and Trowbridge petitioners to Parliament, for example, pointed out that 'the vital principle of trade is peace and confidence, not war and destruction'. Many traders, however, argued that a vote against coercive acts was bound to lead to a general disrespect for law; still others were willing to accept a loss in trade in order to compel colonial submission.[42]

At Bristol, about half of the resident merchants signed either the address or the petition: altogether, forty-five merchants favored coercion, and only thirty-seven favored peace.[43] It is possible to identify sixteen of these merchants as

38 Rudé, *Wilkes and Liberty*, pp. 138–41. It was not possible to establish a connection between the Dissenting leader of independence at Liverpool, Joseph Clegg, and the lawyer, James Clegg.

39 Sainsbury, 'The Pro-Americans of London', 447. Sainsbury found that 31% of the pro-American petitioners were in the merchant category, but of these, only 9% were traders to North America, *Disaffected Patriots*, p. 117. Pro-American merchants often had American family connections, political affinities with the radicals, or were Quakers, pp. 69–73.

40 HO 55/11/4.

41 Clark, *British Public Opinion*, pp. 65–6, 70. G. E. Weare, *Edmund Burke's Connection with Bristol, From 1774 till 1780* (Bristol, 1894), p. 122. Peter T. Underdown, 'The Parliamentary History of the City of Bristol, 1750–1790', University of Bristol M.A. thesis, 1948, pp. 156, 158; Brewer, 'English Radicalism in the Age of George III', p. 331. Sainsbury has a fine discussion of the ideas advanced by Dora Mae Clark, *Disaffected Patriots*, p. 70.

42 *Bath. Chron.* (23, 30 Nov. 1775). *Lond. Eve.-Post* (3–5 Oct. 1775).

43 James Sketchley, *Sketchley's Bristol Directory*, isolates 169 Bristol merchants and companies in a separate section of the directory, pp. 111–16. G. E. Weare, *Edmund Burke's Connection*, pp. 4–5 adds several large mercantile houses and Savadge, 'The West County', pp. 93–4, records the big Dissenting merchants. These lists were compared to HO 55/11/64; 11/9. The total of 62 'coercive' merchants in Table 10.1 is

traders to American and the West Indies, twelve of whom signed the petition, but four leading traders to the colonies signed the coercive address. This requires significant modification of the traditional thesis concerning merchant support of the colonists. And since the merchants were divided, it seems reasonable to conclude that more was at stake in their minds than trade. Insurance brokers, much like lawyers, stood solidly in favor of coercion, and they well symbolize the concerns of the pro-government merchants. At Bristol, six insurance brokers, including Meyler and Maxie, West Indian brokers, and Shimmelpenning and Company, signed the coercive address; only one broker signed the conciliatory petition. Lancelot Atkinson, one of the two ship insurers in Newcastle, signed the coercive address.

It is especially difficult to disentangle trading and religious interests in Bristol, since many of the leading commercial magnates were Dissenters. The most wealthy Presbyterian merchants divided evenly between the coercive and the conciliatory petitions; for example, the Eltons, William Wansey, John Merlott, and James Reed were in favor of coercive measures while Paul and Thomas Farr and Jeremiah and Levi Ames favored conciliation. On the other hand, the big merchants among the Congregationalists, Baptists, and Quakers, including such prominent persons as Robert and William Weare, John Bull, and the entire Champion and Harford families, were far more consistently conciliatory than the Presbyterians. The Presbyterians, however, were the most theologically liberal body in Bristol, and this religious orientation was almost certainly related to a greater degree of social assimilation, especially among the wealthy. The Presbyterians had always been closer to the Anglican Church in ecclesiastical terms – their polity was somewhat more oligarchic and the ordination of ministers less democratic than other Dissenters – and on the whole, they were less averse to occasional conformity than others.[44] On these grounds, some wealthy Presbyterian merchants apparently felt little sympathy for the colonists' grievances. The trading thesis has been formulated far too bluntly; in the minds of many merchants, the issue was authority and law in relation to trade, not merely self-interest, or at a minimum, they expressed differences of political opinion concerning the best way to secure their interests.

derived from the addition of wholesalers, like mercers, and others to this occupational category; Table 10.1 represents the letter cluster only.

44 Michael Watts, *The Dissenters* (Oxford, 1978), pp. 229, 315–16, 482–3. Ronald H. Quilici, 'Turmoil in a City and an Empire: Bristol's Factions, 1700–1775', University of New Hampshire Ph.D. diss., 1976, traces the Presbyterian merchant vote for Brickdale in the 1774 election to the merchants' older age, more established wealth, and their attachment to the faction of Isaac Elton and his son, pp. 246, 258. Family ties, especially among the Quakers, were obviously important: of the four Champions and six Harfords only one (Charles Harford) signed the coercive address; the rest petitioned for peace. On the other hand, a higher proportion of Baptists signed the coercive address; see note 108 below.

John Brewer has provided the most discerning discussion available for why the middling ranks were involved in radical politics, particularly the pro-American variety. He examined the pervasive growth of credit and the concomitant shortage of specie (a problem shared with the colonists). Reliance upon credit made the middling ranks especially vulnerable to trade fluctuations, particularly those produced by war, and so naturally, the decision to wage war was viewed with great concern by these people. Secondly, the tax structure was shifting distinctly toward commodity taxes, and these taxes were borne disproportionately by the middling and lower ranks. The unusual sensitivity of people in these ranks to issues of taxation, and the method and powers of collection, was thus entirely predictable. Thirdly, the growth of the importance of statute law in relation to the well being of the local community meant that the middling ranks were increasingly outspoken concerning the necessity of having representatives in Parliament who were responsive to their needs. A characteristic insistence on independence is found in all three areas of economic and political concern. 'The radicals' pursuit of independence, therefore, became part of a general attack on the social mechanism of patronage and on the system of discretion that enabled the patron to wield power over those he aided.' Sainsbury has documented the way in which the independent London tradesmen tied their sense of economic oppression to the True Whig notion of a political and financial conspiracy. The American conflict threatened the lesser retailers and artisans with 'economic dislocation with no apparent compensating benefits'.[45]

It is thus not surprising that the bulk of support for conciliation with the colonies came from the shopkeepers or retailers and the artisans or skilled craftsmen. A few occupational groups within these categories were prominent. For example, a number of trades in the middling rank were involved with the dissemination of political information and these groups would have had some stake in expressions of popular politics. Brewer has shown how the provincial press played an important role in encouraging confidence in business and credit and argues that this emphasis was aimed especially at the 'middling sort' of Englishman.[46] However, printers of newspapers in the provinces were thoroughly divided over the American conflict, and thus it is not possible to link specifically progressive politics to newspaper publishing. Thomas Fletcher and Francis Hodson of the *Cambridge Chronicle* editorialized on behalf of the Americans and both signed the Cambridge petition for peace. At Leeds, the editor of the *Leeds Mercury*, James Bowling, took a pronounced pro-American

45 Brewer, 'English Radicalism in the Age of George III', p. 347; see also pp. 334, 337–9, 341, 356; Sainsbury, *Disaffected Patriots*, pp. 8–14, 118–19.
46 Neil McKendrick, John Brewer, and J. H. Plumb, *The Birth of a Consumer Society* (London, 1982), pp. 216–17. See also, Kent R. Middleton, 'Commercial Speech in the Eighteenth Century', p. 280, in Donovan H. Bond and W. Reynolds McLeod, *Newsletters to Newspapers: Eighteenth-Century Journalism* (Morgantown, W. V., 1977).

stance and he signed the conciliatory petition, while the radicals at Newcastle were led by the progressive editorials of Thomas Slack, printer of the *Newcastle Chronicle*, who also added his name to the Newcastle petition. Thus many printers, just like a handful of attorneys, had turned to radical causes. But there was no unanimity among printers. Slack's counterpart at Newcastle was Thomas Saint, publisher of the strongly loyalist *Newcastle Courant*, and signer of the address. Samuel Creswell, stationer, bookseller, and printer of Nottingham, wrote numerous editorials against the rebels in the *Newark and Nottingham Journal*, and when opposing documents circulated in Nottingham, he added his name to those who wished the government success.[47]

Many, if not most, printers of newspapers were also booksellers, but there were numerous booksellers and stationers who were not publishers, and among booksellers at Bristol and Newcastle there was a definite proclivity for radical politics. Three booksellers of Bristol and a printseller supported conciliation, while not a single bookseller's name could be located on the coercive address. This however, may have had as much to do with religion as with any liberalizing tendencies in the book trade, since two of the pro-American booksellers were Dissenters.[48] The Newcastle Directory for 1778 listed seven booksellers, and of these, five signed the petition, while Thomas Saint alone, the so-called 'Tory' printer, signed the address. One of these booksellers, Edward Humble, was also a director of a circulating library, as was Richard Fisher, both of whom joined in support of peace, and these men evidently made a connection between their interest in Whig politics, the reading and selling of books, and peace with America.[49] Certainly Thomas Robson did; he was the printer of James Murray's multi-volume history, his numerous sermons and tracts, and also a signer of the petition.

The work of John Money and Linda Colley on taverns and coffeehouses and Brewer's examination of the tradesmen's clubs helps explain the process by which pro-Americanism arose among the shopkeepers and artisans.[50] The connection between club members and the bookseller who sold them political pamphlets as a commercial venture suggests a tie between increasing wealth and radical politics. The well developed infrastructure of communication systems in London that kept the tradesmen, apprentices, and artisans well-informed was thus also characteristic of the large cities in the provinces.

47 *Camb. Chron.* (9 Dec. 1775); *Leeds Merc.* (10, 17, 24, 31 Jan. 1775); *New. Chron.* (7, 21 Oct. 1775); *Nott. New. J.* (28 Jan.; 11, 18 Feb. 1776).
48 J. B. Beckett and Thomas Mullett.
49 One of the Newcastle booksellers, Joseph Atkinson, was also a Dissenter. At Liverpool Thomas Houlston, bookseller, and Egerton Smith, printer, signed the address, while Thomas Cowburne, printer, signed the petition.
50 John Money, 'Taverns, Coffee Houses, and Clubs: Local Politics and Popular Articulacy in the Birmingham Area in the Age of the American Revolution', *HJ* 14 (1971), 15–48; Linda Colley, 'The Loyal Brotherhood and the Cocoa Tree', *HJ* 20 (1977), 77–95.

The moderate means of these groups over against the laborers seems to account for their heightened political activity and interest in independence.[51] Club meetings and the frequenting of public houses, of course, presuppose an element of leisure, and this too, as J. H. Plumb has documented, helps explain the political activity of the middling ranks.[52] The petitions provided further evidence for these connections.

Inns and public houses were major avenues for the dissemination of political ideology, and proprietors at Bristol and Newcastle who favored conciliation were slightly more numerous among petitioners than those who wished for coercion. At Bristol twenty-eight publicans signed the conciliatory petition, compared to eighteen who signed the coercive address (a ratio of 1.5 to 1); at Newcastle it is possible to identify twenty-one proprietors of taverns on the petition to four on the address (a ratio of 5.3 to 1), but given the far greater number of signatures on the Newcastle petition, this is difficult to interpret. Richard Champion recounted how he received from William Burke part of a speech by Lord North hinting at reconciliation, and 'read it to a circle' of his friends. He was astonished that the knowledge of this speech was 'spread over the Town two or three hours after I had read the account', and he received 'Message after Message from grave and gay, old and young' to know more of 'the extraordinary news'.[53] Such news passed rapidly from mouth to mouth and the movement of the communication was facilitated by public houses. At Newcastle, the petition was deposited for one week at Richard Swarley's 'Black Boy' for the purpose of signing, and Swarley himself was, naturally enough, a subscriber to the document.

In Bristol, Newcastle, and Colchester, two to three times as many artisans, supported conciliation over against coercion. These were the same artificers who loudly protested against the oppression of the magistrates at Newcastle and were the group most feared by the upper ranks and commonly denigrated as propertyless rabble. At Bristol they were the same artisans who would by 1781 insist that 'the poor man has an *equal* right, but *more* need, to have representatives in the legislature than the rich one'.[54] The data from Bristol, Newcastle, and Colchester almost perfectly mirror the boroughs of Great Yarmouth, Southampton, and Cambridge, and they directly corroborate Sainsbury's research in London and Marshall's work on Manchester. Was this politicization of the urban artisan a genuinely new phenomenon in the 1760s

---

51 McKendrick, Brewer, and Plumb, *The Birth of a Consumer Society*, pp. 232–3, 253–9. Sainsbury, *Disaffected Patriots*, pp. 22–3, 28–30; but Sainsbury thinks London is to be contrasted to the provinces.

52 McKendrick, Brewer, and Plumb, *The Birth of a Consumer Society*, pp. 280–5.

53 Champion Letterbook, 38083 (4), pp. 520–1: Champion to Mrs. Burke, Nov. 1775.

54 See chap. 9, with notes 46, 98, 132 for divisions in Bristol, Newcastle, and Colchester; see Peter Marshall, *Bristol and the American War of Independence* (Bristol, 1977), p. 24 for a full statement of the radicals' demands.

and 1770s? We now know that in the early eighteenth century popular politics in large urban centers entailed something more than aristocratic feuding or factions contending over merely local, material interests. Nicholas Rogers in particular has demonstrated that for the period before 1760, the earlier interpretation of 'an intrinsically consensual, complacent and deferential society under aristocratic leadership' is by no means an accurate picture of the whole of political life.[55] For example, the amalgam of Dissident Whigs and Tories in London that opposed the Whig oligarchy was not High Church nor royalist in orientation, but populist and libertarian. A similar alliance of Tories and independent Whigs can also be located in York, Worcester, Preston, and other boroughs. But with the exception of London and Westminster, these attempts to promote a broad based opposition to official Whiggism seriously faltered at mid-century.[56] More importantly, the old country program espoused by these groups did not challenge the social base of the oligarchies they opposed. In the period before Wilkes and the American Revolution the heart of urban opposition to the Whig oligarchy cannot be located in the urban artisans; rather, it is located in the Tory and opposition Whig middle ranks, some of whom were sensitive to the small traders. Neither does Rogers think that 'pre-radical' opposition to the Whig oligarchy was grounded in radical ideology (i.e. against the Established Church or the social hierarchy).[57] Outside of London and Westminster, expressions of concern over distinctions of wealth were rare before the period of Wilkes.

In the late 1760s, however, political polarization related to social stratification was increasing, and a more coherent radical platform was extended in a more democratic direction; new issues centering around the working of the law and its accessibility were raised. Scholars agree that the early years of George III's reign witnessed the beginnings of a new urban radicalism, but the precise role the artisan played in the progress of this radicalism has remained obscure. To this date, historians have either assumed that urban artisans in England were politically apathetic during the American Revolution, they have confined artisan radicalism to the metropolis, or they have marshalled only impressionistic evidence for the artisans' behavior, and as a result, very little work has been done on their attitudes, expectations, and aspirations.[58] The social data from

---

55 Nicholas Rogers, 'The Urban Opposition to Whig Oligarchy, 1720–60', pp. 132–3 in Margaret and James Jacob, (eds.) *The Origins of Anglo–American Radicalism* (London, 1984). See also H. T. Dickinson, 'The Precursors of Political Radicalism in Augustan Britain', pp. 68–84 in Clyve Jones, (ed.) *Britain in the First Age of Party, 1680–1750: Essays Presented to Geoffrey Holmes* (London, 1987), and the discussion of Tory radicalism in chap. 1, notes 10 and 18.
56 Rogers finds the continuities in metropolitan popular politics between the 1740s and the 1760s more impressive than the idea of eclipse and subsequent efflorescence, "Aristocratic Clientage, Trade and Independency', p. 105.
57 Rogers, 'The Urban Opposition', pp. 136–7, 145.
58 See the discussion in chap. 1, and notes 30 and 41 above. Rogers, like Sainsbury, has

the petitions of 1775 provides the first quantitative evidence for the collective action of the smaller urban tradesman and artisan and it suggests the reality of an increasing disenchantment among the lower orders with the establishment in Church, law, and local government.

Two other politically disrupted settings invite comparison to the petitions of 1775: the petitioning agitation over the Middlesex election affair, and the rebellion in the American colonies. On the basis of literary evidence, Rudé conjectured that the support for Wilkes from the 'middling sort' was considerable; his examination of land tax returns for Middlesex located numerous pro-Wilkites from the middle ranks. There were also some wealthy merchants who supported Wilkes, but the bulk of support came from petty freeholders and middling and small tradesmen. Rudé successfully refuted Sutherland's thesis that Wilkes depended on the liverymen of the lesser companies, and he showed that Wilkes' support was not derived primarily from the propertyless rabble, (though to be sure, the street demonstrations and riots were led by the lower orders.)[59] But since so few counties and boroughs divided over Wilkes, Rudé discovered little evidence of social division related to radical politics.

The most recent analysis of colonial urban artisans by Gray Nash throws some light on artisan support for conciliation in England.[60] Nash cautions us that 'opportunity' for the artisan in the colonies had more to do with economic security than upward social mobility. At most, the artisan could hope for limited mobility, and what was true of eighteenth-century Philadelphia was probably equally characteristic of Bristol and Liverpool. Thus the concept of economic ambition may help explain the English artisans' concern for peace with America, but it does not fully account for it. A second moral value cherished by the artisan probably accounts for more: self-esteem interpreted in terms of the desire for the social recognition commonly associated with independence. Independence for the artisan, as Nash helpfully describes it, had both

overemphasized the distinction between London and provincial cities in terms of communications networks, and the civic participation of craftsmen, 'The Urban Opposition', pp. 141–2.

59 Rudé, *Wilkes and Liberty*, pp. 144–6, 179, 181–3.

60 Colonial artisans are particularly appropriate for comparison to English artisans since so much more work has been done on the social causes of the Revolution in America; colonial artisans also made up about the same proportion of the population as English artisans; Nash estimates that about half the tax paying inhabitants, and about half the electorate in the seaboard towns and cities, were artisans. Gary B. Nash, *The Urban Crucible: Social Change, Political Consciousness and the Origins of the American Revolution* (Cambridge, Mass., 1979), chaps. 11, 12, and more recently 'Artisans and Politics in Eighteenth-Century Philadelphia', in *The Origins of Anglo-American Radicalism* p. 162. See also Carl Bridenbaugh, *The Colonial Craftsman* (Chicago, 1961); Howard B. Rock, *Artisans of the New Republic: The Tradesmen of New York City in the Age of Jefferson* (New York, 1979); Charles S. Olton, *Artisans for Independence: Philadelphia Mechanics and the American Revolution* (Syracuse, 1975); and on England, I. J. Prothero, *Artisans and Politics in Early Nineteenth-Century London: John Gast and His Times* (Folkestone, 1979).

an economic and a political element and the two were intimately connected. The political independence of an individual presupposed a degree of economic independence sufficient to allow one the exercise of an unconstrained choice.[61]

Unlike some of the tradesmen, the majority of artisans had never been assimilated into society to the extent that they had a sense of possessing a stake in it; few of them held such posts as constables, church wardens, and overseers of the poor. The addresses for coercion uniformly preceded the petitions for peace, and the enthusiastic support for the government's policies espoused by magistrates, clergy, and attorneys must have appeared to many artisans as a portent of greater political control, if not coercion, at home as well as abroad. That the artisans made this connection is borne out by the frequency with which the radical press, in commenting on petitioning, applauded independence as a principle of political behavior.[62] The threat of uncontrollable power exercised by borough elites helped provoke the radical rhetoric against the perceived oppression of city corporations, noted above. The similarity of response between Nonconformists and artisans would also tend to support this conclusion. Politically coherent behavior among artisans is seen in both their voting and petitioning, and this suggests that they were an important consumer of the newspaper editorials, pamphlets, and broadsides of the printers and booksellers. Artisans were behaving in an independent, most outspoken way, though in accordance with the independence encouraged by the radical press and the Dissenting pulpit.

Evidently, radical political ideology was reaching deep into the artisan ranks and it is therefore arguable that the American crisis contributed to the earliest manifestation of what historians have called the 'new radicalism'. The artisans, however, were not in all cases a unified body; they represented a wide range of occupations and income, and religion divided them down the middle. The ease with which non-Dissenting artisans associated with Dissenting radical leadership, however, diminishes the importance of the religious distinction; it appears that a common interest grounded in a lack of political power was more significant. Moreover, there is some evidence that urban artisans were developing a self-conscious, group identity. The organization of craft guilds and workers' combinations analyzed by E. P. Thompson, C. R. Dobson and others, suggests that community interests among artisans could in some settings develop quite apart from the stimulus of religion (though the affinities with the independent behavior of the Dissenters have often been noted).[63] But it will be argued

---

61 Nash, 'Artisans and Politics', pp. 163–4, 166–8.
62 One example among many that could be cited is the *Kent. Gaz.*; see editorials and comments, 2–6, 6–9, 9–13, 13–16, 16–20, 20–3, 23–7 Sept. 1775.
63 E. P. Thompson, 'Patrician Society, Plebian Culture', *Journal of Social History*, 7 (1974), 396–7; C. R. Dobson, *Masters and Journeymen: A Prehistory of Industrial Relations, 1717–1800* (London, 1980), pp. 47–73. For comparisons with the Dissenters' independence, see E. P. Thompson, *The Making of the English Working*

below that the political activity of these skilled craftsmen represents a transitional stage between the old radicalism of the 1760s, and the new radicalism of the 1790s, and that both the colonial crisis and Dissenting religion contributed directly to this development.

Popular agitation over the American crisis involved almost no laborers. 'Plebeian culture' in the case of petitioning led to direct political action, but such culture extended only to skilled artisans, not unskilled workers.[64] Although the data in Table 10.1 are largely made up of petitioners who were also voters or those who were listed in directories and are therefore highly selective, there are several good reasons to believe they provide a reasonably accurate picture of the absence of laborers. Two groups of laborers in particular could have engaged in petitioning agitation, but in fact did not. Nearly 300 resident laborers regularly voted in Bristol elections, but almost without exception, these same people avoided popular political engagements that could have been considered treasonous. A comparison of poll books to petitions indicates that though enfranchised, these laborers were not, on the whole, engaged in popular politics. Second, Dissenting laborers who made up some 10 percent of the adult male population of Dissenters at Bristol, 13 percent at Colchester, 25 percent at Newcastle, and fully one-third at Liverpool, did not petition.[65] As Dissenters these were the very people most motivated to petition, and yet here as well, they refrained from popular politics. Lastly, a sample of more than 500 Anglican register entries at Liverpool was compared to both the address and the petition; this resulted in the addition of only twelve matches, and there was no meaningful pattern in the occupations of these Anglican signers. It is entirely likely that the leaders of the petitioning agitation purposefully avoided these groups and sought out the more respectable signers. There is a plausible social explanation as well, though it must remain conjectural. The engagement of the artisans but not the laborers may be further evidence for an emerging political group consciousness based on a degree of economic and intellectual independence as yet unattained by the lowest orders.

Finally, it is important to account for the large differences between Bristol, Newcastle, and Colchester, on the one hand, and Coventry and Nottingham, and to a lesser extent, Liverpool, on the other. It might be argued that the apparent lack of any differences between petitioners and addressers at Coventry is accounted for by the type of data used, since masters would tend to be representative of a more homogeneous group. But an analysis of Coventry freemen adds very little to this picture. A large letter-cluster sample of the

---

Class (New York, 1963), pp. 30, 36, 51–2.
64 Thompson, 'Patrician Society, Plebian Culture', 397.
65 A high proportion of Dissenting laborers was also found at Yarmouth (43.8%); Southampton (48.2%) and Poole (29.3%) yet here as well, Dissenting laborers were not involved in petitioning against the government.

freemen (approximately 30% of those admitted between 1747 and 1775) was compared to the petition and the two addresses; using this list, the proportion of 'conciliatory' artisans was 4.5 percent greater than that found in Table 10.1, and the proportion of 'coercive' artisans was 5.3 percent greater (a difference of less than 1%). The differences in the proportions of shopkeepers were even less.[66] Moreover, we find almost the identical phenomenon at Nottingham, where the occupational data is drawn from the 1774 poll book. At least part of the explanation for these differences may be found in the religious affiliation of individual petitioners and addressers.

RELIGION, REVOLUTION, AND RADICALISM

One of the earliest, most outspoken addresses of loyalty to the crown came from the Archbishop, the Bishops, and the clergy of the province of Canterbury. They swore allegiance to his Majesty's 'sacred person and government' and reminded him 'that the ecclesiastical part of our constitution is no less excellent than the civil, and that they are so closely and intimately blended with each other, that, as experience has shewn, they must stand or fall together'. They observed, however, that 'a strange licentiousness both of sentiment and conduct, a spirit of frivolous dissipation and ruinous profusion, of disrespect to superiors, and contempt of lawful authority, have made an alarming progress in this nation, and present a very gloomy prospect to every serious and considerate mind'. In light of these developments, the clergy promised to oppose 'these evils' with 'the powerful operation of religious principles', to teach the duties of Christianity, 'which are no less beneficial to society than necessary to salvation', and to pray for the success of 'all your Majesties designs and undertakings' in his extensive dominions.[67] Although it has been claimed that there was no 'specific Anglican attitude' concerning the American revolution and 'no clear-cut' position among the lower clergy,[68] it can be proven that this perspective of the Archbishop and Bishops was shared by the vast majority of clergy throughout the land.

Paul Langford was the first to draw attention to the religious aspect of the pro-government addresses. He demonstrated that many old Tory Members of Parliament who never spoke in the House of Commons were entrusted with presenting the coercive addresses to the king. These were the same country gentlemen who had voted against repeal of the Stamp Act, and they were the ideological successors of the 'Tories'. This identity is established not only by

---

66 'Index of Admissions of Freemen, 1722 –November 1785', Film No. 8257, Coventry City Council. The occupational differences between petitioners and addressers at Bristol, Newcastle upon Tyne, and Colchester are statistically significant at .01 level of probability (using X^2), but not at Liverpool, Coventry, or Nottingham.

67 *Lond. Gaz.* (Jan. 1775); *Brist. J.* (4 Feb. 1775).

68 *Commons, 1754–1790*, 1: 115.

family members, but by geographical location and particularly, High Anglican religious affiliation. The name 'Tory' had, of course, lost its currency by this time, but the former commitment to passive obedience to the king was transformed into trust in the sovereignty of Parliament or, more exactly, the king in Parliament. The colonial crisis thus provoked the rise of a 'new authoritarianism' precisely among those who traced their family lineage to their Tory fathers, and Langford concluded that the religious overtones of the addresses were highly significant. These men not only sustained North's American policies in Parliament, they were the intermediate-level organizers and supporters of coercive addresses to the crown.[69]

The Anglican clergy's support for the government during the petitioning agitation in the fall was the subject of frequent comment. At Bristol 'A Petitioner for Peace' criticized the ministers of the 'gospel of peace' for signing the address.[70] The clergy commonly added 'vicar', 'rector', 'curate', or 'clerk' to their names on the addresses, and, with twenty-nine signatures, the support for coercion among the Bristol clergy was nearly unanimous; James Rouquet was the only clergyman to sign the petition – an act which gained him no little notoriety; and Thomas Newton, Lord Bishop of Bristol, was perhaps the only cleric to abstain. 'Humanus' noted that only two clergymen in the entire borough of Newcastle withstood 'the solicitations, or rather mandates, of power and affluence, for conscience sake'.[71] On the massive Lancashire address, signed by 6273 persons, there were fully sixty-five clerical signatures, and the number of clergy signing the Hampshire address at Winchester was deemed almost miraculous. To one commentator it seemed that 'all the clergy in the diocese' had signed; indeed thirty of the 201 addressers were clergymen, including Prebendaries of the cathedral, Fellows of the college, and many other clergy of the city. This display of loyalty was not lost on the radicals, who took advantage of the opportunity to heap ridicule on the Church: the Hampshire clergy, it was said, had recently made plans to organize a company of grenadiers.[72] Some index of the strength of the clerical turnout in favor of coercion is provided by comparing their response to the clergy's reaction during the agitation over the Middlesex election affair. Rudé counted only eighty clergymen in twelve county petitions in favor of the Middlesex

---

69 Langford, 'Old Whigs, Old Tories', 123–6.
70 Champion Letterbook, 38083 (4), p. 527.
71 *New. Chron.* (29 Dec. 1775). Mr. Ellison of St. Nicholas and Mr. Harding of all Saints. The author was correct; of the thirteen clergy in the directory, these two alone did not sign the address.
72 For Lancashire, *Lond. Gaz.* (5–9 Dec. 1775); 'A Freeholder of Hants', *Lond. Eve.-Post* (14–16 Nov. 1775); another account in *Sal. Win. J.* (13 Nov. 1775); an article in *Lond. Eve.-Post* (7–9 Nov. 1775) lists the thirty clergy and begins 'O ye priests of Piety and Humility'! See *Lond. Gaz.* (7–11 Nov. 1775) and *Lond. Eve.-Post* (5–7 Dec. 1775). The prominence of the clergy in the published defense of the respectability of the Berkshire address is also noteworthy. *Morn. Chron.* (14 Nov. 1775).

electors.[73] Both the numbers and the unanimity of the clerical response in support of the government explain much concerning local fears over a possible resurgence of Toryism. The clerical response also suggests that the American rebellion was perceived to be a far more radical crime than the Middlesex election affair.

Defenders of the Church believed that the Church was seriously in danger, and the near unanimity of the clergy concerning the government's policy of coercion underscores the reality of this fear. A lengthy letter in *Felix Farley's Bristol Journal* began by pondering, 'Can the clergy remain silent spectators, when the church is equally in danger with the state? – The foundation of that venerable edifice must be preserved in order to support the superstructure.' The author connected the attempts to weaken the Church in the previous Parliament (referring to the movement to alter subscription to the Thirty-Nine Articles) with the current attempt to weaken the State: 'These attempts are made by one and the same set of men.'[74] But it was precisely the language of 'the church in danger' and crude references to 'the common enemy' that convinced Low-Churchmen and Dissenters alike that a possible revival of Toryism was afoot. Critics, equally crudely, claimed that the Church was prostituted to the administration; Canadian papists, it was believed, would descend on the colonists, and the encouragement of Catholicism there would lead to Toryism and persecuting principles in England.[75] A new edition of Matthew Taylor's *Book of Martyrs* was projected, and the advertisement at Bristol claimed that 'every true Protestant hath great Reason to be alarmed'. The notice warned that with Catholicism established in Quebec, and 'Popish Emissaries' indefatigable at home, the possibility of persecution was imminent.[76]

In other settings these fears were somewhat muted, but no less powerful. The Established Church was often associated with privilege, and if actual persecution was not feared, oppression was. A religious counterpart to the debate over the town moor at Newcastle is found in the neighboring borough of Morpeth. In the autumn of 1774, a cause between the rector of Morpeth (plaintiff) and the 'Burgesses and Free Brothers' of that town (defendants) concerning the former's claim to the 'tithes of Corn' produced on the waste lands of Morpeth commons came before a special jury at Newcastle. The verdict was given for the defendants on the basis of a liberal construction of a statute of Edward VI, whereby citizens might obtain a seven year exemption from tithes to barren and waste lands. The editor of the *York Courant* concluded that the decision might be 'the Means of encouraging the Improvement of many Thousands of Acres in the Kingdom, which have been hitherto in a

---

73 Rudé, *Wilkes and Liberty*, p. 144.
74 *Brist. J.* (18 Nov. 1775).
75 *Lond. Eve.-Post* (10–12, 21–4 Oct.; 7–9 Nov. 1775).
76 *Brist. J.* (4, 11, 25 March 1775).

great Measure, locked up from the Hand of Industry, by the narrow and Illiberal construction of this Statute in former times, in favour of the Clergy'.[77] At bottom, the issues in Newcastle and Morpeth were identical: the privilege and status of closed bodies had clashed with a new sense of independence among citizens who were eager to apply 'the hand of industry'. The decision on behalf of the burgesses is all the more remarkable when it is remembered that the mutual interdependence between the law and the Church in the eighteenth century was very great. The episode brings us once again to the competing themes of law, order, the established religion, and force on the one hand, and independence, industry, and freedom on the other.

It is difficult for modern historians living in a secular and thoroughly pluralistic age to appreciate the extent to which religion was interwoven with law. The establishment of the Church in England was viewed as the necessary moral foundation for order in society, and respect for the Church was understood as inextricably tied to respect for the law. Ecclesiastical courts had wide jurisdiction in what we would now consider wholly civil matters; the cooperation of common law judges with ecclesiastical discipline was an accepted tradition. A great many Justices of the Peace, for example, were also Anglican clergymen; at the general quarter sessions of the peace for the county of Hampshire in the fall of 1775, five of the eighteen members of the court were clergymen. It is also of some interest that ten members of this court signed the coercive address from the county.[78] It has been estimated that in the early nineteenth century one forth of all magistrates were clergymen, and thus the Dissenters' anti-clericalism discussed in an earlier chapter was unavoidably construed as an attack, not only on the Church, but on law and good government as well.[79] We have noted the prevalence of attorneys' signatures on the coercive addresses, and the increasingly strong alliance between clergymen and lawyers in the late eighteenth century has been thought by some historians to have contributed directly to the harsher workings of the law.[80] Dissenters who took the trouble to

---

77 *York Cour.* (9 Aug. 1774).
78 Compare *Sal. Win. J.* (9 Oct. 1775) with *Lond. Gaz.* (7–11 Nov. 1775). On ecclesiastical courts see G. V. Bennett, 'Conflict in the Church', pp. 156–7 in Geoffrey Holmes (ed.), *After the Glorious Revolution, 1689–1714* (New York, 1969). See also chap. 1 of Harold J. Berman, *Law and Revolution* (Cambridge, Mass., 1974), 'The Interaction of Law and Religion'.
79 Peter Virgin, *The Church in an Age of Negligence* (Cambridge, 1989), p. 94.
80 Diana McClatchey, *Oxfordshire Clergy, 1777–1869: A Study of the Established Church and the Role of the Clergy in Local Society* (Oxford, 1960), pp. 178–201; E. P. Thompson, 'The Role of Law', pp. 258–69, in *Whigs and Hunters: The Origins of the Black Act* (New York, 1975); Paul Lucas, 'A Collective Biography of the Students and Barristers of Lincoln's Inn, 1680–1804: A Study in the "Aristocratic Resurgence" of the Eighteenth Century', *JMH* 46 (1974), 238–9; E. J. Evans, 'Some Reasons for the Growth of English Rural Anti-Clericalism c. 1750–c. 1830', *P&P* 66 (1975), 101; Arthur Warne, *Church and Society in Eighteenth-Century Devon* (Newton Abbot, 1969), p. 9; for the most recent linking of religion and law, Randall McGowan, '"He Beareth Not the Sword in Vain": Religion and Criminal Law in Eighteenth-

examine the addresses may have seen something ominous in the great number of clergymen's signatures interspersed with lawyers' names. A few Dissenters, like Thomas B. Bayley, who organized the Lancashire conciliatory petition, moved beyond the negative critique of anti-clericalism and worked hard for law reform.[81] Others, especially among the middle and lower orders, undoubtedly continued to feel a keen sense of dispossession and alienation. Dissenters and Anglicans alike who had come to resent the power of the Established Church, came by degrees to feel suspicious of the laws that governed them. The radical Dissenters' opposition to clerical oppression readily extended to a critique of law, and this may be one of the reasons that marginalized Anglicans were attracted to the Dissenters in their expressions of popular opposition. It is certainly one of the main reasons the Dissenters seemed so politically disruptive and threatening in the context of a colonial rebellion.

In contrast to the Church, the Dissenters were widely believed to be sympathetic to the Americans, and this belief was not without foundation. The three denominations did not petition the crown as a group, but in early 1775, the Friends did. The Quakers' petition to the crown in March was the first to plea for peace with no reference to trade: their appeal for a cessation of hostilities was grounded simply in the desirability of peace.[82] With their well-known theological commitment to pacifism, the Quakers fell under particular censure, although numerous loyalist essays appeared in the press, purportedly written by Friends, some of which, no doubt, were satirical. 'Obadiah Steadfast', for example, chastised Edmund Burke for his support of the Bristol petition: 'an unruly spirit dwelleth in thee'.[83] Rumors of seditious activity among the older denominations were also common. Notices appeared in the newspapers of a Dissenting minister named Riley 'conveyed' to Newgate 'on a charge of treasonable practices against the state'. It was also rumored that government messengers had left London for the country 'to fetch up two other Dissenting Ministers sixty or seventy miles off'.[84]

In boroughs where Dissenters had traditionally taken a party line in parliamentary politics we might expect them to be prominent in the petitioning

---

Century England', *ECS* 21 (1987/88), 194, 210; and for a general discussion, John Brewer and John Styles, (eds.), *An Ungovernable People: the English and Their Law in the Seventeenth and Eighteenth Centuries* (London, 1980). Peter King, 'Decision-Makers and Decision-Making in the English Criminal Law, 1750–1800', *HJ* 27 (1984), 58, argues that the two-class, patrician-plebeian model does not work (middling men and even laborers! used the law to protect their property) but King does not address the question of the perception of harshness. See note 30 in chap. 5 above.

81 On Bayley, see Brewer, 'English Radicalism in the Age of George III', p. 366, and on law and traders, p. 348.

82 Petition presented 24 March. Text printed *Lond. Chron.* (5–7 Sept. 1775); *York Cour.* (28 March 1775). See Arthur J. Mekeel, *The Relation of the Quakers to the American Revolution* (Washington, 1979), p. 123.

83 *Brist. J.* (28 Oct. 1775) see also 21 Jan., 4 Feb. 1775.

84 *Brist. J.* (28 Oct. 1775); *Read. Merc.* (30 Oct. 1775); *New. Chron.* (28 Oct. 1775).

agitation; this is particularly evident at Bristol (see Table 10.2).[85] The Dissenters' prominence in petitioning is also evident in Coventry, Nottingham, and Taunton, where, because of a lack of documentary evidence, it was impossible to trace the Dissenters in parliamentary elections. More importantly, however, at Newcastle, where Dissenters were inactive in parliamentary politics, and at Colchester, where a variety of circumstances conspired against their outstanding partisanship in elections during the American crisis, they were exceptionally dedicated to petitioning. It is thus clearly the case that petitioning was an important alternative route to political expression for the Dissenters and many Anglicans as well.

Table 10.2: *Nonconformist Signers of Petitions and Addresses*

	Conciliatory Petitions				Coercive Addresses			
	Total Sign.	% Dissent. Sign.	Dissent. Ministers	Anglican Clergy	Total Sign.	% Dissent. Sign.	Dissent. Ministers	Anglican Clergy
Bristol	[519]	29.1	4	1	[540]	14.1	—	29
Newcastle upon Tyne	[784]	24.4	4	—	[102]	9.8	1	12
Liverpool	[279]	14.3	4	2	471	9.3	—	10
Colchester	509	30.1	6	—	125	5.6	—	9
Coventry	406	18.3	3	—	159	5.0	—	3
Nottingham	328	42.7	8	—	230	17.0	—	5
Taunton	[143]	25.9	3	—	191	6.3	—	2

The congruity between ministers and laity is also especially noteworthy; ministers not only led the petitioning agitation, they led their congregations into opposition to the government. However, this congruity is more impressive among the Dissenters than among the Anglicans; in every borough that produced conflicting documents, the Anglican laity were far more seriously divided over the American crisis than were the Dissenters. The uniformity

85 In each borough, all available registers were compared to the petition and the address. In Bristol, a 50% letter cluster sample of the petition and address was used, and in Newcastle, a 60% sample, though the clergy were counted for the entire documents; the conciliatory petition from Taunton has eleven names totally obscured, and thirteen are obscured in the Lancashire petition: hence, brackets are placed around these figures. The available registers for Coventry are quite weak. Vicar Lane Congregational chapel (RG 4/2980) has only 53 entries for the eighteenth century and West Orchard baptismal register (RG 4/3314) begins in 1775, with the Great Meeting house beginning in 1777 (RG 4/2950). Similarly at Taunton, where the Dissenters may have composed two-thirds of the population, the registers were very poorly kept. Conversely, the registers for Nottingham were extremely well kept and full, though they lack occupational data. Sainsbury, partially on the basis of my earlier article, has seriously underestimated the strength of pro-American sentiment among Dissenters, *Disaffected Patriots*, pp. 80–2.

of the Anglican clergy on behalf of coercion, however, suggests a strong element of ideological commitment among the elite. Rudé believed that the strong support Wilkes gathered from a wide range of social classes could be accounted for in part by the 'social aspirations' of London citizens. In the west counties he noted the discontent among a large body of freeholders over the Cider Acts, while in the great trading cities, he believed that discontent was related to the new trade restrictions on American commerce. He also attributed some importance to the Whig theory of secret influence behind the crown and the malevolent machinations of the 'King's Friends'. Smaller freeholders and wage earners, Rudé argued, were also offended by enclosing landlords, turn-pike trusts, and the payment of tithes in kind.[86] All of these considerations undoubtedly also contributed to the division in English society over America, but by 1775 the religious differences in particular stand out. Any account of social divisions in the fall of 1775 must give a large place to the Common-wealthman ideology of the Dissenting pulpit, combined, to be sure, with the discontent Dissenters felt over the failure to find relief from Subscription in 1772, the Quebec Act, longstanding ties with the colonists, and the menacing actions of the Anglican clergy. These distinctly religious motives certainly played a major role in stimulating opposition to the government's colonial policy among Dissenters and Low Churchmen alike.

In Liverpool there was much less unanimity among Dissenting laymen on behalf of reconciliation and a corresponding failure to divide decisively on socio-economic lines; at least this appears to be the case on the basis of the available evidence.[87] Several developments unique to Liverpool may help account for the failure of Nonconformity to exhibit its characteristic opposition to the government. In comparison to the Bristol Dissenters, the Liverpool Non-conformists were overall less well represented in the shopkeeper and merchant categories. Similarly, Liverpool Dissenters were less involved in parliamentary politics and may have had less experience generally in the political process; this contrasts with Bristol, but is not unlike the situation at Newcastle. The petition-ing agitation emerged in the midst of the violent seamen's strike, and in the aftermath of the riots, a garrison was permanently stationed in Liverpool.[88]

---

86 Rudé, *Wilkes and Liberty*, pp. 185–7. Rudé has done work in correlating food prices and disturbances in London with periods of agitation over Wilkes, pp. 188–9.

87 The number of conciliatory petitioners at Liverpool that can be identified from the direc-tory and poll books (excluding non-parochial registers) was far less than the number for the coercive address (44.4% versus 18.6%) which suggests that the occupational differ-ences may be much greater than the current evidence reveals. This observation is based on the assumption that directories normally included only the more well-to-do members of the community. This would seem to be borne out by the fact that only 14.3% of the 279 petitioners at Liverpool voted in the 1780 parliamentary election. However, these same limitations were also characteristic of the data from Bristol and Newcastle where comparable directories and poll books were used.

88 R. B. Rose, 'The Liverpool Sailors' Strike of 1775', *Proceedings of Lancashire and Cheshire Antiquarian Society* 68 (1958), 91.

These developments were hardly conducive to expression of political opposition to the crown. Ideologically, Liverpool Dissenters appear to have been more
politically conservative than other Dissenters on several accounts. We observed
in chapter 8 that as a group they were deeply involved in the slave trade, and
such involvements may well have dampened interest in radical causes. We also
saw in an earlier chapter that opposition to the movement against subscription
in 1772 arose precisely in Liverpool, and even during the conflict with America
there was a lack of unanimity among the Dissenting ministers; three of the
seven ministers of Liverpool did not sign the petition for peace.[89] There was
little continuity between the radical leadership during the Middlesex election
affair and the agitation over coercive measures, and Liverpool was one of the
few boroughs in the country that sent an address to the crown against Wilkes,
as well as one opposing the action of Parliament. Similarly, unlike Bristol and
Newcastle, we find little evidence of radical societies and clubs at Liverpool.
The dominance of a High Anglican corporation, combined with the Dissenters'
lack of training in parliamentary politics, a lack of a continuous radical tradition
stemming from the Middlesex election affair, and an absence of outstanding
ministerial leadership, rendered the Dissenters politically ineffective during the
American crisis. Thomas B. Bayley, a Dissenting layman, member of the
Society of the Supporters of the Bill of Rights, and active participant in the
affairs of Warrington Academy, organized the county opposition to the
address, but he was unable to fully mobilize either the Dissenting ministry or
the laity. Moreover, at Liverpool we find Low-Church Anglican leadership in
the persons of Reverend Daniel Wilson and Reginald Braithwaite, clerk.[90]

The most telling characteristic of Liverpool Dissent, however, is found in the
lack of progressive leadership from the pulpit. In fact, what little evidence we
have suggests that the Dissenting laity were exposed to a pro-government
political ideology. The majority of Dissenters at Liverpool were Presbyterian,
and, as at Bristol, the Presbyterians' more liberal theological orientation may
have been related to a greater degree of social assimilation. The only sermon
known to have been published during the revolutionary period by a Dissenting
minister was politically moderate, indeed pusillanimous. Robert Lewin, Presbyterian minister, hesitated to publish his sermon even after the war was over
because the Dissenting society in Liverpool, he conceded, was 'divided in poli-

89 Robert Lewin, Hugh Anderson, Nicholas Clayton, and Hezekiah Kirkpatrick signed the
   conciliatory petition, but Samuel Medley (Byrom Street), William Harding (Toxteth
   Park) and Philip Taylor (Kaye Street) did not. On the clerical response to the anti-
   subscription campaign of 1772, see The Thompson List, p. 263. If Toxteth Park,
   Warrington, and Gatacre are included, then six ministers altogether signed in 1772. See
   Bradley, *Popular Politics and the American Revolution in England*, p. 123 note 10.
90 The leaders are found clustered at the top of the third column on the first skin of parchment, HO 55/9/3. The two Anglican clergy signed seventh and ninth respectively, in the
   midst of other known leaders, like Abraham Rawlinson, who signed tenth.

tical sentiments'.[91] This sermon never criticized the conduct of the government directly and Lewin's most pointed comments were put in the mouths of others:

> They who consider the late war as impolitic and unjust, will discern many circumstances, both in the beginning, the process, and the termination of it, as awakening calls to these dominions, to confess our errors, and lament our oppression and guilt, no less than thankfully acknowledge heaven's mercy. And all, who confess a divine Providence, may see the hand of God in depriving us of so considerable a part of our empire, and reducing us to a state of comparative weakness, and obliging us with an exhausted treasury to retire from the field, not with triumph, but with mortifying reflections.

But the sins Lewin lists are 'private oppression', not, be it noted, national oppression; his sole focus throughout is on the personal vices of the public, 'extortion, luxury, fondness for pleasure'. Lewin rejoiced in a monarch who 'seems to study the welfare of the public', and exulted in the continued enjoyment of 'our liberty of thinking and acting'. The heart of the sermon was an exhortation to celebrate the cessation of carnage and the prospect of 'wealth and plenty'.[92] Lewin's sermon strongly hints that he provided little or no political direction to the congregation at Benn's Garden during the war; and this concession to the status quo, combined with the lower socio-economic standing of the majority of Liverpool Dissenters, helps in part to account for the inconsistent behavior of the handful of Dissenters who voted, petitioned, and addressed.

If the Liverpool ministers failed to mobilize the laity, four of the seven ministers were in favor of conciliation. Liverpool seems to provide evidence for differing stages of political consciousness among Dissenters. The ministers themselves identified with the American colonists and radical politics of an age gone by – Hezekiah Kirkpatrick named a son born in 1783 Oliver Cromwell Kirkpatrick[93] – but they made little or no effort to stimulate opposition among the laity of their congregations. It may be the case that religion and economic motivation worked as independent variables in some circumstances, and this is possibly the case at Liverpool. On the other hand, the data from Liverpool may suggest that the potency of Dissenting political radicalism and the sharpness of socio-economic divisions were related in a cause-effect nexus. We know that in every setting in which a petition was sent to the crown, Nonconformists clearly stimulated resistance to the government, and they did so in one of at least three ways; the verbal rhetoric of the Nonconformist pulpit stimulated opposition among Dissenters and probably among Anglicans; second, ministers and laity were actually involved in organizing the petitioning agitation; and third, we will find leadership of a different variety in the example that the Dissenting laity provided for non-Dissenting artisans, a topic to which we will return below.

91 Robert Lewin, *A Thanksgiving Sermon on Account of the Late Peace, Preached at Benn's Garden Chapel, Liverpool, on the 29th July, 1784* (Liverpool, 1784), pp. 1–2.
92 *Ibid.*, pp. 10–11; 6, 8, 11, 15, 19.
93 RG 4/1043 under date 1783.

The consistent way in which artisans and Dissenters across boroughs and in different circumstances arrayed themselves against merchants and lawyers suggests the reality of structural, abiding social divisions. Such elements of grass roots support for a radical cause were undoubtedly present both before and after the Revolution, but the American war stimulated their expression and momentarily revealed deep divisions and antagonisms in society. This alone accounts for why conservative interests at home found the rebellion in a distant land so threatening.

Across numerous boroughs in England, irrespective of size, type of franchise, or dominant economy, certain consistent patterns concerning the division of English society over the American crisis stand out. On the side of the government, the most consistent single body was the clergy, joined, not far behind, by the bar. An equally solid source of support for the crown was the city corporation. Government contractors and placemen were as committed to the crown as the clergy and may have supplied a number of loyal signatures about equal in number to the cloth.[94] Individual local officer holders and a large complement of gentlemen, baronets, and esquires, and at least half the merchants in any given setting rounded out the government supporters in the upper ranks. The middling support for the government is less clearly distinguished, although High-Anglican religious ideology may account for much of it. On the whole, the petitioners came from lower social ranks than the addressers. In short, the addressers on the whole were typified by a higher social status, they represented a traditional order established by law, privilege, and government offices, and in most cases, they stood to benefit by the stability of society and by an emphasis on loyalty to the crown, support for Parliament, law, and good order.

The radicalism of the Dissenters and the Anglican artisans cannot be fathomed except by examining their behavior from the local perspective. How radical were those who petitioned in favor of peaceful concessions with the colonists in the fall of 1775? By that date many people believed that even the formed opposition in Parliament encouraged seditious behavior abroad.[95] This chapter has shown that pleading for conciliatory measures usually entailed taking a political stance against local government in the form of the corporation, local law in the persons of attorneys and Justices of the Peace, and religion in the institution of the Church. It meant that petitioners must also be willing to take issue with the considered political judgment of Parliament and the crown. On the whole, the petitioners belonged to lower social ranks than the addressers. In short, a statement of empathy for the colonies in late 1775

---

94 On contractors, see Bradley, *Popular Politics and the American Revolution in England*, pp. 175–6.
95 *Lond. Chron.* (2–4, 23–5 Nov. 1775); *Gen. Eve. Post* (1–3 Aug.; 12–14 Sept. 1775); *Cumb. Pacq.* (17 Aug. 1775); *Suss. Week. Adv.* (4 Sept. 1775).

involved voicing an opinion against every English institution traditionally associated with law, good order, sound religion, and social stability. It is only when the supporters of peaceful concessions are seen from this local angle and through the eyes of the pro-government essayists who wrote for the provincial press that the true dimensions of their radicalism become visible. In Bristol, Liverpool, Coventry, Newcastle upon Tyne, and other large urban centers, political divisions concerning America often bordered on violence and they continued throughout the war.[96] The social and religious divisions that the petitions of 1775 revealed undoubtedly persisted as well, though they cannot be traced in this volume. It is the persistence of this local radical orientation that holds significant promise for future research on the origins of English radicalism and the emergence of class consciousness. But with the evidence we now have, it is possible to posit an artisan radicalism in the 1770s that represents a transitional stage leading to an even more radical movement in the 1790s.

EIGHTEENTH-CENTURY POLITICAL STRUCTURES AND THE FAILURE OF DISSENTING LEADERSHIP

In each of the seven boroughs in Table 10.2 there was a tradition of party rivalry, and it is clear that Nonconformity was one primary cause of pro-American agitation. We will now examine three boroughs where the Dissenters lacked clerical leadership, faced a tradition-bound political environment, and where there was an absence of party rivalry and thus no tradition of opposition politics (Table 10.3). As a result of these circumstances, conciliatory petitions never emerged from these three boroughs, but in two of the three, the Dissenters did not join the Anglicans in support of coercion in any great numbers; Sudbury alone stands as the exception to the rule.

Table 10.3: *Nonconformist Signers of Addresses at Sudbury, Plymouth, and Barnstaple*

	Total Signers	% Dissent. Signers	Dissent. Ministers	Anglican Clergy
Sudbury	140	25.7	—	3
Plymouth	115	7.0	—	—
Barnstaple	149	8.0	—	1

96 On Bristol, see the narrative in Peter Marshall, *Bristol and the American War of Independence* (Bristol, 1977), and Savadge, 'The West Country', pp. 520–48. On Liverpool and Newcastle, see chap. 8 above.

The coercive petition from Sudbury was strident in tone. The address expressed 'detestation and abhorrence of the most unnatural Rebellion' in the colonies – a rebellion that calls 'aloud for the decisive Exertions of Your Majesty's Arms' in the hope that the King's 'Fleets and Armies' would so chastise the Americans that they may be brought back to their senses.[97] Traditionally, the mayor and corporation offered the borough to the highest bidder, and as a result, Sudbury gained a reputation as one of the most venal boroughs in England. As it was 'a large manufactory town', several of the families that belonged to the Presbyterian chapel were in 'plentiful circumstances', and among them was Thomas Fenn, the receiver general of the land tax for part of Suffolk.[98] In 1761 Fenn had an argument with Thomas Fonnereau, a large government contractor, who had cultivated an interest in the borough for some time. This had a decisive influence on borough politics, because with the assistance of some of the 'principal people' in the Presbyterian church,[99] the patronage of the Duke of Grafton, and large amounts of money, Fenn himself became the patron of the borough. The political strength of the Dissenters at this time is demonstrated by the fact that in Fonnereau's unsuccessful attempt to oust Fenn from the receivership, a local correspondent noted in 1763 that the only way to avoid an expensive contest would be to find another receiver general 'agreeable to the general body of Dissenters and freemen'.[100] When Grafton became First Lord in 1766, he supported both of Fenn's nominees, and as a result, Fonnereau was heavily trounced.

Thus a local Dissenter not only drove out an Anglican incumbent, but he secured the return of two government candidates for money in a venal borough with a large proportion of Dissenting voters. This is the context in which the coercive petition was circulated, and along with the names of numerous other Dissenters were the signatures of Thomas Fenn, Esq. and one of his M.P.s, Sir Walden Hamner, who presented the petition. It seems likely that there were Dissenters at Sudbury who would have petitioned for conciliation (had there been such a petition), like the Presbyterian minister, John Lombard, who petitioned for relief from subscription in 1772,[101] but the most that can be said for Lombard is that he abstained from signing the address. The behavior of those Dissenters who did sign the coercive address, however, is difficult to account for on any other basis than that of social deference to the prevailing

---

97 HO 55/11/1; RG 4/1861; 3652; 4018. *Commons, 1715–1754*, 1: 327; *Commons, 1754–1790*, 1: 382. Sir Lewis Namier, *The Structure of Politics, at the Accession of George III* (London, 1929, 2nd edn, 1957), p. 158.

98 This account is derived from the history of Josiah Thompson (ed.), 4: *History of Protestant Dissenting Congregations*, 5 vols., 1772– , MS 38.7–11, 259–61, (hereafter cited as Thompson, History).

99 This crucial connection is noted in Thompson, History, 4: 260–1. The Church was finally split over the issue in 1765.

100 *Commons, 1754–1790*, 2: 448; 1: 383.

101 'A View of English Nonconformity in 1773', *CHST* 5 (1911–12), 373.

pattern of politics. With no tradition of opposition to guide them, and without competent leadership from the ministry, Sudbury Presbyterians appear to have readily capitulated to habit. When William Smith, the reforming Dissenter, was returned for Sudbury in 1784, it was still necessary to ply the electors with the expected gifts, and while this has caused Smith's biographer some embarrassment, it demonstrates the way Sudbury politics worked for Anglican and Dissenter alike.[102]

Plymouth was an important center of Nonconformity, and the borough sustained a close connection to the government through the Admiralty.[103] As a port town it had an enormous amount of government patronage to dispense, and on this basis the government returned whomever it wished. The Dissenters had over 30 percent of the vote in the early part of the century, but this interest was apparently used simply in support of government candidates; there is currently no evidence to link the Dissenters to the movement for independence from the corporation that emerged in 1780.[104] It is possible that the presence of the Dissenters at Plymouth contributed to the mildness of the address, but in any case, only a few Dissenters supported it.

Barnstaple had almost as bad a reputation for venality as Sudbury, and yet here, unlike Sudbury, only a few Dissenters signed the coercive address.[105] This may be related, just as at Plymouth, to the exclusion of Dissenters from offices of trust, but further work must be done to establish this conclusively. Barnstaple Dissenters controlled almost a third of the electorate in 1715, but money, not party rivalry based on ideology, determined the outcome of elections.[106] If corruption was rife in the first half of the century, it was even worse in the second half, yet only a small percentage of Nonconformists signed their names to the coercive address of the mayor, aldermen, and principal inhabitants. Thus while venality may help account for the large proportion of Dissenters who favored coercion at Sudbury, it by no means explains everything. It does seem likely, however, that wherever Dissenters held office

---

102 Richard W. Davis, *Dissent in Politics, 1780–1830: The Political Life of William Smith, M.P.* (London, 1971), pp. 16, 19.
103 HO 55/10/10. RG 4/1216; 1218; 2537; 2159. *Commons, 1715–1754*, 1: 228; *Commons, 1754–1790*, 1: 258.
104 In 1715 there were over 1,500 Presbyterians, Congregationalists, and Baptists, and they had 72 voters in an electorate of about 200. By 1773, however, they had drastically declined. On these and the voting statistics on Barnstaple see James Bradley, 'Nonconformity and the Electorate in Eighteenth-Century England', *Parliamentary History* 6 (1987), 236–61. *Commons, 1754–1790*, 1: 258; 3: 80. John Macbride (M.P., Plymouth, 1784–1790) opposed the administration candidates. He was the son of a Presbyterian minister, but his connection at Plymouth had less to do with his religious heritage than his career in the navy.
105 HO 55/11/33; RG 4/513, and film no. 1238637 from the Genealogical Society of Utah.
106 In 1715 there were 950 Dissenters at Barnstaple, but by 1773 that had declined considerably. They had 100 voters in an electorate of 320 in 1715. *Commons, 1715–1754*, 1: 548, 443, 406; *Commons, 1754–1790*, 1: 225; 2: 391.

in an environment like Sudbury with its characteristic trait of political bartering and its lack of a tradition of party rivalry, their sensitivity to constitutional issues such as those raised by the American Revolution would tend to be dulled. The failure of Dissent in these three boroughs is also related to the size of the cities and the particular stage of their commercial independence.[107]

With few exceptions, however, it is possible to conclude that under a variety of circumstances, many of which were inimical to political principle, the majority of Dissenters gave strong support to conciliatory measures. In each borough, however, there was a small proportion of conservative Dissenters, ranging from a low of 5 percent at Coventry, to more than 25 percent of the coercive addressers at Sudbury. The basis for these Dissenters' support for the government must be explained. Caleb Evans candidly admitted that Baptist laymen, including some members of his own congregation, in addition to several Dissenting ministers he knew personally, supported the North administration; in fact, over 50 percent of the identifiable Dissenters who signed the Bristol address for coercion were Baptists.[108] In a few cases, the basis for the Dissenters' conservatism can be inferred from their social status and employment. Isaac Elton and John Merlott were at once, Presbyterians, esquires, and local office holders, the first an alderman, and the second, a sheriff. We have noted the great number of Dissenters at Bristol who were custom-house officers. Daniel Harson, the collector of customs, was a former Presbyterian minister associated with Tucker Street chapel, and in addition, almost half of the custom-house officers who signed the address were Dissenters.[109] Other Dissenters such as Thomas Bate, who was in the mayor's office, and John Bayly, lieutenant in the Royal Navy, signed the address.[110] At Nottingham, Cornelius Huthwait, Dissenter and alderman, headed the address, and John Greaves Farnsworth, William Johnson, and Thomas Plowman, gentlemen and Dissenters, agreed with the appeal for coercive measures. We have seen how Thomas Fenn's support for the government at Sudbury is explicable in light of his receivership and government connections. The lowest proportion of pro-government Dissenters are found in those boroughs where Dissenters were excluded from office and where there was an outspoken radical ministerial

107 In a study of eighteenth-century Nottingham, Malcolm Thomis has argued that the economic evolution of a city is directly related to its political independence, *Politics and Society in Nottingham, 1785–1835* (Oxford, 1969), pp. 195–6.
108 Caleb Evans, *A Reply to the Rev. Mr. Fletcher's Vindication of Mr. Wesley's Calm Address to Our American Colonies*, p. 85. The Baptist proportion was 54.8%; the Presbyterians had 23.3% and the Quakers 21.9%. The majority of the Baptists who addressed were in the tradesmen and artisan category. See Table 10:4 and the discussion below.
109 Peter T. Underdown, 'Edmund Burke, The Commissary of his Bristol Constituents, 1774–1780', *EHR* 73 (1958), 255–6. Of the ten officers in the 50% letter cluster sample, four were Dissenters. John Ellison, Joseph Grove, and Thomas Miller are identified as custom-house officers in the registers themselves (RG 4/1830, 2497), though William Miles is not.
110 Occupations are confirmed from the Broad Mead registers.

voice, such as at Newcastle and Taunton. We may thus infer a high degree of interaction between structural and ideological influences.

In the majority of cases, however, it is impossible even to guess at the rationale for the Dissenters' support of the government. William Tolladay and Jacob Dansie of Sudbury were good Presbyterians, but they, and a large number of their fellow Dissenters, wished the fleets and armies of the king godspeed. James Berry of Taunton, tradesman, and Timothy Shorey, baymaker of Colchester, whose father was a deacon in the Congregational Church, both supported the government; so did Thomas Sly of Gosford Street, Coventry, and William Treen of Broadgate. The Bristol Quakers are especially difficult to understand; Neville Bath, Peregrine Bowen, and Sampson Sutton were all of the middling rank (a cutler, tanner, and cooper, respectively) yet they thought that force was the best means of bringing the colonists to their senses. In London, the Yearly Meeting of the Society of Friends positively recommended that Quakers avoid any involvement in the agitation concerning America. Thomas Nickleson, Quaker merchant of Poole, had the courage to make a public statement concerning his loyalist politics. For him the issue centered on the support of law and order. Certainly, wealth, status and, in some instances, a pacifist theology played a role in Quaker motivation, but Nickleson and other Quakers defended their position on the basis of a well articulated, clear commitment to political independence.[111] These and a minority of other Dissenters undoubtedly understood themselves to be faithful to their religious principles, but they expressed confidence in the government's coercive policy. These specific illustrations of pro-government Dissenters raise the possibility of a more generalized interdependence of religion and socioeconomic status as causal factors of pro-Americanism.

THE INTERDEPENDENCE OF RELIGIOUS AND ECONOMIC MOTIVATION

If conservative Dissenters were influenced to favor the government either by their wealth, social standing, or employment, high ranking Dissenters in even greater numbers gave their support to conciliation. We have already observed this characteristic independence among Dissenting corporation members at Bristol, Coventry, and Nottingham. Table 10.4 compares all Dissenting petitioners to non-Dissenting petitioners and shows that whatever support there was for peace among the ranks of the elite was derived mostly from the Dissenting elite in the upper two categories. They comprise one-half of all the identifiable elite who supported conciliation. (See the summary in Table 10.5.) These data corroborate the earlier results based on an investigation of Great

---

111 See the attack on the Quakers by 'A Friend to Truth', *Lond. Eve.-Post* (26–8 Sept.; 7–10 Oct. 1775) and the signed response by Thomas Nickleson, *Lond. Eve.-Post* (3–5 Oct. 1775), and another Quaker, *Gen. Eve. Post* (7–10 Oct. 1775). On the London Quakers, none of whom signed the petition, see Sainsbury, *Disaffected Patriots*, p. 117.

Table 10.4: Nonconformist Petitioners' and Addressers' Occupations and All Other Petitioners' and Addressers' Occupations

BRISTOL

	Conciliatory		Coercive	
	Diss.	Other	Diss	Other
1. Gentlemen, Professions	17(21.5)	10 (9.9)	9(28.1)	94(33.8)
2. Merchants	10(12.7)	17(16.8)	5(15.6)	57(20.5)
3. Shopkeepers	19(24.0)	28(27.7)	4(12.5)	47(16.9)
4. Artisans	33(41.8)	43(42.6)	12(37.5)	74(26.6)
5. Laborers	0	2 (2.0)	2 (6.3)	5 (1.8)
6. Others	0	1 (1.0)	0	1 (.4)
	79	101	32	278

NEWCASTLE UPON TYNE

	Conciliatory		Coercive	
	Diss.	Other	Diss.	Other
1. Gentlemen, Professions	4 (4.9)	6 (2.3)	3(30)	29(32.2)
2. Merchants	2 (2.4)	22 (8.3)	4(40)	24(26.7)
3. Shopkeepers	26(31.7)	77(29.3)	2(20)	16(17.8)
4. Artisans	45(54.9)	147(55.9)	1(10)	21(23.3)
5. Laborers	4 (4.9)	11 (4.2)	0	0
6. Others	1 (1.2)	0	0	0
	82	263	10	90

LIVERPOOL

	Conciliatory		Coercive	
	Diss.	Other	Diss.	Other
1. Gentlemen, Professions	7(21.9)	8(16.3)	4(11.1)	60(31.7)
2. Merchants	13(40.6)	16(32.7)	11(30.6)	51(27.0)
3. Shopkeepers	3 (9.4)	12(24.5)	7(19.4)	45(23.8)
4. Artisans	8(25.0)	13(26.5)	14(38.9)	33(17.5)
5. Laborers	1 (3.1)	0	0	0
6. Others				
	32	49	36	189

COLCHESTER

	Conciliatory		Coercive	
	Diss.	Other	Diss	Other
1. Gentlemen, Professions	10(13.3)	3 (4.2)	1	30(56.6)
2. Merchants	5 (6.6)	3 (4.2)	0	1 (1.9)
3. Shopkeepers	20(26.7)	21(29.6)	0	12(22.6)
4. Artisans	29(38.7)	39(54.9)	2	7(13.2)
5. Laborers	3 (4.0)	5 (7.1)	0	0
6. Others	0	1 (1.0)	0	1 (.4)
	75	71	3	53

COVENTRY

	Conciliatory		Coercive	
	Diss.	Other	Diss.	Other
1. Gentlemen, Professions	19(22.4)	7(11.7)	4(25.0)	25(24.0)
2. Merchants	11(12.9)	1 (1.7)	0	8 (7.7)
3. Shopkeepers	15(17.6)	13(21.6)	3(18.8)	35(33.7)
4. Artisans	40(47.1)	39(65.0)	9(56.2)	35(33.7)
5. Laborers	0	0	0	0
6. Others	0	0	1 (.9)	1 (.9)
	85	60	16	104

NOTTINGHAM

	Conciliatory		Coercive	
	Diss.	Other	Diss.	Other
1. Gentlemen, Professions	3 (7.3)	2 (1.6)	0	8 (6.0)
2. Merchants	2 (4.9)	15(11.7)	1	4 (3.0)
3. Shopkeepers	3 (7.3)	25(19.5)	2	36(26.9)
4. Artisans	32(78.1)	86(67.2)	8	85(63.4)
5. Laborers	0	0	0	0
6. Others	1 (2.4)	0	1	1 (.7)
	41	128	12	134

Yarmouth, Southampton, and Cambridge. If the support the conservative Dissenters gave to coercion is explained by their wealth and status, higher social status by no means led the majority of Dissenters over to the government; as Dissenters they maintained an oppositionist stance despite higher social status, and this fact has important implications for the discussion concerning radicalism and the role of religion in the evolution of class or group consciousness.

These data help explain the lesser extent of socio-economic division between petitioners and addressers at Nottingham and possibly at Coventry (Table 10.1), for in these two boroughs the Dissenters had attained a great degree of social acceptance – so much so that they were opposed by Anglican, anti-corporation parties.[112] The Dissenters' support of conciliatory measures was just as strong here as elsewhere, but the overall social differences between petitioners and addressers were definitely muted. At Nottingham, nine gentlemen, a baronet, and two esquires signed the petition, but seven of the gentlemen and one of the esquires were Dissenters. Thus, when the Dissenters with occupations are separated from the non-Dissenting petitioners, the socio-economic contrast between petitioners and addressers is more notable, both at Nottingham, and to a lesser extent, at Coventry. When Nonconformity truly leavened the highest strata of a community, it lost little of its ideological rigor. However, there appears to be little question that the extent of Dissenting support for coercion at Bristol (14% of the total) and at Nottingham (17%, Table 10.2) is related to the greater degree of social assimilation into the highest levels the Dissenters had experienced in these boroughs. This conservatism contrasts quite predictably with the Dissenters' behavior at Newcastle, Colchester, and Taunton, where they were excluded from civic life. At Coventry, because of the very small number of identifiable petitioners among the elite, this interpretation is less compelling, though it seems likely. The specific occupations at Coventry reflect the dominance of the textile industry, and while many different kinds of weavers are distinguished, the nominal nature of these data and their concentration in the artisan category makes finer occupational analysis that might discriminate levels of wealth impossible.[113] The greater division along socio-economic lines in the large seaports of Bristol and Newcastle may be related to more greatly diversified economies, though it will take more detailed research to further illumine the question.

112 Using the available data for all six boroughs in Table 10.4, summarized in Table 10.5, X^2 shows that the occupational differences between Dissenters and Anglicans who petitioned for peace are statistically significant, while those between Dissenters and Anglicans who addressed are not.

113 Coventry and Nottingham were both textile centers; based on occupational data, there was less apparent socio-economic differences here between petitioners and addressers than elsewhere. Yet Colchester was also a cloth manufacturing center and it stands out in this regard.

Table 10.5: *Combined Occupations of Nonconformists and All Other Petitioners' and Addressers' Occupations*

	Conciliatory		Coercive	
	Diss.	Other	Diss.	Other
1. Gentlemen, Professions	60(15.2)	36 (5.4)	21(19.3)	246(29.0)
2. Merchants	43(10.9)	74(11.0)	21(19.3)	145(17.1)
3. Shopkeepers	86(21.8)	176(26.2)	18(16.5)	191(22.5)
4. Artisans	187(47.5)	367(54.6)	46(42.2)	255(30.1)
5. Laborers	8 (2.0)	18 (2.7)	2 (1.8)	6 (.7)
6. Other	10 (2.5)	1 (.1)	1 (.9)	5 (.6)
	394	672	109	848

Table 10.5 shows that proportionately more non-Dissenting petitioners were drawn from the artisan ranks. The contrast with non-Dissenting addressers who were artisans is striking in this regard. Overall, the non-Dissenting artisans comprised 54.6 percent of the petitioners, but among non-Dissenting addressers, artisans comprised only 30.1 percent of the whole (and except for Coventry and Nottingham, this average would have been lower). By comparing the strength of the relationship between religion and petitioning (Table 10.2) and that between socio-economic status and petitioning (Table 10.5) it is clear that both factors were equally strong.[114] More importantly, just as with Yarmouth, Southampton, and Cambridge, religious and economic motivation appear to be interactive. By regrouping the occupational categories in Table 10.5 into high (categories 1 and 2), middle (categories 3 and 4), and low (categories 5 and 6) we discern a clear correspondence between these ranks and the relative strength of the popular response to the government. In each of the three categories religion was important in determining whether or not a person supported or opposed the government's American policy, but religion was considerably more important among the elite than it was among the artisans and laborers.[115] For some Anglicans (certainly the clergy) their religion and socio-

114 Using all available data, the gamma for Table 10.2 is .50 and for Table 10.5 it is .52, thus indicating equally strong associations between religious affiliation and petitioning on the one hand, and socio-economic rank and petitioning, on the other. A gamma of .6 or above is generally thought to indicate a strong correlation, while a gamma of .2 is normally not worthy of attention. See the discussion in John Phillips, *Electoral Behavior*, p. 210 and the reference cited there.

115 The gammas for high, middle, and low ranks are .79, .56, and .55 respectively; these results are almost identical to those tabulated in my earlier study of Yarmouth, Cambridge, Southampton, Bridgwater, and Poole. For the six boroughs in Table 10.5, if category 3 is left by itself and 4 and 5 are combined, the gammas are .79, .68, and .48 respectively.

economic status or their standing in the community, their attitudes toward law, and their assumptions about the social foundations for a well-ordered State were conducive to support for the government. This fact contrasts remarkably with the clergy in the early part of the century. For the Dissenters, a higher socio-economic standing contributed to their support for conciliatory measures, and this suggests that there was a perceived inequity between their social status and the social recognition they received. At Bristol and Nottingham the Dissenters had attained social recognition for themselves, but they were also aware that their fellow Nonconformists in other settings were denied it. At the same time, we see strong support for conciliation among non-Dissenting artisans, and thus at least two distinct groups coalesced to form a pro-American perspective: Nonconformists and skilled artisans and shopkeepers. The religious affiliation of these 'non-Dissenting' artisans is difficult if not impossible to determine. Some of them may have been Dissenters, who failed, for one reason or another, to have their names recorded in the non-parochial registers. It seems likely that many of them were Low-Church Anglicans, since in electoral politics, numerous Anglicans voted with the Dissenters. On the other hand, since Church attendance was on the decline, particularly in large urban areas, these artisans may have been quite thoroughly secularized. It is not unlikely that the pro-American artisans were comprised of all three groups of men. The exact status of the artisans, and the nature of the relationship between these groups, will thus remain problematic, though some attempt to account for the relationship is required.

The economic motives of the middling and artisan ranks examined earlier in this chapter make it entirely plausible that we have two relatively independent strands of motivation intersecting; the one, more religious, supplied the ideology, the intellectual impetus, and the leadership; the other, more economic, supplied the bulk of numbers in a grass roots response. The petitioners, however, seem to provide evidence of an alliance between the Dissenters, non-Dissenting artisans, and Low-Church Anglicans that corroborates the pattern discovered in electoral politics. Because of their ideological tradition and social experience, Nonconformists had a heightened awareness of social inequity, and acting on the basis of this awareness, they became catalysts for change. Dissenting ministers, as the Lord's Remembrancers, led the laity from the pulpit, Commonwealthman ideology was taken to heart by the average Nonconformist, and the seriousness of the Dissenters' conviction was demonstrated in their voting and petitioning behavior. Some artisans had doubtless assimilated true Whig principles directly from the radical press and from Low-Church Anglican clergymen without the intermediation of liberal Dissenters. Though it is not possible to prove that Dissent formed more than a disciplined core around which Low-Church Anglican or secular artisans could rally, it is possible in some cases to infer that the Dissenters stimulated artisan radicalism.

Nottingham and Coventry are the best evidence we have of the Dissenters' influence, because though they held local office and excluded some Anglicans, other citizens in these boroughs were willing to associate themselves with a political option that was everywhere characterized as a specifically Dissenting political position.

The exact mechanism by which Dissenters may have influenced the artisans is not perfectly clear, but the existing evidence at least allows the formulation of a hypothesis. Three overlapping levels of influence may be posited: organizational, ideological, and social. First, it can be documented that the Dissenters were the actual organizers and leaders of the petitioning agitation; this has been firmly established for Bristol, Liverpool, Nottingham, Coventry, Colchester, Great Yarmouth (with the Hurry family), Southampton (with the Bernards), and Poole (with the Joliffes). At Yarmouth, for example, seven of the first ten signers of the petition were Dissenters. In those settings in which the Dissenting ministers or the laity did not promote the petitions by organizing the masses, ministers gave ideological support to radical causes from the pulpit. At Newcastle upon Tyne, Taunton, and Cambridge, Nonconformist clergy did not lead the Dissenters from the hustings, but from the pulpit and in the press, and if, because of structural conditions or legal constraints, they were not first at the polls, they set a radical example by being first to speak against the government and first to sign their names to petitions. We have examined the Dissenters' ideology of independence and resistance to the government at Bristol, Newcastle, Norwich, Nottingham, and Taunton, and to these voices must be added dozen of others in boroughs and towns across the land. The ratio of known radical Dissenting preachers to loyalist Dissenting preachers is four to one. With the possible exception of London, in every documented case of a pro-American petition to the king, the Dissenters were involved in leadership and gave some support to it. Artisans were not afraid of associating with the Dissenters who preached this message of independence; indeed, they appear to have been attracted to it. At Plymouth and Sudbury, where the elite failed to give clear direction to the laity, there was a corresponding lack of radical activity. The role of Dissenting leadership in stimulating resistance to the government's American policy was therefore pivotal, from both a strategic and an ideological viewpoint. Where there was a radical Dissenting voice, there was a measurable response among the Dissenting laity and numerous non-Dissenting artisans. The Dissenting elite did in fact rally the support of Anglicans and artisans.

The American crisis also elicited a strong response among Anglican clergymen. In reaction to High Anglicans, the Low-Church clergy took a distinct position against the government's policy of coercion that is largely indistinguishable from the Dissenters. Low-Church clergymen such as James Rouquet, curate of St. Werburgh and lecturer at St. Nicholas, Bristol,

Benjamin Hutchinson, vicar in Huntingdonshire, Daniel Wilson and Reginald Braithwaite of Liverpool, Dr. Richard Watson, Regius Professor of Divinity at Cambridge, Richard de Courcy, evangelical Anglican of Shrewsbury, Jonathan Shipley, Bishop of St. Asaph, and of course, such well-known radicals as Granville Sharp, enjoyed highly visible profiles in the revolutionary setting.[116] They taught the same political principles from the pulpit as the Dissenting ministers, and they had, therefore, a potential influence on the Low-Church laity. The clergy's actual role in leading the Anglican laity was illustrated by the signatures of a handful of Low-Church Anglican clergy on the petitions for peace in the fall of 1775.

In twelve boroughs it was possible to identify ninety-two Anglican clergymen who supported coercive measures, as over against only seven in the same boroughs who petitioned in favor of peace. This minority of about one in ten, however, clearly reflects a much larger body of pro-American supporters among the Anglican laity.[117] The Anglican support of the Americans above all shows that the orthodox underpinnings of the State were not monolithic. The Anglican clerical leaders were not Whigs simply because they deferred to the great Whig magnates; rather, they heartily embraced the Revolution settlement, they were cautious about the exercise of political power, they were sympathetic toward the American colonists, and they were tolerant toward Protestant Dissenters. Many of them supported Parliamentary reform. But the Low-Church Anglican clergy were not nearly as active in leadership as the Dissenting ministers; it is entirely likely that they served more as a sanction to justify the behavior of some of the Anglican laity, and specifically some Anglican artisans, who were unwilling to follow the lead of the Dissenting minister alone.

But the strong leadership the Dissenters gave to pro-Americanism in their own ranks seems to have worked at a more general, social level as well. The evidence adduced in this study suggests far more than that 'Discontent was often translated into disaffection by Dissent: men were persuaded of a group interest as a sect, against the Church; not yet as a class, against the employer'.[118] We do in fact find evidence that the religious group interest of Dissent directly stimulated a class-like grouping among the artisans. Dissenters

---

116 On these clergymen, see, Caleb Evans, *The Death of a Great and Good Man Lamented and Improved. A Sermon ... Occasioned by the Death of the Rev. James Rouquet* (Bristol, 1776), p. 16; Henry P. Ippel, 'Blow the Trumpet, Sanctify the Fast', *Huntington Library Quarterly* 44 (1980), 46, 57, 59; and 'British Sermons and the American Revolution', *JRH* 12 (1982), 201; Colin Bonwick, *English Radicals and the American Revolution* (Chapel Hill, 1977), pp. 7, 30, 137. Thomas Lacqueur and James Obelkevich have both argued that religion contributed to a communal self-identity that had important political overtones, though the Low-Church, High-Church distinction is neglected.

117 See Bradley, *Popular Politics and the American Revolution in England*, pp. 192–3 and Table 10.2 above.

118 J. C. D. Clark, *English Society, 1688–1832* (Cambridge, 1985), p. 377.

were not the only ones who occasionally felt oppressed by the constricting grip of legal and corporate privilege. Society, while relatively open, was heavily influenced and sometimes controlled by social elites, and lower ranking Anglicans as well as Dissenters experienced pressure from the privileged. This common perception of exclusion, extending in some cases to actual oppression, is illustrated by the ease with which a minority of Dissenters in borough after borough was able to rally a large body of Low-Church Anglicans in opposition to corporations dominated by High Anglicans.[119] Through their experience of inequality under English statutes, the Dissenters had learned both how to utilize the law to their own advantage, and to criticize the law, and they were bolder than others to attack privileged enclaves that were guarded by law. They seem to have been able to communicate both their suspicion of the establishment in Church and State and their boldness to speak out to many of their fellow citizens who were not Dissenters. We found hints of some Anglicans' sense of alienation from the law in William Hogarth's satirical print on power entitled 'Some Principal Inhabitants of the Moon', (1725)[120] and Paul Lucas has connected the increasing severity of the law to the growing alliance between the Church and the bar in the late eighteenth century.[121] Nonconformists were unusually conscious of their inferior legal status, and Anglicans and non-Anglicans alike who experienced various constrictions of opportunity seem to have eagerly identified with the Dissenting interest. Anglican Low-Church support for the principle of religious toleration appears to have had a social counterpart in an antipathy towards oligarchy, privilege, and even the law, at least in its local, High-Church manifestations.[122]

Evidently, the disaffection of Dissent helped solidify a community interest, structured in part on a socio-economic and status related basis. This may even have occurred at Bristol and Nottingham where the Dissenters themselves were often more wealthy than other citizens. Here there were numerous Dissenters among the elite and merchant classes who could have influenced Anglican or secular artisans. Certainly the political writings of the Dissenting ministers like Caleb Evans and George Walker influenced many non-Dissenters, but ideology was not the only dynamic force at work. At Bristol, Dissenters who were

---

119 These observations help explain John Brooke's comment that a large Dissenting population 'always provided a leaven of independence in a constituency'. *Commons, 1754–1790*, 1: 27.

120 See R. S. Neale, *Class in English Society 1680–1850* (Totowa, 1981), p. 160.

121 Paul Lucas, 'A Collective Biography', 238–9. See also Douglas Hay, 'Property, Authority, and the Criminal Law', p. 23 in *Albions Fatal Tree: Crime and Society in Eighteenth-Century England* (New York, 1975), by Douglas Hay *et al.*, on the increased number of convictions in the last half of the century, and the decline in the number of death sentences. See note 80 above.

122 Tories commonly inveighed against oligarchy, and some Dissenters (at Nottingham, for example), had become oligarchic. Somewhat surprisingly, however, even these Dissenters had imbibed the rhetoric of opposition to privilege, and numerous artisans followed their lead.

aldermen, like William Barnes, a wealthy sugar baker, would have commanded much respect, as would the well-to-do clothiers, John and Francis Bull. Other wealthy Dissenters like Champion, Harford, and Noble not only led the people from the standpoint of organizing the petitioning agitation, but as merchants, they had many dependents, not all of whom were Dissenters. In addition, there was J. B. Beckett, bookseller and Dissenter, who sold radical pamphlets, and William Gayner, the one broker who supported conciliation and who was also a Quaker. At Nottingham, a similar picture emerges. Beyond the overwhelming influence of the Dissenting pulpit in favor of conciliation (including George Walker, Peter Emans, Edward Williams, Richard Hopper, Richard Plumb, J. T. Alliston, J. Simpson, and Samuel Stratham), the social status of the Dissenting laity was very impressive, particularly the corporation members: Humphrey Hollins and James Hornbuckle were gentlemen and aldermen; James and John Foxcroft and Jonathan Inglesant were gentlemen and common councilmen. Mark Huish and Matthews Whitlock were both prominent hosiers and common councilmen and they undoubtedly had numerous dependents. The possible influence of the wealthy, however, is much less clear at Newcastle, Colchester, and Coventry.

It might be argued that those artisans who deferred to the leadership and example of Dissenting social superiors could not possibly constitute incipient class radicals. It is true that we do not discern in the mid-1770s a community interest consistently oriented along horizontal class lines. But Dissenters across the nation had earned a reputation for opposing established power structures; this fact was apparently more important to urban tradesmen and artisans than the Dissenters' occasional higher social standing. While economically powerful, the Dissenters at Bristol and Nottingham were apparently not perceived by the artisans as exercising their power in an oppressive way, unlike many entrenched Anglican bodies. Indeed, their higher standing may have held out hope for those who wished to obtain a greater degree of independence. For many years Anglicans in numerous boroughs had accepted the Dissenters' leadership of anti-corporation parties, and since even the wealthiest Dissenters continued to resist the more powerful and seemingly oppressive structures of local and national politics, artisans would have naturally looked to them for leadership. The Dissenters were psychologically, and in some cases, actually marginalized, and they espoused a powerful ideology of independence; religion thereby did function as a transitional mechanism helping discontented artisans to focus their opposition to entrenched vested interests. Religion served as a stimulus whereby artisans gradually became cohesive as a community on a horizontal plane; the basis for the cohesion was, of course, eventually secularized. The threat of uncontrollable power exercised by borough elites helped provoke the Dissenters' radical rhetoric against perceived oppressiveness; shopkeepers and artisans in turn seem to have found this rhetoric convincing because they followed it and associated with the Dissenters, not only where the latter had a higher social status, as at Bristol and Nottingham, but where they were equal, or even perhaps lower in social standing.

Corporation–anti-corporation conflict was important for the emergence of divisions over the American crisis, but not determinative. Whether in office or out, the majority of Dissenters were pro-American; and whether in office or out, High-Anglicans were consistently pro-government. The boroughs of Nottingham and Coventry are particularly revealing in this regard, since the Anglicans who were out of office maintained a pro-government position. It is undoubtedly true that the open door for office at Bristol and Nottingham, and possibly at Coventry, dulled the unanimity of the Dissenters' pro-American-ism. Certainly the greater proportion of conservative Dissenters in these boroughs is readily explicable in these terms. We have seen that where Dissenters were excluded from office, as at Newcastle, Colchester, and Taunton, there were fewer Dissenters in favor of coercion. The Dissenters might be excluded from the corporation, or they might control the corporation; they might be somewhat on the lower side of the social scale, as we find at Liverpool, or on the higher side, as at Bristol; religion might have been interactive with social status, though it might have functioned independently of social status; but the constant in all of this was that the Dissenters, the shopkeepers, and particularly the artisans bravely opposed the government's decision to coerce the colonists.

From Taunton, the center of Commonwealthman ideas in western England, to Newcastle, a great northern entrepôt, English Dissenters in 1775 cast their lot for the Americans and their Revolution. All of the boroughs that sent conciliatory petitions to the crown sustained a large population of Dissenters, and together they comprised approximately one-fourth of the pro-American movement. Writing to Fox in 1777, Burke observed that the Dissenters were electorally important to the Whigs, and in the same year he wrote to Rockingham and listed the various interests that the Whigs must overcome, concluding, 'we contend in a manner against the whole Church'.[123] On this count, Burke was surely correct: in a number of constituencies the Dissenters were 'the main effective part of the Whig strength', and in many settings their greatest opponent was the Anglican Church and its clergy. This is but one of a number of Whig intuitions about English Dissenters that have turned out to be remarkably accurate, and it explains a great deal about contemporary perceptions of two 'parties' in the nation.

Yet Burke seriously underestimated the vitality of Dissenting activity on behalf of the colonists, and it is little wonder that his forays into popular politics were resisted by Lord Rockingham. The social divisions examined in

123 *Burke Correspondence*, 3: 312; Burke to the Marquis of Rockingham, 6 Jan. 1777.

this chapter portray Church, corporation, gentlemen, professions, and law arrayed against Dissent, with its anti-clericalism, shopkeepers, and artisans, and these divisions largely explain why radicalism was politically impotent and why pro-Americanism failed; the opposition to the administration was profoundly divided between the Rockinghams and the radicals. The social composition of provincial urban pro-Americanism made any significant alliance with the proprietary party of Rockingham unworkable, and all the weight of wealth and influence was on the side of the government. But radicalism was far from dead; a new movement with new themes would emerge in less than five years, and when it began, it derived much of its inspiration and many of its provincial leaders from the Dissenters and former pro-Americans.

Conclusion

I

In the aftermath of the popular agitation over Wilkes, and in the midst of the colonists' resistance to the government's coercive measures, the cry of liberty struck a responsive chord in the hearts of English Nonconformists. The gripping themes of liberty and independence emanating from London and from Boston arose at the very time when urban Dissenters were enjoying an unusual degree of social and economic opportunity. Having attained to numerous municipal offices of trust and an economic stature that rivalled that of many Anglicans, the Dissenters found the ideology of resistance to oppression wonderfully well-suited to their own needs. We have seen how, in the quest for their own independence, the Dissenters echoed back the liberating notes of freedom and independence, but with greater volume and more focused intensity than most Anglican Commonwealthmen. Radical Dissenting ministers rejected virtual representation and demanded a reconsideration of the very basis of representative government that tradesmen and artisans found compelling; they called for an equal representation, the necessity of an individual's independent consent, and the right, indeed the sacred duty, of resisting political oppression. Then, as if to illustrate their point, they departed from the ordinary channels of parliamentary elections, and boldly petitioned the crown on behalf of the American colonists.

The unity the Dissenters demonstrated on behalf of pro-Americanism is all the more striking when it is remembered that there was nothing resembling a national party canvass in the 1770s. In fact, in 1740 the Dissenting Deputies had explicitly declined to advise Dissenting voters how to use their votes in parliamentary elections, and this seems to be a policy to which they steadfastly adhered.[1] At Taunton and Nottingham the three denominations comprised more than half of the entire population, and here the support they gave to conciliation is not especially remarkable. But in the majority of boroughs, the proportion of Dissenters who supported conciliation was greater than the Dissenting

---

1 Asked 'what part it will become us to act with reference to the Ensuing General Election?' a subcommittee reported on 28 Jan. 1740/41 that the topic was 'too tender' in nature, and that advice would only be given if it was asked for 'or there should be any case that shall appear to us to be peculiarly circumstantial'. The Protestant Dissenting Deputies, Minutes, 2 vols. (9 November 1732 –20 May 1791), MS 3083-1, 1: 211.

proportion of the entire population, and both the strength and the unity of this support remains impressive. The unity of the elite and the laity is also notable, especially in those boroughs like Bristol, Coventry, and Nottingham where the laity were socially assimilated and enjoyed the benefits of office holding. The pulpit rhetoric of the Dissenting ministry had a profound impact on the politics of ordinary men, and the only documentable instances of the indifference of the laity at Liverpool and Sudbury can be traced to the failure, or at least the passivity, of the Dissenting pulpit.

Through their preaching and political activity, the Dissenting elite not only influenced the body of the laity, their radical political discourse extended to an even larger audience of Anglican and some secularized shopkeepers and artisans, who themselves, for quite different reasons, were well-prepared for the message of liberty. In several boroughs where the Dissenting ministers did not stand forth in the cause of liberty and justice, the laity did: Isaac Diss of Colchester and Thomas B. Bayley of Liverpool are two good examples among many. In every known instance of a petition to the crown concerning America, with the possible exception of London, the Dissenters were active in the leadership and support of political opposition. At London, Bristol, Manchester, Newcastle, Colchester, Nottingham, Yarmouth, Southampton, and Cambridge, the great ground swell of support for the colonists arose from tradesmen and artisans who not only resisted the government, but 'the mandates of power and affluence' in all of their manifestations. The perceived connection between the Dissenting pulpit and the political activity of the laity does not prove the influence of religious ideology, but from the rational coherence of ideology and behavior, we may confidently infer it. Similarly, that the Dissenting leadership appeared in almost every borough with strong support from the lesser shopkeepers and artisans does not prove a cause-effect nexus between religion and social class, or religion and radicalism grounded in economic inequalities. But the consistency of the pattern of Nonconformist leadership across many boroughs, and the predictability of the positive response of the middling and lower orders, allows us to infer a relationship between religious ideology, charismatic leadership, social divisions, and radical behavior. Just as the Dissenters played a prominent role in the leadership of the Industrial Revolution, we may now conclude that they had an equally prominent part in the origins of urban radicalism. The 1770s can no longer be construed as a period in which popular politics receded below the horizon.[2]

2 John Brewer, *Party Ideology and Popular Politics at the Accession of George III* (Cambridge, 1976), p. 268.

II

This study has sought to account for the religious dimensions of the Whig interpretation of party and party continuity in the reign of George III, without at the same time introducing a neo-Whig interpretation. Some insight on this problem has been gained by looking at the religious contribution to parties at the local level. For example, Edmund Burke's understanding of the distinctions between Whig and Tory was traced to his own experience of party politics at Bristol. Burke's experience at Bristol was not unique: other Rockinghams, such as David Hartley at Hull and Sir Charles Saunders at Great Yarmouth, hoped for Dissenting electoral support. We know that Sir William Meredith worked closely with the Dissenting elite at Liverpool and sought support from the Dissenting voters, though without much success. These and other attempts of the Rockingham Whigs in the medium and large freeman boroughs left the impression upon leaders like the Duke of Richmond that the Dissenters had great electoral significance, and there was some validity to their perception.

Dissenters contributed to local Whig party politics throughout the eighteenth century, including the middle period, in at least three closely related configurations. Independent radical political activity was often associated with Dissent, even in the smaller boroughs. For example, the Congregationalist, Martin Dunsford, though a local office holder, was one of the most advanced political radicals at Tiverton, leading the battle to extend the parliamentary franchise to the inhabitants in the 1760s and 1770s.[3] Evidence of this kind of independence was found with the Hurrys at Great Yarmouth, the Bernards at Southampton, and a number of other boroughs. A second, closely related expression was found in the Dissenting backbone of local anti-corporation parties, a phenomenon that was especially characteristic of the larger freeman boroughs. Anti-corporation parties thus often developed in settings where religion was important, but only rarely – if ever – did they develop apart from religion. Therefore, a fully secularized schema such as independency versus oligarchy, even for the middle of the eighteenth century, proves inadequate; it will work for only a handful of boroughs and certainly breaks down in the late eighteenth and early nineteenth centuries. Third, at Bristol the Dissenters were prominent on the corporation, and as a result, no anti-corporation party framework evolved. Bristol demonstrates that strong, well-defined parties could be maintained without anti-corporation structures in those boroughs where religion was prominent. Thus religion could contribute to a balanced and viable local party rivalry even in some boroughs where the Dissenters were not excluded from local office. The phenomenon of constricting oligarchy described by Frank O'Gorman and others was most often Anglican oligarchy, simply because of

---

3 M. L. Banks, *Blundell's Worthies* (London, 1904), p. 91; Martin Dunsford, *Historical Memoirs of the Town and Parish of Tiverton* (Exeter, 1795), p. 255, note 221.

the very small proportion of Dissenters in the nation. But the independent parties were most often associated with Dissent, far more than their small numbers would seem to warrant, because the Dissenters were heavily concentrated in the large open freeman constituencies, and because in these boroughs, they maintained an independent orientation. There is thus an important but little explored ideological interplay between independency and Dissent on the one side, and Anglicanism and oligarchy on the other, that gave a lengthened vitality to party distinctions and appearances.

Throughout the eighteenth century, the importance of the Dissenters' strong political self-identity and independence could be found in two related areas. In some local settings religious convictions provided the focal point, the predictable core of party, around which Low-Church Anglicans could rally. The Dissenting vote thus formed, in effect, a third-party bloc that was commonly submerged in the larger Whig vote. The religion of Dissent provided a powerful catalyst to the electoral orientation of many Anglicans, though to be really effective in the large open boroughs, it required both astute charismatic leadership and a strong contingent of voters in the middle and upper socio-economic ranks, qualities that were lacking at Liverpool. In those constituencies where the Dissenters were insignificant numerically, their mere presence provided a reminder to the Anglican voters of the ancient issues that had divided their forefathers into warring factions. In such circumstances, the Low-Church Anglicans who were sympathetic to the Dissenters could sometimes provide the electoral weight necessary to sway a contest. Trevelyan's insight on the long memory of voters concerning local political loyalties is relevant in this regard. The Dissent-Low-Church alliance is one of the most important yet least studied political phenomenon of the period. Second, with a few exceptions like Newcastle, it appears almost certain that the political influence of the religion of Dissent preceded in time the formation of political parties on the basis of socioeconomic considerations, but in anticipating this tendency toward a later secular basis to party, religion also contributed to it. Local parties in England, however, seldom became wholly secular in the eighteenth century, and they may have had an even greater religious component in the nineteenth century when Nonconformity was much stronger.[4] While much further research remains to be done on this topic, these generalizations open the way for a new, more ideologically based theory of the evolution of party in the late eighteenth century. However, in parliamentary politics, insofar as the Whig interpretation posited a national two-party system, it failed to depict political reality. In the majority of

---

4 Walter L. Arnstein, 'The Religious Issue in Mid-Victorian Politics: A Note on a Neglected Source,' *Albion* 6 (1974), 143. 'Certainly it was the issue of religion that provided an element of continuity – ultimately *the* element of ideological continuity – from the 1680s to the 1910s as long as there were (and whenever there were) Whigs and Tories and later Liberals and Conservatives facing one another across the floor of the House of Commons'.

boroughs there were no party structures, and we have found that in even the open large freeman boroughs of Newcastle, Liverpool, Hull, and Colchester the Dissenters were unable to significantly influence the formation or continuation of local parties. In these boroughs wealth and status were more certain predictors of political support for government candidates than religion. When one considers the entire electorate, however, the relative tardiness and weakness of the effects of wealth on voter preference can be traced to the lack of decisive political options associated with the candidates, and the structural obstacles of the unreformed system.

The picture is far otherwise when one turns to popular politics. Close study of the well-defined issues of the American Revolution, set in the context of an unimpeded opportunity for the public expression of one's opinion in popular petitions, reveals an early and strong connection between religion, socio-economic rank, and radical politics. Just as the Rockingham Whigs contested and represented boroughs where numerous Dissenters resided, they were involved in the popular agitation concerning America in 1775, though rather half-heartedly. In addition to Burke's secret committee at Bristol, William Baker was active on behalf of the London merchants' petition, and Sir George Savile presented the petitions from Newcastle and Halifax. Other Rockinghams who were involved in some facet of the pro-American petitioning agitation included Lord Craven and Lord George Cavendish. Just as in the case of parliamentary contests, these popular activities of the Rockingham Whigs gave the impression to contemporaries – however exaggerated – that there was an ideological and strategic coherence between the opposition at Westminster and local Whig factions. The petitions of 1775 suggested that popular political culture was fundamentally divided on religious and socio-economic lines that to observers looked like parties. Simply because deeply felt opinions on the nature and use of political authority did not surface in parliamentary elections does not mean they were unimportant; they only need to be manifested once for us to be able to posit their abiding presence. We have found in the petitions for peace evidence for the shadowland of political structures Trevelyan intuitively discerned in the nation at large.[5] The conditions described here did not obtain for every parliamentary borough, but they were pervasive enough to leave the impression of relative nationwide uniformity. Clearly, national parties did not exist, but there were discernible and abiding orientations in politics that were related to attitudes toward authority. In a national crisis centered on the single issue of the central government's authority, these latent orientations could distill into two quite well-defined groups. At the moment of distillation, those

5 Trevelyan understood party in terms of the two extraordinary bonds, 'so potent yet so shadowy, which without corporate existence or legal recognition, and with continual change of creed and programme' yet somehow continued 'as a lasting element in public life'. 'The Two-Party System in English Political History,' p. 184 in *An Auto-biography and Other Essays* (London, 1949).

suspicious of political authority naturally appropriated the party language of a previous period. It is true that the terms Whig and Tory were applied to local parties or political clubs in very few boroughs. But few will contest the fact that there was a new emphasis on 'Whig' ideas in the publications of the Commonwealthman radicals in the 1770s and we can now document in the same decade a resurgence of what for want of a better word, must be called conservative or authoritarian ideas.

In the midst of the American Revolution, the terms Whig and Tory were revived, both in the national political forum that found expression in the metropolitan newspapers, and in some boroughs. The reappropriation of the terms was stimulated in part by the petitioning agitation over the use of coercive measures. The connection between petitioning in 1775 and the very origins of the terms Whig and Tory during the 1670s was readily made; the addresses to the crown supporting royal policy in the colonies used the language of 'abhorrence,' which was the same terminology used during the Exclusion Crisis of 1679 when the Tories abhorred the Whig petitioners and stood steadfastly by the royal proclamation against tumultuous petitions. Similarly 'Whigs' associated the addressers with the 'Tory' rebellion of 1745.[6] Nevertheless, in a majority of parliamentary boroughs the old terms were not revived, there was no semblance of party politics, and even less of party continuity. It is also clear that the presence of a local party might not entail the use of the old names, while in many cases, the use of the terms indicated nothing more than political propaganda. But understanding propaganda is important for understanding political behavior, and the majority of Dissenters and many politically active tradesmen and artisans accepted and acted upon the Whig myth of the reign of George III.

The idea of a new-Toryism at the beginning of the reign of George III can hardly be sustained in the traditional Whig terms of the prerogative-hugging designs of the king. But from the angle of local politics, the notion that things remained as they were in town, but were changing at St. James and Westminster, made a good deal of sense, especially when seen through the eyes of the Dissenter. The uniform response of the Anglican clergy and the law simply confirmed their suspicions. However, the Rockingham Whigs were not equipped to marshall national support for their cause, and thus no matter how many isolated Whig factions might oppose the war, these did not constitute a national Whig party. The paternalistically oriented party leaders believed the Dissenting interest was important, but they could never effectively marshall it, and as a result, the greatest effect the Dissenting interest ever had in parliamen-

6 The use of 'Whig' to describe the pro-American petitions, and 'Tory' to describe progovernment addressers is pervasive. *Lond. Eve.-Post* (31 Aug.–2 Sept., 21–24 Oct., 28–30 Nov. 1775); *Morn. Chron.* (20 Sept., 19, 23 Oct 1775); *New. Chron.* (26 Aug., 2 Sept., 9, 30 Dec. 1775).

tary politics was to give a semblance of truth to the claims of Whig historians that there was indeed a great national party. These expressions of independence were harbingers of what a nationwide electorate thinking in terms of party could do, and when nineteenth-century historians looked back on the eighteenth century, they saw it in these terms.

For all of the attention Namier and his colleagues gave to local matters, the school was not adept at social or cultural history. Underlying the characteristic emphases of both the Whig interpretations and the school of Namier are certain assumptions about human nature, history, and historical causation. These assumptions have to some extent dictated both the sources and the methods of the two schools. Political managers in all ages have treated the populace as a force to be manipulated; they have commonly viewed the people as inanimate objects, or alternatively as beasts. Yet Namier and his colleagues studied political connections largely through the eyes of managers and agents, and they came to accept their cynical outlook on the nature of electoral politics. This led Namier to liken the English people on the eve of the American Revolution to hordes of lemmings plunging into the sea, and he finally doubted whether there was any free will in the thinking and actions of the masses. Methodologically, Namier was certainly far-sighted, but in terms of political philosophy, he was unredeemably conservative.[7] His students have taken the same deterministic approach and exaggerated the weaker features of his techniques through narrowing the locus of study even further. Local interests were all controlling in the thought of Namier's students; wherever they looked they found only local, material interests and concerns. Yet in the early modern world of emerging nation states, the political awareness and ideological sophistication of the people of England was truly remarkable.

One example of this fact is found in the petitioning movement of 1775, which in terms of merely the number of people involved, was roughly equivalent to the number of English voters in a general election. It is one thing to read the past in the light of the present and to introduce all manner of innovations before their time; it is another to steadfastly ignore modes of criticism and attempts at new avenues of response that help us account for political change over time. When Dissenters like Priestley and Wallin addressed a nationally dispersed, yet cohesive body of people just before a general election, their thoughts were ranging beyond the local setting, and their political appeals genuinely anticipated a modern approach to elections. When Dissenters in borough after borough risked further social alienation, and in some cases, actual persecution, by protesting against the government on behalf of the

7 Sir Lewis Namier, *England in the Age of the American Revolution*, 2nd edn (London, 1961), pp. 17, 26, 36, 38, 40–1. 'It is only the short-sighted historian who finds the eruptions of the crowd to be "blind".' E. P. Thompson, 'Patrician Society, Plebian Culture,' *Journal of Social History*, 7 (1974), 398.

colonists, they were pressing into a future era when governments themselves would no longer resist popular referendums. If the Nonconformists contributed to the Whig interpretation of the reign of George III through the consistent espousal of True Whig political principles and a pattern of consistent electoral behavior in a handful of large boroughs, they also contributed to a historical development in popular politics that is remarkably similar to the Whig understanding of the benefits accruing from the Revolution settlement, and in particular, the Declaration of Rights.[8] When the unreformed electoral system was unresponsive to their views, they transcended electoral politics in the petitioning agitation of 1775 and stimulated widespread resistance to the government through constitutional, but unsanctioned expressions of opposition.

III

John Cannon has recently argued that the eighteenth century saw little sustained attack on the constitution, the role of the House of Lords, or the hierarchical nature of society. Moreover, he insists that the contribution of the Anglican Church in shaping this 'conformist opinion' has not been sufficiently appreciated. J. C. D. Clark has adopted a similar viewpoint by conceiving of English society as a mutually reinforcing system of monarchy, nobility, and clerical intelligentsia. An alternative conceptualization of the 'confessional state,' according to Cannon and Clark, was not clearly formulated until the early nineteenth century.[9] This thesis is valuable for underscoring the way in which the Anglican elite *conceived* of society and its norms, but does it take sufficient account of the forces of change that were undermining the old order long before it was reconceptualized? The study of Nonconformity helps illumine one way in which an important minority contributed to a different conceptualization of society than the dominant Anglican vision.

The accounts of Cannon and Clark fail to take seriously two intimately related structural elements of eighteenth-century Dissent, one religious, the other social. These essential elements of Nonconformity only attracted the attention of its critics in times of political crisis, particularly in the first two decades of the century and in the 1760s and 1770s, but they were always latent in Dissent. As Nonconformists, the Dissenters were by their very nature against the establishment of the Church, and in the late eighteenth century some of them became outspokenly anti-clerical. Nonconformity amounted to a sustained challenge to the constitution in Church and State that was woven into the

8 Lois G. Schwoerer, 'The Contribution of the Declaration of Rights to Anglo-American Radicalism', pp. 105–24 in Margaret and James Jacob (eds.), *The Origins of Anglo–American Radicalism* (London, 1984).

9 John Cannon, *Aristocratic Century: The Peerage of Eighteenth-Century England* (Cambridge, 1984), pp. 152, 161, 178–79; J. C. D. Clark, *English Society, 1688–1832* (Cambridge, 1985), pp. 89–90, 195, 349–50.

very fabric of English society. Socially, Nonconformity was grounded in an anti-hierarchical sentiment that grew out of their own ecclesiastical polity and quasi-accepted legal status. To the extent that the accounts of Cannon and Clark accurately portray the Anglican elite's view of English society, the genuine radicalism of the Dissenters becomes apparent for the first time: The Nonconformists did pose a radical pluralistic challenge to the Established Church, and by extension, to the foundations of the State. Their radically separated ecclesiastical polity and the more egalitarian social views of a minority thus take us much further than heterodox doctrine in explaining the threat they seemed to pose to the stability of society and government. In the 1770s their unconventional approach to both politics and society represented a significantly different ideal than the dominant Anglican viewpoint.

Increasingly, the Dissenters conceived of themselves as offering an alternative vision of politics, and their vision was not confined to themselves; their sharply focused self-awareness and their numerical concentration in the large open boroughs made the alternative compelling to a wider Anglican and possibly secular audience. Because of the Dissenters' unique position before the law, they were unusually sensitive to questions of legal equity. They well understood that sound religion might be conducive to social order, but religion could also enslave people, and in its established form, they believed it often did. Many Dissenters were deeply offended by those institutions that reflected a mixture of religious and secular authority. The Established Church was not needed for the sound ordering of society; indeed, it was often a clog to justice. In this radical vision, the Church was not a proper pillar of government, but a bloated and arrogant instrument of state control. The radical Dissenters' critique of the Established Church readily extended to an all-embracing criticism of entire areas of legal jurisdiction. In criticizing both the tithes of the Church and the oppressions of the corporation, they located the cause for the inequities in the common human failing of lust for power. But they believed this failure to be especially reprehensible among Anglicans, because with their tithes, the demand for money was hidden beneath a hypocritical religious profession, and in their corporations, the lust took refuge behind religious Tests. Among the Dissenters, the accent was not on the divinely given authority of the magistrate, but on his divinely mandated responsibility for justice and fairness. Monarchy was sometimes praised, but just as often it was merely tolerated, and Dissenters placed their real hope for the future of England in the representative nature of the House of Commons. Radical Dissenting ministers urged their congregations to exercise independent judgment in political matters and they exalted the common person's powers of discrimination and judgment. Whether their minister was orthodox or heterodox, most Dissenting laymen were regularly instructed from the pulpit in the theory of natural rights.

In addition to a different political vision, some Nonconformists held different ideals concerning the nature of English society. The anti-aristocratic rhetoric of Murray, David, and Walker was of a piece with their thoroughgoing anti-clericalism: their thinking and preaching entailed a serious intellectual challenge to the social structure of eighteenth-century England. While Evans and Toulmin accepted the aristocratic ideal, they were quick to criticize its distortions. Other radical ministers, especially Murray, David, and Walker, found no divine sanction for unequal social ranks; rather, rank was merely a social convention that might be tolerated. They lamented the all too common 'proneness to servility' and yet, somewhat inconsistently, they located virtue in the lowest ranks, while they expressed contempt for the higher orders. The language of Murray's *Sermons to Asses* recognized the problem of deference, even among Dissenters, but he was committed to destroying it. Squibs at Bristol crying, 'Cruger, Peach, and Liberty. The Poor Men's Friends', sought to stiffen the resolve of the poor artisans and encourage them to act in a way that would serve their own best interests. If the pulpit had merely reflected rhetoric that was seriously out of touch with reality, the challenge to the social order might have been readily ignored. But the popular element of social disaffection among the artisans gave considerable force to the views of the Dissenting elite. By their actions, these artisans appeared to pose a genuine threat to the highest ranks of the social order.

When Anglican defenders of government read the Dissenters' sermons they believed they discerned a rebellious and seditious spirit; when they saw the names of their less well-to-do neighbors on the petitions for peace, they worried about social disorder and the licentiousness of the lower ranks, and everywhere it was assumed that the rhetoric of the sermons encouraged the disorderly behavior of the artisans. The strength and coherence of political divisions during the Revolution arose in part from the grounding of these views in divergent understandings of the Christian faith. Dissenters saw politics through the lens of a Christianity that freed their conscience from human traditions and church establishments; the Lordship of Christ, for the Dissenter, relativized all human authority. Many Anglicans viewed Christianity as the main restraint to human passion; for them, the fear of God was the foundation for honoring the king and due subordination in society. Each worked back from their political orientation to their own religious convictions and then forward again to a strengthened, more inflexible political viewpoint. These conflicting departures of the elite represented competing Christian views of the state and society, not a Christian versus a secular view, nor an orthodox view at odds with heresy. Clearly, the heterodoxy of some thinkers threatened the orthodoxy of others, but the great majority of pro-American Dissenters were orthodox trinitarians.

If, in the 1770s, we do not find evidence of class groups oriented along a horizontal axis, and if shopkeepers and artisans were not completely free from the influence of higher ranking Dissenters, we have discovered a strong element of consistency in popular politics across several boroughs. This consistency suggests that there was an awareness of similar values, commitments, and interests among those in the highest socio-economic levels, and there were contrasting values, commitments, and interests held by the Dissenters and the middling and lower strata. In their support for government candidates, government policy, and the sway of corporations and magistrates, the borough elite were very familiar with the exercise of force; in their own eyes, they enforced the law for the good of the community, and the reins of power rested comfortably in their hands. In contrast, the attitude toward political power held by the dispossessed and marginalized was often one of suspicion; the Dissenters and artisans frequently saw the magistrates in the light of their own perception of oppression. Even the Dissenting borough elite on the Nottingham corporation were subjected to the ideology of independence and opposition emanating from George Walker's pulpit. It is thus no surprise to find the Anglican elite siding with the government's use of force while the Dissenters sympathized with the colonists; the two parties represented classically different approaches to the use of political power. These major religious and socio-economic divisions within the urban settings of the 1770s are the more important precisely because they cannot be explained on the basis of a specific geographic locale. The reaction of the middle and lower strata to religious, economic, and social inequalities was expressed across geographic boundaries and the wide distribution of these expressions points to both the vitality of urban radicalism and the reality of early expression of class-like struggles.

Not all who signed the petitions for peace would have considered themselves radicals, but the petitions do represent a sizable grass roots base of the population that was sympathetic to radical causes. The petitions divulge the social divisions that radicals hoped to exploit and they do prove the reality of much animosity toward the very things the Dissenting pulpit habitually vilified. The congruence between the behavior of the petitioners and the ideological themes of the pulpit from borough to borough is quite striking: political courage, independence of expression, willingness to question the government's decisions, and antipathy for ensconced and unresponsive power structures, like Church, corporation, and bar. The differences we do find that might seem to suggest inconsistencies between boroughs can be accounted for by the differing stages of economic development among Dissenters. Similarly, where the Dissenters were completely divided, as at Liverpool, the socio-economic divisions between petitioners and addressers were less clear. The overall consistency in radical ideology and political behavior across several boroughs thereby provides a final argument that social divisions were related to political ideology, and that religious and socio-economic motives were interactive.

Some of the conditions surrounding petitioning agitation did change from city to city, but compared to the larger patterns, the differences are insignificant. At Bristol, Newcastle, and Coventry the petitioning agitation was clearly connected to the rise of urban radicalism, as we have shown by the identity of the leaders in the agitation concerning both Wilkes and America. In other boroughs there was little or no connection to earlier manifestations of radicalism. At Colchester, for example, there was no agitation over Wilkes; and, while there was some radical activity at Taunton, the borough was too small to qualify as an important urban center. Nevertheless, the thesis endlessly repeatedly by Namier and his colleagues that radicalism was 'inspired primarily by local, not national issues'[10] needs to be turned on its head; radicalism, while local, was inspired by national, not local issues. The energy, it is true, often came from local resentment over exclusion from office, but the inspiration that ignited local issues came from national crises.

The political divisions were therefore related not only to different understandings of Christianity and contrasting values and interests, they were also connected to an increasing ability on both sides to transcend local concerns. On the one hand, the American crisis helped the Dissenters discern the connections between local injustices in the foreground, and the larger, more universal issues of political morality in the background of international events. On the other hand, corporations, custom houses, and the clergy increasingly conceived of their roles, not merely in local terms, but as instruments of the state, locked in a deadly battle concerning basic issues of political authority, morality, and social subordination. The events of the 1770s thus fused local, national, and international concerns, and among the political literate in the cities, this pointed to the end of provincial introversion. Moreover, previous studies of radicalism have contrasted London and the large cities in the provinces too sharply; the same social and economic forces at work in London were working in the cities as well, and they were slowly transforming the nature of politics and popular participation. The essential structural unity in the concerns of the national government and local authorities not only explains the uniformity of the Dissenters' critique of both, but the power of these forces, when united, goes a long ways toward explaining why the criticisms were unsuccessful. Though the minority failed, society was not as unified politically, socially, or religiously as recent revisionists would have us believe. To the extent that the Dissenters were viewed positively by a larger body of Low-Church Anglicans, they were understood as offering a more hopeful, freer, and different vision of

10 Ian Christie, *Myth and Reality in Late-Eighteenth-Century British Politics* (London, 1970), p. 285.

religious, political, and social reality than that presented by High Anglicans and spokesmen for the 'confessional state.'

Between the Revolution Settlement and the end of the American Revolution, Protestant Nonconformity evolved as an important facet of the alternative political nation. After the accession of George III, the Dissenters' old loyalties shifted away from the House of Hanover. Their dissatisfaction did not represent a uniform alienation in every congregation, but on the whole, the events of the 1760s and 1770s witnessed an increasingly coherent opposition, and the antipathy toward specific policies became in time a permanent undercurrent of criticism toward the state.[11] Gradually a social base for this vision emerged in the same years, but it first came to political expression in the age of the American Revolution. In this period, the latent radicalism of Nonconformity, ever present in its congregational polity, became explicit, and when it aroused the interest of the lower orders it became potentially highly disruptive. The attitudes toward the law, corporations, and the Church that were vividly displayed for the first time in 1775 betray underlying and persistent animosities. The Revolution revealed long standing, pent-up feelings towards those in authority, and these feelings, though manifested but briefly, point to abiding structural fissures in English society. The alternative political nation thought and felt deeply about political matters of authority, justice, and occasionally, social equality. Thus both the theoretical and the social foundations of an alternative vision were present in the 1770s and 1780s, even though they had little immediate effect on the nation at large.

IV

If it can be demonstrated that the Dissenters influenced popular politics in a handful of urban settings in the period 1775–1784, the larger question of the importance of Nonconformity for the whole of English society will remain debatable. Recent research has begun to suggest that Dissent was more important than historians have thought, especially in the early nineteenth century. Although much further work remains to be done, it is becoming increasingly clear that sectarianism must be placed alongside Anglicanism if one hopes to provide a valid picture of the entirety of English society. There is evidence to support both the attractiveness of the Nonconformist alternative vision and its appeal specifically to the lower orders. The attractiveness of Dissent is established by its rapid growth: while antipathy for Dissent among the Anglican intelligentsia increased in the late 1780s and 1790s, popular support for Dissent

---

11 Anthony Lincoln, *Some Political and Social Ideas of English Dissent, 1763–1800* (Cambridge, 1938), pp. 22, 27, 272; John A. Phillips, *Electoral Behavior in Unreformed England* (Princeton, 1982), pp. 294–5, shows the persistence of the anti-administration orientation of the Dissenters in Norwich and Northampton through the end of the century.

grew at a prodigious rate. The Unitarians dwindled to a handful, but old orthodox Dissent, including the Congregationalists and Baptists, and the new variations of Nonconformity, grew rapidly, and thus future work must analyze the
role of alternative structures of worship in the more orthodox setting.[12] The
growth of the theologically orthodox sects suggests that the social nature of
Dissent as an alternative to Anglicanism may have been more important than the
liberal political theory of the so-called 'rational Dissenters'.

Against the widely held assumption concerning the bourgeois character of
nineteenth-century Dissent, Michael Watts' forthcoming chapters on the social
structure of Nonconformity establish for the first time that the majority of these
people were artisans and laborers, not merchants and tradesmen. For example,
in the first three decades of the nineteenth century in Bedfordshire, Essex, and
Buckinghamshire, Congregationalists and Wesleyans mirrored the predominant
laboring complexion of the larger society, with approximately half their
adherents drawn from lower-paid, semi-skilled workers and laborers. But
among Congregationalists in Cheshire and Cambridgeshire, artisans made up
proportionately about 20 percent more of the adherents than the population at
large, and the Congregationalists in Lancashire and Cornwall also attracted a
slightly greater proportion of artisans than the overall population.[13] It seems
likely that the lower orders were attracted to Dissent in part because of the
political transformation it had undergone during the American Revolution;
Dissent appears to have offered the common people an attractive alternative to
the dominant Anglican vision of society.

But if Dissent attracted the lower orders, did it also contribute to their
cohesive social identity? The contribution of Dissent to the formation of early
social group identity is plausibly based on the ideology of independence
espoused publicly by the ministry, the practice of independence in a separated
polity, and, in a few boroughs, an earlier development of economic independence than that found in the population at large, modeled by the laity. We have
discerned two interactive though nevertheless distinct groups in the political
nation that were more oriented towards radical politics than others, namely,
Nonconformists and artisans; it is the thesis of this book that the first not only
stimulated, but served as a compelling role model for the second. Nonconformity functioned as a midwife to radical political behavior among the artisans,
though additional research is needed to clarify the way in which Dissent was a
midwife to class. We can say that before the stratifications of society were
formulated in terms of class, they functioned in such terms, and the early

12 Alan Gilbert, *Religion and Society in Industrial England: Church, Chapel and Social
Change, 1740–1914* (London, 1976), pp. 30–42; Deryck Lovegrove, *Established
Church, Sectarian People: Itinerancy and the Transformation of English Dissent, 1780–
1830* (Cambridge, 1988), pp. 12–13, 162–5.
13 Michael Watts, *The Dissenters*, vol. 2, forthcoming. Further study of specifically urban
Dissenters is needed to determine if this phenomenon obtained in the cities.

embryonic stages of this stratification were nurtured by religious convictions. The self-consciousness of the pro-American leaders was located primarily in the Dissenting middle class, but clearly the cohesiveness of religion was beginning to influence the behavioral coherence of the artisans.

The evidence examined in this study lends a good deal of support to Rudé's understanding of the transitional ideology of protest in the pre-modern, popular strata, that can alternatively be forward-looking, or, depending upon experience, governed by conservative impulses. Rudé described a complex amalgam that drew on both the direct lived experience of the people based in their values and felt needs, and the more highly structured forms of expression supplied by the elite who acted as spokesmen for the common people.[14] This is exactly what we find in the Dissenting pulpit, the election squibs, provincial newspapers, and the acute understanding and response of the artisans. In the 1770s we can speak accurately of a rational congruence between experience, ideology, and behavior. There is much to be said for the American crisis as 'a defensive revolution', for as we have seen, the Dissenting elite themselves often appealed to the mythic past and the ancient constitution to vindicate their injured rights.[15] But the political engagement of the artisans in the 1770s caused hostile observers to react as much to the type of people that were asserting their rights as they did to what they were saying; the leaders of opposition were at one and the same time opposed to the Established Church and supportive of the resistance of the middling and lower sort. The social and political divisions of our period thus require that we understand their rhetoric as genuinely radical, and to the extent that it did encourage the activity of the lower strata of society to distrust and resist the influence of their 'superiors', it was a progressive activity that pointed into the future. In Bristol, Newcastle, Colchester, and Nottingham (and one could add, Norwich, Manchester, Birmingham, and other leading cities), the Dissenters thereby played a crucial role in both the economic and political development of early-modern England.

V

If the Dissenters and their popular activities were important, and if lesser shopkeepers and artisans were genuinely disaffected, why were their efforts in the short run so abortive? One of the principal reasons lies in the fact that the Whig interpretation of an oppressive regime and the machinations of a secret cabinet is a myth. From the highest to the lowest levels of government, there is very little evidence of systematic oppression, and while North's administration may justly be accused of a lack of wisdom concerning colonial policy, it is no longer possible to accuse it of treachery. There was no plot in the imagined

14 George Rudé, *Ideology and Popular Protest*, (London, 1980), pp. 16–31.
15 Pauline Maier, *From Resistance to Revolution* (New York, 1972), p. 35.

cabinet of 'King's friends' to overthrow the constitution, the king's personal involvement in politics was not a new departure, and there was little actual tendency toward arbitrariness in government. Here we must distinguish between the fears and apprehensions of political opponents, the mental world of politics, and reality. The ruling elite, for its part, must be given credit for allowing a large degree of dissent from its policies in England – certainly they allowed far more freedom of expression than the colonists granted Loyalists in America. The government, for example, was remarkably tolerant toward the seditious publication called *The Crisis*, begun in 1775, and the same is true of its handling of seditious expressions of opposition in the provincial press.

If tolerance characterized the government at the central level, the same applies to the administration of justice at the county and borough level; known examples of harsh treatment of Nonconformists are rare. We have seen that Dissenters enjoyed the perquisites of office in a number of municipal and government places at least proportionate to, if not greater than, the general population. In one out of every five boroughs they inhabited, they were active in civic life, and they often found places in the excise, and even on the bench. It is of equally great importance that in our period their social standing was roughly commensurate to that of the majority of Anglicans. Though at Bristol, Norwich, Liverpool, and elsewhere, their trade suffered during the Revolution, the Dissenters' loses did not pinch enough to drive them to open rebellion. All the while, they were protected by the Act of Toleration, and though they were dissatisfied with their legal status, the very complexity of their circumstances in society meant that the majority were neither politically apathetic on the one hand, nor revolutionary on the other. In addition, they had little to fear from the Church, for contrary to the fears the Dissenters expressed, the Church had not suddenly turned 'Tory'. While the majority of Anglican ministers were clearly pro-government in orientation, most of them espoused a doctrine of patriotic loyalty to the king that can only be called moderate Whiggism. Finally, government influence in the form of minor patronage effectively muffled the radical voice at places like Taunton and Portsmouth, and while the Dissenters' voice could be heard in the large boroughs, government gifts had the effect of denying it the force of unanimity.

The Dissenters were remarkably free to express themselves, both in the pulpit and in political pamphlets. Evans, Murray, David, Toulmin, and Walker preached and wrote exactly as they saw fit; the contrast with the freedom of the Loyalists in America could not be greater. Dissenters, unlike the colonists, could and did vote, and this provided a safety valve of unparalleled importance. Sometimes they contributed to major electoral victories, as at Bristol in 1774; often, however, they were defeated. But whether defeated or victorious, they were free to express themselves. The lowest economic orders were not engaged in radical expressions of opposition, and those who were politically engaged, but could not vote, could and did petition. This provided a second alternative political avenue of importance. The great mass of people in the ranks of shopkeepers and artisans therefore had the opportunity to express their frustrations, and though petitioning and publishing proved ineffective, these means of ventilating animosities were undoubtedly very important. Both in terms of social structure and in terms of opportunity for political discourse and popular participation, England was an open society that allowed great freedom to its citizens.

Two further reasons for the failure of the pro-American agitation are found in the wisdom and strength of the central government, and in the disarray of the radical leaders. George III and Lord North handled the petitions astutely; they appeared to receive the petitions sincerely, then quietly let them drop from sight. None of the petitions for peace were printed in the government organ, the *London Gazette*, but all of the loyal addresses were, and this produced the desired appearance of a nation united behind the crown and coercive measures. Thus the successful repression of the petitions for peace was no small factor in the government's success in stemming the radical tide.[16] At the same instant the government displayed a public face of tolerance, it appeared very menacing to radical leaders. A case in point is found in the treatment of John Horne. The government had learned important lessons from the episodes of popular opposition over general warrants and the Middlesex election affair. The combination of vague threats, general toleration of expressions of opposition, and a successful public relations campaign concerning popular opposition shows how eminently well organized the government had become.

The government's astute handling of domestic opposition must be contrasted with the disarray among radicals. Dissension between the followers of Wilkes and the Rockingham Whigs, on the one hand, and internal dissensions within the radical movement itself, on the other, severely hampered the effectiveness of pro-Americanism. The internal dissentions not only meant wasted effort and conflicting tactics among radical leaders, but a loss of public credibility.[17] Tactical errors, such as the London Association's appeal to borough corporations, combined with the failure of the leaders to make their successes more public, compounded the difficulties of a weak united front. The charge of disloyalty was difficult to live down; in spite of the radicals' self-designation as 'patriots,' the dissociation of radicalism from patriotism was inimical to the cause of pro-Americanism, whereas loyalism and support for the war enjoyed a comfortable marriage.[18] In a revolutionary setting, the fact that the govern-

16 Bradley, *Popular Politics and the American Revolution in England: Petitions, the Crown, and Public Opinion* (Macon, Ga., 1986), Chaps. 2, 4.
17 John Sainsbury, *Disaffected Patriots: London Supporters of Revolutionary American 1769-1782* (Kingston and Montreal, 1987), pp. 42–7, 78, 86–7, 96–7.
18 J. H. Plumb, 'British Attitudes to the American Revolution,' p. 82 in *In the Light of History* (London, 1972).

ment's cause was the cause of the powerful and the affluent, was highly intimidating. The Franco-American alliance also had a dampening effect on pro-American sentiment, though the extent of opposition to the war against the colonies even after 1778 remains surprising. These divisions suggest the need for further explanation of the continuities of English radicalism between the American and French Revolutions.

VI

The evidence adduced in this study bears directly upon the conceptual framework of the history of radicalism. Radical opposition to the government in 1775 came primarily from the lower side of the middle class, if it can be called middle class at all. The artisans were shoemakers, tanners, weavers, tailors, cabinet makers, dyers, and breeches makers; the pro-Americans also included some tradesmen, such as butchers, stationers, bakers, and hairdressers. These are the same occupations that we find in the Corresponding Societies of the early 1790s.[19] The petitioners thereby provide evidence for a transitional stage of political engagement in radical causes at a lower social stratum than was heretofore thought possible.[20] At this stage, the artisans were still organized by middle-class radicals, particularly Dissenting leaders; they were thus clearly not as well organized in 1775 as the later Paineite radicals. But the petitioning activity of the artisans in the American Revolution goes beyond the episodes of spontaneous outbreaks of popular feeling in the provinces chronicled by Walter Shelton and John Stevenson. Because of the similarity of the artisans' rational behavior across boroughs, we must conclude that they comprise a socially coherent, and to some extent self-conscious group, that provides us with evidence of abiding structural discontent. Thompson described the London mob of the time of Wilkes as a transitional mob, 'on its way to becoming a self conscious Radical crowd',[21] and that is, I think, what we have in the American crisis in England; evidence of structural class-like divisions that point to the continuities between the middle-class Commonwealthman radicalism of the 1760s and the urban artisan radicalism of the 1790s.

The radical-religious-economic nexus is thus perhaps the most important feature of popular political opposition in the late eighteenth century, and the

---

19 E. P. Thompson, *The Making of the English Working Class* (New York, 1963), pp. 155–56.

20 On the basis of the way in which the artisan radicals of the 1790s depended upon the insights of the American as over against the French Revolution, Arthur Sheps was the first scholar to seriously question the 'old' versus 'new' paradigm of radicalism. 'The American Revolution and the Transformation of English Republicanism,' *Historical Reflections/Reflexions Historiques* 2 (1975), 3–4.

21 Thompson, *The Making*, p. 69.

recently expressed opinion that there was no objective social base to 'reform' is thereby disproven.[22] But the abiding features of the political structures that the radicals opposed are also important for mapping continuities. When the artisan radicals in the 1790s described their opponents, they referred to 'close corporations, or societies partaking of the nature of corporations, or military bodies, or clergy,'[23] and thus the same social groups that supported the government's policy in 1775 opposed the artisans in 1791. The solidarity of the 'old order' of aldermen, priests, lawyers, and the military was even greater in the 1790s than it had been previously, and it was no less intimidating, but part of the growing interdependence in the ruling elite can be accounted for by the growth of Dissent and the heightened ferment in the lower orders. The scope and scale of the alternative political nation was constantly, if slowly, increasing.[24]

The popular agitations of 1775 were by no means ephemeral expressions of discontent. The boroughs that have been studied for the duration of the war show that this was not momentary, but lasting conflict; these generalizations apply to London, Bristol, Norwich, Birmingham, Manchester, Newcastle, Nottingham, Great Yarmouth, and Cambridge.[25] Just as continuity in radical leadership can be traced back from 1775 to the agitation over Wilkes in London, Bristol, Newcastle, and Coventry, it can be traced forward from 1775 to the Association movement in a number of boroughs. Rudé began the process of connecting the leadership of the Wilkes' petitioners with the Yorkshire association movement, and having located three signatures in both petitions from Yorkshire, he commented, 'there were, no doubt, many more'.[26] Indeed there were. A preliminary search shows firm connections in leadership between 1775 and 1779–80 at London, Bristol, Newcastle, Nottingham, Great Yarmouth, and Cambridge. Wyvill's comment that advocates of parliamentary reform in the Association movement were 'without exception, zealous opponents of the American war' can now be shown to have been grounded in fact.[27] Clearly the proximity of the American petitioners to the Wilkes' move-

---

22 Clark, *English Society*, pp. 321, 324; Clark, *Revolution and Rebellion* (Cambridge, 1986), p. 158.
23 Add. Mss. 27808, Place Papers (Notes Respecting the London Corresponding Society), f.55. See also W. D. Rubinstein, 'The End of "Old Corruption" in Britain, 1780-1860,' *P&P* 101 (1983), 59.
24 Brewer, *Party Ideology*, p. 268.
25 See the studies noted above by Sainsbury, Phillips, Marshall, Money, Knox, and Bradley.
26 Rudé, *Wilkes and Liberty* (Oxford, 1962), p. 198. Cannon, *Parliamentary Reform, 1640-1832* (Cambridge, 1973), p. 70, on London. Bonwick doubted whether such connections existed, *English Radicals and the American Revolution* (Chapel Hill, 1977), pp. 112, 137–8, but notes Richard Watson's activity in Cambridge. See Bradley, *Popular Politics and the American Revolution in England*, pp. 134–5. George Walker at Nottingham is another illustrious example that carries us as far forward as the repeal campaign.
27 Bonwick, *English Radicals*, p. 285, note 49.

ment on the one hand and the Association movement on the other invites further comparison and study. Connections outside of London from the 1780s onwards, especially through the Dissenters' involvement in the campaign for the repeal of the Test and Corporation Acts, may ultimately connect the Association movement to the Corresponding Societies of the 1790s.

Further research on leadership and the related problem of organization may help solve some well-known puzzles. Historians have pondered over why the Association movement gained such little support in the counties; for those who wish to stress continuities, it is all the more necessary to account for the radicals' failure to command mass support in the 1780s.[28] The American agitation has illustrated a rapid development of organization, particularly in petitioning and associating, but major tactical errors could still be made, as the London Association amply demonstrated. Given the evidence for urban artisan backing of pro-Americanism, the real failure of the reform movement in the 1780s may be located not only in the well-known differences among the leaders and in the fall-out over the Gordon riots, but in the leaders' failure to work at marshalling the support of the urban artisan.[29] The Association movement focused on the counties, but the counties lacked a concentration of Dissenters, and they obviously lacked a numerous and independent body of artisans. The later successes in the 1790s are exactly where we would expect them to be: in the large industrializing urban centers of Manchester, Sheffield, and Norwich. Wyvill was not only too ideologically moderate, he looked for support in the wrong places. Historians have made too much of the public's lack of interest in radical politics in the 1780s, and it is no longer wishful thinking to say that detailed study of the urban setting in this decade will show tremendous popular ferment.[30] However, differences between the intensive periods of agitation will remain. Clearly the artisans of the 1790s were less indebted to middle-class leadership than they had been, but we can now see that the education of the artisan, the education of the leaders, and the creation of successful organizations were part of a long term, gradual development.

Continuities in the structures of society that provoked discontent, and continuities in the middle and lower levels of society that demanded change and reform require far more study. Historians, in any case, are bound to search for continuities in social structures, for while the vicissitudes of radicalism in the age of the American and French Revolutions were many and varied, ideas and

28 Cannon, *Parliamentary Reform*, p. 142.
29 *Ibid.*, pp. 68–69; Cannon sees this failure clearly, but another insight needs modification: the difficulties of reform in either the 1780s or 1790s can be attributed less to the lack of urbanization, as such, than to the failure of the leaders fully to appreciate the discontent of the urban artisan (p. 124).
30 George Rudé, *Europe in the Eighteenth Century: Aristocracy and the Bourgeois Challenge* (London, 1972). pp. 188, 190: Eugene C. Black, *The Association* (Cambridge, Mass., 1963) p. 83.

programs were more susceptible to rapid change than the development of social structures. The leaders' different emphases depended to some extent on personal differences in religious backgrounds; to some extent, differences could be traced to personalities; and, of course, rapidly changing political exigencies demanded different tactics and programs. But where there was a genuine social base to radical political activity, as we have found in the pro-American artisans of the 1770s, the diverse expressions of radical ideology can be placed in an appropriately relative context. Clearly the same provincial leaders supported both the pro-Wilkes agitation and resistance to the government's American policy, and these diverse causes were often supported by the same body of people. So whether the issue was pro-Wilkes or pro-American, pro-economic reform or pro-parliamentary reform, when the leaders fell out over such issues as strategy and platform, the rank and file remained ready for any good cause.

It cannot be denied that the French Revolution gave an enormous stimulus to radicalism, nor should one minimize the greater involvement of the lower orders and their more advanced ideology grounded in the ideal of equality. But the earlier focus on the first level of leaders and their ideology has obscured important and abiding social-structural continuities. The social and political divisions in England provoked by the American crisis help us conceive of English radicalism in more developmental terms; the debate over the use of political authority in 1775 was a step on the way toward the artisan radicalism of 1791 and 1792. The American conflict reflects slightly deeper social divisions, and in some cases, a slightly more advanced political ideology, than that found in the agitation over the Middlesex electors. The expression of social discontent by artisans and Nonconformists in the 1770s can thus be seen as more coherent and progressively deepening, though not as advanced as the artisan radicalism of the 1790s. Further research on the causes of political and social change will undoubtedly reveal the interdependence of ideology, religion, and socio-economic interests, but even in the setting of two Revolutions, these will best be construed in evolutionary terms.

Appendix 1

Nominal Record Linkage and Letter Cluster Sampling

This study of religious influence on political behavior is based upon identifying single individuals by name in two or more discrete sets of vital, popular, or electoral records. In order to examine a person's political behavior over a span of several elections, it is necessary to link a number of originally unrelated documents and merge them into a single file. In those boroughs where a run of poll books or signed petitions have survived, along with the Dissenters' registers of births or burials, it is possible to identify politically active Nonconformists. Unfortunately, in numerous boroughs the data from the non-parochial registers was inadequate to provide any significant analysis. At Warwick, for example, there was a coercive address circulated with 212 signatures, and while three registers from the Dissenting chapels are available, the earliest register began in 1784 and listed only a handful of early entries. Conversely, at Lancaster the non-parochial registers were excellent, but the coercive petition had only thirty signatures. At Southampton, the absence of occupations in the non-parochial registers rendered it impossible to link the registers to the poll books, while at Coventry, the poll books lacked occupations.[1] However, in this study the baptismal and burial recorders of Dissenters in twelve boroughs were sufficiently well kept to create extended panels or linked files combining registers with poll books or signed petitions and addresses.

Variations in surname spelling and the physical mobility of people from parish to parish have proved to be the two most intractable problems in

1 For Warwick, see HO 55/9/1 and RG 4/3640; 3641; 2808; for Lancaster, see HO 55/11/2 and RG 4/129; 76; 77; 2117. This is a small sample of many boroughs where one finds insufficient evidence to proceed. However, two boroughs in particular show the great potential of record linkage. At Abingdon and Shrewsbury contemporaries went to the trouble to identify all the Dissenters who voted and marked their names with asterisks in the poll books. Of those Dissenters who voted at Abingdon and were identified in the 1768 poll books, fully 65% can be verified by comparing the poll book to the Abingdon Dissenters' birth and baptismal registers. At Shrewsbury, 57% of all the Dissenters who voted in 1747 can be confirmed by the non-parochial registers from Shrewsbury. For a full discussion of Abingdon and Shrewsbury, see James E. Bradley, 'Nonconformity and the Electorate in Eighteenth-Century England', *Parliamentary History* 6 (1987), 236–61.

computer assisted record linkage.[2] The author of the introduction to the Newcastle upon Tyne poll book of 1774 candidly addressed the matter of orthography:

The reader is also to consider that the names of persons very often vary; and though everyone thinks he spells and pronounces his own name right, yet it is not in the power of a clerk, at the time of polling, to spell every man's name exactly as he would do it himself: [in looking for a person's name] he must therefore be ruled more by the sound than the letters .... For what writer could tell the difference in our northern manner of pronouncing Cay and Kay; Carr and Kerr; Leighton, Leaton and Layton; Turnbull and Trumbull; Hindmarsh and Hymers ...'.[3]

Numerous studies have shown that the occupation of individuals was more stable than residence, and in this project as well, occupations were the most important key for the positive identification of individuals in the poll books (see Appendix 2), though in three boroughs, residence supplied valuable supplemental information.[4]

Problems of surname spelling and incomplete or conflicting data were confronted by utilizing the rules for linkage formulated by John Phillips in *Nominal Record Linkage and the Study of Individual Electoral Behavior* (1976).[5] For example, each person's surname was coded by deleting final 'e', 's', 'es', and all double consonants. If the name was still longer than seven characters, it was reduced to seven by deleting, first vowels, then consonants, proceeding from right to left. Given names were abbreviated in a standardized form, or if they were more than five characters, only the first five characters were used. These procedures eliminated most problems in orthography.[6] Naturally, all available information, including the person's occupation, address (where available), and vote were retained. Something of the complexity of a single record is indicated by the fact that the voting portion of the record alone, for a single election, included the year of the election, the individual's occupation code, the occupation group code, the address, the vote summary, (i.e. the identification of the person or persons voted for), the election type, (whether two, three or four man), the first candidate's identification number, the first candidate's political tendency, the second candidate's identification number, his

---

2 On the use of identifying 'keys' such as occupation and residence in nominal record linkage, see W. A. Speck and W. A. Gray, 'Computer Analysis of Poll Books: An Initial Report', *BIHR* 43 (1970), 106–7; Gloria J. A. Guth, 'Surname Spellings and Computerized Record Linkage', *Historical Methods Newsletter* 10 (1976), 15, note 5; John A. Phillips, *Nominal Record Linkage and the Study of Individual Electoral Behavior*, The Laboratory for Political Research (The University of Iowa, 1976), pp. 5–7.

3 *The Poll* (Newcastle upon Tyne, 1774); see, in a similar vein, *The Poll* (Leicester, 1796).

4 Phillips, *Nominal Record Linkage*, p. 13. Residence (parish, district, or adjacent village) were available only for Bristol, Newcastle upon Tyne, and Colchester.

5 The actual linking of records was less fully automated than the process described in this manual.

6 Phillips, *Nominal Record Linkage*, p. 4 with slight modifications.

political tendency, the actual number of votes cast, and the effective vote (i.e. government, opposition, or split).[7] The same process of coding was used with the non-parochial registers; the coded names, designations of jr. or sr., religious denomination, congregation, occupation, dates of register entries (first and last), and in several cases, types of registers, were retained for each individual. The data was analyzed with the Statistical Package for the Social Sciences.

The actual linkage of the poll books themselves was carried out in a semi-automated manner; less than perfect matches of records were accomplished manually, rather than by computer.[8] First, those individuals who had identical names and occupations (or identical names and strictly equivalent occupations) in more than one poll book were linked by the computer.[9] Then lists with possible links were generated for the purpose of manual linkage; these lists of voters had variations in surname spellings, discrepancies in addresses, or analogous, but differently coded, occupations. For example, the computer was programmed to link bookseller with stationer, since this was judged to be a strictly equivalent occupation, but links of persons that involved matching status designations, like esquire, with generic occupation groupings, like merchant, were left for hand linkage in the hope of finding confirming data from addresses. Once all the poll books for a given borough were linked, the entire poll book set was then printed out and merged alphabetically with the data from the non-parochial registers, and in this final step, all of the links with the religious records were also accomplished manually. Lastly, individual voters were tagged in terms of denomination and congregation. By the identification of individuals in more than one election, and by locating the same persons in both the poll books and the registers, the original data set of 20,035 records from six boroughs was reduced to 10,863 linked records.

All of the petitions and addresses to the crown were manually linked to the non-parochial registers, though a computer was used to alphabetize the lists of names. The criterion applied for accepting the identification of a person in both lists was an exact match of Christian and surname, with the date of the register entry falling within specified limits.[10] With the one exception of the coercive address from Newcastle upon Tyne, neither occupational nor residential data

---

7 The full description of the records and variables may be consulted at the Laboratory for Historical Research, University of California, Riverside: 'Eighteenth-Century English Electoral Data, set no. 2'.

8 For a comparable approach, see Michael Katz and John Tiller, 'Record Linkage for Everyman: A Semi-Automated Process', *Historical Methods Newsletter* 5, 4 (1972), 144–50.

9 This procedure presupposes records that are list unique; two or more persons with identical names and occupations in one poll book cannot be linked to other poll books and they were thus eliminated from the linkage process. See Phillips, *Nominal Record Linkage*, p. 7.

10 Only the fathers' names in the baptismal registers and the record of death of adults in the burial registers were used. The birth and baptismal registers were searched for the period after 1745, and the burial registers were searched for the period before 1810.

were available in the petitions. Since, however, for the seven large boroughs studied here, both petitions and addresses were available, the proportion of invalid matches was roughly the same on both lists. In other words, the proportion of common names which were difficult to identify with any degree of certainty is obviously an independent variable and was approximately the same in the petition as in the address. The error rate for these procedures is estimated to be no more than 3 percent.

With over 5,000 voters, Bristol was England's third largest urban constituency, and if one wished to examine the entire voting electorate of the elections of 1754, 1774, 1781, and 1784, one would be required to enter into the computer and then link 22,074 lines of data for the poll books alone.[11] Extracting and collating all of the names from the non-parochial registers in Bristol would prove to be an equally daunting and time-consuming task.[12] The sheer size of the electorates in the large freemen boroughs of Bristol, Liverpool, and Newcastle upon Tyne necessitated the use of sampling, but random sampling of entire populations is obviously incompatible with nominal record linkage. John Phillips has suggested that the problem of sampling and record linkage be resolved by adapting letter-cluster sampling techniques to nominal record linkage.[13] At Bristol, for example, all of the surnames of voters beginning with the letters B, D, E, N, S, U in the 1754 poll book were linked to all of the names beginning with the same letters in the 1774 poll book, and so on, through the 1784 poll book. The letters themselves were selected on the basis of a random number table, and the resulting sample of approximately 25 percent of the resident electorate proved to be, on average, less than .7 percent different than the actual vote of the entire electorate.[14] To achieve sufficiently large samples of approximately 500 voters, letter clusters of 50 percent of the Liverpool and Newcastle electorates were chosen.[15] For the smaller constituencies of Great Yarmouth, Colchester, and Kingston upon Hull, the entire resident electorates were used.

Since the object of this study was to determine the nature of the behavior of Nonconformists, and since non-resident Dissenters could not be identified,

---

11 It is evident why the voters of London, Westminster, and Bristol have not been linked in more than one election before. Norwich and Newcastle upon Tyne, studied by John Phillips and Thomas Knox, were really about the outside limit that one individual could hope to manage in a reasonable time.

12 Several weeks were required to extract and collate a sample of about one-fourth of the names in the non-parochial registers of Bristol alone.

13 John A. Phillips, 'Achieving a Critical Mass While Avoiding an Explosion: Letter Cluster Sampling and Nominal Record Linkage', *JIH* 9 (1979), 493–508.

14 The differences between the total votes cast for the three candidates in 1754 and the 25% letter cluster of 1754 amounted to 1.1%, .5%, and .6%; in 1774, the differences between the overall vote for each candidate and the sample were .4%, .5%, .8%, and .9%. For more extensive tests of accuracy using letter cluster sampling, see Phillips, 'Letter Cluster Sampling', p. 506.

15 See Phillips, 'Letter Cluster Sampling', pp. 501–3 on the size of samples.

resident electorates alone were analyzed in detail. Large numbers of non-residents voted at Bristol, Newcastle upon Tyne, and Colchester, and significant numbers of outvoters turned out at the polls at Liverpool, Great Yarmouth, and Kingston upon Hull. In chap. 8 we found that the vote of non-residents differed dramatically from that of resident voters at Newcastle upon Tyne and Colchester, and these differences, duly noted, had important political implications.[16] But in most of the contests studied in this book, the outcome of elections was not determined by the non-residents. For example, the outvoters for Bristol in 1781 gave the majority (56.1%) to Cruger who, in the event, lost the election; moreover, the pro-Cruger, non-resident vote was supplied almost wholly by London outvoters. In all the other Bristol elections, however, the non-resident vote differed from the resident vote by only several percentage points. Similarly, the differences in political behavior between non-resident and resident voters at Kingston upon Hull were insignificant in all three elections, while at Great Yarmouth, the outvoters were much more strongly oriented in favor of the government candidates (66.8% to 49.3%) only in 1754. At Liverpool in 1761 the votes of the non-residents helped return the opposition candidate, Sir William Meredith (60.2% of the non-residents, versus 34.1% resident), and in this case alone did the outvoters provide the decisive margin.

16 John Phillips, *The Electoral Behavior of Unreformed England* (Princeton, 1982), pp. 186, 190 examined the occupational differences between resident and non-resident voters, and found the same preponderance of people in agricultural trades noted for Colchester in chap. 8. See especially, p. 306.

Appendix 2

Occupational Structure and Socio-Economic Standing

The use of occupations for electoral and social analyses in eighteenth-century studies has taken a major step forward in the past decade. The five-fold classification utilized first by T. J. Nossiter, and subsequently by Thomas Knox, John Phillips, and Frank O'Gorman is now so well established, that if one wishes to contribute to comparative studies, one is compelled to adopt it.[1] But there are good theoretical as well as pragmatic reasons for utilizing this classification that have not heretofore been made sufficiently explicit. This appendix attempts to advance the discussion by analyzing the tables of Joseph Massie and by reconsidering the classification of specific occupational labels, especially at the middling level.

In this project, 456 different occupational labels were encountered in the Anglican registers, non-parochial registers, petitions, and poll books. The historian who wishes to utilize such occupational data for the purpose of social analysis is confronted at the outset by two notoriously difficult problems. First, one must settle upon a small number of general occupational categories that can be related convincingly to social structure. Second, hundreds of specific occupations must be subsumed under half-a-dozen or so occupational categories.

---

1 T. J. Nossiter, *Influence, Opinion and Political Idioms in Reformed England* (Hassocks, Suss., 1975), p. 166; Thomas R. Knox, 'Popular Politics and Provincial Radicalism: Newcastle upon Tyne, 1769–1785', *Albion* 11 (1979), 237, note 23; John A. Phillips, *Electoral Behavior in Unreformed England* (Princeton, 1982), pp. 321–2; Frank O'Gorman, 'The Unreformed Electorate of Hanoverian England: the Mid-eighteenth Century to the Reform Act of 1832', *Social History*, 11 (1986), 42–4. Phillips and others insert a separate category for 'agriculture' that was not found to be useful in this study of urban voters. For an illuminating discussion of eighteenth-century perceptions of ranks and orders in society, with an emphasis on social change and conflict, see Penelope J. Corfield, 'Class by Name and Number in Eighteenth-Century Britain', *History* 72 (1987), 38–61. The work of Serena M. R. Kelly on certain occupations during the early Industrial Revolution will bring much greater precision to our understanding of occupational classification. Studies that use general occupational groupings related to social status with no theoretical rationale can be confusing and occasionally misleading. See Richard B. Sher, 'Moderates, Managers and Popular Politics in Mid-Eighteenth Century Edinburgh: The Drysdale "Bustle" of the 1760s', pp. 181–2 in John Dwyer, Roger A. Mason, and Alexander Murdock, (eds.), *New Perspectives on the Politics and Culture of Early Modern Scotland* (Edinburgh, 1982).

The question of occupational categories as indicators of wealth has recently received a great deal of attention, and there appears to be a growing consensus that such categories as merchant, tradesman, and artisan, may be validly used to classify people in terms of wealth and social status.[2] The second, related question of which occupation belongs in which category will always lead to some disagreement, stemming in part from the different periods of history being studied, and in part from the diverse geographical areas that are sampled. While disagreements on points of detail are inevitable, differences can be minimizcd by a careful explanation of assumptions, definitions, and methodology, and hence each of these questions will be treated at length in this appendix.

In establishing general occupational categories, it has become conventional to utilize the studies of English social structure advanced by Gregory King in 1688, Joseph Massie, in 1756–65 and Patrick Colquhoun in 1801–3.[3] These early social analysts recorded contemporary categories of social status in their tables and they arranged their data in terms that call for close scrutiny. Of the three, the analyses of Massie have been least studied, even though his estimates for the entire nation were recently judged more accurate than those of King.[4]

2 The first study to relate occupational categories to wealth through the study of inventories of probated estates was Jackson Turner Main, *The Social Structure of Revolutionary America* (Princeton, 1965), pp. 68–114. This pioneering work was followed up by the massive documentation of Alice Hanson Jones in *American Colonial Wealth: Documents and Methods*, 3 vols. (New York, 1977), where the same clear relation between wealth and occupation emerged (3:2007–14). For England the first study to link occupational data to probate inventories was Peter H. Lindert, 'English Occupations, 1670–1811', *Journal of Economic History* 40 (1980), where through a comparison of parish registers and probate returns, he concluded that the latter 'give a clear and consistent wealth ranking to the major occupational groups' (p. 694). Phillips compared land tax returns and poor rate records to occupational categories in Norwich and Maidstone and also found a relation between economic and occupational rank, *Electoral Behavior*, p. 199. See also L. D. Schwarz and L. J. Jones, 'Wealth, Occupations, and Insurance in the Late Eighteenth Century: The Policy Registers of the Sun Fire Office', *The Economic History Review* 36 (1983), 371–2, for further evidence of wealth stratification related to occupational classification. Elizabeth Baigent's forthcoming work on Bristol tax returns will undoubtedly throw further light on the topic.

3 For King, see Gregory King, *Natural and Political Observations and Conclusions upon the State and Condition of England*, in *Two Tracts by Gregory King* (ed.) George E. Barnett (Baltimore, 1936), and most recently G. Holmes, 'Gregory King and the Social Structure of Pre-Industrial England', *TRHS* 5th ser., 27 (1977), 58. For Massie, see Peter Mathias, 'The Social Structure in the Eighteenth Century: a Calculation by Joseph Massie', *The Economic History Review* 10 (1957), 30–45. On Colquhoun, see his *Treatise on the Wealth, Power and Resources of the British Empire ...* (1815).

4 While the primary concern of this study is not with Massie's national estimates of the number of people in each category, his work has recently received impressive vindication by an extensive sample of the occupations of 20,494 people in the period 1725–55. Massie's estimates of the number of people in categories for merchants, artisans, and labor are judged 'quite good', and the 'main discrepancies' relate to the professions, farmers, and freeholders. Lindert, 'English Occupations', pp. 688, 707. Mathias' positive but cautious assessment of Massie (pp. 37–41) should be read in light of Lindert's research.

While Massie depends upon King for his major categories, he adds a number of important details that accurately reflect mid-eighteenth-century economic developments, and thus his accuracy and his proximity to the American Revolution makes his assessment the most natural point of departure for this study.

On three occasions between 1756 and 1765, Massie published estimates of the annual income and the taxes of families of different ranks, degrees, or classes. He never utilized specific occupations, but he clearly thought in terms of occupational categories.[5] The following list reproduces Massie's terminology and the order in which he presented his data, though each income for each ranking within the categories is not indicated.

Rank	*Range of yearly income per family in pounds sterling*
1. Temporal, Spiritual, Lords; Nobility, Gentlemen	200 – 20,000
2. Clergy; Law; Liberal Arts; Officers, Civil and Military	50 – 100
3. Common Soldiers	14
4. Freeholders	25 – 100
5. Agriculture	15 – 150
6. Laborers	12.5 – 22.5
7. Manufacturers	18.75 – 30
8. Master Manufacturers	40 – 200
9. Merchants	200 – 600
10. Tradesmen	40 – 140
11. Seamen	20
12. Innkeepers	40 – 100

The specific occupations numbered 2, 11, and 12, and the category 'Freeholders' are to be distinguished from the broader occupational categories, and they will be treated separately. Massie clearly reflects contemporary usage

---

5 Baronets, for example, were not distinguished from knights, and Massie has one category for 'Innkeepers, Alesellers' at £100 and another 'Alesellers, Cottagers' at £40 that it seemed reasonable to conflate. This table is drawn from a broadside entitled *A Computation of the Money* ... (1760). Two of Massie's pamphlets set forth essentially the same categorization, though merchant and master manufacturer are missing from the first: *Calculations of the Present Taxes Yearly Paid By a Family of Each Rank, Degree, or Class* (2nd edn, 1761; first published in 1756); *Brief Observations and Calculations on the Present High Prices* ... (1765). His estimates of wages changed slightly from pamphlet to pamphlet. For example, his London tradesmen's income ranged from £100–300 in his second edition of the *Calculations of the Present Taxes,* and from £100–400 in the broadside of 1760. This is obviously not related to any actual change in income, but reflects the roughness of his estimate.

in the distinctions he makes between generic categories, usage that is readily confirmed from such reference works as R. Campbell's *The London Trades-man* (1747), Richard Rolt's *A New Dictionary of Trade and Commerce* (2nd edn, 1761), Wyndham Beawes' *Lex Mercatoria Redivia: or, The Merchants Directory* (4th edn, 1783), and Samuel Johnson's *A Dictionary of the English Language* (6th edn, 1785). The category of nobility presented few problems for this study, and the second category that was commonly labelled 'profes-sions' was widely assumed to encompass the church, law, medicine, and civil and military officials. To be sure, income in this category could vary radically within various subgroups and from person to person, but it was a recognizable and well defined social group.[6]

It is obvious, however, that Massie did not order his material hierarchically, either from a social or an economic viewpoint, for he placed laborers before manufacturers. The annual average income of laborers reported by Massie comports well with that suggested by Campbell in 1747; both men understood laborers to be non-apprenticed workers who commonly received 2 shillings a week less than the humblest journeyman.[7] In the next category, we find that the manufacturer was not distinguished dramatically from the laborer in income. The eighteenth-century manufacturer was, however, distinguished from the laborer by his apprenticeship in a trade, or by his skill, and the less ambiguous term artisan was preferred. When the term 'manufacturer' was used, it meant simply 'maker', or 'artificer' and nothing was implied about the scale of production.[8] Journeymen had completed a seven year apprenticeship, but not advanced to master; the master manufacturer had not only progressed through an apprenticeship, but completed several years of work and attained to the trade's mark of expertise. Not all, however, who advanced to the status of 'freeman' became masters; many skilled artisans remained in that status their entire life.[9] This added category of master manufacturer does not appear in Gregory King's table and it gives significant point to the difficulty of distin-guishing between artisans and tradesmen, for the question immediately arises, whether this category should be cast with common artisans, their functional

6 Says Johnson, 'The term *profession* is particularly used of divinity, physick, and law'. For the first major study, see Geoffrey Holmes, *Augustan England: Professions, State and Society, 1680–1730* (London, 1982).

7 Campbell sets average laborers' wages in London at 9–12 or 10–12 shillings a week, pp. 222, 262, 273, 319; Massie sets the average at 9 s. in London (£23.8 per year) and 5 s. (£13 per year) in the country. *Calculations of the Present Taxes*, pp. 41–2.

8 See Samuel Johnson under manufacturer, 'a workman; an artificer', and under artisan where manufacturer and artisan are used interchangeably. Rolt too, in the entry for apprentice, distinguishes clearly 'tradesman' from 'artificer'. Massie clearly identifies manufacturers with makers. *Calculations of the Present Taxes*, pp. 8, 38, 40.

9 Some due to abilities; others, because of the nature of their work. For a helpful discus-sion of the length of time between apprenticeship, attaining the freedom of a town, and becoming a master, and the percentage of people involved, see J.F. Pound, 'The Social and Trade Structure of Norwich, 1525–1575', *P&P* 34 (1966), 51.

counterpart, or retail tradesmen, their economic counterpart. Artisans, however, whether apprentice, journeymen, freeman, or master had this in common with the laborer: they usually worked with their hands and thus could be distinguished from merchants and tradesmen, who made their living from trade.

The dictionaries of trade are emphatic in their distinction between merchants or wholesalers, and tradesmen or retailers. The term merchant was 'confined', they say, to those who bought and sold commodities in gross or dealt in the exchange of currency.[10] This distinction was honored even in the breach; it was observed in 1775, with a noticeable air of contempt that 'in the North of England every haberdasher and chandler is a *Merchant*'.[11] Thus, status was attached to the title, and when it was self-ascribed, people knew the difference. But the lexicographer insisted upon more precision: a tradesman, Johnson wrote, is 'a shopkeeper', and, he continued, 'a merchant is called a *trader*, but not a tradesman'. Two points emerge from this survey that are worth emphasizing: In structuring society as he does, Massie records assumptions that were widespread in the mid-eighteenth century about how society was ordered in terms of rank; second, with far more detail than King, he relates social rank to wealth, and in the case of laborers and artisans, these data are readily corroborated from other sources.

For the purposes of this study, Massie's major categories were rearranged and slightly simplified. First, the table was ordered hierarchically and all specific occupations found in his tables were subsumed under generic categories. Thus clergy, and 'persons professing the Law' were grouped under Professions; common soldiers and seamen are listed with laborers; and innkeepers and alesellers fall under tradesmen. In accordance with widespread usage, the categories of Gentry and Professions were united, and on the basis of the largely urban nature of this study, the common category of agriculture, embracing farmer, yeoman, and husbandmen, was separated from the listing. It is questionable whether the yeomen who voted in Bristol elections had anything to do with agriculture, and they, along with the freeholders, were so few in numbers that they were put in a catchall category, labeled 'other'. The incomes in the following list were derived from Massie.

10 See Beawes, p. 31; Rolt agrees: a merchant is not 'at this day' someone who merely buys or sells, but 'only those who traffic in the way of commerce', see the entry, merchant. Under shopkeeper, Rolt has, 'a person who rents, and constantly attends, in an open shop, to sell goods, particularly in the retail way'.
11 *Lon. Eve.-Post*, (30 Nov.–2 Dec. 1775).

	Range of Yearly Income in Pounds Sterling	Average Yearly Income
1. Gentry and Professions	50 – 20,000	482.57
2. Merchants	200 – 600	261.54
3. Tradesmen	40 – 400	53.66
4. Artisans (Masters)	40 – 200	29.61
(Common)	22.5 – 30	
5. Laborers	12.5 – 22.5	14.77
6. Other	—	—

This schematization is broadly compatible with most modern studies of the period, but it is more oriented to socio-economic rank than others, some of which emphasize the difference in types of manufacturing.[12] Massie makes a distinction between artisans working in wool and silk, and those working in wood and iron, and such qualifications are useful when one is assessing change over long periods of time, but they would serve little purpose in the examination of a single generation.

A further step in reducing categories was taken by John Phillips. He carefully discriminated between functional categories and socio-economic categories, and with a precise use of specific occupational labels derived from Campbell's *London Tradesmen*, and data gleaned from tax rolls, he combined gentry, professions, and merchants to form the highest socio-economic rank; tradesmen and a handful of wealthier artisans remain in the middle; and artisans and laborers are combined to form the lower orders.[13] This utilization of occupational data would seem to hold the most promise for social analysis, and it has often been utilized in this study. But the problems involved in linking tradesmen to the middle ranks of society, and artisans to the lower, should be fully recognized. Massie published his tax schemes in order that 'each Person, whether rich, substantial, or poor' might find a tax estimate closely suited to his 'Circumstances and Way of living', and he himself clearly thought in terms of upper, middle and inferior ranks of society.[14] But he never related such distinctions explicitly to his occupational categories nor is there any hint in Massie of horizontal class stratification. His depiction of overlapping incomes

12 L. A. Clarkson, *The Pre-Industrial Economy in England, 1500–1750* (London, 1971), drawing upon Pound (pp. 88–92), utilizes different types of manufacturing, distinguishing textiles, from building, from drink. Lindert also emphasizes the differences between trades, but based on the categories of the 1831 census, he combines retail trade and handicrafts and separates these from manufacturers – an approach that seems less appropriate to the eighteenth century ('English Occupations', p. 688, Table I).
13 Phillips, *Electoral Behavior*, p. 322.
14 Massie, *Calculations of the Present Taxes*, pp. vii, 8. He refers to 'People of the middle or inferior classes' apparently with two groups in mind, and mentions laborers 'among Manufacturers and Working People', p. 8.

between occupational categories suggests, in fact, a classless society, and it has become clear in this study that religion might stratify people as dramatically as wealth. There was, however, in eighteenth-century England an undeniable relation between occupation and socio-economic rank; the issue at stake revolves around the nature of this relationship.

Recent studies of probate inventories provide the strongest evidence yet adduced for linking occupational categories closely to economic rank. This research shows that when the probated inventories of hundreds of individuals with specific occupations are grouped into larger occupational categories, the categories retain their integrity. For example, Lindert's research in probate records in London, 1699–1700, shows that the *difference* between titled gentlemen and merchants in average probated estate was £759.3; between merchants and shopkeepers it was £1406.8; between shopkeepers and building trades, £190.8; and between shopkeepers and manufacturing trades £16.6.[15] The figures were less dramatic in some categories in his sample for the West Midlands in 1700. The *difference* in average probated estate between gentlemen and merchants was £176.5; between merchant and shopkeeper £15.1; between shopkeeper and building trade £110.5; between shopkeeper and manufacturing trade £101.6; between building trade and labor £25.1. Lindert's published samples are small, but he has examined the middle years of the eighteenth century taking larger samples and concludes, 'the probate data clearly imply consistency in the economic meanings of occupational terms in local records over time and space...'.[16] Jones' sample for the thirteen colonies in 1774 was much larger, and the differences between the major categories are just as impressive.[17] On the basis of these data, it would seem reasonable to conclude that the traditional occupational categories do represent valid economic distinctions and that social analysis may proceed on this basis.

Once viable occupational categories have been established, it is necessary to turn to specific occupational labels. Occupational designations were ascribed to people in one of two ways. In the non-parochial registers, the occupations were assigned either by the minister, or by a registrar whose job it was to keep records of births, baptisms, and burials.[18] In neither case is there much evidence that labels were intentionally distorted in an attempt to give oneself, or others, enhanced social standing. The self ascription at the polls might seem to invite such inflation, but in freemen boroughs names were sometimes checked

15 No laborers were sampled for London. Lindert, 'An Algorithm for Probate Sampling', *JIH* 11 (1981), 663, Table 1.
16 Lindert, 'English Occupations', p. 695.
17 Her figures leave out professionals and farmers. See Jones, *American Colonial Wealth*, vol. 3, pp. 2007–14 for the tables.
18 Lindert, who has examined more parish registers than the average genealogist, has a good discussion of this problem, and he discounts any motive that might distort the accuracy of the labels. 'English Occupations', pp. 691, 694.

against registers of freemen to determine if one was qualified to vote, and this, of course, would discourage misrepresentation.[19] On the whole, occupations were added to names simply to identify people more precisely, and the ease with which a person with the same occupation can be identified in the same record over time and in two discrete records such as poll books and registers, suggest that the ascription of labels was not normally in error.[20]

This is not, however, to suggest that occupational labels in the lists were always identical. It was not uncommon for the same occupation to be described by more than one word. In the eighteenth-century, for example, goldsmith was strictly equivalent to silversmith, and a feltmaker was indistinguishable from a hatter.[21] Sometimes phrases were shortened: a brass founder or an iron founder in one list might be simply a founder in another. A more difficult problem was encountered in the use of generic terms such as laborer in one list, and specific terms in another, such as loader, carter, or cartman. 'Shoemaker' seems specific enough, but a shoemaker was commonly called a cordwainer, and patten and clog makers were also 'species of the shoemaker'.[22] But most of these anomalies were easily solved by reference to the trade dictionaries.

Grouping specific occupations in six categories was facilitated by reference to Rolt's *A New Dictionary of Trade and Commerce*, Campbell's *The London Tradesman*, and local newspapers. These sources give detailed accounts of the type of work in which a person was engaged, the materials they used, and the way the product was marketed. Phillips effectively utilized the data in Campbell, and of all the recent work on occupations, his study categorizes the various occupations most convincingly.[23] In different boroughs, however, different trades came to the fore – Bristol for example, was a center for the sugar industry – and constant recourse to local sources and Rolt and Campbell was therefore required. Neither poll books nor registers distinguished journeymen from masters, and this reduced the usefulness of the journeymen's wages provided by Campbell.[24] But in most trades, youth could be apprenticed by their fourteenth year, and thus by the time they were of voting age, they would often

---

19 Phillips discusses the ascription of occupational labels at the Polls. *Electorial Behavior*, pp. 5–6.
20 On the stability of occupational classification over time, see Pound, p. 54.
21 Campbell notes goldsmith 'or, as some call him, silversmith', p. 141. Rolt says the same.
22 Campbell, p. 293. Smiths could be black, white, anvil, anchor, and gun. On occupational equivalencies, see Michael B. Katz, 'Occupational Classification in History', *JIH* 3 (1972), 70–80.
23 Phillips, *Electoral Behavior*, pp. 181–7, 208–10. In this study, newspapers were valuable for establishing the identity of trades that differed in terminology; see, for example, *Felix Farley's Bristol Journal* and the *Reading Mercury and Oxford Gazette*.
24 Campbell supplied journeymen's wages for 132 trades, and the amount necessary to set up and the amount paid to apprentices in 266 trades. Wages in London were higher than in the provinces, but the relative distinctions between trades are still valid.

have completed a seven year apprenticeship.[25] In the freeman boroughs examined in this study, voters would have commonly completed an apprenticeship in order to attain the freedom of the borough, but one cannot assume that all, or even most, freemen were masters.[26] While it is thus impossible to distinguish between journeyman and master, Campbell's tables, and Rolt's manual make it possible in most cases to distinguish between tradesmen and artisans.

The wide range in incomes among the different occupational categories was well depicted by Massie's estimates, but it needs to be emphasized that income levels could vary radically in any given trade. In the professional category, this can be seen in the case of Dissenting ministers' wages; but no occupation, even the commonest, was exempt from such variations. An editorial in the *York Courant* for 3 January 1775, reported that a local shoemaker, 'for some Years past, has exported at least £500 Worth of Shoes, one Year with another, to North America'.[27] If this was common, then artisans *should* have been classed with merchants in the north of England, but this was obviously an exceptional case, and for every wealthy shoemaker, there were a hundred who were poor. As in the case of the minister, so in the case of the shoemaker: what eighteenth century people thought about a particular calling was often more important than the actual income that was attached to the trade. Those occupations at the highest – and at the lowest – level of English society, were by far the easiest to categorize.[28] But there was also little difficulty with most of the occupations that fell under the rubric 'merchant'. Woollen and linen drapers clearly belong in this category, as does the mercer, 'the twin brother' of the draper: all three required over £1,000 to set up, and more important, they dealt principally in wholesale trade, as well as in retail.[29] The trade manuals also assist with less certain occupations, such as agents, bankers, and brokers.[30] The distinction between merchants who on occasion were also retailers, and the third category of tradesmen, who as shopkeepers did not deal in wholesale trade, is reasonable and fairly easy to maintain.

25 For example, youth were bound to plumbers, shoemakers, saddlers, and wax chandlers at 14, and to mercers and coach makers at 15. Campbell, pp. 190, 198, 219, 230, 234, 271, 303.
26 In late sixteenth century Norwich 'approximately 60 per cent of all potential freemen attained their status within five years of the completion of their apprenticeships, and a further 20 per cent had become master craftsmen within ten years'. Pound, p. 51. See, for the eighteenth-century, W. G. Hoskins, *Industry, Trade and People in Exeter 1688–1800* (Manchester, 1935), p. 50.
27 *York Cour.* (3 Jan. 1775).
28 Holmes gives added help with musicians, schoolmasters, mathematicians. See *Augustan England*, pp. 28, 58, 63, 69, 146. And to these can be added organist, drawing master, dancing master, and comedian.
29 Campbell, p. 282. Repeatedly, merchants are distinguished from tradesmen, pp. 284–7.
30 Campbell, 296; Beawes, pp. 45, 355, 492. Though the goldsmiths of London are 'generally bankers' (Rolt, under the entry for goldsmith) it is assumed that in the provinces, they would more commonly be ranked with shopkeepers.

The most difficult distinction to defend in this period of history is that between tradesman and artisan. Throughout the eighteenth century, it was not uncommon for skilled craftsmen to retail their products through their own shops, while others, undoubtedly the majority, with the same occupational label, never engaged in retail trade. It is thus often impossible to distinguish the two. Of 80,000 master manufacturers, Massie estimated that 62,500, or 78 percent, made £40 annually, leaving only 22 percent making £70–200 annually. So the great majority of masters made £10–15 more than the 228,000 common artisans. Of the 162,500 tradesmen, 125,000 or 77 percent made £40 annually, thus ranking the majority of tradesmen with the majority of *master* manufacturers in terms of income.[31] But, and this must be emphasized, according to Massie's figures, for every master artisan who made as much as a tradesman, there were nearly three (2.85) artisans who were considerably below the lowest income level of tradesmen. Thus the important point for this study is the difference in wealth between tradesmen and the great majority of artisans who were not masters.

Phillips has attained greater precision in his classification of tradesmen by merging some artisans, with wages of £50 or more a year, with the tradesmen.[32] This is a useful undertaking, and there are a number of additional categories that may be similarly categorized. It seems reasonable to include in the category of tradesmen some of those who, because of the size of their operation, (represented by a minimum outlay of £500 to set up) may be considered more wealthy, on the average, than most master manufacturers.[33] While they were not often involved in the retail trade, some of these tradesmen did employ laborers and would, with some justification, have considered themselves in the middle ranks of society. On the other hand, brewers, soap boilers, and sugar bakers did not commonly take on apprentices, and hence the label would have tended to be restricted to the master.[34] In addition, there were

31 Massie, *A Computation of the Money*, based on the reconstruction by Mathias, 'The Social Structure', Table 1, pp. 42–3. Lindert says that craftsmen in manufacturing and building trades were in a 'middling wealth position', ('English Occupations', p. 695) which shows how critically definition is needed in this area.

32 Phillips, pp. 183, 206. Those artisans he classes on this basis with the middling ranks also found in this study are cabinet maker, dyer, engraver, instrument maker, and tanner (p. 322).

33 This includes brewer, maltster, distiller, fellmonger, ironmonger, nurseryman, cloth-worker, coach maker, shipbuilder, soap boiler, sugar baker and though Campbell does not mention it, organ builder. Since the sources do not adequately distinguish between the various kinds of smiths, the anchorsmiths and gunsmiths, though requiring £500 to set up, are retained in the artisan category. This consideration also applies to potters who required £1000 to set up but are often indistinguishable in the sources from pot makers and sail makers, who are commonly indistinct from sail cloth makers; the same applies to leather dressers who are indistinguishable from curriers.

34 See Campbell, p. 265. Maltsters are often indistinguishable from brewers. The distillers, Campbell says with some exaggeration, 'all get estates', p. 267. The fellmonger was clearly involved in buying and selling, as was the nurseryman, cloth-worker, iron-

a number of occupations which might not have been thought of as generally oriented towards retail trade, that were in fact characterized by association with a shop.[35] To this group of tradesmen must be added a number of cloth manufacturers who were considered, by eighteenth century observers, to be retailers.[36] Finally, there was a group of lay clerks and minor officials who would not normally be thought of as professional, but would most likely be considered in the middling ranks of society.[37] It also helps to sharpen the distinction between tradesmen and artisan by excluding those that were occasionally retailers, but not commonly so.[38]

There was little difficulty with the category for laborers and a number of people who may not have labored, but were inevitably poor, were included.[39] Although a number of artisans made only laborer's wages, they were retained in the category of artisan.[40] A few occupations defied all categorization[41] and this final group, very few in number, was relegated to category 6, which also included the handful of farmers, yeomen, and husbandmen encountered in the study.

monger, leather dresser or currier, and all required £500 to set up. Campbell, pp. 215, 222, 275. To include cloth-worker seems anomalous, but this tradesman is indistinguishable from a clothier, on which see Rolt. Coach makers and ship builders, who also required £500 to set up, were, like the upholsterer, involved in a considerable amount of subcontracting. It is worth listing those occupations that *normally* were considered retailers, that Campbell notes required £500 to set up: bookseller; chemist; druggist; china factor; goldsmith; grocer; oilman; pawnbroker; printer.

35 These include watchmakers, dry salters, braziers, and furriers, all of whom 'generally keep shops'. See Campbell, pp. 262, 177, 222.
36 Bay, serge, drugget, lace, slea, fearnought, shaloon and stuff makers often employed others and were considered retailers. See Rolt, and for the retailing activities of sergemakers, see Hoskins, *Industry, Trade and People*, pp. 21, 36.
37 Lay clerk, accountant, bookkeeper, scrivener, overseer of poor, writer, coastwaiter, landwaiter, postmaster. The ship's steward, and purser are also included here.
38 This includes tailors, hatters, cappers, glovers, and breeches makers. Hosiers as retailers required £500 to set up shop and were probably related to stockingers in the same way as haberdashers were related to hatters, but hosiers are too frequently united to hatters to justify this distinction. Thus of the four, haberdashers alone should probably be distinguished as retailers.
39 As invalid and pensioner.
40 Examples would be collar makers, stay makers, and pin makers.
41 Such as gamester, singleman, and scotsman.

Bibliography

Manuscript Sources and Poll Books

BRITISH LIBRARY, LONDON

Additional Manuscripts:

Hardwicke Papers, 35626.
Cole Papers, 5813, 5823, 5855.
32736.
Place Papers, 27805.

GUILDHALL LIBRARY, LONDON

The Poll (Abingdon, 1768).
The Poll (Colchester, 1781) Colchester outvoters
The Protestant Dissenting Deputies, Minutes. 2 Vols. 9 Nov. 1732–20
May 1791. MS. 3083-1, microfilm.

INSTITUTE OF HISTORICAL RESEARCH, UNIVERSITY OF LONDON

Poll books of the elections at Bridgwater, Bristol, Colchester, Coventry,
Exeter, Great Yarmouth, Kingston upon Hull, Liverpool, Newcastle
upon Tyne, Nottingham, Reading, Southampton, and Worcester.

PRESBYTERIAN HISTORICAL SOCIETY OF ENGLAND, LONDON

Newcastle: Groat Market (Scots Presbyterian non-parochial register) film
no. D.B. 109.

PUBLIC RECORD OFFICE, CHANCERY LANE, LONDON

Non-Parochial Registers:

Barnstaple: RG 4/2026, 513.
Bath: RG 4/2347.
Brickfield: Brickfield Chapel, Essex, RG 4/1068.
Bridgwater: RG 4/142; RG 6/308.
Bristol:
    Lewins Mead (Presbyterian), RG 4/3507, 1830, 2497.
    Castle Green (Congregational), RG 4/1792.
    Broad Mead and Pithay (Baptist), RG 4/3765, 2871, 1826, 1827,
        1829, 3766, 2697.

The Friars and Temple Street (Quaker), RG 6/305, 1440, 313, 37, 666, 1494, 1565a, 310, 1673, 1417, 128, 177, 10.

The Tabernacle (Calvinistic Methodist), RG 4/2688.

Cambridge: (Congregational) RG 4/3870/ 2.

Colchester:

Lion Walk (Congregational), RG 4/1508, 1509, 2163.

Helen's Lane (Congregational), RG 4/2907.

Eld Lane (Baptist) RG 4/1510, 801.

Colchester Environs:

Bocking (Congregational), RG 4/1500, 1501, 1502.

Coggeshall (Congregational), RG 4/2418, 2419, 802, 1506, 1378.

Dedham (Congregational), RG 4/1511, 1100.

Rochford (Congregational), RG 4/2418.

Witham (Congregational), RG 4/776, 1385.

Coventry:

The Great Meeting House (Presbyterian), RG 4/2950.

Vicar Lane (Congregational), RG 4/2980.

West Orchard (Congregational), RG 4/3314, 3315.

Devizes: (Congregational), RG 4/2591.

Gloucester:

Southgate Street (Congregational), RG 4/768.

Great Yarmouth:

Gaol Street (Presbyterian), RG 4/1973, 2473.

Quaker Meeting, RG 6/1570, 1473, 1410, 689, 597, 557, 1482, 558, 507.

Ipswich:

Tackett Street (Congregational), RG 4/1848.

Kingston upon Hull:

Bowl Alley Lane (Presbyterian) RG 4/3752.

Leominster (Baptist): RG 4/730, 731.

Liverpool:

Benns Garden (Presbyterian) RG 4/1481, 1482, 1042.

Keye Street (Presbyterian) RG 4/972, 1043.

Toxteth Park (Presbyterian) RG 4/1054.

Octagon (Presbyterian) RG 4/3126.

Newington (Congregational) RG 4/1045.

Byrom Street (Baptist) RG 4/1479.

Newcastle:

Silver Street (Scots Presbyterian), RG 4/3215.

Carlisle Street (United Secession), RG 4/2862, 2863.

Close (United Secession), RG 4/4443.

Hanover Square (Unitarian) RG 4/1777.

Postern (Congregational) RG 4/1698.

Tuthill Stairs (Baptist) RB 4/2832.

Nottingham:

High Pavement (Presbyterian), RG 4/1588, 137.

Castle Gate (Congregational), RG 4/1586, 3664.

St. Mary Gate (Congregational), RG 4/1719, 1590.

Friar Lane (Baptist), RG 4/1351.

Broad Street (Baptist), RG 4/1589.

Plymouth:
How Street (Baptist) RG 4/1215.
Norley Street (Congregational) RG 4/2537, 2159.
Batter Street (Presbyterian) RG 4/1091, 1217, 1218.
Poole: RG 4/2270, 464, 121; RG 6/1236, 278, 1340, 429.
Sandwich: RG 4/938.
Southampton: RG 4/610, 624.
Sudbury:
Great Meeting, Friar Street RG 4/1861, 3625.
Taunton:
Pauls Meeting (Congregational), RG 4/1567.
Mary Street Chapel (Baptist), RG 4/2937.
West Ham, Essex: RG 4/1068.

PUBLIC RECORD OFFICE, KEW, SURREY

Home Office Papers: 55/3/4—55/31/6.

SOCIETY OF GENEALOGISTS, HARRINGTON GARDENS, LONDON

Register of the Above Bar Congregational Chapel, Southampton.

DR. WILLIAMS'S LIBRARY, LONDON

Evans, John. List of Dissenting Congregations and Ministers in England
and Wales, 1715-1729. MS 38.4. microfilm.
A List of the Congregational Fund Board Arranged by Counties.
Minute Books of the Body of Protestant Dissenting Ministers of the Three
Denominations in and about the Cities of London and Westminster.
Vols. 1, 2. 11 July 1727–11 April 1797. MS 38.105-106, microfilm.
Minutes of the Congregational Fund Board, microfilm 79-80.
Minutes of the Presbyterian Fund Board, microfilm 82-83.
Thompson, Josiah. List of Protestant Dissenting Congregations in England
and Wales, 1772-1773. MS 38.6, microfilm.
_____. List of Dissenting Congregations in England and Wales, 1772-
1773, with information from a list of 1715. MS 38.5, microfilm.
_____, ed. History of Protestant Dissenting Congregations. 5 vols.
1772–. MS 38.7-11, microfilm.
A View of the Dissenting Interest in London of the Presbyterian and
Independent Denominations from the year 1695 to the 25th of
December 1731, with a Postscript of the Present State of the Baptists.
MS 38.18, microfilm.

BRISTOL CENTRAL LIBRARY

Bristol Elections, 1774-1790. Addresses, Squibs, Songs. Ref. B6979.

BRISTOL RECORD OFFICE

Richard Champion Letterbooks 38083(4).
Parish Registers: P/St Philip and Jacob/R/2b; P/Christ Church/R/1(d); P/St
Stephen/R/le.

CAMBRIDGE CENTRAL LIBRARY

   The Poll (Cambridge, 1774, 1776, 1780).
   The County Poll (Cambridge, 14 Sept. 1780).

CAMBRIDGE COUNTY RECORD OFFICE, SHIRE HALL, CAMBRIDGE

   St. Andrew's Street Baptist Church Book.

ST. ANDREW'S STREET BAPTIST CHURCH ARCHIVES, ST. ANDREW'S
STREET, CAMBRIDGE

   Trust Deeds of 1764 and 1795.

CHELMSFORD, ESSEX RECORD OFFICE

   Colchester Assembly Book, 1763-1797.
   List of Aldermen and Common Councilmen.

CHELMSFORD, ESSEX ARCHEOLOGICAL SOCIETY

   The Poll (Colchester, 1781) Colchester resident voters.

COLCHESTER CENTRAL LIBRARY

   List of Bailiffs and Mayors, E. Col. 1. 352.

COVENTRY, HERBERT ART GALLERY AND MUSEUM

   Index of Admissions of Freemen, 1722-Nov. 1785, film no. 8257.

DORSET COUNTY RECORD OFFICE

   Calcraft Manuscripts: MS poll book of the 1768 Poole election.

GENEALOGICAL SOCIETY OF SALT LAKE CITY, UTAH

   Newcastle: Non-parochial Registers:
      Wall Knoll (Scots Presbyterian), film no. 087983.
      Castle Garth (Scots Presbyterian), film no. 095016.
      Pandon Bank (Unitarian) film no. 095016.
   Parish Registers:
      St. Andrews, film no. 095012.
      St. Nicholas, film no. 095018.
   Liverpool Parish Registers:
      St. George, film no. 093765.
      St. Peter, film no. 093872.
   Kingston upon Hull Parish Registers:
      Holy Trinity, film no. 990828.
      St. Mary, film no. 990838.

MANCHESTER CENTRAL LIBRARY

Samuel Hibbert Ware Miscellany MS q942 .73001 H7.

NEWCASTLE UPON TYNE CENTRAL LIBRARY.

The Register of Freemen of Newcastle upon Tyne: From the Corporation, Guild, and Admissions Book Chiefly of the Eighteenth Century.

NOTTINGHAM, UNIVERSITY OF NOTTINGHAM LIBRARY

Portland Papers, Champion Correspondence PWF2, 713-733.

NORWICH CENTRAL LIBRARY

The Poll (Great Yarmouth, 1777).

NORWICH LOCAL STUDIES LIBRARY

The Poll (Great Yarmouth, 1790).

OXFORD, OXFORDSHIRE RECORD OFFICE

The Poll (Abingdon, 1754).

SHREWSBURY, SHROPSHIRE RECORD OFFICE

S.P.L. Deed 19163.

Index

Aberdeen, 300n
Abingdon, 27, 29, 98n, 114, 190, 316, 431n;
  Dissenting vote, 109-10; and petitioning,
  366; *see also* elections
Abingdon, Willoughby Bertie, 4th Earl of,
  198, 336
Act for Quieting and Establishing Corporations, 70
Act of Navigation, 354
Act of Toleration, 51-2, 66, 253, 425; and
  burials, 55; and marriages, 56; and oaths,
  57; and registration of meetings, 56-7; *see
  also* Cambridge University; Oxford University
Act of Uniformity, 49
Adair, James, 75n, 80n
Addison, William, 340n
addresses and addressers, 25, 318, 338;
  Anglican clergy support of, 346, 348, 350,
  351, 361, 373, 385-9, 390-1, 394,
  402-403, 405, 415; associated with
  oppression, 334, 341, 344-5, 350n, 358;
  compared to clergy and Middlesex, 326-7;
  and corporations, 338, 350, 353, 361-7,
  370-1, 394; country support for, 362; and
  the elite, 373-6, 394; and government
  influence, 318-19, 323, 350, 426; and
  government patronage, 367-9, 370-1, 373,
  394; language of, 321-2, 343, 363; and
  lawyers, 375-6, 388-9, 394, 415; and
  loyalist Dissenters, 395, 398-9, 401; and
  other corporate bodies, 370-1; *see also*
  entry under individual boroughs
Affleck, Edmund, 301, 303, 304, 306, 307,
  308, 309
Ahab, 147n, 153, 164
Aiken, John, 123n
Aldborough, 80n, 102
Alder, Caleb, 270n
Alliston, J.T., 357n, 407
Almon, John, 160
Amaziah, 164
America: as asylum, 142n, 149, 150n
American colonists, 1; and Dissenters, 58
American Revolution, 14, 104, 105, 119,

130, 138, 140, 141, 142, 147-53, 156,
164, 166, 170, 172, 173, 174, 176, 183,
190, 191, 199, 310, 315, 316, 321, 416,
422, 427, 438; and crisis in England, 148;
as defensive revolution, 424; divides
corporations, 366-7; and episcopacy, 59,
148; and George III, 160; influence on
Nonconformists, 7; Nonconformists on
American independence, 149n, 154; as a
political issue, 43, 150, 195, 323, 335-6,
342, 344, 354, 360, 366, 375, 398, 414, in
Bristol, 204, 209, 211-14, 216, 217, 218,
219, 220, 230, 234, 236, 252, 395, in
Colchester, 300, 307, in Great Yarmouth,
241, in Kingston upon Hull, 292-3, in
Liverpool, 278, 281-2, 288-9, 344, 395, in
Newcastle, 258, 261-2, 263, 264, 268,
273, 342, 395, in Norwich, 238, in
Nottingham, 356-7, in Taunton, 353-4;
and public opinion, 1, 17; and representation, 30, 58, 128, 131, 133, 143, 150-2,
157, 214, 335, 354, 410; and ship money,
146; and socio-economic cleavage, 10,
11, 35, 245; and socio-economic divisions
in electorate, 311; Whig sympathy for,
201; *see also* Anglican Church; Nonconformists; petitions
Ames, Jeremiah, 377
Ames, Levi, 377
Amory, Thomas, 351
Anderson, Hugh, 392n
Andover, 72n, 73n, 97n, 362n
Anglican Church, 3, 33, 54n, 59, 95, 108,
158, 162, 171, 216, 381, 417-18, 428;
allows no rivals, 52; and Anglican voters,
110; attacked by Dissenters, 129; and
constitution, 147; in danger, 387; and
Dissenting ideology, 17; and doctrine,
139; and elite's vision of politics, 417,
418, 422, 423; and episcopacy, 139, 148,
157; fears of sedition, 149, 154n, 158;
linked national and local government,
169-70; and moderate Whiggism, 425;
occupational standing, 62-9; and
oligarchy, 412-13; oppressive, 167; as

453

pro-government, 17; and pulpit, 125; and Scripture and political authority, 137; suspects Nonconformists, 14, 59, 87; and Toryism, 425; united against Whigs, 408; *see also* Anglican clergy; Church and State; corporations; High-Church Anglicans; Low-Church Anglicans; pro-Americans; radicals; sermons; Tories

Anglican clergy, 36, 55, 56, 121, 129, 255, 421; and America, 15, 25, 26, 30; and coercive measures, 171; liberal clergy, 60; as magistrates, 172-3, 388; on monarchy, 161-2; and party continuity, 25; *see also* addresses, High-Church Anglicans; pulpit; radicals; sermons; and entry under individual boroughs

Anne, Queen, 52, 58, 118, 201

Annesley, Francis, 228

anti-Catholicism, 150n, 157n, 169n, 219, 263

anti-clericalism, *see* Nonconformists

Apthorp, East, 161

Archer, Andrew, 2nd Baron, 347, 348

Arendt, Hannah, 31

Arianism, 59, 87, 94, 127n, 129n, 131; *see also* Socinianism and Unitarians

aristocracy: clientage of, 370, 381; criticism of, 145, 175, 178, 181-3, 262, 265, 281n, 381, 419

Arminianism, 94

artisans, 2, 10, 18, 35, 37, 46, 120, 327, 380-4, 427; and group identity, 383-4, 423-4; and pro-Americanism in Bristol, 245; and religion, 383; *see also* petitions

Arundel, 97n, 362n

Ashburton, 97n, 102

Association movement, 10, 12, 18, 132, 188, 316, 428-9; at Colchester, 301; at Newcastle, 267

associations, 9, 16, 337-8, 341

Atkinson, Joseph, 379n

Atkinson, Lancelot, 377

Axbridge: and address, 362n, 363

Aylesbury, 84, 97n, 103

Baillie, John, 270n

Baker, Ernest, 199

Baker, John, 299n

Baker, William, 329, 332, 336, 414

Banbury, 72n, 97n

Bance, John, 80n

Baptists, 1n, 13, 44n, 46, 52n, 55, 56, 57, 62n, 65n, 100, 101n, 103n, 114, 140, 164, 171, 175n, 397n, 423; at Bristol, 198, 205-6, 236, 238, 251; at Colchester, 298; General, 1n, 94n, 206; geographic concentration, 93, 94n; at Great Yarmouth,

239; at Kingston upon Hull, 290; at Liverpool, 275; London Baptist Board, 71; losses in London, 93; as loyalists, 398; and office holding, 70-1, 76, 77, 78, 81; Particular, 1n, 94n, 123, 127, 130n, at Newcastle, 256; and social structure, 66; at Taunton, 351

Barnes, William, 366n, 407

Barnstaple, 74n, 82, 97n, 103, 362n; and address, 375, 397-8; *see also* petitions

Barrett, John, 351

Bate, Thomas, 398

Bath, 72n, 73n, 82, 97n

Bath, Neville, 399

Bayley, John, 398

Bayley, Thomas B., 343, 344, 389, 392, 411

Beaufoy, Henry, 43n, 237, 241

Beawes, Wyndham, 439

Bebb, E.D., 39, 92

Beckett, J.B., 379n, 407,

Beckett, James, 368

Beckford, Richard, 210, 222

Beckford, William 43n, 240

Bedford, 98n

Bedford, John Russell, 4th Duke of, 23n

Bedfordshire, 83, 229n, 423

Belsham, William 57

Bentham, Jeremy, 7n

Bentinck, Lord Edward Charles Cavendish, 356n

Benyon, John, 240n

Berkshire, 54n; and addresses and petitions, 362; and petitioning, 336

Bernard family, of Southampton, 107, 404, 412

Berry, James, 399

Berwick-upon-Tweed, 98n, 106

Beverley, 97n, 362n

Bewdley, 74, 97n; and address, 362n, 363-4

Bible, 4, 60; its authority, 135-6, 139, 154; example of wicked kings, 152-3, 164-5; and individual interpretation, 136, 139; and rejection of Church tradition, 136; used by Nonconformists, 130-1, 134, 135, 139, 140, 143n, 145-6, 152-3, 155n, 181, 184

Bideford, Devonshire, 71n

Bilbie, W., 367n

Bill, Charles, 79

Bill of Rights, 146, 173, 317, 340, 417

Bingham, Thomas, 350

Birmingham, 10, 26, 72n, 84, 108, 124, 317n, 424, 428

bishops, 121, 170, 172

Bishop's Castle, 108

Blackburn, 342; and address, 338n

Blackett, John Erasmus, 368

Blackett, Sir Walter, 257-8, 260, 261n, 262n; on America, 263, 266
Blackstone, Sir William, 134
Blackwell, Thomas, 300n
Blaine, 81
Blick, F., 348n
Bloomfield, Bezaleel, 299n, 311
Bocking, 298, 299n, 351
Bodmin,72, 73n, 97n
Bolingbroke, Henry St. John, 1st Viscount, 133n
Bolton, 342; and petition, 336n
Bonwick, Colin, xiv, 7, 8, 10, 42, 127, 138, 147, 148, 160, 167
Boston, England, 74n, 98n
Boston, Mass., 15, 264, 410
Boston Massacre, 148
Boston Port bill, 173; at Bristol, 214
Boston Tea Party, 157
Bowen, Peregrine, 399
Bowes, Andrew, 258, 266, 268-9, 273
Bowling, James, 378
Bowring, John, 15
Bradford, 83
Brailsford, Samuel, 334
Braintree, 298n, 299n, 351
Braithwaite, Reginald, 392, 405
Bramber, 102
Brand Hollis, Thomas, 103
Brewer, John, xii, 6, 8, 9, 13, 26, 40, 108, 172, 316, 369, 378, 379
Brickdale, Matthew, 211-12, 214, 216, 217, 218n, 219, 220, 221, 222, 226, 229n, 232, 234, 243, 245, 377n
Bridgnorth, 97n
Bridgwater, 11, 55n, 76n, 97n, 245, 330, 360, 401n; and address, 328; corporation divided, 366; and petition, 336
Bridport, 76, 96, 98n, 317n
Bright, Richard, 196n
Bristol, 1n, 8n, 10, 17, 19, 27, 30, 37-8, 42, 43, 44n, 45, 46, 54n, 61n, 64n, 86, 88, 96, 98n, 103, 105, 115, 119, 122, 123, 124, 179, 190, 254, 255, 258, 272, 282, 283, 287, 310, 311, 316, 317n, 329, 344, 347, 348, 350, 358, 359, 380, 382, 391, 392, 412, 414, 419, 424, 425, 248, 432n, 434, 435, 443; address and addressers, 321-2, 328, 363, and Anglican clergy, 386, 387, 390, and Nonconformists, 398, 401, and patronage, 368, 370; American issue and violence, 15-16; charitable societies, 209; corporation, 209, 335, divided, 366, 367; elections and electorate, 196, 205, areal analysis of, 248-53, and local politics, 203, 205-9, national issues, 204, 209-12, and party rivalry, 211, 216-20, and politi-

cal clubs, 207-9, popular literature of, 213, 216, 217, 222, 224, reinforces Dissenting pulpit, 213, 214, 222, 224, previous interpretation of, 199-203, 231-3, and trade as issue, 214, and violence, 218, 220; Low-Church Anglicans and party, 242-3, 253; Middlesex election affair, 326, 330-1, connected to America, 421, 428; Nonconformists, 197-8, 199, and America, 236, 237, chapels, 205-207, and corporation, 209, 366, 399, electoral influence of, 207, fund election, 210, lead Union Club, 207, 253, and Low-Church Anglicans, 207, 232, 239, ministers, 205, 233-4, occupational structure, 65-8, office holding, 77, 81, 82, 398, oppose compromise, 211, and partisan behavior, 226, 229-31, 316, compared to Norwich, 238-9, and party rivalry, 221, 234-5, 244, and petitioning, 335, 390, 398, 404, 407, 408, 411, lead petitioners, 331, and political unity of denominations, 238, pulpit marshalls vote, 221-2, 236, 238, and Society of Merchant Venturers, 209, socio-economic motivation, 247, and the vote, 109-10, 116, 200n, 206-7, and wealth, 101; parliamentary reform, 214n; petition and petitioning agitation, 322, 330-7, 389, and Anglican Church, 335, and Nonconformist merchants, 377, and publishing, 379, and socio economic distinctions, 372, 373-7, 380, 384, 385n, 401, 403, 406, 411; popular politics, 202-3; population, 196; radicals and radicalism, 212, 216n, 330-7, 338, annual parliaments, 222, 330n, concern for the poor, 222, 'Independent Society', 330, and radical measures, 331, 380; Society of Merchant Venturers, 200n, 209, 331, 336; Steadfast Society (Loyal and Constitutional Club), 207-9, 210, 216, 217, 231-2, 233, 234, 334, and elections, 208, and High-Anglicanism, 207n; Tories, 210, and America, 212n, Anglican clergy, 233-4, ideological distinctives, 216, 218n, use of broadsides, 216-17, use of term, 215, self-ascribed, 218n; Union Club, 207-9, 210, 216, 229n, 233; voting: Anglican clergy, 207, 233-4, and merchants, 200n, new voters and partisan behavior, 243-4, partisan behavior, 226-8, 230-1, compared to other boroughs, 227-8, 235-6, 236-7, socio-economic distinctions and party, 244-7, 371; Whigs, 210, and America, 218, 219, associated with Dissent, 215, 218, 221-2, and Fox-North Coalition, 232-3, 236-7, and pamphlet

literature, 214-15, 218, principles of, 220, True Whig ideology, 212, use of term, 207, 215, 218, 229n, 233, 234; *see also* American Revolution; Baptists; Congregationalists; elections; Methodists; petitions; Presbyterians; Quakers
Bristol Education Society, 135
broadsides, 14, 42, 49, 122, 200n, 202-3, 212, 213; *see also* newspapers; pulpit; sermons
Brooke, John, xii, 25, 201, 202, 291
Brooksbank, Stamp, 43n, 73n, 80n, 103, 299
Brotherhood, Joseph, 316
Bruce, Lord, *see* Brudenell-Bruce
Brudenell-Bruce, Thomas, 1st Earl of Ailesbury, 79
Buckingham, 72, 97n
Buckinghamshire, 61n, 99n, 229n, 423
Bull, Francis, 407
Bull, John, 377, 407
Burgh, James, 7, 133n, 189
Burke, Edmund, 9, 19, 30, 43n, 122, 124, 134, 196, 199, 200, 202, 204, 209n, 215, 221, 222n, 224, 225, 229n, 231, 234, 243, 245, 252n, 253, 318, 372n, 389, 408, 412, 414; on America, 213-14; on Bristol Nonconformity, 196-7, 198; and Bristol petition, 197; conflict with Henry Cruger, 212, 216, 217, 232; guides petitioning, 331-3, 335-7; and Ireland, 215; as M.P., 212-13; on petitioning, 317, 322; and Whig interpretation of party, 196-7, 216, 234-5, 239, 254
Burke, Richard, 197n, 333
Burke, William, 333, 335, 380
Burnaby, Andrew, 161
Burnet, Gilbert, bishop, 134
Bury St. Edmunds, 62n, 72n, 73n, 97n
Bute, John Stuart, 3rd Earl of, 23n, 111n, 210
Butler, John, bishop, 125, 161
Butler, Richard, 356n
Butterfield, Sir Herbert, xi

Cabbell, J., 353n
Caesar, 155n
Calamy, Edmund, 70
Calhoun, Craig, 35
Calne, 72n, 97n
Calvin, John, 136n
Calvinism, 94, 127, 128, 130, 131n, 136, 140, 189
Cambridge, 57, 82, 98n, 101, 127, 130, 245, 272, 274, 330, 333n, 360, 428; address, 322, 328; corporation divided, 366; and Dissenters, 404; and petition, 378; and socio-economic dvisions, 371-2, 373, 380,

401, 402, 411
Cambridge Chronicle, 378
Cambridge University, 55, 370, 405
Cambridgeshire, 56, 61, 99, 423
Camden, Sir Charles Pratt, 1st Earl, 134
Cameron, Donald, 368n
Campbell, George, 83n, 277, 279, 287
Campbell, R., 439, 441, 443, 444
Canada, 157n, 319
Cannon, John, xiii, 36, 417-18
Canterbury, 83, 98n
Cappe, Newcome, 7, 126, 189
Carlisle, 97n
Carlisle, Frederick Howard, 5th Earl of, 106
Carmarthen, 83; and America, 321
Carruthers, John, 356n
Carter family, of Portsmouth, 75, 101, 114
Carter, Sir John, 321
Cartwright, Major John, 133n, 160, 175n, 357n
Caswall, George, 76, 103, 104
Catholicism, 51, 58, 61, 85, 118, 126n, 137, 148, 150, 157n, 169-70, 275n, 280; in Canada, 387; and Edmund Burke, 198, 214n, 215, 232; *see also* anti-Catholicism
Cavendish, Lord George, 336n, 344n, 414
Champion family, of Bristol, 377
Champion, Richard, 16, 197, 199, 200n, 212n, 221, 222n, 232, 253, 329n, 331, 332, 362n, 376, 380, 407; and petitioning, 333-7, 340
Charles I, 58, 111, 340, 349
Chelmsford and Colchester Chronicle, 101, 299
Cheshire, 99n, 423
Chester, 98n, 362n
Chesterfield, 62n
Chichester, 98n, 106
Chipping Wycombe, 74, 97n
Christ, 135, 137, 139, 147, 153; and Christianity, 419; lordship in relation to state, 138, 143
Christchurch, 72n, 97n, 362n
Christie, Ian, xii, xiii, 27, 201, 241, 258, 266; and 1780 Bristol election, 202, 231-2
Chubb, John, 298n
Church and State, 24, 121; Dissenters criticize union, 169, 171, 184; separation of, 138-9; union of, 387-8
Churchill, Smith, 357
Cicero, 134, 173
Cirencester, 83, 84, 97n, 362n
Clamtree, Thomas, 350
Clapham sect, 292
Clark, J.C.D., xiii, 25, 36, 59, 417-18
Clark, John, 348n, 366n
Clark, Joseph, 82

class, 3, 10, 176n; absence of class struc-
ture, 34; and class-like groupings, 405-8,
411, 420, 427; conflict, 33-4, 38, 372;
consciousness, 34-5, 175, 178-9, 395; and
Nonconformity, 30, 31, 33-5, 405-407,
411; religion and the social cohesion of
lower orders, 423-4; versus community,
35; *see also* radicals
Clayton, Nicholas, 392n
Clegg, James, 375, 376n
Clegg, Joseph, 277, 287, 311, 376n
Clitsom, John, 316, 354n
Cockermouth, 97n, 101, 102
Coe, John, 104
Coercive Acts, 148, 150, 157, 172, 263,
264n
Coggeshall, 298, 299n, 351
Coke, Daniel Parker, 358
Colchester, 17, 43, 45, 46, 83, 98n, 102,
103, 192n, 255, 311, 316, 317, 330n, 358,
367, 399, 407, 411, 414, 421, 424, 432n,
435; and address, 299n, 322, 364; Charter
Club, 350n; corporation-anti-corporation
parties, 299, 301, 302; elections: and
corruption, 299, 302; government and
corporation linked, 302; Nonconformists:
chapels, 298-9, and office holding, 77-8,
298, 299, occupational structure of, 67,
laymen lead independent party, 299, 301,
307, lead petitioning agitation, 300,
350-1, 404, and partisan vote, 302, 307-8,
309, sign petitions, 390, 408; petition and
petitioning agitation, 299n, 322, 350-1,
and corporation, 350, 362, and socio-
economic distinctions, 373-5, 380, 384,
385n, 401, 411; and popular politics, 338;
socio-economic cleavage in, 350; Tories,
299; voting: Anglican clergy as litmus,
303-4, 309, elite and government, 303-4,
371, partisan behavior, 302, and petitioning, 307, outvoters, 306; Whigs and
Dissenters, 299; *see also* elections;
petitions
Coleridge, John, 161, 162
Collett, Thomas, 348n, 366n
Colley, Linda, 86, 112, 379
Colquhoun, Patrick, 62, 437
Colquitt, John, 368
Commonwealthmen, *see* radicals
Congregationalists, 1n, 44n, 52, 56, 57, 95,
100, 101, 103n, 108, 350-1, 265, 397n,
423; at Bristol, 206, 251; at Colchester,
298-9, 399; geographic distribution, 93,
94n; at Great Yarmouth, 239; at Kingston
upon Hull, 290; at Liverpool, 275; losses
in London, 93; at Newcastle, 256n; and
office holding, 70, 77, 78, 81, 115; and

social standing, 62, 67; at Taunton, 351;
and vote, 115
consent, 138-9, 142n, 144, 150-1, 163; and
government as trust, 144-5, 262; *see also*
American Revolution and representation
constitution, 127, 142n, 145-7, 148, 150,
151, 154, 156, 160n, 417; the essence of,
164
Conventicle Act, 51n
Cooper, Miles, 161, 162
Cooper, Samuel, 169, 192
Cornwall, 96, 423
Corporation Act, 69-70, 71, 74, 80; and
corporation and small freeman boroughs,
50, 72-5; and freeholder boroughs, 76;
and large boroughs, 77-80; and medium
freeman boroughs, 75-6; and scot and lot
boroughs, 76; *see also* Test and Corporation Acts
corporations, 17, 21, 27; Anglican dominated, 169, 276, 279; and anti-corporation
parties, 21, 85, 108, 110, 364, 397,
407-408, 412; divided over America,
366-7, 402, 408; and government patronage, 369; linked to Church and Quarter
Sessions, 174; *see also* addresses; Anglican Church; High-Church Anglicans;
local and national politics; Nonconformists
Corresponding Societies, 427, 429
Costerton family, of Great Yarmouth, 364n
Country ideology, 9; *see also* radicals
Courcy, Richard de, 405
Covenanters, 129
Coventry, 15, 16, 55n, 98n, 104, 105, 108,
350, 355, 359, 364n, 399, 407, 431;
corporation-anti-corporation conflict, 346,
347, 348, corporation divided, 366, 367,
370; elections and violence, 346; High
Anglicans, 346, 347; Middlesex election
affair: and America, 347-8, and radicalism, 347; Nonconformists, 346, influence
petitioners, 404, 408, and Low-Church
Anglicans, 347, ministers lead in petitioning, 349, 404, office holding, 78, 346,
366-7, 399, sign petitions, 390, 411, turn
from government, 347, vote, 347; petition
and petitioning agitation, 322n, 327,
336n, 344, 348-9, 395, 398, compared to
Bristol and Newcastle, 348, and High-
Church Anglicans, 348, second address,
349, and socio-economic distinctions,
373-5, 384-5, 401, 402; and popular
politics, 338; pro-Americans, 349; Whigs
and Tories, 346, 349n; *see also* elections;
petitions
Cowburne, Thomas, 379n

Cowen, Robert, 270n
Craner, Joseph, 366n
Craven, William, 6th Baron, 336, 348, 414
Creswell, Samuel, 379
Crewe's Act, 368
The Crisis, 425
Critical Review, 126
Cromwell, Oliver, 146
Crowle, George, 290
Cruger, Henry 198, 202, 209n, 215-20, 221, 222, 224, 225, 226, 229n, 231, 232, 236, 237, 243, 244, 245, 252, 253, 435; on America, 213-14; as M.P., 212-13; as radical, 330-1; *see also* Burke
Cumberland, 54n, 319; and petitioning, 336
Cunliffe, Ellis, 277, 278, 280, 285, 286n, 288

Daken, Thomas, 366n
Dale, Tertius, 357
Dalton, Jacob, 349
Dampier, alderman, 77n
Dampier, Thomas, 161
Daniel, 146
Daniell, Jeremiah, 299
Dansie, Jacob, 399
Dartmouth, 74n, 97n, 338n
Darwall, John, 162
Daubeny, George, 216, 217, 218n, 219, 220, 222, 229n, 232, 252n, 334
Davey, Jonathan, 77
David, Rees, 13, 124n, 130-1, 134, 135, 136, 137, 141n, 142n, 143, 144, 146, 151n, 159, 160, 163, 166, 167, 168, 170, 171, 173, 174n, 182, 183, 187, 189, 310, 419, 425; on American Revolution, 149, 153, 154, 155n; as charismatic leader, 239; on monarchy, 164-5; on petitioning, 186n, 188n; on right of resistance, 157; on social stratification, 181
Davidson, Thomas, 351
Davidson, William, 270n
Davie, Donald, 123
Davis, James, 233n
Davis, Thomas, 46
Deacle, John, 80n
Deane, Thomas, 366n
Declaration of Rights, *see* Bill of Rights
Dedham, 299n, 350, 351
deference, 28, 42, 175, 176, 179, 199; and Calvinism, 136, 189; rejection of, 9, 35, 182-4, 192, 274, 341, 419; strengthening ties of, 25
Defoe, Daniel, 53, 101
Deism, 135n
Delaval, Sir John, 321
Delaval, Thomas, 257, 259, 260, 263, 264,

265, 266, 268, 269, 270, 272n, 273, 339
Delolme, John Louis, 134
Denton, Norfolk, 56n
Derby, 76n, 97n
Derby, Edward Stanley, 11th Earl of, 343
Derbyshire, 83, 132
Devizes, 72, 73, 82, 98n, 114
Devonshire, 84, 96, 102; and address, 263
Diaper, John, 233n
Dickinson, H.T., xv, 8, 24, 316
Dickinson, John, 134
Diss, Isaac, 350-1, 411
Dissenters, *see* Nonconformists
Dissenting Deputies, 16, 29, 52, 55, 56, 59, 410
Diston, Josiah, 73n, 82, 114
Ditchfield, G.M., xv, 24, 60, 113, 117
Dixon, Thomas, 101, 102
Dobson, C.R., 327, 383
Dobson, J., 343
Doddridge, Philip, 55n, 82
Dodson, George, 367n
Donoughue, Bernard, xii
Dorchester, 97n
Dorset, 95
Dover, 79n, 97n
Dudley, 317n
Dunsford, Martin, 81, 412
Durham, 54n, 97n, 132; and Constitutional Club, 259
Durham Act, 243n

East Looe, 74n, 75, 97n
East Retford, 74n, 75, 98n
Easton Grey, Wiltshire, 84
economic reform, 133, 185, 201, 241, 321, 327, 329, 430
Edward I, 146, 151n
Edward VI, 387
Effingham, Thomas Howard, 3rd Earl of, 336, 339, 340n
Egerton, Sir Thomas, 344n
Eglon, 152, 164
Ehud, 152
Elam, Samuel, 198
elections and electorate: and absence of parties, 27; and absence of socio-economic divisions, 11, 34; and American crisis, 195-6, and elite support for government candidates, 311; characteristics of unreformed electorate, 96-7, 100, 311; corruption, 166, 176, 259, 352; cross voting, 226; differences between electoral and popular politics, 120; and Dissenting population distribution, 95-6, 98-9; electors scrutinize Members' votes, 214-15, 218, 263, 281-2, 292-3; floating

vote, 229-30; and franchise, 151; general election (1774), 190; general election (1784), 21; instructing Members of Parliament at Bristol, 215n, 330, 331n, at Newcastle, 257, 259, 260, 261, 267, 339; and localism, 11, 27; outvoters in Colchester, 435, in Newcastle, 266, 435; partisan behavior and double vote, 224-5; partisan behavior at Abingdon, Bristol, Great Yarmouth, Norwich, Shrewsbury, 109-10, 230; partisan behavior defined, 226; partisan vote and issues, 228, and bribes, 228; and partisanship, 22; patronage, 327; secret service money, 352-3, at Bristol, 234, Colchester, 301, Coventry, 346, 347, 349; and socio-economic rank, 66-7, 119; violence, 351, 352; and virtual representation, 151; *see also* party; and entry under individual boroughs
Elisha, 164
elite support for government candidates, 311
Elton, Abraham Isaac, 368n
Elton, Abraham, Jr., 103, 209-10, 352n
Elton, Abraham, Sr., 83n, 209-10
Elton family, of Bristol, 377
Elton, Isaac, Jr., 377n
Elton, Isaac, Sr., 43n, 398, 377n
Emans, Peter, 357n, 407
Encell, John, 316
Essex, 99, 108, 306, 423
Essex Committee, 301
Essex Congregational Union, 16, 350
Established Church, *see* Anglican Church
Estlin, John, 233
Europe, 164
Evans, Caleb, 68, 124n, 127-8, 131, 133, 134, 135, 136, 137, 138, 140, 141, 142n, 143, 145, 146, 147, 148, 153n, 163, 169, 170, 171, 172n, 177, 179, 182, 189, 198n, 199, 206, 214, 233, 238, 310, 317, 335, 359, 398, 406, 419, 425; on administration, 165-6; on American Revolution, 149; as charismatic leader, 236, 239, 253; and origin of political power, 144; and petitioning, 188; and religious liberty, 139; and representation, 150-2, 157; and resistance to government, 154-7
Evans, Hugh, 233n
Evesham, 80n, 97n
Ewin, William, 57
Excise crisis, 109
Exclusion crisis, 113, 118, 415
Exeter, 96, 227, 362n, 364n; and address, 322; partisan vote and America, 228; social standing of Dissent, 287; violence at, 15, 98n, 101, 102, 115, 116
extra-parliamentary meetings, 13-14; *see*

also associations
Eye, 97n
Eyre, James, 348

Falkland, Lucius Cary, 2nd Viscount, 134
Fane, Francis, 352n
Farnsworth, John Greaves, 398
Farr, Paul, 197, 377
Farr, Thomas, 377
Fast and Thanksgiving Day sermons, *see* sermons
fast days, 153, 171, 176, 181, 184, 192
Felix Farley's Bristol Journal, 222, 387
Fellows, John, 367n
Fenn, Thomas, 82, 396, 398
Fifteen, rebellion of, 53, 83, 116, 118, 210
Filmer, Sir Robert, 218n, 341
Finch, Robert Poole, 125
Fisher, Richard, 379
'Five Mile' Act, 51n
Fleming, Sir Michael le, 344n
Fletcher, John, 128, 135, 140, 158, 162, 178, 182
Fletcher, Thomas, 378
Flowers, Mr., 71
Fogo, James, 316
Fonnereau, Thomas, 396
Fordyce, Alexander, 43n, 102, 299, 300, 304
Forster, Francis, 168
Forty-Five, rebellion of, 58, 83, 108, 118, 212, 218, 346n, 358, 415
Foske, Sir Michael, 83
Foskett, Bernard, 233n
Foster, James, 368
Foster, John, 270n
Foster, Nathaniel, 192, 211
Fothergill, John, 129n, 151n, 189
Fowey, 97n
Fox, Charles James, 24n, 58, 196-7, 217, 218n, 220, 232, 237, 279, 298, 398; *see also* Fox-North Coalition
Fox-North Coalition, 201, 218n, 219, 220, 237, 292, 315, 321, 360; impact at Bristol, 226, 232; at Great Yarmouth, 241
Foxcraft, James, 367n, 407
Foxcraft, John, 367n, 407
France, 157, 158
Franco-American alliance, 427
The Freeman's Magazine, 129, 187, 259, 262, 264
French Revolution, 18, 60, 427, 429, 430
Fryer, C.E., 21, 91
Fuller, Richard, 80n
Fuller, William, 114
Furneaux, Philip, 60, 134

Gascoyne, Bamber, Jr., 278, 279n, 281, 282, 283, 285, 286n, 288, 365
Gascoyne, Bamber, Sr., 277, 278, 281
Gayner, William, 407
general warrants, 147; as political issue, 278, 347
gentlemen: and America, 17; support government, 17
Gentlemen's Magazine, 126
George I, 58, 70, 106, 116
George II, 58, 106, 253
George III, 2, 17, 23, 25, 30, 58, 84, 89, 100, 109, 111, 158, 160, 161, 163, 164, 184, 217, 253, 263, 318, 322, 351, 381, 412, 415, 417, 422, 426; and addresses, 319; and king's friends, 23, 201; ministers of, 164; personal rule, 199, 201; *see also* monarchy
Gilbert, Alan, 39, 92
Gipson, Henry, 340n
Glorious Revolution, 8, 118, 127, 146, 147, 155n, 161, 221, 358; and settlement, 253, 317, 405, 417, 422
Gloucester, 82, 83, 98n, 362n, 363n
Gloucestershire, 61n
Glyn, Sir Richard, 347
Glynn, John, 260n
Gordon Riots, 170n, 216, 365n, 429
Gordon, Thomas, 110, 133n, 170, 262
Gould, Nathaniel, 80n
Gould, Nathaniel, cousin, 80n
Gower, John Leveson Gower, 1st Earl of, 98n
Grafton, August Henry Fitzroy, 3rd Duke of, 396
Graham, William, 270n
Gravesend, 82
Gray, Charles, 300, 303, 304n
Great Awakening, 95
Great Marlow, 97n
Great Yarmouth, 132, 169, 190, 192n, 245, 253, 254, 255, 258, 272, 310, 311, 316, 330, 360, 362n, 366n, 412, 428, 434, 435; and address, 328, 364; Nonconformists: and Anglican alliance, 240, failure of clerical leadership, 240, 241, and Fox-North Coalition, 237, laity leads petitioning, 404, oppose government over America, 240, 241-2, popular politics, 240, 241, religious and socio-economic motivation combined, 247, voters, 109-10, compared to Bristol, Northampton, 239, and Norwich, 241; petition and petitioning agitation: and socio-economic distinctions, 371-2, 373, 380, 384n, 401, 402, 411; voting: and Namierian interpretation, 202, and partisan behavior, 242, and socio-economic distinctions, 246-7

Green, Thomas, 347, 348
Greenwood, Matthew, 368
Grenville, George, 210
Grieve, George, 259, 260, 321, 340, 342; and petitioning, 339
Grove, Henry, 351
Guildford, 74, 97n
Gunn, J.A.W., 25
Guthrie, George, 340n
Guy Fawkes day, 127

Habeas Corpus, 146, 160
Hagen, Everett, 85
Halifax: and petition, 336n, 414
Halliday, John, 352, 353
Hallifax, Sir Thomas, 349
Hammond, Francis, 368
Hamner, Sir Walden, 396
Hampden, John, 127, 134
Hampshire, 54n, 229n, 342; and addresses and petitions, 362; and Anglican clergy, 386; and debate over petitions, 325n; and J.P.s, 388; and patronage, 369; petition, 321; and petitioning, 327
Hanbury, Capel, 105
Handasyds, John, 123
Harding, William, 392n
Hardman, John, 43n, 275, 276, 277, 287
Hardwicke, Philip Yorke, 1st Earl of, 56, 57
Hardy, Thomas, 32
Harford family, of Bristol, 377
Harford, Joseph, 77, 197, 221, 331, 376, 407; leads Bristol Whigs, 218n, 253
Harris, alderman, 77n
Harris, John, 368n
Harrison, Jaspar, 340n, 341, 375
Harrison, William, 82
Harson, Daniel, 368, 398
Hartley, David, 43n, 122, 295, 296, 298, 412; and America, 291, 292-4; and parliamentary reform, 293
Harwich, 72n, 97n, 306
Haverfordwest, 62n
Hayes, Thomas, 331n, 334, 335
Hedon, 74n, 97n
Helston, 362n
Hénault, Charles Jean Françoise, 134
Henderson, John, 286
Henley, Henry, 74
Henning family, of Poole, 75
Henry VIII, 171
Hereford, 97n, 362n; and address, 322
Herefordshire: and address, 362
Hertford, 27, 54n, 98n, 101, 108, 115
Hertfordshire, 54n, 99n, 101, 114, 115
Hewitson, John, 342n

Hewitt, James, 347
Hewitt, John, 366n
Hexham, 321, 342
Heywood, Samuel, 83
High-Church Anglicans, 22, 27, 28, 52, 115, 126, 171, 381, 386, 394; influence corporations, 287, 406; and local government, 19, 75, 77, 80, 88, 106, 108; and political theology, 24-25, 111, 125n, 136; and sermons, 162; and Test and Corporation Acts, 71
Higham Ferrers, 75n, 80n
Hindon, 97n, 103
Hoadly, Benjamin, bishop, 70, 134
Hobbes, Giles, 351n
Hobbes, Thomas, 341
Hodson, Francis, 378
Hogarth, William, 99, 167, 406
Hoghton, Henry, 5th Baronet, 43n, 75n, 83, 84, 98n, 102, 103, 116, 290
Hoghton, Henry, 6th Baronet, 116, 124n
Holden, Samuel, 75n
Hollins, Humphrey, 367n, 407
Hollis, Thomas, 154n
Hollis, Thomas Brand, *see* Brand Hollis, Thomas
Holt, Anne, 287
Honiton, 97n, 103
Hopper, Richard, 357n, 407
Hornbuckle, James, 367n, 407
Hornby, Mr., 343
Horne, George, 162
Horne, John, 332
Horsham, 97n
Horton, Sir Watts, 343, 344n
Hoskins, Joseph, 233n
Hotchkin, Charles, 334, 363
Hottoman, François, 341n
Houlston, Thomas, 379n
House of Commons, 153, 353, 361, 362, 418; and American crisis, 195; and money bills, 151
House of Lords, 361, 417; and bishops, 170, 172; and money bills, 151; opposition Lords' protest, 343
Howard, John, 83
Howe, George Augustus, 3rd Viscount, 355
Howe, Thomas, 192n
Howe, Sir William, 355, 356n, 357-8
Huddersfield, 317n
Huish, Mark, 197, 331n, 336n, 367n, 407
Humble, Edward, 379
Hunter, Henry, 123, 189
Hunter, William, 192
Huntingdon: and address, 362n, 363
Huntingdonshire, 405
Hurd, Richard, bishop, 162

Hurry family, of Great Yarmouth, 239, 240, 311, 404, 412
Hurry, Thomas, 240
Hurwich, Judith, 61
Hutchinson, Benjamin, 405
Hutchinson, Thomas, 134
Huthwait, Cornelius, 356, 357n, 398
Hythe, 74n, 97n

ideology, 41; and political behavior, 3, 39-41, 411; and protest, 424; in relation to socio-economic status, 372, 381; *see also* sermons
Ilchester, 98n, 103, 124n
Indemnity Acts, 69, 70
independence, 141-2, 177; of action of Dissenters, 88, 106-9; and artisans, 382-3, 384, 404; and corporations, 388; and Country ideology, 108; Dissenters' use of rhetoric of, 9, 107-8, 410-11, 412-13, 418, 420; and law, 87; its meaning in relation to patronage, 371; Nonconformists nurture, 182; and socio-economic status, 68, 371, 378; *see also* local and national politics; Nonconformist ministers; opposition
Independents, *see* Congregationalists
Industrial Revolution, 31n
Inglesant, Jonathan, 367n, 407
Ipswich, 76, 82, 95, 98n, 306
Ireland, 319n
Israelities, 164-5

Jackson, George, 301n
Jacobites and Jacobitism, 53, 116, 161, 262n, 263n, 280, 362n
James II, 146, 147n
Jebb, John, 175n
Jeffries, Joseph, 354n
Jenkins, Philip, 86
Jenkinson, Charles, 277
Jezebel, 153
Joddrell, Mr., 343
Joel, Thomas, 332, 337
John, King, 157
Johnson, Samuel, 128, 328, 439, 440
Johnson, William, 398
Jolliffe family, of Poole, 75, 404
Jones, Alice, 442
Juvenal, 134

Kenny, Vincent, 81
Kenwood, Mr., 71
Kent, 319
Kent, Bartholomew, 340n
Kentish Gazette, 325, 326
Kidderminster, 123

King, Gregory, 62, 437-8, 439, 440
Kings Lynn, 74n, 97n
Kingston upon Hull, 43, 64n, 65, 97n, 255, 310, 311, 316, 358, 362n, 412, 414, 434, 435; addresses, 294, 295n, 338n; criticism of administration, 293; elections: absence of organizations, 294, corruption in, 291, 294, 310, influence of corporation, 294, lack of issues, 294; Nonconformity: and chapels, 289-90, office holding, 81, 290, politically quiescent, 295, 297, 298, 310; Trinity House, 290, 294, 376; voting: Anglican clergy, 295, elite support for government, 295-7, 371, new voters, 244, partisan behavior, 294-5
Kinnear, Mary, 147, 311, 326
Kippis, Andrew, 189
Kirkpatrick, Hezekiah, 392n, 393
Knaresborough, 97n
Knox, John, 136n
Knox, Thomas, 8, 13, 26, 45, 258, 259, 261-2, 266, 269, 270, 273, 436
Kramnick, Isaac, 31

Lacon family, of Great Yarmouth, 364n
Lady Huntingdon's Connection, 206
Laidler, Matthew, 340n
Lancashire, 83, 99n, 423; address, 339; Anglican clergy and Lancashire address, 346, 386; and divisions over America, 342, 362; petition of 1775, 281, 322, 333-4, 343
Lancaster, 79n, 83, 84n, 98n, 318, 342, 343, 362n, 363n, 431
Langford, Paul, 25, 385-6
Langton, John, 62
Laud, William, archbishop, 157
Launceston, 74n, 97n
law: and authoritarianism, 25; Dissenters attack, 406, 420; Dissenting ministers criticize, 172-4; legal profession, 17, supports coercion, 375-6; oppressive nature of, 167, 173; and order, concern of corporations, 363-4, 388; and reform, 387; and religion interwoven, 42, 388-9, 404; written subordinate to natural, 143, 154, 165, 173
Laxton, Paul, 62
Lecky, W.E.H., 19, 20, 200
Lee, Arthur, 151n
Lee, John, 75n, 80n, 83
Leeds, 198, 317n, 329, 331; petition, 322n, 336, 362n; and petition, 379
Leeds Mercury, 378
Leicester, 83, 98n, 362n, 363n, 364n; and address, 338n
Leicestershire, 56, 99

Leominster, 76, 82, 97n, 103, 104, 119
Lewes, 11, 76n, 98n, 103, 106, 108
Lewin, Robert, 287, 392-3
Lexington and Concord, battles of, 318, 324
liberty and virtue, 141; in America connected to England, 214; civil and religious, 143; *see also* independence; Nonconformist ministers
Lichfield, 97n, 362n; and address, 338n
Lincoln, 97n, 100
Lincoln, Anthony, xi, 7, 123
Lincoln, Bruce, 32
Lindert, Peter, 442
Lippincott, Henry, 216, 217
Liskeard, 74n, 97n
Liverpool, 10, 27, 43, 45, 62, 88, 98n, 105, 169, 255, 266, 307, 310, 311, 316, 317n, 358, 362n, 366, 367, 379n, 382, 411, 412, 413, 414, 425, 434, 435; addresses and addressers, 322, 327-8, 364, and Anglican clergy, 346, 390, compared to voting, 285, and corporation, 279, 342, 365; corporation-anti-corporation conflict, 275-6, 277, 278-9, 281, 285, and Anglicanism, 279, 392; elections: compared to Bristol, Newcastle, 282-3, conservative ambiance, 392-3, and Namierian interpretation, 202, and popular literature, 279, 280, 281, 282-3, rhetoric of oppression, 281-2, trade as issue, 279-80, 288, and violence, 277; inhabitants address, 342-3, addressers as Tories, 344, 345, and patronage, 368-9, 370; Nonconformity: and chapels, 274-5, elite, 277, and inconsistent petitioning, 391-3, 411, 420, and inconsistent vote, 280, 285, 286-7, 310, layman leads petitioning, 343, 392, 404, ministers quiescent, 287, 310, and occupational structure, 63-4, 68, office holding, 77, 81, 274-5, 277, and repeal of Test and Corporation Acts, 61, and slave trade, 287, social status compared, 287-8, 391, versus Church, 282; petition and petitioning agitation, 15, 281, 322, 343-6, 389, and socio-economic distinctions, 373-6, 384, 385n, 391-3, 408, 420, and Wilkes' petition, 344, 392; politics and class, 276; seaman's strike, 15, 281, 325, 343, 391; slave trade, 392; Tories, 275; voting: and Anglican clergy, 286, 289, partisan behavior of, 227, 283-4, 285-6, and socio-economic distinctions, 288-9, 371; Whigs, 275, 280n; *see also* Lancashire; petitions
Lloyd, Posthumous, 349
local and national politics, 414, 416; considered together at Bristol, 202, 213,

219, 224, 233, 236, at Liverpool, 281, at
  Newcastle, 259, 261, 340-1, 364; end of
  provincial introversion, 421; men and
  measures connected at Bristol, 222-3, at
  Kingston upon Hull, 292-3, at Newcastle,
  260; *see also* Anglican Church; independence; opposition; oppression; radicals
Locke, John, 134, 136, 142, 150, 154n,
  155n, 158, 170
Lockyer, Joseph, 98n, 124
Lockyer, Thomas, 98n, 103, 124
Lodge, Richard, 91
Lombard, John, 396
London, 8n, 10, 11n, 12, 14, 15, 16n, 17, 42,
  54, 60, 62n, 71, 79n, 82, 94, 98n, 122,
  123, 124, 159, 167, 196, 210, 229n, 243,
  260, 292, 299n, 306, 317n, 319, 328, 329,
  330n, 332, 333, 336, 338, 343, 344, 379,
  381, 399, 404, 410, 411, 414, 421, 427,
  428, 429, 434n, 435, 442; Dissenting
  decline in, 92-3; patronage and coercive
  address, 368n; and socio-economic
  divisions, 371n,, 372, 376, 380, 391; *see
  also* petitions
London Association, 325, 332, 338, 426,
  429; in Newcastle, 330, 338-40
London Evening Post, 368
London Gazette, 426
London, John, 73n
Long Parliament, 146
Low Church Anglicans, 28 9, 75, 80,
  111-12, 113-17, 118-20, 162-3, 198n,
  207; and American Revolution, 125-6;
  Dissenters example to, 85; ideology of,
  405, 406; influenced by Dissenters, 115;
  and radicalism, 113n; turn against govern-
  ment, 242-3, 253; *see also* Nonconform-
  ists
Lowes, William, 368n
Lowther, Sir James, 102, 336
Lowthian, Samuel, 270n
Loyalists in America, 425
Ludlow, 76n, 97n
Luttrell, Temple, 228, 345, 362
Lyme Regis, 74, 82, 98n
Lymington, 74n, 97n; and patronage, 369;
  and petition, 322n
Lynn, 84

Macaulay, Catherine, 160
Macaulay, Thomas B., 52
Macbride, John, 397n
Maddison, Thomas, 340n
magistrates: and administration, 168-9
Magna Charta, 146, 157, 173
Maidenhead, 362n
Maidstone, 11, 98n, 105, 227, 244, 245; and

partisan vote, 228
Mainwaring, John, 125
Maldon, 76, 97n, 98n, 101, 103, 104, 106,
  298n
Mallard, John, 331n
Malmsbury, 73n, 73n, 97n
Malton, 74n, 216
Manchester, 10, 13, 317n, 318, 342, 343,
  424, 426, 429; and address, 338n; and
  socio-economic divisions, 371, 372, 380,
  411
Manchester Mercury, 343, 344
Manners, Lord Robert, 290, 291, 292, 294,
  295, 297
Mansfield, 133n
Mansfield, William Murray, 1st Earl, 54
Marat, Jean Paul, 262, 341
Markham, William, archbishop, 161
Marlborough, 72n, 79, 97n
Marriage Act (1753), 56
Marshall, Peter, 8, 445, 371, 380
Martin, John, 123, 189
Marx, Karl, 31, 41, 179
Marxism, 31-2, 34, 36
Maskall, Henry, 332
Massie, Joseph, 62, 436, 437-41, 444, 445
Maude, Thomas, 340n, 342
Mauduit, Israel, 124
Maurice, Thomas, 161
Mawbey, Sir Joseph, 325n
Maxwell, Robert, 352n
Mayne, Robert, 304n
Medley, Samuel, 392n
Meech, John, 80
Melhuish, Joseph, 354n
merchants: trading to America, 17; *see also*
  petitions
Meredith, Sir William, 43n, 277-8, 279, 282,
  283, 284, 286n, 288, 412, 435; on
  America, 278; his Tory past, 280, 285
Merlott, John, 377, 398
Methodism, 32n, 53, 54n, 56, 95n, 108; and
  social standing, 61
Methodists, 198; at Bristol, 206; Calvinistic,
  206, 251; at Kingston upon Hull, 290n; at
  Liverpool, 275; at Newcastle, 256
Michison, Robert, 340n, 342n
Middlesex, 82, 92, 122, 362n, 373n; petition
  concerning America, 322n
Middlesex election affair, 12, 18, 27, 129,
  148, 186, 201, 255, 310, 315, 316, 323,
  327, 329, 344n, 346, 349, 350, 360,
  386-7, 391, 410, 428-9, 430; at Bristol,
  204, 209, 211, 326, 330-1; at Coventry,
  326, 347, 348; and Dissenters, 58, 120;
  linked to America through provincial
  leaders, 326; at Liverpool, 379, 392; at

Newcastle, 258-9, 263, 326, 339-40, 341; petitions of, 16, 45, 319; *see also* addresses; petitions

Middleton, Sir William, 3rd Baronet, 83n, 105

Middleton, Sir William, 5th Baronet, 83n

Midhurst, 97n

Milborne Port, 97n

Minehead, 98n, 102

Minster, John, 348n, 366n

Missing family, of Portsmouth, 75, 114

Missing, John, 104-5

Moab, 152, 164

Molesworth, Robert, 1st Viscount, 341n

monarchy, 151; and absolute authority, 263n; danger of criticism, 160; Dissenters devotion to, 148-9, 160, 163; divine right theory, 146, 161; and empire, 354; and God, 136, 137; head of Church, 28, 121; hereditary, 154; limited, 340, 354; and money bills, 151; Nonconformist and Anglican attitudes toward, 159-67; oppressive, 167; passive obedience and non-resistance, 146, 162, 163, 171, 386; and Quebec, 150; as source of law, 143n; tolerated, 418; *see also* Bible; George III

Money, John, xv, 8, 13, 26, 379

Monmouth, 76n, 97n

Monmouthshire, 43, 99n, 105

Montagu, Lord Charles Greville, 328

Montesquieu, Charles de Secondat, Baron, 134, 136, 155n

Monthly Review, 126

More, John, 55n

More, Robert, 108

Morpeth, 74n, 75, 98n, 104, 106, 257, 387-8; and America, 321

Mosley, Edward, 368n

Mouncher family, of Portsmouth, 75

Mullett, Thomas, 379n

Municipal Corporation Act, 80

Murdin, Cornelius, 161

Murray, James, 58, 68, 124n, 128-31, 132, 134, 135, 136, 137, 139, 140, 141, 142n, 143, 145, 146, 147n, 148, 150, 159, 160, 163, 167, 168, 169, 170, 174n, 175, 192, 225, 256, 262, 264, 265n, 270, 272, 310, 317, 359, 379, 419, 425; on administration, 165-6; on American Revolution, 149, 150-2, 154; anti-clericalism, 171-2; on instructing Members, 267; and Kingdom of God, 138; on law, 172-3; on monarchy, 163-6; and Newcastle electors, 265-6; and petitioning, 340; on reform strategy, 186-9; on right of resistance, 155-7; on social stratification, 178-82, 183-4

Naboth, 153, 164

Namier, Sir Lewis, xi, xii, xiii, xiv, 11, 20, 21, 25, 26, 27, 45, 100, 199, 200, 201, 202, 232, 237, 258, 266, 327, 358, 416, 421

Namierian school, 11, 21, 26, 27, 45, 203, 416, 421

Nash, Gary, 35, 382

Nash, Thomas, 347

natural rights, 263n, 418; *see also* law; Nonconformist ministers

Neale, R.S., 34, 167

Netherlands, 55

Netherton-Dudley, 71n

New Shoreham, 80n, 97n

New Windsor, 97n, 362n

New York, 212, 265

Newark and Nottingham Journal, 379

Newcastle Chronicle, 325, 340, 341, 364, 379

Newcastle Courant, 15, 341, 379

Newcastle-Rockingham Whigs, 23

Newcastle, Thomas Pelham-Holles, 1st Duke of, 28, 100, 102, 103, 105, 210, 216, 346, 355

Newcastle under Lyme, 76, 98n

Newcastle upon Tyne, 15, 16, 17, 26, 27, 43, 44n, 45, 46, 88, 97n, 102, 123, 124, 126, 127, 128, 129, 132, 164, 167, 168, 169, 179, 187, 282, 283, 284, 287, 289, 306, 310, 311, 316, 317, 333n, 344, 348, 350, 358, 359, 366, 367, 380, 399, 407, 413, 414, 424, 428, 432, 433, 424, 435; address and addressers, 322, 328, 338n, 364, and Anglican clergy, 339, 386, and the corporation, 339, 362, 364, 375, and patronage, 368-9, 370; Constitutional Club, 259, 339, 341; corporation and politics, 259, 261, 342; elections and electorate: compared to Bristol and Great Yarmouth, 264, magisterial versus burgesses party, 251, 266, 268, 272, 375, 388, past interpretations of, 202, 258, popular literature and constitutional issues in, 260, 261, 262, 263, rhetoric of oppression, 274, scrutiny of Members' voting, 263, and socio-economic distinctions, 265, 266, 271-3, 371; Middlesex election affair, 259, 260, 342; Newcastle Association, 340; Nonconformists: and chapels, 255-6, county voters, 256, fail to vote, 270-71, 309-10, ministers and rebellion, 264, Newcastle Presbytery, 256, and occupational structure, 63-4, 68, and office holding, 81, and petitioning, 340, 390, 404, 408, social status, 270-1, compared to Bristol, Liverpool, and Exeter,

287-8; parliamentary reform, 257, 258, 259; petition and petitioning agitation, 257, 264, 270, 274, 322, 336n, 338, 339-42, 379, and publishing, 379, and socio-economic distinctions, 373-6, 380, 384, 385n, 401, 411; Philosophical Society, 264, 340-1; radicals and radicalism, 227, 258, 264, 266, 330n, 338, 340-1, 364, and artisans and shopkeepers, 272, 274, ideology, 261, and labor, 272, linked to London, 260, 338, past accounts of, 261, and religion, 262, social basis to, 261, 272-4; Tories, 341, burning effigies, 341, and the Crown, 262, and party, 257; Town Moor affair, 257, 259, 261, 339, 340, 387, linked to America, 263, 264-5, 364-5; voting: Anglican clergy, 268, consistency compared to Bristol, Yarmouth, Cambridge, 266, partisan behavior, 227, 267-70, role of outvoters, 266, and new voters, 244, 266; Whigs: as label, 262, and moderate churchmen and Dissent, 262, and party, 257, and principles, 262; Wilkites and Wilkism, 259, 260-1, 264, and local leadership, 260, and congruence in petitioning and voting, 260, 261n, compared to American petitioners and voters, 262; *see also* elections; petitions

Newcome, Joseph, 114
Newnham, George Lewis, 103
Newnham, Nathaniel, 80n, 102
Newnham, Thomas, 75n, 80n
Newport, Gloucestershire, 123
Newport, Isle of Wight, 72n, 97n
newspapers, 8, 44, 126, 128n, 204; and pulpit, 184, 424; and radicalism, 325-6, 333, 337, 340, 342, 344, 349, 378-9, 383, 404; *see also* petitions
Newton, Thomas, bishop, 234, 386
Nickelson, Thomas, 399
Noble, Isaac, 206n, 207
Noble, John, 115, 116, 197, 198n, 209, 253, 354n, 366n, 407
Noble, Luke, 354n
Nonconformist ministers, 12, 13, 30, 36, 60, 112; absence of clerical leadership in electoral politics, 310, 316; on associations, 188; charismatic leadership of, 16, 37, 41, 88, 119, 120, 128, 158, 190, 236, 239, 254, 309-11; and Commonwealthman ideology, 391; confidence in common people, 155, 156, 158, 164, 177, 178, 180-2, 184, 186, 192; criticize crown, 163-6; on electoral corruption, 186-7; encourage petitions, 185-9; on justice, 173; on monarchy, 393; on moral

nature of politics, 140-2; and more advanced radicalism, 14, 18, 58, 60, 159, 175; on natural rights, 141, 142-5, 150, 151, 152n, 156, 174, and common people, 143, 153; and pulpit, 420; pulpit encourages independence, 383, 403, 407, in elections, 186-7; radicalism of pulpit, 182-4; on right of resistance, 154-8; sign petitions, 189, 390, 392; on social inequality, 174-82, 422; *see also* independence; pulpit; sermons

Nonconformists and nonconformity: academies, 55, 102, 104, 278n, 351, 354, 392; alliance with artisans, 32, 37-8, 120, 383, 410, 411, 423, 427, and Low-Church Anglicans, 28, 37, 85, 99, 106, 108, 110-12, 113-20, 387, 403-408, 413, 418, 421, influence Low-Church Anglicans, 158, 242-3, 389, 393; alternative vision of politics and society, 158, 184, 417-22, 423; anti-clericalism, 135n, 138-9, 169-72, 417-18, as an attack on law, 388-9; anti-hierarchical disposition, 418-19; attitudes towards episcopacy, 59; in boroughs, 96-9; and bribery, 97, 99, 103; challenge union of Church and State, 417-8; and Commonwealthmen, 46, 133, 403; and the constitution, 8; in counties, 99; definition of, 1n, 6, 49; Dissenting laborers uninvolved in petitioning, 384, 425; distinctive contribution to radicalism, 137, 154, 192; divide corporations, 366-7; and electoral independence, 311; elite of, 13, 14, 23, 87, 89, 118, 399; fear Anglicans, 170n, 387, 391; and Hanoverian regime, 108-109, 118-20; ideology versus vested interests, 367; and Industrial Revolution, 85-6, 411; and justice, 174; laity, 10, 23, 87, 88, 89, 316; and the law, 20, 49, 84-90, 388-9, 404, 406, 420; lay leadership, 254, 310-11, 334, 343, 350, 411; and loyalism, 57, 61, 123-4, 136, 140, 148, 149, 356, 392-3, compared to pro-Americans, 189-90, 398-9, 404; and marginalization, 87-90; as Members of Parliament, 29, 109, 112, 349, 351n; and middle orders of society, 8, 37; their misperceptions, 162, 425; and moderate radicalism, 42, 148, 160, 174; and numerical decline, 92-5; and numerical growth, 423; and office holding, 36, 72, 74-8, 397-8, 410, 425; and orthodoxy, 4, 18, 130, 131, 174n, 189, 192; and Parliament, 117, 166; and party, 2, 18-22, 27, 29, 106-107, 109-11, 113-17, 197, 412-13, 414-15; and patronage, 104-106, 358, 425; as petitioning pro-Americans,

389-95, 398-9, 408-409, 410-11; polarize society, 182, 192; political influence, 99-106, 190-1, in relation to numbers, 91-2, 95-6; political principles of, 6, 8, 21, 28, 30, 35, 37, 39, 41, 42, 89, 110, 120; and polity, 1n, 4, 59; pre-conditions for radicalism, 310, 395, 398; and radicalism, 2, 5, 7, 87, 403, 411, 414, 417-18, 422; 'rational' Dissent, 4, 11-12, 95, 134, 138n, 351, 377, as explanation for radicalism, 418, 419; their relative freedom, 36-7, 80, 85, 425; and Rockingham Whigs, 29; schoolmasters, 60, 84; and self-interest, 158; sermons and political behavior, 358, 391, 420; social divisions, 2, 8, 17, 119-20; social status compared to Anglicans, 36, 42, 62-9, 410, 423, 425, and improving, 85; as threatening, 158, 234, 389, 419; unity and communal identity, 4, 49, 53, 87-8, 405-407, 413, 418; and violence, 108; as voters, 2, 13, 21, 26, 28, 37, 44, 45, 116, 254, 425; and Whig interpretation, 22; *see also* Act of Toleration; anti-Catholicism; Arianism; Baptists; Bible; class; Congregationalists; electorate; ideology; Methodists; monarchy; Nonconformist ministers; occasional conformity; party; Presbyterians; pulpit; Quakers; radicalism; sermons; subscription campaign; Test and Corporation Acts; Whigs; and entry under individual boroughs
Norfolk, 95
North Briton, 129
North, Frederick Lord (2nd Earl of Guilford), 84, 166n, 212, 216, 217, 218n, 220, 228, 232, 238, 240, 241, 258n, 278, 281, 291, 295, 301, 318, 322, 326, 336, 349, 352-3, 364, 365, 380, 386, 398, 424, 426; recommends addressing, 318-19
North Shields, 84
Northampton, 11, 30, 55n, 56, 98n, 106, 237, 245, 247, 248, 253, 254, 255, 422n; compared to Bristol and Norwich, 239
Northamptonshire, 82, 99n
Northumberland, 99, 102, 105; election of 1774, 341
Northumberland, Hugh Percy, 1st Duke of, 106
Norwich, 11, 13, 27, 30, 44n, 55n, 62n, 71n, 79n, 95, 98n, 101, 109, 110, 119, 124, 127, 130-1, 149, 166, 167, 168, 187, 237, 244, 248, 253, 254, 255, 310, 317n, 364n, 404, 422n, 424, 425, 428, 429, 434n; consistent party support, 230; Dissenters compared to Bristol, 238; Dissenters in office, 77; and Namierian interpretation,

202; partisan vote, 227; and radicalism, 330n; and socio-economic distinctions, 245, 247; *see also* elections
Nossiter, T.J., 436
Nottingham, 10, 13, 17, 44n, 46, 56, 62n, 86, 95, 98n, 101, 103, 124, 127, 131, 132, 134, 137, 166, 167, 168, 175, 188, 190, 192, 197, 311, 316, 317n, 327-8, 329, 331, 346, 358, 359, 364n, 407, 420, 424; address, 379, and Anglican clergy, 356; corporation, 333, and America, 354, 356, divided, 366, 367, 370, and Nonconformists, 355, 356, 367, 399, and petition of, 356, and Whig condidates, 354-5; elections, 355-6; Nonconformists: influence petitioners, 404, 407, 408, ministers lead petitioning, 356-7, 404, and office holding, 78, 357, 398, oppose recruitment, 16, 357, sign petitions, 390, 410, 411, and vote, 355; petition and petitioning agitation, 176, 336, 338, 356-8, inhabitants' petition, 356, and socio-economic distinctions, 373-4, 384-5, 401, 402, 403, 406, 411, and trade, 357; and radicalism, 338; Whigs and Tories, 355, credible use of terms, 356; *see also* petitions
Nottinghamshire, 95, 99n, 132-3, 143
Nowell, Thomas, 161, 162
Nugent, Robert Craggs, 1st Earl (formerly Viscount Clare), 210-12, 222, 224, 226, 229n, 233, 234, 244, 245, 331
nullum tempus bill, 117

Obelkevich, James, 4, 32
occasional conformity, 37, 50, 51, 69-80, 88-9, 94, 191; and social status, 78-9; *see also* office holding under specific denominations
Occasional Conformity Act, 53, 113
Ogilvie, Andrew, 270n
Ogilvie, William, 142n
O'Gorman, Frank, xv, 22, 412, 436
Oldfield, Joshua, 55n, 84n
Oldfield, T.H.B., 85, 291
Oldknow, Thomas, 367n
Oliver, Richard, 332
opposition: and the American rebellion, 15, 119; county, 8; distinguished from Tory, 9; to government's American measures, 321; legitimacy of formed, 316; local, 259, 343; its popular quality, 14; problems faced by Dissenters in, 119-20; in subterranean channels, 120; to Whig oligarchy, 381; *see also* independence; local and national politics
oppression: of America, 152-3; connected, highest to lowest, 167; of corporations,

418, 420; local and national linked, 363-4; myth of, 425; necessity of vigilance against, 141, 147, 155; of poor, 130, 165; rhetoric of, 311, 380; as sin, 141, 156-7

Orton, Job, 114, 123

Ovid, 134

Oxford, 362n

Oxford University, 55, 370

Page, alderman, 77n

Paine, Thomas, 7n, 32, 139, 160

Palmer family, of Great Yarmouth, 364n

Palmer, Samuel, 189

Parliament, 17, 24, 26, 38, 44, 45, 58, 60, 122, 147, 151-2, 156, 175, 201, 293, 317-18, 325, 336, 343, 349, 365, 366, 385, 394; and America, 22; and colonial rebellion, 318; and sovereignty, 152, 156, 166; supremacy, 322, 361, 376, 386

parliamentary reform, 9, 24, 33, 59, 60, 132, 133, 166, 167, 201, 214n, 241, 292n, 293, 315, 321, 327, 331, 357n, 360, 405, 428, 430; issue over reporting debates, 148

party, 3; continuity, 19-26, 30, 113-17; debate over, 20-26; definition, 20; and principles, 20, 24; and radicalism, 395, 397; and religion, 28, 110-12, 118-20; *see also* Anglican Church; elections; Nonconformists; Rockingham Whigs; Tories; Whigs

Paul, St., 136n, 155n

Peach, Samuel, 216, 219, 225, 226, 229n, 330, 331

Pelham, Henry, 28, 100, 346

Pennant, Richard, Lord Penrhyn, 278, 279n, 282, 283, 284-5, 289

Pennsylvania Farmer, 134

Penryn, 97n

people, *see* consent; natural rights; Nonconformist ministers

Percy, Lord Algernon, 321

Perkin, Harold, 32-3, 38

Peterborough, 97n

Peters, L.L., 123, 189

Petersfield, 97n

Petition of Rights, 173; *see also* Bill of Rights

petitions and petitioners, 6, 13, 14, 26, 27, 29, 68, 128; alternative to voting, 311, 317, 329-30, 351, 426; American petitions compared to Middlesex petitions, 319, 323-4, 344, 348, 376, 382, compared to Association movement, 323-4, compared to Coalition petitions, 321, compared to parliamentary reform, 321; American petitions linked to Middlesex election affair, 315, 326, 330, 331; asso-

ciated with sedition, 323-5, 335, 337, 344-5, 348, 349, 353, 358, 363, 384, 394, fears of social upheaval, 345n, 419; and cider act, 188; and clubs and public houses, 379-80; colonial, 318; compared to poll books, 316; concerning America, 16, 45, 132, 160, 316, 360; consistency in voting and petitioning, 327-8; and the constitution, 317, 324, 335, 342; continuity between American and the Association movement, 428; continuity in leadership over Wilkes and America, 326, at Bristol, 331, 421, 428, at Coventry, 348-9, 359, 421, 428, at London, 428, and at Newcastle, 339-40, 421, 428; and debate over petitioning itself, 324-5, 335; and excise crisis, 187; failure of Nonconformist leadership at Barnstaple, 395, 397, 398, Plymouth, 395, 397, 398, and Sudbury, 395-7; geographic distribtuion, 327; language of, 322, compared to language of addresses, 323, 394-5; leadership and organization, 330-7; Low-Church Anglican leadership, 392, 403, 404-405; motives to, 315, 369; nature of, 317, 323; Nonconformist leaders of petitions, 359, 361, 390, 404, at Bristol, 333-4, Coventry, 349, Colchester, 350-1, Liverpool, 343, 393, Newcastle, 340, Nottingham, 357, Taunton, 354; number of, 315, 319, compared to electorate, 315, 319, 321, 360, 416; and patronage, 368-71; and political principles, 358, and meaning in history, 358-9, 416; and the press, 325-6, 333, 335, 378-9; Protestant Association, 170n; public meetings, 333; and public opinion, 316, 326-30; and radicalism, 319, 325-6, 333, 344, 376, 394-5; and socio-economic divisions, 17, 34-5, 37-8, 245, 361, 371-3, artisans in America and during the Middlesex crisis, 382-4, and Dissenting elite, 399-401, economic and religious motivation, 393-4, 398, 399-406, 414, 420-1, and industrial unrest, 327, and lower orders, 384-5, and merchants, 317-18, 372, 376-8, and middling orders, and retailers and artisans, 372, 373, 378-82, 394, 402, 403, 411; and Stamp Act, 187-8, 327; and subscriptions for soldiers, 329, 368; wealth associated with corporations, 361, 364; *see also* addresses; Nonconformists; and entry under individual boroughs

Pharaoh, 164

Philadelphia, 129, 217, 220, 382

Philipps, Sir John, 210, 222

Phillips, John, xiv, 13, 26, 40, 43, 45, 227, 244, 245, 248, 253, 285, 329-30, 432, 434, 436, 441, 445
Phipps, Constantine, 2nd Baron Mulgrave, 257, 259, 260, 264, 265, 270, 272n, 339, 340; changes mind, 264; on Wilkes and America, 263
Pickard, Edward, 123n
Picton, James, 284
Pike family, of Portsmouth, 101
Pilate, 138
Pitt, William, the elder, 1st Earl of Chatham, 24n, 82, 134
Pitt, William, the younger, 21, 24n, 201, 219, 220, 229n, 232, 237, 241, 292, 301
Platt, David, 39
Plowman, Thomas, 398
Plumb, J.H., 380
Plumb, Richard, 357n, 407
Plumptre, John, 355
Plumptre, John, Jr., 355
Plymouth, 75, 82, 97n, 362n; and address, 322, 395, 397, 404; *see also* petitions
Plympton Earle, 74n, 97n
Pole, Charles, 277, 280, 285, 286n, 288
poll books, 13, 29; and socio-economic differences, 17
Pontefract, 97n
Poole, 67n, 75, 98n, 246n, 317n, 329, 330, 360, 384n, 399, 401n; address and patronage, 369; corporation divided, 366; debate over petitioning, 325n; Dissenters lead petitioning, 404
Poole, James, 353n
Popham, Alexander, 352, 353n, 354n
popular politics: contrasted to electoral politics, 414; and national issues, 26-7; and preaching, 42; *see also* petitions
Porteus, Beilby, bishop, 125
Portland, William Henry Cavendish Bentinck, 3rd Duke of, 84, 197n, 198n, 221n, 329n, 334, 335, 336, 337, 348n, 362n
Portsmouth, 75, 78, 98n, 101, 104-5, 114, 119, 425; and America, 321; corporation divided, 366; and Dissent, 321; and independent party, 364
Potter, Christopher, 301, 302, 304, 307, 308, 309
Pread, William, 102
Prentice, Thomas, 192
Presbyterians, 1n, 44n, 49, 52, 95, 96, 97, 100, 101, 103n, 104, 108, 114, 116, 126, 128, 132; 164; at Bristol, 197, 198, 200n, 205, 206, 209, 238, 251, 253n, 265, 377, 397n, 398; at Coventry, 346, 349; geographic distribution, 93, 94n; at Great

Yarmouth, 239, 241, 254; at Kingston upon Hull, 290; at Liverpool, 274-5, 346; losses in London, 93; and office holding, 70, 72n, 76, 77, 78, 81, 377; Scots in Newcastle, 255-6, 264, 271, 298; and social standing, 62-6; at Sudbury, 396-7; at Taunton, 351; United Secession, 256; wealth and social assimilation, 377, 392
press, *see* newspapers
Preston, 83, 98n, 102, 103, 108, 116, 381
Preston family, of Great Yarmouth, 364n
Price, Richard, 7, 45, 57, 123n, 124n, 126, 127, 128n, 132, 133n, 134, 148, 151n, 154n, 159, 160, 175n, 182, 189
Priest, John, 348n
Priestley, Joseph, 7, 45, 57, 58, 126, 127n, 129, 132, 133n, 148, 151n, 154n, 159, 170n, 172n, 182, 189, 242, 416; and national electorate, 190-1, 195
pro-Americans and pro-Americanism, 6, 13, 17, 23, 89, 124, 147-53, 156-7, 189-90, 242, 317n, 361, 403, 427; defined, 147; as Members of Parliament, 362-3; and merchants trading to America, 376; and radicalism, 344; and socio-economic conflict, 372; *see also* Nonconformists
Protestant Dissenters Relief Act, 215
pulpit, 10, 35, 158; and behavior, 122; and popular ideology, 25, 121, 124; and public advocacy, 122; *see also* fast days; ideology; Nonconformist ministers; sermons
Puritan revolution, 125n, 146, 161, 218, 345, 358
Puritanism, 138n, 351

Quakers, 1n, 16, 53-4, 56, 58, 65n, 108, 114, 191; at Bristol, 197, 198, 206, 210, 215, 221, 251; at Bristol, 376, 377, 398n, 399; and Edmund Burke, 214n; at Great Yarmouth, 239; at Liverpool, 275, 279n, 346; at London, 376n, 399; and marginalization, 86; at Newcastle, 256; numerical decline, 93, 94n; and office holding, 69n, 71n, 77; petition, 389; and social standing, 61, 66, 67n; at Taunton, 351; tithe bill, 59; vote, 54, 101, 115; vote at Bristol, 199, 238
Quebec, 148
Quebec Act, 30, 58, 150, 173, 391; at Bristol, 214; galvinizes Dissenters, 197n; at Kingston upon Hull, 293n; at Newcastle, 260, 263, 264n, 271
Queensborough, 75n, 80n

Radcliffe, Ebenezer, 189
radicals and radicalism, 3; absence of class,

10; anti-clericalism as a facet of, 170-2, 180; and artisan or new radicalism, 7-8, 383-4, 395, 403, 423-4, 427-30; and Calvinism, 136; Commonwealthman, 7-10, 60, 127n, 145, 148, 159, 167, 175, 351, 354, 372, 378, 391, 427, compared to Nonconformists, 140n, 142, moderation of, 9, sources of, 133n; and conscience, 138-40, 146; continuities in late eighteenth century, 18, 341, 345, 349, 428-30; and country platform, 133n; definition, 5-6; divisions and impotence, 409, 426; and equality, 430; and evolutionary quality, 430; extension of, 316; and heterodoxy, 59, 135n; ideological sources, 135; and ideology, 12-14; influence of ecclesiastical polity on, 136, 137-9, 142, 170, 184, 418, 422, and two kingdom theory, 138; interpretation of, 7-13, 316; local issues intensify, 159, 167-74; and middle ranks, 9, 378; moderation of pro-Americanism, 9-10; and national issues, 421; and orthodoxy, 127n, 128-9, 134-7; Paineite, 427; perceptions of, 15; and publishing, 378-9, 383; and petitioning, 394-5; and questions of wealth, status, and law, 375-6; reasons for failure, 409, 421, 424-7; and representation, 380; religious independence and political, 142; republicanism, 160, 163-4, 340; right of resistance, 154-8; role of law, 172-4; and social inequality, 175-82; and socio-economic divisions, 12, 14, 17, 382; and symbolism, 341-2; Tory, 5n, 9; trans-Atlantic, 167; Utilitarianism, 7n; Wilkite, 5n, 7n, 9, 16, 133n, connections between Wilkite and pro-Americans, 16, distinctives of Wilkite and artisan, 381-2; working class, 7n; Wyvillite, 133n; *see also* aristocracy; class; ideology; newspapers; Nonconformist ministers; Nonconformists; petitions; and entry under individual boroughs
Ramey, John, 110
Randel, Dr., 55
Rann, Joseph, 348n
Rawlinson, Abraham, 343, 392n
Rawlinson, Henry, 278, 282, 283, 285
Rawson, Thomas, 357
Raymond, John, 80n
Reading, 98n, 227, 46; partisan vote, 228
Rebow, Isaac, 300, 301, 302, 303, 304, 306, 307
Reed, James, 377
Reed, Robert, 340n
Rees, Abraham, 189
Regium Donum, 105

Rehoboam, 164
Reigate, 97n
religion: and ideology, 4-5, 12; non-revolutionary nature, 36; and public opinion, 21; and recent research, 1, 31-2; and socio-economic elements, 32, 35, 36
Restraining Act, 173
Richard, William, 233n
Richardson, James, 270n
Richmond, Charles Lennox, 3rd Duke of, 28, 121, 127, 175n, 195, 332n, 412
Ridley, Matthew, 257-8, 260, 261n, 262n, 268, 269, 273; opposes government over America, 267
Ridley, Matthew, Sr., 257, 263
Rigby, Richard, 306
Riot Act, 57
Rippon, John, 123n
Roberts, Colonel John, 353n
Robbins, Caroline, 7, 351
Robinson, John, 212, 218n, 319
Robinson, Robert, 57, 58, 61, 127n, 134, 130, 172n, 189
Robson, Thomas, 379
Robson, William, 270n
Rochdale, 343
Rochester, 76n, 97n
Rochford, 299n, 351
Rochford, William Henry Zuylestein, 4th Earl of, 356n
Rockingham, Charles Watson-Wentworth, 2nd Marquis of, 197n, 240, 278n, 290, 291, 295, 317n, 331n, 336n, 355, 372n, 408; on popular support, 332
Rockingham Whigs, 2, 18, 24, 85, 113, 127, 133n, 159, 162, 195, 196, 199, 202, 254, 278, 316, 341, 408-409, 426; at Bristol, 209, 213, 215; and Dissenters in electorate, 412, 415-16; legitimate party, 23; and petitions, 322, 330, 331-2, 336, 337, 414
Rogers, John, 123n
Rogers, Nicholas, 8, 370, 381
Rogers, Thomas, 349
Rolt, Richard, 439, 443, 444
Rose, Richard, 119
Rouquet, James, 137n, 335n, 386, 404
Rousseau, Jean Jacques, 129, 134, 135, 262
royal proclamation, 14, 126n, 318, 324, 325, 332; tarred and feathered, 342
Rubinstein, W.D., 85-6
Rudé, George, xiv, 8, 10, 34, 40, 41, 45, 316, 382, 386, 391, 424, 428
Rudkin, Daniel, 350
Rudsdell, Jeremiah, 82
Russell, William, 84
Russell, William, "the patriot," 127

Rutland, 82
Ryder, Dudley, 73n, 80n
Rye, 74, 97n, 362n

Sacheverell, Henry, 53
Sacheverell riots, 108, 171
sacramental tests, *see* Test and Corporation
    Acts
Sainsbury, John, 10, 13, 45, 147, 324, 326,
    328, 372, 376, 378, 380
St. Albans, 27, 98n, 114, 115
St. George's Fields massacre, 147
St. Germans, 80n
St. Ives, 76n, 97n
Saint, Thomas, 341, 379
Salisbury, 72, 73n, 97n; and address, 338n
Saltash, 73, 80n
Salusbury, Thomas, 277
Sandemanians, 256n, 275n
Sands, Thomas, 367n
Sandwich, 76n, 83, 97n
Sandwich, John Montagu, 4th Earl of, 101,
    357
Saul, 165
Saunders, Sir Charles, 240, 412
Savadge, W.R., 200
Savile, Sir George, 100, 290, 291, 292, 295,
    336n, 414
Savile, Richard Lumley, 100
Sayre, Stephen, 337
Scarborough, 72n, 97n
Schism Act, 113
Schism bill, 53n
Scotland, 55, 256, 271, 319n, 363n
Scott, John, 189; and national electorate,
    190-1
Scott-Naylor suit, 56
Scrope, John, 210
Sedley, Sir Charles, 355
Seed, John, 89
Seneca, 134
Septennial Act, 166
sermons, 14, 18; Anglican, 25, 126n, 161-2;
    Dissenting, 41-2, 120, 121, 130, 132, 419;
    Fast and Thanksgiving Day, 25, 126, 358;
    influence on laity, 152-3, 419; and news-
    papers, 424; theological basis, 124; *see
    also* fast days; pulpit; ideology
Sewell, Thomas, 115
Shackleton, Richard, 197n
Shaftesbury, 98n, 103
Shaftesbury, Anthony Ashley Cooper, 3rd
    Earl of, 58
Sharp, Granville, 145n, 151n, 160, 175, 405
Sheffield, 429
Shelton, Walker, 427
Shields, James, 270n

Shipley, Jonathan, bishop, 405
Shirley, Thomas, 295
shopkeepers: and artisans, 17, 35; *see also*
    artisans; petitions
Shore, Samuel, 83
Shorey, Timothy, 399
Shrewsbury, 29, 74, 75, 98n, 109, 114, 190,
    253, 362n, 405, 431n; Dissenting vote,
    109-10; *see also* elections
Sidney, Algernon, 127, 134
Simpson, J., 357n, 407
Slack, Thomas, 341, 364, 379
slave trade, abolition, 60
slavery, 175
Sly, Thomas, 399
Smith, Egerton, 379n
Smith, John, of Ailesbury, 84
Smith, John, of Easton Grey, 84
Smith, Jarrit, 211
Smith, Joseph, 197
Smith, Robert, 358n
Smith, William, 260, 339, 340, 397
Smollett, Tobias, 351
Smyth, Sir Robert, 300, 302, 304, 307, 308,
    309; and parliamentary reform, 301
society: not unified, 421; open quality, 3,
    36, 85, 406, 425, 426
Society for Constitutional Information, 83
Society of Supporters of the Bill of Rights,
    7n, 325, 339, 343, 392
Socinianism, 131n
Soden, James, 348
Solomon, 135, 164
Somerset, 96, 99n, 116
South Molton, 362n
Southampton, 11, 82, 98n, 107, 245, 330,
    360, 362, 412, 431; and address, 328, 364;
    Dissenters lead petitioning, 404; and
    patronage, 369; petition, 322n, 328; and
    socio-economic divisions, 371-2, 373,
    380, 384n, 401, 402, 411
Southwark, 82, 97n, 190, 373n; and debate
    over petition, 325n; petition, 322n
Span, Samuel, 331
Sparkes, Emmanuel, 297
Speke, George, 75n
Spence, Thomas, 32, 129, 142n, 179, 180n
Spufford, Margaret, 62
Stafford, 74n, 98n
Staffordshire, 99n; and addresses and
    petitions, 362; and debate over petition,
    325n; petition, 322n, 336;
Stamford, 97n
Stamp Act, 148, 150n, 156, 157, 315, 385;
    at Bristol, 214; *see also* petitions
Stanhope, James, 1st Earl of, 70
Stanley, Edward (Lord Stanley), 343, 344n,

345
Stanton, Thomas, 351n
Stebbing, Henry, 161
Stevenson, John, 427
Steyning, 80n, 97n
Stinton, Mr., 71
Stockbridge, 80n
Stockport, Cheshire, 71n
Story, John, 340n
Stratham, Samuel, 357n, 407
Stuart dynasty, 161, 218
subscription campaign (1772), 23, 58, 59,
   60, 61, 84, 112, 117, 148, 170, 205, 270,
   278, 287, 297, 357n, 387, 391, 392, 396;
   see also petitions
Sudbury, 76, 82, 95, 98n, 103, 106, 119; and
   addresses, 395-7, 398, 399, 404, 411
succession, 118
Suffolk, 82, 95
Sunderland, 341
Surtees, Aubone, 368
Sussex, 99n
Sutherland, Lucy, 382
Sutton, Sampson, 399
Swarley, Richard, 380
Sweeting, Mr., 353n
Swift, Jonathan, 70
Sykes, Norman, xi
Symonds, Thomas, 334, 375

Tabor family, of Colchester, 298
Tacitus, 134
Tamworth, 97n
Tarleton, Banastre, 278, 279n, 284-5, 286n,
   288
Taunton, 10, 12, 13, 46n, 96, 98n, 104-5,
   108, 124, 131, 167, 168, 188n, 311, 316,
   358, 359, 362n, 367, 399, 401, 421, 425;
   address and corporation, 353, 364, 365-6,
   376; corporation-anti-corporation conflict, 352, 353; elections, 352-3, and corruption, 352, 353; Nonconformity: and
   chapels, 351, and government, 352, 353,
   and Low-Church Anglicans, 352, and
   petitioning, 354, 404, and pro-Americans,
   353, 408, 410; petition and petitioning
   agitation, 322n, 353-4; and popular
   politics, 338; Whigs and Tories, 351, 353;
   see also petitions
Tavistock, 97n
taxes, 179-80, 183, 188
Taylor, Henry, 75, 114
Taylor, John, 84
Taylor, Matthew, 387
Taylor, Philip, 392n
Taylor, Walter, 82
Tenison, Thomas, 70

Test Act, 70, 80-1, 207n; and custom house
   and excise officers, 81-2; and Justices of
   the Peace, 83-4; and the military, 82-3;
   and receiverships, 82
Test and Corporation Acts, 24, 33-4, 37, 42,
   50-2, 69, 71, 85, 169, 170, 367, 418; and
   education, 55, 86; influence on elections,
   97; and repeal campaign, 29, 59-61, 80,
   83, 84, 87, 88, 132, 171, 241, 429; and
   'Sheriff's Cause', 54; *see also* Corpora-
   tion Act; Test Act
Thirsk, 97n
Thirty-Nine Articles, 52, 58, 60, 84, 148,
   170, 205, 287, 387; *see also* subscription
   campaign
Tholfsen, Trygve, 41
Thomas, John, 233n
Thomas, John, bishop, 161
Thomond, Percy Wyndham O'Brien, Earl
   of, 352n
Thompson, E.P., 12, 32-3, 36, 383, 427
Thompson, Josiah, 80, 95
Thornton, Henry, 291
Thornton, Samuel, 290, 291, 292, 294, 296,
   298
Tiberius Caesar, 166n
Tierney, George, 301
Tillingshaft, Stephen, 368
tithes, 171, 179-80, 418
Tito family, of Poole, 75
Tiverton, 46n, 72, 73, 81, 98n, 106, 412
Tolladay, William, 399
Tolles, Frederick B., 86
Tooke, John Horne, 160
Tories and Toryism, 53, 165; and address-
   ing, 362n, 385-6, 387; advocate petition-
   ing, 323; and corporations, 74; differences
   from Whigs, 110-11, 117, 118; dislike of
   Dissent, 20, 58, 108; and exclusion from
   high politics, 33n; identity, 25n; and
   industrialization, 69n, 86; and law, 20;
   link to High Church, 110-112, 115, 116;
   origins, 415; and party, 19, 22, 195; and
   radicalism, 203n, 350n, 381; regarding the
   Crown, 162; resurgence of, 22, 23n, 24-6,
   30, 199, 201, 234, 387, 415; versus local
   Whig parties, 115, 116; and Whig
   historians, 2; and Whigs at Bristol, 201-3;
   see also High-Church Anglicans; radicals;
   Whigs; and entry under individual
   boroughs
Totnes, 74, 97n
Tottenham Park, 79
Touchet, Samuel, 103, 124n
Toulmin, Joshua, 12, 124n, 131, 134, 137,
   141n, 142n, 145, 146n, 150n, 151, 166,
   167, 168, 177, 178n, 189, 317, 351, 354,

359, 365, 366n, 419, 425; on American
  Revolutioin, 149, 154, 155n, 156-7; and
  goal of government, 144
Towers, Joseph, 16, 58, 107, 120; on
  petitioning, 188n, 189
Townley, Richard, 343, 344
Townshend, Charles, 240, 241, 277
Townshend duties, 124n, 129, 148, 200-1,
  212
Treen, William, 399
Trenchard, John, 110, 133n, 170
Trevelyan, G.M., 19-20, 26, 112, 413, 414
Trevelyan, Sir John, 258, 266, 268, 269
Trinitarianism, 136, 159
Troeltsch, Ernst, 31
Trotter, Robert, 104
Trowbridge, 317n
Truro, 72n, 97n
Tucker, Josiah, 128, 161, 171, 188n, 211,
  222, 244, 335n
Turner, William, 189
Twekesbury, 97n
Tyssen, Samuel, 300n, 302n, 304n
Tyzack, Nicholas, 260, 339, 340n

Underdown, Peter, 200, 202, 232
Unitarians, 1n, 52, 59, 62, 87, 94, 131, 205,
  206, 423; at Liverpool, 274; and
  marginalization, 86n; at Newcastle,
  256-7; at Taunton, 351
Unwin, John, 299n
Usk, 81

Virgil, 134
Virginia, 175n
Voltaire, 134
Vowler, Henry, 84, 101, 115

Wakefield, 56
Wakefield, George, 78
Wales, 319n
Walker, George 12, 124n, 128n, 131-3, 134,
  137, 140, 141, 142n, 143, 145, 146, 147,
  150n, 151n, 159, 160, 163, 167, 168,
  170n, 171, 181, 182, 189, 192, 317, 326n,
  359, 406, 407, 419, 420, 425, 428n; on
  administration, 166; on American Revolution, 154, 155n; drafts petition, 188,
  357; on monarchy, 163-4; and origin of
  political power, 144; and reform strategy,
  185-7, 188; on social stratification,
  175-8, 183
Wallin, Benjamin, 189, 242, 416; and
  national electorate, 190-1, 195
Wallingford, 80n, 97n; petition, 322n
Wallis, John, 331
Walpole, Horace, 19n, 200, 358

Walpole, Richard, 240
Walpole, Sir Robert (1st Earl of Orford), 9,
  28, 100, 346
Walsh, John, xv
Wansey, William, 377
Ward, W.R., 32
Wareham, 80n, 96, 97n
Waring, Walker, 347, 348
Warren, Matthew, 351
Warwick, 98n; and address, 362n, 363, 431
Warwickshire, 61, 82
Watkins, Edmund, 81
Watson, Richard, 405, 428n
Watts, Michael, xv, 62, 86, 423
Weare, G.E., 199-200
Weare, John Fisher, 334
Weare, Robert, 377
Weare, William, 377
Webb, Francis, 82
Webb, Robert, 352n
Weber, Max, 31, 33n
Weddell, William, 291
Wedderburn, Alexander, 318, 324n
Wells, 74n, 75, 98n
Wendover, 97n
Weobley, 97n
Wesley, John, 16, 58n, 125, 128, 130, 150,
  171n, 178, 198, 206, 335, 341; on
  America, 216-17, 231-2; on Dissenters,
  158
Wesleyans, 423; *see also* Methodists
West Ham (Essex), 82
West Indies, 377
Westbury, 97n, 109; and petitioning, 336
Westbury, Warminster, and Trowbridge
  petition, 376
Western Baptist Association, 16
Westminster, 17, 42, 82, 97n, 112, 196, 243,
  381, 434n
Westmorland, 54n, 229n
Wetherell, Charles, xiv
Wetheringsett, Suffolk, 57n
Weymouth and Melcombe Regis, 76, 80,
  82, 97n
Wheater, Richard, 82
Whigs, 53, 161; attached to king, 163; defi-
  nition of, 28, and in relation to Dissent
  and religion, 110-13, 115, 117, 118-20,
  121, 191, 195, 196, 408; of early years of
  George III, 163; historians, 2, 18-19, 21,
  22, 105; influence, 122, 124-6; independent allied with Tories, 381; interpretation
  of, 19-20, 22, 27, 30, 39, 412-14, 417;
  and Low-Church Anglicans, 405; myth,
  58, 105; myth of secret cabinet, 158, 165,
  391, 415, 424-5; origins of interpretation
  at Bristol, 198; as a party, 195; and party

continuity, 2, 19, 23n, 30, 111, 120; party
labels, 20, 30, 111, 201, revived in Amer-
ican conflict, 112, 117, 379, 412, 415;
principles, 16, 21, 117, 121; and social
control, 125; and Tories at Bristol, 199,
200-3, 207; true, 133n, 142; *see also*
Nonconformists; party; Rockingham
Whigs; Tories; and entry under individual
boroughs
White family, of East Retford, 98n
White family, of Portsmouth, 75, 101
White, Richard, 299n
White, Thomas, 340n, 342n
Whitechurch, 97n
Whitefield, George, 206
Whitehaven, 101, 317n
Whitelock, Matthews, 367n, 407
Wigan, 74n, 342, 362n
Wikoff, Peter, 217, 218
Wilberforce, William, 291, 292, 294, 295,
296, 297, 298
Wilkes, John, 8, 45, 58, 60, 129, 175n, 259,
319, 325, 326, 332, 336, 339, 340, 381,
426, 427
Wilkin, Simon, 77
William I, 127
William III, 145, 146
Williams, Edward, 357n, 407
Williams, William, 84
Wilson, Daniel, 392, 405
Wilson, Thomas, 197n
Wilton, 72, 73, 97n
Wilton, Samuel, 189
Winchester, 74n, 97n, 321, 362n, 373n, 386;
and Constitutional Club, 364; debate over
petitioning, 325n; and independent party,
364
Witham, 299n, 351
Wolverhampton, 317n
Wooldridge, Thomas, 325n, 336-7
Worcester, 27, 44n, 79n, 98n, 105, 366, 381;
and address, 364n; and corporation, 365;
petition, 322n, 338
Worcestershire, 363n; and address, 362
Wright, Thomas, 233n
Wyvill, Christopher, 428, 429

Yeo, Edward Roe, 347, 348
York, 56, 98n, 292, 362n, 366, 381; and
corporation, 365; debate over petitioning,
325n
York Courant, 387, 444
Yorkshire, 83, 99, 100, 132, 281
Yorkshire Association, 83
Young, George, 340n

Zedekiah, 146, 164